Communications
in Computer and Information Science 1981

Rationale

The CCIS series is devoted to the publication of proceedings of computer science conferences. Its aim is to efficiently disseminate original research results in informatics in printed and electronic form. While the focus is on publication of peer-reviewed full papers presenting mature work, inclusion of reviewed short papers reporting on work in progress is welcome, too. Besides globally relevant meetings with internationally representative program committees guaranteeing a strict peer-reviewing and paper selection process, conferences run by societies or of high regional or national relevance are also considered for publication.

Topics

The topical scope of CCIS spans the entire spectrum of informatics ranging from foundational topics in the theory of computing to information and communications science and technology and a broad variety of interdisciplinary application fields.

Information for Volume Editors and Authors

Publication in CCIS is free of charge. No royalties are paid, however, we offer registered conference participants temporary free access to the online version of the conference proceedings on SpringerLink (http://link.springer.com) by means of an http referrer from the conference website and/or a number of complimentary printed copies, as specified in the official acceptance email of the event.

CCIS proceedings can be published in time for distribution at conferences or as post-proceedings, and delivered in the form of printed books and/or electronically as USBs and/or e-content licenses for accessing proceedings at SpringerLink. Furthermore, CCIS proceedings are included in the CCIS electronic book series hosted in the SpringerLink digital library at http://link.springer.com/bookseries/7899. Conferences publishing in CCIS are allowed to use Online Conference Service (OCS) for managing the whole proceedings lifecycle (from submission and reviewing to preparing for publication) free of charge.

Publication process

The language of publication is exclusively English. Authors publishing in CCIS have to sign the Springer CCIS copyright transfer form, however, they are free to use their material published in CCIS for substantially changed, more elaborate subsequent publications elsewhere. For the preparation of the camera-ready papers/files, authors have to strictly adhere to the Springer CCIS Authors' Instructions and are strongly encouraged to use the CCIS LaTeX style files or templates.

Abstracting/Indexing

CCIS is abstracted/indexed in DBLP, Google Scholar, EI-Compendex, Mathematical Reviews, SCImago, Scopus. CCIS volumes are also submitted for the inclusion in ISI Proceedings.

How to start

To start the evaluation of your proposal for inclusion in the CCIS series, please send an e-mail to ccis@springer.com.

Ana I. Pereira · Armando Mendes ·
Florbela P. Fernandes · Maria F. Pacheco ·
João P. Coelho · José Lima
Editors

Optimization, Learning Algorithms and Applications

Third International Conference, OL2A 2023
Ponta Delgada, Portugal, September 27–29, 2023
Revised Selected Papers, Part I

Editors
Ana I. Pereira ⓘ
Instituto Politécnico de Bragança
Bragança, Portugal

Armando Mendes ⓘ
University of Azores
Ponta Delgada, Portugal

Florbela P. Fernandes ⓘ
Instituto Politécnico de Bragança
Bragança, Portugal

Maria F. Pacheco ⓘ
Instituto Politécnico de Bragança
Bragança, Portugal

João P. Coelho ⓘ
Instituto Politécnico de Bragança
Bragança, Portugal

José Lima ⓘ
Instituto Politécnico de Bragança
Bragança, Portugal

ISSN 1865-0929   ISSN 1865-0937 (electronic)
Communications in Computer and Information Science
ISBN 978-3-031-53024-1   ISBN 978-3-031-53025-8 (eBook)
https://doi.org/10.1007/978-3-031-53025-8

Preface

The volumes CCIS 1981 and 1982 contains the refereed proceedings of the III International Conference on Optimization, Learning Algorithms and Applications (OL2A 2023), a hybrid event held on September 27–29.

OL2A provided a space for the research community in optimization and learning to get together and share the latest developments, trends and techniques as well as develop new paths and collaborations. OL2A had the participation of more than four hundred participants in an online and face-to-face environment throughout three days, discussing topics associated with areas such as optimization and learning and state-of-the-art applications related to multi-objective optimization, optimization for machine learning, robotics, health informatics, data analysis, optimization and learning under uncertainty and 4th industrial revolution.

Six special sessions were organized under the topics Learning Algorithms in Engineering Education, Optimization in the SDG context, Optimization in Control Systems Design, Computer Vision Based on Learning Algorithms, Machine Learning and AI in Robotics and Machine Learning and Data Analysis in Internet of Things. The event had 66 accepted papers. All papers were carefully reviewed and selected from 172 submissions. All the reviews were carefully carried out by a scientific committee of 115 PhD researchers from 23 countries.

The OL2A 2023 volume editors,

September 2023

Ana I. Pereira
Armando Mendes
Florbela P. Fernandes
Maria F. Pacheco
João P. Coelho
José Lima

Organization

General Chairs

Ana I. Pereira   Polytechnic Institute of Bragança, Portugal
Armando Mendes   University of the Azores, Portugal

Program Committee Chairs

Florbela P. Fernandes   Polytechnic Institute of Bragança, Portugal
M. Fátima Pacheco   Polytechnic Institute of Bragança, Portugal
João P. Coelho   Polytechnic Institute of Bragança, Portugal
José Lima   Polytechnic Institute of Bragança, Portugal

Special Session Chairs

João P. Teixeira   Polytechnic Institute of Bragança, Portugal
José Cascalho   University of the Azores, Portugal

Technology Chairs

Paulo Medeiros   University of the Azores, Portugal
Rui Pedro Lopes   Polytechnic Institute of Bragança, Portugal

Program Committee

Ana Isabel Pereira   Polytechnic Institute of Bragança, Portugal
Abeer Alsadoon   Charles Sturt University, Australia
Ala' Khalifeh   German Jordanian University, Jordan
Alberto Nakano   Federal University of Technology – Paraná, Brazil
Alexandre Douplik   Ryerson University, Canada
Ana Maria A. C. Rocha   University of Minho, Portugal
Ana Paula Teixeira   University of Trás-os-Montes and Alto Douro,
                                   Portugal
André Pinz Borges   Federal University of Technology – Paraná, Brazil

Jorge Igual	Universitat Politécnica de Valencia, Spain
Jorge Ribeiro	Polytechnic Institute of Viana do Castelo, Portugal
José Boaventura-Cunha	University of Trás-os-Montes and Alto Douro, Portugal
José Cascalho	University of the Azores, Portugal
José Lima	Polytechnic Institute of Bragança, Portugal
José Ramos	Nova University Lisbon, Portugal
Joseane Pontes	Federal University of Technology – Ponta Grossa, Brazil
Josip Musić	University of Split, Croatia
Juan A. Méndez Pérez	University of Laguna, Spain
Juan Alberto García Esteban	University de Salamanca, Spain
Júlio Cesar Nievola	Pontifícia Universidade Católica do Paraná, Brazil
Kristina Sutiene	Kaunas University of Technology, Lithuania
Laura Belli	University of Parma, Italy
Lidia Sánchez	University of León, Spain
Lino Costa	University of Minho, Portugal
Luca Davoli	University of Parma, Italy
Luca Oneto	University of Genoa, Italy
Luca Spalazzi	Marche Polytechnical University, Italy
Luis Antonio De Santa-Eulalia	Université de Sherbrooke, Canada
Luís Coelho	Polytechnic Institute of Porto, Portugal
M. Fátima Pacheco	Polytechnic Institute of Bragança, Portugal
Mahmood Reza Khabbazi	University West, Sweden
Manuel Castejón Limas	University of León, Spain
Marc Jungers	Université de Lorraine, France
Marco Aurélio Wehrmeister	Federal University of Technology – Paraná, Brazil
Marek Nowakowski	Military Institute of Armoured and Automotive Technology in Sulejowek, Poland
Maria do Rosário de Pinho	University of Porto, Portugal
Martin Hering-Bertram	Hochschule Bremen, Germany
Matthias Funk	University of the Azores, Portugal
Mattias Bennulf	University West, Sweden
Michał Podpora	Opole University of Technology, Poland
Miguel Ángel Prada	University of León, Spain
Mikulas Huba	Slovak University of Technology in Bratislava, Slovakia
Milena Pinto	Federal Center of Technological Education Celso Suckow da Fonseca, Brazil
Miroslav Kulich	Czech Technical University Prague, Czech Republic
Nicolae Cleju	Technical University of Iasi, Romania

Contents – Part I

Machine Learning

Learning Algorithms in Engineering Education

Machine Learning and Data Analysis in Internet of Things

Optimization

Optimization in the SDG Context

Contents – Part II

Machine Learning and AI in Robotics

Machine Learning

A YOLO-Based Insect Detection: Potential Use of Small Multirotor Unmanned Aerial Vehicles (UAVs) Monitoring

Guido S. Berger[1,2,3]([⊠]), João Mendes[1,2], Arezki Abderrahim Chellal[1,2,3], Luciano Bonzatto Junior[5], Yago M. R. da Silva[7], Matheus Zorawski[1,2], Ana I. Pereira[1,2], Milena F. Pinto[1,7], João Castro[6], António Valente[3,4], and José Lima[1,2,4]

[1] Research Centre in Digitalization and Intelligent Robotics (CeDRI), Instituto Politécnico de Bragança, Bragança, Portugal
{guido.berger,joao.cmendes,arezki,matheuszorawski,apereira,jllima}@ipb.pt
[2] Laboratório Associado para a Sustentabilidade e Tecnologia em Regiões de Montanha (SusTEC), Instituto Politécnico de Bragança, Bragança, Portugal
[3] Universidade de Trás-os-Montes e Alto Douro, Vila Real, Portugal
avalente@utad.pt
[4] INESC Technology and Science, Porto, Portugal
[5] Federal University of Technology, Paraná, Curitiba, Brazil
[6] Centro de Investigação de Montanha (CIMO), Bragança, Portugal
jpmc@ipb.pt
[7] Centro Federal Tecnológica Celso Suckow da Fonseca, Rio de Janeiro, Brazil
milena.pinto@cefet-rj.br

Abstract. This paper presents an approach to address the challenges of manual inspection using multirotor Unmanned Aerial Vehicles (UAV) to detect olive tree flies (Bactrocera oleae). The study employs computer vision techniques based on the You Only Look Once (YOLO) algorithm to detect insects trapped in yellow chromotropic traps. Therefore, this research evaluates the performance of the YOLOv7 algorithm in detecting and quantify olive tree flies using images obtained from two different digital cameras in a controlled environment at different distances and angles. The findings could potentially contribute to the automation of insect pest inspection by UAV-based robotic systems and highlight potential avenues for future advances in this field. In view of the experiments conducted indoors, it was found that the Arducam IMX477 camera acquires images with greater clarity compared to the TelloCam, making it possible to correctly highlight the set of Bactrocera oleae in different prediction models. The presented results in this research demonstrate that with the introduction of data augmentation and auto label techniques on the set of images of Bactrocera oleae, it was possible to arrive at a prediction model whose average detection was 256 Bactrocera oleae in relation to the corresponding ground truth value to 270 Bactrocera oleae.

Keywords: Unmanned aerial vehicles · Object classification · Insect detection · Olive fly · YOLOv7 algorithm

A. I. Pereira et al. (Eds.): OL2A 2023, CCIS 1981, pp. 3–17, 2024.
https://doi.org/10.1007/978-3-031-53025-8_1

1   Introduction

Unmanned Aerial Vehicles (UAVs) are robotic platforms that have been increasingly used in the field of precision agriculture, providing flexibility, cost efficiency, and high spatial and temporal resolution [1,2]. According to recent literature, UAVs are commonly applied in the context of agriculture to perform tasks such as the identification of invasive plants [3], diseases [4], spraying [5], yield estimation [6], and among others.

In addition, UAVs can carry different types of sensors such as LiDAR, multispectral cameras, hyperspectral, or even thermal sensors [7], whose purpose is to collect information related to the specific needs of different crop cultures to optimize potential solutions to the problems that are faced in agricultural production. In this sense, UAVs are versatile, flexible, and adaptable to different contexts [8–10].

In the last decade, UAVs have been used to collect data in monitoring forest insect pests and diseases (FIPD), whose objective is to control and monitor potential local pests and thus minimize the damage caused to the crop. For this, the UAV equipped with multispectral or hyperspectral sensors is used to produce class maps, for example, to discriminate the regions potentially affected by certain pests over time [11].

However, the method depends on sensors with a high financial cost and an adequate platform to support operations with a high flight ceiling. In this sense, developing methodologies based on robotic systems by UAVs that detect the incidence of pests between sets of trees is highly intriguing and desirable in precision agriculture [12].

The olive fly known as Bactrocera oleae is one of the most harmful pests in the field of olive growing, which mainly responsible for causing depreciation in the quality of the olive and, consequently, economic losses on the commercialization of the product in question. Current methods for monitoring olive fly populations involve field visits by an expert who conducts visual inspections of traps installed over the tops of olive groves [13,14].

The manual inspection process is a complex and time-consuming task due to sending one or more specialists on foot to assess all the traps along the olive-growing region [15]. Furthermore, with the expansion of cultivation, manual intervention to diagnose pest infestations is becoming increasingly difficult, with increasing efforts by farmers to monitor unforeseeable infestations [16].

To deal with manual inspection problems, we present a proof of concept to detect olive flies (Bactrocera oleae) by small multirotor UAVs in this work. In this sense, computer vision techniques based on You Only Look Once (YOLO V7) detect insects trapped in a yellow chromotropic trap. The main objective of this research is to contribute to advancing and developing future automatic pest monitoring systems by small-scale UAVs. The main contributions to this work are highlighted in the following topics:

- Evaluate the performance of detecting and quantify olive flies (Bactrocera oleae) by different prediction models created from YOLOv.7;

- To investigate the feasibility of proof of concept considering the future use of UAVs for detecting Bactrocera oleae in yellow chromotropic traps;
- Provide information that advances with state-of-the-art in the field of automation of pest insect inspection by robotic systems based on UAVs;

The remainder of this paper is organized as follows. Section 2 presents related works within the theme of this research. The materials used and the methodology applied to the theme of this work are described in Sect. 3. In Sect. 4, the results observed by the experiments are presented, and finally, in Sect. 5, the conclusions and future directions of this work are presented.

2   Related Works

The constant monitoring of insect pests in agriculture is essential to neutralize a given infestation at the best time, optimizing the strategy of controlling and managing inputs on a given crop. In practice, the monitoring and management of a wide range of insect pests are usually carried out by capturing insects in traps that are positioned under the canopy of trees, thus making it possible to estimate the population density of pests by qualified operators who regularly visit the site and evaluate the number of insect species captured in each trap [17].

Monitoring insect pests by manual procedures is often costly and time-consuming and thus can lead to uncertainties about situational awareness in the field. The delay in recognizing pests can prevent farmers from making local assessments promptly, which could result in massive damage to production and crop quality. To overcome these problems, electronic traps (E-Trap) can be used as management and decision-making systems by positioning near the trap's vision sensors that identify and classify insects using computer vision resources [18].

Different technological resources can be combined with the E-Trap, whose objective is to advance with precision in sampling insects trapped in traps. In this sense, optoacoustic sensors can be used to modulate the wingbeat of insects and identify when they are close to the trap [19]. On the other hand, in other works, LASER sensors are used to produce a barrier that indicates when an insect is trapped in a given trap [20]. The information can be treated by computer vision resources such as Deep Learning (DL), Machine Learning (ML), or Convolutional Neural Networks, which classify and quantify the incidence of insects trapped in traps [21,22].

However, the use of E-Traps on a large scale considerably increases the costs of the monitoring operation, given the wide range of electronic resources that are normally integrated into the embedded system of each electronic trap, such as GPS, RF transmitters, 3G-4G-5G connection, vision sensors, detection sensors and more [23,24]. In addition, it is necessary to maintain the devices to verify incidences of transmission failures constantly, occlusion in captured images, replacement of batteries, or even damage caused by adverse weather events [18,25].

In the context of robotics, the application of UAVs to detect incidences of pest attacks is mainly employed in operations that depend on a high flight ceiling, large UAVs, and costly sensors, such as multispectral or hyperspectral. In this type of inspection, the biophysical parameters of the vegetation are projected on two-dimensional or three-dimensional maps, and through Artificial Intelligence resources, inferences are created of regions potentially attacked by insect pests [1,26].

Usually, the focus for insect pest detection solutions is directed at detecting the effects of pests concerning crop damage or the preventive insect detection strategy when using E-Traps on a large scale. Few works in the literature address the use of UAVs in low-altitude, i.e., close to treetop level.

The work presented by [27], proposes using a multirotor UAV to identify insects by ultraviolet light, using computational vision resources to analyze migratory patterns of certain species of invasive insects. In [28], the authors proposed a strategy based on deep learning to detect the pest Brassica chinensis in low-altitude aerial images in greenhouses. In [29], the authors explore the feasibility of an aerial survey method to locate cocoons of the eastern moth, Monema Flavescens Walker, for accurate detection of cocoons in the winter to avoid defoliation in the subsequent summer.

Also presented in [30] is an approach that evaluates using a multirotor UAV for fruit fly counting. In this work, Deep Learning (DL) techniques were used to count and classify males and females of the species Drosophila suzukii. For this, static images of insect traps commonly used to capture the insect in question were collected. The results indicate the potential use of UAVs to monitor insect traps autonomously.

In this sense, the development of pest monitoring methods by small multirotor UAVs operating at low altitudes, i.e., at treetop level, is still a field lacking information and a great opportunity to be explored. This study contributes to the possibilities of future applications in swarms of small multirotor UAVs whose future applications could reduce inspection time in large growing regions as well as grant inspection flexibility in areas of difficult access.

3   Materials and Methods

The main objective of the methodology used for this research is to evaluate the potential of the YOLOv7 algorithm in detecting and quantify olive grove flies (Bactrocera oleae) by small multirotor UAVs. The strategy to validate the methodology applied in this work consists of two stages, as described in the following subsections.

3.1 Experimental Setup in an Indoor Environment

As part of the proposed methodology, two digital cameras are used, whose characteristics are presented in Table 1. These cameras are used to capture images of Bactrocera oleae trapped in a yellow chromotropic trap, normally used to inspect insect pests in olive groves.

Table 1. Hardware characteristics.

Model	Resolution	FOV
DJI Tello	5MP (2592×1936)	82.6°
Arducam Autofocus 477p	12.3MP (4056×3040)	75°

The Arducam Autofocus IMX477 camera was used in this methodology because it has features that allow it to be quickly loaded onto a small UAV. In addition, this camera can perform manual or automatic focus adjustment, making it ideal for capturing small images, such as insects trapped above the yellow chromotropic trap. On the other hand, the second camera used in this work is native to the UAV Tello and, therefore, already integrated into the embedded system of the aircraft itself, which we call TelloCam.

The Jetson Nano embedded system acquires images from the Arducam camera, while the images captured by TelloCam are transmitted via Wi-Fi to a local computer. The Tello_Driver library was used for this, which interfaces with the Robot Operating System (ROS). UAV Tello's interface with ROS allows adding of new features and read sensors into the aircraft, such as the front camera, Inertial Measurement Unit (IMU), flight status, and others.

A yellow chromotropic trap containing a set of approximately 270 Bactrocera oleae is selected as a target for the cameras used in the experiment. Each camera, i.e., Arducam and TelloCam, acquires 45 images of the yellow chromotropic trap in different positions and angles to be subsequently used to create prediction models by YOLOv7.

These images are acquired from different perspectives when considering that the UAV in flight may not remain just under the frontal region of the trap. To keep the yellow chromotropic trap in a predetermined position, a Universal Robots - UR3 robotic arm was used (see Fig. 1) as it can produce controlled movements with high precision and high repetibility.

The methodology for capturing the images followed procedures, as illustrated in Fig. 2. In this sense, the following steps were adopted:

– Each camera used in the experiment remains fixed on a table, keeping its orientation guided in front of the target object, centered on the yellow chromotropic trap. A laser meter with an accuracy of approximately 2 mm was used to determine the distance between the camera and the trap.

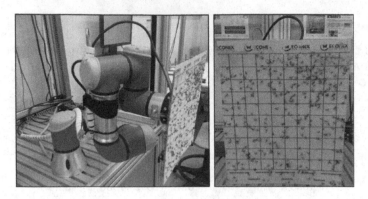

Fig. 1. Yellow chromotropic trap positioned next to the UR3 robotic arm. (Color figure online)

- The UR3 robotic arm was programmed to perform a set of predetermined movements so that the cameras used in the experiment acquired a set of images under angles of 25°, 35°, and 45° of the yellow chromotropic trap.
- For each angle, i.e., 25°, 35°, or 45°, a total of five movements are performed. For each movement, the camera acquires an image, totaling five images. Taking the 25° angle as an example, the movement order starts with the trap positioned at 0° and subsequently at 25° up, down, left, and right. Then the same process is repeated for the angles at 35° and 45°.
- Each camera used in the experiment was positioned at an initial distance of 20 cm in relation to the yellow chromotropic trap. After completing the image capture process, the camera is back more than 20 cm, and the image capture process is repeated. The maximum distance between the cameras and the trap was 60 cm. The distances of 20 cm, 40 cm, and 60 cm are used in total.

At the end of the procedures conducted indoors, 90 images were taken by the cameras used in the experiment. The information acquired in a controlled environment, i.e., with little or no disturbance from the external environment, was used as a database to train different models in the YOLOv7 algorithm, aiming for images well framed to the central focus of the cameras that are easily distinguishable in the pictures. Then, the *labelImg* software was used to produce notes (label) of Bactrocera oleae on the images obtained. Figure 3 illustrates the positioning of the cameras when used for image acquisition.

The algorithm chosen for detecting and quantify insects used in this research was You Look Only Once (YOLO), widely known and adopted in computer vision systems. The YOLOv7 architecture provides a faster and more resilient network architecture, as well as an improved method for feature integration, improved object recognition performance, a more robust loss function, and a higher label assignment and model training efficiency [31]. YOLOv7 outperforms its predecessors regarding inference time and object detection accuracy and thus was selected for use in this research.

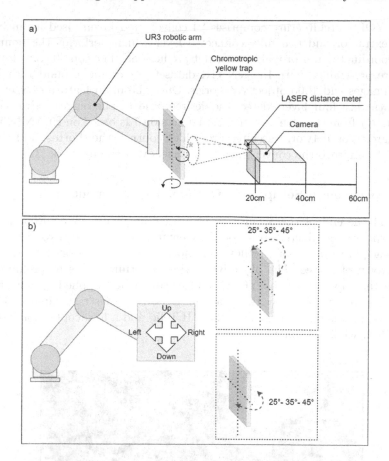

Fig. 2. a) camera positioning in relation to the trap; b) predetermined angles performed by the UR3.

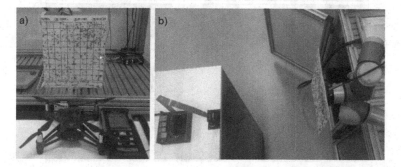

Fig. 3. Procedures adopted for image acquisition. a) Tello camera b) Arducam Autofocus 477p.

The YOLO architecture comprises 24 convolution layers used as an image feature extractor and two fully connected layer which performs the bounding boxes' coordinates and probability output predictions. The top 20 convolutional layers are pre-trained with ImageNet1K dataset, which has around 1.2 million labeled images and 1000 object categories. Once the main feature extraction is trained, the last four layers detect the desired object. The biggest advantage of the YOLOv7 from the oldest version is that version 7 is based on ELAN (efficient layer aggregation network) architecture, which controls the shortest and longest gradient to improve the convergence and efficiency of the network [32].

3.2 Experimental Setup in an Outdoor Environment

Finally, at the end of the acquisition of images in an indoor environment, an experiment was conducted in an outdoor environment, where two UAVs were used to acquire images of a yellow chromotropic trap positioned at the level of the crown of a tree. The objective of this experiment was to preliminarily evaluate the capacity of the YOLOv7 algorithm when applied to detect and classify Bactrocera oleae by two different UAVs, as illustrated in Fig. 4. The UAVs used in this experiment were the DJI Tello and a hexacopter commanded by the Pixhawk 2.4.8 control board.

Fig. 4. Acquisition of images by UAVs in an external environment. a) Hexacopter with Arducam autofocus 477p b) DJI Tello EDU.

4   Results

Initially, the degree of variability of the labels in the images captured by Arducam and TelloCam was analyzed by the distances corresponding to 20 cm and 40 cm. In this sense, a total of 60 images were grouped, considering the different degrees of positioning (25°, 35°, and 45°) and in the different perspectives, that is, inferior, superior, right, left, and frontal, as mentioned in Sect. 3. Table 2 presents the mean and standard deviation values around the number of labels annotated in the images captured by the Arducam and Tello UAV cameras under the distances of 20 cm and 40 cm.

Based on the results presented in Table 2, it is observed that for both cameras (Arducam and TelloCam), the results around the mean of fly detection were far from the ground truth value. The ground truth listed in Table 2 refers to the manual counting of insects contained in the yellow chromotropic trap used in the experiments of this research. Comparing the results of the two cameras, it is noted that the images produced by Arducam had a standard deviation ratio lower than that of TelloCam, indicating more concise label annotations.

Table 2. Degree of the variability of the labels contained in the images.

Distance (cm)	Groundtruth	Arducam		TelloCam	
		Average	STD	Average	STD
20 cm	270	166	17	182	20
40 cm		212	15	195	16

As can be seen, the results presented in Table 2 are quite outdated in relation to the manual count number, evidencing the difficulties in carrying out the classification only by image resources captured by the cameras. Based on the results presented, the upper and lower limits of the baseline were calculated. The baseline corresponds to the mean of the values of the labels contained in the set of images, i.e., for Arducam, it was the mean of the values at 20 cm (166 labels) and 40 cm (212 labels), while for TelloCam, it was the mean of the values of 20 cm (182 labels) and 40 cm (195 labels).

By defining the baseline values and their limits, we proceed to the network training by YOLOv7. For this, 25 images labeled as training sets and the remaining as validation sets were used. The default pattern of the YOLOv7 algorithm (git and data) was used, changing only the number of batches to 4. The entire training process was carried out with Google Colab resources with GPU support (Tesla T4) and CUDA version 12.0. Based on this training, two algorithms linked to Arducam and TelloCam images were generated. The result obtained by this method is shown in Fig. 5.

The results demonstrate the existence of a significant variation in the detection of flies by Arducam in relation to TelloCam, as shown in Fig. 5. Different degrees of confidence were used to verify which confidence index is closest to the Baseline value.

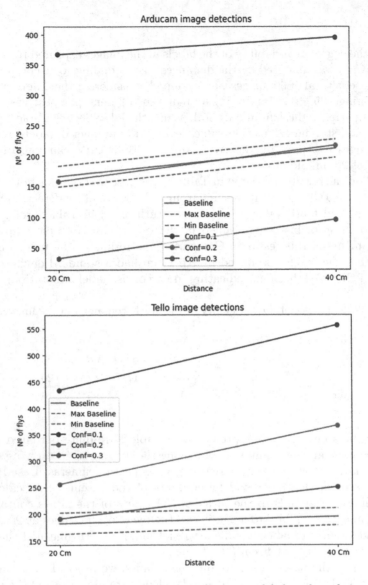

Fig. 5. Results of Arducam and TelloCam prediction models based on their confidence indices

Analyzing the Arducam results, it was verified that the model with a confidence level of 0.2 presented predictions of fly detection within the limits of its Baseline for distances between 20 cm and 40 cm. In the case of the UAV Tello, its image predictions exceed the maximum boundary of its Baseline, suggesting vast inconsistency in the detection of insects in the region of 20 cm.

The models that showed the best fly detection results, i.e., Arducam with the confidence rate model at 0.2 and TelloCam with the confidence rate model at 0.3, were used to be trained on the images acquired by the UAVs in the outdoor environment, whose objective is to establish a quantitative relationship between the detection of flies and the number of labels that were added to the images. The same models were also used on pictures collected at a distance of 60 cm indoors from a frontal perspective. Table 3 presents the results obtained by the experiment.

Table 3. Results obtained by the prediction models Arducam and TelloCam.

	Fig. 6(a) Arducam image	Fig. 6 Arducam image no background	Fig. 6(b) TelloCam	Fig. 6(b) TelloCam no background	60 cm indoor no background
Labels	197	197	202	202	222
Arducam model	133	117	232	188	156
TelloCam model	157	196	259	297	225

For Fig. 6(a), the prediction model that best approached the number of annotations was TelloCam when applied to the image without background, while for the Fig. 6(b) the best prediction model was Arducam when applied to the image without a background. For images at 60 cm, the TelloCam prediction model had a better effect than the Arducam model. In this preliminary experiment, it was noted that the origin of the images did not produce significant influences on the fly detection models on the trap, as shown in Fig. 7.

Fig. 6. Images acquired by UAVs in an external environment. (a) Arducam image; (b) TelloCam image

Fig. 7. Fly detection models on the trap

Then, and seeking to improve the Bactrocera oleae detection models, four new prediction models were elaborated. The first one, called Hybrid, was developed based on combining all the images from the Arducam and TelloCam cameras, having these with their respective captions.

Subsequently, twenty more training images were added, corresponding to images generated by zoom and cropped to highlight only a few sets of Bactrocera oleae, thus creating a new model called Hybrid 2.0.

For the Hybrid 3.0 model, data augmentation techniques were used on the set of camera images, artificially increasing the training images by geometric transformations, i.e., randomly cropping, rotating, and translating the images. Finally, over 30 images were added to the Hybrid 3.0 model using pseudo labeling techniques, whose objective is to automatically label the new images to be used in the composition of the last prediction model, called Hybrid 4.0.

At the end of the development of the four prediction models, these were used to perform the detection of Bactrocera oleae in front of the images collected by the UAVs in an external environment (Fig. 4) as well as under the images 60cm away conducted in an internal environment. The results that indicate the detection performance of the hybrid models are shown in Table 4.

Table 4. Results obtained by the prediction models.

	Fig. 6(a) Arducam image	Fig. 6(a) Arducam image no background	Fig. 6(b) TelloCam	Fig. 6(b) TelloCam no background	60 cm indoor no background
Hybrid	76	317	176	320	308
Hybrid2.0	122	281	181	291	283
Hybrid3.0	238	245	259	258	243
Hybrid4.0	250	242	248	275	263

Based on the results presented, the model became more robust when zoomed images of Bactrocera oleae were introduced on the training set, making it possible to identify a higher number of flies in relation to the ground truth value. On the other hand, introducing the data augmentation technique on the Hybrid 3.0 model showed greater consistency concerning previous models, considering the results presented in Fig. 6(a) and Fig. 6(b) without background, where the average detection of 249 flies was obtained.

Finally, the introduction of the auto label made it possible to smooth out the difference in fly detection between previous predictions, presenting results that list the Hybrid 4 model as the most accurate among the other models, considering that an average of 256 flies were detected by the Hybrid 4 model. Bactrocera oleae in relation to the ground truth value, which corresponds to an amount of 270 flies.

5 Conclusions and Future Work

This work presents an approach to address manual inspection problems by using a small multirotor UAV to detect olive flies (Bactrocera oleae). The YOLOv7 algorithm was employed for insect detection in yellow chromotropic traps, contributing to the development of automatic pest monitoring systems using drones. The study evaluated the performance of YOLOv7 in detecting and quantify olive flies using different camera images in a controlled environment, investigating the algorithm's capabilities at varying distances and angles. The outcomes suggested that this research brings a contribution to advancing automation in pest insect inspection using UAV-based robotic systems.

Future developments from this work include refining identification and quantification algorithms for improved accuracy and efficiency in identifying olive flies. Also, field testing and real-world deployment to evaluate system performance under diverse conditions, such as wind and lighting disturbances. In this sense, the integration with decision support systems and data analytics will be also implemented to enhance the pest management strategy and to explore autonomous navigation. In addition, field tests and real-world deployment to evaluate the performance of the system under various conditions, such as wind and lighting disturbances, or even when applied to another pest insect species, such as the Asian wasp or even the chestnut gall wasp.

Acknowledgment. The authors are grateful to the Foundation for Science and Technology (FCT, Portugal) for financial support through national funds FCT/MCTES (PIDDAC) to CeDRI (UIDB/05757/2020 and UIDP/05757/2020), SusTEC (LA/P/ 0007/2021), Oleachain "Skills for sustainability and innovation in the value chain of traditional olive groves in the Northern Interior of Portugal" (Norte06-3559-FSE-000188) and Centro Federal de Educação Tecnológica Celso Suckow da Fonseca (CEFET/RJ). The authors thank Marta Sofia Madureira from the Agrobio Tecnologia - Insects Laboratory, part of the Mountain Research Center (CIMO), for the technical support provided throughout this work.

References

1. Duarte, A., Borralho, N., Cabral, P., Caetano, M.: Recent advances in forest insect pests and diseases monitoring using uav-based data: a systematic review. Forests **13**, 911 (2022)
2. de Castro, G.G.R., Pinto, M.F., Biundini, I.Z., Melo, A.G., Marcato, A.L.M., Haddad, D.R.: Dynamic path planning based on neural networks for aerial inspection. J. Control Autom. Elect. Syst. **34**(1), 85–105 (2023)
3. Papp, L., et al.: Monitoring invasive plant species using hyperspectral remote sensing data. Land **10**(1) (2021)
4. Bouguettaya, A., Zarzour, H., Kechida, A., Taberkit, A.M.: A survey on deep learning-based identification of plant and crop diseases from uav-based aerial images. Cluster Comput. **26**(2), 1297–1317 (2023)
5. Wang, G., Lan, Y., Qi, H., Chen, P., Hewitt, A., Han, Y.: Field evaluation of an unmanned aerial vehicle (uav) sprayer: effect of spray volume on deposition and the control of pests and disease in wheat. Pest Manag. Sci. **75**(6), 1546–1555 (2019)
6. Feng, A., Zhou, J., Vories, E.D., Sudduth, K.A., Zhang, M.: Yield estimation in cotton using uav-based multi-sensor imagery. Biosyst. Eng. **193**, 101–114 (2020)
7. Berger, G.S., et al.: Sensor architecture model for unmanned aerial vehicles dedicated to electrical tower inspections. In: Optimization, Learning Algorithms and Applications: Second International Conference, OL2A 2022, Póvoa de Varzim, Portugal, 24–25 October 2022, Proceedings, pp. 35–50. Springer, Cham (2023). https://doi.org/10.1007/978-3-031-23236-7_3
8. Radoglou-Grammatikis, P., Sarigiannidis, P., Lagkas, T., Moscholios, I.: A compilation of uav applications for precision agriculture. Comput. Netw. **172**, 107148 (2020)
9. Ramos, G.S., Pinto, M.F., Coelho, F.O., Honório, L.M., Haddad, D.B.: Hybrid methodology based on computational vision and sensor fusion for assisting autonomous uav on offshore messenger cable transfer operation. Robotica **40**(8), 2786–2814 (2022)
10. Melo, A.G., Andrade, F.A.A., Guedes, T.P., Carvalho, G.F., Zachi, A.R.L., Pinto, M.F.: Fuzzy gain-scheduling pid for uav position and altitude controllers. Sensors **22**(6), 2173 (2022)
11. Ma, L., et al.: Model-based identification of larix sibirica ledeb, damage caused by erannis jacobsoni djak based on uav multispectral features and machine learning. Forests **13**(12), 2104 (2022)
12. Aslan, M.F., Durdu, A., Sabanci, K., Ropelewska, E., Ültekin, S.S.G.: A comprehensive survey of the recent studies with uav for precision agriculture in open fields and greenhouses. Appli. Sci. **12**(3), 1047 (2022)
13. Vizzarri, V.: Testing the single and combined effect of kaolin and spinosad against bactrocera oleae and its natural antagonist insects in an organic olive grove. Life **13**(3), 607 (2023)
14. Rossini, L., Bruzzone, O.A., Contarini, M., Bufacchi, L., Speranza, S.: A physiologically based ode model for an old pest: Modeling life cycle and population dynamics of bactrocera oleae (rossi). Agronomy **12**(10), 2298 (2022)
15. de Castro, G.G.R., et al.: Adaptive path planning for fusing rapidly exploring random trees and deep reinforcement learning in an agriculture dynamic environment uavs. Agriculture **13**(2), 354 (2023)
16. Velusamy, P., Rajendran, S., Mahendran, R.K., Naseer, S., Shafiq, M., Choi, J.-G.: Unmanned aerial vehicles (uav) in precision agriculture: applications and challenges. Energies **15**(1), 217 (2021)

17. Skendžić, S., Zovko, M., Živković, I.P., Lešić, V., Lemić, D.: The impact of climate change on agricultural insect pests. Insects **12**(5), 440 (2021)
18. Preti, M., Verheggen, F., Angeli, S.: Insect pest monitoring with camera-equipped traps: strengths and limitations. J. Pest. Sci. **94**(2), 203–217 (2021)
19. Sciarretta, A., Calabrese, P.: Development of automated devices for the monitoring of insect pests. Current Agricul. Research J. **7**(1) (2019)
20. Sun, Y., Lin, Y., Zhao, G., Svanberg, S.: Identification of flying insects in the spatial, spectral, and time domains with focus on mosquito imaging. Sensors **21**(10), 3329 (2021)
21. Li, W., Zheng, T., Yang, Z., Li, M., Sun, C., Yang, X.: Classification and detection of insects from field images using deep learning for smart pest management: A systematic review. Eco. Inform. **66**, 101460 (2021)
22. Sütö, J.: Embedded system-based sticky paper trap with deep learning-based insect-counting algorithm. Electronics **10**(15) (2021)
23. Hadi, M.K., Kassim, M.S.M., Wayayok, A.: Development of an automated multidirectional pest sampling detection system using motorized sticky traps. IEEE Access **9**, 67391–67404 (2021)
24. Rigakis, I.I., Varikou, K.N., Nikolakakis, A.E., Skarakis, Z.D., Tatlas, N.A., Potamitis, I.G.: The e-funnel trap: automatic monitoring of lepidoptera; a case study of tomato leaf miner. Comput. Electronics Agricult. **185**, 106154 (2021)
25. Guo, Q., Wang, C., Xiao, D., Huang, Q.: Automatic monitoring of flying vegetable insect pests using an rgb camera and yolo-sip detector. Precision Agric. **24**(2), 436–457 (2023)
26. Yu, R.: Three-dimensional convolutional neural network model for early detection of pine wilt disease using uav-based hyperspectral images. Remote Sensing **13**(20) (2021)
27. Stumph, B., et al.: Detecting invasive insects with unmanned aerial vehicles. In: 2019 International Conference on Robotics and Automation (ICRA), pp. 648–654 (2019)
28. Zhao, R., Shi, F.: A novel strategy for pest disease detection of brassica chinensis based on uav imagery and deep learning. Int. J. Remote Sens. **43**(19–24), 7083–7103 (2022)
29. Park, Y.-L., Cho, J.R., Lee, G.-S., Seo, B.Y.: Detection of monema flavescens (lepidoptera: Limacodidae) cocoons using small unmanned aircraft system. J. Econ. Entomol. **114**(5), 1927–1933 (2021)
30. Roosjen, P.P.J., Kellenberger, B., Kooistra, L., Green, D.R., Fahrentrapp, K.: Deep learning for automated detection of drosophila suzukii: potential for uav-based monitoring. Pest Manag. Sci. **76**(9), 2994–3002 (2020)
31. Yuan, W.: Accuracy comparison of yolov7 and yolov4 regarding image annotation quality for apple flower bud classification. Agri Engineering **5**(1), 413–424 (2023)
32. Wang, C.-Y., Bochkovskiy, A., Liao, H.-Y.M.: Yolov7: trainable bag-of-freebies sets new state-of-the-art for real-time object detectors. In: Proceedings of the IEEE/CVF Conference on Computer Vision and Pattern Recognition, pp. 7464–7475 (2023)

A Comparison of Fiducial Markers Pose Estimation for UAVs Indoor Precision Landing

Luciano Bonzatto Junior[1,6]($\boxtimes$), Guido S. Berger[2,3], Alexandre O. Júnior[2], João Braun[2,3,4], Marco A. Wehrmeister[6], Milena F. Pinto[5], and José Lima[2,3,4]

[1] Instituto Politécnico de Bragança, Braganca, Portugal
[2] Research Centre in Digitalization and Intelligent Robotics (CeDRI),
Instituto Politécnico de Bragança, Campus de Santa Apolonia, Bragança, Portugal
`{guido.berger,alexandrejunior,jllima}@ipb.pt`
[3] Lab. para a Sustentabilidade e Tecnologia em Regiões de Montanha (SusTEC),
Braganca, Portugal
[4] INESC TEC - INESC Technology and Science, Porto, Portugal
[5] Centro Federal Tecnológica Celso Suckow da Fonseca, Rio de Janeiro, Brazil
`milena.pinto@cefet-rj.br`
[6] Universidade Tecnológica Federal do Paraná, Paraná, Brazil
`lucjun@alunos.utfpr.edu.br`

Abstract. Cooperative robotics is exponentially gaining strength in scientific research, especially regarding the cooperation between ground mobile robots and Unmanned Aerial Vehicles (UAVs), where the remaining challenges are equipollent to its potential uses in different fields, such as agriculture and electrical tower inspections. Due to the complexity involved in the process, precision landing by UAVs on moving robotic platforms for tasks such as battery hot-swapping is a major open research question. This work explores the feasibility and accuracy of different fiducial markers to aid in the precision landing process by a UAV on a mobile robotic platform. For this purpose, a Tello UAV was used to acquire images at different positions, angles, and distances from ArUco, ARTag, and ArUco Board markers to evaluate their detection precision. The analyses demonstrate the highest reliability in the measurements performed through the ArUco marker. Future work will be devoted to using the ArUco marker to perform precision landing on a mobile robotic platform, considering the necessary adjustments to lessen the impact of errors intrinsic to detecting the fiducial marker during the landing procedure.

Keywords: Unmanned Aerial Vehicles · Position Tracking · Fiducial Marker

1 Introduction

Unmanned Aerial Vehicles (UAVs) are robotic platforms widely used in various research fields, meeting demands in the field of agriculture [1], infrastructure

© The Author(s), under exclusive license to Springer Nature Switzerland AG 2024
A. I. Pereira et al. (Eds.): OL2A 2023, CCIS 1981, pp. 18–33, 2024.
https://doi.org/10.1007/978-3-031-53025-8_2

inspection and monitoring [2], goods delivery [3], cooperative robotics [4], and others. The applicability of UAVs, especially multirotors, is due in part to their ability to hover at a specific point, to have high maneuverability, and to present a reasonable payload ratio that can be transported [5].

In addition, the high degree of autonomy and reliability of multirotor UAVs currently allow remote operations to be conducted with minimal operator intervention, leading to a recent paradigm shift in applications involving multiple robots, namely UAVs and UGVs (Unmanned Ground Vehicles) whose purpose is to automate the inspection process both indoors and outdoors [6,7].

Remote operations provide greater autonomy and capabilities in decision-making, given that the nature of the tasks allows the operation of multiple robots for extended periods. However, prolonged operations by multirotor UAVs have still been a problem considering that the average flight time of a multirotor UAV is, on average, 20 to 30 min [5,8].

In this sense, several works have been explored to prolong the flight time of multirotor UAVs. For this, autonomous precision landing systems have been presented as one of the main research topics related to recharging or replacing UAV batteries [6]. In this sense, algorithms based on fiducial markers have been presented in several studies in the literature, whose objective is to provide UAV location estimates for situational awareness and autonomous decision-making [9,10].

However, few works address the evaluation of detection capabilities by fiducial markers when applied to precision landing operations by multirotor UAVs in an indoor environment, making this topic highly intriguing and, above all, desirable in the field of research related to cooperative robotic operations between UAV-UGV in an indoor environment [11].

This work presents a methodological approach to analyzing the performance of a set of fiducial markers when applied to precision landing operations by multirotor UAVs in an indoor environment. In this sense, the fiducial markers, i.e., ArTag, ArUco, and ArUco board, are positioned at different distances and angles, whose main objective is to investigate the ability of a UAV Tello to correctly detect the set of markers used in this experiment, aiming at future operations of precision landing.

The subsequent sections of this paper are structured as follows: Sect. 2 present a comprehensive overview of the background necessary to fully comprehend the proposed work, along with a review of related literature. Section 3 elaborates on the methodology proposed for this study. The findings of the fiducial marker comparison in the proposed scenario are presented in Sect. 4. Finally, in Sect. 5, we offer concluding remarks and outline potential avenues for future research.

2   Background and Related Works

Computer vision-based localization tasks enable vehicles to determine their positions without relying on GNSS. This is particularly crucial for precision missions or operations in GNSS-denied environments. Therefore, computer vision is an alternative sensing method that aids robot localization. As stated in Coelho et al. [12], algorithms using computer vision through a camera can detect artificial features, such as fiducial markers, extract their characteristics, and estimate the position and relative orientation of the robot.

Fiducial markers are reference points easily distinguishable for object tracking, motion capture, augmented reality, and visual localization [10]. A wide range of fiducial marker packages is available, including open-source options. Some open-source packages are also available to the robotics community as ROS packages, such as ARTag, ArUco markers, Artrack, etc. [13]. A good general overview of fiducial markers used for robot pose estimation is provided by Kalaitzakis et al. [10].

The project implementation involves using two types of markers: ArUco and ARTag, along with an ArUco board, a collection of ArUco markers. While these markers share some common characteristics, they rely on precise detection and interpretation packages. For the ARTag markers is used the Ar Track Alvar package [14], which is based on ALVAR [15], a set of SDKs that offer a range of tools for developing augmented reality applications using marker-based 2D imaging, multi-marker, or 3D point cloud-based tracking. As for the ArUco markers, use the ArUco library from OpenCV, which provides a set of functions for marker detection, tracking, and pose estimation.

Several studies have compared the detection of markers at different angles and distances. For instance, Jurado-Rodriguez et al. [16] developed a system to design, detect and track personalized fiducial markers. The study compared the accuracy, response time, and occlusions of six different types of markers, capturing photos of the markers at three different distances using a camera with a resolution of 1280×720 pixels. Their experiment concluded that the custom markers, while experiencing a slight loss in accuracy and detection speed compared to usual markers, were a valid option for commercial and research applications.

Similarly, in [17], a UAV delivery system was developed using an optical flow module for hover and cruise while using visual processing for target detection. This strengthens the use case of fiducial markers in UAV applications where accurate and reliable target detection is crucial.

In Kalaitzakis et al. [10], the authors presented a review and experimental comparison of four types of fiducial markers (ARTag, AprilTag, ArUco, and STag) for their localization performance in autonomous systems and robotics applications. The study investigated location accuracy, robustness under varying lighting conditions and motion blur, and computational performance. The experiments used different tag configurations and employed the Logitech C270 Webcam and Raspberry Pi camera for data acquisition. The fiducial markers were rotated during the experiment, and photographs were captured at various distances. This approach enabled the evaluation of measurement errors and the determination of detection rates for each type of fiducial marker. The results indicated that AprilTag, ArUco, and STag demonstrated high detection rates, AprilTag had the best orientation measures, and STag had the best position measures.

However, not all environments may be suitable for vision-based localization. As indicated in [18], methods like the precise cable-guided landing of tethered drones can prove helpful in degraded environments where GNSS and vision are not feasible. This draws attention to the need for alternative strategies in addition to the fiducial marker-based approaches to achieve precision in landing.

3 Proposed Approach

This work aims to investigate the capacity of the UAV Tello when used to detect different models of fiducial markers, i.e., ARTag, ArUco, and ArUco Board, whose main objective is to evaluate the accuracy of the information provided by the fiducial markers to the UAV, considering its application in scenarios of precision landing operations in an indoor environment. In this sense, the methodology adopted in this work considered evaluating the detection of fiducial markers by the Tello UAV at predetermined distances and angles, aiming to investigate the possible limits of detection by the aircraft.

The fiducial markers type used in this experiment were selected because they are widely referenced in the literature in several applications involving UAVs, are open source, and are already integrable with the ROS platform.

The marker needs to be large enough to be detected on the flight ceiling, and also small enough to prevent occlusion as the UAV approaches at the time of landing. With this, it was defined that the dimensions of the ARTag and ArUco are 8×8 cm, with a white margin of approximately 1 cm, while the ArUco marker measures 8×8 cm with an internal space of approximately 9 mm. As the Tello camera has a field of view of 82.6°, these markers will stop being detected at approximately 5 cm. These markers are shown in Fig. 2.

Tello UAV integrates with the ROS platform through the Tello_driver library, providing the ability to adapt new features to the aircraft and analyze and transmit its image capture data to a local computer. In addition, the system utilizes the ur_rtde library API to establish a connection with UR3, allowing access to robot data such as position, velocity and force, as well as enabling the transmission of control commands to manipulate the robot. With this, a specialized code was created that sends precise position commands to UR3 and saves the images returned by the Tello_driver after the movement is completed, in this way, the UAV and the marker were positioned and the system acquired the images automatically.

As the objective of this work is to evaluate the ability of the UAV Tello to detect the different models of fiducial markers when applied to precision landing operations, and considering that the UAV Tello has only one camera pointing forward, it was adapted in the frontal region of the aircraft a 3×3 cm mirror positioned at 70° perpendicularly to the Tello camera, whose main function is to reflect the image from the front camera to the lower region of the UAV. With this, the objective was to extract results as close as possible to the UAV Tello application scenario, i.e., when used in precision landing operations. Figure 1 illustrates the mirror's adaptation under the UAV Tello's frontal region.

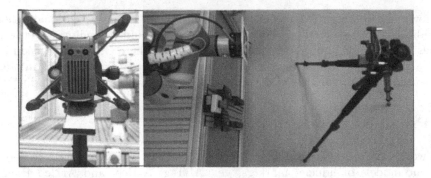

Fig. 1. Mirror's adaptation under the UAV Tello's.

Fig. 2. Fiducial Markers used (ARTag being arranged on the left, ArUco in the center and the ArUco board on the right)

To evaluate the detection accuracy of the markers in different situations, a set of experiments was carried out based on the principles of photogrammetry. In this experiment, several photographs were captured for each fiducial marker, acquiring images in predefined positions and angles. From these images, it was possible to calculate the error associated with each measurement obtained, thus allowing us to determine which fiducial marker has the lowest mean error in all situations. To ensure precision in moving the markers, a robot from Universal Robotics - UR3 was used. In order to acquire the images, a set of procedures was performed, as shown in Fig. 4.

- In a controlled environment, i.e., without interference from external factors, the UAV Tello was positioned with the optical center of its camera pointed toward the front of the UR3 robot. Under the end of the UR3 is positioned the fiducial marker used during the experiments.
- A LASER gauge accurate to approximately 2 mm was used to guide the distance between the Tello UAV camera and the fiducial markers. In addition, the LASER meter was used to orient the fiducial markers to the center of the mirror, keeping them centralized under the image captured by the UAV Tello.
- A tripod was used to guide the UAV Tello in front of the UR3 robot.
- Four ranges of distances were determined to perform the acquisition of UAV Tello images in relation to the fiducial markers. These bands comprise 75, 100, 125, and 150 cm distances.

For image acquisition, a script was developed in which the Tello UAV captures a set of 5 images at the moment each position of the UR3 robot is assumed. In total, nine positions were programmed for the UR3, as shown in Fig. 3. The actions adopted for image acquisition are:

- The Tello UAV remains centered 75 cm away from the fiducial marker.
- Initially, the UR3 robot goes to position one and remains with the fiducial marker at point $(0,0)$, that is, in the center of the Tello UAV camera.
- The UR3 goes to the fist position (P1).
- The fiducial marker is rotated to $30°$, $20°$, $10°$, $0°$, $-20°$, $-30°$, $-10°$ in pitch and yaw, and finally, at $0°$, $-15°$, $-30°$, $-45°$, $-60°$, $-75°$ in roll. As 0 in each of them is the same angle, this gives a total of 18 angles in each position. As five photos were taken at each angle, in total, a set of 90 images are acquired by the UAV in position one.
- Then, the UR3 goes to position two, and the procedures adopted in position one are repeated until the nine pre-established positions are completed. Upon completing the nine positions (see Table 1), the UAV Tello is moved to the following distance on the z-axis, 1 m away from the fiducial marker.

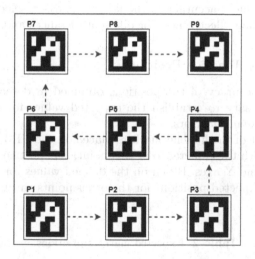

Fig. 3. Positions assumed by the UR3 robot.

Table 1. Set of predetermined positions for UR3 robot.

	P1	P2	P3	P4	P5	P6	P7	P8	P9
X	0.360	0.360	0.360	0.360	0.360	0.360	0.360	0.360	0.360
Y	−0.150	0.070	0.290	0.290	0.070	−0.150	−0.150	0.070	0.290
Z	0.080	0.080	0.080	0.080	0.080	0.080	0.080	0.080	0.080

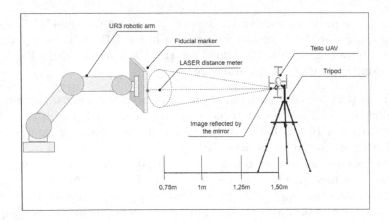

Fig. 4. Procedures adopted for data acquisition.

4   Results and Discussion

This section discusses the results obtained through the methodology adopted to classify the measurement accuracy of the fiducial markers selected for this case study, identifying their effectiveness for different distances and angles.

4.1   Performance Towards Position

To determine the accuracy of the positions obtained in detecting the fiducial markers, it is necessary to establish the expected values for each position to calculate the measurement errors.

The center point of the fiducial markers placed on the UR3 is assumed to be precisely aligned with the camera, so at this point, is expect to get the values of $(0,0)$ m for the X and Y axes. Based on the defined values for the UR3 motion (see Table 1), the expected positions for the other points can be determined, as shown in Table 2.

Table 2. Expected markers positions.

	A	B	C	D	E	F	G	H	I
X	−0.220	−0.220	−0.220	0.000	0.000	0.000	0.220	0.220	0.220
Y	−0.160	0.000	0.160	−0.160	0.000	0.160	−0.160	0.000	0.160

Figure 5 shows the values obtained by detecting the fiducial markers (blue dots) and the expected position (i.e., red dots). It can be seen that the measurements follow an error pattern. The measures have a downward and leftward shift in all positions, showing an intrinsic error in the system.

As mentioned in Sect. 3, the mirror has an angle of 70° concerning the y-axis of the camera. With this, the image suffers a distortion, causing an intrinsic error in the measurements of this coordinate that grows along the distance between the marker and the camera, as a consequence also of the decrease of accuracy in detecting the fiducial markers at long distances. It is possible to see this error more clearly in Fig. 7, Fig. 6 and Fig. 8, which show that the error in the measurements at 0.75 m is closer to zero than the of 1.5m. This error is less prominent on the X-axis, as the mirror angle on this axis is close to 0°. This offset can be calculated based on these angles and must be considered during the UAV precision landing.

Note that the ArUco and the ARTag suffer little interferences in the X and Y axis measurements about the position and angle of the marker. In contrast, with the ArUco board, a significant variation in the error with the yaw rotations is presented.

On the z-axis, it is possible to verify sudden changes in the error in the position changes in all graphs, showing a significant interference in the measurement of the three markers. Besides, both the ArUco and the ArUco board suffer more interference from the angle of the marker.

4.2 Performance Towards Orientation

In the case of orientation measurements, the expected values align with the predefined ones for the UR3 rotation, as presented in Sect. 3 and Table 3. Subsequently, the error is calculated for each measurement, presented in Fig. 9, Fig. 10, and Fig. 11. Notably, the results obtained from the three markers exhibit striking similarities, with most measurements yielding errors between −10 and 10°.

However, when considering yaw and pitch measurements taken from a distance of 1m, it becomes apparent markers exhibit errors surpassing 10° on multiple occasions. Hence, to determine more accurate outcomes, it is crucial to compare the standard deviation and average error (Table 4, Table 5, and Table 6).

None of the markers showed a significantly high average error, with the largest recorded error being 5.704°. However, it is important to mention that the standard deviation revealed some problematic values.

We see that in the pitch measurements of the ArUco board at the four distances, the standard deviation is greater than 20°, showing that the measurements were too dispersed in relation to the average, showing a problem in the detection of the marker. In ArUco and ARTag we see a less disperse behavior, with a maximum of 9.701 and 8.797 respectively.

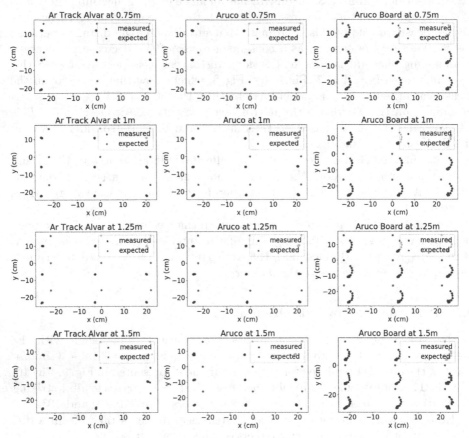

Fig. 5. Positions measured with the fiducial markers (ARTag being arranged on the left, ArUco measurements in the center and the ArUco board on the right) at different distances (0.75, 1, 1.25, and 1.5 m).

Table 3. Expected Marker Angles.

Pitch	Yaw	Roll	Pitch	Yaw	Roll	Pitch	Yaw	Roll
$-30°$	$0°$	$0°$	$0°$	$0°$	$0°$	$0°$	$-30°$	$0°$
$-20°$	$0°$	$0°$	$0°$	$0°$	$-15°$	$0°$	$-20°$	$0°$
$-10°$	$0°$	$0°$	$0°$	$0°$	$-30°$	$0°$	$-10°$	$0°$
$10°$	$0°$	$0°$	$0°$	$0°$	$-45°$	$0°$	$10°$	$0°$
$20°$	$0°$	$0°$	$0°$	$0°$	$-60°$	$0°$	$20°$	$0°$
$30°$	$0°$	$0°$	$0°$	$0°$	$-75°$	$0°$	$30°$	$0°$

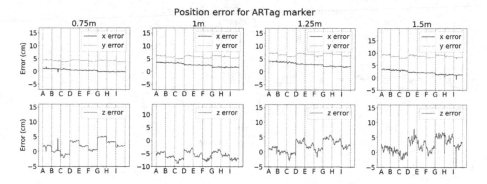

Fig. 6. ARTag position measurement error.

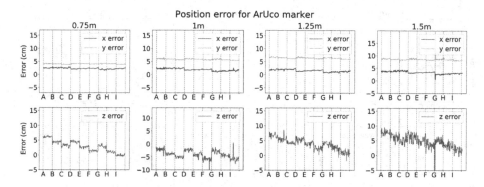

Fig. 7. ArUco position measurement error.

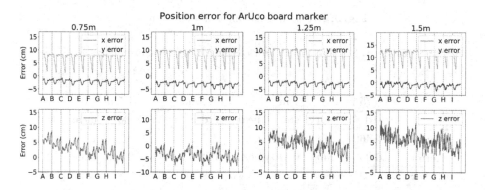

Fig. 8. ArUco board position measurement error.

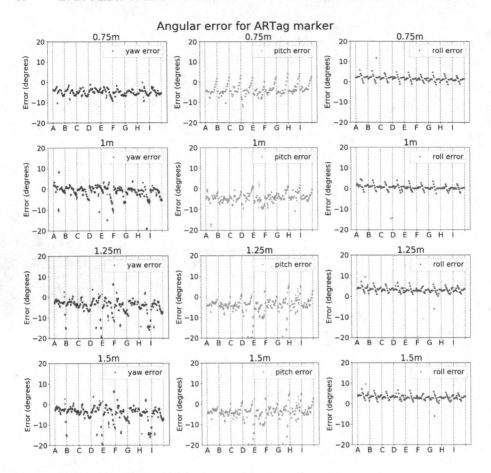

Fig. 9. ARTag angular measurement error.

Table 4. Std and mean error of the ARTag measurements.

	ARTag							
	0.75 m		1 m		1.25 m		1.5 m	
	std	mean	std	mean	std	mean	std	mean
x_error	0.460	0.376	0.692	2.497	0.719	2.858	0.794	2.089
y_error	0.263	4.140	0.416	5.684	0.446	6.638	0.469	8.599
z_error	1.799	1.832	1.345	−5.848	1.863	1.868	2.281	2.274
yaw_error	1.506	−4.852	3.158	−1.207	5.269	−4.857	8.797	−5.704
pitch_error	3.074	−3.782	3.586	−4.751	5.334	−4.645	6.761	−5.535
roll_error	1.385	1.646	1.402	0.424	1.262	3.168	1.449	1.444

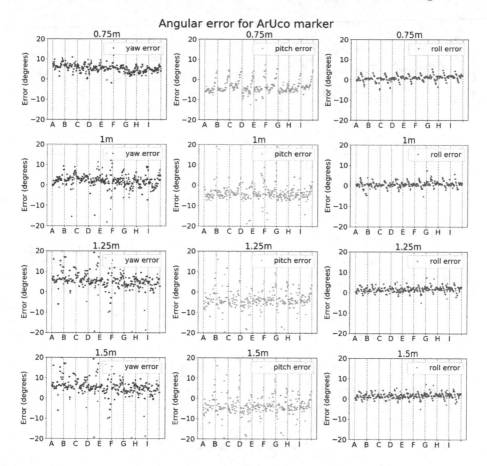

Fig. 10. ArUco angular measurement error.

Table 5. Std and mean error of the ArUco measurements.

	ArUco							
	0.75 m		1 m		1.25 m		1.5 m	
	std	mean	std	mean	std	mean	std	mean
x_error	0.247	2.201	0.493	1.821	0.408	1.519	0.403	3.309
y_error	0.127	3.997	0.317	5.778	0.221	6.349	0.252	8.474
z_error	1.867	2.899	2.266	−4.052	1.488	3.869	1.851	4.843
yaw_error	1.798	5.360	7.720	1.825	4.567	4.858	6.401	4.506
pitch_error	3.871	−3.139	9.701	−3.711	4.399	−3.193	5.903	−2.205
roll_error	1.459	0.949	1.689	0.745	1.450	1.605	1.375	1.502

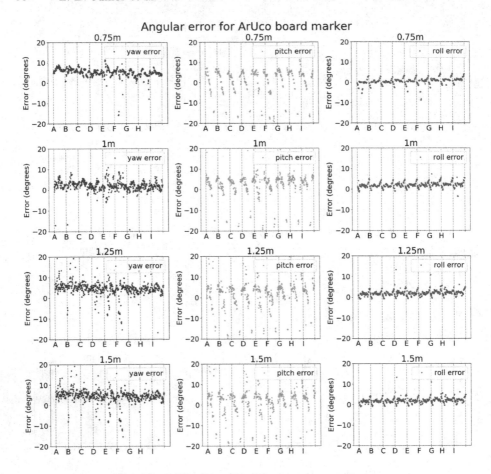

Fig. 11. ArUco Board angular measurement error.

Table 6. Std and mean error of the ArUco board measurements.

	ArUco board							
	0.7 5m		1 m		1.25 m		1.5 m	
	std	mean	std	mean	std	mean	std	mean
x_error	0.687	−2.091	0.755	−3.101	0.713	−2.845	0.715	−1.056
y_error	2.020	6.964	2.037	8.383	2.076	9.177	2.072	11.234
z_error	2.239	**2.874**	2.459	−3.553	1.892	4.353	**2.234**	5.647
yaw_error	2.447	5.154	9.840	1.901	2.836	4.003	5.862	3.597
pitch_error	25.102	3.235	23.782	**3.849**	25.055	**3.322**	25.375	5.594
roll_error	1.683	0.546	1.588	1.988	1.228	2.005	1.280	1.181

4.3   Overall Performance of the Fiducial Markers

Upon examining the error tables (Table 4, Table 5, Table 6), the best and worst values for each marker type are indicated in green and red, respectively. Based on these results, it can be concluded that the ArUco board marker consistently shows the weakest results among the three markers. It also shows that the ArTag and ArUco markers have similar results, as they both have many of the best values.

A closer look at the values reveals that the ArTag and ArUco markers have similar standard deviation and mean error values. However, ArUco has a slightly lower mean error than ArTag and also has a more consistent result by having lower standard deviations.

Comparing the ArUco board with the ArUco, where the detection method is the same, shows that using more than one marker made the results worse, especially on rotation. This worsening is associated with the size of the markers. In the ArUco board, the internal markers are about 3.5 cm, half that used in the regular ArUco, which makes the measurements much worse the further away the camera is from the marker. This fact is also demonstrated in Kalaitzakis et al.

5   Conclusions and Future Work

This research focused on investigating different fiducial markers suitable for a reliable UAV-to-UGV landing, considering the requirements of marker size and flight ceiling restrictions. Besides, it employed computer vision techniques to extract and interpret marker features. For this step, it was considered different positions and rotations of both the UAV and UGV.

Overall, it can be concluded that the ArUco board marker exhibited the weakest performance in both position and rotation measurements. ArUco and markers displayed similar levels of accuracy, with the ArUco marker showing better accuracy and consistency. Within the tested range of 0.75 m to 1.5 m, the markers achieved a positional accuracy, in the worst case, of approximately 3 cm on the x-axis, 5 cm on the z-axis, and 8 cm on the y-axis. Note that these results can be further improved by accounting for the error associated with the system. By implementing appropriate error treatment techniques, particularly for the y-axis measurements, the error in the vertical direction is expected to be reduced.

Considering the requirements of dimensions and the indoor flight ceiling restrictions, this work demonstrated the feasibility and effectiveness of employing these techniques, showcasing their potential to enhance the landing process between these heterogeneous vehicles.

Further research and refinement in marker design, placement, and error correction techniques can significantly enhance the overall performance and expand the practical applications of these markers in diverse indoor landing scenarios. Considering challenges such as occlusion, position error, and illumination, future investigations will be performed into optimal marker placement strategies, taking into account the layout of indoor environments and potential occlusion points, which would further improve the reliability and accuracy of marker-based localization. Developing advanced error correction techniques, such as machine learning algorithms and computer vision approaches, can effectively mitigate the adverse effects of position errors and illumination changes, ensuring the consistent and precise localization of autonomous systems. The outcomes of this research work open up several possibilities for future improvements, ultimately contributing to the advancement and widespread adoption of autonomous systems in various domains.

Acknowledgment. The authors are grateful to the Foundation for Science and Technology (FCT, Portugal) for financial support through national funds FCTMCTES (PIDDAC) to CeDRI (UIDB/05757/2020 and UIDP/05757/2020), SusTEC (LA/P/ 0007/2021), Oleachain "Skills for sustainability and innovation in the value chain of traditional olive groves in the Northern Interior of Portugal" (Norte06-3559-FSE-000188), Centro Federal de Educação Tecnológica Celso Suckow da Fonseca (CEFETRJ), Fundação de Amparo à Pesquisa do Estado do Rio de Janeiro (FAPERJ), and Coordenação de Aperfeiçoamento de Pessoal de Nível Superior (CAPES). The project that gave rise to these results received the support of a fellowship from "la Caixa" Foundation (ID 100010434). The fellowship code is LCF/BQ/DI20/11780028.

References

1. de Castro, G.G.R., et al.: Adaptive path planning for fusing rapidly exploring random trees and deep reinforcement learning in an agriculture dynamic environment uavs. Agriculture **13**(2), 354 (2023)
2. Sharma, R., Arya, R.: Uav based long range environment monitoring system with industry 5.0 perspectives for smart city infrastructure. Comput. Indus. Eng. **168**, 108066 (2022)
3. Benarbia, T., Kyamakya, K.: A literature review of drone-based package delivery logistics systems and their implementation feasibility. Sustainability **14**(1) (2022)
4. Berger, G.S., et al.: Sensor architecture model for unmanned aerial vehicles dedicated to electrical tower inspections. In: Optimization, Learning Algorithms and Applications: Second International Conference, OL2A 2022, Póvoa de Varzim, Portugal, 24–25 October 2022, Proceedings, pp. 35–50. Springer (2023). https://doi.org/10.1007/978-3-031-23236-7_3
5. Mohsan, S.A.H., Khan, M.A., Noor, F., Ullah, I., Alsharif, M.H.: Towards the unmanned aerial vehicles (uavs): a comprehensive review. Drones **6**(6) (2022)
6. Grlj, C.G., Krznar, N., Pranjić, M.: A decade of uav docking stations: a brief overview of mobile and fixed landing platforms. Drones **6**(1) (2022)
7. Niu, G., Yang, Q., Gao, Y., Pun, M.-O.: Vision-based autonomous landing for unmanned aerial and ground vehicles cooperative systems. IEEE Robot. Autom. Lett. **7**(3), 6234–6241 (2022)
8. Liu, Q., et al.: Joint power and time allocation in energy harvesting of uav operating system. Comput. Commun. **150**, 811–817 (2020)
9. Kalaitzakis, M., Carroll, S., Ambrosi, A., Whitehead, C., Vitzilaios, N.: Experimental comparison of fiducial markers for pose estimation. In 2020 International Conference on Unmanned Aircraft Systems (ICUAS), pp. 781–789 (2020)

10. Kalaitzakis, M., Cain, B., Carroll, S., Ambrosi, A., Whitehead, C., Vitzilaios, N.: Fiducial markers for pose estimation: overview, applications and experimental comparison of the artag, apriltag, aruco and stag markers. J. Intell. Robot. Syst. **101**, 1–26 (2021)
11. Bautista, N., Gutierrez, H., Inness, J., Rakoczy, J.: Precision landing of a quadcopter drone by smartphone video guidance sensor in a gps-denied environment. Sensors **23**(4) (2023)
12. Coelho, F.O., Carvalho, J.P., Pinto, M.F., Marcato, A.L.: Ekf and computer vision for mobile robot localization. In: 2018 13th APCA International Conference on Automatic Control and Soft Computing (CONTROLO), pp. 148–153. IEEE (2018)
13. Quigley, M., et al. Ros: an open-source robot operating system. In: ICRA Workshop on Open Source Software, Kobe, Japan, vol. 3, p. 5 (2009)
14. VTT Technical Research Centre of Finland. Alvar aalto museum (Accessed 2023)
15. Alvar: Artoolkit for java. http://virtual.vtt.fi/virtual/proj2/multimedia/alvar/index.html. (Accessed 5 June 2023)
16. Jurado-Rodríguez, D., Muñoz-Salinas, R., Garrido-Jurado, S., Medina-Carnicer, R.: Design, detection, and tracking of customized fiducial markers. IEEE Access **9**, 140066–140078 (2021)
17. Shi, Y.-L., Zou, S.-Z.: A design of an indoor delivery uav. J. Phys: Conf. Ser. **2457**, 012036 (2023)
18. Lima, R.R., Rocamora, B.M., Pereira, G.A.S.: Continuous vector fields for precise cable-guided landing of tethered uavs. IEEE Robot. Autom. Lett. (2023)

Effect of Weather Conditions and Transactions Records on Work Accidents in the Retail Sector – A Case Study

Lucas D. Borges[1,2](✉) , Inês Sena[1,2] , Vitor Marcelino[1,2] ,
Felipe G. Silva[1,2] , Florbela P. Fernandes[1,2] , Maria F. Pacheco[1,2] ,
Clara B. Vaz[1,2] , José Lima[1,2] , and Ana I. Pereira[1,2]

[1] Research Center in Digitalization and Intelligent Robotics (CeDRI),
Instituto Politécnico de Bragança, Campus de Santa Apolónia,
5300-253 Braganca, Portugal
[2] Laboratório Associado para a Sustentabilidade e Tecnologia em Regiões de
Montanha (SusTEC), Instituto Politécnico de Bragança, Campus de Santa Apolónia,
5300-253 Braganca, Portugal
{lucasborges,ines.sena,vitor.marcelino,gimenez,fflor,pacheco,clvaz,
jllima,apereira}@ipb.pt

Abstract. Weather change plays an important role in work-related accidents, it impairs people's cognitive abilities, increasing the risk of injuries and accidents. Furthermore, weather conditions can cause an increase or decrease in daily sales in the retail sector by influencing individual behaviors. The increase in transactions, in turn, leads employees to fatigue and overload, which can also increase the risk of injuries and accidents. This work aims to conduct a case study in a company in the retail sector to verify whether the transactions records in stores and the weather conditions of each district in mainland Portugal impact the occurrence of work accidents, as well as to perform predictive analysis of the occurrence or non-occurrence of work accidents in each district using these data and comparing different machine learning techniques. The correlation analysis of the occurrence or non-occurrence of work accidents with weather conditions and some transactions pointed out the nonexistence of correlation between the data. Evaluating the precision and the confusion matrix of the predictive models, the study indicates a predisposition of the models to predict the non-occurrence of work accidents to the detriment of the ability to predict the occurrence of work accidents.

Keywords: Predictive Analysis · Correlation Analysis · Weather Conditions · Transactions Records

1 Introduction

The retail sector while appearing to pose little risk of injury or death, especially when compared to jobs in agriculture and construction, is involved in a wide

A. I. Pereira et al. (Eds.): OL2A 2023, CCIS 1981, pp. 34–48, 2024.
https://doi.org/10.1007/978-3-031-53025-8_3

range of demanding work activities and is exposed to various hazards [4, 20]. In 2020, this sector in Portugal was considered the second economic activity with the highest number of accidents at work [23].

However, there is a gap in work safety, mainly in the retail sector, regarding the occurrence and the best predictors for predicting work accidents. Nevertheless, several underlying studies on the analysis of work accidents already indicate some factors that may be related to work accidents in this sector. These factors include mental fatigue [2], job turnover [8], unsafe working conditions [7], sleep [21], and human errors [3], among others.

Some studies reveal that weather change has significant implications for people's everyday lives [1], directly impacting the mental and physical well-being of individuals [6]. In recent years, there has been an increase in global temperatures [18], which can impair cognitive skills and the ability to perform mental tasks, leading to a greater likelihood of injuries and accidents in the workplace [6, 11].

Parnaudeau et al. [18] state that the weather can impact companies' sales in several different economic sectors because the weather influences people's financial decision-making. Other studies also reveal the weather impacts consumption and the number of daily sales in the retail sector [5, 25], as well as the ease of physically getting to stores, the desire to carry out other activities, and the underlying demand for particular products [26].

However, this impact also has consequences for the employee since several factors can affect his psychology in high sales volumes, such as anxiety and stress, work overload, and interpersonal relationships, among others [22]. In addition, some studies support that employees in this sector feels stress levels [20]. The work stress will lead to low job satisfaction, which is not favorable for the organization since job satisfaction is a condition that companies should strive for, as it affects organizational output such as turnover intention, absenteeism, and, in turn, productivity, and commitment [22]. Moreover, some researchers argue that satisfied employees are more often safe, and employee attitudes and work-related stress are significantly related to accidents, health, and safety at work [13].

The main objective of this work is to study whether the weather conditions and the company's transaction records are related to the occurrence of work accidents in the retail sector. This case study is based on information from the history of accidents and transaction diary records between the years 2019 and 2022, provided by a Portuguese company in the retail sector, and the weather conditions collected through an Application Programming Interface (API). To this end, it is intended to apply correlation and predictive analysis in different datasets created with the information mentioned to achieve the listed objective.

Since the company consists of several stores spread throughout the country, and the weather varies between geographic areas [25], the results obtained are presented by each district of mainland Portugal.

The paper proceeds as follows. Section 2 describes the dataset and the analysis methods applied. Section 3 presents the results obtained by the district for each dataset. Finally, Sect. 4 summarizes the study's findings and suggests future research directions.

2   Methodology

The main objective of this study is to evaluate the impact of weather conditions and transaction records on retail accidents through correlation and prediction analyses. As the company under study has several stores distributed in different regions, it is intended to analyze the results by districts of mainland Portugal.

Thus, this section will present the datasets used and the analysis methods applied.

2.1   Dataset Characterization

The company under study provided information on the latitude, longitude, accident history, and transaction records between 1 January 2019 and 31 December 2022 of 298 Portuguese stores. The recording of accidents and transactions is standardized for all stores of this company, which validates the store grouping in this analysis.

Weather data was obtained from an external source, accessed through an application programming interface (API). The API used is the Open-Meteo API, which provides access to weather data from around the world, allowing users to retrieve historical weather data for a specific location and period [17]. For data collection, requests were made to the API using the latitude and longitude of the stores, the initial and final date and the weather variables to be studied as parameters. In this way, it was possible to associate each variable value set to the correct stores. Thus, a set of data was obtained including the store, district, date, temperature (°C), relative humidity (%), and precipitation (mm) values.

After obtaining the three main databases to be used, different datasets were developed to study the impact of weather conditions and transaction records on occupational accidents of a Portuguese retail company.

Weather Conditions and Accident History. The association of these two datasets was carried out using the date of the accident and the geographic coordinates. The presence or absence of accidents in each district for each day was identified while the average value of each weather variable (temperature, precipitation, and relative humidity) was recorded. These results in a dataset comprising three input variables (temperature, precipitation, and relative humidity) and one output variable (0 for non-occurrence of work accidents and 1 for occurrence).

Transactions Records and Accident History. For this dataset, the stores' transaction records in the same district were added daily, and the occurrence or non-occurrence of work accidents was recorded for each. The result is a dataset with an input variable (total number of transactions) and the same binary output variable as the previous dataset.

Weather Conditions, Transactions Records, and Accident History.
Since the company's transaction record is found daily, its combination with
weather conditions was performed similarly to the previously obtained datasets.
The weather conditions were used as input variables and the values were averaged per day and district; the sum of the transactions registered per day for
each district along with the occurrence or non-occurrence of work accidents was
taken into account. A dataset was obtained with the same output variable as the
previous ones but with four input variables (temperature, precipitation, relative
humidity, and the total number of transactions).

2.2   Methods

To assess whether weather conditions and the recording of transactions impact
the occurrence of work accidents, two different approaches were used, correlation
analysis and predictive analysis for each of the datasets formed.

Correlation Analysis – is a statistical technique that allows one to observe
whether there is any relationship between two variables, by calculating different
coefficients, depending on the data type [24].

Pearson's correlation coefficient is widely used to calculate the linear relationship between two variables and ranges from -1 (perfect negative correlation) to
$+1$ (perfect positive correlation) [16]. Spearman and Kendall coefficients are non-
parametric methods for measuring the relationship between two ordinal variables
that may not be linear [12]. The calculation of these two correlation coefficients is
based on ranks or orders of variable values, however, it has the same correlation
magnitude range and scale as the Pearson coefficient [12].

None of the above methods can be used when working with dichotomous
data [12,16]. To overcome this situation, the Point-Biserial correlation coefficient
can be used, which can measure the relationship between a continuous variable
and a dichotomous (binary) variable, the magnitude scale varies on the same
scale as the other correlation coefficients [9].

Table 1 classifies the relationship between the variables according to the considered magnitude scale.

Table 1. Magnitude values of coefficient and their characteristics. Adapted from [15].

Absolute magnitude of the coefficient	Interpretation
0–0.30	no correlation
0.31–0.50	week correlation
0.51–0.70	moderate correlation
0.71–0.90	strong correlation
> 0.90	very strong correlation

Predictive Analysis – uses statistical and Machine Learning techniques to predict future events based on historical data. In this case, it is intended to verify whether it is possible through weather conditions and the transaction records of a company to predict the occurrence of work accidents.

In general, classification algorithms create models capable of analyzing data characteristics and detecting patterns and relationships between features and classes. During training, the models analyze previous data and create rules to classify new data based on the recognized patterns. In this case, to train the models' ability to predict classes 0 (non-occurrence of work accidents) and 1 (occurrence of work accidents) [10], the following algorithms were applied and compared in one iteration for each district and dataset using Python language with Scikit-Learn library [19]:

- **Multilayer Perceptron (MLP):** is an approach to artificial neural networks, which are inspired by the functioning of the human brain. Therefore, it consists of several layers of interconnected artificial neurons capable of learning complex patterns in input data to perform classification. During training, synaptic weights are adjusted to optimize the model's performance [10]. This model was implemented the default settings.
- **Decision Tree (DT):** creates a decision tree to classify the data. It recursively divides the data based on specific features, creating branches and leaves representing different classes to optimize the classification process [10]. This model was implemented with the default settings.
- **Gradient Boosting (GB):** combines multiple weak learning models and trains the models sequentially, with each one correcting the errors made by the previous model. The final result is a weighted combination of the individual models capable of performing accurate classifications and improving overall performance [10]. This model was implemented with 100 estimators.
- **Logistic Regression (LR):** uses the logistic function to model the relationship between the independent variables and the probability of occurrence for each class. It estimates the coefficients of the predictors using optimization techniques, enabling the prediction of classification probabilities [10]. This model was implemented with the default settings.
- **Random Forest (RF):** constructs multiple independent decision trees and combines their predictions to perform classification. Each tree is trained on a random sample of the training data and uses a random selection of features at each split. The final classification is determined by a majority vote of the individual trees [10]. This model was implemented with 100 estimators.
- **Support Vector Machines (SVM):** consists of machine learning algorithms that seek to find the best hyperplane of separation between the data classes. They map the data into a high-dimensional space and identify a hyperplane that maximizes the margin between the classes. Support vectors are the data points closest to the hyperplane and are essential for determining the decision boundary [10]. This model was implemented with the default settings.

It used a confusion matrix for each algorithm to evaluate the classification models' performance, which obtained good *Precision* [14], which indicates:

- **True Negatives** (TN): non-accident samples that the model correctly identified as non-accident.
- **False Negatives** (FN): accident samples that the model identified as non-accident.
- **True Positives** (TP): accident samples that the model correctly identified as accident.
- **False Positives** (FP): non-accident samples that the model identified as accident.

The *Precision*, defined in Eq. 1, is calculated to evaluate the total correct predictions for a specific class [14]:

$$Precision = \frac{TP}{TP + FP} \tag{1}$$

3   Results

The obtained results are presented and analyzed, by district, for each dataset used to achieve the listed objective, studying the impact of weather conditions and transaction records on the work accidents of a company in the retail sector in Portugal. For this purpose, Fig. 1 shows the districts of mainland Portugal that will be analyzed.

Fig. 1. Mainland Portugal Districts.

To apply the six classification algorithms mentioned in Sect. 2, each dataset must be divided into a training set (80% of the data) and a test set (20% of the data).

3.1   Weather Conditions and Accident History

After preparing the dataset, it was observed that the weather variables were continuous while the occurrence of work accidents was dichotomous. For this reason, the Point-Biserial correlation coefficient was applied to study the relationship between the occurrence of work accidents and each weather variable. The results are shown in Fig. 2.

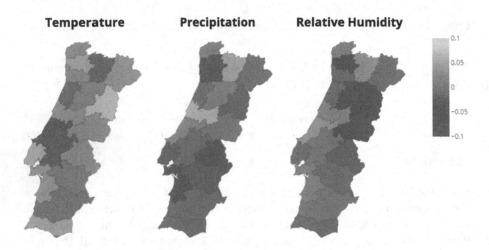

Fig. 2. Point-Biserial correlation between weather conditions and occurrence of work accidents.

Observing Fig. 2, it can be noted that the relationship between the three input variables with accidents is weak, showing coefficient values close to zero. The correlation with the variable temperature is mostly positive, so they follow a directly proportional relationship, when the temperature increases the number of accidents also increases. On the other hand, precipitation and relative humidity mostly show districts with negative correlations, indicating that the number of accidents increases when the value of these variables decreases.

Figure 3 presents the precision values achieved for each district by each algorithm.

Precision values range from approximately 0.55 to 0.99. The Logistic Regression, Multilayer Perceptron, Random Forest, and Support Vector Machines presented around 0.60 as a minimum *Precision* value. This indicates that the performance of the models in predicting accidents varies between districts and independent variables. Districts such as Beja, Bragança, Guarda, Portalegre, and Vila Real have relatively high *Precision* values, close to or greater than 0.98. This suggests that the model accurately predicts accidents in these districts based on the independent variables provided. On the other hand, districts such as Lisbon,

Multilayer Perceptron   **Decision Tree Classifier**   **Gradient Boosting Classifier**

Logistic Regression   **Random Forest Classifier**   **Support Vector Machines**

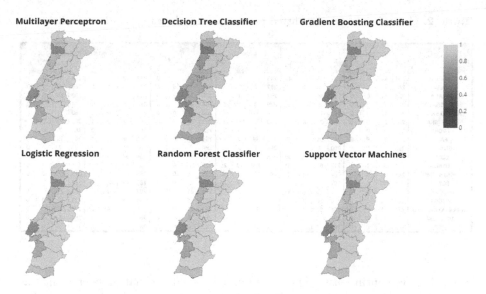

Fig. 3. Precision of fitted prediction models using weather conditions.

Porto, and Setúbal have lower *Precision* values, ranging from 0.55 to 0.78. This highlights that the fitted models have greater difficulty predicting accidents in these districts than the others.

Most districts' *Precision* values for different independent variables are relatively close. This suggests the model's predictive performance is consistent across different weather variables in these districts.

Confusion matrices were calculated for each district and model to show the quality of accident prediction, presented in Table 2.

Through the analysis of the confusion matrices, it can be seen that for all districts and adjusted models, the false positive rate is higher than the true positive rate (correct prediction of the occurrence of work accidents). The true negative rate (correct prediction of the non-occurrence of work accidents) is higher than the false negative rate. This reveals that the model predicts more efficiently the events that were not accidents, which means that despite having obtained high *Precision* values, these models are not efficient in predicting the occurrence of work accidents, which can be justified due to the imbalance of existing accident records compared to non-accident related records. Despite having lower accuracy, Lisboa, Porto and Setúbal districts had a greater number of true positives, indicating greater aptitude than the other districts in predicting the occurrence of accidents.

3.2 Transactions Records and Accident History

Once again it was observed differences between the data type to be compared. While the occurrence of work accidents is a dichotomous variable, transaction

Table 2. Confusion matrices of fitted prediction models using weather conditions.

District	Multilayer Perceptron				Decision Tree Classifier				Gradient Boosting Classifier				Logistic Regression				Random Forest Classifier				Support Vector Machines			
	TN	FN	TP	FP	TN	FN	TP	FP	TN	FN	TP	FP	TN	FN	TP	FP	TN	FN	TP	FP	TN	FN	TP	FP
AVEIRO	248	44	0	0	201	39	5	47	243	43	1	5	248	44	0	0	242	43	1	6	248	44	0	0
BEJA	288	4	0	0	288	4	0	0	287	4	0	1	288	4	0	0	288	4	0	0	288	4	0	0
BRAGA	258	34	0	0	236	34	0	22	257	34	0	1	258	34	0	0	254	34	0	4	258	34	0	0
BRAGANÇA	284	8	0	0	281	8	0	3	279	8	0	5	284	8	0	0	284	8	0	0	284	8	0	0
CASTELO BRANCO	280	12	0	0	267	12	0	13	274	12	0	6	280	12	0	0	278	12	0	2	280	12	0	0
COIMBRA	263	29	0	0	235	25	4	28	260	28	1	3	263	29	0	0	262	28	1	1	263	29	0	0
ÉVORA	285	7	0	0	284	7	0	1	283	7	0	2	285	7	0	0	285	7	0	0	285	7	0	0
FARO	253	39	0	0	215	36	3	38	253	39	0	0	253	39	0	0	249	38	1	4	253	39	0	0
GUARDA	290	2	0	0	290	2	0	0	290	2	0	0	290	2	0	0	290	2	0	0	290	2	0	0
LEIRIA	258	34	0	0	219	32	2	39	255	33	1	3	258	34	0	0	254	34	0	4	258	34	0	0
LISBOA	174	115	2	1	114	61	56	61	150	104	13	25	175	117	0	0	133	75	42	42	175	117	0	0
PORTALEGRE	285	7	0	0	284	6	1	1	285	7	0	0	285	7	0	0	285	7	0	0	285	7	0	0
PORTO	184	108	0	0	107	53	55	77	158	90	18	26	184	108	0	0	135	67	41	49	184	108	0	0
SANTARÉM	271	21	0	0	234	21	0	37	268	21	0	3	271	21	0	0	267	21	0	4	271	21	0	0
SETÚBAL	227	65	0	0	173	50	15	54	220	64	1	7	227	65	0	0	209	59	6	18	227	65	0	0
VIANA DO CASTELO	271	21	0	0	264	18	3	7	270	20	1	1	271	21	0	0	269	21	0	2	271	21	0	0
VILA REAL	286	6	0	0	277	6	0	9	283	6	0	3	286	6	0	0	286	6	0	0	286	6	0	0
VISEU	282	10	0	0	269	10	0	13	281	10	0	1	282	10	0	0	282	10	0	0	282	10	0	0

records behave continuously. Thus, the Point-Biserial correlation coefficient was also applied in this case. The results obtained are shown in Fig. 4.

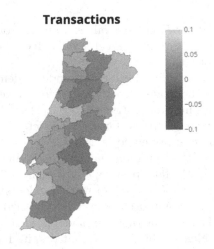

Transactions

Fig. 4. Point-Biserial correlation between transaction records and occurrence of work accidents.

Examining Fig. 4, it can be seen that except in the district of Portalegre, with a coefficient equal to -0.0021, all districts present a positive correlation between transactions and the occurrence of work accidents ranging between 0.0037 and 0.072. These coefficient values indicate non-consistently correlations.

Finally, we proceeded to calculate the prediction of the occurrence of work accidents with the total number of transactions. Figure 5 presents the achieved precision values for each tested algorithm.

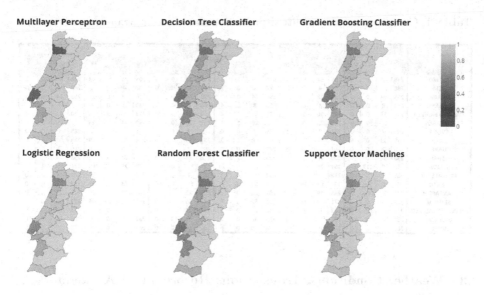

Fig. 5. Precision of fitted prediction models using transaction records.

Based on Fig. 5, it can be seen that except for the MLP algorithm, which presented a minimum value of 0.37, the *Precision* varies from approximately 0.50 to 0.99. It is noted, in this case, the same pattern found in the analysis that used weather conditions, where the districts Beja, Bragança, Guarda, Portalegre, and Vila Real, this time in the company of the district Évora, present the highest *Precision* values, ranging between 0.95 and 0.98. In the same way, the districts where the models presented the worst performance were Lisbon, Porto, and Setúbal, with their *Precision* ranging from 0.37 to 0.78. Again, the adjusted models did not present significant differences in *Precision* values.

Table 3 shows the confusion matrices achieved by each model for each district.

The confusion matrices of the transaction-based models also show an imbalance in predicting the occurrence and non-occurrence of work accidents. The true positive rates (correct prediction of the occurrence of work accidents) are lower than the false positive rates. In comparison, the true negative rates (correct prediction of the non-occurrence of work accidents) are higher than the false negative rates. Again the imbalance between the volume of information on accident occurrence and the non-occurrence of work accidents may cause this effect on the metric, although the districts of Lisbon, Porto and Setúbal again present a greater number of true positives.

Table 3. Confusion matrices of fitted prediction models using transaction records.

District	Multilayer Perceptron				Decision Tree Classifier				Gradient Boosting Classifier				Logistic Regression				Random Forest Classifier				Support Vector Machines			
	TN	FN	TP	FP	TN	FN	TP	FP	TN	FN	TP	FP	TN	FN	TP	FP	TN	FN	TP	FP	TN	FN	TP	FP
AVEIRO	248	44	0	0	205	34	10	43	241	43	1	7	248	44	0	0	205	33	11	43	248	44	0	0
BEJA	288	4	0	0	287	4	0	1	287	4	0	1	288	4	0	0	287	4	0	1	288	4	0	0
BRAGA	258	34	0	0	236	28	6	22	256	34	0	2	258	34	0	0	236	28	6	22	258	34	0	0
BRAGANÇA	284	8	0	0	280	8	0	4	280	8	0	4	284	8	0	0	280	8	0	4	284	8	0	0
CASTELO BRANCO	280	12	0	0	273	10	2	7	276	11	1	4	280	12	0	0	273	9	3	7	280	12	0	0
COIMBRA	263	29	0	0	240	24	5	23	262	28	1	1	263	29	0	0	240	24	5	23	263	29	0	0
ÉVORA	285	7	0	0	284	7	0	1	285	7	0	0	285	7	0	0	284	7	0	1	285	7	0	0
FARO	253	39	0	0	224	32	7	29	250	38	1	3	253	39	0	0	224	32	7	29	253	39	0	0
GUARDA	290	2	0	0	287	2	0	3	287	2	0	3	290	2	0	0	287	2	0	3	290	2	0	0
LEIRIA	258	34	0	0	230	28	6	28	253	32	2	5	258	34	0	0	230	28	6	28	258	34	0	0
LISBOA	1	0	117	174	109	79	38	66	151	112	5	24	175	117	0	0	109	79	38	66	174	116	1	1
PORTALEGRE	285	7	0	0	282	7	0	3	282	7	0	3	285	7	0	0	282	7	0	3	285	7	0	0
PORTO	0	0	108	184	105	63	45	79	153	92	16	31	184	108	0	0	105	63	45	79	184	108	0	0
SANTARÉM	271	21	0	0	245	19	2	26	267	21	0	4	271	21	0	0	245	19	2	26	271	21	0	0
SETÚBAL	227	65	0	0	171	52	13	56	221	62	3	6	227	65	0	0	171	52	13	56	227	65	0	0
VIANA DO CASTELO	271	21	0	0	252	20	1	19	266	21	0	5	271	21	0	0	252	20	1	19	271	21	0	0
VILA REAL	286	6	0	0	281	6	0	5	282	6	0	4	286	6	0	0	281	6	0	5	286	6	0	0
VISEU	282	10	0	0	262	10	0	20	274	10	0	8	282	10	0	0	262	10	0	20	282	10	0	0

3.3 Weather Conditions, Transactions Records, and Accident History

Finally, transaction records data were merged with weather conditions to adjust accident prediction models for better results. Figure 6 shows the achieved *Precision* values.

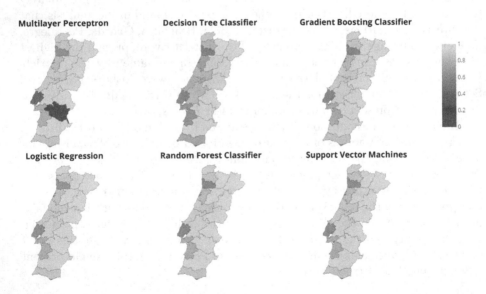

Fig. 6. Precision of fitted prediction models using weather conditions and transactions records.

As shown in Fig. 6, again the MLP model performed worse than the other models but with greater discrepancy this time. The performance of this model in the Évora district called attention, with a *Precision* of 0.027, which can be considered an outlier among the other results. Except for the Évora district, the minimum *Precision* of this model was 0.40 while that of the other models ranged between 0.53 and 0.60. As in the previous models, the maximum *Precision* value was 0.99.

The confusion matrices obtained by each algorithm can be analyzed in Table 4.

Table 4. Confusion matrices of fitted prediction models using weather conditions and transactions records.

District	Multilayer Perceptron				Decision Tree Classifier				Gradient Boosting Classifier				Logistic Regression				Random Forest Classifier				Support Vector Machines			
	TN	FN	TP	FP	TN	FN	TP	FP	TN	FN	TP	FP	TN	FN	TP	FP	TN	FN	TP	FP	TN	FN	TP	FP
AVEIRO	248	44	0	0	203	40	4	45	242	44	0	6	248	44	0	0	244	43	1	4	248	44	0	0
BEJA	288	4	0	0	287	4	0	1	288	4	0	0	288	4	0	0	288	4	0	0	288	4	0	0
BRAGA	258	34	0	0	230	29	5	28	257	34	0	1	258	34	0	0	257	34	0	1	258	34	0	0
BRAGANÇA	284	8	0	0	272	7	1	12	282	8	0	2	284	8	0	0	284	8	0	0	284	8	0	0
CASTELO BRANCO	280	12	0	0	271	11	1	9	278	12	0	2	280	12	0	0	280	12	0	0	280	12	0	0
COIMBRA	263	29	0	0	234	27	2	29	262	28	1	1	263	29	0	0	261	29	0	2	263	29	0	0
ÉVORA	1	0	7	284	278	7	0	7	283	7	0	2	285	7	0	0	285	7	0	0	285	7	0	0
FARO	253	39	0	0	211	36	3	42	253	39	0	0	253	39	0	0	251	39	0	2	253	39	0	0
GUARDA	290	2	0	0	290	2	0	0	290	2	0	0	290	2	0	0	290	2	0	0	290	2	0	0
LEIRIA	258	34	0	0	221	31	3	37	258	32	2	0	258	34	0	0	258	34	0	0	258	34	0	0
LISBOA	1	0	117	174	100	57	60	75	155	104	13	20	175	117	0	0	134	90	27	41	175	117	0	0
PORTALEGRE	285	7	0	0	283	7	0	2	284	7	0	1	285	7	0	0	285	7	0	0	285	7	0	0
PORTO	184	108	0	0	110	62	46	74	150	87	21	34	184	108	0	0	139	75	33	45	184	108	0	0
SANTARÉM	271	21	0	0	242	20	1	29	269	21	0	2	271	21	0	0	271	21	0	0	271	21	0	0
SETÚBAL	227	65	0	0	173	48	17	54	222	64	1	5	227	65	0	0	218	59	6	9	227	65	0	0
VIANA DO CASTELO	271	21	0	0	255	18	3	16	270	21	0	1	271	21	0	0	270	21	0	1	271	21	0	0
VILA REAL	286	6	0	0	277	6	0	9	283	6	0	3	286	6	0	0	286	6	0	0	286	6	0	0
VISEU	282	10	0	0	270	10	0	12	282	10	0	0	282	10	0	0	282	10	0	0	282	10	0	0

Based on the analysis of the confusion matrices, it can be observed that the aforementioned problem remains. The true positive rates are also lower than the false positive rates. In comparison, the true negative rates are higher than the false positive rates, evidencing a greater predisposition of the model to correctly predict the non-occurrence of work accidents to the detriment of the accident occurrence predictions. Again, Lisboa, Porto and Setúbal districts had a greater number of true positives, also indicating greater aptitude than the other districts in predicting the occurrence of accidents.

4 Conclusions and Future Work

The main objective of the present study was to discover whether the transaction records for the stores of a retail company and the weather conditions of each district of Mainland Portugal influence the occurrence of work accidents and if they can be used as predictors to predict the occurrence of work accidents.

The primary analysis took into account the Point-Biserial correlation coefficient between the occurrence (value equal to 1) or non-occurrence (value equal to 0) of accidents in a district with average weather conditions (temperature, precipitation, and relative humidity) and the total number of transactions in stores in this district. All results pointed to an insignificant correlation (ranging from -0.06 to 0.07), so in practice, it makes no sense to distinguish whether the correlation is positive or negative.

After the first analysis, 18 classification models were adjusted, for each district of Mainland Portugal, consisting of six machine learning algorithms for three different sets of input variables, always maintaining the output variable: occurrence or non-occurrence of work accidents.

All fitted models are performed similarly by the district. However, it should be noted that the districts of Beja, Bragança, Guarda, Portalegre, and Évora presented the highest precision values, always above 0.97. However, through the analysis of the confusion matrices of each model, the non-identification of the accident event is visible.

The Lisbon, Porto, and Setúbal districts achieved the lowest precision values, ranging between 0.37 and 0.78, which means that different approaches should be explored in future work. However, it is the districts that manage to achieve some assertiveness in predicting the occurrence of an accident, however, compared to the other districts, they reduce the accuracy of the non-occurrence of an accident.

Thus, through the analysis of the confusion matrix of each model, it is possible to verify a greater ability to predict the non-occurrence of accidents at work than the occurrence of accidents at work, which can be explained by the proportion of non-accident data being much higher compared to accident data.

The next steps of this work are based on exploring strategies to increase the model's performance in predicting the occurrence of work accidents. One hypothesis is implementing data balancing techniques to improve the fitted models, such as the Synthetic Minority Oversampling Technique (SMOTE), Class Weighting, Oversampling, and Undersampling.

Acknowledgement. The authors are grateful to the Foundation for Science and Technology (FCT, Portugal) for financial support through national funds FCT/MCTES (PIDDAC) to CeDRI (UIDB/05757/2020 and UIDP/05757/2020) and SusTEC (LA/P/0007/2021). This work has been supported by NORTE-01-0247-FEDER-072598 iSafety: Intelligent system for occupational safety and well-being in the retail sector.

References

1. Adam-Poupart, A., et al.: Climate change and occupational health and safety in a temperate climate: potential impacts and research priorities in quebec, canada. Ind. Health **51**(1), 68–78 (2013)
2. Al-Libawy, H., Al-Ataby, A., Al-Nuaimy, W., Al-Taee, M.A., Al-Taee, A.M.: A fatigue prediction cognitive model for naturalistic typing environment. In: 2017 10th International Conference on Developments in eSystems Engineering (DeSE), pp. 227–231. IEEE (2017)
3. Alkhaldi, M., Pathirage, C., Kulatunga, U., et al.: The role of human error in accidents within oil and gas industry in bahrain. In: 13th International Postgraduate Research Conference (IPGRC): Conference Proceedings, pp. 822–834. University of Salford (2017)

4. Anderson, V.P., Schulte, P.A., Sestito, J., Linn, H., Nguyen, L.S.: Occupational fatalities, injuries, illnesses, and related economic loss in the wholesale and retail trade sector. Am. J. Ind. Med. **53**(7), 673–685 (2010)
5. Badorf, F., Hoberg, K.: The impact of daily weather on retail sales: an empirical study in brick-and-mortar stores. J. Retail. Consum. Serv. **52**, 101921 (2020)
6. Berry, H.L., Bowen, K., Kjellstrom, T.: Climate change and mental health: a causal pathways framework. Int. J. Public Health **55**, 123–132 (2010)
7. Chi, S., Han, S., Kim, D.Y.: Relationship between unsafe working conditions and workers' behavior and impact of working conditions on injury severity in us construction industry. J. Constr. Eng. Manag. **139**(7), 826–838 (2013)
8. Choi, Y., Choi, J.W.: The prediction of workplace turnover using machine learning technique. Inter. J. Bus. Analy. (IJBAN) **8**(4), 1–10 (2021)
9. Gupta, S.D.: Point biserial correlation coefficient and its generalization. Psychometrika **25**(4), 393–408 (1960)
10. Hastie, T., Tibshirani, R., Friedman, J.: The Elements of Statistical Learning. SSS, Springer, New York (2009). https://doi.org/10.1007/978-0-387-84858-7
11. Im Kampe, E.O., Kovats, S., Hajat, S.: Impact of high ambient temperature on unintentional injuries in high-income countries: a narrative systematic literature review. BMJ Open **6**(2), e010399 (2016)
12. Kendall, M.G.: Rank correlation methods. Griffin (1948)
13. Kim, C.W., McInerney, M.L., Alexander, R.P.: Job satisfaction as related to safe performance: a case for a manufacturing firm (2002)
14. Mendes, J., Lima, J., Costa, L., Rodrigues, N., Brandão, D., Leitão, P., Pereira, A.I.: Machine learning to identify olive-tree cultivars. In: Optimization, Learning Algorithms and Applications: Second International Conference, OL2A 2022, Póvoa de Varzim, Portugal, 24–25 October 2022 Proceedings, pp. 820–835. Springer (2023). https://doi.org/10.1007/978-3-031-23236-7_56
15. Miot, H.A.: Correlation analysis in clinical and experimental studies (2018)
16. Montgomery, D.C., Runger, G.C.: Applied statistics and probability for engineers, 5th edn. John Wiley & Sons, New York (2010)
17. Open-Meteo.com: Open-meteo: Open-meteo api. https://open-meteo.com/, Accessed March 2023
18. Parnaudeau, M., Bertrand, J.L.: The contribution of weather variability to economic sectors. Appl. Econ. **50**(43), 4632–4649 (2018)
19. Pedregosa, F., et al.: Scikit-learn: machine learning in Python. J. Mach. Learn. Res. **12**, 2825–2830 (2011)
20. Putz Anderson, V., Schulte, P.A., Novakovich, J., Pfirman, D., Bhattacharya, A.: Wholesale and retail trade sector occupational fatal and nonfatal injuries and illnesses from 2006 to 2016: Implications for intervention. Am. J. Ind. Med. **63**(2), 121–134 (2020)
21. Samy, L., Macey, P.M., Alshurafa, N., Sarrafzadeh, M.: An automated framework for predicting obstructive sleep apnea using a brief, daytime, non-intrusive test procedure. In: Proceedings of the 8th ACM International Conference on PErvasive Technologies Related to Assistive Environments, pp. 1–8 (2015)
22. Sandroto, C.W., Fransiska, J.: The importance of emotional intelligence for the sales associates profession as a mediation between job stress and job satisfaction. Inter. J. Manag. Econ. **57**(4), 331–342 (2021)
23. dos Santos (FFMS), F.F.M.: Pordata. https://www.pordata.pt/portugal, Accessed 4 March 2023
24. Smith, A., Johnson, B.: Title of the article. Journal Name (2018)

25. Štulec, I., Petljak, K., Naletina, D.: Weather impact on retail sales: how can weather derivatives help with adverse weather deviations? J. Retail. Consum. Serv. **49**, 1–10 (2019)
26. Tran, B.R., et al.: The impact of weather on retail sales. FRBSF Econ. Lett. **2022**(23), 1–5 (2022)

Exploring Features to Classify Occupational Accidents in the Retail Sector

Inês Sena[1,2,3](✉) , Ana Cristina Braga[3] , Paulo Novais[3] ,
Florbela P. Fernandes[1,2] , Maria F. Pacheco[1,2] , Clara B. Vaz[1,2] ,
José Lima[1,2] , and Ana I. Pereira[1,2]

[1] Research Center in Digitalization and Intelligent Robotics (CeDRI),
Instituto Politécnico de Bragança, Campus de Santa Apolónia,
5300-253 Bragança, Portugal
[2] Laboratório Associado para a Sustentabilidade e Tecnologia em Regiões de
Montanha (SusTEC), Instituto Politécnico de Bragança, Campus de Santa Apolónia,
5300-253 Bragança, Portugal
{ines.sena,fflor,pacheco,clvaz,jllima,apereira}@ipb.pt
[3] ALGORITMI Research Centre, LASI, University of Minho, Campus de Gualtar,
4710-057 Braga, Portugal
acb@dps.uminho.pt, pjon@di.uminho.pt

Abstract. The Machine Learning approach is used in several application domains, and its exploitation in predicting accidents in occupational safety is relatively recent. The present study aims to apply different Machine Learning algorithms for classifying the occurrence or non-occurrence of accidents at work in the retail sector. The approach consists of obtaining an impact score for each store and work unit, considering two databases of a retail company, the preventive safety actions, and the action plans. Subsequently, each score is associated with the occurrence or non-occurrence of accidents during January and May 2023. Of the five classification algorithms applied, the Support Vector Machine was the one that obtained the best accuracy and precision values for the preventive safety actions. As for the set of actions plan, the Logistic Regression reached the best results in all calculated metrics. With this study, estimating the impact score of the study variables makes it possible to identify the occurrence of accidents at work in the retail sector with high precision and accuracy.

Keywords: Workplace Accidents Classification · Machine Learning algorithms · Score Impact

1 Introduction

Over the years, accidents at work have been the subject of numerous studies to understand, prevent, and reduce them. Among the most adopted strategies in various sectors to fight workplace accidents, investigating these incidents and implementing preventive safety measures stand out [4].

© The Author(s) 2024
A. I. Pereira et al. (Eds.): OL2A 2023, CCIS 1981, pp. 49–62, 2024.
https://doi.org/10.1007/978-3-031-53025-8_4

These events can occur due to several factors. Several theories in the literature explain the causes of accidents, such as the accident proneness theory, domino theory, injury epidemiology, and macro-ergonomic theory, among others. However, if the causes are known, accidents can be predicted through predictive models that can identify patterns and trends that help to understand the leading causes of accidents at work and to develop effective prevention strategies [17].

Although there is still a need for more information regarding predicting accidents at work, some studies already demonstrate the successful application of Machine Learning techniques in predicting accidents in different business sectors. Ajavi et al. (2020) conducted a study focused on predicting accidents in energy infrastructures, exploring the methods of Particle Swarm Optimization (PSO), Decision Tree, Random Tree, and Gradient Boosting Machine (GBM) [1]. They built four predictive analysis models for the occurrence of accidents and the frequency index, in which the GBM-PSO was the model that presented the best predictive capacity [1].

Another relevant study is Kakhki et al. (2020), who developed a predictive model using Random Forest, Decision Tree, and Naive Bayes methods to predict accidents in agricultural installations, more specifically with grain elevators, achieving an accuracy between 80% and 95% [8].

In addition, other business areas already have studies with the application of Machine Learning methods for the prediction of accidents at work, such as the steel industry [9], construction [10,19], agribusiness [7], among others. It was found, after an extensive bibliographic review, that a business sector that has not carried out studies on this subject is the retail trade sector, which, although it seems to have a low risk of injuries or deaths compared to sectors such as agriculture and construction, is a sector that is involved in a variety of challenging work activities and exposed to various hazards [3,16]. It occupied the second place of economic activity in Portugal during the year 2020, with high records of accidents at work, compared to other sectors [18].

That way, it is essential to emphasize the importance of research in this area since the safety of employees is a priority in any economic activity. However, one of the main problems is the need for more knowledge about which data, variables, or parameters drive the occurrence of an accident. In addition, companies in the retail sector have a large amount of information that can be used to implement models for predicting accidents at work, from accident histories, information about the work environment, and employee demographic data, among others. However, it is necessary to study and analyze the amount and type of data inserted in Machine Learning models since the learning capacity of the model depends mainly on the dataset used.

Thus, this study aims to apply different Machine Learning algorithms in a new database approach to classify the occurrence or non-occurrence of accidents at work in the retail sector. This new approach comprises using only impact scores per database. Two databases were used in this case: preventive safety actions and action plans. Being a large company, it is distributed throughout the country in different stores, each with varying work units. Thus, the impact score calculation will be based on the number of records for each store and work unit.

To demonstrate the effectiveness of this new approach, the occurrence (1) or non-occurrence (0) of accidents will be associated with the score of each store and unit, taking into account the period from January to May 2023. Subsequently, it intended to apply each set of data to several Machine Learning methods and observe whether it is possible to classify the occurrence of accidents at work in the retail sector through the two designed impact scores.

The paper is organized into four sections. The Sect. 2 presents a discussion of the methodology, in particular, datasets, pre-processing, theoretical concepts of classification algorithms, and the applied performance evaluation metrics. The Sect. 3 aims to compare the achieved results for each data set. Finally, Sect. 4 concludes the study and indicates possible directions for future research.

2   Methodology

This section presents the collected databases and the process of designing the datasets to be used. The pre-processing techniques applied to improve the data quality will also be demonstrated, like the approach to achieve the best results for the listed objective.

2.1   Characterization of Datasets

For the present study, it is intended to use three databases made available by the Portuguese flap company:

- **Accident history**, which contains information about the general character-istics of the injured workers (age, length of service, etc.), the conditions of the accident (place, time, sector, function served at the time of the accident, etc.), the damage caused (severity, type of injury, etc.) and the cause of the accident.
- **Preventive safety actions** are records of risk situations or unsafe conditions observed by members of the Occupational Safety and Health (OSH) team when they visit the stores.
- **Action plans** are drawn up after the intervention of third parties or employ-ees to correct and improve the working conditions observed during an audit of your workplace.

The obligation to create action plans to solve the problems that persist in the employee's well-being and working conditions has existed in the company since 2008, a period to be considered in this study. However, the observation and registration by the company of preventive safety actions to improve employees' conditions and quality of work is relatively recent, being practiced only from August 2022, counting 8681 registrations of action plans and 7757 preventive security actions. Each record will be associated with the occurrence of accidents through the company's accident history recorded between January 2023 and May 2023.

Considering the number of records in each database, the impact score will be calculated for each store and 16 work units. After obtaining the score, it will be related to the occurrence or not of accidents. It should be noted that, due to the records period, it is only possible to obtain the score for 78 stores, considering the set of preventive security actions, and for 316 stores according to the group of action plans.

For each dataset, the average of records per work unit $(\bar{r}_{uw})$ was considered considering the records per work unit of each store (r_{uws}) and the number of work units (n_{uw}), as shown in Eq. (1):

$$\bar{r}_{uw} = \frac{\sum r_{uws}}{n_{uw}} \tag{1}$$

Subsequently, the score (X) was calculated for each data set, in which the number of records was counted for each store and work unit, and the Eq. (2) was applied:

$$X = \frac{n_{uw} - \bar{r}_{uw}}{n_{uw}} \tag{2}$$

The values obtained were arranged using min-max character scaling, a normalization approach that scales the character to the fixed range of [0,1], as shown in Eq. (3).

$$X_{score} = \frac{X - X_{min}}{X_{max} - X_{min}} \tag{3}$$

Then, each store and work unit's X_{score} was linked to the history of accidents, associating the occurrence or non-occurrence of an accident, the store, and the corresponding work unit. Since not all the stores had accidents during this period, it was only possible to obtain the impact of observation on the occurrence of accidents in 71 stores for preventive safety actions and 283 stores for action plans.

Finally, the datasets used in this study will have the information of store, work unit, and impact score and an output parameter (accident (1) or not an accident (0)).

2.2   Pre-processing Data

Data pre-processing is a significant initial step when using Machine Learning (ML) algorithms to classify events or information. This is because the data quality directly impacts the model's learnability.

Some issues that may affect learning the desired model can be identified by closely examining the datasets. These problems include an imbalance between output variables and data typology. Therefore, it is necessary to apply pre-processing techniques to deal with these issues before using the data in the developed model.

The balance of the data set is crucial to improve the performance of ML algorithms since it is essential that each class has the same number of samples and, thus, has equal relevance in the analysis, avoiding any bias [23]. In this research, the data related to the non-occurrence of accidents is significantly higher than in the other classes. This can lead the algorithms to favor this class and generate predictions with high values but inaccurate and distorted. Therefore, it is essential to use confusion matrices to validate the prediction results.

In this way, the Synthetic Minority Oversampling Technique (SMOTE) technique will be applied, whose main objective is to increase the number of minority samples by inserting n synthetic minority samples among the k samples that are closest to a given sample with lower dimension [23].

The one-hot encoding technique was applied since Machine Learning algorithms tend to obtain better results when dealing with numerical data [14], and datasets contain categorical typology information. This technique consists of removing the categorical variable and dividing it into n new binary variables, depending on the number of categories in the data.

2.3 Machine Learning Techniques

To find out if an impact score can replace the information from a database, it is intended to calculate the correlation coefficient between the two variables, applying different ML algorithms – to conclude if obtaining a relationship with the accident event is possible.

The strength of the association varies between -1 and $+1$, indicating a strong relationship between variables. If the correlation coefficient is near 0, it represents a weaker relationship between variables [2].

Different types of coefficients can be calculated, such as Pearson, Spearman, Kendall Tau, and others. The selection of the coefficient to be calculated depends on the data type. In this case, as the data sets have a non-Gaussian distribution, the Kendall-Tau Correlation was chosen, which is a non-parametric method that measures the association between two variables X, Y based on ratings of sampled observations from X and Y [21]. In addition, it should be used when the same classification is repeated many times on a small dataset, as in the present case [2] (Table 1).

Table 1. Interpretation of the correlation coefficient values based [2].

Correlation Coefficients	Relation Interpretation
[-1, -0.9[or]0.9, 1]	Perfect
[-0.9, -0.7[or]0.7, 0.9]	Strong
[-0.7, -0.4[or]0.6, 0.4]	Moderate
[-0.3, -0.1[or]0.3, 0.1]	Weak
[-0.1, 0[or]0.1, 0]	None

To identify the occurrence of accidents, it is intended to apply and compare different classification algorithms to understand whether it is conceivable to predict the occurrence of accidents through the impact score. Thus, the following algorithms were used:

- **Decision Tree (DT)**, is a versatile Supervised Learning algorithm applicable for both classification and regression and for categorical and continuous dependent variables [23]. Its main objective is to develop a tree structure that identifies the values of test samples through training samples [13]. It is easy to understand and interpret and is often used to support decision-making since each branch represents a choice between several alternatives. Each node represents a [11] decision. This algorithm uses a recursive partitioning technique, building a decision tree composed of several nodes created and divided based on specific criteria. This process is interrupted when the training dataset is adjusted to the predictions [1].
- **K-Nearest Neaighbor (KNN)**, classifies an observation by analyzing the k nearest [23] observations. The algorithm uses the nearest neighbor technique to assign a classification to a new sample point based on its proximity to a set of previously classified points [14]. This method involves two main parameters, the value of k and the distance function. The value of k is determined through several executions with different values, selecting the one that minimizes the number of errors found and provides greater forecast accuracy. The distance function used by KNN is the Euclidean distance, which represents the distance physics between two-dimensional points [14].
- **Random Forest (RF)**, is a popular Machine Learning approach that uses multiple independent decision trees that are built from previously selected variables [1]. Each decision tree is trained using a portion of the original training data. It performs the divisions considering only a random subset of the input variables. The final categorization is defined through the classifier's output that obtains the most votes from the trees [1,23].
- **Logistic Regression (LR)**, is an algorithm used for classification capable of estimating discrete values based on a set of dependent variables [23]. It calculates the probability of an event by fitting the data into a logical function. As a result, the algorithm's output is always between 0 and 1 [23].
- **Support Vector Machine (SVM)**, is a widely used Machine Learning algorithm with a solid theoretical basis, which seeks to find a hyperplane that separates the training data into different classes, maximizing the margin between them [13]. Different kernels, such as linear, RBF, and sigmoid, can be applied for this task. However, proper training parameters are essential to ensure satisfactory prediction accuracy. In general, SVM is recognized for its effectiveness in classifying binary sentiments and its ability to deal with classification and regression problems, outperforming many other statistical and ML methods [13].

To implement the datasets in the five referred algorithms, it is necessary to divide them into training (70%) and testing (30%). To evaluate the performance of each applied algorithm, specific metrics per class were used, including accuracy, precision, recall, and F_{score}. To calculate them, it is necessary to identify the following:

- True Positives (TP) - data that were accidents and the model predicted as an accident.
- True Negatives (TN) - non-accident samples that the model correctly projected as non-accident.
- False Positives (FP) - data representing accidents and the model projected as non-accidents.
- False Negatives (FN) - accidents samples and the model predict as a non-accident.

Accuracy is a metric widely applied in problems of this nature. It returns a general value of how much the model is correctly predicting the class concerning the entire data set (as defined in Eq. (4)) where:

$$Accuracy = \frac{TP + TN}{TP + FP + TN + FN} \tag{4}$$

The *Precision*, defined in Eq. (5), refers to the model's reliability when correctly predicting a specific class [5].

$$Precision = \frac{TP}{TP + FP} \tag{5}$$

The *Recall* measures the number of true positives that were classified correctly, using Eq. (6), [5].

$$Recall = \frac{TP}{TP + TN} \tag{6}$$

The F_{score} is the harmonic mean of *Precision* and *Recall*, as can see in Eq. (7), which reaches its best value at one and its worst at zero [5].

$$F_{score} = \frac{2 \times Precision \times Recall}{Precision + Recall} \tag{7}$$

The referred metrics are based on the confusion matrix generated for each algorithm. The confusion matrix for the specific case study is based on the occurrence of accidents [5].

All the algorithms presented in this work were tested, trained, and implemented on a computer equipped with an 11th Gen Intel(R) Core(TM) i7-1185G7 processor, with a RAM 16 GB memory and Python version 3.10.6 in Google Colab. For this study, different libraries were used, such as the Numpy library (version 1.22.4) [6] and Pandas (version 1.5.3) [20] for efficient data manipulation and analysis, the Scipy library (version 1.10.1) [22] to calculate the correlation, the Imbalanced-learn library (version 0.10.1) [12] for data imbalance, and finally, the Scikit-learn library (version 1.2.2) [15], also known as sklearn, for creating robust predictive models and evaluating performance through appropriate metrics.

3   Results

In this section, the results obtained from the relationship between the impact score and the occurrence of accidents will be presented, as well as the values of the performance evaluation metrics obtained by each iteration of the classification algorithms applied to the dataset. These results enable an understanding of whether it is possible to predict the occurrence of accidents through the calculated impact score.

3.1   Preventive Security Actions

As previously mentioned, this database is recent in the company, containing a reduced period of recording information. However, the impact score of recording preventive safety actions was calculated between August and December 2022 and connected to accidents from January 2023 to May 2023. Therefore, the dataset has three input variables (store identification, identification of the work unit for each store, and impact score) and an output variable (accident or not an accident), as shown in Table 2.

Table 2. Distribution of data by output variables.

Predict Label	Number of data
Not an accident	536
Accident	84

As mentioned in Sect. 2.3, the Kendall-Tau coefficient calculates the association between impact score and crash occurrence. The value 0.0984 refers to a fragile association between them. However, it reveals a positive association, referring to a level of agreement between the impact score (X_{score}: continuous variable) and the occurrence of accidents (0 and 1).

Although there is a fragile association between the variables, the possibility of predicting the occurrence of accidents through the impact score was studied. In this way, different classification algorithms were applied with five cross-validations, and the performance results can be analyzed in Table 3.

Through Table 3, it is possible to observe high accuracy values. However, it is worth noting the lack of assertiveness in identifying the occurrence of accidents. Thus, the algorithms that achieved the highest accuracy values, RF and SVM, could not classify any accidents. However, the remaining algorithms were able to identify a small number of cases. The run time of the prediction models tested was 0.17 s.

The inability of the algorithms to predict the occurrence of accidents can be justified due to the imbalance of information between the outputs, which may hamper the performance of the models in identifying accidents at work. To this end, the SMOTE method was applied, balancing the data from the minority class according to the majority class [23].

Table 3. Results obtained for preventive security actions by the metrics for each algorithm.

Learning algorithms	Predict Label	$Precision$	$Recall$	F_{score}	$Accuracy$
Logistic Regression (LR)	Not an accident	0.87	0.91	0.89	0.80
Logistic Regression (LR)	Accident	0.23	0.16	0.18	0.80
Decision Tree (DT)	Not an accident	0.86	0.89	0.88	0.78
Decision Tree (DT)	Accident	0.12	0.10	0.10	0.78
Random Forest (RF)	Not an accident	0.86	1.00	0.92	0.86
Random Forest (RF)	Accident	0.00	0.00	0.00	0.86
Support Vector Machine (SVM)	Not an accident	0.86	1.00	0.92	0.86
Support Vector Machine (SVM)	Accident	0.00	0.00	0.00	0.86
K-Nearest Neighbors (KNN)	Not an accident	0.85	0.90	0.88	0.78
K-Nearest Neighbors (KNN)	Accident	0.04	0.03	0.03	0.78

Once the data set was modified, the association between the two variables was calculated again using the Kendall-Tau coefficient, showing an increase in the coefficient value to 0.1422, revealing a weak positive association between the variables. Thus, the prediction tests were repeated for the balanced data set. In Table 4, the results of the metrics calculated to evaluate the performance of each of the tested algorithms with a cross-validation of five are presented. The run time of the prediction models tested was 0.16 s.

Table 4. Results obtained for preventive security actions balanced data by the metrics for each algorithm.

Learning algorithms	Predict Label	$Precision$	$Recall$	F_{score}	$Accuracy$
Logistic Regression (LR)	Not an accident	0.88	0.88	0.88	0.88
Logistic Regression (LR)	Accident	0.88	0.88	0.88	0.88
Decision Tree (DT)	Not an accident	0.88	0.73	0.80	0.82
Decision Tree (DT)	Accident	0.77	0.90	0.83	0.82
Random Forest (RF)	Not an accident	0.93	0.65	0.77	0.80
Random Forest (RF)	Accident	0.73	0.95	0.83	0.80
Support Vector Machine (SVM)	Not an accident	0.88	0.89	0.88	0.88
Support Vector Machine (SVM)	Accident	0.89	0.88	0.88	0.88
K-Nearest Neighbors (KNN)	Not an accident	0.90	0.65	0.75	0.79
K-Nearest Neighbors (KNN)	Accident	0.73	0.93	0.81	0.79

Observing Table 4, the increase in assertiveness in detecting the occurrence of accidents is notorious, in addition to the increase in accuracy values, in almost all the cases, except Random Forest.

The SVM and LR were the ones that obtained the best results, and the Support Vector Machine was more assertive in identifying the occurrence of accidents, maintaining the accuracy of the LR in detecting non-occurrence. On the other hand, the RF showed the highest precision in the non-occurrence of accidents and the lowest for the classification of accidents, like the KNN.

3.2   Actions Plans

In Table 5, the distribution of the amount of data of the output variables of the dataset that relates the impact score of action plans and the occurrence of accidents is presented.

Table 5. Distribution of data by output variables.

Predict Label	Number of data
Not an accident	1795
Accident	174

The relationship between the impact score and the output variable was also calculated using the Kendall-Tau coefficient for this data set. Thus, a correlation of 0.0131 was obtained, a fragile association between the variables.

However, the occurrence of accidents was also identified based on the impact score of the action plans registered by the company through the implementation of the data set in the different selected classification algorithms. In Table 6, the results obtained by the metrics after cross-validation of five can be seen. The run time of the prediction models tested was 1.58 s.

Table 6. Results obtained for actions plan data set by the metrics for each algorithm executed.

Learning algorithms	Predict Label	Precision	Recall	F_{score}	Accuracy
Logistic Regression (LR)	Not an accident	0.92	0.94	0.93	0.87
Logistic Regression (LR)	Accident	0.19	0.15	0.16	0.87
Decision Tree (DT)	Not an accident	0.91	0.96	0.94	0.88
Decision Tree (DT)	Accident	0.15	0.08	0.10	0.88
Random Forest (RF)	Not an accident	0.91	1.00	0.95	0.91
Random Forest (RF)	Accident	0.28	0.02	0.03	0.91
Support Vector Machine (SVM)	Not an accident	0.91	1.00	0.95	0.91
Support Vector Machine (SVM)	Accident	0.00	0.00	0.00	0.91
K-Nearest Neighbors (KNN)	Not an accident	0.91	0.98	0.94	0.89
K-Nearest Neighbors (KNN)	Accident	0.18	0.04	0.07	0.89

Observing Table 6, the high accuracy values achieved by the tested algorithms are noted. However, the little assertiveness in the classification of "Accident" is noticeable. In this case, the RF and the SVM were the ones that achieved the highest accuracy values. However, the Support Vector Machine could not identify any accidents occurring.

Once again, this lack of ability to predict an accident can be explained by the sharp difference in data between the two possible outputs. In this way, SMOTE was also applied to this set, which allows for increasing the number of data representing the occurrence of accidents depending on the size of the non-occurrence class.

The previous calculations were repeated, starting with the Kendall-Tau correlation coefficient, which increased to 0.026, keeping the fragile association between the two variables. Subsequently, the occurrence of accidents was classified using the same algorithms and five cross-validations. The results obtained by the metrics can be seen in Table 7. The run time of the prediction models tested was 1.24 s.

Table 7. Results obtained for actions plan balanced dataset by the metrics for each algorithm executed.

Learning algorithms	Predict Label	$Precision$	$Recall$	F_{score}	$Accuracy$
Logistic Regression (LR)	Not an accident	0.92	0.93	0.93	0.92
Logistic Regression (LR)	Accident	0.93	0.92	0.92	0.92
Decision Tree (DT)	Not an accident	0.91	0.65	0.76	0.79
Decision Tree (DT)	Accident	0.73	0.93	0.82	0.79
Random Forest (RF)	Not an accident	0.96	0.51	0.66	0.74
Random Forest (RF)	Accident	0.66	0.98	0.79	0.74
Support Vector Machine (SVM)	Not an accident	0.90	0.93	0.92	0.92
Support Vector Machine (SVM)	Accident	0.94	0.90	0.91	0.92
K-Nearest Neighbors (KNN)	Not an accident	0.92	0.73	0.81	0.83
K-Nearest Neighbors (KNN)	Accident	0.78	0.94	0.85	0.83

Observing Table 7, one can indicate a high increase in the accuracy of the algorithms in classifying the occurrence of accidents, maintaining assertiveness in identifying non-occurrence. Random Forest was the algorithm that reached the highest precision values in class "not an accident" prediction and the lowest for class "accident" identification, compared to the other algorithms, reaching the most insufficient precision. SVM and LR were the ones that achieved the best accuracy results, with Logistic Regression standing out in the remaining evaluation metrics.

The attempt to classify the occurrence of accidents by merging the two scores is worth noting since they are complementary information. However, it was impossible due to the information discrepancy in the two databases.

4   Conclusions and Future Works

This study aimed to calculate an impact score for the two databases that identify risk situations and unsafe conditions in the company's work areas and, consequently, to understand whether, through the score obtained, it is possible to predict the occurrence of accidents on work.

To this end, the impact score was obtained by calculating the average of the records for each dataset per store and work unit. An impact score was obtained through the annual records and then normalized using the min-max feature scaling that establishes a scale of values between 0 and 1 depending on the maximum and minimum values obtained.

By achieving the impact score for each database, a connection was made with the history of accidents between January and May 2023, associating the occurrence or not of accidents at work for each store and work unit with an impact score reached.

With the creation of the two datasets, the Kendall-Tau coefficient was calculated to understand the association between the impact score and the occurrence of accidents. A fragile association was observed between the set of action plans and the event of the accident, and a weak positive association between the impact score of preventive safety actions and the occurrence of accidents.

Afterward, the occurrence of accidents was classified through the achieved impact scores. First, the original datasets were used. However, the results could have been better for their classification due to the data imbalance between the two output variables. In this way, the SMOTE technique was applied, which allows for increasing the information of the minority class as a function of the majority class, equalizing the amount of data for each category.

Thus, five classification algorithms were applied to observe whether it is possible to identify the occurrence of accidents through the impact scores obtained in this study. For the data set of preventive safety actions, the Support Vector Machine was the most assertive in identifying the occurrence of accidents, maintaining high values of accuracy and precision in the classification of the non-occurrence of accidents. As for the action plan dataset, the Logistic Regression algorithm reached the best results in all analyzed metrics.

For both cases, Random Forest was the algorithm that obtained the best precision in predicting class "not an accident" but the lowest values when identifying class "accident".

Thus, it can be concluded that it is possible to classify the occurrence of accidents at work in the retail sector through the impact score obtained by the records of preventive safety actions and action plans carried out by the safety and health team leader and the company's employees.

For future work, it is intended to explore these results further and test this approach in other company databases to find other impact scores that can predict the occurrence of accidents at work in the retail sector.

Acknowledgement. The authors are grateful to the Foundation for Science and Technology (FCT, Portugal) for financial support through national funds FCT/MCTES (PIDDAC) to CeDRI (UIDB/05757/2020 and UIDP/05757/2020), ALGORITMI UIDB/00319/2020 and SusTEC (LA/P/0007/2021). This work has been supported by NORTE-01-0247-FEDER-072598 iSafety: Intelligent system for occupational safety and well-being in the retail sector. Inês Sena was supported by FCT PhD grant UI/BD/153348/2022.

References

1. Ajayi, A., et al.: Optimised big data analytics for health and safety hazards prediction in power infrastructure operations. Saf. Sci. **125**, 104656 (2020)
2. Akoglu, H.: User's guide to correlation coefficients. Turkish J. Emerg. Med. **18**(3), 91–93 (2018)
3. Anderson, V.P., Schulte, P.A., Sestito, J., Linn, H., Nguyen, L.S.: Occupational fatalities, injuries, illnesses, and related economic loss in the wholesale and retail trade sector. Am. J. Ind. Med. **53**(7), 673–685 (2010)
4. Cioni, M., Savioli, M.: Safety at the workplace: accidents and illnesses. Work Employ Soc. **30**(5), 858–875 (2016)
5. Grandini, M., Bagli, E., Visani, G.: Metrics for multi-class classification: an overview. arXiv preprint arXiv:2008.05756 (2020)
6. Harris, C.R., Millman, K.J., et al,: Array programming with NumPy. Nature **585**(7825), 357–362 (Sep2020). https://doi.org/10.1038/s41586-020-2649-2,https://doi.org/10.1038/s41586-020-2649-2
7. Kakhki, F.D., Freeman, S.A., Mosher, G.A.: Evaluating machine learning performance in predicting injury severity in agribusiness industries. Saf. Sci. **117**, 257–262 (2019)
8. Kakhki, F.D., Freeman, S.A., Mosher, G.A.: Applied machine learning in agro-manufacturing occupational incidents. Procedia Manufact. **48**, 24–30 (2020)
9. Koc, K., Ekmekcioğlu, Ö., Gurgun, A.P.: Accident prediction in construction using hybrid wavelet-machine learning. Autom. Constr. **133**, 103987 (2022)
10. Koc, K., Gurgun, A.P.: Scenario-based automated data preprocessing to predict severity of construction accidents. Autom. Constr. **140**, 104351 (2022)
11. Kumar, V., Garg, M.: Predictive analytics: a review of trends and techniques. Int. J. Comput. Appl. **182**(1), 31–37 (2018)
12. Lemaître, G., Nogueira, F., Aridas, C.K.: Imbalanced-learn: a python toolbox to tackle the curse of imbalanced datasets in machine learning. J. Mach. Learn. Res. **18**(17), 1–5 (2017), https://jmlr.org/papers/v18/16-365.html
13. Liu, Y., Bi, J.W., Fan, Z.P.: Multi-class sentiment classification: the experimental comparisons of feature selection and machine learning algorithms. Expert Syst. Appl. **80**, 323–339 (2017)
14. Oyedele, A., et al.: Deep learning and boosted trees for injuries prediction in power infrastructure projects. Appl. Soft Comput. **110**, 107587 (2021)
15. Pedregosa, F., et al.: Scikit-learn: machine learning in Python. J. Mach. Learn. Res. **12**, 2825–2830 (2011)
16. Putz Anderson, V., Schulte, P.A., Novakovich, J., Pfirman, D., Bhattacharya, A.: Wholesale and retail trade sector occupational fatal and nonfatal injuries and illnesses from 2006 to 2016: Implications for intervention. Am. J. Ind. Med. **63**(2), 121–134 (2020)

17. Sanmiquel, L., Rossel, J.M., Vintró, C.: Study of Spanish mining accidents using data mining techniques. Saf. Sci. **75**, 49–55 (2015)
18. dos Santos (FFMS), F.F.M.: Pordata. https://www.pordata.pt/portugal Accessed Jan 6 2023
19. Shirali, G.A., Noroozi, M.V., Malehi, A.S.: Predicting the outcome of occupational accidents by cart and chaid methods at a steel factory in Iran. J. Public Health Res.**7**(2), jphr-2018 (2018)
20. pandas development team, T.: pandas-dev/pandas: Pandas (Feb 2020). https://doi.org/10.5281/zenodo.3509134, https://doi.org/10.5281/zenodo.3509134
21. Valencia, D., Lillo, R.E., Romo, J.: A kendall correlation coefficient between functional data. Adv. Data Anal. Classif. **13**, 1083–1103 (2019)
22. Virtanen, P., et al.: SciPy 1.0 Contributors: SciPy 1.0: Fundamental Algorithms for Scientific Computing in Python. Nature Methods **17**, 261–272 (2020). https://doi.org/10.1038/s41592-019-0686-2
23. Zhu, R., Hu, X., Hou, J., Li, X.: Application of machine learning techniques for predicting the consequences of construction accidents in China. Process Saf. Environ. Prot. **145**, 293–302 (2021)

Resource Dispatch Optimization for Firefighting Using a Differential Evolution Algorithm

Marina A. Matos[(✉)] , Rui Gonçalves , Ana Maria A. C. Rocha ,
Lino A. Costa , and Filipe Alvelos

ALGORITMI Research Centre/LASI, University of Minho, Campus de Gualtar,
4710-057 Braga, Portugal
mmatos@algoritmi.uminho.pt, {arocha,lac,falvelos}@dps.uminho.pt

Abstract. The incidence of forest fires has shown an upward trend in recent years. This increase can be attributed to rising ambient temperatures and population growth, which act as the primary catalysts for these disasters. The application of optimization techniques has significantly contributed to addressing forest firefighting challenges, enabling improvements in the efficiency and promptness of firefighting operations. This study focuses on a specific resource dispatch problem to combat forest fires, which involves assigning 7 resources to extinguish 20 ignitions. The main objective is to minimize the total area burned by these ignitions in a minimum period of time. To solve this problem, the differential evolution algorithm adapted to this context was applied. Furthermore, a statistical analysis was performed to evaluate the performance of differential evolution when different selection and crossover operators are tested. The preliminary results show that the current-to-best selection and exponential crossover operators are the most suitable to solve the resource dispatch problem for forest firefighting.

Keywords: Forest Fires · Single-objective Optimization · Resource Dispatch Problem · Differential Evolution

1 Introduction

In recent years, forest fires have been increasingly frequent on our planet. This is due to the fact that ambient temperatures have been rising over the years, leading to high-risk situations for the health of living beings and forests. In 2017 fire season, there were several fires around the world. Canada, United States, Chile, Portugal, Spain, South Africa, Ireland and Greenland were the most

This work has been supported by FCT Fundação para a Ciência e Tecnologia within the R&D Units Project Scope UIDB/00319/2020 and PCIF/GRF/0141/2019: "O3F - An Optimization Framework to reduce Forest Fire" and the PhD grant reference UI/BD/150936/2021.

A. I. Pereira et al. (Eds.): OL2A 2023, CCIS 1981, pp. 63–77, 2024.
https://doi.org/10.1007/978-3-031-53025-8_5

affected countries in this catastrophic year. In turn, in 2018 the total burned area exceeded 1 million hectares, thus surpassing the year 2017. In this year, the most affected regions were Greece, England, Sweden and North America [7]. Australia also experienced a series of severe wildfires due to unusually high temperatures between 2019 and early 2020 [5].

Unfortunately, every year around 4 million square kilometers of land (roughly the size of the European Union) burn around the world [17]. In Europe, more than 5500 square kilometers of land burned in 2021 [20]. According to the Global Forest Fire Information System, between 2012 and 2021 an average of 448 million hectares of land burned each year, with 1.4 million hectares corresponding to the European Union and the United Kingdom [22].

With the increase in the number of forest fires in recent years, more and more decision-support strategies for fighting forest fires have been studied. The main objectives of firefighting decisions are to reduce the burned area, protect living beings, structures and the environment. The number, skills, and level of preparedness of firefighting teams are relevant factors. The performance of the fighting team is a very important factor in firefighting, and the better and faster it is, the less damage will be caused [2]. Fire suppression management involves identifying how many and which combat resources need to be deployed for each forest fire in order to best and quickly extinguish the fire.

Several optimization strategies have been used in the engineering area to solve fire suppression problems aiming to find the best trajectory and position of fighting vehicles, find the shortest route, decide the number of resources to dispatch, among others. In Zeferino et al. [24], a mathematical optimization model was developed to identify the optimal location of various aircraft in order to maximize the coverage of high-risk areas. The research focused on a case study conducted in Portugal. Chan et al. [6] introduced the Firefly algorithm in their study as a means to allocate a limited number of drones and firefighters across multiple zones. The performance of the Firefly algorithm was evaluated under various configurations. Their findings demonstrated that when a relatively small percentage of drones, ranging from 10% to 20% of the total number of zones, were deployed, the algorithm achieved optimal performance levels of 80% to 95% in the majority of cases. In the study conducted by Granberg et al. [10], a mathematical model was developed to address the problem of dispatching firefighting and rescue services. This problem involved determining the optimal allocation of firefighters to vehicles and devising an efficient dispatch strategy for emergency situations. The researchers employed both exact and heuristic solution methods to solve the developed model, using data from the Skåne region in Sweden. The results showed that the exact solution method was time-consuming in certain scenarios, while the heuristic approach generally produced fast and near-optimal solutions in the majority of cases. The study demonstrated the effectiveness of different solution techniques for addressing the firefighting and rescue service dispatch problem.

To effectively mitigate forest fires, it is imperative to develop decision-support systems for forest fire management that use advanced techniques for monitoring, detection and control. These initiatives aim to improve the understanding of forest fire dynamics and implement measures to minimize their occurrence and impact [2]. The strategic planning of forest firefighting resources, including determining the appropriate quantity and type of resources required to suppress a specific fire, is a highly significant field of study. These research efforts have the potential to minimize the damage caused by forest fires and to provide valuable support to decision makers involved in firefighting operations. By understanding the optimal allocation and utilization of firefighting resources, decision-makers can make informed choices and take effective actions to combat forest fires, ultimately reducing the overall impact and devastation caused by these incidents.

The resource dispatch problem refers to a simulation that determines resource utilization, including when, where, and what resources will be used in a given scenario. In the context of forest firefighting, this problem involves making decisions about which methods to apply and which firefighting resources should be deployed to fight a specific fire and at what time they should be used. By addressing the resource dispatch problem, authorities can optimize their response strategies, ensuring the timely and appropriate allocation of firefighting resources to effectively manage and extinguish forest fires [1,3,16].

Several algorithms have been applied to solve the resource dispatch problem, such as particle swarm optimization, genetic algorithm, among others. Baisravan et al. [12,13] have proposed several decision support strategies to minimize the total burned area using the Genetic Algorithm (GA). The GA developed an ideal line of fire in order to reduce the total area burned, also providing the best places to attack the firefighting teams. In addition, homogeneous and heterogeneous environmental conditions were considered. Monte-Carlo simulations were used to develop robust strategies under uncertain conditions. Naziris et al. [18] developed a model to protect historic buildings from fires, where they presented a generic model of resource selection and allocation. For this, they applied the differential evolution and particle swarm optimization algorithms. The case study was based on the monasteries of Mount Athos, where good results were obtained, showing the efficiency of the presented model. Zhou and Zhang [26] proposed a model event response tree-based method for dispatching different types of firefighting assets based on the fire suppression index. This index evaluates the effect of fire suppression considering time, cost and dispatch effect resources. To validate this method, historical fire data from Nanjing Laoshan National Forest Park was used and the results were compared to a mixed integer programming (MIP) method. The results showed that both methods were effective. In addition, the proposed model was clear and intuitive for firefighters to make decisions regarding the various dispatch processes of forest firefighting vehicles.

This paper focuses on solving the resource dispatch problem for forest firefighting. The objective function to be minimized is the extent of burned area, using a Differential Evolution (DE) algorithm, implemented in the *Python* programming language. Taking advantage of the DE algorithm, the study aims to improve the decision-making process in the dispatch of resources for forest firefighting operations. A resource dispatch problem involving 7 firefighting resources to extinguish 20 ignitions of a forest fire is used to evaluate the performance of DE in solving this type of problem. Furthermore, several DE variants were tested, followed by a statistical analysis to determine the most suitable operators to achieve the best results in this particular problem. In addition, a comparison of solutions between DE and GA is made.

This paper is organized as follows. The differential evolution algorithm is described in Sect. 2 and in Sect. 3 the problem definition is presented. The implementation details, the testing of DE variants, the best solution found and the comparison of solutions between DE and GA are presented in Sect. 4. Finally, the conclusions of this study and future work are shown in Sect. 5.

2 Differential Evolution

Differential evolution is a widely adopted evolutionary algorithm that has become popular for its effectiveness in solving complex optimization problems. It was first proposed by Storn and Price [21] and is known for its simplicity and efficiency. This stochastic search algorithm is population-based and uses mutation, crossover and selection operators to iteratively guide the population towards the global optimum [23]. DE is specifically designed to optimize real-valued functions with real parameters. The algorithm starts by randomly initializing a population of candidate solutions for a given optimization problem. By applying crossover and mutation operators, new individuals are created in each generation of the evolutionary process. The crossover operator combines the target individual with a mutated individual, resulting in an experimental individual that incorporates successful solutions from the previous generation. The experimental individual is then compared with the target individual, and the one with the lowest function value is selected to move on to the next generation. The mutation, crossover and selection processes continue until a stopping criterion is reached, such as reaching the maximum number of generations, reaching the maximum number of function evaluations, reaching a specific fitness value or reaching a predetermined computation time. By improving the population based on the successful individuals and favoring those with the lowest function values, differential evolution aims to converge to the optimal solution of the optimization problem at hand [11].

The DE has only three control parameters that need to be adjusted: mutation, crossover and selection [9]. As with all evolutionary algorithms, the DE starts with an initial set of potential solutions (initialization), which are evolved (using mutation, crossover and selection operators) until a stopping criterion (termination) is achieved [8,19]. In each iteration, for each parent x_i, $i = 1, \ldots, NP$, a mutant vector v_i is created by means of a differential mutation operator. Then, the mutant is crossed-over with the parent and yields an offspring u_i. The selection is based on a competition between x_i and u_i.

Initialization

In the initialization of the algorithm, an initial population of NP individuals is generated in the search space to be evaluated by the DE operators, usually with random values.

Mutation

In the mutation phase, individuals with better fitness are selected and modified by introducing more genetic material into the population to create new individuals. Mutation aims to add diversity and avoid getting stuck in local optima. In the case of DE, a new individual is created by adding a scaled differential term to a base vector (individual). In addition, another aspect that influences the mutation and performance of the algorithm is the mutation factor F, usually a range between 0 and 2 is considered. This factor controls the rate of evolution of the population by determining the size of the perturbation of the differential term. The higher the value of F, the greater the probability of escaping from local optimum.

Mutation has several variants, and the mutant vector v_i used in this paper is presented below [25].

- **DE/rand/1:**
$$v_i = x_{r_1} + F\left(x_{r_2} - x_{r_3}\right)$$

- **DE/best/1:**
$$v_i = x_{\text{best}} + F\left(x_{r_1} - x_{r_2}\right)$$

- **DE/current-to-best/1:**

$$v_i = x_i + F_1\left(x_{\text{best}} - x_i\right) + F_2\left(x_{r_1} - x_{r_2}\right)$$

where $x_{r_1}, x_{r_2}, x_{r_3}$ are randomly selected individuals from the current population $\{1, \ldots, NP\}$, distinct from each other and also from individual x_i (i.e. $r_1 \neq r_2 \neq r_3 \neq i$) and F, F_1 and F_2 are real constants, $F, F_1, F_2 \in [0, 2]$.

Crossover

The crossover phase intends to improve the diversity of the population. Two populations (current and mutated) are used and a new experimental population is created. There are several crossover operators, the most commonly used being the binomial and the exponential. In binomial crossover a random number is generated between 0 and 1 in which, if it is less than the crossover control parameter (CR, crossover probability), the element is removed from the mutated individual. Otherwise, the element from the current individual is copied to the experimental individual. On the other hand, in the exponential crossover procedure an initial starting point is generated, and the opposite of binomial crossover occurs.

Thus, the offspring vector u_i is computed either from the elements of target vector $x_i = x_{i,1}, \ldots, x_{i,n}$ or the elements of the mutant vector $v_i = v_{i,1}, \ldots, v_{i,n}$ as follows:

$$u_{i,j} = \begin{cases} v_{i,j}, & \text{if } \text{rand}_{i,j} \leq CR \text{ or } j = j_{\text{rand}} \\ x_{i,j}, & \text{otherwise} \end{cases}$$

where $i = \{1, \ldots, NP\}$, $j = \{1, \ldots, n\}$, n is the dimension of a single vector, $\text{rand}_{i,j} \sim U(0, 1)$ is a uniformly distributed random number which is generated for each j and $j_{\text{rand}} \in \{1, \ldots, n\}$ is a random integer used to ensure that $u_i \neq x_i$ in all cases.

Selection

In the selection phase of the algorithm, a mechanism is used to select the individuals who will form the next generation. A comparison is made based on their objective values between the experimental and current individuals. The individuals with the lowest function value (when considering a minimization problem) are selected to form the next generation. This survival criterion can also be called "objective function based criterion" or "greedy criterion".

Thus, the new target vector is obtained and its value is computed as follows:

$$x_i = \begin{cases} u_i, \text{ if } f(u_i) < f(x_i) \\ x_i, \text{otherwise} \end{cases}$$

where $f(u_i)$ is the objective function value of the trial vector and $f(x_i)$ is the objective value of the parent vector.

Termination

In the termination phase, the algorithm stops when a stopping condition is reached. Typically, this can be the maximum number of generations or the maximum number of function evaluations, for example.

The DE steps are presented in Algorithm 1.

Algorithm 1. DE algorithm

Require: NP, F, CR

  $\{x_1, x_2, \ldots, x_{NP}\} \longleftarrow$ **Initialization**

  while stopping criterion is not met **do**

    for each point x_i of the population **do**

      Mutation(F)

      Crossover(CR)

      Selection

    end for

  end while

Several approaches have been proposed to solve optimization problems using DE. Researchers continue to explore and develop DE variants and hybrid algorithms that better handle constraints and improve DE performance in constrained optimization scenarios. According to the literature, DE has been widely applied in resource dispatching problems, however, as far as we know, no application of this algorithm to forest firefighting resource dispatching problems has been done. Naziris et al. [18] present an optimization-based metaheuristic approach to solve the budget dispatch problem related to fire safety improvement for a group of historic buildings. The motivation behind this research is the development of a generic resource selection and allocation (SRA) model specifically tailored to the improvement of fire protection measures in historic buildings. The model is formulated as a variant of the knapsack problem and is solved using metaheuristics. The proposed approach is evaluated and compared using two metaheuristic optimization algorithms, namely particle swarm optimization and differential evolution. Real test cases are used to evaluate the effectiveness of the approach, focusing on updating the fire protection measures in the 20 monasteries of Mount Athos. The study demonstrates the efficiency and applicability of the approach based on metaheuristic optimization in solving the SRA model for various budget scenarios. The results show the adaptability and suitability of the approach in optimizing the selection and allocation of resources for different networks of historic buildings and cultural heritage structures. In the article by Li et al. [14], an effective three-layer DDE structure with adaptive resource allocation that increases search efficiency and improves computational efficiency has been proposed. Three methods (general performance indicator, fitness evaluation allocation and load balance strategy) were applied to obtain the results. In addition, theoretical analyzes were carried out to show how this structure can be effective. With the results obtained, they verified the efficiency of the proposed structure.

3 Problem Definition

In this paper, the resource dispatch problem for fighting forest fires is described. The problem involves 7 resources, denoted as A, B, C, D, E, F and G, which are dispatching to extinguish 20 ignitions of a forest fire, identified as I_i (where i ranges from 1 to 20). The considered time ranges from 0 to 100 min, with 10 min intervals spanning multiple instants of time. At time 0, resources are stationed at the base or fire station and need to be strategically dispatched to fight the fires over this time interval. Resources for fighting forest fires are vehicles equipped with water tanks. These vehicles have a total water capacity of 9000 liters. The specific capacities of each resource water tank, measured in liters (l), are given in Table 1. At the beginning of the time interval, all resources are fully charged with water, so their tanks are at maximum capacity.

Table 1. Resource capacity

Resource	A	B	C	D	E	F	G
Capacity	500	1000	3000	1500	1000	500	1500

The locations of the ignitions and the base (fire station) are known, as well as the travel times between the base and each ignition point. Additionally, the travel time between each ignition point is also known. It is important to note that the travel times remain constant regardless of the capacity of the firefighting means used. However, the fire spreads over time causing the burned area to increase. The burned area (in ha) of each ignition is known for each instant of time and, increasing over time, with some ignitions growing at a slower rate than others. Similarly, the amount of water (in liters) required to extinguish each ignition varies with time and is related to the burned area. That is, at each instant of time, the larger the burnt area, the greater the amount of water needed to extinguish an ignition. The data used for the problem were generated for the simulation of a real situation of 20 ignitions and are fully described in [15].

To solve the resource dispatch problem, several assumptions need to be considered. Some ignition and resource assumptions are considered. The following ignition assumptions are considered: each ignition can only be extinguished once; a given ignition can be extinguished by one or more resources; if the water capacity of the assigned resources is sufficient to extinguish a given ignition, it will be extinguished immediately. Regarding the resources, it is assumed that, each resource has a maximum capacity of water in its tank, which can be used until it runs out; each resource can only be assigned to one ignition at a time, during each instant of time. Given these assumptions, the resource dispatch problem can be effectively addressed and optimized to dispatch available firefighting resources for maximum efficiency and effectiveness in fighting forest fires.

The objective of this problem is to minimize the total burned area (TBA) by effectively extinguishing the ignitions. To solve the resource dispatch problem, the differential evolution algorithm is used as the chosen solution methodology.

4   Experimental Results

4.1   Implementing Details

In this study, the differential evolution algorithm is implemented in the *Python* programming language. The implementation is based on the adaptation of the DE algorithm from the pymoo framework [4], which is a *Python* library providing several single-objective optimization algorithms. To solve the resource dispatch problem, a permutation representation is used (more details in [15]). This representation consists of ordering a sequence of forest firefighting actions, indicating the order in which resources must be dispatched to extinguish the ignitions. The permutations, which represent potential solutions of the problem, were generated in an array of dimension equal to the number of resources multiplied by the number of ignitions. This array indicates the order each resource must combat the ignitions, i.e., defines the combat priority of each resource. After implementing the DE algorithm and adapting it to the resource dispatch problem for fighting forest fires, different variants of the DE algorithm are tested. The objective is to identify the configuration that presents the best performance in solving the problem of dispatching firefighting vehicles effectively. Variants of the DE algorithm involve exploring various combinations of algorithm parameters, such as population size, mutation rate, crossover rate, and selection strategy, where considered to identify the most effective configuration that can help decision makers to make informed choices and improve dispatching resources strategies for forest firefighting.

In this work, the DE algorithm was configured with specific parameters. The population size was set to 20, the maximum number of generations was set to 1000 and the maximum number of function evaluations was 100000. The crossover probability, which determines the probability of mating occurring during crossover, was fixed at 0.3 and the mutation factor was 0.5. Several crossover operators were tested, including binomial/uniform, exponential, hypercube and linear crossovers. For selection, three different strategies were tested, random selection, best selection and current-to-best selection. These selection strategies determine how individuals are chosen from the population for the next generation based on their fitness values. The type of mutation applied was the polynomial mutation (default) and the mutation probability was 0.1. To ensure robustness and reliability of the results, the experiment was conducted with 30 independent runs. This statistical analysis allows a comprehensive evaluation of the performance of different DE variants and provides significant information about the effectiveness of the algorithm in solving the problem of dispatching resources to combat forest fires.

The numerical experiments were carried out on a PC 11th Gen Intel(R) Core(TM) i7-1165G7 @ 2.80 GHz, 2803 Mhz, 4 Nucleus(s), 8 Processor(s) Logic(s), 16 Gb RAM. The code was implemented in *python* (version 3.9.13) using *VScode* (Version 1.79.1).

4.2 Testing DE Variants

In this section, the strategy used to test the different DE variants is described. The DE variants were obtained by combining Random, Best and Current-to-best selection with Binomial, Exponential, Hypercube and Line crossover. The mutation operator in all test was the polynomial mutation. All DE variants were assessed in terms of total burned area. First, the selection operator was varied, keeping the binomial crossover (DE/Selection/1/Crossover) and polynomial mutation. From the three different selections, the current-to-best selection performed the best. Afterwards, the four different crossover operators were tested, maintaining the polynomial mutation and the current-to-best selection. It turns out that the crossover operator with the best performance was the exponential crossover. Table 2 summarizes the statistics for 30 independent runs of the several DE variants assessed. The total burned area (TBA_{av}), in ha, the number of generations ($ngen_{av}$), the number of objective function evaluations (nfe_{av}), the total used water (UW_{av}), in l, and the execution time ($Time_{av}$), in s, are presented. In addition, the standard deviation of the total burned area (TBA_{sd}) is also reported.

Table 2. Statistics for different variants of DE

DE/Selection/1/Crossover		TBA_{av}	TBA_{sd}	UW_{av}	$ngen_{av}$	nfe_{av}	$Time_{av}$
Selection	Crossover						
Random	Binomial	1279.5	21.4	5319.9	59.2	1164.0	69.7
Best	Binomial	1268.3	15.2	5268.8	66.7	1314.0	74.0
Current-to-best	Binomial	1267.1	20.9	5305.5	70.4	1388.7	35.2
Current-to-best	**Exponential**	**1266.5**	**32.9**	**5250.1**	**98.2**	**1944.7**	**46.3**
Current-to-best	Hypercube	1270.6	25.9	5293.8	70.3	1386.7	35.9
Current-to-best	Line	1273.7	22.6	5332.6	59.8	1176.0	31.0

Based on these performance data statistics, a statistical analysis was conducted. The one-tailed t-student test for was used and the p-values computed. A significance level of 5% was considered, meaning that if the p-value is less than 0.05, the differences between the TBA values are considered statistically significant. This statistical analysis provides a rigorous evaluation of the performance of the different DE operators, allowing for a comprehensive comparison and identification of the operators that yield the most significant improvements in solving the resource dispatch problem for forest firefighting.

Testing Selection

Table 3 presents the results of the statistical analysis performed to evaluate the different selection operators used in the DE algorithm. In the lower triangular part of the table, the p-values corresponding to the comparisons between the selection operators are displayed. These p-values indicate the significance of the differences between the TBA values obtained with each selection operator. In the upper triangular part of the table, the average differences between the TBA values of the selection operators are displayed. These differences provide information about performance variations between selection operators. By examining the p-values and mean differences, it is possible to determine which selection operators have statistically significant differences in terms of their impact on TBA values. This analysis helps to identify the selection operators that contribute to better or worse performance in solving the resource dispatch problem for fighting forest fires using the DE algorithm. After the statistical analysis between the selection operators, it was verified that between the operators random and best, and random and current-to-best, there were significant differences (p-value < 0.05). However, the combination of best selection and current-to-best selection obtained a p-value > 5%. Therefore, the chosen operator was the current-to-best because it was the one that obtained a lower value of TBA (see Table 2) compared to the remaining selection operators.

Table 3. Statistical analysis for selection DE operator

	Random	Best	Current-to-best
Random	–	**11.165**	**12.384**
Best	0.012	–	1.218
Current-to-best	0.013	0.398	–

Testing Crossover

A statistical analysis was performed to compare the DE crossover operators, maintaining the current-to-best selection and the polynomial mutation. The results of this analysis are shown in Table 4. The table shows the p-values corresponding to the paired comparisons of crossover operators in the lower triangle. The p-values indicate whether there are statistically significant differences between the TBA values obtained with each crossover operator. In this case, as all p-values are greater than 0.05, no significant differences are observed between the crossover operators. However, based on the average TBA values shown in Table 2, the exponential crossover was chosen since it has the lowest average TBA value. The negative values presented in Table 4 indicate that the operators in the leftmost column obtained lower TBA values compared to the operators in the corresponding row.

Table 4. Statistical analysis for crossover DE operator

	Binomial	Exponential	Hypercube	Line
Binomial	–	0.557	−3.519	−6.568
Exponential	0.469	–	−4.076	−7.125
Hypercube	0.282	0.298	–	−3.048
Line	0.123	0.166	0.315	–

Overall, the statistical analysis allows for a comprehensive assessment of the performance of DE crossing operators, providing insights into their effectiveness in solving the problem of deploying resources to combat forest fires. After statistical analysis, it was found that the best operators for this problem were current-to-best selection and exponential crossover, that means DE/current-to-best/1/exp.

4.3   Best Result Analysis

The best solution found by the DE algorithm, based on the previously selected operators (current-to-best selection and exponential crossover), among the 30 independent runs, is presented in Table 5. This table includes the optimal value obtained for the total burned area (TBA = 1211.6 ha) and the amount of water used to extinguish the ignitions in the optimal solution (UW = 5088.3 l). Additionally, it presents the number of generations (ngen = 132), the number of function evaluations (nfe = 2620) performed by DE during the optimization process, and the execution time of the algorithm (Time = 46.8 s), indicating its efficiency in finding a high-quality solution within a reasonable time. Thus, this table offers a comprehensive view of the performance and efficiency of the DE algorithm in solving the resource dispatch problem for forest firefighting, considering the selected operators.

Table 5. Best solution found using current-to-best, exponential crossover and polynomial mutation operators (DE/current-to-best/1/exp)

TBA	UW	ngen	nfe	Time
1211.6	5088.3	132.0	2620.0	46.8

Table 6 presents the best solution found by DE, where at each instant of time the resource assigned to each ignition is shown. The symbol $\rightarrow$ represents that the resource of combat is traveling.

Table 6. The best resource dispatch solution found by DE (TBA = 1211.6)

R	t					
		10	20	30	40	50
A	Base	$\rightarrow$	I_{14}	I_{13}	I_{16}	
B	Base	$\rightarrow$	I_4	$\rightarrow$	I_3	
C	Base	$\rightarrow$	I_6	I_{12}	I_{16}	
D	Base	I_9	$\rightarrow$	I_{17}	I_{18}	I_{15}
E	Base	$\rightarrow$	I_{20}	$\rightarrow$	I_{10}	I_2
F	Base	$\rightarrow$	I_8	I_5		
G	Base	I_7	I_{19}	I_{11}	$\rightarrow$	I_1

In the beginning, all the resources are at the Base. At $t = 10$, the resources D and G are assigned to ignitions I_9 and I_7, respectively. At $t = 20$ resources A, B, C, E, F and G are assigned to extinguish ignitions I_{14}, I_4, I_6, I_{20}, I_8 and I_{19}, respectively. In addition, resource D is traveling. The ignitions I_{13}, I_{12}, I_{17}, I_5 and I_{11} are extinguished at the instant of time $t = 30$. At the instant of time $t = 40$, resources B, D and E are dispatched to ignitions I_3, I_{18} and I_{10}, respectively, extinguishing them. Resources A and C are assigned to ignition I_{16}. Resource A ran out of water in its tank, so resource C is needed to finish extinguishing this ignition. From this instant of time, resource F was not assigned to any more ignitions, as it did not have enough water to extinguish any other remaining ignitions. Finally at instant of time $t = 50$, the ignitions I_{15}, I_2 and I_1 were extinguished by the resources D, E and G, respectively. In this solution, it took only 5 instants of time for the 7 resources to extinguish all ignitions.

4.4 Comparison Between de and GA

In this section, the performance between DE and GA algorithms is analyzed. The comparison is based on the average values, among 30 runs, obtained by DE and GA. Table 7 presents the performance of the algorithms in terms of the average values of TBA, UW, nfe and Time, where the lower values are indicated in bold. The optimization results when solving this problem by GA can be found in [15].

Table 7. Comparison between DE and GA average results

TBA_{av}		UW_{av}		nfe_{av}		$Time_{av}$	
DE	GA	DE	GA	DE	GA	DE	GA
1266.5	**1249.9**	**5250.1**	5891.2	1944.7	**1584.7**	46.3	**16.1**

It can be seen that in terms of average TBA, GA outperformed DE. In contrast, the average value of UW was lower in DE than in GA. However, it should be noted that UW was not being optimized. DE obtained the highest average nfe value while GA was the least time-consuming. The difference between the average TBA values achieved by DE and GA is 16.6. A statistical analysis was performed between the TBA values for both algorithms, which showed that the p-value for the TBA mean difference test was greater than 0.05, meaning that there were no significant differences between the performance of the two algorithms.

5   Conclusions

The occurrence of forest fires has increased in recent years. Therefore, the importance of studying new decision-making approaches for forest firefighting means is very significant.

In this paper a problem of dispatching forest firefighting resources was studied. The effective dispatch of firefighting resources plays a vital role in forest firefighting management. In order to control the fire in the shortest possible time, resources must be dispatched efficiently and effectively. The goal was to minimize the TBA by assigning 7 combat resources to extinguish 20 ignitions. For this, the differential evolution algorithm was applied. The DE algorithm is a powerful optimization technique that can be used to efficiently and effectively dispatch firefighting resources, leading to a reduction in the total burned area caused by ignitions. Furthermore, a statistical analysis was performed between the variants of DE (DE/selection/1/crossover) for the forest firefighting resource dispatch problem. This analysis revealed that the best DE variant for this particular problem was DE/current-to-best/1/exp. These operators showed superior performance and effectiveness in minimizing the total burned area and obtaining optimal solutions. An optimal solution value of TBA = 1211.6 ha was found. Additionally, a statistical analysis and comparison of the average solutions between the DE and GA algorithms was performed, where it was found that there were no significant differences, although GA had a lower average TBA value when compared to DE.

In the future, it is intended to solve this type of problems using a multi-objective strategy, for example, minimizing the total burned area and the used simultaneously. Moreover, to validate this strategy, a problem with real data will be solved.

References

1. Alvelos, F.: Mixed integer programming models for fire fighting. In: Gervasi, O., et al. (eds.) Computational Science and Its Applications - ICCSA 2018, pp. 637–652. Springer, Cham (2018). https://doi.org/10.1007/978-3-319-95165-2_45
2. Attri, V., Dhiman, R., Sarvade, S.: A review on status, implications and recent trends of forest fire management. Arch. Agric. Environ. Sci. 5(4), 592–602 (2020)

3. Bélanger, V., Lanzarone, E., Nicoletta, V., Ruiz, A., Soriano, P.: A recursive simulation-optimization framework for the ambulance location and dispatching problem. Eur. J. Oper. Res. **286**(2), 713–725 (2020)
4. Blank, J., Deb, K.: Pymoo: multi-objective optimization in Python. IEEE Access **8**, 89497–89509 (2020)
5. Boer, M.M., de Dios, V.R., Bradstock, R.A.: Unprecedented burn area of Australian mega forest fires. Nat. Clim. Chang. **10**(3), 171–172 (2020)
6. Chan, H., Tran-Thanh, L., Viswanathan, V.: Fighting wildfires under uncertainty: a sequential resource allocation approach. In: Proceedings of the Twenty-Ninth International Conference on International Joint Conferences on Artificial Intelligence, pp. 4322–4329 (2021)
7. Coogan, S.C., Robinne, F.N., Jain, P., Flannigan, M.D.: Scientists' warning on wildfire-a Canadian perspective. Can. J. For. Res. **49**(9), 1015–1023 (2019)
8. Dragoi, E.N., Curteanu, S.: The use of differential evolution algorithm for solving chemical engineering problems. Rev. Chem. Eng. **32**(2), 149–180 (2016)
9. Georgioudakis, M., Plevris, V.: A comparative study of differential evolution variants in constrained structural optimization. Front. Built Environ. **6**, 102 (2020)
10. Granberg, T.A.: Optimized dispatch of fire and rescue resources. In: de Armas, J., Ramalhinho, H., Voß, S. (eds.) Computational Logistics: 13th International Conference, ICCL 2022, Barcelona, Spain, 21–23 September 2022, Proceedings, vol. 13557, pp. 132–146. Springer, Cham (2022). https://doi.org/10.1007/978-3-031-16579-5_10
11. Hassan, S., Hemeida, A.M., Alkhalaf, S., Mohamed, A.A., Senjyu, T.: Multi-variant differential evolution algorithm for feature selection. Sci. Rep. **10**(1), 1–16 (2020)
12. HomChaudhuri, B., Kumar, M., Cohen, K.: Genetic algorithm based simulation-optimization for fighting wildfires. Int. J. Comput. Methods **10**(06), 1350035 (2013)
13. HomChaudhuri, B., Zhao, S., Cohen, K., Kumar, M.: Generation of optimal fireline for fighting wildland fires using genetic algorithms. In: Dynamic Systems and Control Conference, vol. 48920, pp. 111–118 (2009)
14. Li, J.Y., Du, K.J., Zhan, Z.H., Wang, H., Zhang, J.: Distributed differential evolution with adaptive resource allocation. IEEE Trans. Cybern. **53**(5), 2791–2804 (2022)
15. Matos, M.A., Rocha, A.M.A.C., Costa, L.A., Alvelos, F.: Resource dispatch optimization for firefighting based on genetic algorithm. In: Gervasi, O., et al. (eds.) Computational Science and Its Applications - ICCSA 2023 Workshops, pp. 437–453. Springer, Cham (2023). https://doi.org/10.1007/978-3-031-37108-0_28
16. Mendes, A.B., e Alvelos, F.P.: Iterated local search for the placement of wildland fire suppression resources. Eur. J. Oper. Res. **304**(3), 887–900 (2023)
17. Naderpour, M., Rizeei, H.M., Khakzad, N., Pradhan, B.: Forest fire induced Natech risk assessment: a survey of geospatial technologies. Reliab. Eng. Syst. Saf. **191**, 106558 (2019)
18. Naziris, I.A., Lagaros, N.D., Papaioannou, K.: Selection and resource allocation model for upgrading fire safety of historic buildings. J. Manag. Eng. **32**(4), 05016004 (2016)
19. Pant, M., Zaheer, H., Garcia-Hernandez, L., Abraham, A., et al.: Differential evolution: a review of more than two decades of research. Eng. Appl. Artif. Intell. **90**, 103479 (2020)
20. San-Miguel-Ayanz, J., et al.: Forest fires in Europe, Middle East and North Africa 2021 (KJ-NA-31-269-EN-N (online), KJ-NA-31-269-EN-C (print)) (2022). https://doi.org/10.2760/34094

21. Storn, R., Price, K.: Differential evolution-a simple and efficient heuristic for global optimization over continuous spaces. J. Global Optim. **11**(4), 341 (1997)
22. Vieira, D., Borrelli, P., Jahanianfard, D., Benali, A., Scarpa, S., Panagos, P.: Wildfires in Europe: burned soils require attention. Environ. Res. **217**, 114936 (2023)
23. Wu, G., Shen, X., Li, H., Chen, H., Lin, A., Suganthan, P.: Ensemble of differential evolution variants. Inf. Sci. **423**, 172–186 (2018). https://doi.org/10.1016/j.ins.2017.09.053, https://www.sciencedirect.com/science/article/pii/S0020025517309714
24. Zeferino, J.A.: Optimizing the location of aerial resources to combat wildfires: a case study of Portugal. Nat. Hazards **100**(3), 1195–1213 (2020)
25. Zeng, Z., Zhang, M., Chen, T., Hong, Z.: A new selection operator for differential evolution algorithm. Knowl.-Based Syst. **226**, 107150 (2021)
26. Zhou, K., Zhang, F.: An event-response tree-based resource scheduling method for wildfire fighting. Forests **14**(1), 102 (2023)

A Pattern Mining Heuristic for the Extension of Multi-trip Vehicle Routing

Leila Karimi[iD], Connor Little[(✉)], and Salimur Choudhury[iD]

School of Computing, Queen's University, Kingston, ON K7L 3N6, Canada
{leila.karimi,connor.little,s.choudhury}@queensu.ca

Abstract. Multi-trip vehicle routing problem with a variable number of wagons significantly reduces the number of vehicles and drivers needed to service customers. It is often hard to solve these problems in acceptable CPU times using exact algorithms when the problem contains very big real-world data sets. We use meta-heuristic algorithms to get a solution close to the optimal solutions for vehicle routing problems with a dynamic capacity of a vehicle. First, local search heuristics applied with genetic algorithms are proposed. Then, a pattern-mining algorithm is developed to improve the solutions found from the genetic algorithm. We perform detailed experiments on Solomon instances for vehicle routing problem with time windows (VRPTW). Our experiments establish the effectiveness of the algorithms.

Keywords: Vehicle routing problem · Multi-trip · Various capacity · Pattern mining · Genetic algorithm

1 Introduction

A variation of the classical vehicle routing problem with time windows (VRPTW) [27] where vehicles can be planned for more than one trip within a workday is known as the Multi-Trip Vehicle Routing Problem with Time Windows (MTVRPTW) [5]. MTVRPTW emerges when the number of vehicles and drivers is limited. Despite of the importance of MTVRPTW and its daily use in the supply chain, fewer papers have studied this variant compared to other types of VRP. In this study, we take into account a specific variant of MTVRPTW, where the capacity of a vehicle is constructed at the beginning of the workday.

A variant of the classical vehicle problem known as the multi-trip vehicle routing problem with variable numbers of wagons and time windows (MTVRP-VW-TW) [13] allows for the determination of a vehicle's capacity based on the route's overall demand as the vehicle is getting ready to depart the depot. In this case, one, two, or three wagons could be connected to create a vehicle that is prepared to serve customers. Therefore, three different capacities are possible for each vehicle, and the capacity remains constant throughout the day for all

© The Author(s), under exclusive license to Springer Nature Switzerland AG 2024
A. I. Pereira et al. (Eds.): OL2A 2023, CCIS 1981, pp. 78–92, 2024.
https://doi.org/10.1007/978-3-031-53025-8_6

routes. This considerably reduces waste of the capacity of a vehicle when it is not required and less number of vehicles and drivers can be assigned to service all customers. The ability to serve customers at varied distances is significantly impacted by adjusting a vehicle's capacity. While the number of wagons per vehicle does not directly influence the objective function which is the minimization of the total distances and the number of vehicles, it does change which routes are feasible. By allocating wagons to specific vehicles, more efficient routes could be constructed. For some cases, adding more wagons allows us to have a longer route since return trips to the depot can be omitted and for some other cases, a shorter route can be built with fewer wagons added. Additionally, the introduction of wagons allows more parameters for routers to control, allowing the problem to be more analogous to real-world scenarios, at the cost of higher complexity.

The Vehicle Routing Problem with time window (VRPTW) is an NP-hard problem in general [17], and it is typically challenging to obtain an optimal solution, especially as the problem becomes more complex and relevant to the real world. In the case of multi-trip VRPTW, the problem is solved by up to 40 customers optimally [5,11] and up to 10 customers for MTVRP-VW-TW [13]. The majority of studies to solve VRP used heuristic techniques due to memory, time, and cost limitations and it can be applied to a wider range of customers. Among meta-heuristic algorithms, a genetic algorithm is a successful one. Operators for crossover and mutation can be added to enhance the genetic algorithm. A number of operators to apply to traveling salesman problems and their variants are introduced in [2]. In this paper, we use local search operators defined in [18] to improve the effectiveness of the genetic algorithm.

The goal of many research work on VRP is to aim to have high-quality solutions for heuristic techniques. A new technique called pattern injection local search is introduced in [3] to seek the effectiveness of the solution. The algorithm explores high-quality patterns and injects them into the solution. So, high-order neighborhoods are discovered by pattern mining and injection.

The main contribution of this work is to develop a meta-heuristic algorithm to solve MTVRP-VW-TW while the algorithm provides a near-optimal solution. MTVRP-VW-TW is only solved optimally by up to 10 customers in [13] and this is the first meta-heuristic algorithm presented to solve the problem. Our algorithm solves the problem more effectively and closes to the optimal solution while it is faster than the exact algorithms. Genetic algorithm and pattern mining local search are used to create the meta-heuristic algorithm. Extensive experiments are performed on Solomon instances [1].

The rest of the paper is organized as follows. The related work is presented in Sect. 2. We describe the problem definition in Sect. 3. The construction heuristic is in Sect. 4. The genetic algorithm to solve MTVRP-VW-TW is described in Sect. 5. The pattern mining heuristic is in Sect. 6. The detailed experimental study is discussed in Sect. 7. Finally, we conclude with a discussion in Sect. 8.

2   Related Work

A wide range of Vehicle Routing Problems has been studied as a result of the requirement to find optimal solutions to logistic and distribution problems. One of the main challenges related to logistic and distribution problems is the execution time for finding the optimal solutions that exponentially rise when the number of customers increases. Multi-trip vehicle routing problem (MTVRP) is one of these essential daily needs of distribution products whose exact algorithms are ineffective. Instead, various heuristic algorithms are developed to solve these problems in terms of time and efficiency.

First, Fleischmann [9] used a Bin Packing Problem algorithm to assign the routes to vehicles with multiple uses. Later, Brandão and Mercer [7] presented a tabu search algorithm for MTVRP. A hybrid genetic algorithm for MTVRP is proposed in [8]. They introduced a new local search operator to swap customers between trips as well. A hybrid particle swarm optimization algorithm and a hybrid genetic algorithm are developed in [31]. They found a near-optimal solution for small instances and up to 200 customers are evaluated. Pan et al. [23] modeled multi-trip time-dependent vehicle routing problem with time windows. Two Ready time and duration functions are defined to accelerate the local search operators.

A heterogeneous fleet vehicle routing problem ($HVRP$) is a variant of VRP. The vehicles are of different capacities located at the depot, and a fixed cost is associated with each vehicle. [22] takes into account the three-dimensional (3D) loading constraints that must be satisfied given the vehicle's capacity. They used a local search and simulated annealing to find a solution. Gendreau et al. [10] proposed a tabu search for heterogeneous fleet vehicle routing problems. Berghida and Boukra [6] developed a quantum-inspired algorithm for a VRP with heterogeneous fleet mixed backhauls and time windows. Penna et al. [24] solved the problem using a hybrid heuristic that mixed a local search with a variable neighborhood search. An updated version of the green VRPTW is presented in [20]. To optimize the routing of a mixed vehicle fleet made up of electric and conventional vehicles, they suggested an iterative local search algorithm. [16] is a survey on heterogeneous vehicle routing problems and their variants. Additionally, the paper compares the metaheuristic algorithms that have been suggested. Prins [25] developed the heterogeneous VRP for a limited number of each vehicle type and the potential for each vehicle to make multiple trips added to the problem. They described a few heuristics to solve the problem. Memetic algorithm and simulated annealing approaches for multi-trip heterogeneous vehicle routing problems coordinated with production scheduling are presented in [30]. A hybrid differential evolution algorithm combining a genetic operator with a fuzzy logic controller for multi-trip vehicle routing problems with backhauls and heterogeneous fleets has been developed in [26]. Vieira et al. [29] proposed two metaheuristic algorithms based on unified hybrid genetic search and variable neighborhood search to evaluate the instances for the heterogeneous site-dependent multi-depot multi-trip periodic vehicle routing problem.

In this paper, we consider a new variant of VRP called MTVRP-VW-TW which is presented in [14] for the first time. The problem is to make various capacities for the vehicles by attaching wagons to them based on the routes that they are going. The vehicle configuration is made at the beginning of each workday and vehicles can have more than one route daily. In contrast to heterogeneous VRP, there are a limited number of trailers and wagons. There is no extra cost for a trailer when wagons are attached to it. This gives vehicles three different capacities. The problem in this paper allows the vehicle to change configuration daily. A mathematical model and branch and price algorithm are proposed in [14]. The algorithm is implemented for small instances. In this paper, we are developing a heuristic algorithm to run the problem for larger instances while the solution can be effective.

Arnold et al. [3] introduced a new algorithm called pattern injection local search (PILS). The algorithm explores high-order local-search neighborhoods and injects them into the solution. This is done in two stages, pattern extraction, and pattern injection. The application of the algorithm is studied on two metaheuristics [4] and [28] for the capacitated vehicle routing problem. PILS notably improves the performance of each metaheuristic. In [19], PILS is applied to genetic Algorithms on the multiobjective capacitated pickup and delivery problem with time windows. They introduced various inter-route and intra-route mutations to see how they affect the final solution. We use the pattern mining exploration applied to the genetic algorithm presented in [19] on MTVRP-VW-TW and evaluate the performance of the algorithm on large instances.

3   Problem Definition

The Multi-Trip Vehicle Routing Problem with a Variable Number of Wagons and Time Windows is presented in a complete directed graph $G = (N, A)$, where A is a set of arcs $\{(i, j) : i \neq j, i, j \in N\}$ and N is a set of nodes including customers and depot $\{0\}$. A traveling time is associated with each arc of A. We consider the traveling time as the distance between every two nodes. Each customer has a demand that should be met within a time window $[a_i, b_i]$, a_i is the earliest point in time and b_i is the latest point in time where the customer may be visited. If the vehicle arrives before the time window, should wait, and if this is after the time window, the customer can not be visited. A customer's whole demand should be satisfied at a single vehicle visit. Each client has a service time. A set of vehicles is used to service customers. There are a set of wagons with a capacity of q for each one that is combined to build a vehicle's capacity. Hence, an organization of a vehicle is several wagons added to the vehicle. The number of wagons attached to a vehicle is up to three. Therefore, the capacity associated with a vehicle can be q, $2q$, or $3q$. At the beginning of the workday, vehicle configurations are built and stay the same during the day. A route is a closed path that visits various customers. It starts and ends at the depot. Each vehicle can have multiple routes during a workday which is called a tour. Tours start and end at the depot as well. Each customer should be visited exactly once. The time windows of the customers should be satisfied. The starting of a vehicle's subsequent route should occur after the completion of its former route. There are limitations on the number of vehicles, wagons, and routes.

The objective function is a hierarchical cost function. The two objectives we aim to minimize are the number of vehicles and the total distance traveled. A weight of 10000 was assigned to the number of vehicles while a weight of 1 was applied to the distance traveled. This ensures the number of vehicles takes priority in the algorithm. If a solution is invalid it is assigned a cost of infinity.

4 Construction Heuristic

The construction heuristic is built using a random sequential insertion algorithm. This algorithm was chosen as it provided a lot of variance in the initial population, while also being very fast. The algorithm begins with a single route seeded with a random customer. A new customer is inserted into a random possible location in the route while the demand of the customer and the remaining capacity of the vehicle is checked. If there is not enough capacity to service the customer demand and the number of added wagons is less than three, then we can add a new wagon to the vehicle. When a vehicle is back at the depot, it can start a new route. If there are no valid locations to insert a new customer, a new vehicle is added and the process is repeated. The number of vehicles is always initially set to be large enough to be constructed. A 2-opt algorithm is implemented after inserting a customer to improve the solution. Algorithm 1 generates the initial solutions.

This algorithm was chosen when compared against parallel insertion heuristics, cheapest insertion, and furthest insertion. Random sequential insertion produced relatively fit individuals with a much more diverse population.

5 Genetic Algorithm

Genetic algorithms aim to be effective and flexible in a wide range of circumstances. A review of genetic algorithms are presented in [21] and [15]. Karakatič and Podgorelec [12] provided a survey of genetic algorithms for multi-depot vehicle routing problems. They discussed the weakness and strengths of approaches, operators, and settings. Following, we described the initial population, evaluation, selection, crossover, and mutation of genetic algorithms for our problem.

Initial Population: The initial population is generated by the construction heuristic explained above.

Evaluation: The objective is to minimize the total distances of all tours. Hierarchical evaluation is used: $\alpha * numbervehicles + \beta * totaldistance$. α and β were chosen to weight the number of vehicles significantly higher than the distance, ensuring that fewer vehicles were always prioritized.

Algorithm 1. Sequential Insertion

Input: Insertion Heuristic H, Insertion Operator I, Local Search Operator O
Output: A feasible solution

1: *routes* ← []
2: Let *requests* be a set of nodes to insert
3: **while** True **do**
4:    *newRoute* ← []
5:    **while** Not all *requests* are inserted **do**
6:       *tempRoute* ← *newRoute*
7:       Choose *request* with H
8:       Insert *request* into *newRoute* with I
9:       Improve *newRoute* with O
10:       **if** *newRoute* is feasible **then**
11:          Remove *request* from *requests*
12:       **else**
13:          Append *tempRoute* to *routes*
14:          break
15:       **end if**
16:    **end while**
17:    **if** *requests* is empty **then**
18:       return *routes*
19:    **end if**
20: **end while**

Selection: The binary tournament selection with replacement is applied for parent selection. Offspring selection uses the new offspring and old population together, which are taken and sorted by linear rank. Multi-pointer selection is employed to select a new population fairly.

Crossover: We used the crossover operation described in the thesis [19]. Parents are solutions including a variety of tours. To make a solution from these two parents, each iteration, one tour is randomly taken from one of the parents. In the beginning, the solution is empty. Eventually, randomly taken tours are appended to it. We check if there are common customers in the taken tour and the solution that we are building, they will be removed. The rest of the tour is appended to the solution. We continue until there are no more tours from any parent to be added. As the final step, if ithere are small (2 nodes or less) routes, we remove it. We then reinsert those nodes into other routes. This crossover operation will be called route copy crossover with ejection.

Mutation: Inter-route and intra-route operations are used to improve the solution. Inter-route operations including single-pair relocation, double-pair relocation, customer relocation, best-customer relocation, route ejection, and route divide are applied. And for intra-route, 2-opt and 4-opt are applied. With the 4-opt a Monte-Carlo algorithm is employed as the search space can be too large to fully cover in a reasonable time.

6   Pattern Mining Heuristic

Pattern mining local search was created by Arnold and Sörensen [4] in 2019. It is a multi-step process that aims to use historical solution data to improve upon newer solutions. The algorithms can be broadly broken down into two steps: pattern mining and pattern extraction.

The first step is pattern mining. Patterns are ordered sequences of customers. As solutions are learned and updated within the genetic algorithm, patterns can be extracted from a solution. Every iteration a subset of the solutions is chosen and for given lengths patterns are collected and stored in a heap. This is done in an exhaustive fashion using a sliding window over the routes of a given solution. A maximum number of patterns are stored and sorted by frequency.

The second step is pattern insertion. Once a sufficient number of patterns have been extracted they will be forcefully added back into a new solution. A branch and bound inspired algorithm is used, as seen in Algorithm 2. This algorithm selects a solution and a pattern. All nodes from the pattern are removed from the solution, reducing the solution to fragments. These fragments either originate from the depot and are beginning fragments, do not interact with the depot and are middle fragments, or end at the depot and are ending fragments. These fragments, alongside the chosen pattern, are iteratively combined to produce a new solution.

We need the following notation to describe the following algorithm:

- R: A pattern, which is a subset of the solution.
- R_beg: A set which contains all patterns which begins at the depot.
- beg: A single pattern which begins at the depot.
- R_mid: A set which contains all patterns which does not contain the depot.
- mid: A single pattern which does not contain the depot.
- R_end: A set which contains all patterns which ends at the depot.
- end: A single pattern which ends at the depot.
- R_comp: A set which contains all patterns which begins and ends at the depot.
- B: The best solution known.
- F: A function which returns the objective function for a given solution.
- len: the length of a pattern

Pattern mining and insertion have many benefits over other heuristics. One such benefit is that it is able to make much higher-order moves than would otherwise be possible. This allows a larger search space to be explored. It is also a learning-based algorithm with minimal overhead once learned.

The integration into the genetic algorithm is shown in Fig. 1.

Algorithm 2. Pattern Insertion

Input: R_{beg}, R_{mid}, R_{end}, R_{comp}, Best Solution B, Evaluation Function F
Output: Best Solution B

1: **if** $F(R_{beg}) + F(R_{mid}) + F(R_{end}) + F(R_{comp}) \leq F(B)$ **then**
2:    **if** $len(R_{beg}) == 0$ **then**
3:       return R_{comp}
4:    **else**
5:       $beg \leftarrow random\_choice(R_{beg})$
6:       **for** $mid \in R_{mid}$ **do**
7:          $R_{beg2} \leftarrow R_{beg} - beg + (beg + mid)$
8:          $R_{mid2} \leftarrow R_{mid} - mid$
9:          $candidate \leftarrow Pattern\_Insertion(R_{beg2}, R_{mid2}, R_{end}, R_{comp}, B, F)$
10:         **if** $F(candidate) < F(B)$ **then**
11:            $B \leftarrow candidate$
12:         **end if**
13:       **end for**
14:       **if** $len(R_{beg}) \neq 1 || len(R_{mid}) = 0$ **then**
15:          **for** $end \in R_{end}$ **do**
16:             $R_{beg2} \leftarrow R_{beg} - beg$
17:             $R_{end2} \leftarrow R_{end} - end$
18:             $R_{comp2} \leftarrow R_{comp} + (beg + end)$
19:             $candidate \leftarrow Pattern\_Insertion(R_{beg2}, R_{mid}, R_{end2}, R_{comp2}, B, F)$
20:             **if** $F(candidate) < f(B)$ **then**
21:                $B \leftarrow candidate$
22:             **end if**
23:          **end for**
24:       **end if**
25:    **end if**
26: **end if**
27: return B

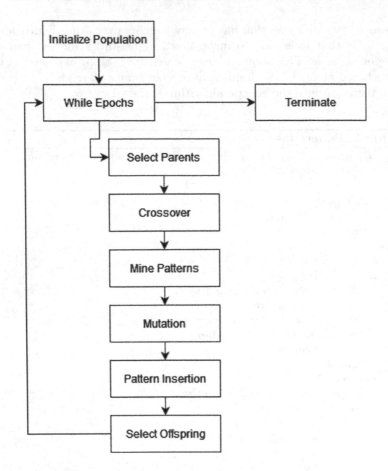

Fig. 1. Workflow for pattern insertion heuristic genetic algorithm

7   Results

All instances were run on an i7-9750H CPU with 16 GB of RAM. Our work was done in two separate experiments. The first was a comparison of pattern mining on the 50 node Solomon instances [1] unaltered. The second was a comparison that introduced multiple trips and wagons. 3 trips were allowed per vehicle and the capacity of each vehicle is set to 0. To compensate for the lack of capacity, wagons can be allocated which increased a vehicle's capacity by the original capacity divided by 3. This allows the algorithm to decide how to weigh each vehicle. In all cases, we used the same genetic algorithm. The parameters can be found in Table 1.

The number of epochs and the population size were chosen empirically. The population was chosen to be large enough to still contain diversity while small enough to allow multiple iterations such that the populations always converged before finishing. When comparing against the standard iteration of the

Table 1. Model Parameters

Parameter	Value
Parent Selection	Binary tournament with replacement
Offspring Selection	$(\mu + \lambda)$ with Multi Pointer Selection
Intra Route Mutation Operator	2-opt and 4-opt
Inter Route Mutation Operator	Ejection Search, Single Pair Search, Customer search, Best Customer Search, Route Swap Search, Route Divide
Xover Operation	Route Copy Crossover w Ejection
Construction Heuristic	Random Sequential Insertion
Population	50
Epochs	100
Mutation Rate	100%
Xover Rate	30%
α	10000
β	1
Max Time (<50 nodes)	1200 s
Max Time (100 nodes)	3600 s
Pattern Extraction Rate[a]	20%
Pattern Insertion Rate[a]	20%
Pattern Size[a]	50%
Max Heap Size[a]	200%
Number of trips[b]	3
Number of wagons[b]	Number of vehicles * 3
Capacity of wagons[b]	capacity/3

[a]Only included in the pattern mining version of the problem.
[b]Only included in the experiment with wagons and multi-trip.

Solomon instances the pattern mining greatly outperformed the non-pattern mining instances. The results can be seen in Tables 2 and 3. The greatest difference was in the clustered instances (C) which improved distance 39.11% and reduced the number of vehicles by 25.72%. Randomly distributed instances (R) were improved by a distance of 18.06% but also increased vehicles by 4.54%. Lastly, randomly distributed and clustered data (RC) improved distance by 6.65% and improved vehicles by 4%. Overall the pattern mining heuristic was beneficial when appended to the genetic algorithm framework.

Table 2. Solomon 50 Instances without Pattern Mining

Class of Problem	Average Distance	Average Number of Vehicles
C	738.73	6.92
R	862.54	4.4
RC	980.64	6.25
All	833.33	6.18

Table 3. Solomon 50 Instances with Pattern Mining

Class of Problem	Average distance	Average Number of Vehicles
C	449.82	5.14
R	706.75	4.6
RC	915.34	6.0
All	635.33	5.37

When introducing wagons and multi-trip similar results were seen. The results are slightly higher than the previous experiment as some vehicles are given smaller capacities (one wagon) compared to the vehicles used in Tables 2 and 3. Tables 4 and 5 display our findings. Clustered instances were improved by a distance of 23.28% and the number of vehicles was reduced by 12.16%. Randomly distributed instances improved by 9.33% and 11.57% respectively. Finally, the class RC was improved by 8.58% in terms of distance but increased vehicles by 12.18 %. Similar to the previous experiment, the overall contribution of the pattern extraction heuristic was positive. When working with clustered instances the difference is most apparent. R and RC instances still had improvement most often, but the difference between them was inconsistent.

A third experiment was run on larger instances to determine how the heuristic would scale. We tested the Solomon 100-node instances with the following modifications. Unlike the 50-node instances, the 100-node instances were unlikely to converge, so a strict limit of 1 h was set. This meant that the pattern mining variation would perform fewer epochs as it contains more computation. Secondly, to convert the problem into a multi-trip variation with wagons each instance was assigned 3 trips, its capacity was divided by 3, and the number of wagons was set to 3 times the number of vehicles. This allows the algorithm to weigh how much each vehicle should carry. The algorithms were run on the first 5 instances of each distribution, I.E. C101, C102, C103, C104, C105, R101, etc. Tables 6 and 7 display the results.

Table 4. Solomon 50 Instances with Wagons without Pattern Mining

Class of Problem	Average Distance	Average Number of Vehicles
C	738.53	7.07
R	903.89	4.75
RC	1109.56	7.22
All	886.71	7.03

Table 5. Solomon 50 Instances with Wagons with Pattern Mining

Class of Problem	Average distance	Average Number of Vehicles
C	566.59	6.21
R	819.47	4.2
RC	1014.33	8.1
All	764.58	6.51

Table 6. Multi-trip Solomon 100 Instances with Wagons without Pattern Mining

Class of Problem	Average Distance	Average Vehicles
C1	2963.82	18.4
R1	2746.07	26.6
RC1	3553.46	27.4
All	3087.79	24.13

When viewing how the heuristic performed, overall there is a marginal difference. The pattern mining heuristic made slightly shorter trips but required slightly more vehicles. More interesting is how the algorithm interacted with each distribution. It has the opposite effect as the 50-node instances. The new heuristic performed significantly worse on clustered instances while performing moderately better on random instances, and the best on random clustered instances. This coincides with the work done by Little [19] on the dynamic instances. When not all data is analyzed, clustered data tends to produce counter intuitive patterns, while randomly distributed data with frequent clusters improves the patterns that are found. Based on the 50-node experiments, this dissonance between data types is removed when sufficient time is given to exploration, reversing the impact that the distribution has on the result.

Table 7. Multi-trip Solomon 100 Instances with Wagons with Pattern Mining

Class of Problem	Average distance	Average Number of Vehicles
C1	2913.20	20.6
R1	2665.21	26.0
RC1	3266.47	26.2
All	2948.30	24.26

8   Conclusion and Future Work

This work designed a new algorithm for MTVRP-VW-TW. The problem is a variant of standard VRP where each client should be served in a time frame and a vehicle can perform more than one trip throughout the period of a workday while the capacity of vehicles is built at the start of the day. The genetic algorithm is one of the best-known metaheuristics to solve VRPs. Here, we introduce a new metaheuristic using genetic algorithms and pattern mining to solve the problem fast and effectively for large instances. With pattern mining insertion, we are able to find solutions that are better than previously known solutions. We implemented the algorithm on Solomon's instances for 50 and 100 customers to see the effectiveness of the algorithm. Then, the comparison of the results with the previous ones is done. And, we show using the genetic algorithm we can find near-optimal solutions in a reasonable time for a large number of customers.

Future work would involve expanding on the problem to create a proper benchmark and exploring other metaheuristics. Possible metaheuristics could include variable neighbourhood search, which could incorporate the patterns learned into the neighbourhoods searched, or tabu search.

References

1. Solomon's benchmark instances (2008). https://www.sintef.no/projectweb/top/vrptw/solomon-benchmark/. Accessed 30 Mar 2023
2. Abdoun, O., Abouchabaka, J., Tajani, C.: Analyzing the performance of mutation operators to solve the travelling salesman problem. arXiv preprint arXiv:1203.3099 (2012)
3. Arnold, F., Santana, Í., Sörensen, K., Vidal, T.: PILS: exploring high-order neighborhoods by pattern mining and injection. Pattern Recogn. **116**, 107957 (2021)
4. Arnold, F., Sörensen, K.: Knowledge-guided local search for the vehicle routing problem. Comput. Oper. Res. **105**, 32–46 (2019)
5. Azi, N., Gendreau, M., Potvin, J.Y.: An exact algorithm for a vehicle routing problem with time windows and multiple use of vehicles. Eur. J. Oper. Res. **202**(3), 756–763 (2010)
6. Berghida, M., Boukra, A.: Quantum inspired algorithm for a VRP with heterogeneous fleet mixed backhauls and time windows. Int. J. Appl. Metaheuristic Comput. (IJAMC) **7**(4), 18–38 (2016)

7. Brandão, J.C.S., Mercer, A.: The multi-trip vehicle routing problem. J. Oper. Res. Soc. **49**, 799–805 (1998)
8. Cattaruzza, D., Absi, N., Feillet, D., Vidal, T.: A memetic algorithm for the multi trip vehicle routing problem. Eur. J. Oper. Res. **236**(3), 833–848 (2014)
9. Fleischmann, B.: The vehicle routing problem with multiple use of vehicles. Fachbereich Wirtschaftswissenschaften, Universität Hamburg (1990)
10. Gendreau, M., Laporte, G., Musaraganyi, C., Taillard, É.D.: A Tabu search heuristic for the heterogeneous fleet vehicle routing problem. Comput. Oper. Res. **26**(12), 1153–1173 (1999)
11. Hernandez, F., Feillet, D., Giroudeau, R., Naud, O.: An exact method to solve the multitrip vehicle routing problem with time windows and limited duration. TRISTAN **7**, 366–369 (2010)
12. Karakatič, S., Podgorelec, V.: A survey of genetic algorithms for solving multi depot vehicle routing problem. Appl. Soft Comput. **27**, 519–532 (2015)
13. Karimi, L., Nawrin Ferdous, C.: Branch and price algorithm for multi-trip vehicle routing with a variable number of wagons and time windows. Algorithms **15**(11), 412 (2022)
14. Karimi, L., et al.: Algorithms for multi-trip vehicle routing and device to device communications. Ph.D. thesis, Lethbridge, Alta.: Department of Mathematics and Computer Science (2022)
15. Katoch, S., Chauhan, S.S., Kumar, V.: A review on genetic algorithm: past, present, and future. Multimedia Tools Appl. **80**, 8091–8126 (2021)
16. Koç, Ç., Bektaş, T., Jabali, O., Laporte, G.: Thirty years of heterogeneous vehicle routing. Eur. J. Oper. Res. **249**(1), 1–21 (2016)
17. Lenstra, J.K., Kan, A.R.: Complexity of vehicle routing and scheduling problems. Networks **11**(2), 221–227 (1981)
18. Little, C., Choudhury, S., Hu, T., Salomaa, K.: Comparison of genetic operators for the multiobjective pickup and delivery problem. Mathematics **10**(22), 4308 (2022)
19. Little, C., et al.: An exploration of heuristics applied to genetic algorithms on the capacitated pickup and delivery problem with time windows. Master's thesis (2023)
20. Macrina, G., Pugliese, L.D.P., Guerriero, F., Laporte, G.: The green mixed fleet vehicle routing problem with partial battery recharging and time windows. Comput. Oper. Res. **101**, 183–199 (2019)
21. Mitchell, M.: An Introduction to Genetic Algorithms. MIT Press, Cambridge (1998)
22. Pace, S., Turky, A., Moser, I., Aleti, A.: Distributing fibre boards: a practical application of the heterogeneous fleet vehicle routing problem with time windows and three-dimensional loading constraints. Procedia Comput. Sci. **51**, 2257–2266 (2015)
23. Pan, B., Zhang, Z., Lim, A.: Multi-trip time-dependent vehicle routing problem with time windows. Eur. J. Oper. Res. **291**(1), 218–231 (2021)
24. Penna, P.H.V., Subramanian, A., Ochi, L.S., Vidal, T., Prins, C.: A hybrid heuristic for a broad class of vehicle routing problems with heterogeneous fleet. Ann. Oper. Res. **273**(1), 5–74 (2019)
25. Prins, C.: Efficient heuristics for the heterogeneous fleet multitrip VRP with application to a large-scale real case. J. Math. Model. Algorithms **1**(2), 135–150 (2002)
26. Sethanan, K., Jamrus, T.: Hybrid differential evolution algorithm and genetic operator for multi-trip vehicle routing problem with backhauls and heterogeneous fleet in the beverage logistics industry. Comput. Ind. Eng. **146**, 106571 (2020)
27. Solomon, M.M., Desrosiers, J.: Survey paper-time window constrained routing and scheduling problems. Transp. Sci. **22**(1), 1–13 (1988)

28. Vidal, T., Crainic, T.G., Gendreau, M., Lahrichi, N., Rei, W.: A hybrid genetic algorithm for multidepot and periodic vehicle routing problems. Oper. Res. **60**(3), 611–624 (2012)
29. Vieira, B.S., Ribeiro, G.M., Bahiense, L.: Metaheuristics with variable diversity control and neighborhood search for the heterogeneous site-dependent multi-depot multi-trip periodic vehicle routing problem. Comput. Oper. Res. **153**, 106189 (2023)
30. Yağmur, E., Kesen, S.E.: Multi-trip heterogeneous vehicle routing problem coordinated with production scheduling: memetic algorithm and simulated annealing approaches. Comput. Ind. Eng. **161**, 107649 (2021)
31. Zhen, L., Ma, C., Wang, K., Xiao, L., Zhang, W.: Multi-depot multi-trip vehicle routing problem with time windows and release dates. Transp. Res. Part E: Logistics Transp. Rev. **135**, 101866 (2020)

Time-Dependency of Guided Local Search to Solve the Capacitated Vehicle Routing Problem with Time Windows

Adriano S. Silva[1,2,3,4,5](✉) (ID), José Lima[1,3] (ID), Adrián M. T. Silva[4,5] (ID),
Helder T. Gomes[2,3] (ID), and Ana I. Pereira[1,3] (ID)

[1] Research Centre in Digitalization and Intelligent Robotics (CeDRI), Instituto Politécnico de Bragança, 5300-253 Bragança, Portugal
{adriano.santossilva,jllima,apereira}@ipb.pt
[2] Centro de Investigação de Montanha (CIMO), Instituto Politécnico de Bragança, 5300-253 Bragança, Portugal
htgomes@ipb.pt
[3] Laboratório Associado para a Sustentabilidade e Tecnologia em Regiões de Montanha (SusTEC), Instituto Politécnico de Bragança, 5300-253 Bragança, Portugal
[4] Laboratory of Separation and Reaction Engineering - Laboratory of Catalysis and Materials (LSRE-LCM), Faculty of Engineering, University of Porto, 4200-465 Porto, Portugal
adrian@fe.up.pt
[5] ALiCE - Associate Laboratory in Chemical Engineering, Faculty of Engineering, University of Porto, 4200-465 Porto, Portugal

Abstract. Research have been driven by the increased demand for delivery and pick-up services to develop new formulations and algorithms for solving Vehicle Routing Problems (VRP). The main objective is to create algorithms that can identify paths considering execution time in real-world scenarios. This study focused on using the Guided Local Search (GLS) metaheuristic available in OR-Tools to solve the Capacitated Vehicle Routing Problem with Time Windows using the Solomons instances. The execution time was used as a stop criterion, with short runs ranging from 1 to 10 s and a long run of 360 s for comparison. The results showed that the GLS metaheuristic from OR-Tools is applicable for achieving high performance in finding the shortest path and optimizing routes within constrained execution times. It outperformed the best-known solutions from the literature in longer execution times and even provided a close-to-optimal solution within 10 s. These findings suggest the potential application of this tool for dynamic VRP scenarios that require faster algorithms.

Keywords: VVRP · Metaheuristic · Scheduling Problems

1 Introduction

One of the century's biggest challenges is global warming, which is now a matter of reaching public authorities and mobilizing nongovernmental organizations

© The Author(s) 2024
A. I. Pereira et al. (Eds.): OL2A 2023, CCIS 1981, pp. 93–108, 2024.
https://doi.org/10.1007/978-3-031-53025-8_7

worldwide. The emission of greenhouse gases is one of the main responsible of the environmental issue. In this regard, the logistics sector must find the smartest solutions to move goods around sustainably. The transportation sector accounts for about 21% of greenhouse gas emissions, emphasizing the urgent need to optimize transportation tasks. Aligned with the environmental need to decrease gas emissions from this activity, there is an increasing demand for more efficient transportation services. According to most updated surveys, e-commerce is growing significantly, requiring delivery services to ship goods purchased online [1]. Increasing demand for this service will also affect the number of trucks travelling on the road, overcoming more emissions. The example mentioned here is only one from a variety of services depending on transportation, and services of this kind will probably increase over the years due to economic development [2]. For almost 70 years, researchers have been studying route optimization to solve a wide range of problems, creating the class of Vehicle Routing Problems (VRP).

Several formulations were created and studied through the years, each attempting to reach similarities with real-life problems [3,4]. The capacity and time constraints are the most explored in the literature, with several algorithms developed to optimize routes so vehicles can provide services [5]. The Capacitated Vehicle Routing Problem with Time Windows (CVRPTW) is the most known formulation that approaches time and capacity as constraints [6]. At first, the objective of the problems was solely focused on reducing distances to save resources. However, in the current scenario, the objective is to consider the environmental impacts of vehicle emissions during the trips [7]. This consideration, at first, is not hard to implement, considering that both cost and emission will be reduced by shortening travelled distances. On the other hand, in problems where time windows are flexible and can be changed, one can choose the proper time window to provide a determined service based on the traffic [8]. For instance, if the vehicle needs to visit the city centre, the responsibility for decision-making regarding the time window to perform this visit can avoid travelling in hours of traffic, avoiding higher carbon emissions [9]. More sophisticated formulations include a deeper analysis of roads and traffic, considering travelling speed and real-time information on traffic to plan the routes more sustainably [10]. Despite the strong literature on this topic, several authors consider static formulations. Considering the increased competitiveness in the sector and the stochastic nature of demands for transports, the development of dynamic formulations represents the unavoidable end [11]. For this purpose, developing faster algorithms to find the shortest path is required, which is often neglected in most works devoted to route optimization [12].

Therefore, in this work, the Guided Local Search metaheuristic available in OR-Tools was tested to solve the Capacitated Vehicle Routing Problem with Time Windows to find optimal distances ensuring feasible execution time. To perform this evaluation, data available in Solomons instances of the CVRPTW were used. The stop criterion was based on execution time since this is the most important parameter considering dynamic operations. The performance of GLS to solve the instances was measured in execution times ranging from 1 to 10 s to evaluate the best execution time to find the best route. The rest of the paper is organized as follows: Sect. 2 brings relevant literature for this topic, Sect. 3 shows the methodology considered to perform this study, Sect. 4 brings the numerical results obtained, and Sect. 5 brings the conclusions and future work.

2 Related Literature

The most updated literature regarding the development of algorithms to solve the Capacitated Vehicle Routing Problem was gathered upon search in the Web of Science and Scopus database using the keyword "Vehicle Routing Problem". Figure 1 shows the evolution of the most relevant author's keywords found in both databases from 2014 to 2022.

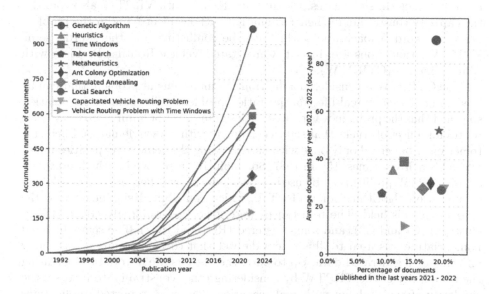

Fig. 1. Authors keywords evolution from 1992 to 2022

The analysis of the most relevant keywords among the published studies reveals a sharp increase devoted to algorithms development since 2004, with Genetic Algorithms dominating the scenario. Regarding the formulation, time windows appear amongst the most relevant keywords in the field, demonstrating the relevance of this constraint in VRP. In the next sections, the most updated literature regarding the algorithms used to solve the CVRPTW and the scenarios in which the formulation was applied will be discussed in more detail.

2.1 Capacitated Vehicle Routing Problem with Time Windows Formulations

Vehicle Routing Problems (VRP) consist of a class of problems devoted to finding the optimal route for a fleet of trucks to serve a determined set of customers. The VRP is the most important problem in delivering or picking up goods and services. Several formulations arose in the last decades from the need to develop problems mimicking real transportation problems. The formulations often attempt to cover actual complications from the real system, which depends on the quality of the service required, customer characteristics, and goods being transported [13]. The most typical complications approached are the vehicles performing multiple routes, the capacities, and the customers accepting the delivery in a specified time window. The simplest formulation is the Capacitated Vehicle Routing Problem (CVRP). A set of trucks at the central depot needs optimal paths to service customers with known demands [14]. Another formulation commonly considered in the literature is the Vehicle Routing Problem with Time Windows which considers the time window for a determined customer in route planning. In some cases, the authors dealing with VRPTW also consider the capacity constraints in their formulation without identifying in the problem name the word "capacitated", which can be conflicting. In other words, some VRPTW formulations are, in fact, Capacitated Vehicle Routing Problem with Time Windows (CVRPTW).

The CVRPTW is considered a distribution management problem that can be used to model many real-life transportation problems. The pioneer formulation specified that the problem was related to designing a set of minimum-cost vehicle routes for a fleet of trucks that serves customers with known demands. Each customer must be served only once without exceeding the vehicles' capacities under allowable delivery times [15]. In 1987, Solomon [16] introduced in the literature a set of VRPTW problems to be used as benchmarks by other authors developing optimization algorithms for CVRPTW, which contributed significantly to the progress in this field. The 6 instances were generated randomly (R1 and R2), clustered (C1 and C2), and semi-clustered (RC1 and RC2). The semi-clustered nomenclature was used to illustrate a dataset that contains a mix of randomly and clustered generated data. Up to date, the authors are devoted to increasing the complexity of the VRPTW by considering other constraints to increase the similarity of the problem with real scenarios. The most reported applications include (but are not limited to) industrial or municipal refuse collection [17], just-in-time delivery [18], school bus routing [19], and postal deliveries [20].

For instance, Masmoudi et al. [17] have proposed an extension of the traditional CVRPTW by studying the utilization of plug-in hybrid electric vehicles powered by two different power sources (electricity and compressed natural gas). Their model approached the realistic fuel consumption of the truck during the route, considering multiple load-outs to be used in other routes. For school bus routing, Hasan et al. [19] have considered the design of another variant of CVRPTW. In their problem, School Bus Routing Problem (SBRP), the authors have considered optimizing transportation costs by minimizing the fleet of vehicles and time spent to complete the task. In their approach, the authors have considered a decision variable related to the student's presence at the bus stop, so the bus will only perform a stop if the student reaches the spot at the correct time. Regarding just-in-time delivery, Nishi et al. [18] have proposed the design of a problem formulation to solve the conflict-free route planning for automated vehicles used in just-in-time delivery to minimize delays or earliness in the total completion time. In their problem, the vehicle can idle at the nodes waiting for the dispatching confirmation of the next delivery task to arrive in the stipulated time window. The time-space in their problem is dynamic, meaning the pickup and delivery tasks are dynamically scheduled. Sitek et al. [20] have proposed a CVRPTW with alternative pick-up, delivery, and time windows for postal delivery services. The problem was formulated by combining VRP variants such as the CVRP, VRPTW, and Vehicle Routing Problem with Pickup and Delivery (VRPPD). The difference in their approach is the introduction of alternative delivery points and parcel lockers incorporated into the distribution network.

2.2 Optimization Algorithms

Many decision problems in business, economics and logistics are too difficult to be solved by exact methods within a reasonable amount of time. Nonetheless, in cases where simply obtaining a feasible solution is not satisfactory, one should investigate procedures and strategies to obtain the best possible solution using exact methods. However, in most cases, the high number of customers considered in CVRPTW, added to the complexity of real-life data, does not allow for solving the problem with exact methods. In this scenario, heuristic and metaheuristic algorithms emerge as tools to find feasible solutions within a reasonable execution time. Both metaheuristic and heuristic algorithms can return feasible solutions but are not necessarily optimal [21].

The exact methods reported in the literature to solve the CVRPTW can be divided into column generation, dynamic programming, and Lagrange relaxation-based methods. These methods perform poorly in solving the VRP class of problems due to the execution time, which can take days to find a moderately decent solution. Authors dealing with exact methods often explore alternatives to decrease the execution time by adapting the space-time of the algorithm or exploring acceleration techniques to reinforce the algorithm's performance. For instance, Yang et al. [22] presented an augmented Lagrangian algorithm to solve the VRP with mixed backhauls and time windows (VRPMBTW). Their experiments based on a 9-node simple network and real-world Chicago sketch network demonstrated that their algorithm performs better than linear Lagrangian relaxation models, with lower conversion times. Regarding the column generation method, Fahram et al. [23] showed a column generation approach to solve the location-routing problem with time windows (LRPTW). Their branch-and-price algorithm performance was reinforced with acceleration techniques and a heuristic approach. Their results demonstrated that column generation acceleration and stabilization combined with a two-stage heuristic based on the problem characteristics can improve significantly the results for bigger instances. Regarding dynamic programming, Kok et al. [24] proposed an algorithm to solve the CVRPTW considering the legislation rules for drivers working hours. The authors proposed a methodology to include the break scheduling for drivers without increasing the algorithm's time complexity. Their computational solutions overcame the benchmark instances with 18% fewer vehicles and 5% fewer travel distances.

The utilization of non-exact algorithms is far more active than exact algorithms in the literature. In this regard, several heuristic algorithms have been reported to solve the CVRPTW and variants in the last few years. The formal definition states that heuristic is a technique that seeks good solutions (near optimal) with a reasonable computational cost without being able to guarantee optimal or how close to optimal the solution is. Heuristic algorithms are often developed to solve specific problems and cannot be used to solve other problems [25]. The heuristic algorithms used to solve the CVRPTW can be classified as route-building and route-improving algorithms depending on the mechanism considered to achieve the solution. Route-building heuristics operate by assembling the route from scratch, whereas route-improving heuristics produce an improved solution using an existing solution. The first class of algorithms was more explored in the past by modifications in savings heuristics and insertion heuristics. Nowadays, route-improving heuristics are mainly used due to the more expressed optimization achieved via this strategy. For instance, Tas et al. [26] presented one heuristic for solving the VRP with Flexible Time Windows (VRPFlexTW). Their algorithm operates in three instances, starting with the generation of a feasible solution, going to the solution improvement using the Tabu Search algorithm, and finishing with the scheduling of the proposed solution.

The last class of algorithms is metaheuristics, considered power techniques that can be applied to various problems. This is the algorithms class currently used to solve different formulations of CVRPTW. Algorithms in this class are known for their capacity to guide and modify the operations of subordinated heuristics by combining the concepts of exploring and exploiting the search space. A random solution is generated to initiate the algorithms and then subjected to modifications through exploit and explore operations until the stop condition is met. Ant Colony Optimization (ACO), Particle Swarm Optimization (PSO), Genetic Algorithm (GA), Simulated Annealing (SA), and Tabu Search (TS) are examples of algorithms reported in the literature. Kaabachi et al. [27] developed an improved ACO algorithm to solve the multi-depot CVRPTW considering the vehicle's speed to minimize fuel consumption. Their IACO overcame the regular ACO by improving the method to generate the first solution. Marinakis et al. [28] has presented a new variant of the PSO algorithm to solve the CVRPTW by exploring different adaptative strategies to evaluate performance improvement. The algorithm has one strategy for initialization (Greedy Randomized Adaptative Search Procedure), movement of the particles from one solution to another (Adaptative Combinatorial Neighborhood Topology), and another adaptative procedure to calculate the parameter of the PSO. The tests performed with benchmarks from the literature revealed that their algorithm is one of the best-performing algorithms to solve the CVRPTW.

2.3 Stochastic and Dynamic Scenarios

The literature is enriched with diverse formulations that are far more complex than the first formulation of the CVRPTW presented decades ago. In addition, the algorithms reported in the literature address previously reported weaknesses and drawbacks pointed out by other authors. The advance in formulations and solutions proposed in the literature is clearly increasing the attention of companies dealing with the transportation sector to the potential optimization of services provision.

Despite the quality and number of works published, formulations and algorithms are developed considering the problem in a static scenario. In this approach, the information required to run the optimization algorithm is known before the execution, and routes obtained in the optimization procedure are scheduled. Considering the dynamic nature of real transportation operations, the formulations and algorithms need to be explored in a more dynamic scenario in which not all information is known before the execution (i.e. routes may change during the execution).

Authors dealing with dynamic formulations of VRP have reported that the algorithm's performance is unaffected by the paradigm shift between static and dynamic scenarios. In other words, the best algorithms in static scenarios will perform similarly in dynamic runs. This can be explained by the fact that altering the formulation from static to dynamic does not affect the algorithm's search mechanism but changes how the algorithm is triggered to find the optimal path. In a typical dynamic test, the algorithm would be responsible for planning the route during truck stops, requiring faster algorithms since truck stops might take less than one minute.

The threats are related to premature utilization of the algorithms in real-life scenarios. Before advancing towards applying the algorithm for a particular case, there is the need to increase the complexity of the simulated scenario considered to run the experiments, trying to cover as much as possible the adversities. Another aspect that should be considered is the accessibility of the proposed solution for the final users. In other words, the algorithm proposed should be able to run dynamically considering the most generic input to finding the solution (i.e. distance matrix and time-windows matrix, for example).

3 Methodology

This work aims to explore the influence of the algorithm's execution time in the performance of GLS, the finest metaheuristic available in OR-Tools, to solve the Solomons instances of CVRPTW. Most studies in the literature deal with algorithm development and tuning to achieve optimized paths, considering static scenarios. However, the future and dynamic formulations of route optimization problems will demand faster algorithms. In this scenario, the influence of the execution time on the algorithm's performance will be important to determine the most feasible execution time to optimize routes. The instances used here to perform the study, from Solomons [16], are widely studied in the literature and comprised of 6 instances divided into randomly generated sets (R1 and R2), clustered sets (C1 and C2), and finally, semi-clustered sets (RC1 and RC2). Sets R1, C1 and RC1 have a limited scheduling horizon and can only accommodate a small number of customers per route (approximately 5 to 10). On the other hand, sets R2, C2 and RC2 have a longer scheduling horizon and can accommodate more customers with the same vehicle (over 30). The number of vehicles ascribed to perform the paths is not fixed in all datasets.

To evaluate the influence of the execution time on the algorithm's performance, we explored execution times from 1 to 10 s. Another long run of 6 min was also performed to evaluate the long-term solution achieved with the algorithm and compare the result with the distances obtained in short runs. The algorithm was also designed to search for the optimized path based on the distance travelled and the minimum number of trucks to execute the paths. The set of solutions obtained for all datasets studied was further gathered and processed to identify patterns and compare the algorithm's performance according to the execution time. Figure 2 brings the overview of the work performed.

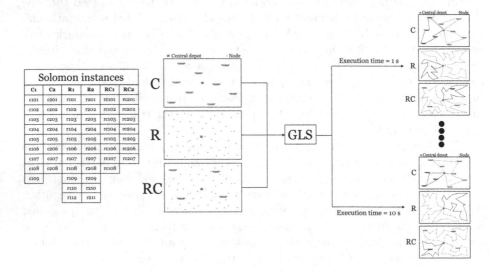

Fig. 2. Representation of the study performed.

3.1 Mathematical Formulation of the CVRPTW

The CVRPTW is one of the most important formulations of VRP problems, being recognized as a basic distribution management problem that can be used to model many real-world problems in the logistics field. In brief, the problem can be summarized as designing a set of minimum-cost routes for a fleet of trucks to perform the delivery or pick-up services to a set of customers with known demands and time windows to receive the visit. The customers must be assigned once, and only once, to a determined vehicle without exceeding the vehicle's capacity and respecting the customer's time windows.

The mathematical formulation of CVRPTW states that the problem is represented by a directed graph $G = (V, C)$, in which the fleet of homogeneous vehicles is denoted by $V = \{1, 2, \ldots, k\}$ and the set of customers is denoted by C. The graph has $|C| + 1$ vertices, where the central depot is represented by the vertex 0 (trucks depart and arrive at this site), and the customers are denoted $1, 2, 3, \ldots, n$. The CVRPTW is comprised of multiple objectives, such as minimizing total travel time, the number of vehicles used to perform the task, and total travel distance. The set of edges N represents the connection between the central depot and the customers and is denoted by A. All edges begin and terminate in vertex 0 at the central depot. Each edge (i, j) is associated with a cost c_{ij} and a time t_{ij} that can include the service time at customer i, where $i \neq j$. The vehicles have limited capacity Q, the customers have demanded d_i, and they need to be visited within the timestamp defined by the time window $[a_i, b_i]$. The vehicle must arrive at the customer before b_i and after a_i. However, in the latter case, the vehicle needs to wait until a_i to execute the service. The central depot also has a time window $[a_0, b_0]$, and the vehicles must not leave the central depot before a_0 nor arrive after b_0.

The parameters $Q, a_i, b_i, d_i, c_{i,j}$ are non-negative integers, whereas the parameter t_{ij} is assumed to be positive integers. It is assumed that both c_{ij} and t_{ij} satisfy the triangular inequality. The formulation contains two sets of decision variables x_{ijk} and y_{ijk}. For each arc (i, j), where $i \neq 0, j \neq 0, i \neq j$, each vehicle k we define as $x_{ijk} = 1$, if and only if the arc (i, j) is traversed by vehicle k in the optimal solution. The variable will assume null value ($x_{ijk} = 0$) otherwise. The other decision variable, y_{ijk}, is defined for each vehicle k and each vertex i, and represents the time vehicle k starts the service for customer i. If the vehicle k does not start the service to the customer i, the decision variable y_{ijk} does not mean anything. Considering that $a_0 = 0$ for all trucks we assume that $y_{ijk} = 0$, for all k. The goal of the problem is to design a set of routes, one for each vehicle so that each customer is visited only once. All routes should begin and end at the central depot (vertex 0), and time windows and capacity constraints are respected. In this regard, the mathematical formulation, based on the literature of the CVRPTW [29], is the one that follows:

$$\text{Minimize} \sum_{k \in V} \sum_{i \in N} \sum_{j \in N} c_{ij} x_{ijk} \tag{1}$$

Subject to:

$$\sum_{i \in C} d_i \sum_{j \in N} x_{ijk} \leq Q, \forall k \in V \tag{2}$$

$$\sum_{k \in V} \sum_{j \in N} x_{ijk} = 1, \forall i \in C \tag{3}$$

$$\sum_{j \in N} x_{0jk} = 1, \forall k \in V \tag{4}$$

$$\sum_{i \in N} x_{i0k} = 1, \forall k \in V \tag{5}$$

$$\sum_{i \in N} x_{ihk} - \sum_{j \in N} x_{hjk} = 0, \forall h \in C, \forall k \in V \tag{6}$$

$$a_i \leq y_{ik} \leq b_j, \forall i \in N, \forall k \in V \tag{7}$$

$$y_{ik} + t_{ij} - K(1 - x_{ijk}) \leq y_{jk}, \forall i, j \in N, \forall k \in V \tag{8}$$

$$x_{ijk} \in \{0, 1\}, \forall i, j \in N, \forall k \in V \tag{9}$$

The constraint 2 states that vehicles cannot carry more load than their capacity, and constraint 3 guarantees that each customer is visited exactly once. The next three constraints 4, 5, and 6 are related to the continuity of the route, ensuring that each vehicle leaves the central depot, and leaves again after performing the service to a determined customer, and arrives back at the central depot. Constraint 7 ensures that time windows are respected, and constraint 8 states that a vehicle traversing from i to j cannot arrive at j before $y_{ijk} + t_{ij}$. Finally, constraints 9 are the integrality constraints for the decision variable x_{ijk}.

4   Numerical Results

The numerical results obtained for solving the Solomon instances of the CVRPTW using the GLS metaheuristic available in OR-Tools will be discussed in this section. The main goal is to assess the impact on the algorithm's performance upon increasing the execution time to feasible levels. It is important to highlight that the tests performed in this study are important for the development of faster algorithms required for real-life dynamic applications of VRP. In this scenario, the execution time should be as lower as possible, still keeping the performance of the algorithm acceptable. The short runs (execution times from 1 to 10 s) were compared to the results obtained in a long run of 6 min to evaluate how good the fast solutions are compared to time-expensive solutions.

4.1   Optimal Distances

The Solomon instances considered for this work are the most famous dataset for testing algorithms to solve the CVRPTW. In total, there are 6 big datasets comprised of 9 (C1), 8 (C2), 12 (RC1), 8 (RC1), and 8 (RC2) sub-datasets to be studied. For all sets, the GLS performance to solve the CVRPTW was evaluated by increasing the execution time. To facilitate the representation of the results, the average distance found for each dataset will be reported, such as performed by other authors. Figure 3 brings an overview of the best solution found in this work compared to other solutions reported in the literature using metaheuristic algorithms. The comparison was performed with the works from Rochat and Taillard ([30], RT), Taillard et al. ([31], TB), Chiang and Russel ([32], CR), Potvin and Bengio ([33], PB), and Thangia et al. ([34], TH).

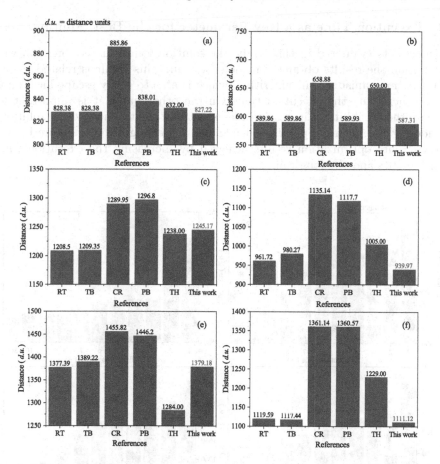

Fig. 3. Results obtained and compared to the literature for instances (a) C1, (b) C2, (c) R1, (d) R2, (e) RC1, and (f) RC2. The interval in X-axis is not proportional to the actual interval.

The results showed that for instances C1, C2, R2, and RC2 the GLS metaheuristic available in OR-Tools was able to overcome the best reported in the literature. Even for instances R1 and RC1, the algorithm used in the present study was able to overcome the results obtained by 2 other authors [32,33]. Considering the sum of the best solutions achieved by each algorithm reveals that GLS has the second best performance compared to literature, losing only to the algorithm used by authors in RT [30] (6085.44 *d.u.* from RT *vs* 6089.97 *d.u.* using GLS). The minimum number of trucks found in this work was the same as reported in the literature, 10 for C1, 3 for C2, 12 for R1, 3 for R2, 12 for RC1, and 3 for RC2. Despite the routes being assembled considering the same number of vehicles, the difference in distance observed here is related to the route assembly process that is able to find the shortest paths compared to the literature.

4.2   Execution Time as a Key Parameter for the Best Solution

For most sets evaluated in this study, the solution found in the long run was better than the results obtained in the short run. This result is related to the operation mechanism of the algorithm, which is able to easily escape local minima by increasing the execution time. On the other hand, it is important to evaluate the feasibility of increasing the execution time to improve the solution, considering the future application demanding faster algorithms. Figure 4 summarizes route optimization results achieved by increasing the execution time from 1 to 10 s and the long run.

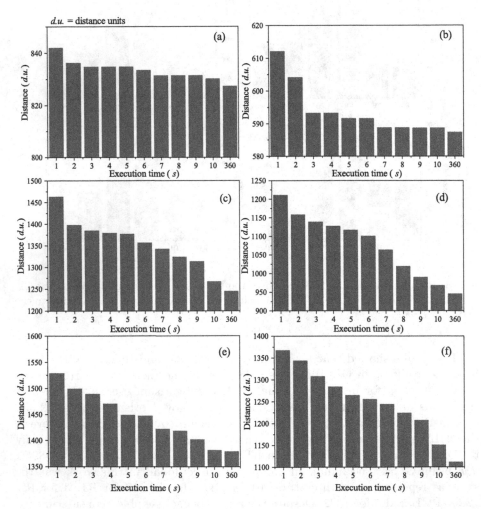

Fig. 4. Shortest distance obtained using GLS changing execution time for instances (a) C1, (b) C2, (c) R1, (d) R2, (e) RC1, (f) RC2. The interval in X-axis is not proportional to the actual interval.

The results demonstrate how powerful execution time increase can be to improve the route optimization results, allowing to achieve higher resource savings in delivery or pick-up services. It is important to highlight that distance shortening obtained with increased execution time is not linear. In other words, the resource savings achieved upon a determined execution time increase might not be efficient or feasible. For instance, despite the better results obtained in the long run, utilizing this approach for real scenarios would not be possible due to the delayed time to execute the algorithm. The numerical results also show that the algorithm has higher difficulty to improve distance shortening for sets C1, R1, and RC1 compared to the other sets, which is related to the smaller time windows in the first class of sets. Nonetheless, the optimization obtained by increasing the execution time from 1 to 10 s is more noticeable compared to increasing the execution time from 10 to 360 s.

The results obtained for the experiment also reveal a versatile behavior of the GLS algorithm, that is able to return satisfying solutions in terms of distance shortening in long runs, but also significant optimization with faster execution time. In other words, if one is more interested in distance savings, no matter the execution time the algorithm could be used with larger execution times. In contrast, aiming for dynamic scenarios and the need for faster algorithms, the GLS could also be used with an execution time of 10 s to return the most efficient solutions, accounting for both distance shortening and fast execution time. It is complicated to compare the algorithm in terms of execution time with the literature due to the lack of information regarding this particular aspect in published studies dealing with the CVRPTW solution. Most authors devoted to the development of algorithms for this purpose are more worried about the capacity of their algorithm to beat others reported in the literature and do not discuss and evaluate aspects to increase the potential feasibility of their solution for real scenarios.

5   Conclusions and Future Work

The GLS metaheuristic available in OR-Tools was able to return better solutions compared to the literature for almost all Solomons instances in the long run. Furthermore, the tests performed for short runs, with execution times lower than 10 s, revealed that increasing the execution time from 1 to 10 s returns significant savings in distance travelled. In this scenario, the utilization of this tool in a dynamic scenario would not be hindered by the execution time, since the algorithm is able to return satisfying solutions within 10 s of execution time. Moreover, the algorithm has also proven its performance in finding the shortest path with increased execution time used in the long run.

For future studies, the evaluation of other metaheuristic algorithms available in OR-Tools, such as SA and TS, will be performed. For instance, other studies already reported that GLS is the finest metaheuristic in OR-Tools, but in that case, CVRP was approached. In addition, the dependency in distance shortening upon increasing the algorithm's execution time will be compared to the time windows and capacities from each Solomons instance to observe the correlations that could be important in real scenarios. Once the relevant parameters are accounted for, the algorithm will be tested using a realistic dataset from a scenario that could be approached by CVRPTW: the waste collection task.

Acknowledgements. This work has been supported by FCT - Fundação para a Ciência e Tecnologia within the R&D Units Project Scope: UIDB/05757/2020, UIDP/05757/2020, UIDB/00690/2020, UIDB/50 020/2020, and UIDB/00319/2020. Adriano Silva was supported by Doctoral Grant SFRH/BD/151346/2021 financed by the Portuguese Foundation for Science and Technology (FCT), and with funds from NORTE 2020, under MIT Portugal Program. The authors are grateful to Sociedade Ponto Verde for the finantial support through the project "A digitalização como ferramenta para melhorar a sustentabilidade do processo de recolha seletiva".

References

1. Sitek, P., Wikarek, J., Rutczyńska-Wdowiak, K., Bocewicz, G., Banaszak, Z.: Optimization of capacitated vehicle routing problem with alternative delivery, pick-up and time windows: a modified hybrid approach. Neurocomputing **423**, 670–678 (2021)
2. Praveen, V., Keerthika, P., Sivapriya, G., Sarankumar, A., Bhasker, B.: Vehicle routing optimization problem: a study on capacitated vehicle routing problem. Mater. Today: Proc. **64**, 670–674 (2022)
3. Leite, G., Marcelino, C., Pedreira, C., Jiménez-Fernández, S., Salcedo-Sanz, S.: Evaluating the risk of uncertainty in smart grids with electric vehicles using an evolutionary swarm-intelligent algorithm. J. Clean. Prod. **401**, 136775 (2023)
4. Mendes, R.S., Wanner, E.F., Martins, F.V., Deb, K.: Aggregation or selection? clustering many objectives for vehicle routing problem with demand responsive transport. In: 2021 IEEE Congress on Evolutionary Computation (CEC), pp. 1257–1264. IEEE (2021)
5. Laporte, G.: The vehicle routing problem: an overview of exact and approximate algorithms. Eur. J. Oper. Res. **59**(3), 345–358 (1992)
6. Tanel, A., et al.: Capacitated vehicle routing problem with time windows. In: Durakbasa, N.M., Gençyılmaz, M.G. (eds.) Digitizing Production Systems: Selected Papers from ISPR2021, 07–09 October 2021, pp. 653–664. Springer, Cham (2022). https://doi.org/10.1007/978-3-030-90421-0_56
7. Andelmin, J., Bartolini, E.: A multi-start local search heuristic for the green vehicle routing problem based on a multigraph reformulation. Comput. Oper. Res. **109**, 43–63 (2019)
8. Çimen, M., Soysal, M.: Time-dependent green vehicle routing problem with stochastic vehicle speeds: an approximate dynamic programming algorithm. Transp. Res. Part D: Transp. Environ. **54**, 82–98 (2017)
9. Cokyasar, T., Subramanyam, A., Larson, J., Stinson, M., Sahin, O.: Time-constrained capacitated vehicle routing problem in urban e-commerce delivery. Transp. Res. Rec. **2677**(2), 190–203 (2023)
10. UCT in capacitated vehicle routing problem with traffic jams. Inf. Sci. **406–407**, 42–56 (2017)
11. Real-time collaborative feeder vehicle routing problem with flexible time windows. Swarm Evolution. Comput. **75**, 101201 (2022)

12. Silva, A.S., Lima, J., Pereira, A.I., Silva, A.M.T., Gomes, H.T.: Execution time experiments to solve capacitated vehicle routing problem. In: Gervasi, O., et al. (eds.) ICCSA 2023. LNCS, vol. 14111, pp. 273–289. Springer, Cham (2023). https://doi.org/10.1007/978-3-031-37126-4_19

13. Silva, A.S., et al.: Capacitated waste collection problem solution using an open-source tool. Computers **12**(1) (2023)

14. Silva, A.S., et al.: Solving a capacitated waste collection problem using an open-source tool. In: Gervasi, O., Murgante, B., Misra, S., Rocha, A.M.A.C., Garau, C. (eds.) ICCSA 2022. LNCS, vol. 13378, pp. 140–156. Springer, Cham (2022). https://doi.org/10.1007/978-3-031-10562-3_11

15. Raff, S.: Routing and scheduling of vehicles and crews: the state of the art. Comput. Oper. Res. **10**(2), 63–211 (1983)

16. Solomon, M.M.: Algorithms for the vehicle routing and scheduling problems with time window constraints. Oper. Res. **35**(2), 254–265 (1987)

17. Amine Masmoudi, M., Coelho, L.C., Demir, E.: Plug-in hybrid electric refuse vehicle routing problem for waste collection. Transp. Res. Part E: Logist. Transp. Rev. **166**, 102875 (2022)

18. Nishida, K., Nishi, T.: Dynamic optimization of conflict-free routing of automated guided vehicles for just-in-time delivery. IEEE Trans. Automat. Sci. Eng. (2022)

19. Hashi, E.K., Hasan, M.R., Zaman, M.S.U.: GIS based heuristic solution of the vehicle routing problem to optimize the school bus routing and scheduling. In: 2016 19th International Conference on Computer and Information Technology (ICCIT), pp. 56–60. IEEE (2016)

20. Sitek, P., Wikarek, J., Rutczyńska-Wdowiak, K., Bocewicz, G., Banaszak, Z.: Optimization of capacitated vehicle routing problem with alternative delivery, pick-up and time windows: a modified hybrid approach. Neurocomputing **423**, 670–678 (2021)

21. Baldacci, R., Mingozzi, A., Roberti, R.: Recent exact algorithms for solving the vehicle routing problem under capacity and time window constraints. Eur. J. Oper. Res. **218**(1), 1–6 (2012)

22. Yang, S., Ning, L., Shang, P., (Carol) Tong, L.: Augmented Lagrangian relaxation approach for logistics vehicle routing problem with mixed backhauls and time windows. Transp. Res. Part E: Logist. Transp. Rev. **135**, 101891 (2020)

23. Farham, M.S., Süral, H., Iyigun, C.: A column generation approach for the location-routing problem with time windows. Comput. Oper. Res. **90**, 249–263 (2018)

24. Kok, A.L., Hans, E.W., Schutten, J.M.J.: Optimizing departure times in vehicle routes. Eur. J. Oper. Res. **210**(3), 579–587 (2011)

25. Reeves, C.: Modern Heuristic Techniques for Combinatorial Problems. Wiley, London (1995)

26. Taş, D., Jabali, O., Van Woensel, T.: A vehicle routing problem with flexible time windows. Comput. Oper. Res. **52**, 39–54 (2014)

27. Kaabachi, I., Jriji, D., Krichen, S.: An improved ant colony optimization for green multi-depot vehicle routing problem with time windows. In: 2017 18th IEEE/ACIS International Conference on Software Engineering, Artificial Intelligence, Networking and Parallel/Distributed Computing (SNPD), pp. 339–344 (2017)

28. Marinakis, Y., Marinaki, M., Migdalas, A.: A multi-adaptive particle swarm optimization for the vehicle routing problem with time windows. Inf. Sci. **481**, 311–329 (2019)

29. Kallehauge, B.: Formulations and exact algorithms for the vehicle routing problem with time windows. Comput. Oper. Res. **35**(7), 2307–2330 (2008). Part Special

Issue: Includes Selected Papers Presented at the ECCO 2004 European Conference on Combinatorial Optimization

30. Rochat, Y., Taillard, É.D.: Probabilistic diversification and intensification in local search for vehicle routing. J. Heuristics **1**, 147–167 (1995)
31. Taillard, É., Badeau, P., Gendreau, M., Guertin, F., Potvin, J.Y.: A Tabu search heuristic for the vehicle routing problem with soft time windows. Transp. Sci. **31**(2), 170–186 (1997)
32. Chiang, W.C., Russell, R.A.: A reactive Tabu search metaheuristic for the vehicle routing problem with time windows. INFORMS J. Comput. **9**(4), 417–430 (1997)
33. Potvin, J.Y., Bengio, S.: The vehicle routing problem with time windows Part II: genetic search. Informs J. Comput. **8**(2), 165–172 (1996)
34. Thangiah, S.R., Potvin, J.Y., Sun, T.: Heuristic approaches to vehicle routing with backhauls and time windows. Comput. Oper. Res. **23**(11), 1043–1057 (1996)

Federated Learning for Credit Scoring Model Using Blockchain

Daniel Djolev$^{(\boxtimes)}$, Milena Lazarova●, and Ognyan Nakov

Technical University of Sofia, Sofia 1000, Bulgaria
daniel.djolev93@gmail.com, {milaz,nakov}@tu-sofia.bg

Abstract. In the last years technologies have emerged in a very disruptive way, modelling and navigating a big part of human life. Recently blockchain and machine learning technologies reached a new level of maturity. From low penetrated tech, blockchain become in the bottom of the digital crypto currencies and many projects out of them. At the same time, machine learning is becoming more powerful and strong technology and many companies start to adopt it as a solution for non-trivial technical problems leveraging on the tones of data they use and generate in their daily functioning. Both blockchain and machine learning technologies have become a big part of our life and different studies show how much potential they have. The paper presents a system architecture approach for building a decentralized FELScore platform based on federated learning paradigm and blockchain technology for credit score modelling. The main goal is to provide a platform for distributed machine learning that several financial institutions could leverage on without having the need to exchange real customer or product data and without the requirement to trust each other. To further improve the security of the federated learning the proposed approach uses blockchain technology.

Keywords: Credit Score · Federated Learning · Smart Contract · Blockchain

1 Introduction

Credit scores are used by financial institutions to assess the risk profile of their customers which usually wants to take a credit product. Credit scoring has been done for many years and is also a mandatory step in the credit application of a customer, also supervised by national and central banks as a strong requirement in the credit risk processes. The credit score can be a number or a vector of numbers which assess the creditability of a person. There are different approaches for calculation of credit scores which utilization depends on the capability of the credit organization [1]. The first group of approaches are based on using a credit score matrix which evaluates the credit score by following different rules and weights on input features and rely on assumptions for the data used. The other group of approaches utilizes more sophisticated data-driven algorithms and data modelling techniques to create a score model [2]. Different algorithms can be used as statistical learning models (linear discriminant analysis, logistic regression, naïve Bayes), various machine learning algorithms and complex neural network architectures.

A. I. Pereira et al. (Eds.): OL2A 2023, CCIS 1981, pp. 109–122, 2024.
https://doi.org/10.1007/978-3-031-53025-8_8

No matter what is the credit score modeling approach it requires data for the credit score evaluation that are acquired by three different sources – data obtained from the customer, data gathered from the national bureaus and data which the financial organization has for this customer. This is valid for Eastern Europe, but in different countries can be specific because the availability of data can vary in the different regions based on the financial infrastructure of the country, the data privacy regulations in place and the existence of central credit reporting repositories. The first two data sources are mandatory while the third one might not always be available as it requires the person in question to be an existing customer of the financial institutions which is not necessarily true in any case. Due to that fact for the credit score modeling data dependency, the financial institutions usually give better credit conditions for their existing customers versus new customers and the approval credit rate for an existing customer is usually far big than the approval rate for new customers. That's why, the third data source based on own data of the financial organization can significantly increase the accuracy of the credit scoring. Therefore, many organizations invest a lot to analyze and assess the possibilities of utilization as much as possible of their internal data into the analytical credit scoring algorithms and thus to significantly decrease the credit risk level.

Artificial intelligence is aiming to unlock the computer power to solve complex tasks applying different approaches to do that, from statistics to machine learning, neural networks and deep learning architectures aimed to mimic the human brain structure and functionality. Many different machine learning algorithms are used to solve the credit scoring that is regarded as supervised learning problem: k-nearest neighbor, decision trees, support vector machines, random forests, boosting, bagging, artificial neural networks, as well as several deep learning models can be used: restricted Boltzmann machines, deep belief neural networks, deep multilayer perceptron, convolutional neural networks.

Federated learning is a concept proposed by McMahan [3] as a collaborative machine learning environment that allows training data decentralization. In contrast to the centralized distributed machine learning approach where all training data are available to all participants in the distributed training environment, the federated learning is based on model sharing rather than data sharing among the participants. Each participant trains a machine learning model only based on its own private data and contributes to a centralized data model by providing a sub-model aggregated by a centralized server to obtain a general model. Even if data privacy is ensured by the federated learning approach, the main concerns for proper model aggregation and data reliability still remain as the centralized server is a single point of failure [4, 5].

Blockchain starts its history since 1991 when Stuart Haber and W. Scott Stormetta propose their idea for implementation of secure time-stamping of documents in order to solve the problem with the authenticity and ability for backdating or tampering of the documents [6]. Then the technology is being amended and developed by different people over the years, but the very significant moment is the introduction of Bitcoin as the first crypto currency based on the fundamental of blockchain by S. Nakamoto in 2009 [7]. Bitcoin sets an example for many further developed crypto currencies by defining the basic set of principles of building a digital currency on the decentralized network utilizing peer-to-peer paradigm. The blockchain itself is a data structure that consists of connected data blocks where each block contains a hash of the previous one which prevents the system to not been modified after the block is written in the chain. This feature of blockchain is also used by Nakamoto in order to define the crypto transactions as one block in the chain, which is playing a role as a public general ledger, not centralized, but copied to each participant. Each transaction is validated by the community of peers and a "consensus model" is introduced where the transaction is confirmed only if minimum of the half plus one of the total participants are voted for its validity. To stimulate the validation and voting the scope of work to be done is defined based on a Proof of Work algorithm which aims to solve a complex math task requiring computing power. Thus, each of the participants receives incentive or coin for the time and energy spent. The next innovation to the basic principle used by Bitcoin is the development of Ethereum [8] which adds significant strength by providing ability to build applications over the blockchain and thus unlocks a lot of opportunities out of the simple mining. Ethereum provides the possibility to run complete programs called Smart Contracts over the blockchain which can maintain a particular state.

The architecture of a blockchain network as shown on Fig. 1 and Fig. 2 typically is a decentralized model where multiple nodes participate in the validation and maintenance of the blockchain's public ledger ensuring transparency and reducing the risk of a single point of failure.

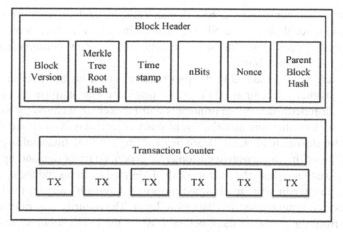

Fig. 1. Blockhain architecture simplified (Source: [9]).

Consensus protocols play a crucial role in maintaining agreement among network participants about the state of the blockchain. Apart from Proof of Work (PoW) used in Bitcoin, other consensus mechanisms like Proof of Stake (PoS), Delegated Proof of Stake (DPoS), and Practical Byzantine Fault Tolerance (PBFT) have emerged, each with its own strengths and limitations.

In a Proof of Stake (PoS) blockchain validators are chosen to create new blocks and validate transactions based on the number of coins they hold and are willing to "stake" as collateral, incentivizing honest behavior and reducing the need for intensive computational work. Blockchain networks often use Merkle trees – a data structure that

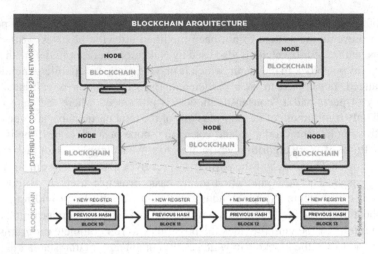

Fig. 2. Blockhain architecture network (Source: [10]).

efficiently summarizes large amounts of data, reducing the size and complexity of the stored information. Merkle trees assist in verifying the integrity of data quickly and securely.

To maintain data consistency across the network, blockchain systems use cryptographic hashing algorithms, such as SHA-256 (used in Bitcoin), which convert data into fixed-length hash values. Any change in the data will result in a completely different hash, ensuring data immutability.

The research work presented in the paper introduces a novel system architecture designed to construct a decentralized FELScore platform. The platform relies on a combination of both federated learning principles and blockchain technology to develop a reliable system for credit score models. The primary objective is to create a collaborative environment for distributed machine learning enabling multiple financial institutions to participate without sharing sensitive customer or product data or demanding to rely on mutual trust. To enhance both the security of the federated learning and the improvement in the accuracy of credit score models, the proposed approach includes the blockchain technology as a communication and data store layer. The security improvements inherently comes from the nature of the blockhain, while the credit score accuracy can be improved by the fact that multiple participant's data instead of data of only one single entity are used for the data model scoring.

2   Related Work

Credit score evaluation is an important aspect in credit markets that requires different financial institutions to adopt quantitative models with persistent hidden heterogeneity of data coming from various sources [11]. Apart from the statistical and machine learning methods used for credit score modelling [1], the attempts on improving the discrimination performance of credit scoring methods are focuses on utilizing additional information related to creditworthiness coming from social networks, financial networks, legal judgments, e-commerce platforms [12, 13].

In order to adapt to the requirements for utilization of data from different sources as well as the data privacy and security requirements, decentralized distributed score modelling approaches are used. A federated learning prototype is suggested for credit risk assessment of mortgages in [14]. The authors demonstrated that federated learning can be efficiently utilized by financial institutions of different sizes holding various own data that benefit significantly from the collaboration with other institutions.

Even if federated learning concept provides a secure and data preservation for distributed machine learning there are many problems related to its application in terms of data confidentiality and model security especially in the fintech industry [15].

In [16] a decentralized credit scoring method based on vertical federated learning is present aimed at addressing the challenges of preserving data privacy during collaborative modeling in a credit scoring. The suggested approach is based on L1 regularization and distributed proximal gradient descent with homomorphic encryption to deal with redundant and irrelevant information during the collaborative modeling process. Federated optimization algorithm for distributed machine learning in case of evenly distributed data over an extremely large number of nodes is suggested in [17].

Blockchain empowered federated learning approaches are suggested and implemented to provide secure and reliable sharing in case of lack of trust between the participants [18]. Blockchain based federated learning framework with committee consensus is suggested in [19] that uses global model storage and local model update exchange with a committee consensus mechanism reducing the amount of consensus computing and malicious attacks. Data sharing model based on the federated learning and the blockchain concepts is proposed in [20] using an incentive mechanism based on reputation points and a smart contract for the automatic distribution of profits on the blockchain. Full-fledged blockchain-based federated learning protocol implemented in the Ethereum smart contract is presented in [21]. The protocol includes client registration, training, aggregation, and reward distribution and suggests incentive mechanism, reputation system, peer-reviewed model, commitment hash and model encryption to deal with the shortcomings of the assumption of a trusted environment of the general vanilla federated learning.

Trustworthy federated learning empowered by blockchain can be used in different cases where there is a need different parties which don't trust to each other to train centralized models without giving access to each other's data and without exchanging private information as is the case in many application areas in the fields of healthcare, finance, energy, government, and defense. Decentralized paradigm for big data-driven cognitive computing (D2C) that builds on federated learning and blockchain for is described in [22] to deal with the problem of poisoning attacks, performance, and inadequate data resources in data-driven intelligent manufacturing. A Chained Distributed Machine learning approach (C-DistriM) is presented in [23] and evaluated for training healthcare models to predict two-year lung-cancer survival. Blockchain-based federated learning approach is used for privacy-aware and efficient vehicular communication networking for autonomous vehicles [24]. In [25] data privacy and fairness of financial recommendation systems based on blockchain is described.

3   Credit Scoring Based on Federated Learning and Blockchain

Machine learning as a subset of artificial intelligence consists of algorithms which learn patterns and behavior or find hidden relationships between different data features in a big amount of data which cannot be manually performed. Linear regression is one of the simplest supervised learning algorithms used to calculate a linear prediction model based on annotated training data. The suggested FELScore platform for credit score modeling is based on basic linear regression to demonstrate the use of distributed learning supported by smart contracts.

A typical machine learning modeling run on a centralized server that both stores the training data and the machine learning algorithm. The relationship model between the input and the output data after the training is accomplished in the case of linear regression is given by the slope and intercept values provided by the model. The trained model can be represented as a matrix of the estimated coefficients or weights and bias or intercept and can further be used to predict the output, i.e. a credit score value, based on provided input data.

In order to evaluate the credit score of a customer a bank or financial credit institution have to provide at least two input datasets – (1) data collected from the customer and (2) data collected from the central bureau. For an existing financial institution customer a third dataset can be used to enrich the input data: (3) data available at the financial organization for this customer. In such cases the data provided by the national bureau usually is a single point of failure. In order to provide a fully real time credit scoring process to support digital loan sales the evaluated credit score and the respective credit decision based on it need to be performed within very short timeframes (seconds to minutes). Utilization of the data available at the national credit bureau is under serious data governance with the respective quality controls in the sources as well as in the centralized database. The data exchange between the financial institutions and the credit bureau and the data governance applied is a challenge for all the participants. Data privacy is another major challenge which is very hard to be maintained due to different levels of access to the national bureau and strong access control that have to be established to fully prevent unintended data access. Last but not least, central bureau requires only a defined scope of data to be presented from the banks in the central database and usually this are only customer and product data, but neither transactional, nor behavior or data from customer's interactions with the digital channels, contact center, etc. All these challenges lead to the suggestion of utilization of federated learning approach that provides credit score modeling to be maintained in a distributed environment with the relevant data protection and security.

In the federated learning the training of a machine learning algorithm is distributed to multiple servers (Fig. 3). Each of the servers performs its own training over the model and the data which it hosts are not shared [26]. Thus, each server receives a model from the central server, trains the model using its own dataset and then sends back the trained model to the central server. In Fig. 3 the federated learning paradigm is represented for the case of linear regression model by the weights and the biases of the model. The centralized server aggregates the received sub-models by applying an average and sends a next version of the model to the servers for a new training iteration. The training iterations repeat until the required quality of the model is achieved. In the distributed training environment, the training data access is strictly controlled by each of the servers and the data do not leave its premises in any case since the training only requires sub-models to be shared and exchanged in the network.

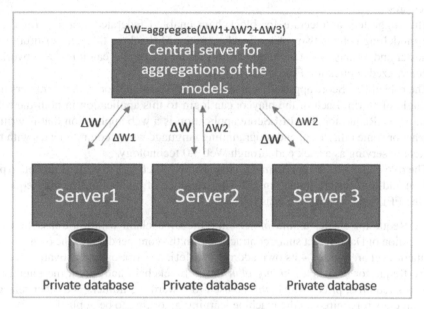

Fig. 3. Federated learning paradigm.

To apply the federated learning for credit score modeling the "servers" could be the servers in the premises of each of the financial institutions and other organizations that work together in the data distributed environment thus allowing better risk score models to be gained based on external data.

The important aspect in the utilization of the described federated learning approach for credit score modeling is who can be given the role of a centralized aggregation server. The federated learning approach needs such a role due to the requirement to provide centralized model store and aggregation of the sub-models.

On the other hand, even if there is no private data exchanged between the parties, the existence of a centralized server still puts the whole "system" at risk as being a single point of failure. The risk of malicious attacks or hijacking the centralized server can corrupt the model fairness and accuracy. For the credit score modelling the central server could be either the national credit bureau or some other financial regulator but, in both cases, the added value of playing that role have to be outlined.

The proposed approach for credit score modelling includes blockchain technologies in the distributed learning environment for further security and model protection. The role of the central server typically used in the federated learning models to calculate the sub-model aggregations and to coordinate the process of data/models exchange is distributed among the other players and uses the blockchain principles in order to enforce the needed trust and transparency between the players while keeping the privacy of the information. The centralized server in the suggested architecture is replaced by a smart contract deployed on Ethereum blockchain network that acts as "controlling" function to trace all the required steps in the training and data exchanging process and logs into the blockchain the required footprint and the respective identifiers in order to ensure further proof.

The suggested architecture for blockchain enabled federated learning for credit score modelling defines two roles of each participant (bank or financial institution) – Requester and Trainer. The common platform where the parties can join the network is a decentralized application FELScore (Fig. 4).

The role of FELScore application is to "connect" the requestors and the trainers into the single platform. Each of the players can login to this application in both the roles of Trainer or Requestor. The FELScore application is a web application that is written on React or some other front end programming language which communicates with the blockchain serving as a back end through Web 3.0 technology.

The role of the Requester is to make a request to the network to train its model, to pay its price and to receive a trained mode. The sequence of interactions of the Requestor with the FELScore application is as follows:

1. The Requestor creates a *data project* into the blockchain within a transaction and execution of DataProject smart contract. Within the contract data for the owner of the data project are written – its own address (wallet), description and activation fee.
2. The Requestor creates a *training plan* in the blockchain and sets it the number of rounds required, prices which will be used to reward the trainers and other relevant parameters if required by the machine learning algorithm to be applied.
3. The Requestor signs and uploads an initial data model to the IPFS – distributed public storage where the physical files are stored and obtains CID (identifier of the file) for the uploaded file which is also a parameter of the training plan. Only the CID is written into the transaction since blockchain avoids storing large files.

All the parameters are required for creation of the training plan using a defined smart contract DataTrainingPlan. The identifier of the contract is important for the trainers as they have to know it in order to be allowed to join it within the network. In the FELScore application all the trainers can see the available data projects and data training plans and can be aware of their respective contract identifier.

The participants with a role of Trainer can join some of the available training plans within the available data projects in the platform FELScore. The Trainer has to participate into the training rounds, to train the models with the data which it has under its ownership and to receive an incentive (token) for the job done following the steps:

1. The Trainer selects a data project and a training plan which he wants to join.
2. The Trainer runs its training nodes by providing the identifier of the respective smart contract of the training plan.

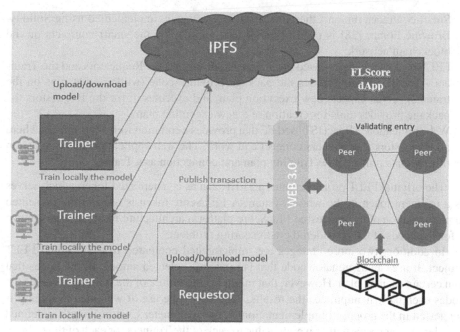

Fig. 4. FELScore platform architecture.

3. The Trainer downloads the model from IPFS by CID which has been written into the respective training plan.
4. The Trainer trains the model with its own data, uploads its "delta" version of the trained model into IPFS and waits for the next training round.
5. One of the training nodes is selected randomly to perform the sub-models aggregation and this selection happens at the time of joining the training plan. Thus, the selected node collects all the CIDs of the "delta" models, downloads them from IPFS, applies aggregation of the model and finally uploads the aggregated model into IPFS.
6. All the Trainer nodes perform the contract rounds defined in the training plan and receive a reward (FELScore token) for each iteration.

Finally, the last uploaded aggregated model is available for the Requestor for downloading.

The proposed architecture consists from the most commonly used components in an architecture for federated learning using blockchain – federated learning network (ensured by different participants), federated learning orchestrator (randomly selected trainer node), consensus mechanism (natively come from the blockchain), incentive mechanism (the FELScore token).

4 FELScore Platform Implementation and Experimental Results

To validate the suggested FELScore platform architecture for credit score modeling it is implemented using an open-source project FELT (FEderating Learning Token) [27]. The implementation of the system comprises:

– Smart contracts: run on Ethereum or other blockchain, implemented using Solidity, Brownie library [28] is used to build, test, and deploy the smart contracts on the blockchain network;
– FELT package: Python-based programs which support the Requestors and the Trainers – for the Training nodes the package provides code (worker) that runs on the trainer's server, expects new execution plan, and executes it; for the Requestors the package provides tools for creation of a new execution plan;
– Web application: a ReactJS based FE that provides a common web environment where all Requestors and Trainers connect and work. The web application allows creation of new Data project, new Training plan and connection as a Trainer.

The original FELT project creates a FELToken as a generalized token which serves as a payment token in the whole system. A FELScore token is used in the presented implementation of the suggested FELScore platform architecture in order to customize it for the needs of the considered credit scoring problem.

In addition, two more changes are implemented compared to the original FELT project. It uses an aggregator node that is randomly selected among all the nodes that join certain training plan. However, that might lead to failure of the training if one of the nodes eventually manipulates the results. That's why the use of weighted averaging is suggested in the proposed implementation. A new parameter CustomWeigth is defined in order to assign a particular weight value to each of the Trainers for each of the training iterations. A metrics is required that can be used in order to evaluate which participant participate positively and which negatively to the aggregation during each round. That's why the calculation of the CustomWeigth parameters is based on evaluation of the mean squared error (MSE) of each model. MSE is a metric which is used to measure the performance and accuracy of a model's prediction. It can give an indication of what's the level of matching between the model predictions and the observed values of a regression problem. The error is estimated by the respective node using a subset of its data. The bigger the error, the smaller the CustomWeight parameter of the Trainer. Then in the aggregation all the trainers' results are weighted using the calculated trainer's CustomWeight. So basically the CustomWeight is calculated as 1 divided by the MSE of the respective trainer's model:

$$Custom\,Weight = 1/MSE \qquad (1)$$

In the original FELT project the first rows of the training dataset which all the trainers have at their own premises are always used. In this way the results of the same node with its same first training dataset rows are the same and the FL interactions are meaningless. To overcome this, in the implemented worker programs randomness is introduced by using random 1000 records for each interaction.

In order to validate the suggested concept, the described implementation is experimentally evaluated using local blockchain that runs with ganache technology that provides a local Ethereum network for development purposes [29].

The sequence diagram of the implementation of the FELScore platform is presented on Fig. 5.

First some configurations are made, as setting a wallet address. The blockchain is created using Brownie library. A test Requestor is built by a python script ("create_plan.py") when the local blockchain is ready. Then a test Data project and a test Training plan are created with the following parameters: Linear Regression model; number of iterations (rounds) – 3; reward – 10, for each submission of a model by Trainers.

When the Requestor is ready and the Training plan is published on the working ganache blockchain, Trainers' instances or so-called worker nodes are running. The workers are started with a command that contains the address of the network returned after successful blockchain start. Each of the workers has a unique sequential identifier. In our test scenario two worker nodes are started that are identified as node1 and node2. The worker node is a python program which uses web3.0 python libraries to connect to the blockchain on the specified network address. Once the worker nodes connect to the blockchain network, they start listening for training plans, and if a training plan is running on the blockchain, the worker nodes perform the training, sequentially, waiting for each other to finish the respective round.

Each worker node is using its private data for the model training. The described implementation of the blockchain based federated learning for credit score modeling is tested using the Home Credit Default Risk dataset available at Kaggle [30] that comprises both training and test datasets for credit applications.The dataset contains clients credit application data and a binary target value of the clients' repayment abilities. The goal of the credit score model training is to learn from the training dataset to predict the target value of a customer repayment ability. The training dataset is split into two files with around 90k rows per file for each of the two worker nodes. After completion of each round either of the two worker nodes, on a random basis, is selected to perform the final model aggregation and upload.

The experimental results obtained for the model prediction based on the suggested FELScore platform architecture are based on utilization of linear regression model and average aggregation of the sub-models and serve as a proof of concept of the possibility to use the suggested approach for credit score modeling (Table 1).

Using the original aggregation function without aggregation weights for 3 rounds of 2 worker nodes provides final model with Mean Squared Error 0.516 while the MSE drops to 0.395 with the modified aggregation function and CustomWeigth on every iteration based on the error of each submitted model.

The results show that even when only two worker nodes are used, and the model is trained for only 3 rounds the modified aggregation with weighted average on each round significantly improves the model MSE.

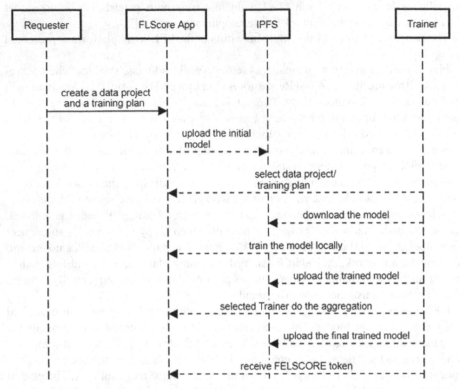

Fig. 5. FELScore platform sequence diagram

Table 1. FELScore experimental results for credit score modeling.

Experiment #	Number of worker nodes	Number of rounds	Number of training samples	Prediction model MSE
1	2	3	90k	0.516
2	2	3	90k	0.39

5 Conclusion

Federated learning provides an approach for distributed training of different machine learning models that can be utilized by banks and other financial institutions to increase the quality of credit scoring models used for assessment of the customers creditability based on other parties' data. The improvement of the creditability assessment and credit scoring using federated learning is especially important for non-existing customers where data from other sources are of vital importance for model accuracy.

The traditional federated learning schema requires a centralized server that in the suggested FELScore platform is replaced by adding a blockchain smart contracts in order to facilitate, log and trace the whole process of training model aggregation. The proposed FELScore platform also uses blockchain to provide means of incentives of all participants and motivation for participation in the federated learning by ensuring native payments of crypto tokens (FELScore token). In this way the single point of failure of the centralized federated learning server, which in the case of credit score modeling is usually a national credit bureau, is eliminated and moreover the participants can contribute to the model training by securing the private customers data and still providing them to the other parties in terms of the sub-models shared the distributed environment.

Further research directions are aimed at evaluation of the suggested FELScore platform for credit score modeling implementing various machine learning algorithms and different approaches for model aggregation that weights the sub-models at each iteration based on the model accuracy.

Acknowledgements. The research presented in the paper is funded by the project BG-RRP-2.004-005-C01 "Improving the research capacity and quality to achieve international recognition and resilience of TU–Sofia".

References

1. Dastile, X., Celik, T., Potsane, M.: Statistical and machine learning models in credit scoring: a systematic literature survey. Appl. Soft Comput. **91** (2020)
2. Wang, X., Xu, M., Pusatli, Ö.T.: A survey of applying machine learning techniques for credit rating: Existing models and open issues. In: Arik, S., Huang, T., Lai, W.K., Liu, Q. (eds.) ICONIP 2015. LNCS, vol. 9490, pp. 122–132. Springer, Cham (2015). https://doi.org/10.1007/978-3-319-26535-3_15
3. McMahan, B., Moore, E., Ramage, D., Hampson, S., Arcas, B.: Communication-efficient learning of deep networks from decentralized data. In: Proceedings of the Artificial Intelligence and Statistics, pp. 1273–1282. Ft. Lauderdale (2017)
4. Cheng, K., et al.: SecureBoost: a lossless federated learning framework. IEEE Intell. Syst. **36**(6), 87–98 (2021)
5. Zhang, K., Song, X., Zhang, C., Yu, S.: Challenges and future directions of secure federated learning: a survey. Front. Comput. Sci. **16** (2022)
6. Haber, S., Stornetta, W.: How to time-stamp a digital document. J. Cryptol. **3**(2). Springer, Heidelberg (1991)
7. Nakamoto, S.: Bitcoin: a peer-to-peer electronic cash system. Decentraliz. Bus. Rev. (2008)
8. Wood, G.: Ethereum: a secure decentralised generalised transaction ledger. Ethereum Project Yellow Paper **151**, 1–32 (2014)
9. Zheng, Z., et al.: An overview of blockchain technology: architecture, consensus, and future trends. In: IEEE International Congress on Big Data (BigData Congress 2017), pp. 557–564 (2017)
10. https://www.stefanjunestrand.com/blog/what-is-blockchain, last accessed 2023/07/29
11. Chatterjee, S., Corbae, D., Dempsey, K., Ríos-Rull, J.: A quantitative theory of the credit score. National Bureau of Economic Research, No. w27671 (2020)

12. Zhou, J., Wang, C., Ren, F., Chen, G.: Inferring multi-stage risk for online consumer credit services: an integrated scheme using data augmentation and model enhancement. Decis. Supp. Syst. **149**, 113611 (2021)
13. Li, Y., Wang, X., Djehiche, B., Hu, X.: Credit scoring by incorporating dynamic networked information. Eur. J. Oper. Res. **286**(3), 1103–1112 (2020)
14. Dash, B., Sharma, P., Azad, A.: Federated learning for privacy-preserving: a review of PII data analysis in fintech. Int. J. Softw. Eng. Appl. **13**(4) (2022)
15. Lee, C., Fernández, J., Menci, S., Rieger, A., Fridgen, G.: Federated learning for credit risk assessment. In: Proceedings of the 56th Hawaii International Conference on System Sciences, pp. 386–395 (2023)
16. He, H., Wang, Z., Jain, H., Jiang, C., Yang. S: A privacy-preserving decentralized credit scoring method based on multi-party information. Decis. Supp. Syst. **166**, 113910 (2023)
17. Konečný, J., McMahan, H., Ramage, D., Richtárik, P.: Federated optimization: distributed machine learning for on-device intelligence. arXiv preprint arXiv:1610.02527 (2016)
18. Zhu, J., Cao, J., Saxena, D., Jiang, S., Ferradi, H.: Blockchain-empowered federated learning: challenges, solutions, and future directions. ACM Comput. Surv. **55**(11), 1–31 (2023)
19. Li, Y., Chen, C., Liu, N., Huang, H., Zheng, Z., Yan, Q.: A blockchain-based decentralized federated learning framework with committee consensus. IEEE Network **35**(1), 234–241 (2020)
20. Wang, Z., Yan, B., Dong, A.: Blockchain empowered federated learning for data sharing incentive mechanism. Procedia Comput. Sci. **202**, 348–353 (2022)
21. Oktian, Y.E., Stanley, B., Lee, S.: Building trusted federated learning on blockchain. Symmetry **14**(7) (2022)
22. Qu, Y., Pokhrel, S., Garg, S., Gao, L., Xiang, Y.: A blockchained federated learning framework for cognitive computing in Industry 4.0 networks. IEEE Trans. Indust. Inf. **17**(4), 2964–2973 (2020)
23. Zerka, F., et al.: Blockchain for privacy preserving and trustworthy distributed machine learning in multicentric medical imaging (C-DistriM). IEEE Access **8**, 183939–183951 (2020)
24. Pokhrel, S., Choi, J.: Federated learning with blockchain for autonomous vehicles: analysis and design challenges. IEEE Trans. Commun. **68**(8), 4734–4746 (2020)
25. Wang, J., Wu, Q.: Research on the blockchain-based privacy protection for Internet financial product recommendation systems. In: Proceedings of the 2020 IEEE International Conference on Computer Science and Management Technology, Shanghai, pp. 310–313 (2020)
26. McMahan, H., Moore, E., Ramage, D., Arcas, B.: Federated learning of deep networks using model averaging. arXiv preprint arXiv:1602.05629 2 (2016)
27. FELT. FEderating Learning Token, FELT Labs. https://github.com/FELT-Labs/federated-learning-token. Accessed 12 June 2023
28. Brownie Library. https://eth-brownie.readthedocs.io. Accessed 11 June 2023
29. Ganache. https://trufflesuite.com/docs/ganache. Accessed 11 June 2023
30. Home Credit Default Risk Dataset. https://www.kaggle.com/competitions/home-credit-default-risk/data. Accessed 11 June 2023

PhishVision: A Deep Learning Based Visual Brand Impersonation Detector for Identifying Phishing Attacks

Giovanni Graziano[1,2], Daniele Ucci[1], Federica Bisio[1], and Luca Oneto[2(✉)]

[1] aizoOn Technology Consulting, Turin, Italy
[2] University of Genoa, Genoa, Italy
luca.oneto@gmail.com

Abstract. With the rapid growth of online space and the rising number of interconnected devices, security threats related to both personal and corporate data have increased considerably. Phishing attacks are commonly used to target corporate networks and gain initial access into security perimeters. The campaigns associated to these attacks span different propagation media and, in the case of web pages, attackers mimic real pages to trick users into downloading malicious software or sharing their credentials. In this paper we propose PhishVision, a framework for visually detecting phishing websites by identifying the main logo that characterizes them and comparing it with a set of logos which PhishVision protects. In case of presence of multiple logos, the framework is able to reconstruct which logo identifies the page while ignoring the others. The framework has been designed to have a lower false positive rate, fast detection times, and works in near-real-time fashion to provide a phishing detection service to Security Operation Centers. Its operators can use it make informed decisions about potential phishing activities by offering a comprehensible grey box explanation about how the framework has reached its conclusions. PhishVision achieves 0.997 ROC AUC on a test set of 404 screenshots, including both benign and malicious samples.

Keywords: Deep Learning · Explainability · Brand Impersonation · Phishing

1 Introduction

With the rapid growth of online space and the rising number of interconnected devices, security threats related to both personal and corporate data have increased considerably [8]. One of the most disruptive and expensive form of data breaches are ransomware, which makes different forms of extorsion demands until a ransom is paid. Very often, these attacks are delivered through phishing campaigns [22], costing an estimated average of $4.91M per data breach [13]. Phishing campaigns span many different propagation media, from web pages to

A. I. Pereira et al. (Eds.): OL2A 2023, CCIS 1981, pp. 123–134, 2024.
https://doi.org/10.1007/978-3-031-53025-8_9

e-mails, including QR codes [29] and mobile applications [18]. In particular, in the cases involving web pages, attackers imitate real pages to trick users into downloading malicious software or sharing their credentials. In the last year, phishing attacks targeting corporate networks have continued to be performed to gain initial access into security perimeters [8]. Thus, it is of paramount importance to identify phishing attacks occurring in a monitored network by means of automated solutions, to reduce possible human errors that still play a critical tole in most security breaches [20].

Both in academia and industry, several approaches have been developed ranging from the simplest, yet ineffective, ones based on blacklists [5,26] to solutions employing Machine Learning (ML) techniques. The latter leverage, e.g., URL features [3,9,21] or HTML based heuristics [19,23,31]. However, such approaches suffer from low explainability and are susceptible to HTML code obfuscation that can be employed to avoid detection [4,27]. Other ML-based solutions explore ways for detecting phishing pages based on a set of brands and their respective websites, widely known in literature as *protected set*, to identify web pages that attempt to mimic their appearance [1,2,6,10,16,17]. In literature, protected set is a loose term whose semantics change depending on the context in which it is used. For example, it may indicate a set of webpages whose layout and appearance a model learns to recognize [1], or a set of logos that a classifier can identify [6,16,17]. In other scenarios, the protected set describes a list of URLs that phishing pages might try to mimic, as in [3,9,21]. However, all these works have in common a protected set through which a model is able to identify possible brand identities that spoofed pages are going to emulate in various ways. For this reason, many phishing detection systems focus on identifying pages that, according to specific features, try to imitate a page of the protected set. Nevertheless, previous ML solutions have non-negligible false positive rates and do not work in near-real-time fashion.

In this work we propose PhishVision, a framework for visually detecting phishing websites by identifying the main logo that characterizes them and comparing it with a set of logos which PhishVision protects (i.e., our definition of protected set). Indeed, a company logo is the most recognizable visual feature of a website, not only for humans but also for an ML-based vision system. In case of presence of multiple logos, the framework is able to reconstruct which logo identifies the page, while ignoring the others. Although some previously referenced works have already employed similar methodologies [1,16,17], PhishVision has been designed to have a lower false positive rate, faster detection times, and works in near-real-time fashion to provide a Phishing Detection Service (PDaaS) to Security Operation Centers (SOCs). PhishVision has been implemented by leveraging an Object Detection (OD) framework, YOLOv7 [30], which was further optimized to better perform on this specific domain, alongside being refactored into a more modular configuration. The proposed algorithm significantly improves the accuracy and efficiency of phishing website detection. Moreover, despite being developed to contrast phishing websites, a similar approach could be used to identify phishing emails, with minimal modifications.

The works mostly related to PhishVision are [16] and [17], but they use a further brand predictor component for classifying detected logos, through an additional layer of neural networks, significantly increasing the overall computational cost. Conversely, PhishVision uses directly its OD model to accurately classify logos, without leveraging any additional component. It is worth noting that the employed approach drastically reduces the room for web page obfuscation attacks: in fact, an attacker may obfuscate the code of the web page to avoid detection by means of code analysis but, in any case, page visual similarity must be maintained in order to deceive a victim.

Summarizing, the advantages of the main contribution of the paper, PhishVision, are twofold (i) it reduces the false positive rate by focusing on identifying the logo rather than the entire page, which is a more reliable indicator of brand identity and is akin to how humans recognize brands, and (ii) it provides a service that SOC operators can use to make informed decisions about potential phishing activities offering a comprehensible grey box explanation about how the model reaches its conclusions by including information about recognized brands and confidences in its predictions.

The rest of the paper is organized as follows. Section 2 presents a comprehensive overview of PhishVision, its threat model of reference, its internal architecture, and its implementation details. Section 3 reports obtained results. Finally, Sect. 4 concludes our work and Sect. 5 presents future experiments to be carried out.

2   PhishVision

The idea behind PhishVision is to establish, using visual features alone, whether a web page is representative of a particular company or institution. Once identified, it is simpler to check whether the domain name associated to such web page belongs to the list of legitimate domains associated to that brand or to an attacker. As further discussed in Sect. 2.1, phishing pages have high visual similarity to the corresponding targeted pages and the logo plays a crucial role in detecting phishing attacks. The proposed framework is able to accurately identify when a web page contains a logo from the protected set. In case of multiple logos, the algorithm is able to reconstruct the logo of the company that owns the page, while ignoring any secondary logos.

In the next sections, we will present the threat model, the PhishVision architecture, and the framework implementation details.

2.1   Threat Model

The phishing web pages that PhishVision is able to identify are websites in which the attacker mimics one of the pages belonging to a brand of the protected set, in order to deceive victims. The attacker might spread a malicious URL to the phishing web page through various means in other to reach as many victims as possible. When such a URL is intercepted by a SOC operator, through the monitoring tools he uses, PhishVision can be queried to verify if such link is malicious.

Given a set of protected brands B and web pages W^b corresponding to each brand $b \in B$, PhishVision is able to identify whether a suspicious web page $\overline{w}$ is imitating a page belonging to a protected brand. The service returns both the targeted brand and the prediction confidence. More formally, the final output of the model can be interpreted as the likelihood $p = P[\overline{w} \in W^b]$, with $p \in [0,1]$, that $\overline{w}$ is using a protected logo to imitate the brand b.

2.2   Architecture

PhishVision consists of three main components: a crawler, an OD model, and a brand predictor.

The crawling module is in charge of following suspicious URLs and capturing a screenshot of the page, which is then fed to the OD model. However, in case

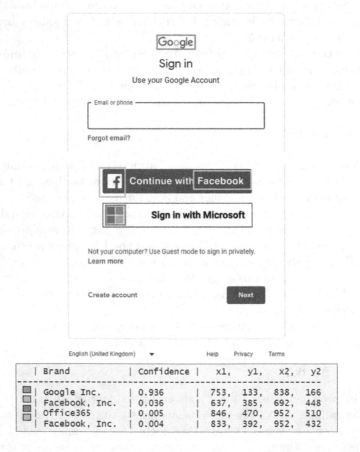

Brand	Confidence	x1,	y1,	x2,	y2
Google Inc.	0.936	753,	133,	838,	166
Facebook, Inc.	0.036	637,	385,	692,	448
Office365	0.005	846,	470,	952,	510
Facebook, Inc.	0.004	833,	392,	952,	432

Fig. 1. Real-world example of PhishVision correctly identifying the main logo in a phishing page, targeting Google. Facebook and Microsoft logos are also identified as secondary logos and this can be easily noticed by the assigned low confidence.

that the URL domain is contained in the whitelist of known protected domains, no further action is taken, and the service simply flags the page as not phishing.

The second component is the core of PhishVision: the OD model is a deep Convolutional Neural Network (CNN) capable of identifying the logos in a web page $L = \{l_1, l_2, ..., l_n\}$. Each l_i can be represented using three components: its bounding box $(x_i^1, y_i^1, x_i^2, y_i^2)$, the brand b_i associated to the logo, and a prediction confidence p_i.

Given the list of identified logos, the brand prediction module selects one of these as the main logo, and assigns a targeted brand b and prediction confidence p to the input URL. As an example, consider a login page containing multiple single signs on options, each with the respective logo, as depicted in Fig. 1. The brand predictor component is responsible for choosing which one of the detected logos is actually associated to the brand that hosts the page. In addition, as shown in Fig. 1, PhishVision predictions can be easily interpreted by security operators through brand-enclosing bounding boxes and their corresponding confidences, so that analysts can make informed decisions about potential phishing activities. In case the web page owner is not in the protected set, the brand predictor should output that no brand was identified.

2.3   Implementation

Once either a URL or a domain name is submitted to PhishVision to be analyzed, the first step consist in comparing the extracted domain with the domains associated with the logo brands contained in the protected set. If it is not the case, the corresponding web page is rendered using *Selenium*[1], a browser automator, and a screenshot is taken. Additionally, Selenium is able to interact with the page to dismiss popups, since these are sometimes used to block parts of the page in order to interfere with phishing detection techniques. The screenshot is then fed forward to the logo detector.

For this component, various OD models were considered preliminarily and model selection procedure clearly indicated YOLOv7 as the top performing OD architectures for this problem. Although the network architecture was not changed, YOLOv7 was refactored into a more modular design, abstracting part of the code, which allowed for some improvements that permitted faster training, such as a faster label assignment algorithm, an improved caching strategy, and better transfer of the weights of the detection head to leverage transfer learning.

---

[1] www.selenium.dev.

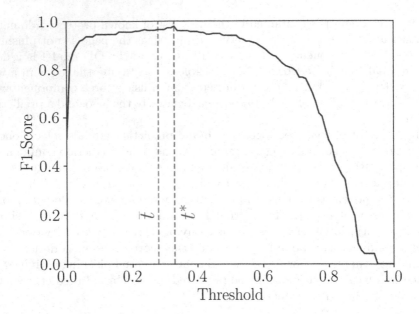

Fig. 2. F1-score obtained on varying the threshold t in the interval $[0, 1]$. The dashed red line shows the threshold t^* through which it is possible to achieve the highest F1-score in the test phase, namely $t^* = 0.33$. It is worth noting that t^* is close to $\bar{t} = 0.28$, that is the threshold that maximizes the F1-score during validation phase. (Color figure online)

In particular, the label assignment algorithm used is SimOTA [12], a simpler and faster version of OTA [11], which was further vectorized to improve efficiency, resulting in a 21% faster loss calculation over YOLOv7. Furthermore, the caching algorithm was modified to cache part of the dataset in RAM, and part on disk memory, which enables caching for large datasets which do not fit entirely in memory. Since in the original YOLOv7 model the weights of the head were completely reinitialized when transferring weights from pretrained models, the efficiency of fine tuning was impaired in the experiments conducted. Therefore the weight transfer strategy was modified to maintain the weights that identified bounding box location.

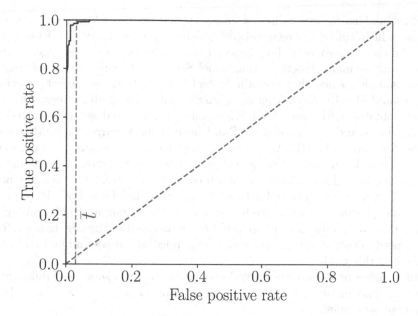

Fig. 3. PhishVision ROC curve. The dashed green line corresponds to the threshold $\bar{t} = 0.28$ obtained in the validation phase. (Color figure online)

These modifications, combined with the usage of a fast single shot detector such as YOLOv7 and the removal of the additional neural network that performs brand prediction that other solutions propose, result in a system that is faster both in training and in prediction time, allowing us to achieve phishing detection in near-real time even on limited hardware.

Empirical analysis were conducted discovering that it is sufficient for the brand predictor to simply assign the brand b with highest confidence p_b if it surpasses a threshold $p_b > t$, otherwise deciding for no brand, because the OD model is sufficiently accurate in the classification task.

3   Experimental Results

In order to extensively test the proposed detection system, it was necessary to construct a custom dataset to train the modified YOLOv7 model: the datasets that are currently available and contain screenshots of phishing websites, labelled with the logo bounding box, are the Phishpedia benign dataset [16] and the LogoSENSE dataset [6]. However, both suffer from some problems that make them impractical for the training of PhishVision. Phishpedia is not limited to a set of protected websites, but instead collects one screenshot from each site resulting in a different logo every time. LogoSENSE labelled every logo on the page, not just the main one.

After identifying 8 brands that are frequently targeted by phishing attacks [28], Selenium was used to take screenshots of their websites (see

Sect. 2.2), and more screenshots were selected from the Phishpedia phishing dataset, which collects screenshots of phishing pages. However, Phishpedia misses labels for logo bounding boxes. For each screenshot, the logo bounding box was manually labelled using Label Studio[2]. We call this set of images positive samples, since they contain protected logos that the object detection model should identify. Collecting both crawled and Phishpedia screenshots, the dataset contains 2,012 positive images, using a protected set constituted by the following brands: Facebook, PayPal, Chase Bank, Orange Bank, Microsoft, Google, Amazon, and DHL. Analogously, a negative set is required as well, to let the framework learn that, in some real-world cases, screenshots do not contain any (known) logo. This dataset was much easier to acquire, as it does not need any labeling. The screenshots for this set were collected from both Phishpedia benign and phishing datasets, excluding web pages belonging to the protected set. A total of 3,323 images were selected to be included in the negative set. The dataset used in these experiments will be expanded and made public in a future extension of this work.

The training procedure tested various hyperparameter sets, used image augmentation, and examined different combinations of loss functions and label assignment strategies.

The detector performed better when optimized using SGD over Adam [7], and using a cosine annealing learning rate scheduler increased the validation mean Average Precision (mAP). Using SimOTA [12] as the label assignment strategy made YOLOv7 converge to a higher mAP, and the YOLO loss [24] performed better than Focal loss [14] on this problem. An interesting aspect of data augmentation is that not all image augmentation techniques yielded better results. In particular, translations and reflections along both the X and Y axis resulted in an object detection model that often assigned high confidences to secondary logos, therefore resulting in false positives. However, other geometric transformations, color augmentations, and the usage of random noise allowed for data augmentation that did not hinder the results.

Another important component that improved detection performance was pretraining the model on positive samples alone, and successively introducing negative samples. This was done because training YOLOv7 on the entire dataset caused the OD model to assign low confidence to the logos detected, whereas the method employed increased the separation between true positives and false positives.

The YOLOv7 model was trained starting from a pretrained checkpoint with input image size of 640 × 640 pixels, after which it was used in the framework for testing.

The validation set was made up of 404 screenshots, 270 of which were negative samples. The test set also included 404 screenshots, 270 of which were negative samples, and it was distinct from the validation set.

Figures 2 and 3 show the excellent performance of PhishVision in detecting phishing websites: the framework achieves 0.997 ROC AUC and, using a thresh-

---

[2] https://labelstud.io.

old $\bar{t} = 0.28$, it generates only 8 false positives (FP) and 2 false negatives (FN). Threshold $\bar{t} = 0.28$ has been selected because it maximizes the F1-score on the validation set. However, it can be easily noticed that the maximum F1-score on the test set corresponds to $t^* = 0.33$, that is very close to $\bar{t}$.

Figure 1 shows an example of a detected phishing site where multiple logos were present: PhishVision is able to correctly identify that the target brand is Google, and assigns the other logos a lower confidence. Such detections can be easily verified by analysts and can support their decisions: indeed, the Google logo is identified with a confidence $0.936 > \bar{t}$ and security operators can possibly double check the framework output. Even in cases where multiple logos are present but the main logo is not part of the protected set, PhishVision is able to identify the location of the primary logo, but assigns it a low confidence. Other logos - even ones present in the protected set - are assigned an even lower confidence, and the page is correctly marked as not phishing.

4   Conclusion

In this paper we proposed PhishVision, a framework that leverages deep learning for phishing attacks visual brand impersonation detection by identifying the main logo that characterizes them and comparing it with a set of logos which PhishVision protects. The framework was designed to have low false positive rate, low response times, and to offer a comprehensible grey box explanation about how its internal model reaches conclusions about submitted input, in order to use it as a near-real time phishing detection service which security operators can query to better understand if a link is a phishing attempt, in a secure and autonomous way.

To achieve these objectives, various object detection models were tested to select one that could identify logos in a screenshot with good accuracy and low prediction times, ultimately landing on YOLOv7, a state of the art single-stage object detection model. This model was further optimized to lower training times and trained on a custom dataset of screenshots of phishing and benign sites. An important contribution of this work is identifying how an object detection model can be used to classify logos into the brands in the protected set, which allows the proposed model to avoid expensive computations that are present in other state of the art models. PhishVision can then use the object detection model to identify logos in a screenshot that belong to the protected set, and use this information to detect phishing websites.

Experimental evaluations show very promising results with a 0.997 ROC AUC on a test set of 404 screenshots of real-world websites, with only 8 false positives and 2 false negatives. On a NVidia® Tesla® P100 GPU, the 404 screenshots are evaluated in just 101 seconds, therefore achieving real-time phishing detection on GPU.

5 Future Work

Although the proposed model shows promising results and achieves good performance on the test dataset, further experiments should be carried out to test its capabilities in real-world scenarios.

The protected set used in this work contains 8 brands, however future experiments will test the efficacy of the model with larger protected sets. Given that YOLO achieves good results with 91 classes—the standard in object detection datasets [15]—and has been expanded to 9000 classes [25], the performances shown in this paper are not expected to be significantly impacted.

Moreover, eXplainable Artificial Intelligence (XAI) and adversarial attack techniques will be used both to understand how the model derives its predictions and to ensure that the framework is resilient to active attackers, since a malevolent actor may attempt to build a phishing page in such a way that it evades computer vision techniques. Both of these topics are of utmost importance in cybersecurity analytics, however their role is often understudied.

Finally, an extension and future implementation of this work will study how it can be applied to phishing emails, since these are a common way to spread malicious links. Phishing email share similarities to phishing websites, since they are also characterised by visual similarity to legitimate emails, and usually present a logo of the target institution, therefore the logic behind PhishVision should work in similar way to detect phishing emails.

Acknowledgments. This work is partially supported by project SERICS (PE00000014) under the MUR National Recovery and Resilience Plan funded by the European Union - NextGenerationEU.

References

1. Abdelnabi, S., Krombholz, K., Fritz, M.: Visualphishnet: zero-day phishing website detection by visual similarity. In: ACM SIGSAC Conference on Computer and Communications Security (2020)
2. Afroz, S., Greenstadt, R.: Phishzoo: detecting phishing websites by looking at them. In: IEEE International Conference on Semantic Computing (2011)
3. Ahmed, A.A., Abdullah, N.A.: Real time detection of phishing websites. In: IEEE Annual Information Technology, Electronics and Mobile Communication Conference (2016)
4. AlEroud, A., Karabatis, G.: Bypassing detection of URL-based phishing attacks using generative adversarial deep neural networks. In: International Workshop on Security and Privacy Analytics (2020)
5. Bell, S., Komisarczuk, P.: An analysis of phishing blacklists: google safe browsing, openphish, and phishtank. In: Australasian Computer Science Week Multiconference (2020)
6. Bozkir, A.S., Aydos, M.: Logosense: a companion hog based logo detection scheme for phishing web page and e-mail brand recognition. Comput. Secur. **95**, 101855 (2020)

7. Diederik, P.K., Ba, J.: Adam: a method for stochastic optimization. Tech. rep. (2017)
8. ENISA. Enisa threat landscape 2022. Tech. rep. (2022)
9. Feroz, M.N., Mengel, S.: Phishing url detection using url ranking. In: IEEE International Congress on Big Data (2015)
10. Fu, A.Y., Wenyin, L., Deng, X.: Detecting phishing web pages with visual similarity assessment based on earth mover's distance (emd). IEEE Trans. Depend. Secure Comput. 3(4), 301–311 (2006)
11. Ge, Z., Liu, S., Li, Z., Yoshie, O., Sun, J.: Ota: optimal transport assignment for object detection. In: IEEE/CVF Conference on Computer Vision and Pattern Recognition (2021)
12. Ge, Z., Liu, S., Wang, F., Li, Z., Sun, J.: Yolox: exceeding yolo series in 2021. arXiv preprint arXiv:2107.08430 (2021)
13. IBM. Cost of a data breach report 2022. Tech. rep. (2022)
14. Lin, T.Y., Goyal, P., Girshick, R., He, K., Dollár, P.: Focal loss for dense object detection. In: IEEE International Conference on Computer Vision (2017)
15. Lin, T.Y., et al.: Microsoft coco: common objects in context. In: European Conference on Computer Vision (2014)
16. Lin, Y., Liu, R., Divakaran, D.M., Ng, J.Y., Chan, Q.Z., Lu, Y., Si, Y., Zhang, F., Dong, J.S.: Phishpedia: A hybrid deep learning based approach to visually identify phishing webpages. In: USENIX Security Symposium (2021)
17. Liu, R., Lin, Y., Yang, X., Ng, S.H., Divakaran, D.M., Dong, J.S.: Inferring phishing intention via webpage appearance and dynamics: a deep vision based approach. In: USENIX Security Symposium (2022)
18. Marforio, C., Jayaram Masti, R., Soriente, C., Kostiainen, K., Čapkun, S.: Evaluation of personalized security indicators as an anti-phishing mechanism for smartphone applications. In: CHI Conference on Human Factors in Computing Systems (2016)
19. Moghimi, M., Varjani, A.Y.: New rule-based phishing detection method. Expert Syst. Appl. 53, 231–242 (2016)
20. Moore, S.: 7 top trends in cybersecurity for 2022 - gartner inc. Tech. rep. (2023)
21. Nguyen, L.A.T., To, B.L., Nguyen, H.K., Nguyen, M.H.: A novel approach for phishing detection using url-based heuristic. In: International Conference on Computing, Management and Telecommunications (2014)
22. PhishLabs, F.: Ransomware Attacks: Why Email is Still the Most Common Delivery Method. Tech. rep, Fortra (2023)
23. Rao, R.S., Ali, S.T.: Phishshield: a desktop application to detect phishing webpages through heuristic approach. Procedia Comput. Sci. 54, 147–156 (2015)
24. Redmon, J., Divvala, S., Girshick, R., Farhadi, A.: You only look once: unified, real-time object detection. In: IEEE Conference on Computer Vision and Pattern Recognition (2016)
25. Redmon, J., Farhadi, A.: Yolo9000: better, faster, stronger. In: IEEE Conference on Computer Vision and Pattern Recognition (2017)
26. Sheng, S., Wardman, B., Warner, G., Cranor, L., Hong, J., Zhang, C.: An empirical analysis of phishing blacklists. In: International Conference on Email and Anti-Spam (2009)
27. Song, F., Lei, Y., Chen, S., Fan, L., Liu, Y.: Advanced evasion attacks and mitigations on practical ml-based phishing website classifiers. Int. J. Intell. Syst. 36(9), 5210–5240 (2021)
28. Vade. Phishers' favorites. 2022 year-in-review. Tech. rep. (2023)

29. Vidas, T., Owusu, E., Wang, S., Zeng, C., Cranor, L.F., Christin, N.: Qrishing: the susceptibility of smartphone users to QR code phishing attacks. In: Financial Cryptography and Data Security (2013)
30. Wang, C.Y., Bochkovskiy, A., Liao, H.Y.M.: Yolov7: trainable bag-of-freebies sets new state-of-the-art for real-time object detectors. arXiv preprint arXiv:2207.02696 (2022)
31. Xiang, G., Hong, J., Rose, C.P., Cranor, L.: Cantina+ a feature-rich machine learning framework for detecting phishing web sites. ACM Trans. Inf. Syst. Secur. **14**(2), 1–28 (2011)

Call Centre Optimization Based on Personalized Requests Distribution

Elizaveta Tarasova[(✉)] ⓘ and Dmitry Ivanov ⓘ

ITMO University, S. Petersburg, Russian Federation
el.u.tarasova@gmail.com

Abstract. The paper is devoted to the assignment problem in the framework of optimizing the call centre work based on a scheduling theory online model. A multi-criteria problem is considered, which includes not only formal theoretical indicators of the obtained schedules (average delay), but also taking into account the human factor (client satisfaction and operator fatigue). The paper proposes a new approach and DCSF algorithm (Deadline, Compatibility, and Safe Factor) for optimizing assignment within the call centre. An important feature of this work is the algorithm personalization, achieved by taking into account the individual customers and operators parameters. The paper also uses the concept of calculating deadlines based on the client's readiness to wait and the concept of taking into account the safety factor. These approaches are used for the first time to manage the call centre work.

Keywords: Queuing system optimization · Online schedule model with deadlines · Personalized Assignment · Multi-criteria problem

1 Introduction

Assignment models are widely used to improve the efficiency of various technical, economic, administrative and other systems by optimizing resource consumption. Many studies based on the queuing theory are devoted to improving the service quality, increasing the operator's efficiency, minimizing service time, queue length and waiting time.

The base model describes the system "applications - executors" in which the executor processes incoming applications. This setting is applicable to various queuing systems, including call centres. Queuing systems within the framework of the selected job are usually built according to two types, "Man - man" and "Man - machine". In these cases, it is necessary to take into account individual characteristics and different criteria, both for clients and for clients. Recent research in this area has focused on the influence of the human factor, which can have a strong influence on the system efficiency, but at the same time is difficult to formalize. At the same time, the classical assignment problem is considered within the framework of an offline model, that is, under conditions of complete certainty of the initial data. However, many applied jobs involve changing the

© The Author(s), under exclusive license to Springer Nature Switzerland AG 2024
A. I. Pereira et al. (Eds.): OL2A 2023, CCIS 1981, pp. 135–147, 2024.
https://doi.org/10.1007/978-3-031-53025-8_10

applications set during the work of performers, which leads to the online problem consideration.

However, most of the studies in this paper are based on highly specialized and poorly scaled models. We offer a new approach to optimize the call centre work based on online planning and accounting for personalization both on the part of the client and the operator. As part of this study, the following work was carried out:

- the call centre model was developed based on the job of assignment, optimization, online planning (through deadlines) and personalization;
- the new method and algorithm for managing the work of a call centre has been developed. The algorithm is based on assignment based on weights, prediction of individual parameters and the human factor consideration;
- the performance of this system was tested on the basis of synthetic data.

It should be emphasized that this paper presents the first stage of a large-scale study, based primarily on the development and testing of a new concept and methodology. At the same time, due to the strong results obtained, this work is important not only from the point of view of the technical development of this area, but also from the point of view of social significance. This is because taking into account the human factor potentially improves the quality of life for both customers and operators.

2   Related Work

Some considered works are devoted to optimization for the assignment problem based on the methods of scheduling theory. In [14], a bipartite graph is used to solve the assignment problem. This ignores the edges that conflict in terms of assignment and solves a simplified B&B problem. In another study [2], devoted to modelling the call centre work, the introduction of two ribs of flexibility is used, based on the introduction of several schedule formats (both in duration terms of the scheduling and the size of the planned cell) and the different quality assumption of service for different periods of time while maintaining the minimum average over the total time period under consideration. According to a study [15], this approach reduces the inventory of operators from 36.8% to 7.5% and reduces the overall cost by 3–10%.

The work [13] is devoted to the minimizing problem the weighted average execution time on identical parallel processors in an online formulation. The possibility of reducing the weighted average job completion time using the weighted shortest processing time based on Smith's algorithm (WSPT) is considered. The study [20] proposed an LJSF algorithm for single-processor online scheduling with deadlines based on the safety factor and job size, relative to others. The algorithm is based on taking into account the job size and the safety factor for each of the available jobs at the assignment time:

$$K_i = \frac{D_i - time}{p_i}, \tag{1}$$

where D_i is the due date of job i, *time* is the current time on the processor, p_i is the job i duration.

There are also studies devoted to optimization in terms of increasing the satisfaction level of the performer. For example, in [10], an approach is presented to improve the quality of the system by adding a significance level to various indicators from the point of the performer view (satisfaction of the teacher, supervisor, school administrator).

It is possible to reduce the personal parameters of clients to the operation standard parameters in terms of scheduling theory. For example, in [19], the study proposed the concept of applying the model with due dates for queuing systems with multi-criteria problem. The concept is based on reducing the "readiness to wait" parameter of the client to the deadline:

$$D_i = r_i + w_i \tag{2}$$

where D_i is the predicted due date for client (call) i, r_i is the time when client i enters the system, w_i is the predicted readiness to wait for client i. The key feature of the developed method is the combination of the individual characteristics of the system elements with the classical parameter of the scheduling theory, which made it possible to develop a generalized algorithm for optimizing the queuing system based on personalization.

Another optimization approach is to focus on finding the best pair to assign in terms of various parameters of both sides. For example, in [21], the jobs distribution based on a pre-trained model is proposed: each employee is assigned such a subset of questions k from the available ones so that the quality is maximum. The paper [17] considers the use of the ELECTRE III decision-making system for solving a multicriteria assignment problem (by the example of appointing referees for football matches in Italy). The introduction of min-max thresholds for various criteria in the assignment is shown, as opposed to the usual scheme of reducing the choice with the minimization of one indicator (often - monetary or temporary).

For the best assignment, it is required to identify a number of customers and operators characteristics, according to which the assessment will be carried out, as well as predicting such individual parameters as readiness to wait, fatigue, etc. For systems in which the client and the contractor have a set of parameters, in various studies they are divided into groups [1,9]. At the initial stage, clustering is carried out according to the available data, but then, as the interactions history between operators and customers accumulates, the number of known parameters increases, which leads to the reorganization of groups. Also, based on the selected characteristics, it is possible to divide clients into groups of complexity. The study [5] proposes a naive Bayesian classification algorithm that distributes customers among four levels of risk (according to bank default) based on personal data and transactions. The work [16] is devoted to the search for relationships between personal factors and service efficiency, absenteeism, staff turnover in call centres. According to this study results, the service quality negatively correlates only with openness to new experience (ambition), other parameters do not have a significant impact within call centres, since there is no personal communication between operators and teamwork. The article [18] conducted a study on the distribution of investors among eight categories: cautious, self-confident, optimist, prudent, realist, individualist, integrator and well-balanced. The third (optimist) and sixth (individualist) categories accounted for 45.8% and 21.5% of the entire sample, so two of the eight categories accounted for already 2/3 of all clients.

The work [11] is devoted to improving the accuracy of determining personal characteristics (extroversion, emotional stability, accommodating, conscientiousness, openness to experience) through the analysis of chats and the further use of this information to create a recommended products list. Based on data from a UK online gift shop, the paper shows an 18.67% improvement in characterization accuracy.

One of the objective functions considered optimizing the call centre work is customer satisfaction. There are various approaches to determine this objective function and calculate the level of satisfaction at the end of the interaction with the client. This problem occurs in various human-to-human queuing systems. For example, the study [2] considers the measurement of student satisfaction in the library help chat depending on the operator. The work [4] includes a review and formulation of the shortcomings of modern banking call centres from the point of view of the client. The work [12] explores what factors (both on the part of the client and on the part of the site) affect client satisfaction. The article [8] analyses the relationship between customer satisfaction and certain service factors. According to this study, perceptions are affected by empathy, competence, and tangibility, but not by responsiveness, reliability, credibility, and service quality assurance. At the first contact, the most important thing is efficiency and understanding of the problem.

In work [6], in contrast to the concept of "first in - first out", the system management is demonstrated based on indicators determined on the basis of how long the client is willing to wait before hanging up and whether the client will call again. The study shows that when applying this concept, the waiting time was reduced by 29%, throughput increased by 6%. The main ideas isolated from the considered works, on the basis of which the development of the optimization method was carried out:

- prediction of the maximum waiting time of the client to optimize scheduling;
- increasing or decreasing the priority of customer service depending on a number of factors;
- analysis of factors influencing customer satisfaction during communication;
- analysis of factors affecting the quality of work, fatigue, and churn among operators;
- dividing clients into groups for conducting various conversation scenarios;
- selection and forecasting of individual indicators of clients.

3 Deadline, Compatibility, and Safe Factor Algorithm

The call centre system contains several stages of interaction with customers (see Fig. 1), optimization takes place in a dedicated area at the level of creating a schedule for the customer queue and assigning a "client-operator".

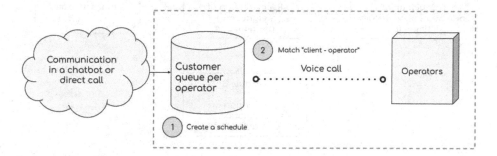

Fig. 1. The system of interaction with customers within the call center.

System management is reduced to solving the following jobs:

- predicting the deadline for starting and ending a conversation based on the client's willingness to wait;
- selection of the most suitable operator for each client;
- increasing customer satisfaction from the call through assignment based on selected parameters in terms of individual characteristics and time in the system;
- prevention of operator burnout by taking into account the level of fatigue in the assignment.

The operators in the size M participating in the system operation are given. For each client, the history of interaction is known (if it was), on the basis of which, for each request $v_i i \in N$, the client group is determined (according to individual characteristics and psychological type), the type of request, the predicted execution time p'_{ij}, for each of the available operators j, willingness to wait for this type of call w_i, processing complexity h_{ij} for each operator j.

A multi-criteria problem is considered with the following objective functions, on the basis of which the quality and effectiveness of the assignment made will be evaluated:

1. Minimizing the average delay in working with each client relative to the predicted deadlines:

$$f_1 = \frac{\sum_{i=1}^{N} max(0, \tau_i + p_i - D_i)}{N'} \rightarrow min \qquad (3)$$

where τ_i is the start time of work with job i, p_i is the actual execution time of job i (time of talking with client i), $N' = |\{v_i : \tau_i + p_i > D_i\}|$ is the number of

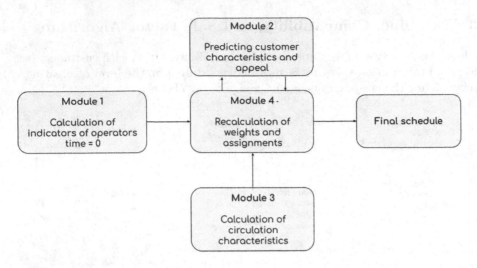

Fig. 2. Scheme of the optimization system.

late jobs (number of clients, the conversation with which is completed after the deadline).

2. Maximizing customer satisfaction based on tracking late or ahead of deadlines and choosing the right operator:

$$f_2 = \frac{\sum Sat(D_i - (\tau_i + p_i), Match)}{|Sat(D_i - (\tau_i + p_i), Match)|} \rightarrow max \qquad (4)$$

where $Match$ is a matrix showing the success of the assignment by groups of clients and operators.

3. Minimization of fatigue (burnout) of operators:

$$f_3 = \sum_{j=1}^{M} \frac{\sum_{i=1}^{N_j} h_{ij}}{|V'_j|} h_{lvl_j}^{-1} \rightarrow min \qquad (5)$$

where N_j are calls processed by operator j, h_{ij} is the complexity of call i for operator j, h_{lvl_j} is the fatigue level of operator j.

System optimization is based on the following ideas: analysis of the client's recent actions to select a qualified operator; maintaining a "flexible" assignment and allowing for a decrease in the quality of service at certain intervals while maintaining the overall quality for the period under review; the use of psychological types to improve the quality of the client-operator dialogue during the assignment.

Figure 2 shows a diagram of the call centre management and optimization system, consisting of 4 modules.

The result of the system operation is the schedule of all operators, on the basis of which the values of the objective functions f_1, f_2, f_3 are calculated.

Module 1 includes the calculation of the characteristics of operators at time zero: the psychological type of each operator $M_j(\psi)$, where ψ are possible psychological types, the predicted execution time $\overline{p_{ij}}$ for each type of call, the level of stress resistance h_{lvl_j};

Module 2 recalculates the predicted execution time $(\overline{p_{ij}})$ each time the processing of the call by the operator j is completed;

Module 3 calculates the characteristics of the call and determines the client group at the time of entering the system: predicting the readiness to wait w^i_{type} of the client i according to the current type of call at the time of arrival depending on the time of the call, the complexity of the client's client μ_i, psychological type (group) of client $V_i(\psi)$; Module 4 is the basis of the system operation and recalculates all weights of the graph of possible assignments (Fig. 15.3) to select the optimal client-operator pair at the moment one of the operators is released $time = \min_{\tau_i}(\max_{\tau_i} \tau_{ij} + p_{ij})$ and assignment of the call to the operator.

The cost G_{ij} of each edge is a function of a linear combination of weights g_k and coefficients λ_k and safety factor $K_i = \frac{D_i - time}{p_i}$ [20], where $D_i = r_i + w_{ij}$, r_i is the time the client i entered the system, $time$ is the current time in the system:

$$G_{ij} = K_i \sum_{k=1}^{4}(\lambda_k g_k), \sum_{k=1}^{4} \lambda_k = 1 \tag{6}$$

To determine the cost G_{ij} of each edge, the functions g_k are given:

1. Weight by customer waiting time stock:

$$g_1 = w_{ij} - (time - \tau_{ij}) - \overline{p_{ij}}, \lambda_1 > 0. \tag{7}$$

2. Weight by execution time:

$$g_2 = \overline{p_{ij}}, \lambda_2 > 0. \tag{8}$$

3. Weight according to the compatibility of psychological types:

$$g_3 = Match(v_i(\psi), m_j(\psi)), \lambda_3 < 0. \tag{9}$$

4. Weight by operator release time:

$$g_4 = max(\overline{p_{i'j}} + \tau_{i'j}) - time, \lambda_4 > 0, \tag{10}$$

where $v_{i'}$ is the current job of the operator j.

So the general algorithm is as follows:

- before starting work, the characteristics of operators are calculated (module 1);
- with each arrival of a new client, its characteristics are calculated (module 3);
- when the operator is released, the weights are recalculated (module 4) and assigned according to the minimum weight G_{ij};
- the actual processing time of the job (call) is sent to correct the forecast of the job execution time (module 2).

4 Experiments

4.1 Simulation and Testing

To analyse the effectiveness of the algorithm DCSF, we simulated the operation of a call centre on synthetic data and tested it. Testing included finding the optimal weights for the algorithm and comparing the algorithm with others suitable for this call centre model. The implementation of the algorithm, testing and results are posted on GitHub [7].

Testing was carried out on synthetic data generated for this model by the method described in [3], for a model with delivery. For each job, the delivery time value was chosen uniformly from the given range, similarly, the execution time and arrival time $r_i \in [1; r_{max}], p_i \in [1; t_{max}], q_i \in [1; q_{max}]$. The following values were set: $t_{max} = 50, q_{max} = r_{max} = Kn$, where n is the number of jobs. The coefficient K was chosen from the range $[10; 25]$, the values of this range were noted by the author of the method as the most difficult for the problem under consideration. 20 groups of examples of 30 tests with different parameters were generated. The distribution of psychological types for each appeal was also added. The distribution of 9 psychological types for each appeal was also added. 10 operators were introduced (with three different psychological types). Also, the algorithm also requires a psychological type matching matrix. Data on psychological types and comparison of psychological types (successful matching) were provided by the company as part of a research project. For jobs (calls to the call centre), 4 types were identified, which differ in duration time (depending on operator) and complexity. As part of the simulation, it is assumed that when a call comes into the system, it is known what type of job the call belongs to, what psychological type the client belongs to. Estimated processing time is determined by job type. The actual time is generated and is equal to p_i. The predicted time will affect the assignment, and the actual time will affect the objective functions and the resulting schedule.

When testing, the following objective functions were taken into account to evaluate the effectiveness of the solutions obtained: the average delay time, the average success rate of the client-operator assignment, equal to the compatibility coefficient between their psychological types, and the average operator fatigue.

To evaluate the efficiency of the algorithms, several stages of testing and comparison of the results obtained on them were carried out:

1. Algorithm FIFO - stage 1: the assignment is made according to the principle "first in - first out", that is, the first released operator will be assigned to the client who called before the others.
2. Algorithm ABoM (Assignment Based on Match) - stage 2: assignment according to the principle of the largest compatibility coefficient between their psychological types of the client and the operator, that is, when the operator is released, one of the waiting clients is selected, the most suitable for the compatibility of psychological types with the released operator, in the case when there are several such clients, the client is selected from them principle "first in - first out".

3. Algorithm DCSF (Deadline, Compatibility, and Safe Factor) - stage 3: based on the new method and algorithm proposed in Sect. 3.

At stage 3, the values of the objective functions depended on the choice of the coefficients λ_k. Then λ is the vector of coefficients for the weights g_i, which are calculated at the assignment stage. Each set of coefficients will be called a "configuration". At the same time, g_4 was skipped at this stage, so the vector will consist of three elements. At the same time, g_4 was skipped at this stage, so the vector will consist of three elements. Since g_4 is used in the case when the assignment takes into account not only the released operator, but also the rest. This situation was omitted from testing because it creates a large amount of computation, resulting in a delay in assignment.

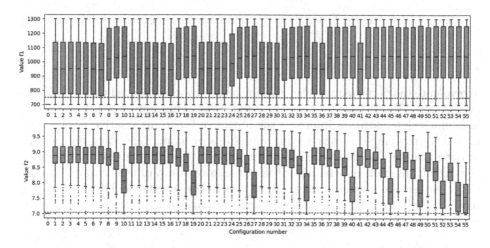

Fig. 3. Boxplots for f_1 and f_2 in different configuration (Stage 3, DCSF).

56 different configurations were considered, each of which satisfies the condition: $\sum_{k=1}^{3} \lambda_k = 1$. For each configuration, the algorithm was tested (stage 3) and the values of the three objective functions were considered for all tests. Based on the testing (see Fig. 3), configuration 16 $\lambda = (0.10, 0.50, 0.40)$ was chosen as the most balanced in terms of objective functions f_2.

At the same time, the objective function f_3 responsible for operator fatigue was not taken into account, since the values obtained were close for all configurations (see Fig. 4). Difference in the maximum, minimum, spread, median and average is no more than 1%.

For further testing, configuration 16 was used for all tests. Of the selected best configurations, this one was the most balanced in terms of functions f_1 and f_2.

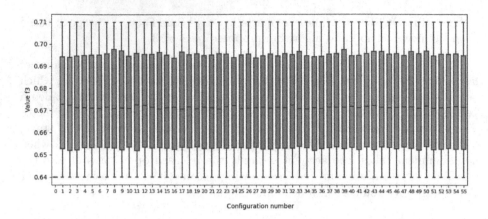

Fig. 4. Boxplots for f_1 and f_2 in different configuration (Stage 3, DCSF).

4.2   Result and Discussion

To evaluate the performance, the DCSF algorithm was compared with two others (FIFO and ABoM) based on objective functions. The graphs (see Fig. 5) show how much the algorithm improves the objective functions relative to the algorithms. Improvement means getting values less or more, depending on the type of optimization - minimization or maximization. The histograms in the figure show the number of cases falling within the improvement ranges. Negative values of the percentage of improvement mean that in these tests the DCSF algorithm received the values of the objective functions than with the one with which the comparison was made.

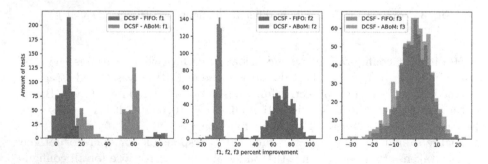

Fig. 5. Comparison of DCSF algorithm with FIFO and ABoM algorithms based on percentage improvement.

An important observation is that the deterioration in objective function f_1 is observed only when compared with the DCSF algorithm on no more than 40 examples out of all and does not fall below 6%. This circumstance is due to the fact that the algorithm is looking for a balance between customer satisfaction and indicators in terms of the schedule (for example, deadlines). However, a good indicator is that this situation is observed in a small percentage of all tests. At the same time, a significant part of the tests falls within the improvement range of up to 20% when compared with FIFO and in the range from 50% to 67% when compared with ABoM.

Relative to objective function f_2, there is a deterioration of up to 23% when compared with the ABoM algorithm. This is also due to the search for a balance between the best assignment and other indicators. Since in the ABoM algorithm the decision to assign is based only on the best matching, it is quite obvious that, according to this indicator, the algorithm should get results no worse than the DCSF algorithm. This means that, as for any multicriteria problem, it is required to consider the results for all objective functions in a compartment. However, despite this, a few tests can be observed for which the algorithm improves the value by more than 20%. At the same time, for objective function f_2, significant improvements are observed relative to the FIFO algorithm: at least 35%, maximum 110%, on average - 65%.

From the point of view of objective function f_3, it is difficult to identify an algorithm that performs significantly better. This is due to the fact that, in fact, no algorithm takes into account operator fatigue when assigning. Potentially, in the future, the algorithm will also take into account this factor through the level of operator fatigue at the time of assignment. However, at this stage of implementation, this factor was omitted.

Thus, the DCSF algorithm balances between objective functions, showing significant improvements in each of them.

5   Conclusion

The developed optimization model allows you to determine the rules for the operation of a queuing system based on the call centre model and is focused on improving the efficiency of this system in terms of assigning calls to operators. The application of the developed model will potentially increase the economic efficiency of the call centre by increasing customer satisfaction and reducing operator burnout.

An analytical review of current methods for optimizing queuing systems, including call centres, was carried out, and the characteristics of customer and operator profiles were highlighted to assess the effectiveness of the operator-client system when making calls to the call centre. Also, a system model was developed that describes the call centre work in terms of interaction with the client, and an assignment algorithm was developed based on a personalized approach and taking into account the current system load. The developed model relates to multicriteria optimization of assignment in the condition of incomplete data. Further, based on the generated synthetic data based on the selected methodology, simulation and experimental verification of the DCSF algorithm's performance were carried out. When compared with other algorithms, the algorithm showed significant improvements in two of the three objective functions.

For the third target function based on operator fatigue, all tested algorithms obtained similar results. This is due to the fact that the algorithms do not take into account the level of operator fatigue at the time of the assignment. This point is one of the factors that will be improved in the subsequent development of this study. It also plans to test on real data to evaluate the effectiveness of work in an applied situation and introduce finer personalization settings.

Acknowledgment. This research is financially supported by the Russian Science Foundation, Agreement 17-71-30029 (https://rscf.ru/en/project/17-71-30029/), with co-financing of Bank Saint Petersburg.

References

1. Adiana, B., Soesanti, I., Permanasari, A.: Analisis segmentasi pelanggan menggunakan kombinasi rfm model dan teknik clustering. Jurnal Terapan Teknologi Informasi **2**, 23–32 (12 2018). https://doi.org/10.21460/jutei.2018.21.76
2. Barrett, K., Logan, J., Pagotto, S., Greenberg, A.: Teaching and user satisfaction in an academic chat reference consortium. Commun. Inform. Literacy **14** (12 2020). https://doi.org/10.15760/comminfolit.2020.14.2.2
3. Carlier, J.: The one-machine sequencing problem. Europ. J. Oper. Res. **11**, 42–47 (1982). https://doi.org/10.1016/S0377-2217(82)80007-6, https://www.sciencedirect.com/science/article/pii/S0377221782800076, third EURO IV Special Issue
4. Elhag, S., Alshahrany, E., Alsharif, Z.: An automated experience-based business process reengineer: Case study bank call center. Int. J. Sci. Res. (IJSR) p. 5 (12 2018). https://doi.org/10.21275/ART20202691
5. Hassan, M.: Customer profiling and segmentation in retail banks using data mining techniques. Int. J. Adv. Res. Comput. Sci. **9**, 24–29 (12 2018). https://doi.org/10.26483/ijarcs.v9i4.6172
6. Hathaway, B., Emadi, S., Deshpande, V.: Personalized priority policies in call centers using past customer interaction information. SSRN Electron. J. (12 2020). https://doi.org/10.2139/ssrn.3596178
7. Ivanov, D., Tarasova, E.: Deadline, compatibility and safe factor algorithm. GitHub (2023). https://github.com/DmitriiIvanov1998/DCSF
8. Khurana, D.S.: Relationship between service quality and customer satisfaction: an empirical study of Indian banking industry. IUP J. Bank Manage. **13**, 51 (12 2014)
9. Kostić, S.M., Duričić, M., Simić, M.I., Kostić, M.V.: Data mining and modeling use case in banking industry, pp. 1–4 (2018). https://doi.org/10.1109/TELFOR.2018.8611897
10. Lee, S.M., Schniederjans, M.J., Cole, J.P.: A multicriteria assignment problem: a goal programming approach. Interfaces **13**, 75–81 (1983). http://www.jstor.org/stable/25060447
11. Marwade, A., Kumar, N., Mundada, S., Aghav, J.: Augmenting e-commerce product recommendations by analyzing customer personality, pp. 174–180 (12 2017). https://doi.org/10.1109/CICN.2017.8319380
12. Medyawati, H., Mabruri, A.: Website quality: case study on local government bank and state own bank in bekasi city. Procedia - Social and Behavioral Sciences **65**, 1086–1091 (2012). https://doi.org/10.1016/j.sbspro.2013.02.121, https://www.sciencedirect.com/science/article/pii/S1877042813004163, international Congress on Interdisciplinary Business and Social Sciences 2012 (ICIBSoS 2012)

13. Megow, N., Schulz, A.: On-line scheduling to minimize average completion time revisited. Oper. Res. Lett. **32**, 485–490 (12 2004). https://doi.org/10.1016/j.orl. 2003.11.008

14. Richards, B.A., Lillicrap, T.P.: Dendritic solutions to the credit assignment problem. Curr. Opinion Neurobiol. **54**, 28–36 (2019). https://doi. org/10.1016/j.conb.2018.08.003, https://www.sciencedirect.com/science/article/ pii/S0959438818300485, neurobiology of Learning and Plasticity

15. Robbins, T.: Complexity and flexibility in call center scheduling models (12 2017)

16. Sawyerr, O., Srinivas, S., Wang, S.: Call center employee personality factors and service performance. J. Serv. Market. - J SERV MARK **23**, 301–317 (12 2009). https://doi.org/10.1108/08876040910973413

17. Scarelli, A., Narula, S.: A multicriteria assignment problem. J. Multi-Criteria Decision Anal. **11**, 65–74 (12 2002). https://doi.org/10.1002/mcda.317

18. Segura, A., Strehlau, S.: Personality-based segmentation of Brazilian private banking clients. Latin American Bus. Rev. **13** (12 2012). https://doi.org/10.1080/ 10978526.2012.749086

19. Tarasova, E., Bochenina, K.: A conceptual framework for personality-sensitive scheduling models, pp. 1–4 (2022). https://doi.org/10.1109/ICOA55659.2022. 9934181

20. Tarasova, E., Grigoreva, N.: Accounting for large jobs for a single-processor online model. In: 2022 8th International Conference on Optimization and Applications (ICOA), pp. 1–5. https://doi.org/10.1109/ICOA55659.2022.9934593, https://doi. org/10.1109/ICOA55659.2022.9934593

21. Zheng, Y., Wang, J., Li, G., Cheng, R., Feng, J.: Qasca: a quality-aware task assignment system for crowdsourcing applications, pp. 1031–1046 (12 2015). https://doi. org/10.1145/2723372.2749430

AquaVitae: Innovating Personalized Meal Recommendations for Enhanced Nutritional Health

Henrique S. Marcuzzo[1,2(✉)] , Maria J. V. Pereira[1] , Paulo Alves[1] ,
and Juliano H. Foleis[2]

[1] CeDRI, Instituto Politécnico de Bragança, IPB, Bragança, Portugal
{henrique.marcuzzo,mjoao,palves}@ipb.pt
[2] DACOM, Universidade Tecnológica Federal do Paraná, UTFPR, Curitiba, Brazil
julianofoleiss@utfpr.edu.br

Abstract. In this study, we present an advanced recommendation system specifically engineered to aid nutritionists in developing personalized, optimized nutritional plans. Our system operates by amassing a broad range of data including users' preferences, dietary restrictions, and specific nutritional requirements, which it then utilizes to craft a diverse assortment of meal choices individually tailored to each user. A key innovation of our system is its ability to facilitate continuous diet monitoring, eliminating the need for repeated consultations to update the nutritional plans. This allows for real-time dietary adjustments and provides nutritionists with more accurate data for subsequent plans. Additionally, the system prioritizes the inclusion of thermogenic foods to maximize nutritional efficiency, while simultaneously providing a pleasurable experience for the users. This combination of sophisticated data collection and innovative food recommendations underscores the potential of our system to improve the process of nutritional counseling and the generation of nutritional plans, bringing notable benefits to both practitioners and clients alike.

Keywords: Recommendation System · Thermal-Based · Nutritional Plan · Food Ranking

1   Introduction

This article delves into the intricacies of a state-of-the-art recommendation system poised to revolutionize the field of nutrition and dietetics. This system offers an advanced Recommendation Service (RS) that aims to enhance the realm of personalized nutritional planning.

Recognizing the complexity and diversity of dietary needs and preferences, the RS is engineered to offer custom-made, diversified meal suggestions. It intelligently employs the insights drawn from crucial studies, such as [12], to dynamically adapt to specific dietary restrictions and nutritional plan rules. Through

A. I. Pereira et al. (Eds.): OL2A 2023, CCIS 1981, pp. 148–161, 2024.
https://doi.org/10.1007/978-3-031-53025-8_11

this personalized approach, the RS enriches the dietary experience of the users, thereby fostering a sustainable and enjoyable commitment to healthful living.

An integral aspect of the recommendation system's design is the emphasis on thermal-based foods within meal suggestions. These food items are widely recognized for their significant contribution to a balanced and nutritious diet as is intended to be proved in Aquae Vitae Project context. By ensuring their inclusion, the system exhibits our unwavering commitment to deliver diverse, healthful, and palatable meal options to the users. Additionally, the final plan can be validated by a nutritionist to ensure optimal results.

This trailblazing recommendation system encapsulates the future of personalized, data-driven nutritional planning. By leveraging the power of artificial intelligence and advanced data analytics, it enhances the efficacy of dietary management, making it more user-centric, responsive, and interconnected.

It is noteworthy that while many dietary recommendation systems exist, in this specific project, we intend the plans to be generated based on a dynamic food table that emphasizes thermal-based foods. More crucially, this system is primarily designed to assist nutritionists in their recommendation and monitoring tasks, rather than to be autonomously used by patients. In essence, it functions as a supportive tool for nutritionists rather than a standalone system for patients. Furthermore, it allows the inclusion of new foods, particularly prioritizing thermal-based foods, and facilitates remote monitoring of patients' daily diets.

2   Related Work

In this work, we focus on developing a Recommendation System (RS) for personalized meal plans. Our goal is to provide relevant and adaptable recommendations, considering dietary rules and restrictions, and individual preferences. For this, we reviewed a series of studies related to deep learning in RS, the collection of explicit and implicit feedback, and the observation of user micro-behaviors.

The role of deep learning in enhancing the efficiency of RSs has been thoroughly explored in different sectors. Renowned studies such as [8,13] suggest that deep learning techniques are capable of learning high-dimensional representations of data, thus improving the accuracy of recommendations, regardless of their application domain.

Feedback collection, both explicit and implicit, is universally recognized as a critical factor for the success of RSs across various fields. The study by [14] demonstrated how different machine learning techniques influence this aspect differently. In a similar vein, [10] delved into the exploration and exploitation approaches, proposing a balanced mechanism for systems that progressively accumulate knowledge.

Furthermore, the understanding of users' micro-behaviors becomes a paramount aspect when tailoring personalized recommendation systems. Microbehaviors refer to the subtle and often quick actions or reactions of users when they interact with a platform or service. These can be as intricate as the time spent hovering over an item, the sequence of clicks, or even subtle hesitations before making a choice. Such behaviors provide a deeper insight into user preferences and can be pivotal in refining recommendation algorithms.

In the realm of harnessing these micro-behaviors, the study [7] stands out. This particular research introduced the MKM-SR algorithm, which is a fusion of two significant algorithms: M-SR and KM-SR. While the specifics of what each algorithm (M-SR and KM-SR) does were not detailed in your initial information, the MKM-SR's prowess lies in its ability to effectively combine the strengths of both, resulting in superior performance when compared to other state-of-the-art methods.

To deal with data density, the embedding technique, which reduces the dimensionality of data, was proposed by [5]. This approach proved effective in improving the performance of a session-based RS.

Finally, we will apply the rule-based and scoring method to our RS as proposed by [4,11]. This method showed good performance in cross-validation, especially when compared to the classification method.

Rule-based systems, at their core, operate on a set of predefined rules. These rules are explicit statements that specify a certain action or outcome based on certain conditions. In the context of a recommendation system, these rules could be formulated based on user behaviors, attributes, or other contextual factors. For instance, if a user prefers vegan meals and exercises regularly, a rule might recommend high-protein vegan dishes to that user. The strength of rule-based systems lies in their transparency and ease of modification. They can be particularly effective when domain knowledge is strong and well-defined, allowing for precise, logic-based recommendations.

3   Development of the Recommendation System

The dietary plan recommendation system is a complex structure designed to provide personalized nutritional advice. The system takes into account various factors such as user preferences, consumption history, and dietary restrictions prescribed by a nutritionist. This is carried out in two main steps: food ranking and filling out the nutritional plan.

3.1   Food Ranking

The food ranking process is an integral part of our recommendation system, working as a personalization tool that assigns scores to foods based on multiple user-related factors. The primary factors considered here are the user's stated preferences and their consumption history.

The process initiates by examining foods that the user has explicitly mentioned as liked or preferred. Such foods are assigned a positive score, indicating their high suitability for the user's meal plans. On the contrary, foods the user has marked as disliked or not preferred are given negative scores, implying these are not ideal for inclusion in the user's diet, unless absolutely necessary due to their nutritional value.

Further, the system takes into account the food category specified by the user. Foods within the same category are assigned higher scores. For example, if a user indicates a preference for 'fruits,' other food items within the 'fruits' category receive a higher score, considering that the user might also enjoy them due to the similarity in taste, texture, or nutritional content.

An innovative aspect of the food ranking process is its approach to deal with frequently consumed foods. While it is essential to consider the user's past consumption, it's also necessary to avoid over-recommendation of any specific food item, as it may lead to dietary monotony and reduce user adherence to the meal plan. Hence, foods that have been consumed frequently by the user in a specific timeframe are assigned a penalty in the form of negative points. This method encourages dietary diversity, promoting a more varied and balanced diet, and enhancing the overall nutritional value of the meal plan.

Overall, the food ranking step is a dynamic and adaptive process that leverages user data to generate a personalized, varied, and nutritionally balanced dietary plan. Crucially, this ranking system ensures that foods prohibited due to allergies or specific restrictions set by the nutritionist are excluded, ensuring a safe and tailored approach for each user.

3.2   Grouping and Making Meal Recommendations

Next comes the process of filling out the nutritional plan. This involves gathering information about meal types included in the plan and the items allowed for consumption. The items for each meal are ranked based on the sum of the scores of the foods that make up these items.

The grouping of meal items and subsequent meal recommendations are a crucial part of the dietary recommendation system. This process involves categorizing and selecting food items to provide a diversified and personalized diet plan.

Grouping of Meal Items. After evaluating and scoring all meal items based on user preferences, consumption history, and dietary restrictions, the items are sorted and divided into three distinct groups. The decision to employ these specific percentage-based groupings was taken with the overarching aim of striking an optimal balance between catering to users' immediate preferences and ensuring they benefit from a wider variety of nutritional options. By so doing, we intended not only to align with immediate likes and dislikes but also to gradually introduce and normalize a broader spectrum of dietary choices, ensuring a more holistic approach to nutrition.

- The first group consists of the top 10% of items with the highest scores. These items represent those most closely aligned with the user's immediate preferences and nutritional needs. They serve as the bedrock of the meal plan, ensuring user satisfaction and adherence.

– The second group includes items that rank between the top 10% and 30% in terms of their scores. While these items might not be the immediate favorites, they are still well-suited to the user's dietary profile and introduce an element of diversity without straying too far from known preferences.
– The third group comprises items that fall between the 30% and 60% range. This category acts as a bridge, incorporating items that might be less familiar or less frequently consumed but still meet the broader nutritional requirements. Introducing these items in a controlled manner ensures the meal plans don't become monotonous and encourages users to explore and adopt a broader range of foods over time.

By structuring our system in this manner, we hope to foster a more diversified diet that caters not only to taste but also to comprehensive nutritional health.

Making Meal Recommendations. Once the meal items have been grouped, the system proceeds to make meal recommendations. A single item is randomly selected from each group for each meal. This method ensures that the meals consist of a mixture of highly preferred, moderately preferred, and lesser preferred foods, promoting a balanced and varied diet.

Determining Quantity. After selecting an item from each group, the system determines the quantity to be included in the meal. This decision is based on the user's nutritional limits for each meal, as defined by their dietary restrictions or goals. For example, if the user's total daily caloric limit is 2000 cal, a specific meal may only account for 30% of this daily total. This percentage signifies the caloric cap for that meal.

If the total calories of the selected items surpass this meal-specific cap, the system will adjust the quantities to ensure the user's caloric limit for that meal is not exceeded. It's crucial to highlight that the adjustment is done at the meal level, rather than the daily level, offering a more precise and responsive dietary recommendation.

By taking into account both the preference scores and nutritional limits per meal, the system can provide meal recommendations that cater to the user's tastes while helping them adhere to their dietary goals on a meal-to-meal basis. This approach ultimately creates a more personalized, balanced, and manageable meal plan for the user.

3.3 Technical Aspects of the Recommendation System

Delving deeper into the technical aspect, the model is divided into two main steps: ranking the foods based on user preferences and consumption history, and appropriately filling the meals of the nutritional plan with items containing the ranked foods.

To rank foods, the system begins by evaluating user-specified preferences. While foods from the same category as the specified food may receive higher scores due to the user's inclination, the algorithm does not restrict itself to a single item from each category. It aims to maximize the diversity of food choices but acknowledges that multiple items from the same category can be included if they align with the user's preferences. In contrast, less favored foods are assigned a negative score.

The evaluation doesn't stop there. Before finalizing the nutritional plan, the system meticulously categorizes and assesses the types of meals and permissible foods. Each food item undergoes a scoring process that aggregates several parameters: user preferences, nutritional value, historical consumption patterns, and its relevance within the broader context of the dietary plan. The user's consumption patterns play a pivotal role. Foods consumed frequently in a short duration receive a penalty to foster variety, while those consumed occasionally are given scores. Prohibited foods, for various reasons, are entirely excluded.

When the system curates meals with multiple items, it doesn't treat the meal in isolation. It calculates a cumulative score by summing up scores of individual components, ensuring the combined foods align perfectly with the user's preferences and dietary requirements.

By implementing such an exhaustive ranking process, the system can produce meal plans that are diversified, aligned with user preferences, and nutritionally sound. Yet, a vital final touch remains: all meal plans are reviewed and validated by a nutritionist, ensuring the recommendations aren't merely algorithmically sound but also nutritionally balanced, catering to the individual's specific needs.

This integrative approach ensures that every meal recommendation is an ideal mix of taste, variety, and nutrition, paving the path for a fulfilling and healthful eating experience.

3.4   Normalization Process

The normalization process in the dietary recommendation system ensures that the recommended diet aligns with the user's daily caloric intake limit and balanced meal proportions.

Mitigating Excess Calories. The first normalization process involves adjusting the percentage of permitted calories for each meal if the total exceeds 100%.

For instance, if breakfast items summed up to 40%, lunch items to 35%, snacks to 15%, and dinner to 20% of the daily caloric intake, the total would amount to 110%. This is clearly over the 100% daily limit. The system mitigates this issue by proportionally scaling down each meal's caloric content so that the overall daily intake does not exceed 100%.

Calculating Daily Caloric Intake. The second normalization process calculates the number of calories that can be consumed per day based on the information provided in the nutritional plan. Every individual's caloric need is different, and it depends on factors like age, sex, weight, height, and physical activity level.

The system uses this information to calculate the daily caloric intake in a way that it aligns with the user's specific nutritional needs. If the user's daily caloric need is estimated to be 2000 cal, for example, the system will recommend foods in such a way that the total calorie content of the foods recommended for breakfast, lunch, snacks, and dinner does not exceed 2000 cal.

These normalization processes are crucial for the effectiveness of the dietary recommendation system. They ensure that the recommended diet not only caters to the user's food preferences and dietary restrictions but also aligns with their specific nutritional needs and goals.

3.5 Final Recommendations

After the normalization process, the system makes recommendations for days on the nutritional plan with no previously registered foods. The recommendations are executed by invoking a method that sorts the meal items in descending order of their scores. The items are then divided into three groups based on their scores, and an item is randomly selected from each group to be recommended. The quantity of the selected item is determined based on the nutritional limits established for the patient, and the recommended item is inserted into the database.

3.6 Overview

This comprehensive process ensures the recommendation system provides diverse and suitable food choices that cater to the user's tastes and nutritional needs. The intricacies of the recommendation system are visually mapped out in Fig. 1. It's important to note that the diagram should be interpreted from left to right.

At the foundation of this system lies the food table, which acts as a crucial database. This table encompasses several entries, each detailing different foods, their nutritional values, possible allergens, and other pertinent information.

To clarify certain terms:

- **Food**: Refers to the individual food items, like "apple" or "chicken breast" Each food is detailed in the table with its associated attributes.
- **Item**: An item refers to a collection of foods that are meant to be consumed together during a specific part of the day. For instance, an item for breakfast might include "scrambled eggs", "whole-grain toast" and "orange juice".
- **Meal**: Represents the broader categorization of consumption throughout the day. It encompasses different items for various parts of the day, such as "Breakfast", "Lunch", "Dinner" and so forth.
- **Diary**: This refers to the record of meals consumed by a user over a specific period, allowing the system to understand consumption patterns and preferences over time.

By having a robust and detailed food table, the system can efficiently navigate through various foods, items, and meals to curate the best possible recommendations, ensuring every meal aligns with the user's preferences and nutritional requirements.

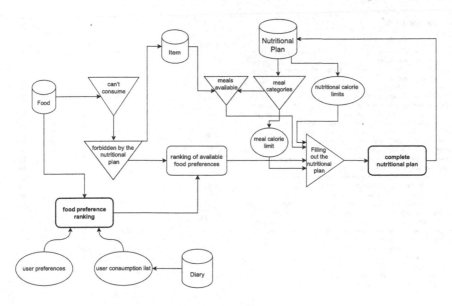

Fig. 1. Recommendation System process overview.

4   Tests and Results

For every functionality in the Backend (BE), an endpoint was established. This design decision ensured that the Frontend (FE) under development could seamlessly interact with the backend systems. Comprehensive endpoint testing was then executed on the entire system. This testing was particularly focused on both the nutrition plan management and recommendation subsystems.

The primary aim was not only to analyze and ensure that the system was functioning as anticipated but also to evaluate the code coverage rate with these tests. Such an evaluation helps in determining the efficiency of the tests. Moreover, the performance of these endpoints was scrutinized based on their response times. By centering the tests around the endpoints, we ensured that the Backend was robust and ready for integration with the ongoing Frontend development.

With the coverage and performance tests, the system was able to achieve 96% coverage, as can be observed in Fig. 2, indicating that the developed tests were efficient in covering almost the entire system. The response times for the recommendation system's endpoints were also satisfactory, with a median of less than 20 ms, as seen in Fig. 3. It's important to note that these response times can vary depending on the hardware running the software. For this test, the system was run on a 9th generation i5 processor with 16GB of DDR4 RAM at 1400MHz.

Tests were also conducted on the creation of meal plans with the aim of analyzing the variety of meal options for each of the generated nutritional plans. The results indicate that the recommendation system is functioning as expected, pro-

Coverage report: 96%

Module	statements	missing	excluded	coverage ↑
src/modules/domain/biochemical_data/entities/biochemical_data_entity.py	48	20	0	58%
src/core/utils/image_utils.py	40	15	0	62%
src/modules/domain/specificity/services/specificity_type_service.py	19	7	0	63%
src/modules/app/app_service.py	3	1	0	67%
src/core/constants/enum/periods.py	13	4	0	69%
src/core/utils/pagination_utils.py	108	31	0	71%
src/modules/domain/nutritional_plan/entities/nutritional_plan_entity.py	28	8	0	71%
src/modules/domain/meal/dto/food_can_eat_at/food_can_eat_at_dto.py	18	5	0	72%
src/modules/domain/diagnosis/entities/diagnosis_entity.py	19	5	0	74%
src/modules/domain/plan_meals/entities/meals_of_plan_entity.py	19	5	0	74%
src/modules/domain/meal/services/food_can_eat_at_service.py	16	4	0	75%
src/modules/domain/anthropometric_data/services/anthropometric_data_service.py	94	21	0	78%
src/modules/domain/specificity/entities/specificity_entity.py	18	4	0	78%
src/modules/domain/diary/entities/diary_entity.py	15	3	0	80%
src/modules/domain/meal/entities/food_can_eat_at_entity.py	15	3	0	80%
src/modules/infrastructure/auth/tests/test_auth_e2e.py	54	11	0	80%
test/utils/database_config_test_utils.py	59	12	0	80%
src/modules/domain/forbidden_foods/entities/forbidden_foods_entity.py	16	3	0	81%
src/modules/domain/plan_meals/dto/meals_of_plan/meals_of_plan_dto.py	17	3	0	82%
src/modules/domain/specificity/entities/specificity_type_entity.py	11	2	0	82%
src/modules/domain/appointment/services/appointment_service.py	61	10	0	84%
src/modules/infrastructure/user/user_service.py	87	14	0	84%
src/modules/app/app_controller.py	7	1	0	86%
src/modules/domain/nutritional_plan/dto/nutritional_plan_dto.py	22	3	0	86%
src/modules/domain/food/interfaces/food_interface.py	15	2	0	87%
src/core/middlewares/limit_upload_size.py	17	2	0	88%
src/modules/domain/antecedent/dto/antecedent/antecedent_dto.py	18	2	0	89%
src/core/utils/json_utils.py	10	1	0	90%

Fig. 2. Code coverage report from *pytest-cov*

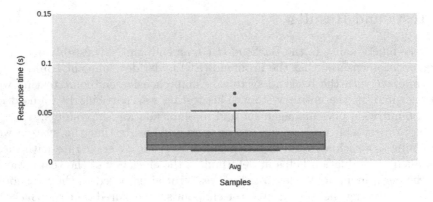

Fig. 3. Response time distribution of the system end-points

viding accurate meal suggestions based on the user's preferences and nutritional needs.

Four scenarios were created with different inputs, and in each case, the system adjusted its recommendations for the nutritional plan based on the provided data:

1. Using only daily caloric intake data, the system generated meal options aimed at meeting the caloric goal, and the result of a full day can be observed in Fig. 4.

meal_date	meal_description	meal_start_time	meal_end_time	food_description	amount
	Ao acordar	09:00:00+00	09:30:00+00	Chá de hortelã	0,5
				Limonada com gengibre	0,5
				Suco de melancia com hortelã	0,5
	Pequeno-almoço	10:30:00+00	11:00:00+00	Sanduíche natural com queijo e peito de peru	0,5
				Biscoitos integrais com geleia de frutas sem açúcar e queij	0,5
				Salada de frutas com iogurte e coco ralado	0,5
	Meio da Manhã	11:30:00+00	12:00:00+00	Sanduíche de frango desfiado com cenoura e alface	0,5
				Biscoitos integrais com geleia de frutas sem açúcar e queij	0,5
				Smoothie de morango e banana	0,5
2023-04-21	Almoço	13:00:00+00	14:00:00+00	Sanduíche de pão sírio com pasta de grão-de-bico e legum	1
				Omelete de legumes com macarrão de abobrinha e salada	0,5
				Bife de alcatra ao molho de cogumelos com arroz selvager	0,5
	Lanche da tarde	16:00:00+00	16:30:00+00	Sanduíche integral com atum e salada	0,5
				Salada de grão-de-bico com atum e vegetais	0,5
				Biscoitos integrais com geleia de frutas sem açúcar e queij	0,5
	Jantar	21:00:00+00	22:00:00+00	Tofu grelhado com purê de mandioquinha e brócolis no va	1
				Salada de grão-de-bico com atum e vegetais	1
				Torrada integral com queijo quark e frutas	2,5
	Ceia	23:30:00+00	00:00:00+00	Biscoitos integrais com geleia de frutas sem açúcar e queij	0,5
				Sanduíche integral com atum e salada	0,5
				Bowl de frutas com chia e mel	0,5

Fig. 4. Nutritional plan without any input.

meal_date	meal_description	meal_start_time	meal_end_time	food_description	amount
	Ao acordar	09:00:00+00	09:30:00+00	Chá de hortelã	0,5
				Suco de melancia com hortelã	0,5
				Suco verde detox	0,5
	Pequeno-almoço	10:30:00+00	11:00:00+00	Pão com ovo e tomate	0,5
				Overnight oats com frutas	0,5
				Torradas com queijo cottage e geleia de frutas sem açúcar	0,5
	Meio da Manhã	11:30:00+00	12:00:00+00	Parfait de iogurte, frutas e chia	0,5
				Iogurte com frutas e granola	0,5
				Pão com ovo e abacate	0,5
2023-04-21	Almoço	13:00:00+00	14:00:00+00	Filé de peixe ao molho de alcaparras com purê de batata-c	1
				Risoto de cogumelos com lombo suíno grelhado e salada c	0,5
				Ovos mexidos com abacate e torrada integral	0,5
	Lanche da tarde	16:00:00+00	16:30:00+00	Sanduíche integral com atum e salada	0,5
				Parfait de iogurte, frutas e chia	0,5
				Iogurte com frutas e granola	0,5
	Jantar	21:00:00+00	22:00:00+00	Tortilha de batata-doce com espinafre e queijo	1
				Sanduíche de pão sírio com pasta de grão-de-bico e legum	1
				Estrogonofe de frango com arroz integral e salada de pepi	2,5
	Ceia	23:30:00+00	00:00:00+00	Overnight oats com frutas	0,5
				Smoothie de morango e banana	0,5
				Parfait de iogurte, frutas e chia	0,5

Fig. 5. Nutritional plan with consumption history data only.

2. With caloric intake data and user consumption history, the system adapted its suggestions to better match the user's preferences, and the result of a full day can be observed in Fig. 5.
3. With caloric intake data and user preferences, the system was able to prioritize meals that aligned with the user's tastes, and the result of a full day can be observed in Fig. 6.
4. With caloric intake data, user preferences, and consumption history, the system provided a comprehensive and personalized meal plan, and the result of a full day can be observed in Fig. 7.

meal_date	meal_description	meal_start_time	meal_end_time	food_description	amount
2023-04-21	Ao acordar	09:00:00+00	09:30:00+00	Chá de hortelã	0,5
				Limonada com gengibre	0,5
				Suco verde detox	0,5
	Pequeno-almoço	10:30:00+00	11:00:00+00	Torrada integral com queijo quark e frutas	0,5
				Sanduíche natural com queijo e peito de peru	0,5
				Pão com ovo e tomate	0,5
	Meio da Manhã	11:30:00+00	12:00:00+00	Crepioca com queijo e espinafre	0,5
				Sanduíche natural com queijo e peito de peru	0,5
				Mingau de aveia com frutas secas e canela	0,5
	Almoço	13:00:00+00	14:00:00+00	Frango grelhado com batata-doce assada e salada de tom	1,5
				Filé mignon suíno com polenta e salada de espinafre e ma	0,5
				Estrogonofe de frango com arroz integral e salada de pepi	1
	Lanche da tarde	16:00:00+00	16:30:00+00	Pão com queijo cottage e tomate	0,5
				Pão com ovo e tomate	0,5
				Sanduíche natural com queijo e peito de peru	0,5
	Jantar	21:00:00+00	22:00:00+00	Risoto de cogumelos com lombo suíno grelhado e salada (	0,5
				Tortilha de batata-doce com espinafre e queijo	1,5
				Torrada integral com queijo quark e frutas	2,5
	Ceia	23:30:00+00	00:00:00+00	Sanduíche integral com peito de peru, queijo cottage e rú(	0,5
				Mingau de aveia com frutas secas e canela	0,5
				Iogurte com frutas e granola	0,5

Fig. 6. Nutritional plan with user preferences only.

meal_date	meal_description	meal_start_time	meal_end_time	food_description	amount
2023-04-21	Ao acordar	09:00:00+00	09:30:00+00	Chá de hortelã	0,5
				Água aromatizada com pepino e limão	0,5
				Suco de melancia com hortelã	0,5
	Pequeno-almoço	10:30:00+00	11:00:00+00	Bowl de iogurte, aveia e frutas com amêndoas	0,5
				Overnight oats com frutas	0,5
				Torradas com pasta de grão-de-bico e tomate	0,5
	Meio da Manhã	11:30:00+00	12:00:00+00	Sanduíche integral com atum e salada	0,5
				Iogurte com frutas e granola	0,5
				Sanduíche integral com peito de peru, queijo cottage e rú(	0,5
	Almoço	13:00:00+00	14:00:00+00	Frango assado com batata doce e salada de espinafre	1
				Filé mignon suíno com polenta e salada de espinafre e ma	0,5
				Tortilha de batata-doce com espinafre e queijo	1,5
	Lanche da tarde	16:00:00+00	16:30:00+00	Pão com ovo e tomate	0,5
				Mingau de aveia com frutas secas e canela	0,5
				Bowl de iogurte, aveia e frutas com amêndoas	0,5
	Jantar	21:00:00+00	22:00:00+00	Sanduíche de pão sírio com pasta de grão-de-bico e legum	1
				Estrogonofe de frango com arroz integral e salada de pepi	1
				Tortilha de batata-doce com espinafre e queijo	1,5
	Ceia	23:30:00+00	00:00:00+00	Mingau de aveia com frutas secas e canela	0,5
				Sanduíche natural com queijo e peito de peru	0,5
				Bowl de iogurte, aveia e frutas com amêndoas	0,5

Fig. 7. Nutritional plan with user preferences and consumption history.

- **Note 1:** Please note that the results are in Portuguese, as the system is being developed with a focus on the audience in Portugal. Therefore, the meals are provided in the local language.
- **Note 2:** Another important point to highlight is that the results are currently being provided in a spreadsheet format because the frontend is still under construction. As a result, there is no screen available to directly view the nutritional plan within the application.
- **Note 3:** For each meal, there are always three options provided. Additionally, portions are consistently based on 100g quantities.

- **Note 4:** It's imperative to highlight that due to the initial scarcity of registered data in the system, we turned to ChatGPT specifically to exploit its random data generation capability. This strategic move was made to enrich our database with diverse meal combinations at a time when acquiring access to comprehensive meal databases proved challenging. Now, with more extensive databases at our disposal, we're in the process of further enhancing the data quality and variety within our system.

In summary, the tests conducted on the recommendation system affirm its functionality within the designed scenarios. Even with minimal information, it was possible to generate diverse nutritional plans. The API tests comprehensively covered the system, and the performance tests indicated satisfactory response times.

When comparing the generated meal plans, there were indeed observable differences. As preferred foods were added and certain foods appeared in the user's consumption history, meals containing these same foods were recommended more frequently and ranked higher. However, due to the limited amount of data entered into the database for testing and the element of randomness that the system also adopts when recommending meals, this trend was not very pronounced.

The main constraint applied to the meal plans was the daily caloric intake. The system then distributed these calories across meals made throughout the day and the amount to be consumed at each one. This validates the system's ability to customize meal plans based on both user preference and dietary restrictions.

While supplementary unit tests could enhance software security and facilitate continuous integration and delivery, they are not deemed essential for the project's initial phase.

5   Conclusion and Future Work

In this research, our primary objective was the development of an innovative recommendation system intended to assist nutritionists in their daily tasks, and to enhance the patients' experience with their nutritional plans. The system is designed to populate nutritional plans with meal suggestions that are personalized to each patient's profile and dietary requirements.

This research involved an in-depth exploration of various techniques used in recommendation systems, as referenced in works such as [1–4,11]. The studies [6,9] were particularly insightful in providing guidance on the essential elements a nutritional assistant system should encompass.

The process of system modeling and development has demonstrated promising results in achieving, and even exceeding, the outlined goals. The structure of our system allows for easy addition of new functionalities while maintaining excellent performance of the existing ones. Moreover, the generated plans allow to enrich the system over the time.

Our future endeavors for the recommendation system include automating the creation and importation of new meals into the system's database. Moreover, as the system accumulates more data, we plan to apply machine learning and artificial intelligence algorithms to improve the scoring metrics for food items and meals. This strategy promises not only to maintain variety but also to increase the accuracy of recommendations and better meet the needs of both patients and nutritionists.

In conclusion, this work represents an earnest attempt to contribute to the intersection of technology and nutrition. The recommendation system developed is a humble step towards a future where nutritional advice is not only more personalized but also scientifically accurate. This would potentially make it more beneficial to patients and aid nutritionists in monitoring their progress more effectively.

References

1. Halverson, R.: An empirical investigation comparing if-then rules and decision tables for programming rule-based expert systems. In: [1993] Proceedings of the Twenty-sixth Hawaii International Conference on System Sciences. vol. iii, pp. 316–323 vol 3 (1993). https://doi.org/10.1109/HICSS.1993.284327
2. Ishibuchi, H., Nakashima, T., Murata, T.: A fuzzy classifier system that generates fuzzy if-then rules for pattern classification problems. In: Proceedings of 1995 IEEE International Conference on Evolutionary Computation. vol. 2, pp. 759–764 vol 2 (1995). https://doi.org/10.1109/ICEC.1995.487481
3. Ishibuchi, H., Sotani, T., Murata, T.: Tradeoff between the performance of fuzzy rule-based classification systems and the number of fuzzy if-then rules. In: 18th International Conference of the North American Fuzzy Information Processing Society - NAFIPS (Cat. No.99TH8397), pp. 125–129 (1999). https://doi.org/10.1109/NAFIPS.1999.781667
4. Kardan, A.A., Ebrahimi, M.: A novel approach to hybrid recommendation systems based on association rules mining for content recommendation in asynchronous discussion groups. Inf. Sci. **219**, 93–110 (2013)
5. Li, Y., Chen, W., Yan, H.: Learning graph-based embedding for time-aware product recommendation. In: Proceedings of the 2017 ACM on Conference on Information and Knowledge Management, pp. 2163–2166. CIKM '17, Association for Computing Machinery, New York, NY, USA (2017). https://doi.org/10.1145/3132847.3133060, https://doi-org.ez48.periodicos.capes.gov.br/10.1145/3132847.3133060
6. Mazuelos, A.G.F., Pelaez, N.R.Y., Cerna, E.A.: Technological solution for the development and validation of a healthy diet in times of pandemic. In: 2021 IEEE 1st International Conference on Advanced Learning Technologies on Education and Research (ICALTER), pp. 1–4 (2021). https://doi.org/10.1109/ICALTER54105.2021.9675087
7. Meng, W., Yang, D., Xiao, Y.: Incorporating user micro-behaviors and item knowledge into multi-task learning for session-based recommendation, pp. 1091–1100. SIGIR '20, Association for Computing Machinery, New York, NY, USA (2020). https://doi.org/10.1145/3397271.3401098, https://doi-org.ez48.periodicos.capes.gov.br/10.1145/3397271.3401098
8. Ong, K., Haw, S.C., Ng, K.W.: Deep learning based-recommendation system: an overview on models, datasets, evaluation metrics, and future trends, pp. 6–11. CIIS 2019, Association for Computing Machinery, New York, NY, USA

(2019). https://doi.org/10.1145/3372422.3372444, https://doi-org.ez48.periodicos. capes.gov.br/10.1145/3372422.3372444

9. Rubilar, D., Aguilera, A.: Automated menu recommendation system focused on clinical nutrition. In: 2019 IEEE CHILEAN Conference on Electrical, Electronics Engineering, Information and Communication Technologies (CHILECON), pp. 1–7 (2019). https://doi.org/10.1109/CHILECON47746.2019.8988061

10. Silva, T., Silva, N., Werneck, H., Pereira, A.C.M., Rocha, L.: The impact of first recommendations based on exploration or exploitation approaches in recommender systems' learning. In: Proceedings of the Brazilian Symposium on Multimedia and the Web, pp. 173–180. WebMedia '20, Association for Computing Machinery, New York, NY, USA (2020). https://doi.org/10.1145/3428658.3430971, https://doi-org. ez48.periodicos.capes.gov.br/10.1145/3428658.3430971

11. Song, H., Zhang, H., Xing, Z.: Research on personalized recommendation system based on association rules. In: Journal of Physics: Conference Series. vol. 1961, p. 012027. IOP Publishing (2021)

12. Willett, W.C., Stampfer, M.J.: Current evidence on healthy eating. Annu. Rev. Public Health **34**, 77–95 (2013)

13. Zhang, S., Yao, L., Sun, A., Tay, Y.: Deep learning based recommender system: a survey and new perspectives. ACM Comput. Surv. **52**(1) (February 2019). https://doi.org/10.1145/3285029, https://doi-org.ez48.periodicos.capes. gov.br/10.1145/3285029

14. Zhao, Q., Harper, F.M., Adomavicius, G., Konstan, J.A.: Explicit or implicit feedback? engagement or satisfaction? a field experiment on machine-learning-based recommender systems, pp. 1331–1340. SAC '18, Association for Computing Machinery, New York, NY, USA (2018). https://doi.org/10.1145/3167132.3167275, https://doi-org.ez48.periodicos.capes.gov.br/10.1145/3167132.3167275

Barriers to Organizations to Adopt Digital Transformation for Driving Eco-Innovation and Sustainable Performance

Zornitsa Yordanova(✉)

University of National and World Economy, Sofia, Bulgaria
zornitsayordanova@unwe.bg

Abstract. This article presents a literature review on the barriers faced by organizations in adopting digital transformation for eco-innovation and sustainable performance to address the surprisingly little research that has explored the connection between digitalization and eco-innovation. Through a systematic review of relevant literature, the article identifies and categorizes key barriers into three categories: technological, organizational, and environmental. Technological barriers include issues related to technological readiness, data management, interoperability, and cybersecurity. Organizational barriers encompass challenges related to organizational culture, leadership, change management, and resistance to change. Environmental barriers involve external factors such as regulatory frameworks, legal constraints, and stakeholder pressures. The review reveals that these barriers can significantly impede organizations' efforts to drive eco-innovation and sustainable performance. The article concludes by proposing avenues for future research and practical implications for organizations seeking to overcome these barriers. This contributes to the literature on digital transformation, eco-innovation, and sustainable performance, and provides insights for scholars and practitioners in this field.

Keywords: Digital Transformation · Eco-innovation · Sustainable Performance · Emerging Technologies · Technology Management

1 Introduction

Digital transformation has emerged as a critical driver of innovation and sustainability in organizations across various industries [1]. It involves leveraging digital technologies and capabilities to transform business models, processes, and strategies to achieve better performance and create value in a rapidly evolving digital landscape [2]. In the context of sustainability, digital transformation offers significant potential to drive eco-innovation, which refers to developing and implementing novel solutions that simultaneously address environmental challenges and create economic value [3]. Organizations are increasingly adopting digital transformation initiatives to foster eco-innovation and achieve sustainable performance outcomes. However, despite the potential benefits, organizations face various barriers and enablers that influence their ability to effectively adopt

© The Author(s), under exclusive license to Springer Nature Switzerland AG 2024
A. I. Pereira et al. (Eds.): OL2A 2023, CCIS 1981, pp. 162–171, 2024.
https://doi.org/10.1007/978-3-031-53025-8_12

and implement digital transformation for sustainability [4]. Understanding these barriers and enablers is critical for organizations to successfully navigate the complexities of digital transformation and achieve sustainable outcomes.

One clear research gap in the literature is the lack of a comprehensive framework that integrates the concepts of digital transformation, eco-innovation, and sustainable performance. While there are studies that separately examine these concepts, there is a need for a holistic framework that elucidates the interconnections and dynamics among these factors [5]. Such a framework could provide a more nuanced understanding of how digital transformation can drive eco-innovation and ultimately contribute to sustainable performance in organizations. This article aims to provide a comprehensive literature analysis of the barriers faced by organizations in adopting digital transformation for driving eco-innovation and sustainable performance. The analysis will draw on existing research and empirical evidence to shed light on the key challenges associated with digital transformation for sustainability. The findings of this analysis will contribute to the growing body of knowledge in the field of digital transformation, sustainability, and innovation, and provide insights for practitioners and policymakers on how organizations can effectively embrace digital transformation for sustainable outcomes.

The article is organized as follows. First, a review of relevant literature on digital transformation, eco-innovation, and sustainable performance is presented. This will be followed by an in-depth analysis of the barriers to organizations adopting digital transformation for sustainability. Subsequently, the article will highlight the key findings from the literature analysis and discuss their implications for practice and future research. The article will conclude with a summary of the main insights and recommendations for organizations seeking to leverage digital transformation for driving eco-innovation and sustainable performance.

2 Theoretical Background: Eco-Innovation and Sustainable Performance

Eco-innovation, which involves the development and implementation of new ideas, processes, products, or business models that contribute to environmental sustainability, has gained significant attention in recent years due to the increasing global concern about climate change, resource depletion, and environmental degradation. Sustainable performance refers to the ability of organizations to achieve economic, social, and environmental goals simultaneously, ensuring long-term viability and a positive impact on society. The concept of eco-innovation and sustainable performance has been widely discussed in the scientific literature, with research focusing on various aspects such as drivers, barriers, impacts, and outcomes. In this literature scientific analysis, we will review and analyze the existing research on eco-innovation and sustainable performance, with a particular emphasis on the relationship between these two concepts and their implications for businesses, society, and the environment.

2.1 Drivers of Eco-innovation and Sustainable Performance

Numerous drivers have been identified in the literature that promotes eco-innovation and sustainable performance. One of the key drivers is the growing awareness and concern about environmental issues, such as climate change and resource scarcity, which have led to increased pressure on organizations to adopt sustainable practices and reduce their environmental impact [6]. Additionally, regulatory and policy frameworks, including environmental regulations, standards, and incentives, have been identified as significant drivers that shape the adoption of eco-innovation and sustainable performance in organizations [7]. Moreover, customer demand for environmentally-friendly products and services, as well as changing consumer preferences and values towards sustainability, have also been identified as drivers that influence organizations to innovate and perform sustainably [8]. Furthermore, strategic motivations, including competitive advantage, reputation enhancement, and stakeholder engagement, have been identified as drivers that encourage organizations to adopt eco-innovation and sustainable performance practices [9].

2.2 Barriers to Eco-innovation and Sustainable Performance

Despite the drivers, organizations face several barriers to the adoption of eco-innovation and sustainable performance. One of the key barriers is the perception of higher costs associated with eco-innovation and sustainability practices, including investments in new technologies, process changes, and certifications, which may deter organizations from adopting such practices [10]. Additionally, a lack of awareness, knowledge, and expertise in eco-innovation and sustainability among organizational members can hinder the adoption of sustainable practices [11]. Moreover, organizational culture, structures, and processes, which may prioritize short-term economic goals over long-term sustainability objectives, can act as barriers to eco-innovation and sustainable performance [12]. Furthermore, regulatory and policy challenges, such as inconsistent or insufficient regulations, lack of enforcement mechanisms, and limited access to incentives, can also impede the adoption of eco-innovation and sustainable performance practices [13].

In conclusion, eco-innovation and sustainable performance are critical concepts that organizations need to embrace to address pressing environmental and societal challenges. Literature on this topic highlights that eco-innovation and sustainable performance practices can bring multiple benefits to organizations, society, and the environment. From a business perspective, organizations can achieve competitive advantages, such as improved market positioning, customer loyalty, and innovation capabilities. From a societal perspective, eco-innovation and sustainable performance can contribute to social outcomes, such as the creation of green jobs, community development, and stakeholder engagement. From an environmental perspective, these practices can lead to positive environmental outcomes, such as reduced emissions, waste reduction, and resource conservation. However, implementing eco-innovation and sustainable performance practices also comes with challenges. These challenges include financial constraints, regulatory barriers, lack of awareness and knowledge, and resistance to change [14]. Organizations need to overcome these challenges through strategic planning, stakeholder engagement, innovation, and collaboration with partners and stakeholders. Additionally, policymakers, governments, and institutions play a crucial role in creating an enabling environment that promotes eco-innovation and sustainable performance practices through supportive policies, regulations, and incentives. Furthermore, future research in this area could explore the role of different organizational factors, such as organizational culture, leadership, and employee engagement, in driving eco-innovation and sustainable performance.

3 Research Design

3.1 Systematic Literature Review

This study will adopt a literature analysis approach to elicit the barriers and enablers of digital transformation of eco-innovations for organizations. The research involves a systematic review of relevant literature from the Scopus database. The search strategy is designed to capture articles that are related to the intersection of digital transformation, eco-innovation, and organizational context. The inclusion and exclusion criteria are defined to ensure that only relevant and high-quality literature is included in the analysis.

The inclusion and exclusion criteria for this literature analysis study on barriers and enablers of digital transformation of eco-innovations for organizations are as follows:

Inclusion Criteria:

- Articles.
- Literature that focuses on the barriers to digital transformation in the context of eco-innovation for organizations.
- Literature that provides empirical evidence, conceptual frameworks, or theoretical perspectives related to barriers and enablers of digital transformation for eco-innovation and sustainable performance.
- Literature that is written in English, as this is the language of the study.

The only exclusion criterion is limiting literature that does not specifically focus on digital transformation, eco-innovation, or barriers and enablers in the context of organizations.

3.2 Data Collection and Analysis

The data collection process involved systematically reviewing and analyzing the identified literature. The data was extracted from the Scopus dataset using the following keywords:

"digital transformation" AND "eco-innovation" OR "sustainable", limited to: 1.) subject area: Business, Management and Accounting and Social Sciences (to focus on the managerial context); 2.) articles only; 3.) Journals only as a source; 4.) English language. This is the formula for the Boolean search:

(TITLE-ABS-KEY ("digital transformation") AND TITLE-ABS-KEY ("eco-innovation" OR "sustainable")) AND (LIMIT-TO (SUBJAREA, "BUSI") OR LIMIT-TO (SUBJAREA, "SOCI")) AND (LIMIT-TO (DOCTYPE, "ar")) AND (LIMIT-TO (SRCTYPE, "j")) AND (LIMIT-TO (LANGUAGE, "English")).

The data set amounted to 409 documents, published between 2016 and 2023. There is a huge increase in the number of the publications in this area in 2022.

Afterward, the analysis involved identifying and categorizing key themes or patterns in the literature related to barriers and enablers of digital transformation of eco-innovations for organizations.

4   Results and Discussion

4.1   Digital Transformation for Driving Eco-Innovation And Sustainable Performance

Digital transformation is revolutionizing the way organizations operate, and its potential for promoting eco-innovation and sustainable performance has gained significant attention in the literature. This literature scientific analysis aims to explore the current state of research on digital transformation as a driver of eco-innovation and sustainable performance, with a focus on identifying key findings, trends, and gaps in the existing literature.

Numerous studies have highlighted the significant impact of digital transformation on organizations' eco-innovation and sustainable performance. Digital technologies, such as the Internet of Things (IoT), artificial intelligence (AI), big data analytics, and blockchain, are enabling organizations to optimize resource utilization, enhance environmental monitoring and reporting, and develop innovative solutions to address environmental challenges [15]. For example, digital technologies are being used to optimize energy management, reduce waste, and promote circular economy initiatives, such as product-sharing, remanufacturing, and recycling [16]. Digital transformation is also driving sustainable business models, such as servitization, where organizations shift from selling products to providing services, resulting in extended product lifecycles, reducing environmental footprints, and increasing customer satisfaction [17].

Additionally, digital transformation is facilitating collaboration and knowledge sharing among organizations, academia, government, and civil society, leading to the co-creation of eco-innovations and the development of sustainable performance metrics and reporting frameworks [18]. Moreover, digital platforms and marketplaces are emerging as enablers of circular economy initiatives, where organizations can collaborate and exchange resources, products, and services to promote sustainability [19]. Digital-enabled services, such as remote work, virtual events, and teleconferencing, are also contributing to reducing environmental footprints, as they reduce the need for physical travel and promote sustainable work practices ([20].

However, despite the potential benefits of digital transformation for driving eco-innovation and sustainable performance, there are also challenges and barriers that organizations need to overcome. Despite the growing body of literature on digital transformation for driving eco-innovation and sustainable performance, there are several gaps and areas for further research. First, there is a need for more empirical studies that investigate the actual impact of digital transformation on eco-innovation and sustainable performance in different organizational contexts and sectors [21]. Many existing studies are based on conceptual frameworks, case studies, and qualitative research, and there is a need for more quantitative research that can provide robust evidence on the relationships between digital transformation, eco-innovation, and sustainable performance. Second, there is a need for research that explores the role of digital leadership, organizational culture, and change management in driving digital transformation for sustainability [22]. Organizations need leaders who can navigate the complex landscape of digital transformation, foster a culture of innovation and learning, and effectively manage change to ensure successful outcomes ([23]. Understanding the key drivers and barriers of digital leadership, organizational culture, and change management in the context of sustainability can provide valuable insights for organizations seeking to embark on a digital transformation journey. Third, there is a need for research that explores the ethical implications of digital transformation for sustainability, including issues such as data privacy, security, and fairness [24]. As organizations collect and analyze vast amounts of data to drive eco-innovation and sustainable performance, ethical considerations become critical to ensure that the use of data aligns with sustainability principles and does not result in unintended negative consequences [25]. Research on the ethical implications of digital transformation for sustainability can provide guidance for organizations in developing responsible and sustainable digital strategies.

4.2 Barriers to the Digital Transformation of Eco-Innovation and Sustainable Performance of Organizations

The digital transformation of eco-innovations has gained significant attention in recent years as organizations strive to adopt sustainable practices and leverage digital technologies for innovation and performance improvement. However, despite the potential benefits, several barriers hinder the successful implementation of digital transformation in the context of eco-innovations. In this section, we discuss the key barriers identified in the literature and provide insights into their implications for organizations.

One of the prominent barriers to the digital transformation of eco-innovations is the lack of organizational readiness. Organizations often face challenges in terms of their internal capabilities, resources, and cultural mindset to embrace digital technologies and integrate them into their eco-innovation processes [26]. For instance, organizations may lack the necessary technical infrastructure, data management capabilities, and digital literacy among their workforce, which can impede the adoption and utilization of digital tools for eco-innovation initiatives [27]. Furthermore, organizational culture and resistance to change may hinder the acceptance and integration of digital technologies into established eco-innovation practices [28]. Overcoming these organizational readiness barriers requires investment in technology infrastructure, upskilling of employees, and fostering a culture that promotes openness and innovation.

Another significant barrier to the digital transformation of eco-innovations is the regulatory and policy environment. Organizations operating in the eco-innovation space face a complex landscape of regulations, standards, and policies that can either facilitate or hinder the adoption of digital technologies [29]. For instance, strict regulations related to data privacy, intellectual property rights, and environmental compliance can create barriers to the collection, sharing, and analysis of data required for digital transformation initiatives. Inconsistent or unclear policies related to digital innovation and sustainability may also create uncertainty and reluctance among organizations to invest in digital technologies for eco-innovations. Addressing these regulatory and policy barriers requires active engagement with relevant stakeholders, collaboration with policymakers, and advocating for supportive regulations and policies that promote the digital transformation of eco-innovations [30]. Furthermore, the lack of collaboration and partnerships can hinder the digital transformation of eco-innovations. Many eco-innovation challenges require interdisciplinary approaches and collaborative efforts among different stakeholders, including academia, industry, government, and civil society [31].

However, organizations may face barriers in terms of building and maintaining partnerships, such as differences in interests, priorities, and cultures among stakeholders. Limited access to networks, platforms, and resources for collaboration can also hinder the adoption of digital technologies for eco-innovation initiatives [32]. Overcoming these collaboration barriers requires fostering a collaborative mindset, building strong partnerships, and leveraging digital technologies to enable effective collaboration among diverse stakeholders. In addition, financial constraints can be a significant barrier to the digital transformation of eco-innovations. Implementing digital transformation initiatives often requires substantial investments in technology infrastructure, software, talent, and training [33]. Small and medium-sized enterprises (SMEs) and startups, in particular, may face financial limitations, which can hinder their ability to adopt and leverage digital technologies for eco-innovations. Limited access to funding, lack of business models, and uncertainties about the return on investment can create barriers to the adoption of digital technologies for eco-in innovations. Overcoming financial barriers requires exploring alternative funding options, such as public-private partnerships, crowdfunding, and grants, and developing viable business models that can generate revenues from digital eco-innovations [34]. Moreover, the lack of digital skills and talent can also be a significant barrier to the digital transformation of eco-innovations. Organizations need a skilled workforce that is proficient in digital technologies and can effectively utilize them for eco-innovation initiatives [14]. Additionally, the rapid pace of technological advancements and the need for continuous upskilling can further exacerbate the digital skills gap [35]. Addressing the digital skills and talent gap requires investment in education and training programs, partnerships with academic institutions, and talent development initiatives that equip the workforce with the necessary digital skills for eco-innovation.

In conclusion, the digital transformation of eco-innovations is a complex and multifaceted process that can offer significant benefits to organizations in terms of sustainability performance and innovation outcomes. However, several barriers can hinder the successful implementation of digital transformation initiatives in the context of eco-innovations. The identified barriers include the lack of organizational readiness, regulatory and policy environment, collaboration and partnerships, financial constraints, and digital skills and talent gap. Overcoming these barriers requires proactive efforts from organizations, policymakers, and other stakeholders to address the challenges and create an enabling environment for the digital transformation of eco-innovations. Strategies such as investing in technology infrastructure, fostering a culture of innovation, advocating for supportive regulations and policies, building strong collaborations and partnerships, exploring alternative funding options, and investing in education and training programs can help organizations overcome these barriers and leverage digital technologies for eco-innovations.

Amongst the major challenges for companies in driving eco-innovations and these endeavors' digitalization is finding well-prepared human resources [36]. Companies are addressing these challenges through internal training and development; collaboration with universities and research institutions and skill-based hiring [37]. The transition from digital production (Industry 3.5) to digital company (Industry 4.0) and moving to the next technological generation of Industry 5.0 based on the accession of digital and social instruments in techniques across all business processes and activities have also been intensively discussed in the literature recently [38].

5 Conclusion

Barriers can be summarized into the following main categories:

- Lack of organizational readiness and culture: Organizations may face challenges in terms of their readiness and culture to embrace digital transformation for sustainability, including resistance to change, lack of awareness or understanding of the potential benefits, and reluctance to disrupt existing processes and practices.
- Limited resources and investment: Limited financial resources and investment in digital technologies, as well as the costs associated with implementation and maintenance, can pose barriers to organizations in adopting digital transformation for sustainability.
- Data and technology-related challenges: Issues related to data quality, availability, interoperability, and security, as well as the complexity of integrating and managing multiple digital technologies, can be barriers to digital transformation for sustainability.
- Legal and regulatory constraints: Organizations may face legal and regulatory constraints related to data privacy, intellectual property, and other legal or regulatory requirements that can impede the adoption of digital transformation for sustainability.
- Lack of well-prepared human resources handling and moving forward

In conclusion, this study sheds light on the significant barriers hindering organizations from embracing digital transformation to drive eco-innovation and sustainable performance. By addressing issues related to technological constraints, organizational culture, and resource allocation, companies can overcome these obstacles and unlock the full potential of digital technologies to achieve their sustainability objectives. For future research, it is imperative to delve deeper into the dynamic interplay between digital transformation and eco-innovation, exploring the role of leadership, policy frameworks, and collaborative networks in fostering a more sustainable and resilient business landscape. Additionally, comparative studies across industries and regions could provide valuable insights into tailored strategies that address unique challenges and opportunities in different contexts, ultimately advancing the understanding and adoption of eco-innovations in the era of digital transformation. COVIDization had also its impact on the trends of eco-innovations and their digitalization in companies [39]. All sectors have been partially impacted, not only the ecologically obvious [40].

Acknowledgment. The paper is supported by the UNWE Research program, project NID NI 7/2022 .

References

1. Bharadwaj, A., El Sawy, O.A., Pavlou, P.A., Venkatraman, N.: Digital business strategy: toward a next generation of insights. MIS Q. **37**(2), 471–482 (2013)

2. Verhoef, P.C., et al.: Digital transformation: a multidisciplinary reflection and research agenda. J. Bus. Res. **122**, 889–901 (2021)
3. Schaltegger, S., Hansen, E.G., Lüdeke-Freund, F.: Business models for sustainability: origins, present research, and future avenues. Organ. Environ. **29**(1), 3–10 (2016)
4. Paula, F.D.O., De Macedo-Soares, T.D.V.A.: The role of firm alliance portfolio diversity to leverage sustainable business model innovation. Int. J. Innov. Manag. **26**(06), 2250041 (2022)
5. Bocken, N.M., Short, S.W., Rana, P., Evans, S.: A literature and practice review to develop sustainable business model archetypes. J. Clean. Prod. **65**, 42–56 (2014)
6. Antikainen, M., Uusitalo, T., Kivikytö-Reponen, P.: Digitalisation as an enabler of circular economy. Procedia Cirp **73**, 45–49 (2018)
7. Triguero, A., Moreno-Mondéjar, L., Davia, M.A.: Drivers of different types of eco-innovation in European SMEs. Ecol. Econ. **92**, 25–33 (2013)
8. Hockerts, K.: The effect of experiential social entrepreneurship education on intention formation in students. J. Social Entrepreneurship **9**(3), 234–256 (2018)
9. Jayaraman, K., Jayashree, S., Dorasamy, M.: The effects of green innovations in organizations: influence of stakeholders. Sustainability **15**(2), 1133 (2023)
10. Ch'ng, P.C., Cheah, J. and Amran, A.,: Eco-innovation practices and sustainable business performance: the moderating effect of market turbulence in the Malaysian technology industry. J. Clean. Prod. **283**, 124556 (2021)
11. Valero-Gil, J., Surroca, J.A., Tribo, J.A., Gutierrez, L. and Montiel, I., 2023. Innovation vs. standardization: the conjoint effects of eco-innovation and environmental management systems on environmental performance. Res. Policy **52**(4), p.104737
12. Peyravi, B., Jakubavičius, A.: Drivers in the eco-innovation road to the circular economy: organiational capabilities and exploitative strategies. Sustainability **14**(17), 10748 (2022)
13. Zhao, S., Teng, L. and Ji, J.: Impact of environmental regulations on eco-innovation: the moderating role of top managers' environmental awareness and commitment. J. Environ. Plann. Manage. 1–28 (2023)
14. Grama-Vigouroux, S., Saidi, S., Uvarova, I., Cirule, I. and Sellami, M., 2023. Drivers and barriers of national innovation ecosystems for implementing sustainable development goals: a latvian case study. IEEE Trans. Eng. Manage.
15. Zhou, Y.: The application trend of digital finance and technological innovation in the development of green economy. J. Environ. Public Health (2022)
16. Han, Y., et al.: Exploring how digital technologies enable a circular economy of products. Sustainability **15**(3), 2067 (2023)
17. Rothenberg, S., Ryen, E.G., Sherman, A.G.: The Evolution of research on sustainable business models: Implications for management scholars. J. Environ. Sustain. **7**(1), 3 (2019)
18. Weck, M., Gelashvili, T., Pappel, I., Ferreira, F.: Supporting collaboration and knowledge sharing in building SLEs for ageing well: Using cognitive mapping in KMS design. Knowl. Manag. Res. Pract. **20**(6), 865–877 (2022)
19. Cantú, A., Aguiñaga, E., Scheel, C.: Learning from failure and success: the challenges for circular economy implementation in SMEs in an emerging economy. Sustainability **13**(3), 1529 (2021)
20. Li, C., Guo, S., Cao, L., Li, J.: Digital enablement and its role in internal branding: a case study of HUANYI travel agency. Ind. Mark. Manage. **72**, 152–160 (2018)
21. Jaiswal, J., Tiwari, A.A., Gupta, S. and Agarwal, R.: Frugal innovation: a structured literature review of antecedents, enablers, implications and directions for future research. Innovation, pp.332–361 (2022)
22. Zhang, X., Xu, Y., Ma, L.: Research on successful factors and influencing mechanism of the digital transformation in SMEs. Sustainability **14**(5), 2549 (2022)
23. Press, J.: IDeaLs (innovation and design as leadership): Transformation in the Digital Era. Emerald group publishing (2021)

24. Muñoz, P., Cohen, B.: Entrepreneurial narratives in sustainable venturing: beyond people, profit, and planet. J. Small Bus. Manage. **56**, 154–176 (2018)
25. Moorkens, J.: Ethics and machine translation. Machine translation for everyone: empowering users in the age of artificial intelligence **18**, 121 (2022)
26. Marrucci, L., Iannone, F., Daddi, T., Iraldo, F.: Antecedents of absorptive capacity in the development of circular economy business models of small and medium enterprises. Bus. Strateg. Environ. **31**(1), 532–544 (2022)
27. Fornasiero, R., et al.: Paths to innovation in supply chains: the landscape of future research. Next Generation Supply Chains: A Roadmap for Research and Innovation, pp.169–233 (2021)
28. Lippolis, S., Ruggieri, A., Leopizzi, R.: Open Innovation for sustainable transition: The case of Enel "Open Power". Business Strategy and the Environment (2023)
29. de Jesus Pacheco, D.A., ten Caten, C.S., Jung, C.F., Navas, H.V.G., Cruz-Machado, V.A.: Eco-innovation determinants in manufacturing SMEs from emerging markets: systematic literature review and challenges. J. Eng. Tech. Manage. **48**, 44–63 (2018)
30. Batra, G., Uitto, J.I., Feinstein, O.N.: Environmental Evaluation and Global Development Institutions: A Case Study of the Global Environment Facility (p. 184). Taylor & Francis (2022)
31. Dentchev, N., et al.: Embracing the variety of sustainable business models: a prolific field of research and a future research agenda. J. Clean. Prod. **194**, 695–703 (2018)
32. Ashfaq, M., Tandon, A., Zhang, Q., Jabeen, F. and Dhir, A.: Doing good for society! How purchasing green technology stimulates consumers toward green behavior: A structural equation modeling–artificial neural network approach. Business Strategy and the Environment (2022)
33. Lin, H.: Government–business partnerships for radical eco-innovation. Bus. Soc. **58**(3), 533–573 (2019)
34. Jesic, J., Okanovic, A., Panic, A.A.: Net zero 2050 as an EU priroty: modeling a system for efficient investments in eco innovation for climate change mitigation. Energy, Sustain. Society **11**(1), 1–16 (2021)
35. Raghavan, A., Demircioglu, M.A., Orazgaliyev, S.: COVID-19 and the new normal of organizations and employees: an overview. Sustainability **13**(21), 11942 (2021)
36. Hojnik, J., Ruzzier, M., Ruzzier, M.K., Sučić, B., Soltwisch, B.: Challenges of demographic changes and digitalization on eco-innovation and the circular economy: qualitative insights from companies. J. Clean. Prod. **396**, 136439 (2023)
37. Jabbour, C.J.C., Neto, A.S., Gobbo, J.A., Jr., de Souza Ribeiro, M., de Sousa Jabbour, A.B.L.: Eco-innovations in more sustainable supply chains for a low-carbon economy: a multiple case study of human critical success factors in Brazilian leading companies. Int. J. Prod. Econ. **164**, 245–257 (2015)
38. Nikolay, S., Fahri, I.: "The IM (Possible) Transition Towards the Digital Economy in Bulgaria," Economic Alternatives, University of National and World Economy, Sofia, Bulgaria, issue 1, pp. 142–150, March (2022)
39. Radev, R.: Identifying strategies as a ploy for overcoming negative effects of COVIDization of economy. Econ. Alternatives **4**, 489–503 (2021)
40. Blagoev, D.: Impact of the wood sector on climate changes (following the example of bulgaria). current trends and challenges for forest-based sector: carbon neutrality and bioecoNOMY, p.125 (2023)

Interpretable Structural Analysis
for Evolutionary Generative Design
of Coastal Breakwaters

Denis O. Sidorenko, Nikita O. Starodubcev, Maiia Pinchuk,
and Nikolay O. Nikitin[✉]

Nature Systems Simulation Lab, ITMO University, Saint Petersburg, Russia
nnikitin@itmo.ru

Abstract. This paper presents an interpretable approach for the generative design of coastal breakwaters that combines evolutionary optimization and structural analysis of solutions. It allows both to improve the convergence of optimization for breakwaters structure and analyze the sensitivity of each sub-part of the solution to various changes. We conduct experiments on synthetic harbour configuration to validate this approach. The results confirm the effectiveness of our method in generating high-quality and explainable breakwater designs.

Keywords: generative design · coastal breakwaters · structural analysis

1 Introduction

Generative design problem focuses on improving physical object properties by generating unseen configurations [31]. For instance, [16] aims to improve the strength of a ship hull form; [22] targets to increase the compliance of a car wheel.

The example worth considering is the design of coastal protective structures, also called breakwaters [7]. The main goal is to produce a breakwaters configuration providing maximum infrastructure protection from waves and storm surges. The design of coastal breakwaters is a complex and challenging problem due to the high variability of a meta-ocean environment and the necessity to balance configuration efficiency and its sustainability [26].

Traditional approaches to the breakwaters design rely on manual modelling with the involvement of expert engineers. On the other hand, automated approaches, which are based on various optimization techniques [12], show more promising results. As an example, evolutionary algorithms have wide application in design of various mathematical structures [18,23]. In [21], an evolutionary algorithm is used to find an optimal structure of breakwaters using a wind wave model to evaluate its efficiency. Surrogate-assisted approaches can be applied [29] to reduce the computational cost of the optimization.

Although evolutionary algorithms provide encouraging results for optimizing breakwaters, two main problems remain relevant. Firstly, there are difficulties in

A. I. Pereira et al. (Eds.): OL2A 2023, CCIS 1981, pp. 172–185, 2024.
https://doi.org/10.1007/978-3-031-53025-8_13

finding a balance between exploration and exploitation. Often hyperparameters tuning cannot handle with this difficulty since it requires high resource and time requirements. Secondly, evolutionary approaches lack interpretation since they work as a black box. However, the sensitivity of each configuration element is a crucial factor for engineers to make a final decision. In addition, it is critical to determine whether an optimized structure contains any sub-components that can be eliminated while maintaining the desired quality of the solution.

This paper presents a novel hybrid optimization approach that combines optimization based on interpreted structural sensitivity analysis (SA) and cutting-edge evolutionary approaches to design coastal breakwaters. In addition to the interpretability, the proposed approach significantly increases the exploitation rate, which allows to obtain more efficient breakwaters configurations.

To evaluate the effectiveness of this approach, we conducted a series of experiments using a synthetic harbour configuration consisting of multiple land polygons, sea routes, and control points. The results of these experiments confirm that the proposed approach can improve the quality and interpretability of the optimization result.

2   Related Works

Memetic algorithms (MAs) are gaining popularity every year. These algorithms use a local search technique to improve the quality of solutions generated by the evolutionary algorithm. MAs can guide the search in the direction of the global optimum [9], which in turn can ensure that the convergence rate is large enough to prevent any deviation in the evolution process. Memetic algorithms tend to obtain better performance than just genetic algorithms in various complex real-world problems [8,13,15,19,35].

Incorporating a local search method in a genetic algorithm can improve the exploiting ability of the search algorithm and at the same time, its ability to explore will not be limited [9]. If the proper balance between global exploration and local exploitation capabilities can be adjusted, the algorithm can produce solutions with high accuracy [17].

The choice of a local optimization algorithm is crucially important since it can affect convergence and computational costs a lot. Sensitivity analysis can help identify critical control points and verify and validate a model [4]. Also, SA gives insights about the sensitivity of each component of a model, which makes it possible to evaluate the contribution of each component to the final metric and makes the model more interpretable [32].

Since sensitivity analysis can be adapted to graph structures to analyze the impact of every substructure in a graph, it is possible to base a local optimization on structural sensitivity analysis. Notably, in [34], filter methods were incorporated in evolutionary algorithms to improve classification performance. Filter methods are introduced as local learning procedures in the evolutionary search to add or delete features from the chromosome, which can be interpreted as an optimization using local structural sensitivity analysis.

Starting with the most basic and standard sensitivity analysis algorithms, variance-based methods and notably [27] method is widely used when it is feasible to calculate it. This method can be adapted for application on configuration optimization tasks if the graphs representing breakwaters are appropriately encoded. The search space can be successfully explored with the help of a combination of Sobol analysis and Monte-Carlo algorithm [10]; however, the computational cost would be too high. In [11], the derivative-based global sensitivity method was described; however, it does not apply to coastal protective structures design in this particular case because of the too high computational cost too. On the other hand, One-factor-at-a-time (OAT) method is easily interpreted and simple [33], but applicable to breakwaters design since the search space is much smaller and it is possible to change the configuration of breakwater without too much computing overhead.

Sensitivity analysis algorithms have proven their efficiency in optimizing graph structures. Researchers have suggested many pruning algorithms based on sensitivity analysis to obtain the optimal structure of neural networks [14,20,24]. Although many articles about sensitivity analysis approaches exist, most results are limited to specific model structures and on a case-by-case basis. In [6], a formal, systematic approach to sensitivity analysis for arbitrary linear Structural Causal Models was developed; however, there is still a need to develop distinct approaches for some problems since every domain of knowledge requires specific actions to be considered during optimization with sensitivity analysis.

3   Problem Statement

In this paper, we consider the optimization of coastal breakwaters. The objective is to find an optimal configuration (coordinates of vertices in each polygon) that provides minimum wave height estimated by a wind wave simulator. Wave heights field is determined by the bathymetry and strength/direction of the wind. Moreover, the found configuration should satisfy the spatial constraints.

More formally, the optimization problem can be written as the following:

$$\begin{cases} \mathbf{X} = \arg\min_{\mathbf{X} \in \mathbb{D}} \mathcal{F}(\mathbf{X}), \\ \mathcal{C}(\mathbf{X}) = 1, \end{cases} \tag{1}$$

where $\mathbb{D} = [a, b]^n$ is the search space representing possible spatial coordinates of a breakwaters configuration; n - search space dimension (corresponds to the number of vertices in polylin); $\mathcal{F}$ - fitness function that shows the wave height at target points; $\mathcal{C}$ - binary constraints function. To be more precise, a polyline is defined as a set of Euclidean points, e.g. $\mathbf{X} = [[a_1, b_1], ..., [a_n, b_n]]$. Specific examples of restrictions are the following: ship fairways, lands, marine structures. We provide an example of the problem in Fig. 1.

Various generative design and topology optimization approaches are used in the literature to resolve similar problems [30]. Some involve additional steps - sensitivity analysis of solutions [3]. However, they cannot be directly applied to

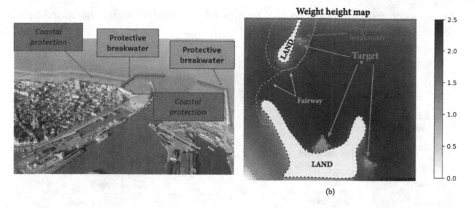

Fig. 1. Example of the coastal breakwaters optimization problem. Left part represents the real-world case for harbour protection, right part describes the representation of problem considered in the paper.

the geometrically-encoded breakwater structures because (1) the evolutionary optimizer should be used to preserve the high diversity of obtained solution; (2) the specific breakwaters design task makes it necessary to use more task-specific perturbations for structures. At the same time, it is promising to take insights from applying structural analysis techniques of machine learning pipelines [1].

For these reasons, we propose an approach of the flexible structural sensitivity analysis algorithm in the solution search procedure. Since the structure of breakwaters is defined as a geometrical system represented as a set of polylines, we can explore each of the objects in the system separately and not violate the restrictions imposed on the problem.

4   Proposed Approach

The main idea of the proposed approach is to combine the potential of genetic algorithms and sensitivity-based local optimization. We add the sensitivity analysis algorithm to the GEFEST [28] framework with expectations of synergy results. The GEFEST uses an evolutionary optimization algorithm that iteratively improves the geometrically-encoded solutions by selecting the most promising candidates and generating new solutions through mutation and crossover for polylines, polygons, vertices, and edges. The module interaction scheme between the proposed approach and the framework is shown in Fig. 2. After we have received a ready-made solution from the genetic algorithm, we can initialize the sensitivity analysis algorithm, which will try to improve the resulting structure qualitatively.

Implementation of a sensitivity assessment software module for physical objects described below as pseudocode and allows leading:

- improve the quality of modelling using generative design compared to using the classical evolutionary approach;

– bring some explainability to the results of generative design obtained from the "black box".

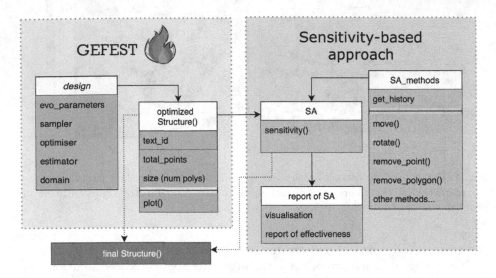

Fig. 2. Structural schema of interaction between GEFEST core and proposed sensitivity-based approach

The sensitivity analysis algorithm consists of methods for transforming individual physical structure polylines, which are described below and shown in Fig. 3.

Moving: Within this method, at each iteration of the sensitivity analysis, it is proposed to move the polygon by a step depending on the sum of the lengths of all sides of the considered polygon. Thus, the larger the object (polygon), the larger the step we will use to move.

At one iteration, this method can analyze the change in the quality metric for object movement in eight directions: north, northeast, east, southeast, south, southwest, west, and northwest. The proposed method assumes an adaptive approach to moving the polygon. If there is no improvement in the quality metric at the first iteration of moving the polygon, the step will be halved. The method can make double the movement step. However, the selected displacement step may need to be less significant for the quality of the entire structure to be improved.

Rotation: This method uses the rotation of each polygon around its centre of mass. The user can define a set of polygon rotation angles. By default, there is exploring of all rotation angles every 45°C.

Geometry Transformation: It is assumed that the polygons of the physical structure may contain such vertices, which negatively influence the quality

Algorithm 1. Proposed Sensitivity Analysis algorithm

```
1:  procedure SA.ANALYSIS()
2:      Input: InitStructure ← GENETICALGORITHM()
3:      initFitnes ← REALMODEL(InitStructure)
4:      procedure MOVE(initFitnes, InitStructure)
5:          while stepFitnes < initFitnes do
6:              for polygon in InitStructure do
7:                  movingStep ← FUNCTION(length(polygon))
8:                  newStruct ← MOVING(polygon, movingStep)
9:                  stepFitnes ← REALMODEL(newStructure)
10:                 if stepFitnes> =initFitnes then
11:                     movingStep ← movingStep/2
12:                     repeatLoop(3attempts)
13:         return stepFitnes, newStructure
14:     procedure ROTATE(initFitnes, structure) ←MOVE()
15:         while stepFitnes < initFitnes do
16:             for polygon in structure do
17:                 newStructure ← ROTATING(polygon)
18:                 stepFitnes ← REALMODEL(newStructure)
19:         return stepFitnes, newStructure
20:     procedure FIND COMBO(initFitnes, structure) ←ROTATE()
21:         polygons ← STRUCTURE.POLYGONS()
22:         uniqueCombinations ← PERMUTATION(polygons)
23:         while stepFitnes < initFitnes do
24:             for combination in uniqueCombinations do
25:                 stepFitnes ← REALMODEL(combination)
26:         return stepFitnes, newStructure
27:     procedure REBUILD(initFitnes, structure) ←FIND COMBO()
28:         while stepFitnes < initFitnes do
29:             for polygon in structure do
30:                 newStructure ← CHANGEGEOMETRY(polygon)
31:                 stepFitnes ← REALMODEL(newStructure)
32:         return newStructure
33:     ImprovedStructure ← REBUILD()
34:     Output ImprovedStructure
```

metric. In this method, the geometric shape of the polygon can be changed in the way shown in Fig. 3.

Combination: Within the method, it is supposed to analyze the need for the physical structure of all polygons generated by the framework. A physical structure consisting of n polygons can be obtained in the evolutionary optimization process. It is assumed that there are such polygons that do not affect the quality metric or that their influence is not significant.

4.1   Sensitivity Analysis Algorithm

We propose the "one iteration" of sensitivity analysis as a final approach. The process of obtaining the improved physical structure is shown in Fig. 3. The initial structure for the sensitivity analysis algorithm is an optimized physical structure from the generative design tool. After the structure is initialized, the object sequentially goes through the analysis stages for testing sensitivity by changes. The sensitivity criterion is the wave height, but in other cases, it might be defined by the user for each specific task. One iteration of the sensitivity analysis is a minor change to an object, such as a rotation, displacement and others. After each iteration, the object is evaluated using a physical process simulator and receives a new quality metric. Without a qualitative increase, the changes made to the object at the previous iteration are cancelled, and the analysis process continues. Physical structure sensitivity analysis continues until all available transformation methods in various variations have been applied and evaluated. The user receives a qualitatively improved "Final Structure" at the algorithm's output which means any further changes in the structure will negatively affect the quality metric.

Thus, the time and memory computational complexity of the sensitivity analysis algorithm is near-linear.

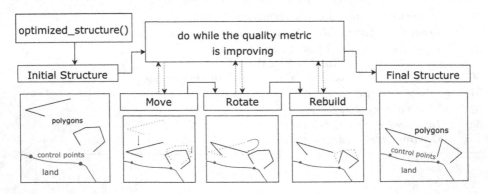

Fig. 3. The workflow of the proposed algorithm for structural sensitivity analysis. The search space is defined as a set of possible transformations that do not violate the restrictions for the allowed area. The breakwaters are represented as black lines at subplots.

5   Experimental Studies

5.1   Experimental Setup

Finding the optimal configuration of breakwaters was chosen as the basis for the experiments. Land boundaries limit the search area for solutions. Also, it has control points for the estimation of the quality metrics. In addition, sea routes have been added to the solution search field for the plausibility of the experiment. Final breakwaters should not intersect with any limitations. Schematically all restrictions are shown in Fig. 4.

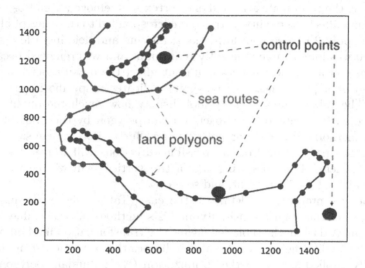

Fig. 4. Search space, encoding of solutions, target points, and constraints.

Our approach is implemented as a part of the GEFEST framework, which is a modular generative design tool. The quality metric is wave height, which is measured at control points. The SWAN wind wave model [2] was chosen as a simulator of interaction between breakwaters and marine environment [5] for calculating quality metrics. Evolutionary optimization parameters: population size - 15, number of generations of evolution - 80 (we choose relatively small values to maintain the case with limited computational time available). A series of 30 independent experiments with the parameters described above was launched to prove the sustainable effectiveness of the sensitivity analysis algorithm. A single-criteria evolutionary optimizer was chosen for this series of experiments. In each experiment, the effectiveness of applying sensitivity analysis was tested after 20 generations of evolution, after 40, after 60, and after the stopping criteria satisfied.

5.2 Application for Test Case

Ensuring the interpretability of results is a fundamental aspect of our approach. Figure 5 shows the explainability of results for one specific case of modelling breakwaters. In this case, the iterative application of polygon transformation algorithms made it possible to improve the overall quality metric by 21%.

The transparent and dotted line polygons are the initial configuration of the physical structure obtained by the sensitivity analysis algorithm from the generative design framework. The bright line shows the configuration of the polygons transformed by the developed algorithm.

It can be seen that poly_1 was rotated to improve the quality metric, slightly shifted along the coordinate grid, and one vertex was removed from this polygon, which did not affect the quality metric and corresponded to the concept of redundancy. The poly_2 needed transformations: moving and deleting a few vertices. The poly_0 was found to be inherently redundant and was removed because its absence inside the physical structure did not affect the quality metric.

Each symbol placed near the polygons indicates a specific impact on the polygon. The values under each symbol display how much the quality metric will worsen with specific other impacts on the polygon by the available transformation methods. Hence, using poly_2 as an illustration, we can say that any movement of this polygon from all possible directions will worsen the quality metric by at least 4.2%, removing any of the vertices will worsen the quality metric by at least 54.5% percent, and so on.

In order to interpret the details of the case, Table 1 shows the impact on the polygons of the applied sensitivity analysis methods and the values of their contribution. A dash in the table cell means the transformation method does not improve the quality metric. A zero value indicates that a particular method was successfully applied as part of the optimization (the redundant polygon vertex or the entire polygon was removed). However, the action did not change the quality metric. This strategy for modelling objects of generative design allows objects to be closest to reality and have the possibility of real production in the industry.

Table 1. Contribution to improving the quality metric of SA methods for each polygon (removing points and polygons is successful if changing the quality metric is ≥0)

Polygon	Improvement for a specified method of SA,%			
	move	rotate	remove poly	remove point
poly 0	–	–	0	–
poly 1	3	7.6	–	0
poly 2	–	10.4	–	0

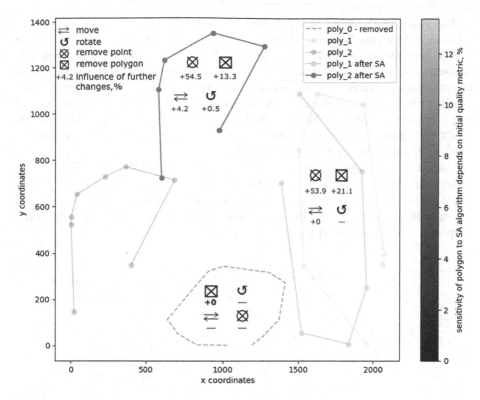

Fig. 5. The improvement and interpretation of breakwater configurations using a proposed approach. The dashed lines represent the polygons that were removed after sensitivity analysis (SA). The semi-transparent lines represent the polygons with adjusted positions. The icons and numbers represent the sensitivity of the objective function to various factors in the final solution.(Color figure online)

5.3 Validation of Algorithm

As mentioned above, to prove the algorithm's stability, 30 independent experiments were launched using the proposed sensitivity analysis algorithm. Figure 6 compares the proposed algorithm and existing genetic algorithm in the GEFEST framework.

The X-axis displays the gradation of the wave height, and the Y-axis displays the optimization process. The picture should be considered as three processes: continuous evolutionary optimization using the generative design framework (yellow box plots), the evolutionary optimization process, which took the same amount of time as the sensitivity analysis algorithm (green box plots), the sensitivity analysis process (pink box plots). The process displayed in green deserves an additional explanation since this is just a continuance of the work of the genetic algorithm and, in essence, is an auxiliary indicator for comparing the results of genetics and sensitivity analysis at the same time of the algorithms.

According to the work of the genetic algorithm, for each new epoch, a set of individuals is supplied from the best individual parents who have undergone evolutionary processes. Thus, after [20,40,60,80], the best individuals are simultaneously submitted to the sensitivity analysis and the genetic algorithm, where the evolutionary process occurs. In Fig. 6, we can see that the sensitivity analysis algorithm has better results than the genetic algorithm (comparing green and pink box plots), especially at the initial stages of evolution. When the genetic algorithm is fully completed, sensitivity analysis remains an effective approach to qualitatively improving the physical structure.

Comparative analysis of fitness improvement values is shown in Table 2. To confirm the enhancement provided by the sensitivity analysis approach we utilize paired t-test [25]. Obtained $p_{value} = 0.033$ enables us to reject the null hypothesis at a significance level of 0.05. In other words, there is a statistical improvements compared to the baseline approach.

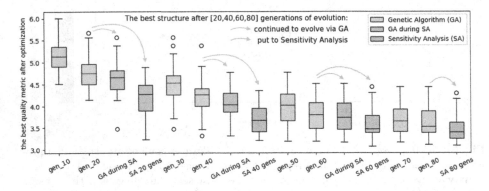

Fig. 6. Experimental comparison of baseline evolutionary approach and proposed hybrid approach based on sensitivity analysis. Three scenarios involved the SA after each 20 generations are considered.

Table 2. Comparison of average effectiveness between near-SOTA solution GEFEST and proposed SA-based approach with the same evaluation time

Method	Improvement for a specified number of gens,%			
	20	40	60	80
GEFEST	2.8±4.7	4.1±6.7	1.2±3.0	–
Evo+SA	**12.4±7.9**	**11.9±8.7**	**5.0±6.2**	**4.2±6.6**

6   Conclusion

In the paper, a hybrid optimization approach for coastal breakwaters is proposed. It combines the evolutionary exploration of search space of geometrically-encoded solutions and the improvement of solutions using structural sensitivity analysis.

The experimental results demonstrate the potential of the hybridization of evolutionary approach structural analysis to enhance the design of coastal breakwaters, providing decision-makers with a more comprehensive understanding of the optimized structures and their sensitivity to changes. As seen from the experiments, the SA-based approach is more effective for optimization runs with a small number of generations. Since the simulation of wind waves interacting with breakwaters is computationally expensive, reducing total optimization time can be helpful for practical applications.

The main limitation of the proposed approach is the fast increase of time complexity for structural analysis in high-dimensional search spaces (a large number of breakwaters or breakwater segments). However, the approach can be effectively paralleled since many operations in the proposed SA algorithm are independent.

Acknowledgment. This research is financially supported by The Russian Scientific Foundation, Agreement #22-71-00094.

Data and code availability. All methods and algorithms described in the paper are available as a part of the open-source framework GEFEST (https://github.com/aimclub/GEFEST). The scripts for experimental studies and obtained results are available in the separate repository https://github.com/ITMO-NSS-team/OL2A_2023_gd_with_sa_paper.

References

1. Barabanova, I.V., Vychuzhanin, P., Nikitin, N.O.: Sensitivity analysis of the composite data-driven pipelines in the automated machine learning. Procedia Comput. Sci. **193**, 484–493 (2021)
2. Booij, N., Holthuijsen, L., Ris, R.: The "swan" wave model for shallow water. Coast. Eng. **1**, 668–676 (1996)
3. Cho, S., Jung, H.S.: Design sensitivity analysis and topology optimization of displacement-loaded non-linear structures. Comput. Methods Appl. Mech. Eng. **192**(22–24), 2539–2553 (2003)
4. Christopher Frey, H., Patil, S.R.: Identification and review of sensitivity analysis methods. Risk Anal. **22**(3), 553–578 (2002)
5. Christou, M., Swan, C., Gudmestad, O.: The interaction of surface water waves with submerged breakwaters. Coast. Eng. **55**(12), 945–958 (2008)
6. Cinelli, C., Kumor, D., Chen, B., Pearl, J., Bareinboim, E.: Sensitivity analysis of linear structural causal models. In: International Conference on Machine Learning, pp. 1252–1261. PMLR (2019)

7. Elchahal, G., Younes, R., Lafon, P.: Optimization of coastal structures: application on detached breakwaters in ports. Ocean Eng. **63**, 35–43 (2013)
8. Fernández-Navarro, F., Hervás-Martínez, C., Gutiérrez, P.A.: A dynamic over-sampling procedure based on sensitivity for multi-class problems. Pattern Recogn. **44**(8), 1821–1833 (2011)
9. Hart, W.E.: Adaptive global optimization with local search. Ph.D. thesis, Citeseer (1994)
10. James, F.: Monte Carlo theory and practice. Rep. Prog. Phys. **43**(9), 1145 (1980)
11. Kucherenko, S., Iooss, B.: Derivative based global sensitivity measures. arXiv preprint arXiv:1412.2619 (2014)
12. Kundapura, S., Hegde, A.V.: Current approaches of artificial intelligence in breakwaters-a review. Ocean Syst. Eng. **7**(2), 75–87 (2017)
13. Lacroix, B., Molina, D., Herrera, F.: Region based memetic algorithm for real-parameter optimisation. Inf. Sci. **262**, 15–31 (2014)
14. Lauret, P., Fock, E., Mara, T.A.: A node pruning algorithm based on a Fourier amplitude sensitivity test method. IEEE Trans. Neural Netw. **17**(2), 273–293 (2006)
15. Lee, J., Kim, D.W.: Memetic feature selection algorithm for multi-label classification. Inf. Sci. **293**, 80–96 (2015)
16. Liu, X., Zhao, W., Wan, D.: Multi-fidelity co-kriging surrogate model for ship hull form optimization. Ocean Eng. **243**, 110239 (2022)
17. Lobo, F.G., Goldberg, D.E.: Decision making in a hybrid genetic algorithm. In: Proceedings of 1997 IEEE International Conference on Evolutionary Computation (ICEC 1997), pp. 121–125. IEEE (1997)
18. Maslyaev, M., Hvatov, A.: Solver-based fitness function for the data-driven evolutionary discovery of partial differential equations. In: 2022 IEEE Congress on Evolutionary Computation (CEC), pp. 1–8. IEEE (2022)
19. Nalepa, J., Blocho, M.: Adaptive memetic algorithm for minimizing distance in the vehicle routing problem with time windows. Soft. Comput. **20**, 2309–2327 (2016)
20. Nielsen, A.B., Hansen, L.K.: Structure learning by pruning in independent component analysis. Neurocomputing **71**(10–12), 2281–2290 (2008)
21. Nikitin, N.O., Polonskaia, I.S., Kalyuzhnaya, A.V., Boukhanovsky, A.V.: The multi-objective optimisation of breakwaters using evolutionary approach. In: Developments in Maritime Technology and Engineering, pp. 767–774. CRC Press (2021)
22. Oh, S., Jung, Y., Kim, S., Lee, I., Kang, N.: Deep generative design: integration of topology optimization and generative models. J. Mech. Des. **141**(11), 767–774 (2019)
23. Pavlenko, A., Chivilikhin, D., Semenov, A.: Asynchronous evolutionary algorithm for finding backdoors in boolean satisfiability. In: 2022 IEEE Congress on Evolutionary Computation (CEC), pp. 1–8. IEEE (2022)
24. Qiao, J.-F., Zhang, Y., Han, H.-G.: Fast unit pruning algorithm for feedforward neural network design. Appl. Math. Comput. **205**(2), 622–627 (2008)
25. Raschka, S.: MLxtend: providing machine learning and data science utilities and extensions to Python's scientific computing stack. J. Open Source Softw. **3**(24) (2018). https://doi.org/10.21105/joss.00638, https://joss.theoj.org/papers/10.21105/joss.00638
26. Richardson, S., Cuomo, G., Dimakopoulos, A., Longo, D.: Coastal structure optimisation using advanced numerical methods. In: From Sea to Shore-Meeting the Challenges of the Sea: (Coasts, Marine Structures and Breakwaters 2013), pp. 1184–1194. ICE Publishing (2014)

27. Sobol, I.M.: Global sensitivity indices for nonlinear mathematical models and their Monte Carlo estimates. Math. Comput. Simul. **55**(1–3), 271–280 (2001)
28. Starodubcev, N.O., Nikitin, N.O., Andronova, E.A., Gavaza, K.G., Sidorenko, D.O., Kalyuzhnaya, A.V.: Generative design of physical objects using modular framework. Eng. Appl. Artif. Intell. **119**, 105715 (2023)
29. Starodubcev, N.O., Nikitin, N.O., Kalyuzhnaya, A.V.: Surrogate-assisted evolutionary generative design of breakwaters using deep convolutional networks. In: 2022 IEEE Congress on Evolutionary Computation (CEC), pp. 1–8. IEEE (2022)
30. Tyflopoulos, E., Tollnes, F.D., Steinert, M., Olsen, A., et al.: State of the art of generative design and topology optimization and potential research needs. In: DS 91: Proceedings of NordDesign 2018, Linköping, Sweden, 14th-17th August 2018 (2018)
31. Vajna, S., Clement, S., Jordan, A., Bercsey, T.: The autogenetic design theory: an evolutionary view of the design process. J. Eng. Des. **16**(4), 423–440 (2005)
32. Wolkenhauer, O., Wellstead, P., Cho, K.H., Ingalls, B.: Sensitivity analysis: from model parameters to system behaviour. Essays Biochem. **45**, 177–194 (2008)
33. Xu, M., Yang, J., Gao, Z.: Using one-at-a-time sensitivity analysis designs for genetic algorithm solving continuous network design problems. In: 2009 International Joint Conference on Computational Sciences and Optimization, vol. 2, pp. 114–118. IEEE (2009)
34. Zhu, Z., Ong, Y.S., Kuo, J.L.: Feature selection using single/multi-objective memetic frameworks. In: Goh, CK., Ong, YS., Tan, K.C. (eds.) Multi-objective memetic algorithms, Studies in Computational Intelligence, vol. 171, pp. 111–131. Springer, Heidelberg (2009). https://doi.org/10.1007/978-3-540-88051-6_6
35. Zhu, Z., Xiao, J., He, S., Ji, Z., Sun, Y.: A multi-objective memetic algorithm based on locality-sensitive hashing for one-to-many-to-one dynamic pickup-and-delivery problem. Inf. Sci. **329**, 73–89 (2016)

An Example of Ontology in Medical Diagnosis: A Case Study

Antonela Prnjak⑩, Marko Rosić ⑩, Goran Zaharija⑩, Divna Krpan$^{(\boxtimes)}$ ⑩, and Monika Mladenović ⑩

Faculty of Science, University of Split, Split, Croatia
{antonela.prnjak,marko.rosic,goran.zaharija,divna.krpan, monika.mladenovic}@pmfst.hr

Abstract. The widespread use of AI tools in recent years has put even more emphasis on the interaction between humans and computers in terms of information exchange and knowledge representation. Appropriate knowledge representation is important in the context of human-computer interaction because the knowledge has to be represented in a manner that is understandable to humans while still being useful for computers. This paper describes the approach of knowledge representation using ontologies and provides a use case example of using this approach in medical diagnosis.

Keywords: Ontologies · Knowledge Representation · Artificial Intelligence

1 Introduction

With the increased complexity of machine learning models, there is a growing need to develop models that can be interpretable and explainable [1].

Knowledge integration in machine learning models is standard practice, usually done through labeling and feature engineering (data-driven approach). However, there is an increased interest in using formal knowledge representations to further integrate knowledge in machine learning models (knowledge-driven approach) [2]. Knowledge representation is a well-established scientific field that has been used in Artificial Intelligence for decades. Over that time, many formalisms for knowledge representation have been developed. Four main styles of symbolic representation in AI have been: (a) logic, (b) production rules, (c) procedures, and (d) semantic networks and frames [3]. Some of these formalisms are focused on declarative (*what?*) knowledge, while others are concerned with procedural (*how?*) knowledge. The final choice of formalism depends on the particular use case and the type of knowledge that must be expressed.

With an additional focus on explainability, the use of ontologies in information systems has become increasingly popular in various fields [4]. One of the examples is ML models for automated driving, which require knowledge representation that needs to be both understandable to human (safety) engineers and amenable to computer-aided processing. Ontologies as a knowledge representation are particularly suitable for describing the semantic contents of data, including the semantic interplay of contents [5].

A. I. Pereira et al. (Eds.): OL2A 2023, CCIS 1981, pp. 186–196, 2024.
https://doi.org/10.1007/978-3-031-53025-8_14

Ontologies are organized representations of concepts, categories, and connections within a particular domain. They have their roots in philosophy but were later popularized by computer science and artificial intelligence. They are an effective technique for categorizing knowledge and information, enabling machines to discover and comprehend intricate connections among numerous different entities [6]. By providing a formal and clear framework, ontologies help organize and explain concepts and connections within a certain knowledge area [7]. Ontologies are useful for organizing knowledge because they can capture and explain the underlying semantics of a domain. By offering a standard vocabulary and supporting interoperability across different systems, ontologies aid in more effective and intelligent information processing and open new possibilities for study and development in several fields. Ontologies are essential for structuring and making sense of vast amounts of structured and unstructured data in the context of the exponential rise of data and information.

Using ontologies can provide a common vocabulary of an area and define the meaning of the terms and relationships between them. There are many benefits for using ontological knowledge representation such as: (a) sharing a common understanding of the structure of information, (b) reuse of domain knowledge, (c) explicit domain assumptions, (d) separation of domain and operational knowledge, and (e) ability to analyze domain knowledge [8].

2 Ontologies

Ontologies have their roots in philosophy, where the term "ontology" refers to the study of the nature of existence and reality. Aristotle was one of the many ancient Greek philosophers who tried to categorize and order the world around them. Ontology was significantly developed and enlarged in the twentieth century with the rise of formal logic and analytic philosophy. The idea of formal languages and logical frameworks that might accurately and formally define knowledge and information was investigated by philosophers. In computer science and artificial intelligence, these ideas formed the basis for creating databases, the Semantic Web, and ontologies.

In the 1960s and 1970s, during the beginning of AI research, attempts were made to formalize knowledge in a structured and machine-understandable style. Researchers like Marvin Minsky and John McCarthy were among the first to look at formal logic, frames, and semantic networks to represent knowledge [9]. The goal of these early AI systems was to enable robots to think, understand, and communicate similarly to humans. In the 1980s, the focus shifted to how domain-specific information is represented in so-called "expert systems." These systems are based on the idea that knowledge from human specialists in a certain subject may be captured and expressed as a set of rules, hypotheses, and heuristics. It has become normal practice to capture domain knowledge and draw inferences from it using inheritance hierarchies, rule-based languages like Prolog, and frame-based systems [9].

Early in the 1990s, ontologies were initially considered in computer science, particularly in the setting of artificial intelligence. The goal was to develop a formal, structured knowledge representation system that computers could understand and use. One of the earliest major initiatives in this sector was the Knowledge Interchange Format (KIF), developed in 1989 by John McCarthy and his collaborators. Knowledge representation was formalized and organized using the KIF language. Tom Gruber first used the term "ontology" in the context of computer science in his 1991 work "The Role of Common Ontology in Achieving Sharable, Reusable Knowledge Bases" [7]. Gruber defined ontology as "a clear statement of an idea." The World Wide Web's growth in the late 1990s and early 2000s accelerated the idea of ontologies as a formal method for expressing knowledge. Tim Berners-Lee envisioned a "Semantic Web," where content on the Web would be organized and accessible to both humans and machines, allowing for greater interactions and services. The need for a uniform, machine-readable vocabulary to convey information led to the development of the ontology language standards RDF (Resource Description Framework) and RDFS (RDF Schema) [10].

The capabilities of RDF and RDFS were expanded with the introduction of more expressive ontology languages in the early 2000s, such as the Web Ontology Language (OWL). When OWL was defined by the World Wide Web Consortium (W3C) in 2004, it immediately gained popularity as a method for expressing intricate knowledge and reasoning tasks on the Semantic Web. Ontology tools, such as Protégé, Jena, and Cogui, were created during this period to make designing, altering, and maintaining ontologies easier [11].

Ontologies have become an essential part of various areas and applications, from e-commerce to healthcare to natural language processing and information retrieval. The creation of ontologies has resulted in a vast network of machine-readable knowledge that can be easily shared and reused. Ontologies are becoming increasingly important as networked data, Big Data, and the Internet of Things are introduced, along with their capacity to organize and make sense of enormous amounts of data [12].

2.1 Components of Ontologies

Ontologies are made up of several parts that work together to describe information in a formal and organized way. These elements, which include classes, properties, and individuals, aid in defining the ideas, connections, and particular occurrences inside a domain. Understanding the purpose and function of each component is crucial to building a solid ontology that effectively reflects the semantics of the domain it represents [11].

Classes: Classes are the basic building blocks of an ontology, representing the most important concepts or categories within the domain. They act as a guide for classifying, arranging, and establishing a hierarchy for the different entities. Classes can be arranged in a hierarchical structure, with more general classes (e.g., "animal") at higher levels and more specific subclasses below (e.g., "cat"). As a result of this configuration, subclasses can inherit relationships and attributes from their superclass. Classes help to categorize ideas clearly, which is important for establishing the general structure and organization of information inside an ontology. Classes also make reasoning and querying easier.

Properties: Properties are the attributes or characteristics associated with the classes and individuals in an ontology. They represent the relationships between the different components and can be used to describe the different aspects of the entities within the domain. Properties can be divided into two main types: object properties and data type properties. Object properties describe relationships between individuals of different classes, while data type properties relate individuals (classes) to specific data values, such as numbers or strings. For example, if we have two concept classes, "person" and "cat", we can define an object property "hasOwner" to describe the relationship between a person and their pet. Data properties, on the other hand, describe characteristics of a concept class using data values. For example, we can define a data property "has Age" to describe the age of a person or a pet. Properties play a critical role in capturing the relationships and dependencies between different entities, allowing for a more detailed representation of knowledge within the domain.

Individuals: Individuals, also called instances, are the specific elements or entities within the domain that instantiate the classes defined in the ontology. They represent real-world examples or occurrences of the concepts and categories described by the classes. Individuals can be assigned properties that reflect their attributes and relationships with other individuals. The role of individuals in ontology is to ground the knowledge representation in concrete "examples" so that it is possible to reason about and query specific instances within the domain. For example, within the concept of "cat", individual instances might include "Bengal", "Persian cat", and "Sphynx".

Axioms or rules: Axioms are the logical statements that define the relationships between different components within an ontology. They impose constraints on the relationships between concepts and properties, thus ensuring the consistency and coherence of the ontology. Rules can also be used to specify how concepts and properties can be combined to form more complex statements and queries. For example, two concept classes that have no overlap are "Dog" and "Cat" so we can define the axiom: Dog DisjointClasses Cat.

Together, classes, properties, and individuals form the backbone of an ontology and provide a systematic and coherent representation of knowledge within a domain. By structuring and defining concepts, relationships, and instances formally and explicitly, ontologies enable machines and software applications to understand, process, and reason about complex information and relationships efficiently and meaningfully.

2.2 Ontology Languages and Tools

Ontologies are used to structure and formalize the representation of knowledge and concepts. Depending on the complexity of the domain and the needs of the specific application, ontology languages, and tools are crucial for producing and managing structured and formal knowledge representations in various ways. It is possible to specify classes, attributes, and connections in a knowledge domain using ontology languages. RDF and RDFS provide a basis for knowledge representation, while OWL expands on this with more expressive expressions, making it appropriate for modeling complicated domains and facilitating complex reasoning. On the other hand, Protégé, Jena, Cogui, and JSON LD are popular tools for ontology construction and administration that offer a user-friendly interface and a set of APIs for ontology editing, querying, and reasoning. The most popular ontology languages and tools are discussed in this article.

RDF (Resource Description Framework) is a data model and language based on graphs that are used to express data about resources on the World Wide Web. Using triples - which are made up of a subject, a predicate, and an object - RDF offers a mechanism to define resources. The object is the value of the property or other resource, the predicate is an individual or resource, and the subject is a thing. While RDF is a versatile and lightweight model for encoding straightforward knowledge structures, several more sophisticated constructions and expressive features offered by OWL are absent from RDF [10].

RDFS (RDF Schema) is an addition to RDF that adds a fundamental schema language for specifying classes, properties, and their connections. Class hierarchies, property domains, ranges, and certain fundamental restrictions may all be defined using RDFS. In contrast to OWL, which has more sophisticated capabilities for expressing complicated connections and restrictions, RDFS has less expressive capacity.

OWL (Web Ontology Language) is a Semantic Web language created to describe in-depth and complicated information about objects, collections of objects, and connections across various domains. OWL offers a mechanism to declare the classes, characteristics, and axioms that characterize the knowledge domain and is based on Description Logic (DL). By adding new constructs and characteristics like class disjointness, cardinality restrictions, and property constraints, OWL builds on RDF and RDFS and increases its expressive capabilities. OWL makes efficient inference and reasoning possible, making it appropriate for applications requiring sophisticated semantic capabilities.

Protégé is a knowledge management system and free, open-source ontology editor created by Stanford University. With Protégé, users may create and manage ontologies using a user-friendly interface and a variety of ontology languages, such as OWL and RDF. Additionally, it offers tools for ontology reasoning, debugging, and visualization.

A Java framework called Jena is used to create Semantic Web apps. For use with RDF and OWL ontologies, Jena offers a set of APIs that include ontology parsing, querying, and reasoning. A rule-based inference engine and support for SPARQL, a potent query language for RDF data, are also included in Jena. Jena is a well-liked option for developers creating ontology-based applications because of its numerous capabilities and APIs.

Ontology-based intelligent assistants may be created using the open-source Cogui framework. Users may engage with sophisticated knowledge structures using an intuitive and natural interface designed to be user-friendly. Users may engage with knowledge directly through natural language questions and conversations, eliminating the need to learn and utilize complicated software interfaces. The ontology language used by Cogui is OWL, and it offers a number of capabilities for querying, reasoning, and ontology visualization.

Although JSON is not an ontology language, JSON-LD (Linked Data) is a lightweight JSON-based format for describing linked data, including RDF and RDF-like structures. JSON-LD is a popular option for developers who like working with JSON over XML-based formats like OWL and RDF/XML because it enables RDF data to be encoded in a familiar and simple-to-use JSON format. But JSON-LD doesn't offer OWL's degree of expressiveness and inference power.

3 Example: Medical Diagnosis

Ontologies play an important role in artificial intelligence because they provide a systematic and structured way to represent complex knowledge domains. In the following, we'll discuss some examples of the use of classes, properties, and individuals in the context of AI applications.

Consider an AI application that aims to help physicians diagnose diseases based on patients' symptoms and medical history. In this scenario, the ontology might include the following components:

- Classes: Heart Disease, Symptoms, Treatments, Patients
- Object Properties: hasSymptom, diagnosed With, prescribed Treatment
- Datatype Properties: age, gender, FirstName
- Individuals: specific medical conditions (e.g., Arrhythmia, Diabetes), symptoms (e.g., Fever, Fatigue), treatments (e.g., Antiviral Medication, Insulin Therapy), and patients
- Axioms: visible by querying ontology structure and knowledge base (e.g., patients older than 55 years).

In this example, done within Cogui, the classes represent the main concepts within the medical domain, such as different medical conditions, symptoms, and treatments. The properties capture relationships between these concepts, such as the symptoms associated with particular medical conditions and the treatments prescribed for patients diagnosed with specific conditions. The individuals represent concrete instances of these concepts, such as specific patients, conditions, symptoms, and treatments.

3.1 Ontology (System) Elements

"A set of system elements can be any collection of objects called object elements. Elements of the system can be abstract or concrete, and a finite countable set of elements from 1 to N for some finite number N will be considered."

Figure 1 shows how one class – *Attributes* - can be broken down into more detailed subclasses establishing structure and organization of information. Let us imagine an example to say that a set of attributes from the figure above describes a person. *Ana is a 61-year-old woman who is passionate about hiking in nature. She got into hiking primarily because of her cholesterol levels, which she developed in her youth due to a poor diet.* We start with the basic attributes to describe the patient's condition. As the system evolved, the need for new attributes grew, and they were gradually added at each stage. In the example of heart disease, when considering complex relationships (N-relationships), we need to look at multiple symptoms (their values) that must have a common link to infer the disease. For example, if the cholesterol level is high, the heart rate is irregular, and the ECG is incorrect, we can conclude that there is heart disease, such as arrhythmia. If the complex relationship described above is true, it may be this disease, but nothing can be determined without one of these three components. If we add another symptom, the original relationship expands, or more precisely, they form a new relationship and can indicate another disease. Figure 2 shows the hierarchy.

Systems with multiple levels can combine lower-level elements (atomic elements) into higher-level elements - structured elements (Fig. 3).

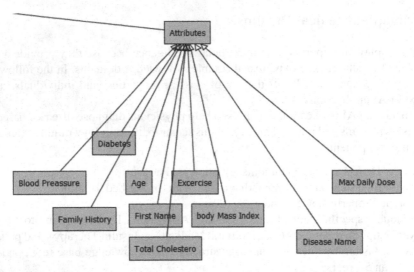

Fig. 1. Grouping attributes of symptoms, diseases, and treatment into higher gender attribute

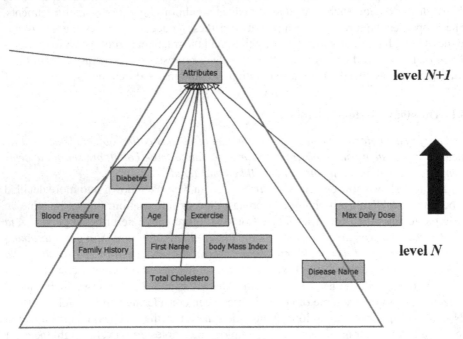

Fig. 2. Hierarchy

3.2 System Description

Why do we need to describe the system? To demonstrate how the system should function, with the purpose of obtaining a representative. We describe the system in terms of entities - anything that can be uniquely determined, identified, and distinguished so that the entity

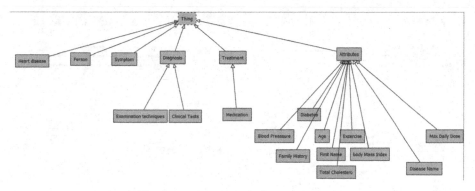

Fig. 3. Joining elements at a higher level

can be any real or abstract object that is the subject of current consideration. An entity in the represented system is a person. Each person is described by some attributes (age, gender, age…) and symptoms (cholesterol, pulse, activity…). We can infer diseases from these symptoms and then confirm them through clinical studies or examinations. After that, we can prescribe therapy if necessary and warn about other possible risks (Figs. 4, 5 and 6).

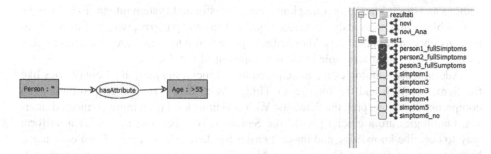

Fig. 4. Instance of a class "Person"

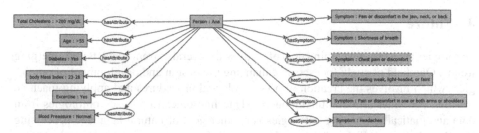

Fig. 5. Enquiry

This example shows how ontologies can be used to model and express domain-specific knowledge in a structured and machine-readable form in AI systems. Ontologies

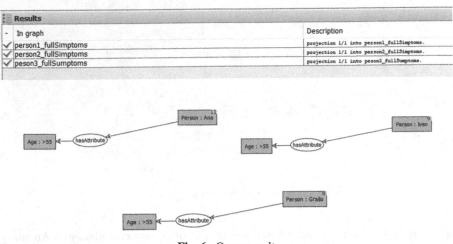

Fig. 6. Query results

enable AI systems to understand, query, and process complicated information by defining concepts, relationships, and instances within a domain, which enables smarter and more efficient decision-making processes.

4 Future

Ontologies are a fast-developing field of study with several current projects and emerging trends. One field of study focuses on enhancing the design and development of ontologies, which involves the creation of novel tools and procedures and applying machine learning and other artificial intelligence (AI) technologies to produce ontologies from data automatically. Creating ontologies is another goal of natural language processing (NLP) techniques, which are also used to extract information from unstructured text data and discover ideas and connections within text data. This strategy has the potential to greatly broaden the use of ontologies since they may collect knowledge from a variety of sources and disciplines, promoting knowledge transfer and system integration. To make it possible to find previously unnoticed relationships and patterns, which in turn lead to new insights and applications, knowledge capture and integration are projected to play an increasingly significant role in the development of ontologies.

Additionally, ontologies are anticipated to be crucial in emerging technologies like the Semantic Web and the Internet of Things. With data arranged so computers can comprehend and interpret, the Semantic Web envisions a smarter, more connected Internet. Ontologies are a crucial part of the Semantic Web because they offer a uniform way to describe knowledge and make it easier for data to be integrated and exchanged between various systems. Ontologies, which may depict the connections between networked devices and the data they create, are anticipated to make it possible for the Internet of Things to handle and analyze the enormous volumes of data more effectively [12]. This will enable handling and analyzing IoT data more effectively, providing fresh perspectives and applications in fields like smart cities, healthcare, and transportation.

5 Conclusion

The investigation of existence and being was first referred to as "ontology" in philosophy. In the 1990s, the term was adopted by the computer science and artificial intelligence communities to refer to structured models of knowledge and information within a specific domain providing a common vocabulary and understanding between users and systems, facilitating seamless communication, collaboration, and knowledge sharing.

The Semantic Web, the Internet of Things, biology, computer science, and other areas extensively use ontologies today. OWL, RDF, Protégé, or Cogui, among other ontology languages and tools, are available for creating and maintaining ontologies. One of its fundamental advantages is the capacity to capture and describe the semantics of a domain, fostering consistency, clarity, and system interoperability. Ontologies are crucial for organizing and making sense of enormous volumes of structured and unstructured data, allowing for more intelligent and effective information processing. Throughout this paper, we emphasized the value of ontologies in structuring knowledge and enabling various applications across multiple areas, including computer science and healthcare.

Ontologies play a bigger role in research and development across several disciplines as data and information volumes increase. In order to create effective ontologies that support their particular domain of interest, researchers and practitioners can benefit from having a solid understanding of the principles underlying ontology modeling and engineering, as well as the tools and languages available for creating and managing ontologies.

References

1. Roscher, R., Bohn, B., Duarte, M.F., Garcke, J.: Explainable machine learning for scientific insights and discoveries. IEEE Access **8**, 42200–42216 (2020). https://doi.org/10.1109/ACCESS.2020.2976199
2. Rueden, L. et al.: Informed machine learning - a taxonomy and survey of integrating prior knowledge into learning systems. IEEE Trans. Knowl. Data Eng., 1–1 (2021). https://doi.org/10.1109/tkde.2021.3079836
3. Koenraad De Smedt: Knowledge representation techniques in artificial intelligence: an overview. In: van der Veer, G.C., Mulder, G. (eds.) Human-Computer Interaction, pp. 207–222. Springer, Heidelberg (1988). https://doi.org/10.1007/978-3-642-73402-1_13
4. Roussey, C., Pinet, F., Kang, M.A., Corcho, O.: An introduction to ontologies and ontology engineering. In: Falquet, G., Métral, C., Teller, J., Tweed, C. (eds.) Ontologies in Urban Development Projects, pp. 9–38. Springer, London (2011). https://doi.org/10.1007/978-0-85729-724-2_2
5. Herrmann, M., et al.: Using ontologies for dataset engineering in automotive AI applications. In: 2022 Design, Automation & Test in Europe Conference & Exhibition (DATE), pp. 526–531 (2022). https://doi.org/10.23919/DATE54114.2022.9774675
6. Studer, R., Benjamins, V.R., Fensel, D.: Knowledge engineering: principles and methods. Data Knowl. Eng. **25**, 161–197 (1998). https://doi.org/10.1016/S0169-023X(97)00056-6
7. Gruber, T.R.: A translation approach to portable ontology specifications. Knowl. Acquis. **5**, 199–220 (1993). https://doi.org/10.1006/knac.1993.1008

8. Salem, A.-B.M., Cakula, S.: Using ontological engineering for developing web-based AI ontology. In: Proceedings of the 6th International Conference on Communications and Information Technology, and Proceedings of the 3rd World conference on Education and Educational Technologies, pp. 220–225. World Scientific and Engineering Academy and Society (WSEAS), Stevens Point, Wisconsin, USA (2012)
9. Russell, S.J., Norvig, P.: Artificial Intelligence a Modern Approach, Pearson (2021)
10. Staab, S., Studer, R. (eds.): Handbook on Ontologies. Springer, Heidelberg (2004). https://doi.org/10.1007/978-3-540-24750-0
11. Noy, N.F., McGuinness, D.L.: Ontology Development 101: A Guide to Creating Your First Ontology. Stanford Knowledge Systems Laboratory, Technical Report KSL-01-05 and Stanford Medical Informatics Technical Report SMI-2001-0880 (2001)
12. Suárez-Figueroa, M.C., Gómez-Pérez, A., Motta, E., Gangemi, A. (eds.): Ontology Engineering in a Networked World. Springer, Heidelberg (2012). https://doi.org/10.1007/978-3-642-24794-1

Text Chunking to Improve Website Classification

Mohamed Zohir Koufi[1,3]($\boxtimes$), Zahia Guessoum[1], Amor Keziou[2],
Itheri Yahiaoui[1], Chloé Martineau[3], and Wandrille Domin[3]

[1] CReSTIC, EA 3804, University of Reims Champagne-Ardenne, Reims, France
`mohamed-zohir.koufi@univ-reims.fr`,
`{zahia.guessoum,itheri.yahiaoui}@univ-reims.fr`
[2] LMR - UMR9008, University of Reims Champagne-Ardenne, Reims, France
`amor.keziou@univ-reims.fr`
[3] Olfeo, Paris, France
`{zkoufi,cmartineau,wdomin}@olfeo.com`

Abstract. Website classification is a crucial task in various applications such as web search, content filtering, and recommendation systems. Effectively categorizing long web pages into different categories based on their content is essential for providing accurate and personalized user experiences. Traditional transformer-based models, such as BERT and RoBERTa, have significantly advanced the field of natural language processing. However, such models face limitations when handling long sequences due to their fixed-length input restrictions resulting from their quadratic complexity. This paper presents a simple weighted stratified split approach (WSSA), to address the limitations of BERT and RoBERTa, in processing long text sequences for website classification. WSSA consists into chunking web pages into smaller chunks, then a new train chunk dataset is generated by a weighted stratified split following the distribution of the categories in the whole chunk dataset. This train chunk dataset is then used to train the models. Our approach improves the accuracy of BERT and RoBERTa models, surpassing the performance of Longformer and BigBird models. The proposed solution enables efficient processing and data augmentation, with reasonable fine-tuning times for BERT and RoBERTa models. Inference times remain efficient, showcasing the practicality of these models in real-time website classification tasks. The combination of WSSA with the index web page performs exceptionally well, highlighting its effectiveness in addressing the long text sequence limitation and improving transformer-based models for website classification.

Keywords: Website Classification · NLP · Transformers · Machine Learning · Data Splitting

1 Introduction

Website classification plays a vital role in various applications such as web search, content filtering, and recommendation systems. It involves categorizing long web

© The Author(s), under exclusive license to Springer Nature Switzerland AG 2024
A. I. Pereira et al. (Eds.): OL2A 2023, CCIS 1981, pp. 197–216, 2024.
https://doi.org/10.1007/978-3-031-53025-8_15

pages into different categories according to their content. However, websites are not just individual pages, but complex structures with interconnected pages that contain significant a lot of textual information. This information can be diverse and heterogeneous, including page content, meta tags, and other metadata. This makes processinglong text sequences a unique and challenging problem to website classification.

Traditional approaches [1,7,8,11,14–19,24,25,30] to website classification have relied on feature engineering techniques, shallow models and traditional machine learning classifiers like SVM, Naive Bayes...). However, these methods may struggle to capture the complex relationships and nuances within web content.

Recently, transformer-based models like BERT (Bidirectional Encoder Representations from Transformers) and RoBERTa (Robustly Optimized BERT Pre-training Approach) have shown impressive results in NLP tasks NLP tasks such as sentiment analysis, text classification, and question answering. But these models face challenges when dealing with long text sequences, as their quadratic complexity becomes computationally expensive and memory-intensive. One specific area where the limitation of long text sequences poses a significant hurdle is website classification. So, new adaptations to the transformers architecture have been introduced to address this limitation [2,3,5,6,9,10,13,20,21,23,27–29]. However, most of of the proposed methods use transformer architecture and are task oriented, which lead us to the question whether it is really a matter of architecture or could there be a simpler way to address this issue?

In this paper, we proposed a statistical-based approach called the Weighted Stratified Split Approach (WSSA) to address the challenges associated with processing long sequences in website classification. The WSS technique splits websites into smaller, stratified chunks, facilitating efficient processing of long sequences and providing an opportunity for data augmentation from the original dataset. Our approach relied solely on the dataset we provided to fine-tune the models. By evaluating the performance of these models on both the WSSA-generated dataset and a baseline dataset, we assessed their effectiveness in website classification tasks. We considered two scenarios: website classification using only the index web page and classification incorporating information from neighboring web pages. This allowed us to analyze the models' ability to leverage contextual information and assessed their performance in real-world website classification scenarios. In addition to evaluating their accuracy, we also investigated the fine-tuning and inference times of the models. Understanding the computational costs associated with these models is crucial for determining their practicality in real-time website classification applications.

This paper is organized as follows: We first start with a review of the existing related works in Sect. 2. In Sect. 3, We introduce the basic data stratified splitting method, followed by our new weighted stratified splitting approach. We first present the different considered steps with an overview graphic and we then present the considered models for our study. At the end of this section, we introduce our website classification method through an aggregating strategy.

Section 4 presents the used datasets and the experimental scenarios with the final results. Finally, we conclude with a summary of our results and future objectives.

2   Related Work

Several works have been proposed to address the challenges of large-text classification, and they can be categorized into two approaches. The first approach focuses on improving the attention mechanisms to handle large texts, while the second approach focuses on enhancing the scalability of models to classify large texts. The Longformer model, proposed by Beltagy et al. [2], uses a "sliding window" mechanism to efficiently process sequences up to 4,096 tokens, while maintaining a global context. Similarly, the BigBird model, proposed by Zaheer et al. [29], extends this idea with sparse attention patterns, enabling it to handle sequences up to 8,192 tokens, for both models the exact complexity is not mentioned in the papers. Transformer-XL, proposed by Dai et al. [5], incorporates a segment-level recurrence mechanism to capture long-term dependencies beyond a fixed context length, while compressive transformers, Rae et al. [21], apply random projections to compress long sequences, while this approach can potentially reduce the computational complexity of attending to long text sequences, the exact complexity would depend on the specifics of the compression function and how it's implemented. The BP-Transformer, introduced by Ye et al. [28], leverages binary partitioning to model long-range context effectively, and blockwise self-attention, this model yields $O(k \cdot n \log(n/k))$ connections where k is a hyperparameter to control the density of attention. Qui et al. [20], divides sequences into blocks for more efficient computation of self-attention. While these methods efficiently handle long sequences by partitioning them, they may face challenges in capturing fine-grained dependencies across partitions.

Wang et al. [27] propose Linformer, which introduces a self-attention mechanism with linear complexity, reducing computational overhead for long sequences, the Linformer reduces the overall self-attention complexity from $O(n^2)$ to $O(n)$. Kitaev et al. present Reformer [10] that utilizes reversible layers and sparse factorizations to improve transformer efficiency, this model reduces the complexity from $O(n^2)$ to $O(n \log n)$. Performers by Choromanski et al. [3] rethink the attention mechanism to reduce memory consumption and increase scalability, the complexity is same as in [27]. Roe et al. [23] improve computational efficiency by leveraging sparsity patterns with efficient content-based sparse attention and routing transformers. Kitaev et al. [9] develop an adaptive attention span, allowing transformers to dynamically adjust the attention window and enhance efficiency in handling long-range dependencies. While these approaches offer improved scalability and memory efficiency for processing longer sequences, they may introduce additional complexity and require careful parameter tuning.

The reviewed approaches offer different solutions to solve the challenges of handling long sequences. Techniques like attention modifications, sequence partitioning, model efficiency improvements, and specialized architectures show advancements in scalability, memory efficiency, and computational complexity. However, these approaches also have limitations. Some techniques may introduce additional computation complexity and excessive resources or require careful parameter tuning, making them less straightforward to implement. Furthermore, partitioning approaches may face challenges in capturing fine-grained dependencies across partitions, and efficient models may sacrifice some modeling capacity. Therefore, it is important to carefully consider the trade-offs between computational efficiency, modeling capacity, and the specific requirements of the task at hand when choosing an approach for handling long sequences.

In this paper, we propose an original approach to benchmark Longformer and BigBird on website classification tasks. Moreover, we propose a statistical approach to overcome the long sequence limitation of traditional transformer-based models (BERT and RoBERTa). We apply transformer-based models on the index and neighboring web pages of websites. This approach provides valuable insights into the application of machine learning in website classification and expand the current state of knowledge in the field.

3   Data Splitting and Website Classification Approach

In this section, we present the basic split method that will be used as a baseline to compare with ourweighted stratified split approach and then we follow up with our method for website classification.

3.1   Basic Split (BS)

Before we begin, it is noteworthy to know that there are two types of basic data splitting [22]. The first type is a basic split with non-stratified data and the second type is with stratified data. The main difference between the two lies in how the subsets are created and whether they preserve the distribution of categories in the original dataset.

Basic Non-Stratified Split (BNSS). In a non-stratified split, the subsets are created without considering the distribution of categories in the original dataset. This can result in imbalanced class distributions, which can introduce biases and lead to inaccurate evaluation results, especially when the categories are not evenly represented in the dataset. Non-stratified splitting may be appropriate when the distribution of categories is not a critical factor or when the dataset is well-balanced, with approximately equal instances per category. However, in scenarios where class imbalance exists or accurate representation of class distributions is essential, non-stratified splitting can pose challenges and hinder reliable model training, evaluation, and generalization performance assessment.

Basic Stratified Split (BSS). In a stratified split, subsets are created while preserving the proportion of each category from the original dataset in each subset. This approach aims to maintain the distribution of categories in the subsets, thereby avoiding biases and ensuring accurate representation of the underlying data. Stratified splitting is particularly crucial when dealing with imbalanced datasets, where there is a substantial difference in the number of instances across categories. In classification tasks, stratified splitting is commonly employed to generate training, validation, and test sets that accurately reflect the distribution of categories in the data. By utilizing stratified splitting, the resulting subsets enable reliable model training, evaluation, and assessment of generalization performance. Stratified splitting is a commonly used technique in data analysis, including text document classification, to ensure that the distribution of classes/categories in the original dataset is preserved across the subsets. This section presents the methodology for performing a basic stratified split.

Let D be the dataset consisting of N text documents, each labeled with a class or category. Let C be the set of all unique classes/categories in the dataset, with $|C|$ denoting the total number of unique classes. In this paper we use the basic stratified split as our baseline.

Training Set. Let D_{train} be the training set, which contains a fraction of the total dataset for training the classification model. We define the size of the training set as T, representing a percentage $(0 < T < 100)$ of the total dataset size. To convert T to its decimal form t, we have: $t = \frac{T}{100}$.

For each class c in C, it is crucial to ensure that the proportion of documents from class c, in the training set (D_{train_c}), is similar to the proportion of class c in the original dataset.

Mathematically, we achieve this by setting $D_{\text{train}_c} = \frac{t \times N}{N_c} \times D_c$, where:

- N is the total number of documents in the original dataset D,
- N_c is the number of documents belonging to class c in D, and
- D_c represents the subset of documents in D that belong to class c.

Test Set. Let D_{test} be the test set used for final evaluation and measuring the model's generalization performance. The size of the test set is usually similar to that of the validation set: $T = V = \frac{v}{100} \times N$, where v is the percentage representing the size of the test and validation sets with respect to the total dataset size N.

To maintain the class distribution of the original dataset, we ensure that each class c in C is appropriately represented in the test set. Mathematically, this is achieved by setting $D_{\text{test}_c} = \frac{v}{100} \times D_c$, where D_{test_c} represents the subset of documents in the test set that belong to class c, and D_c is the subset of documents in the original dataset D that belong to class c.

By following this methodology, a stratified split of the text document dataset can be performed, ensuring that the proportion of each class in the training and test sets is representative of the original dataset. This helps to avoid biases and ensures that the subsets accurately reflect the distribution of categories in the data.

3.2 Our Weighted Stratified Split Approach - WSSA

When we began our study, we used a basic stratified split based on the categories and the number of web pages in each category. However, we soon discovered that this approach resulted in a significant imbalance, with larger web pages being disproportionately included and favored in the training set, where predominantly smaller websites were represented. To effectively address this data imbalance challenge, we propose a novel approach that balances the data distribution between the train and test sets by taking into account the weight of each website.

Our weighted stratified split approach addresses the challenge of data imbalance and the limitation of maximum sequence length in traditional transformer-based models for website classification tasks. In website classification, we deal with long web pages containing heterogeneous and extensive textual information, making it challenging to process efficiently. Transformers like BERT and RoBERTa have a maximum sequence length of 512 tokens, potentially leading to the loss of valuable context from longer web pages texts. To overcome this limitation and balance the data distribution, we devise the WSSA approach. By chunking web pages into smaller, stratified blocks and calculating the weight of each website based on the number of generated chunks, we ensure that long web pages do not dominate the training set. This approach not only allows us to retain valuable context but also helps maintain a balanced representation of each category in the training and test sets. By leveraging the WSSA approach, we aim to enhance the accuracy of website classification models while ensuring the retention of important information from long text sequences. The approach takes into account the weights of websites to create a more balanced and informative dataset. Our method ensures a more equitable representation of both large and small web pages in both the training and test sets, thereby mitigating bias and promoting fair evaluation of the classifiers.

We first start with the full dataset without any split. We then chunk all web pages into multiple chunks of a maximum sequence of 500. We calculate the length of each subdivided web page blocks, which we use to calculate the weight of each web page. The weight of each website will be defined as the sum of the weights of all of its web pages.

We follow up by calculating the frequency of each of our categories. To do so, we group the dataset by the categories and sum all of the frequencies and group by each category together. Now that we have our main statistics that take in consideration the length of the web pages, we shuffle then split our dataset using the frequencies of each category in which we take 0.7 of the frequency of each category into the train set and the rest into test set. It is noteworthy to know that all generated chunks fall under the same source websites and have the same category of it.

In other words, to calculate the weight w_i of each website D_i in the dataset, we count the number of generated blocks N_i associated with that website. The primary key for identifying neighboring web pages is the website name. Mathematically, we have

$$w_i = \frac{N_i}{\sum_{i=1}^{N} N_i}, \tag{1}$$

where, N_i represents, for each website D_i, the number of generated blocks from all of its web pages. The denominator $\sum_{i=1}^{N} N_i$ represents the total number of generated blocks from all web pages in the dataset.

Therefore, to obtain the frequency f_{C_ℓ}, for each category C_ℓ, we sum the weights w_i of each website D_i belonging to the same category, namely,

$$f_{C_\ell} = \sum_{i=1}^{N} w_i \, \mathbf{1}_{\{D_i \in C_\ell\}}, \tag{2}$$

$\mathbf{1}_{\{D_i \in C_\ell\}}$ being the indicator function, taking value 1 when $D_i \in C_\ell$, and zero elsewhere. We give, in Table 1, an example for computing the frequency of each category, for a dataset with 9 websites and 2 categories (C_1 and C_2).

Table 1. Category frequencies from weighted sums

Cat	D_i	N_i	w_i	f_{C_ℓ}
C_1	D_1	3	0.1304	0.4781
	D_2	2	0.0869	
	D_3	2	0.0869	
	D_4	4	0.1739	
C_2	D_5	1	0.0434	0.5219
	D_6	2	0.0869	
	D_7	1	0.0434	
	D_8	3	0.1304	
	D_9	5	0.2173	

To construct the train set, we select a proportion (say 0.7) times the weighted size $f_{C_\ell} \times N$ websites from each category C_ℓ. Define the limits

$$\lim_{C_\ell} = 0.7 \times f_{C_\ell} \times N, \quad \text{for all } \ell = 1, \ldots, L, \tag{3}$$

L being the total number of categories. For the example in Table 1, specifically, we select $0.7 \times 0.4781 \times 9 = 3.012 \approx 3$ websites from C_1 and $0.7 \times 0.5219 \times 9 = 3.2880 \approx 3$ websites from C_2. We randomly select websites (without replacement) and accumulate the frequencies of each category, according to formula

(2), until we reach the limit $\lim_{C_\ell}$, for each respective category. For example, one possible outcome for the train set, for the example in Table 1, might be $D_{\text{train}} = \{D_1, D_2, D_3, D_6, D_7, D_9\}$. Figure 1 summarizes our proposed WSSA approach.

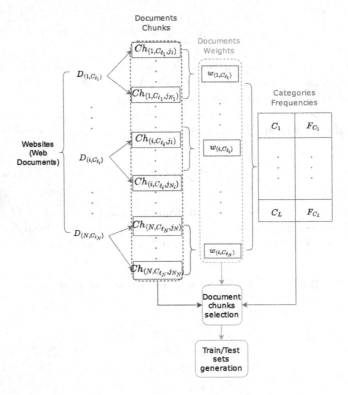

Fig. 1. Overview of our proposed weighted stratified approach (WSSA). Left to right: $D_{(i,C_{\ell_i})}$ refers to the ith document/website in the dataset from C_{ℓ_i} category; $Ch_{(i,C_{\ell_i},j_i)}$, $j_i = 1, \ldots, N_i$, refers to the jth block chunk from i^{th} document $D_{(i,C_{\ell_i})}$; $w_{(i,C_{\ell_i})}$ refers to the ith website's weight; $\{C_1, \ldots, C_L\}$ and $\{f_{C_1}, \ldots, f_{C_L}\}$ refers to the categories in the dataset, respectively, their obtained frequencies.

3.3   Considered Models for Web Page Classification

In the following, we briefly present the considered models for our classification task, we consider BERT, RoBERTa, Longformer and BigBird.

BERT. Based on the Transformer architecture [26], Devlin et al. [6] proposed a new language model called Bidirectional Encoder Representations from Transformers (BERT). The latter is a pre-training technique for natural language processing (NLP) developed by Google. It is based on a transformer language model and has a variable number of encoder layers and self-attention heads. Unlike traditional NLP techniques that rely on annotated language corpora, BERT uses unannotated text from the web to achieve state-of-the-art results on a range of NLP tasks. As a result, it has become a popular NLP research baseline and final task architecture.

RoBERTa Model. RoBERTa (Robustly Optimized BERT approach) by Yinhan et al. [13] is a language representation model based on the Transformer architecture. It builds upon the success of BERT and aims to address some of its limitations by optimizing the pretraining process. RoBERTa follows a similar approach to BERT, where it is pretrained on a large corpus of unlabeled text in a self-supervised manner. During pretraining, the model learns to predict masked words within sentences and to understand the relationships between different parts of the text. This process allows RoBERTa to capture rich contextual representations of words and sentences.

However, RoBERTa introduces several modifications and enhancements to the BERT architecture. It extends the training duration, uses larger minibatches, and removes the next sentence prediction objective. Additionally, RoBERTa utilizes dynamic masking, which means that the masked words are randomly selected for each training epoch, enabling the model to gain a deeper understanding of the text. The extensive training of RoBERTa on a massive amount of data from various sources leads to improved performance on a wide range of natural language processing (NLP) tasks, including text classification, named entity recognition, question answering, and more. Its robustness and effectiveness have made it a popular choice among researchers and practitioners in the NLP community.

Longformer Model. Beltagy et al. [2] introduced a variation to the RoBERTa model where they utilize a combination of local and global attention mechanisms to capture extensive context while maintaining computational efficiency. Longformer introduces a novel attention pattern, the "sliding window" attention, which allows the model to attend to a larger context without incurring excessive computational overhead. By incorporating a sparse attention mechanism, Longformer extends the reach of the context window and enables the modeling of long-range dependencies in a more efficient manner.

BigBird Model. Proposed by Zaheer et al. [29], addresses both the computational and memory limitations of traditional NLP models. It introduces a sparse attention mechanism that enables efficient modeling of long-range dependencies by attending to only a subset of tokens. By leveraging random attention patterns and utilizing locality-sensitive hashing, BigBird significantly reduces the computational complexity of self-attention, making it feasible to process long sequences. Additionally, BigBird incorporates global and block contextual information.

3.4   From Web Pages/Chunks to Website Classification

This paper seeks to investigate the optimal strategy for aggregating post-classification results based on web pages. To accomplish this goal, we first formalize our problem into an aggregation-like scenario, where each web page is considered as a classifier that aims to categorize its corresponding website. As such, each web page is treated as a voter that generates a single ballot containing the probabilities for each category. In this paper, we applied the majority voting strategy (MVS) in order to aggregate the web pages results.

The MVS is a simple but effective technique used in machine learning to combine the outputs of multiple classifiers in order to improve overall prediction accuracy. In this strategy, each classifier is trained on the same dataset, and their individual predictions are combined using a voting scheme. Figure 2 sums up the architecture of our approach.

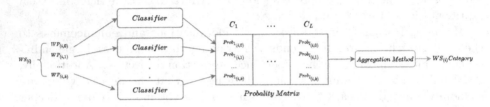

Fig. 2. Overview of the website classification architecture.
Left to right: $WS_{(i)}$ refers to the ith website in the dataset, $WP_{(i,k)}$ refers to the k^{st} web page (or chunk block) from i^{th} website $WS_{(i)}$. $\{C_1, \ldots, C_L\}$ refers to the categories in the dataset. $\left[Prob1_{(i,0)}, \ldots, Prob1_{(i,k)}\right]$ refers to the predicted probabilities by the classifier of the k^{st} web page (or chunk block) with respect to each category. P_{WS_i} is the full probability matrix for all web pages (or chunk block) of WS_i. $WS_{(i)}Category$ is the final predicted category.

4   Experiments

In our experiments we compare the implemented approaches of automatic website classification through two main case studies. In the first case, we evaluate the performance of our classifiers over the text we gathered from the index page of each website to which we refer by depth = 0. In the second case study, we want to know how the classifiers would perform on the index web page of each website and also the gathered information from their neighboring web pages in a +1 radius to which we refer to as depth = 1. In each of our experiments we used a cross validation step and a class majority voting aggregator to get the final website category since we are classifying websites and not web pages. In the following we provide the used datasets, the evaluation metrics and our experimental results.

4.1   Datasets

From the Olfeo's[1] URLs dataset, we selected 10 categories and we consider only the websites in English language. The crawler we designed is made in a way to crawl the target website and also its neighboring web pages per each website. After crawling the data we end-up with a dataset of 96741 web pages for 3368 unique websites, Table 2 sums-up a general view of our dataset by categories and the generated chunks of 500 tokens for each category. Figure 3 shows the data distribution for all datasets showing how the category proportions are similar to the original dataset. We follow by the text extraction from the raw HTML was performed using the same HTML tags as [19], and we additionally extracted text from the metadata tags, which often contained short texts such as the title and description of the web page, with a length ranging from 7 to nearly 100 tokens.

We compare various models for automatic website classification through two case studies. The first case evaluates the performance of classifiers based on text obtained from the index page of each website, while the second case considers both the index page (depth 0) and the information from the surrounding web pages within a radius of +1 (i.e. depth 1), these webpages are obtained from the links inside the index web page where we only consider the first top 50 links to crawl. The objective of these two cases is to determine the effect of including additional information from surrounding web pages on the classifiers performance. Moreover, in order to compare the effectiveness of our proposed Weighted stratified split approach we generate a baseline database and evaluate the models on each of them. For each dataset, 70% of the data is used as training data from which we take another 10% for the validation data and finally the last 30% are used as test data. The datasets we use in this paper are described as below:

1. **Basic Split Baseline Data (BSBD).** To generate this dataset we use the BS on the whole dataset. We split the data (i.e. web pages) following a stratified strategy in order to counter the imbalanced data bias as said in the beginning. It is noteworthy that when depth is 0 there is no need for an aggregation step since we classify only the index web pages in this dataset and no chunking has been performed the web pages were fed as it is.
2. **Frequential Split Approach Dataset (WSSAD).** To generate this dataset we first take the original dataset and generate text chunks of 500 token each, as shown in Table 2. We then perform our proposed WSSA on the resulted chunks of web pages to generate the train and test sets.

The tables present the distribution of websites in the generated train/test sets using BSBD and WSSAD methods. Table 3 shows the number of websites

---

[1] https://www.olfeo.com/ (visited on: 07/07/2022).

for each category in the training and test sets, along with the overall dataset size. Additionally, Table 4a and b provide data distribution details for the BSBD and WSSAD datasets, respectively, showing the distribution of web pages and chunked blocks in the training and test sets for each category.

Table 2. Crawled dataset and chunked blocks

Category	Websites	Web pages	Chunks
tourism_hotel	756	20051	51300
business_services	587	16918	47658
bank_insurance	543	13623	37106
education	367	10327	28010
fashion_beauty	196	7261	17917
cars_motor	194	6481	18572
home_garden_interior	188	6432	15555
escort_services	185	6204	16135
consumer_services	202	5696	14624
counterfeit	150	3748	8865
Size	**3368**	**96741**	**255742**

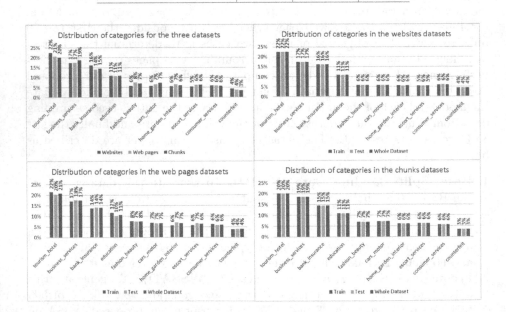

Fig. 3. Data distribution for categories in each dataset

Table 3. Websites for each generated train/test set after BS and WSSA

Category	$BSBD_{tr}$	$BSBD_{te}$	$WSSAD_{tr}$	$WSSAD_{te}$
tourism_hotel	529	227	543	213
business_services	411	176	396	191
bank_insurance	380	163	378	165
education	257	110	257	110
fashion_beauty	137	59	140	56
cars_motor	136	58	133	61
home_garden_interior	132	56	124	64
escort_services	129	56	126	59
consumer_services	141	61	130	72
counterfeit	105	45	104	46
Size	**2357**	**1011**	**2331**	**1037**

Table 4. Data distribution for BSBD and WSSAD

(a) Web pages distribution for train/test sets in BSBD

Category	$BSBD_{tr}$	$BSBD_{te}$
tourism_hotel	6107	13944
business_services	4836	12082
bank_insurance	3905	9718
education	3318	7009
fashion_beauty	2154	5107
cars_motor	1976	4505
home_garden_interior	1590	4842
escort_services	1646	4558
consumer_services	1767	3929
counterfeit	1091	2657
Size	28390	68351

(b) Chunked blocks distribution for train/test sets in WSSAD

Category	$WSSAD_{tr}$	$WSSAD_{te}$
tourism_hotel	35910	15390
business_services	33360	14298
bank_insurance	25974	11132
education	19606	8404
fashion_beauty	12541	5376
cars_motor	13000	5572
home_garden_interior	10885	4670
escort_services	11291	4844
consumer_services	10235	4389
counterfeit	6205	2660
Size	179007	76735

4.2   Evaluation Metrics

In this section we present the main metrics we use to evaluate our models. After establishing the confusion matrix for each experiment. We then measure the accuracy. We then follow with a comparison inter-classifiers over the same datasets with the Cochran's Q test in order to establish that the obtained results are consistently significant.

Cochran's Q Test. Cochran's Q test can be regarded as a generalized version of McNemar's test that can be applied to evaluate multiple classifiers. In a sense, Cochran's Q test is analogous to ANOVA for binary outcomes. To compare more than two classifiers, we can use Cochran's Q test, which has a test statistic Q that is approximately, (similar to McNemar's test), distributed as χ^2 with L1 degrees of freedom, where L is the number of models we evaluate (since L = 2 for McNemar's test, McNemar's test statistic approximates a χ^2 distribution with one degree of freedom). More formally, Cochran's Q test tests the hypothesis that there is no difference between the classification accuracies (i.e. $p_i : H0 = p_1 = p_2 == p_L$.).

Let $\{D_1, \ldots, D_L\}$ be a set of classifiers who have all been tested on the same dataset. If the L classifiers don't perform differently, then the following Q statistic is distributed approximately as chi-square with $L - 1$ degrees of freedom:

$$Q_C = (L - 1) \frac{L \sum_{i=1}^{L} G_i^2 - T^2}{LT - \sum_{j=1}^{N_{ts}} (L_j^2)} \tag{4}$$

Here, G_i is the number of objects out of $N_t s$ correctly classified by $D_i = 1, \ldots L$; L_j is the number of classifiers out of L that correctly classified object $z_j \in Z_{ts}$, where $Z_{ts} = z_1, \ldots z_{N_{ts}}$ is the test dataset on which the classifiers are tested on; and T is the total number of correct number of votes among the L classifiers [4, 12]:

$$T = \sum_{i=1}^{L} G_i = \sum_{j=1}^{N_{ts}} L_j \tag{5}$$

To perform Cochran's Q test, we typically organize the classifiers predictions in a binary $N_{ts} \times L$ matrix. The ijth entry of such matrix is 0 if a classifier D_j has misclassified a data example (vector) z_i and 1 otherwise (if the classifier predicted the class label $l(z_i)$ correctly) [4].

4.3 Classification Results

All the experiments are implemented using Python and run through the super calculator ROMEO[2]. Transformer models were fine-tuned using huggingface library (version 4.29.2). Due to resources limitations we used a max sequence length for Longformer and BigBird of 1024 with a training and validation batch size equal to 4 (low GPU memory) and the learning rate was 1e−5. For BERT and RoBERTa the max sequence length is by default 512, the training batch size was 16 and the validation batch size was 32 and the learning rate for both models was 5e−5. For the rest of the parameters we kept the default ones. All the models were fine-tuned for 40 epochs (Table 5).

---

[2] https://romeo.univ-reims.fr/.

Table 5. Model Fine Tuning Time (with FT for Fine Tuning and IT for Inference Time)

Depth	Clf	BSBD		WSSAD	
		FT (mn)	IT (s)	FT (mn)	Inf (s)
0	**BERT**	15,8	0,0033	14,9	0,0012
	RoBERTa	4,9	0,0032	13,1	0,0012
	Longformer	26,7	0,0208	126	0,0203
	BigBird	54,6	0,0210	498	0,0891
1	**BERT**	48,7	0,0033	216	0,0011
	RoBERTa	48,3	0,0031	216	0,0012
	Longformer	204	0,0206	2880	0,0203
	BigBird	288	0,0207	8640	0,0908

Table 6. Accuracies after MVS

Depth	Clf	BSBD	WSSAD
0	**BERT**	**89,55%**	93,09%
	RoBERTa	88,33%	**93,10%**
	Longformer	89,15%	92,96%
	BigBird	82,77%	91,59%
1	**BERT**	**90,70%**	91,90%
	RoBERTa	89,96%	**92,14%**
	Longformer	87,60%	90,71%
	BigBird	85,42%	86,59%

The results in Table 6 present the accuracies obtained after applying the Majority Voting Strategy (MVS) to aggregate the predictions of classification models. The focus here is on the performance of the models on the Weighted stratified split approach (WSSAD), as compared to the Basic Split Baseline Dataset (BSBD).

Across different depths and classifiers, the accuracies achieved on the WSSAD dataset consistently outperform those obtained on the BSBD dataset. Notably, the accuracies on WSSAD are higher for most combinations of depth and classifier. For instance, considering the results at depth 0, both BERT and RoBERTa models achieve higher accuracies on WSSAD (93.09% and 93.10%, respectively) compared to BSBD (89.55% and 88.33%, respectively). This improvement is also observed for the Longformer and BigBird models, where the accuracies on WSSAD (92.96% and 91.59%, respectively) surpass those on BSBD (89.15% and 82.77%, respectively).

Moving to depth 1, we see a similar trend. BERT and RoBERTa models attain higher accuracies on WSSAD (91.90% and 92.14%, respectively) compared to BSBD (90.70% and 89.96%, respectively). While the Longformer model exhibits a slightly lower accuracy on WSSAD (90.71%) compared to BSBD (87.60%), the BigBird model demonstrates a noteworthy increase in accuracy on WSSAD (86.59%) compared to BSBD (85.42%).

These results highlight the effectiveness of the stratified split approach employed in the WSSAD dataset. By considering the content and context of web page chunks, the WSSAD dataset provides a more comprehensive representation of web pages, enabling the classification models to make more accurate predictions. The consistently higher accuracies obtained on the WSSAD dataset demonstrate its value in improving the performance of classification models for web page classification tasks.

Therefore, the frequential based split approach in the WSSAD dataset showcases its significance in enhancing the accuracy of classification models.

4.4   Cochran's Q Test Results

In our study, we formulate the following hypotheses for the Cochran's Q test:

- **Null Hypothesis (H0):** There are no significant differences in the performances of the classifiers on the classification task. In other words, the classifiers predictions are consistent across instances, and any observed differences are due to random fluctuations.
- **Alternative Hypothesis (H1):** There are significant differences in the performances of the classifiers on the classification task. This suggests that certain classifiers demonstrate superior or inferior performance compared to others, and the observed differences are not solely attributable to chance.

By subjecting our data to the Cochran's Q test, we aim to rigorously assess the significance of these differences and gain a deeper understanding of the relative strengths and weaknesses of the classifiers under consideration. This statistical analysis will enable us to make informed decisions about the most effective classifiers for our task.

The table presented below displays the outcomes of the Cochran's Q tests conducted for all classifiers across each dataset. Our initial focus is on comparing the classifiers across different datasets at varying depths. To ensure the applicability of the Cochran's Q test for classifiers trained on different datasets, we create two new test datasets. Subsequently, we evaluate the fine-tuned BERT and RoBERTa models on these newly generated test datasets. This approach allows us to comprehensively assess the performances of the classifiers, facilitating fair and meaningful comparisons even when dealing with varying training datasets.

Table 7. Cochran's Q test results

(a) Cochran's Q test inter-datasets

Depth	Dataset	Cochran's Q	p-value
0	**BSBD**	45.887	5.99e−10
0	**WSSAD**	50.464	6.36e−10
1	**BSBD**	3.674	0.2988
1	**WSSAD**	131.372	2.97e−15

(b) Cochran's Q test For BERT and RoBERTa

Depth	Dataset	Cochran's Q	p-value
0	**$BSBD_{new}$**	87.38	3.22e−12
0	**$WSSAD_{new}$**	90.55	7.47e−12
1	**$BSBD_{new}$**	85.40	6.06e−13
1	**$WSSAD_{new}$**	140.592	5.31e−21

The results of the Cochran's Q test, as presented in Table 7, provide valuable insights into the performance of classifiers across different datasets and depths.

In the inter-dataset comparison (Table 7a), we observe significant differences in the performances of classifiers between the "BSBD" and "WSSAD" datasets at Depth 0 and Depth 1. At Depth 0, both datasets show a low p-value (5.99e−10 for "BSBD" and 6.36e−10 for "WSSAD"), indicating that there are significant differences in classifier performances between these datasets. Similarly, at Depth 1, the p-value remains low for both datasets (3.674 for "BSBD" and 2.97e−20 for "WSSAD"), further emphasizing significant differences in classifier performances across the two datasets. These findings suggest that the choice of the dataset has a substantial impact on classifier performance, and different datasets may yield varying results.

In the comparison between BERT and RoBERTa on the same dataset (Table 7b), we find significant differences in their performances at both Depth 0 and Depth 1. For both depths, the p-values are much smaller than 0.05, indicating significant variations in classifier performances between the two models. The Cochran's Q test results show that the choice of the model significantly influences the classification accuracy on the given dataset.

Overall, the Cochran's Q test highlights the importance of dataset selection and model choice in the performance evaluation of classifiers. It demonstrates that different datasets and models can lead to notable variations in classifier performances. Therefore, researchers and practitioners should be cautious in their dataset and model selection to make informed decisions when working on natural language processing tasks, ensuring accurate and reliable evaluations of classifiers.

5 Conclusion

One of the most known open issue in the research community is processing large-scale text sequences in many NLP tasks. In this paper, we proposed a novel simple statistical approach, namely Weighted Stratified Split Approach (WSSA), for website classification. We evaluated its performance using popular language models, including BERT, RoBERTa, Longformer and BigBird, on the WSSAD dataset. We compared the results to the baseline dataset (BSBD) and observed that BERT and RoBERTa achieved high accuracies. However, their maximum sequence length limitation hampered their performance on longer web pages.

To address this limitation, we introduced the WSSA split, which divides web pages into stratified chunks, allowing for the retention of contextual information while maintaining a balanced distribution of categories. WSSA approach outperforms Longformer and BigBird models, which struggle with longer texts and complex web page content.

WSSA achieves high accuracies with Longformer and RoBERTa for depth-0 classification tasks and surpasses BigBird for depth-1 classification tasks. However, we acknowledge the slight discontinuities introduced by the chunking process and the dependency of the majority voting strategy on individual model accuracies and noisy chunks. We also notice that the best results are obtained through the combination of index web pages, RoBERTa model and our WSSAD dataset. This result shows how efficient website classification can be done while being low-cost in resources and time consumption unlike other models.

Overall, our study demonstrates the effectiveness of the WSSA split in improving website classification accuracy and overcoming the limitations of BERT and RoBERTa models. These findings have implications for applications such as information retrieval and content filtering. Finally, our future work aims to explore optimizations to the WSSA approach and its performance on other classification tasks and larger datasets.

Acknowledgement. This work is part of the RAPID project METIS which was funded by the French Ministry of the Armed Forces, Defence Innovation Agency (Reference number: 202906117).

References

1. Bartík, V.: Text-based web page classification with use of visual information. In: 2010 International Conference on Advances in Social Networks Analysis and Mining, pp. 416–420. IEEE (2010)
2. Beltagy, I., Peters, M.E., Cohan, A.: Longformer: the long-document transformer (2020)
3. Choromanski, K., et al.: Rethinking attention with performers. arXiv preprint arXiv:2009.14794 (2020)
4. Cochran, W.G.: The comparison of percentages in matched samples. Biometrika **37**(3/4), 256–266 (1950)

5. Dai, Z., Yang, Z., Yang, Y., Carbonell, J., Le, Q.V.: Transformer-XL: attentive language models beyond a fixed-length context. In: Proceedings of the 57th Annual Meeting of the Association for Computational Linguistics, pp. 2978–2988 (2019)
6. Devlin, J., Chang, M.W., Lee, K., Toutanova, K.: BERT: pre-training of deep bidirectional transformers for language understanding. arXiv preprint arXiv:1810.04805 (2018)
7. Espinosa-Leal, L., Akusok, A., Lendasse, A., Björk, K.-M.: Website classification from webpage renders. In: Cao, J., Vong, C.M., Miche, Y., Lendasse, A. (eds.) ELM 2019. PALO, vol. 14, pp. 41–50. Springer, Cham (2021). https://doi.org/10.1007/978-3-030-58989-9_5
8. Janaki Meena, M., Chandran, K., Karthik, A., Vijay Samuel, A.: A parallel ACO algorithm to select terms to categorise longer documents. Int. J. Comput. Sci. Eng. 6(4), 238–248 (2011)
9. Kitaev, N., Kaiser, u., Levskaya, A.: Adaptive attention span in transformers. In: Proceedings of the 2020 Conference on Empirical Methods in Natural Language Processing (EMNLP), pp. 2911–2922 (2020)
10. Kitaev, N., Kaiser, u., Levskaya, A.: Reformer: the efficient transformer. In: Proceedings of the 37th International Conference on Machine Learning, ICML 2020 (2020)
11. Kumar, J., Santhanavijayan, A., Janet, B., Rajendran, B., Bindhumadhava, B.: Phishing website classification and detection using machine learning. In: 2020 International Conference on Computer Communication and Informatics (ICCCI), pp. 1–6 (2020). https://doi.org/10.1109/ICCCI48352.2020.9104161
12. Kuncheva, L.I.: Combining Pattern Classifiers: Methods and Algorithms. Wiley (2014)
13. Liu, Y., et al.: ROBERTa: a robustly optimized BERT pretraining approach. CoRR abs/1907.11692 (2019). http://arxiv.org/abs/1907.11692
14. Meena, M.J., Chandran, K., Karthik, A., Samuel, A.V.: An enhanced ACO algorithm to select features for text categorization and its parallelization. Exp. Syst. Appl. 39(5), 5861–5871 (2012)
15. Mohammad, R.M., Thabtah, F., McCluskey, L.: Intelligent rule-based phishing websites classification. IET Inf. Secur. 8(3), 153–160 (2014)
16. Özel, S.A.: A web page classification system based on a genetic algorithm using tagged-terms as features. Exp. Syst. Appl. 38(4), 3407–3415 (2011)
17. Panwar, A., Onut, I.-V., Miller, J.: Towards real time contextual advertising. In: Benatallah, B., Bestavros, A., Manolopoulos, Y., Vakali, A., Zhang, Y. (eds.) WISE 2014. LNCS, vol. 8787, pp. 445–459. Springer, Cham (2014). https://doi.org/10.1007/978-3-319-11746-1_33
18. Qi, X., Davison, B.D.: Knowing a web page by the company it keeps. In: Proceedings of the 15th ACM International Conference on Information and Knowledge Management, pp. 228–237 (2006)
19. Qi, X., Davison, B.D.: Web page classification: features and algorithms. ACM Comput. Surv. (CSUR) 41(2), 1–31 (2009)
20. Qiu, J., Ma, H., Levy, O., Yih, W., Wang, S., Tang, J.: Blockwise self-attention for long document understanding (2019)
21. Rae, J.W., Potapenko, A., Jayakumar, S.M., Lillicrap, T.P.: Compressive transformers for long-range sequence modelling. In: International Conference on Learning Representations (ICLR) (2020)
22. Reitermanova, Z.: Data splitting. In: WDS, vol. 10, pp. 31–36. MatfyzPress, Prague (2010)

23. Roy, A., Saffar, M., Vaswani, A., Grangier, D.: Efficient content-based sparse attention with routing transformers. arXiv preprint arXiv:2003.05997 (2020)
24. Shabudin, S., Sani, N.S., Ariffin, K.A.Z., Aliff, M.: Feature selection for phishing website classification. Int. J. Adv. Comput. Sci. Appl. **11**(4) (2020)
25. Vaghela, S.D., Patel, P.: Web page classification techniques - a comprehensive survey. IJIRSET **6**, 17472–17479 (2014)
26. Vaswani, A., et al.: Attention is all you need. In: Advances in Neural Information Processing Systems, vol. 30 (2017)
27. Wang, S., Li, Z., Khabsa, M., Fang, H., Ma, H., Tang, J.: Linformer: self-attention with linear complexity. arXiv preprint arXiv:2006.04768 (2020)
28. Ye, Z., Guo, Q., Gan, Q., Qiu, X., Zhang, Z.: BP-transformer: modelling long-range context via binary partitioning. arXiv preprint arXiv:1911.04070 (2019)
29. Zaheer, M., et al.: Big bird: transformers for longer sequences (2020)
30. Zhong, S., Zou, D.: Web page classification using an ensemble of support vector machine classifiers. J. Netw. **6**(11), 1625 (2011)

Automatic Speech Recognition for Portuguese: A Comparative Study

Pedro Henrique Borghi[1,2] (iD), João Paulo Teixeira[2,3](✉) (iD),
and Diamantino Rui Freitas[1] (iD)

[1] Faculty of Engineering, University of Porto (FEUP), 4200-465 Porto, Portugal
{borghi,dfreitas}@fe.up.pt
[2] Research Centre in Digitalization and Intelligent Robotics (CeDRI), 5300 Bragança, Portugal
joaopt@ipb.pt
[3] Associate Laboratory for Sustainability and Technology (SusTEC), Instituto Politécnico de
Bragança, Campus de Santa Apolónia, 5300-253 Bragança, Portugal

Abstract. This paper provides some comparisons of Automatic Speech Recognition (ASR) services for Portuguese that were developed in the scope of the Safe Cities project. ASR technology has enabled bi-directional voice-driven interfaces, and its demand in Portuguese is evident due to the language's global prominence. However, the transcription process has complexities, and a high accuracy depends on the ability of capturing speech variability and language intricacies, while being rigorous in terms of semantics. The study first describes ASR services/models by Google, Microsoft, Amazon, IBM, and Voice Interaction regarding their main features. To compare them, three tests were proposed. Test A uses a small dataset with six audio recordings to evaluate in terms of word hit rate the accuracy of online services, with IBM outperforming others (pt-BR: 93.33%). Tests B and C utilize the Mozilla Common Voice database filtered by a keywords' set to compare online and offline models for Brazilian and European Portuguese regarding accuracy (Ratcliff-Obershelp algorithm), Word Error Rate, Match Error Rate, Word Information Loss, Character Error Rate and Response-Request Ratio. Test B highlights the higher accuracy of Google Cloud (pt-PT: 94.90%) and Azure (pt-BR: 98.11%). Test C showcases the potential of Voice Interaction's real-time application despite its lower accuracy (pt-PT: 78.81%). The tests were carried out using a framework developed using Python 3.x on a Raspberry Pi 4 model B with a server desktop and the REST APIs from the companies' repositories.

Keywords: Automatic Speech Recognition · Portuguese · Language Model · Transcription · Mozilla Common Voice · ASR accuracy

1 Introduction

Automatic Speech Recognition (ASR) systems have revolutionized the way we interact with electronic technology, enabling seamless voice-driven interfaces and applications [1]. ASR technology has undergone significant advancements, with major industry players such as Google, Microsoft, Amazon, and IBM actively exploring its potential. In this

A. I. Pereira et al. (Eds.): OL2A 2023, CCIS 1981, pp. 217–232, 2024.
https://doi.org/10.1007/978-3-031-53025-8_16

paper, a review of available ASR services in the context of the Portuguese language is presented, shedding light on the challenges faced and the progress achieved.

Portuguese, being one of the most widely spoken languages globally, demands no less accurate and efficient ASR models. With approximately 250 million native speakers distributed across Portugal, Brazil, Mozambique, Angola, and many other countries, the need for robust Portuguese ASR systems becomes evident.

The design of ASR models entails a complex interplay of acoustic and linguistic components. High accuracy in this speech-to-text transcription is notoriously challenging to achieve due to several factors. One primary factor lies in the inherent variability of speech signals, including different accents, speaking rates, and background noise. Moreover, the complexity of natural language, with its vast vocabulary and intricate grammar, further amplifies the difficulty in accurate transcription [1, 2].

ASR architectures have evolved over time naturally to address these challenges. Modern ASR systems commonly employ deep learning techniques, such as recurrent neural networks (RNNs) and convolutional neural networks (CNNs). These architectures effectively capture temporal dependencies and hierarchies within the speech signals, improving transcription accuracy. However, high accuracy remains challenging due to the intricacies involved in modelling the nuances of speech and language [1, 2].

In this review, ASR services of major companies were explored, but not only, as a smaller Portuguese one, Voice Interaction, was also considered, by examining their approaches, techniques, and achievements in building robust ASR systems for Portuguese speakers. By evaluating the strengths and limitations of these services, the aim is to provide insights into the current state-of-the-art in ASR technology for Portuguese.

To conduct the analysis, the Mozilla Common Voice database was used, a rich and diverse collection of multilingual speech data, including substantial contributions from Portuguese speakers. Leveraging this comprehensive dataset, the performance and capabilities of various ASR services were explored, considering factors such as accuracy, response time, features, pricing, and model customization. Through this comparative study, the authors aim to contribute to the understanding of the advancements, challenges, and potential future directions in the field of automatic speech recognition for the Portuguese language, while helping to speed up the search for ASR services.

The study was developed under the scope of project Safe Cities – Innovation for Building Urban Safety, which, among others, had the aim to elaborate, experiment and deploy a voice processing module using Speech-to-Text, Text-to-Speech, and Speaker Identification for emergency calls scenarios.

2 Speech Processing Service Suppliers

To experience speech transcription and synthesis services available commercially, a list of suppliers is surveyed identifying the provided services, with a focus on available models in the Portuguese language.

2.1 Google Cloud

The transcription service provided by Google Cloud Platform[1] has three basic modes: synchronous recognition Representational State Transfer (REST) and Google Remote Procedure Call (gRPC), asynchronous recognition (REST and gRPC) and streaming recognition (gRPC). In synchronous mode, the audio file, with a maximum duration of one minute, is sent to the Application Programming Interface (API), which processes it completely and then returns the text. In asynchronous mode, audio of a maximum of 480 min is sent to the API that can periodically return the text while processing the audio. In streaming recognition, the audio is sent through a stream bidirectional gRPC used for real-time recognition, provisional results are sent and updated while the transmission is active. API calls are counted every 15 s, rounded up to 15 s at the end of the period.

Synchronous Recognition. Although this method is of the blocking type, the API takes approximately 15 s to process 30 of audio, which may take longer in case of low audio quality. Still, it can be considered as suitable for real-time application. Before executing the API call, the configuration parameters according to Table 1 must be set: sampling rate [Hertz], language (Best Current Practice 47 (BCP-47); Table 2), maximum alternatives, profanity filter, speech context, phrases, boost, timestamps, model, diarization, channel count, automatic scoring, and word confidence level.

Table 1. Audio Formats Supported by Google Cloud API [3].

Codec	Name	Losses	Usage notes
MP3	MPEG Audio Layer III	Yes	Beta feature
FLAC	Free Lossless Audio Codec	No	16-bit or 24-bit for streams
LINEAR16	Linear PCM	No	16-bit linear PCM. The header must contain the sampling frequency
MULAW	μ-law	Yes	8-bit PCM encoding
AMR	Adaptive Multi-Rate Narrowband	Yes	Sampling frequency must be equal to 8 kHz
AMR_WB	Adaptive Multi-Rate Wideband	Yes	Sampling frequency must be equal to 16 kHz
OGG_OPUS	Opus encoded audio frames in an Ogg container	Yes	Sampling frequency must be 8 kHz, 12 kHz, 16 kHz, 24 kHz or 48 kHz
SPEEX_WITH_ HEADER_BYTE	Speex wideband	Yes	Sampling frequency must be equal to 16 kHz
WEBM_OPUS	WebM Opus	Yes	Sampling frequency must be 8 kHz, 12 kHz, 16 kHz, 24 kHz or 48 kHz

---

[1] https://console.cloud.google.com/.

In conjunction with the configuration, the audio file is provided either directly (pointing to a file on local storage) or indirectly by passing the Uniform Resource Identifier (URI) address of a file present in Google Cloud Storage. In the first case, the file is first sent to the cloud and then processed. For gRPC request, the audio must be Protocol Buffer version 3 (Proto3) compatible and be provided as binary. For REST request, audio must be JavaScript Object Notation (JSON) compliant and be provided as Base64-encoded.

Table 2. Google Cloud STT API resources available for Portuguese [4].

BCP-47	Model	Automatic Punctuation	Diarization	Boost	Word-Level confidence	Profanity Filter	Spoken punctuation
pt-BR	Command and search		✔	✔		✔	✔
pt-BR	Default		✔	✔		✔	✔
pt-BR	Enhanced phone call	✔	✔	✔	✔	✔	✔
pt-BR	Phone call	✔	✔	✔	✔	✔	✔
pt-PT	Command and search			✔		✔	✔
pt-PT	Default			✔		✔	✔

The limit for each API request using local files is 10 MB. For files present in Google Cloud Storage, there is no size limit. However, there is a general limit on the number of requests per minute, which is 900, and processing per day, 480 h of audio. Using adaptation in speech models, the sentence limit per request is 5000, the maximum character limit is 100,000 and the maximum character limit is 100. These limits are shared across all IP addresses and applications of a single Speech to Text (STT) project. It is still possible to request extraordinary quotas from the company as needed [5].

The API returns the audio containing the transcription results and the billing time. The results present the recognition alternatives containing the complete text, the confidence level for the best hypothesis and the list of words in the text with the respective configured characteristics (time stamps, confidence level, etc.). It also presents the marking of channel; the final recognition time in the audio; and the language code.

Streaming Recognition. Streaming transcription requests happen in a bidirectional way, where consecutive pieces of audio are sent, and provisional excerpts of the respective transcript are received. At the end of the transmission, a final text is returned, which corresponds to the best hypothesis of all audios. In other words, as more content is presented throughout the broadcast, the context is enriched, and the word alternatives become more appropriate.

Unlike synchronous recognition where a single request is made, multiple API calls are required here. The first takes only the configuration information. The following only batches the audio in bytes. The configuration parameters are general characteristics (contains the same configuration parameters presented in synchronous recognition), single sentence, and partial results.

As a continuous feedback to the streaming recognition, the API sends: the transcription hypotheses ordered by accuracy; an end-of-audio indication, i.e. when it is not, the hypotheses correspond to partial results and may change over time; stability, a probability that the hypotheses will change (parameter different from the confidence level of the hypothesis); the relative duration to the audio beginning; channel numbering in case of multichannel transcription; the language code BCP-47; and billing time.

2.2 IBM

IBM's[2] speech-to-text transcription service can be accessed through APIs that communicate with IBM Watson. Synchronous and asynchronous acknowledgments via HTTP REST interface and streaming via WebSocket interface are available. The transcription models offered are divided into two generations: In the so-called old generation with broadband and narrowband models and in the current generation, with multimedia and telephony models. For broadband and multimedia models, the minimum audio sampling frequency required is 16 kHz while in narrowband and telephony models is 8 kHz. In general, current generation models provides better yields and transcription accuracy [6].

In addition to the text, the service can return different aspects of the audio, all contained in a response with JSON format and 8-bit Unicode Transformation Format (UTF-8) characters. The communication interface also allows the user to specify different parameters of the sent and request audio, such as service metrics, and linguistic customization and acoustic models. In the case of the Portuguese language, it is limited to Brazilian Portuguese models, which are: Broadband, Narrowband, Telephony, and Telephony + Low Latency. All of these require sampling frequency greater than 8 kHz and have linguistic, grammar and acoustic customization, except for Broadband, which requires higher sampling frequency ($\geq$16 kHz), and the latter, which doesn't support acoustic customization [7].

The process of sending audio to the API is limited to a maximum of 100 MB and a minimum of 100 B per request. The system automatically identifies the ends of the audio and in the case of multiple channels, aligns them all to a mono channel for transcription. In synchronous communication mode, only final result is returned while partial results can be obtained using the WebSocket interface. It is even possible to send an audio stream through the same HTTP interface using pieces of the audio as it arrives. Although the small batches shipment, the return is received after the last piece is finished. The service is completed when no more than 15 s of audio is sent within a 30 s period or when no speech is detected within 30 s. The formats supported by both the HTTP and WebSocket interfaces are shown in Table 3.

According to the information provided by IBM on their website, there are several advantages to using the WebSocket interface instead of HTTP. A major advantage is the reduction of communication latency, since the service sends the transcription results directly to the client, while in HTTP, the process goes through four different requests

---

[2] https://www.ibm.com/cloud.

Table 3. Summary of supported audio types [8].

Format	Losses	Content type specification	Required parameters	Optional Parameters
A-law	Yes	Yes	Sampling Frequency	None
Basic Audio	Yes	Yes	None	None
FLAC	No	No	None	None
G. 729	Yes	No	None	None
LINEAR 16	No	Yes	Sampling Frequency	Channels; Endianess
MP3/MPEG	Yes	No	None	None
mu-law	Yes	Yes	Sampling Frequency	None
Ogg	Yes	No	None	Codec: opus or vorbis
WAV	Yes/No	No	None	None
WebM	Yes	No	None	Codec: opus or vorbis

and connections. Another significant advantage is the possibility of establishing a single authentication for an indefinite period, while in HTTP, for each request it is necessary to perform a new authentication.

Synchronous and Streaming Recognition. The API request format contains the following parameters: audio, format (Table 3), template, language customization identifier, acoustic customization identifier, base model version, customization weight, inactivity interval, keywords, keyword threshold, maximum alternatives, threshold of alternative words, word confidence level, timestamps, profanity filter, smart formatting, speaker labels, grammatical model, redaction, audio metrics, end-of-sentence silence time, end-of-sentence separation of transcription, speech detection sensitivity, background audio suppression, and low latency.

Language customization offers the possibility to expand and specify the vocabulary that the model can recognize, once the base model is trained for generic uses. When creating such a model, it must provide examples relating to the desired domain, either by listing words or sentences. In addition, it is possible to create a grammatical model. Its main function is to limit the vocabulary according to the grammatical characteristics provided, making the search domain of the service smaller and with faster responses. In the customized acoustic model, audio segments recorded in the environment and in the desired human conditions must be provided to be integrated into the base model, such as distance from the microphone, users of the transcription service and the place of use. The training the language model takes a few seconds, while the acoustic model takes a time proportional to the audios sent.

2.3   Amazon Web Services (AWS)

Batch and Streaming Transcription. AWS[3] speech-to-text conversion service is based on creating and executing transcription jobs managed by its online platform. Transcriptions can be performed over audio files uploaded to AWS storage or streaming. In both cases, the parameterization of the service can be performed by API through the boto3 library for Python. The supported audio formats are shown in Table 4, with the most recommended being lossless [9]. Regarding sampling frequency, values from 8 kHz can be used for low fidelity and from 16 kHz to 48 kHz for high fidelity.

Table 4. Audio Formats Supported by AWS streaming and batch transcription service [9].

Format	Losses	Batch	Streaming
FLAC	No	Yes	Yes
MP3	Yes	Yes	No
MP4	Yes	Yes	No
Ogg	Yes	Yes	Yes
WebM	Yes	Yes	No
AMR	Yes	Yes	No
WAV	No	Yes	No
LINEAR16	No	-	Yes

Among the languages supported by the service are European and Brazilian Portuguese. Associated with each language there are several specific features that can be activated to integrate the models (see Table 5). Both variations are available in batch transcription mode, but only the Brazilian Portuguese model supports streaming. The digit transcription feature automatically converts the speech of numbers into their respective symbols and formats, such as times, dates, and fractions. Acronyms can be more easily recognized when indicated within a custom model. However, support for training customizable models in Portuguese is unavailable yet, so acronyms are transcribed when the paused pronunciation of separate letters occurs. The redaction feature, when enabled, automatically identifies, and hides sensitive information such as credit card numbers and passwords. Also, for batch transcripts it is possible to request analysis of interactions between models and input, such as time stamps, sentiment analysis, categorization, problem detection, input characteristics and sensitive data.

For all languages supported by the AWS transcription service, input audio channel identification, vocabulary customization, language identification, speaker differentiation, and vocabulary filtering features are available [11].

Regarding usage limits, AWS sets a list of standard parameters such as number of custom language models per account, number of concurrent transcription jobs, maximum and minimum audio file duration (14,400 s and 500 ms), maximum audio file size (2 GB), custom vocabulary size (50 KB), etc. [12].

---

[3] https://aws.amazon.com/.

Table 5. Characteristics associated with the language for the Portuguese models [10].

BCP-47	Speech Input	Digits	Acronyms	Model language custom	Redaction	Call analysis
pt-BR	Batch only	No	Yes	No	No	Yes
pt-PT	Batch, streaming	No	Yes	No	No	Yes (only batch)

2.4 Microsoft Azure

Microsoft Azure's speech processing services is the speech-to-text conversion, capable of performing speech recognition over audio files or broadcasts in real time. This service, available online on the Azure platform[4], is used in Microsoft applications such as Cortana and in Office products. In addition, it can be associated with other speech processing services such as text-to-speech translation and synthesis.

Based on intensive training on Microsoft databases, the available standard models can also be adapted according to acoustic, language and pronunciation characteristics. Thus, ambient noise conditions and specific vocabulary can be considered, enabling the acquisition of better results. Customizations options available for European Portuguese model are related to text and pronunciation, while for Brazilian Portuguese are related to audio as well [13].

Azure speech-to-text processing services allows to perform real-time speech-to-text conversions from streaming or local file, batch-file speech-to-text conversion, multi-device conversation transcription and translation, speech recognition, speaker identification and speaker differentiation in real-time multi-speaker calls, creation and management of custom models, and pronunciation evaluation. To use all the features mentioned, Azure provides the Speech Command Line Interface (CLI) tools, Speech Software Development Kit (SDK), Speech Studio and Speech API.

By default, the audio format should be WAV, sampled at 8 kHz or 16 kHz, mono and PCM. However, Speech CLI and Speech SDK can make use of the GStreamer tool to handle other audio formats, decompressing and allowing to be sent as pure PCM. These formats are MP3, Opus/Ogg, FLAC, ALAW (WAV container), MULAW (WAV container) and any other unknown formats.

2.5 Voice Interaction

Audimus Server. Voice Interaction's Audimus Server solution contains an offline speech recognizer that can receive any type of media file, generating a set of acoustic and linguistic data that can be used in various applications, such as automatic subtitling and speaker identification for example (see Fig. 1). Transcription results can be obtained in a variety of text formats. According to [14], the audio analysis and conversion time is less than its duration, being suitable for construction of real-time continuous processing

---

[4] https://azure.microsoft.com/.

applications. The models offered have different training vocabularies, and it is also possible to adapt them to a local context. Furthermore, the models are available in European, Brazilian and African Portuguese. An interesting feature is the automatic alignment of the transcript to the original audio, allowing a practical identification of words.

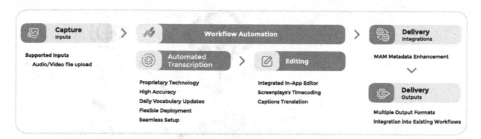

Fig. 1. Illustration of the Audimus Server basic processes [14].

2.6 Mozilla Common Voice Database

Mozilla Common Voice is an initiative to help teach machines how real people speak. Common Voice is a publicly available voice dataset powered by the voices of volunteer contributors around the world.

Currently, most voice datasets are owned by companies, which stifles innovation. These voice datasets also represent other English-speaking white males. It means that voice-enabled technology simply doesn't work in many languages. Each input in the dataset consists of a single MP3 and the corresponding text file. Many of the 18,243 h recorded in the dataset also include demographic metadata such as age, gender, and accent, which can help train the accuracy of speech recognition engines. The dataset currently consists of 14,122 validated hours in 87 languages [15]. For Portuguese language, 112 h of speech files are currently available, including 84 h validated. There are 2038 different voices, mostly male (75%) and aged between 19 and 29 Years (39%).

3 Methodology and Results

As a vital part of the transcription device designed in the context of the Safe Cities project, laboratory tests were carried out with the objective of performing a comparison among the main transcription services available commercially with a focus on available models in the Portuguese language.

To carry out the laboratorial tests, the team set up a Raspberry Pi 4 Model B 8 GB RAM running Raspberry Pi OS (64-bits), with an USB microphone, internet connection via Wi-Fi, touch screen interface and loudspeakers, as Fig. 2 illustrates. Further, it was noticed that a heatsink case was needed on extensive tests due to the increased Raspberry Pi power dissipation. The algorithms developed were implemented using Python 3.x on Visual Studio Code software and stored on GitHub platform with copy on a local device.

The REST APIs were used by getting Python SDKs from the providers repositories at their webpages or directly via PIP, the Package Installer for Python. Therefore, it was possible to communicate with the online transcription services to carry out the experimental tests.

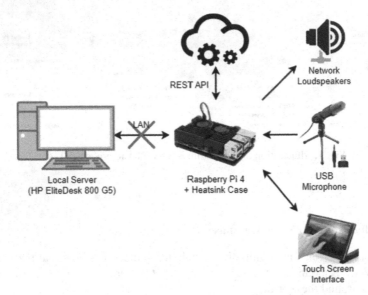

Fig. 2. Functional diagram used on experimental phase.

At a later stage, Voice Interaction's transcription system were explored at the Local Server, running Windows 10 Pro (64-bits) OS, but without integrating with the Raspberry Pi.

Test A. In order to experience speech transcription and synthesis services from the most popular companies on the market, a set of tests was carried out. In addition to validate the performance of services, it was possible to build an organizational system of the authentication mechanisms and of the dependencies services update to standardize the entries to receive the audio files with the same format and under the same conditions. Also, the output text was normalized to be compared with the reference and later integration into the message to be sent via the network.

The set of audios used was obtained through recordings from different mobile phones. The set is composed by voices from six volunteers with characteristics described in Table 6. Recording conditions did not restrict participants in terms of recording environment, speech rate, or voice volume. The main goal was to evaluate the performance of transcription services when dealing with every-day and unconditioned speech recordings. Therefore, the recordings collected contained diverse noises, such as blowing on the microphone, clipping, hiss and sounds of urban activity. The recordings showed changes in the voice volume due to a change in the speaker's position in relation to the microphone. Despite this, measurements of the signal-to-noise ratio was considered only a note from the perception of the audio quality.

Table 6. Characteristics of the subjects whose voices compose the audio set of the test A.

Subject	Gender	Age	Recording Condition	Duration [s]
A	Male	26	Poor	30
B	Female	26	Good	30
C	Male	26	Poor	25
D	Male	20	Good	27
E	Female	22	Good	34
F	Female	55	Good	36

Each volunteer read a text that contains phrases related to emergency scenarios. The text is spoken in Portuguese:

"Atenção! Por favor, dirijam-se à saída mais próxima seguindo as indicações refletivas de segurança. Carreguem consigo apenas o necessário, evitando ter as mãos ocupadas. Mantenham a calma e cuidado para não obstruir a passagem dos demais. Se afastem do fogo e de estruturas comprometidas. Não utilizem os elevadores. Estejam atentos às sinalizações e aos profissionais de segurança. Ajudem crianças e pessoas com movimentação debilitada."

The recordings were then used in the speech-to-text transcription services of Google Cloud, IBM, AWS and Azure without any type of pre-processing, that is, without treatment of the presence of noise, cuts or gains and attenuations. The texts obtained were compared by visual inspection to the reference by the following criteria:

1. a transcribed word is considered correct if it fully corresponds to the reference or if it presents divergence only in gender or number (singular/plural);
2. words added in the transcript do not weigh negatively or positively, that is, they are disregarded;
3. words similar to the reference where there is no great loss of meaning (e.g., signs and signals) are considered correct;
4. the score is disregarded in all cases;
5. words are considered wrong when they diverge from the reference and there is a loss of meaning in the sentence.

According to the criteria, the accuracy (Acc) for the test A is defined as the ratio of correct words (CW) and the maximum ($TotW = 65$),

$$Acc = \frac{CW}{TotW} 100 \qquad (1)$$

Then, the comparative report between the results from reference text and texts obtained from the audio transcripts was obtained. The overall results are presented in Fig. 3 while Table 7 presents the average results.

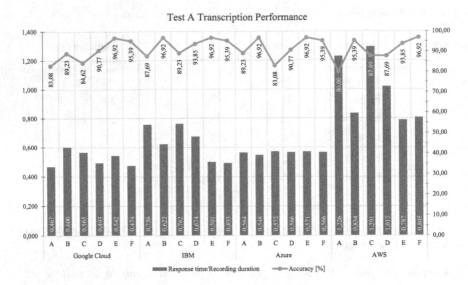

Fig. 3. Transcription performance measures for Test A.

From Fig. 3 a similar performance of the four services in terms of accuracy can be observed, except in case of the IBM service which presented superior performance when comparing inner subjects. Additionally, in the cases of poor-quality recordings (subjects A and C), the hit rate is always lower than other recordings, indicating a certain sensitivity degree to noise conditions.

Table 7. Average transcription performance by company tried in the test A.

Company	Response time/ Recording duration	Accuracy [%]	Correct Words in 65
Google Cloud	0.524	90.00	58.50
IBM	0.635	93.33	60.67
Azure	0.565	92.05	59.83
AWS	0.993	90.26	58.67

Regarding the response time of the services, except for AWS, all companies satisfy the basic condition of real-time processing. The main justification for AWS does not attend this requirement is the fact of transcription dynamics request to send the file to AWS Cloud storage adding time to responses to confirm each API operation.

Test B. Test B includes the use of data present in the CommonVoice (CV) platform of Mozilla considering only the Portuguese recordings in version 7.0 (latest version when acquired). Of the total of 94,265 recordings, 1500 were selected, which had at least one of the words related with some safety scenarios presented in Table 8.

Unlike the first test, where a paragraph reading is used, the CV recordings are one or two short sentences, with an average duration of approximately 5 s. As in test A, no treatment of noise and adverse events of the recordings were applied since it is intended to observe once again the resilience of the services under these conditions.

Table 8. Set of Portuguese words used to filter the CV data used in the test B.

Atenção	Sinalização	Acidente	Devagar	Escadas	Fila	Indicações
Calma	Segurança	Cautela	Sinais	Saída	Por favor	Fogo
Cuidado	Iluminação	Alerta	Incêndio	Ajuda	Chamas	Perigo

As a criterion to determine the accuracy in test B, the Ratcliff-Obershelp algorithm was used [16], which uses the number of matching characters (K) between two strings with lengths S_1 and S_2 to measure their similarity (SIM).

$$SIM = \frac{2K}{S_1 + S_2} \tag{2}$$

In addition, common measures for evaluating transcription systems, [17], were used, where H is the number of hits, S is the number of substitutions, D is the number of deletions, I is the number of insertions, N_1 is the number of words from reference sentence, N_2 is the number of words from STT output, $N = \max(N_1, N_2)$ and CER is calculated as WER taking each character as it was a different word, hence the subscript c:

- WER: Word Error Rate

$$WER = \frac{S + D + I}{H + S + D} = \frac{S + D + I}{N_1} \tag{3}$$

- MER: Match Error Rate

$$MER = \frac{S + D + I}{H + S + D + I} = \frac{S + D + I}{N} = 1 - \frac{H}{N} \tag{4}$$

- WIL: Word Information Loss

$$WIL = 1 - \frac{H^2}{N_1 N_2} \tag{5}$$

- CER: Character Error Rate

$$CER = \frac{S_c + D_c + I_c}{H_c + S_c + D_c} \tag{6}$$

The tests were carried out on models for Brazilian and European Portuguese (when available) from the companies Google Cloud, IBM, AWS and Microsoft Azure. The summary of the results obtained in this second test is presented in Table 9, with the better ones highlighted in bold. Another common metrics for ASR models like Phoneme Error Rate and Speaker Diarization Error Rate were not explored because there was just one speaker per audio file, as well as the manipulation depth of available services is not enough for phoneme level exploration.

Table 9. Results of the performance of the transcription models of the test B.

Company	BCP-47	Accuracy [%]	WER [%]	MER [%]	WIL [%]	CER [%]	Response/ Duration
IBM	pt-BR	92.87	18.23	17.06	24.18	8.11	0.722
AWS	pt-BR	95.44	14.64	13.90	20.25	6.43	3.772
Google Cloud	pt-BR	96.27	11.84	11.42	15.54	5.30	0.282
Azure	pt-BR	**98.11**	6.76	6.35	9.68	2.76	0.490
Google Cloud	pt-PT	**94.90**	15.50	14.93	21.50	7.11	0.279
Azure	pt-PT	94.17	20.65	18.19	26.02	8.49	0.478

The results obtained at this stage indicates that the services of the companies tested so far: Google Cloud, IBM, AWS and Azure, have similar accuracy performances (maximum difference of 5.24%), despite the Google and Azure stand out from the rest. In addition, Google and Azure generally presented an average superiority in performance for the parameters explored. Moreover, the availability of models in European Portuguese, customization, potential speaker identification service, well established text-to-speech service, and the possibility to containerize the services, are strong indicatives that Google and Azure are the most suitable suppliers in this preliminary analysis.

Test C. The test of the offline speech to text engine from Voice Interaction (VI) was conducted taking the same database used for testing online services previously i.e., CommonVoice from Mozilla at version 7.0 for Portuguese. The filtered version was applied to the Voice Interaction STT system by placing these sentences on the engine folder at the Local Server. The system automatically converts the audio files into text files, placing these in a different folder.

By analysing the results using the same metrics as before i.e., WER (Word Error Rate), MER (Match Error Rate), WIL (Word Information Loss), CER (Character Error Rate) and Accuracy (via Ratcliff-Obershelp algorithm), the data for Voice Interaction from Table 10 were obtained. Compared with Azure's online service, it is clear the gap of efficiency between these transcription services. From Table 10, the WER for VI indicates that approximately half of the words in the sentences have some error, fact reinforced by MER which indicates a mismatch between reference and result words around 45%. Although the overall accuracy form VI shown a difference over 15% compared to Azure's, it is possible to say that this system sustains a response over duration ratio close to 1, what demonstrates the potential of following a possible real time application, even if that is not a main requirement for the present scenario.

Table 10. Comparison between Azure's (online) and VI's (offline) speech to text services.

Company	BCP-47	Accuracy [%]	WER [%]	MER [%]	WIL [%]	CER [%]	Response/ Duration
Azure	pt-PT	94.17	20.65	18.19	26.02	8.49	0.478
Voice Interaction	pt-PT	78.81	51.12	45.45	58.21	26.47	1.079

It is interesting to point out that the VI engine was not retrained or acoustic adapted to better fits our emergency vocabulary and recording environment from the database which led the performance to lower levels when compared with specific models.

4 Conclusion

In conclusion, the laboratory tests conducted to compare the main transcription services available commercially for the Portuguese language have provided valuable insights. The tests were carried out using a Raspberry Pi device equipped with the necessary components and using Python 3.x. The REST APIs provided by the transcription suppliers were utilized for the experimental tests without any acoustic or vocabulary adaptations, nor requesting retraining to the companies.

In Test A, recordings from different mobile phones were used to evaluate the performance of speech transcription services provided by Google Cloud, IBM, AWS, and Microsoft Azure. The results showed that the services had similar accuracy, with IBM outperforming the others.

In Test B, data from the CommonVoice of Mozilla were used, and transcription models for Brazilian and European Portuguese were evaluated. The Ratcliff-Obershelp algorithm was employed to determine the accuracy, and measures such as WER, MER, WIL, and CER were also considered. The results indicated that the models from Google Cloud and Microsoft Azure exhibited higher accuracy compared to IBM and AWS.

Test C involved the evaluation of Voice Interaction's offline speech-to-text engine using the same database as in Test B. The results showed a significant gap in efficiency between these two transcription services. While Voice Interaction had a lower accuracy and higher error rates compared to Microsoft Azure, it demonstrated the potential for real-time applications.

Future work includes expanding the database of recorded speech segments by integrating other databases, testing additional suppliers, and exploring different parameterizations and signal conditions. Overall, the findings suggest that Google Cloud and Microsoft Azure are the most suitable providers based on the evaluated criteria. It is worth noting that the performance of the Voice Interaction engine could be improved through retraining request or by adapting the model for specific domains and environments.

Acknowledgements. The authors are grateful to the Foundation for Science and Technology (FCT, Portugal) for financial support through national and community funds (FSE), in the form of a doctoral scholarship with reference 2022.12371.BD. The authors are also grateful to the Safe Cities – Innovation for Building Urban Safety project for financial support in the form of a research grant with reference POCI-01-0247-FEDER-041435. The authors are also grateful to the Foundation for Science and Technology (FCT, Portugal) for financial support through national funds FCT/MCTES (PIDDAC) to CeDRI (UIDB/05757/2020 and UIDP/05757/2020) and SusTEC (LA/P/0007/2021).

References

1. Medeiros, E., Corado, L., Rato, L., Quaresma, P., Salgueiro, P.: Domain adaptation speech-to-text for low-resource European Portuguese using deep learning. Fut. Internet **15**(5), 159 (2023). https://doi.org/10.3390/fi15050159
2. de Lima, T.A., Da Costa-Abreu, M.: A survey on automatic speech recognition systems for Portuguese language and its variations. Comput. Speech Lang. **62**, 101055 (2020). https://doi.org/10.1016/J.CSL.2019.101055
3. Introduction to audio encoding | Cloud Speech-to-Text Documentation | Google Cloud. https://cloud.google.com/speech-to-text/docs/encoding. Accessed 12 Jul 2022
4. Language support | Cloud Speech-to-Text Documentation | Google Cloud. https://cloud.google.com/speech-to-text/docs/languages. Accessed 12 Jul 2022
5. Working with quotas | Documentation | Google Cloud. https://cloud.google.com/docs/quota#requesting_higher_quota. Accessed 12 Jul 2022
6. Speech to Text - IBM Cloud API Docs. https://cloud.ibm.com/apidocs/speech-to-text?code=python#introduction. Accessed 12 Jul 2022
7. Language support for customization | IBM Cloud Docs. https://cloud.ibm.com/docs/speech-to-text?topic=speech-to-text-custom-support. Accessed 12 Jul 2022
8. Supported audio formats | IBM Cloud Docs. https://cloud.ibm.com/docs/speech-to-text?topic=speech-to-text-audio-formats. Accessed 12 Jul 2022
9. Data input and output - Amazon Transcribe. https://docs.aws.amazon.com/transcribe/latest/dg/how-input.html. Accessed 12 Jul 2022
10. Supported languages and language-specific features - Amazon Transcribe. https://docs.aws.amazon.com/transcribe/latest/dg/supported-languages.html. Accessed 12 Jul 2022
11. Amazon Transcribe features - Amazon Transcribe. https://docs.aws.amazon.com/transcribe/latest/dg/feature-matrix.html. Accessed 12 Jul 2022
12. Guidelines and quotas - Amazon Transcribe. https://docs.aws.amazon.com/transcribe/latest/dg/limits-guidelines.html. Accessed 12 Jul 2022
13. Language support - Speech service - Azure Cognitive Services | Microsoft Docs. https://docs.microsoft.com/en-us/azure/cognitive-services/speech-service/language-support?tabs=speechtotext#speech-to-text. Accessed 12 Jul 2022
14. VoiceInteraction | Audimus.Server. https://www.voiceinteraction.ai/platforms/audimus_server.html. Accessed 12 Jul 2022
15. Common Voice. https://commonvoice.mozilla.org/pt/datasets. Accessed 12 Jul 2022
16. Pattern Matching: the Gestalt Approach | Dr Dobb's. https://www.drdobbs.com/database/pattern-matching-the-gestalt-approach/184407970?pgno=5. Accessed 19 Sept 2022
17. Morris, A.C., Maier, V., Green, P.: From WER and RIL to MER and WIL: improved evaluation measures for connected speech recognition. In: ICSLP 8th International Conference on Spoken Language Processing, INTERSPEECH 2004, Korea (2004)

Comparative Analysis of Windows for Speech Emotion Recognition Using CNN

Felipe L. Teixeira[1,2] (iD), Salviano Pinto Soares[2,4,5] (iD), J.L. Pio Abreu[6,7] (iD),
Paulo M. Oliveira[2,8] (iD), and João P. Teixeira[1,3(✉)] (iD)

[1] Research Centre in Digitalization and Intelligent Robotics (CEDRI), Instituto
Politécnico de Bragança, Campus de Santa Apolónia, 5300-253 Bragança, Portugal
{felipe.lage,joaopt}@ipb.pt
[2] Engineering Department, School of Sciences and Technology, University of
Trás-os-Montes and Alto Douro (UTAD), Quinta de Prados, 5000-801 Vila Real,
Portugal
{salblues,oliveira}@utad.pt
[3] Associate Laboratory for Sustainability and Technology (SusTEC), Instituto
Politécnico de Bragança, Campus de Santa Apolónia, 5300-253 Bragança, Portugal
[4] Institute of Electronics and Informatics Engineering of Aveiro (IEETA), University
of Aveiro, 3810-193 Aveiro, Portugal
[5] Intelligent Systems Associate Laboratory (LASI), University of Aveiro, 3810-193
Aveiro, Portugal
[6] Hospital da Universidade de Coimbra, 3004-561 Coimbra, Portugal
pioabreu@icloud.com
[7] Faculty of Medicine, University of Coimbra, 3000-548 Coimbra, Portugal
[8] INESC-TEC, Universidade de Trás-os-Montes e Alto Douro (UTAD), Vila Real,
Portugal

Abstract. The paper presents the comparison of accuracy in the Speech
Emotion Recognition task using the Hamming and Hanning windows
for framing the speech and determining the spectrogram to be used as
input of a convolutional neural network. The detection of between 4
and 10 emotional states was tested for both windows. The results show
significant differences in accuracy between the two window types and
provide valuable insights for the development of more efficient emotional
state detection systems. The best accuracy between 4 and 10 emotions
was 64.1% (4 emotions), 57.8% (5 emotions), 59.8% (6 emotions), 48.4%
(7 emotions), 47.8% (8 emotions), 51.4% (9 emotions), and 45.9% (10
emotions). These accuracy is at the state-of-the art level.

Keywords: Speech Emotion Recognition · Hamming · Hanning · CNN

1 Introduction

This work was carried out as part of the "GreenHealth -Digital Strategies Based
on Biological Assets to Improve Well-being and Promote Green Health" project,

A. I. Pereira et al. (Eds.): OL2A 2023, CCIS 1981, pp. 233–248, 2024.
https://doi.org/10.1007/978-3-031-53025-8_17

where the identification of emotional states is a key part of the diagnosis of schizophrenia [1]. Understanding the emotional state of an individual plays a crucial role in several areas, such as psychology. Speech is an essential tool in human communication and has been recognised as a valuable source of information about the subject's emotional state. Thus, the study and investigation of prosodic [2] [3]and acoustic speech characteristics can yield valuable results about human emotions, contributing to more accurate clinical diagnoses, advances in technology development, and more effective social interactions. It is generally not possible to quantify human emotions, but it is essential to know how to interpret them in order to maintain social interactions. The best way to interpret emotions is through facial expressions or voice [4], however a study conducted by [5] concludes that human hearing is more effective in detecting emotions in a conversation than vision when faced with facial expressions. The methodology for this conclusion was simple: the subjects recorded the reading of a text, and afterwards, the voice was changed, concluding that if the voice was high and fast, the story was more exciting, and if it was slower and monochordic, it was more boring. Emotions in speech can vary depending on the style of the speaker, however, speech signals are more susceptible to emotional influences and acoustic interference than other communications [6]. It is possible to identify some emotional "nuances" regardless of the language spoken. In the study by [7] they concluded that the voice transmits 24 non-verbal emotions (tested in several countries and different cultures). The evolution of machine learning techniques and tools has enabled significant advances in analysing and identifying emotions. This study tested convolutional neural networks (CNN) to explore the relationship between emotional state and speech spectrogram using public databases (EmoDB, Emovo, Ravdess, and Savee). The main reason for choosing these tools is that they are effective in dealing with sequential data (speech) due to their ability to learn hierarchical representations through temporal dependencies (in speech, the information obtained in each frame is crucial to detecting emotional states). On the other hand, these tools also show great performance in several tasks, such as natural language processing and complex pattern recognition. Speech Emotion Recognition (SER) may be considered a branch of Automatic Speech Recognition (ASR), exploiting the same kind of signal, feature extraction processes, and potential application of diverse machine learning techniques, such as deep learning (DL) architectures, that are also applied in the field of Natural Language Processing (NLP). DL approaches developed in ASR or NLP, like several models of convolutional neural networks (CNN) and recurrent neural networks (RNN), are evaluated for SER practical applications [8]. Some existing approaches use convolutional neural networks (CNN) to learn salient affective features for speech emotion recognition [9], another approach is presented by [10] that proposes a concatenation of CNN and Recurrent Neural Networks without using traditional parameters and is responsible for creating a spectrogram type image. A SER scheme was also presented in [11] where they compare three procedures to adapt deep neural networks (DNN) with layers of LSTM and CNN, where the acoustic parameters (3D Log-Mel spectra) are defined as inputs and each class corresponds to the emotion. Another model for emotion recognition is shown in [12] which consists of a DNN with convolutional and LSTM layers. A CNN with three blocks with several convolutional layers, a pooling layer (for parameter extraction), two additional dense layers, and a softmax layer as output, fed with spectrograms obtained from audio, is presented by [13]. With a similar approach, [14] proposed using paralleled recurrent networks, extracting features learned from LSTM and computed Mel spectrograms. They applied a CNN to extract features from the image, so with two sets of features for the same utterance applied to a softmax classifier, they obtained the respective emotions. Another identical approach is presented by [15] where RNN and DL fed by spectrograms and MFCCS are proposed. The DL network is composed of 4 layers (input, output, and 2 hidden layers) fully connected to each other, and already the recurrent model is formed by gated recurrent units (GRU). Since the pre-trained nets are not specific for all cases, it is necessary to retrain them, so transfer learning was applied. Transfer learning has become a popular method in speech and audio processing to make use of existing deep learning models that have been trained on large datasets. It has been shown to be effective in improving model performance across a range of tasks and domains, both in terms of training time and total accuracy. When there is a lack of data available for the objective task, this strategy is extremely beneficial [16].

The features merely have greater significance in emotion recognition since the features for emotions differ from each other. According to what was studied in [17] the parameters that can be promising for the detection of the emotional state through speech are the linear prediction cepstral coefficients (LPCC), linear spectral features (LSF), pause rate, fundamental frequency (F0), intensity (I), formants (F1, F2, and F3), duration of pauses and sentences, and Mel-frequency cepstral coefficients (MFCCs). The work of [18] also states that various parameter sets such as LPC, LPCC, and MFCC contribute significantly to emotion recognition [18]. On the other hand, [19] highlights the importance of the raw spectrogram, stating that it is more promising since the "manually created" features are uncorrelated. In this work, this approach was experimented. This paper is organised into six chapters. In the present chapter, the Introduction, is provided a theoretical approach to the problem under study. In the subsequent chapter, is contextualised the state of the art. The third chapter describes the implemented procedures, while the fourth chapter provides detailed insights into the utilised databases and their relevant characteristics. The fifth chapter presents the achieved results. Finally, in the Conclusion chapter, we summarise the main findings and discuss their implications.

2   Related Works

The detection of emotional states is an important field in areas such as psychiatry, and the amount of work aiming to identify emotions has been growing in recent years. There are several possible approaches, the most common being facial expression or speech analysis.

There are several possible approaches, the most common being facial expression or speech analysis. However, an alternative approach gaining attention is the use of spectrograms for emotional state detection. The spectrograms offer a visual representation of sound frequency content over time, providing valuable insights into emotional cues, and are widely used as input for CNN.

Liang et al. [20] manually extracted the colour, direction, and brightness maps of the spectrogram. These features were normalised by taking the average of a small sub-matrix. Further, PCA was used to remove redundancy from the feature set. There is another work by Ozseven [21] in which the spectrogram feature was extracted using texture analysis. The texture analysis identifies the structural characteristics of an image. The texture is described as a spatial variation of the pixel intensity. These features are complementary to the traditional acoustic features. Hence, these features significantly improve the result when combined with the acoustic features. However, these features can be extracted automatically using a deep neural network.

Combining spectrograms and CNN allowed [22] to state that they are robust parameters for emotion identification. In [23] also combined spectrograms with deep convolutional neural networks (DCNN), and in both cases, the implemented systems improved when compared with other parameters. Combining spectrograms and CNN allowed [22] to claim that they are robust parameters for emotion identification, in [23] also combined spectrograms with deep convolutional neural networks (DCNN) and claimed in both cases that the implemented systems improved when compared with other parameters.

In the work of [24], they combined CNN and LSTM and concluded that implementing the spectrogram allowed for a 6.62% increase in emotion identification. In [25], they applied spectrograms extracted from sentences to CNN (GoogLeNet), used the IEMOCAP database, and obtained a 68% rate for the classification of 4 emotions with the 10-fold cross-validation method (9 parts of the dataset for training, and tested with 1 part at a time). In [24] adopted a 2D CNN and LSTM network to learn high-level features from log-mel spectrograms. They used the EmoDB and IEMOCAP dataset, and obtained the maximum 95.9% accuracy, but the databases were tested individually.

In [23] proposes a systematical approach to implement an effectively emotion recognition system based on deep convolution neural networks (DCNNs) that achieves about 40% classification accuracy, they used IEMOCAP dataset (80% train set). In the work of [26] the authors present an implementation to detect emotion recognition based on DNN applied directly to spectrograms, they used the IEMOCAP dataset to test and obtained 68%. In the same way, the authors of [27] also used the same approach with CNN, and their accuracy was 84.3% with Emo-DB dataset (75% of subjects to train and 5 folds cross validation). Based on phonemes sequence and the spectrogram as inputs of CNN improve the accuracy in IEMOCAP dataset to detect emotional state, in work developed by [28], the authors experimented three methods and obtained an overall accuracy of 73.9%, if they used only spectrogram the accuracy was 71.3%.

3   Research Design and Procedures

To achieve the objectives proposed by this work, it was necessary to design a methodology applied to the problem in question, starting with the starting point of any work related to artificial intelligence algorithms, the dataset. Subsequently, the methods and algorithms used to classify emotional states will be discussed and finally, the methodology itself will be presented.

3.1   Dataset

As a starting point for any artificial intelligence application, the dataset to be used is undoubtedly one of the main weights for its success. In this way, obtaining a dataset that guarantees security in the application of AI methods is one of the processes that require more attention from the programmer, in the end, it is from this that all the learning of the algorithm will emerge, allowing a good generalization or on the other hand not guaranteeing sufficient characteristics for correct functioning. As detecting emotional states through voice has been studied for several years, obtaining this type of dataset is facilitated, with some databases already available online. In this way, the first step is to take into account the research and collection of publicly available datasets. For this purpose, 4 datasets were used (see Table 1).

One of the most used in the area of SER is EMO-DB, a German database containing 535 audios of varying duration, recorded by 5 male and 5 female professional speakers. These audios are categorized into seven emotions. To ensure consistent speech quality, all audio files were recorded at a 16 kHz sampling rate, saved in wav format, with mono-channel and 16 bits per sample [29].

EMOVO is composed of voices of up to 6 actors who played 14 sentences simulating 6 emotional states (disgust, fear, anger, joy, surprise, sadness) plus the neutral state. These emotions are the well-known Big Six found in most literature on emotional speech. The recordings were made with professional equipment in the Fondazione Ugo Bordoni laboratories [30].

RAVDESS is also very often used in developed work. This dataset includes 1440 audio files, recorded by 12 male and 12 female actors speaking English scripts with 8 different emotions. All recorded audio files have a 48 kHz sample rate and a 16-bit resolution [29].

SAVEE is also utilized in this study and was recorded by 4 males at the Centre for Vision, Speech and Signal Processing (CVSSP), University of Surrey. Each speaker was asked to speak 120 phonetically balanced English sentences in 7 emotional categories, in a total of 480 utterances [29].

In Table 1 the "Ang" is anger, "Dis" is disgut, "Hap" is happiness, "Sad" is sadness, "Neu" is neutral, "Fe" is "fear", "Sur" is surprise, "Ca" is calm, "Bor" is boredom, "Anx" is anxiety, "Sub" is subjects, and "Ut." means utterances.

3.2   Features

An SER system is an outcome of two stages: (i) a front-end processing unit that extracts the features from the data and (ii) a back-end unit that classi-

Table 1. Databases applied and their information.

Dataset	# Sub.	Language	Age	Emotional State (# Sentences)										# Ut.
				Ang	Dis	Hap	Sad	Neu	Fe	Sur	Ca	Bor	Anx	
Emo-DB [31]	10	German	29.7	127	46	71	62	79	0	0	0	81	69	535
Emovo [32]	6	Italian	23–30	84	84	84	84	84	84	84	-	-	-	588
Ravdess [33]	24	English	20–30	192	192	192	192	96	192	192	192	-	-	1440
Savee [34]	4	English	29.5	60	60	60	60	120	60	60	-	-	-	480
Total	44	-	-	463	382	407	398	379	336	336	192	81	69	3043

fies the speech utterances into emotion categories. The dimensionality reduction techniques are an intermediate step between the front-end and back-end processing units, applied to reduce the classifiers' high computational and storage complexities due to a high number of dimensions. These techniques also eliminate redundant features and preserve decorrelated features. There are two ways of dimensionality reduction: (i) feature selection and (ii) feature transformation [35] [36].

The speech signals were segmented into frames of 256 samples (Sampling frequency of 44.1 kHz) with a 50% overlap, corresponding to windows of about 6 ms duration, producing a broadband spectrogram.

The spectrogram of a sequence is the magnitude of time-dependent Fourier Transform (FT) versus time, known as the Short-Time Fourier Transform (STFT). It describes the spectral changes under a joint time-frequency domain [37], in others words the spectrum is a sound representation in time domain, taking consideration of its decomposition into different partials and their respective intensities [38], or spectrogram is a time-frequency representation of the signal. The time-varying short-time Fourier transforms (STFT) magnitude spectrum is displayed as an image [35]. The STFT was used to transform speech signals in the spectrogram, In Fig. 2 it is possible to see two spectrograms of happy and anger emotional states. The critical parameters for STFT are:

– Hanning (Hann) Window
  • Divide the signal into 256-sample segments and window each segment with a periodic Hann window;
  • the coefficients of a Hann window are generated by Eq. 1;
  • Specify 128 samples of overlap between adjoining segments. This length is equivalent to 50% of the window length;
  • Specify 256 DFT points and centre the STFT at zero frequency (with the frequency expressed in Hertz);

$$w(n) = 0.5(1 - \cos\left(2\pi\frac{n}{N}\right)), 0 \leq n \leq N \qquad (1)$$

– Hamming Window
  • Divide the signal into 256-sample segments and window each segment with a periodic Hann window;
  • the coefficients of a Hamming window are generated by Eq. 2;

- Specify 128 samples of overlap between adjoining segments. This length is equivalent to 50% of the window length;
- Specify 256 DFT points and centre the STFT at zero frequency (with the frequency expressed in Hertz);

$$w(n) = 0.54(0.46 - \cos\left(2\pi\frac{n}{N}\right)), 0 \le n \le N \tag{2}$$

Figure 1 illustrates the smooth and symmetrical variation of the Hanning and Hamming windows.

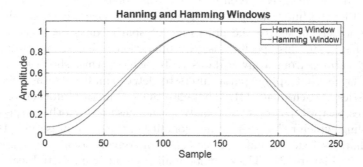

Fig. 1. Characteristics of Hanning and Hamming windows.

Other windows could be used, such as Blackman, Kaiser, and rectangular. As the rectangular window is the absence of a window that typically produces worse results, the other windows present similarities to the windows applied in this work. However, in other work comparing windows, the windows used here tend to be more advantageous [39, 40].

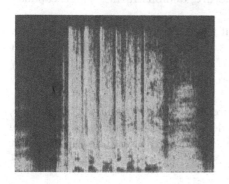 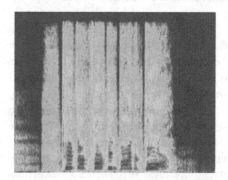

(a) Spectrum extracted from the happy emotional state

(b) Spectrum extracted from the anger emotional state

Fig. 2. Spectral difference between two emotional states.

The implementation of this work involves a CNN capable of autonomously extracting features, which takes the spectrogram as input and is expected to obviate the need for any additional features.

3.3 Convolutional Neural Networks CNN

Several algorithms have proven capable of carrying out this type of identification, machine learning algorithms such as support vector machines (SVM), Gaussian mixture models (GMM), K-nearest neighbor (KNN), or artificial neural networks (ANN). However, this algorithm is being used increasingly with computational advances and the advances presented by convolutional neural networks.

Inspired by the functioning of the human brain's visual cortex, this type of network is largely linked to the processing of spatial data, such as images or spectrograms, as in this specific case. Its operation is based on automatically extracting features from a given dataset. To achieve this, she resorts to convolutional layers that apply spatial filters to detect small patterns and specific characteristics of each image [41]. These layers can identify information regarding textures, shapes, colors, etc. Usually, after these are another type of layer called pooling, which reduces the dimensionality of the data, preserving the most relevant characteristics. Usually at the "end" of convolutional processes are the fully-connected layers [29]. These combine all previously extracted features and perform the final classification. Usually, these layers are connected with the final neurons corresponding to the number of classes in the problem.

Emphasizing that all these processes are optimized for each iteration in the training set by adjusting the weights of the filters and the connections between the layers using optimization algorithms, such as gradient descent. This allows the network to adapt to the training data and improve its generalization ability, that is, its ability to correctly classify new spectrograms that were not presented during training.

During the last few years, exceptional performances have been seen in various tasks related to images by this type of structure, demonstrating a high capacity to capture spatial hierarchies in the data.

Considering that spectrograms represent the temporal and frequency content of audio signals as two-dimensional images, using structures such as CNN for their classification becomes a viable choice, essentially considering their ability to learn local patterns in lower layers and progressively combine them to identify complex patterns in higher layers.

Another reason we chose these structures was their translation invariance, meaning they can identify patterns regardless of their specific location in the spectrogram. Emotion-related spectrogram features can manifest in different temporal and frequency positions, and CNNs can effectively extract these features regardless of their exact position.

In this way, a CNN was created and trained from scratch. To choose the structure to use, several combinations were tested. It was noticed that smaller networks converged faster and presented better results, in this way, the chosen structure is constituted only by a convolutional layer. The images are introduced at the original scale (875,656,3) and resized to our network's input dimensions (224,224,3). After this resize, the convolutional layer comes into play, consisting of 64 filters of dimensions (3,3) that produce 64 feature maps of the initial image. Then a max-pooling layer is used to highlight the most present feature in the patch. Finally, a fully-connected layer is used with the softmax function to classify the probability of each of the categories in percentage. The architecture implemented and described here is summarised in Fig. 3.

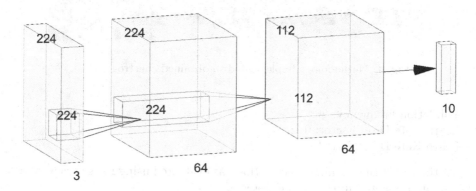

Fig. 3. Developed architecture.

3.4 Methodology

The applied methodology in this work was based on using four databases (EmoDB, Emovo, Ravdess and Savee). To implement CNN, the entire sound spectrogram was extracted with two types of windows (Hamming and Hann). After extraction, a matrix was built with the total number of shuffled samples (all the subjects of the 4 databases see Table 1) and divided into two sub-matrices: a training matrix with 80% of the samples and a test matrix with 20%.

The experiments demonstrated here were carried out to develop a simplified network that could achieve good results while reducing the required computational power and processing time. The use of four databases aimed to extend the amount of data, but mainly to obtain different environments at the moment of recording and the largest amount of emotions catalogued. These experiments are an initial approach to the development of a tool to detect emotional states in a natural context. In Fig. 4 it is possible to see the approach until obtaining the final spectrogram corresponding to each subject.

After obtaining the spectrograms, the convolutional network was trained using the following training parameters:

- Initial Learn Rate: 0.0001;
- Batch Size: 32;
- Max Epochs: 20;

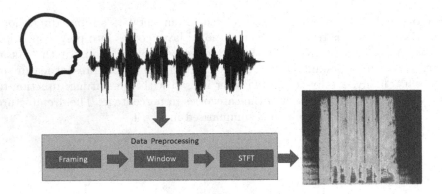

Fig. 4. Methodology implemented to obtained spectrogram.

- Validation Frequency: 20;
- Learn Rate Drop Factor: 0.1;
- Learn Rate Drop Period: 10;

At the end of the training process, this was evaluated using its accuracy, with the results presented in the next chapter.

4   Results

The spectrograms of all sound files were extracted with two types of windows (Hamming and Hann) according to what was mentioned in Subsect. 3.2 and organised by the respective emotions. They were applied to a pre-trained convolutional network, and the results shown in Table 4 were obtained. Table 3 presents the number of subjects used for training and testing according to the number of categories implemented.

In Table 4 the quantities of categories were filled according to the number of subjects in each category, that is, for the 4 categories, the 4 categories with more subjects were used, for the 5 categories, the 5 categories with more samples were used, and so on until the totality of categories (emotions) was used. The values correspond to the accuracy of the test set (20% of the subjects) and are expressed in percentage (%).

According Table 4, the hanning windows generally show the best results.

The best values are mostly reached with the Hann window to classify 4, 5, 6, 7 and 9 emotions. The maximum accuracy varies between 64.1% for the 4 classes, and 48.4% for the 7 classes, to classify nine emotional states the obtained accuracy was 51,4%. For the classification of eight and ten emotional states, the Hamming window presents the best results (47.8% and 45,9% correspondly, being 2.5% and 4% higher). The analysis of the values obtained can be done with the help of the graph shown in Fig. 5 (Table 2).

In this work, the results are presented by the accuracy measure. On the one hand, obtaining other measures such as F1 score, recall, and precision would be

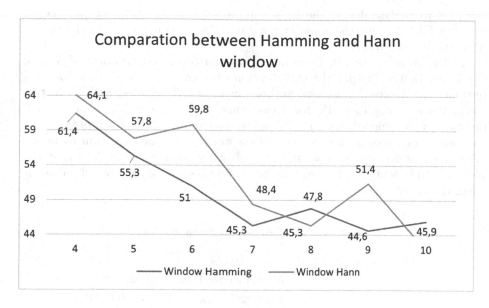

Fig. 5. Obtained accuracy in set train with CNN.

Table 2. Subset formation with the emotional states.

Subset	S4	S5	S6	S7	S8	S9	**S10**
Emotional Categories	Anger Disgust Happiness Sadness	S4 ¦ Neutral	S5 + Fear	S6 + Surprise	S7 + Calm	S8 + Boredom	S9 + Anxiety

Table 3. Number of utterances used in each set.

	# of emotions	S4	S5	S6	S7	S8	S9	S10
Set	**Train**	1318	1622	1891	2160	2314	2379	2434
	Test	330	405	473	540	579	595	609
	Total	1648	2027	2364	2700	2893	2974	3043

Table 4. Obtained results with different windows for classification in test set.

Window	Subsets of Categories (emotional states)						
	S4	S5	S6	S7	S8	S9	S10
Hamming	61.4	55.3	51	45.3	47.8	44.6	45.9
Hann	64.1	57.8	59.8	48.4	45.3	51.4	41.9

complex to analyse due to the large and varied number of classes (between 4 and 10). Furthermore, the accuracy measure allows comparison with the results obtained in other works.

In the state of the art, there are works that obtained accuracy of 68 [25, 26] up to 73.9 % [28] for the classification of 4 emotions, for 5 emotions [23] obtained 40 %. For 7 emotions, authors such as [27] achieved 84.3 %, in this work, the accuracy of 64.1% for 4 emotions, 59.8 % for 6, and 51.4 % for 9 emotions was achieved, The Table 5 shows the values of accuracy obtained in this work compared with other developed works, using spectrogram as input. Although our results are close to those of other authors, we believe that the method implemented can be equally promising because if only one database is used, the accuracy increases.

Table 5. State of Art comparasion results.

# Emotions	This Work	Others Works			
		Acc	Author	Tool	Dataset
4	64.1	73.9	[28]	CNN	IEMOCAP
		68	[25]		
		68	[26]	LSTM	
5	57.8	40	[23]	deepCNN	
6	59.8	-			
7	48.4	84.3	[27]	deepCNN	Emo-DB
8	47.8	-			
9	51.4	-			
10	45.9	-			

The results of the emotion analysis reveal accuracy percentages ranging between 64.1% (S4), 57.8% (S5), 59.8% (S6), 48.4% (S7), 47.8% (S8), 51.4% (S9), and 45.9% (S10). These values highlight the importance of the chosen window type, evidencing its significant impact on the model's performance. Notably, our results reached levels comparable to the state of the art for some of the emotions analysed.

5   Conclusion

European (non-tonal) languages were used in this work. To do this type of analysis for tonal languages, the model must be trained with datasets of these languages.

The use of the different windows influences the classification of the implemented system. Being that the most promising window in this study was the

Hann for emotional state detection in the majority, it presented superior results up to 8.8% from 4 to 7 emotional categories.

For 4 and 7 emotions, this work achieved an accuracy below the state of the art. However, for five emotions, our results were superior. For the remaining emotions, we did not find any papers analyzed in the state of the art, which makes a direct comparison with our results impossible.

Comparing with the state of the art, our values are justified due to the number of subjects used in each classification (see Table 3), and the different nature of the data since the recording environment of the database, although controlled, was not exactly the same.

The initial experiment of using the full VGG16 layers was carried out however, the training time was unbearable, and with the reduction of the layers, the model was simplified and the time of each training was considerably reduced.

The next step in the evolution of this work will be to combine what has been demonstrated here with the acoustic parameters studied in [17].

Acknowledgements. This research was funded by the European Regional Development Fund (ERDF) via the Regional Operational Program North 2020, GreenHealth-Digital strategies in biological assets to improve well-being and promote green health, Norte-01-0145-FEDER-000042; Foundation for Science and Technology (FCT, Portugal) support from national funds FCT/MCTES (PIDDAC) to CeDRI (UIDB/05757/2020 and UIDP/05757/2020) and SusTEC (LA/P/0007/2021).

The authors are grateful for financial support from UTAD.

The authors would also like to thank João Mendes for his collaboration throughout the work.

References

1. Lopes, R.P., et al.: Digital technologies for innovative mental health rehabilitation. Electronics (Switzerland) **10**(18), 1–15 (2021)
2. Teixeira, J.P., Freitas, D.: Segmental durations predicted with a neural network. In: 8th European Conference on Speech Communication and Technology, EUROSPEECH 2003, pp. 169–172 (2003)
3. Teixeira, J.P., Freitas, D., Braga, D., Barros, M.J., Latsch, V.: Phonetic events from the labeling the European Portuguese database for speech synthesis, FEUP/IPB-DB. In: 7th European Conference on Speech Communication and Technology, EUROSPEECH 2001, Scandinavia, pp. 1707–1710 (2001)
4. Teixeira, F.L., Teixeira, J.P., Soares, S.F.P., Abreu, J.L.P.: F0, LPC, and MFCC analysis for emotion recognition based on speech. In: Pereira, A.I., Košir, A., Fernandes, F.P., Pacheco, M.F., Teixeira, J.P., Lopes, R.P. (eds.) Optimization, Learning Algorithms and Applications, OL2A 2022. Communications in Computer and Information Science, vol, 1754, pp. 389–404. Springer, Cham (2022). https://doi.org/10.1007/978-3-031-23236-7_27
5. Kraus, M.W.: Supplemental material for voice-only communication enhances empathic accuracy. Am. Psychol. **72**(7), 644–654 (2017). http://supp.apa.org/psycarticles/supplemental/amp0000147/amp0000147_supp.html

6. Hamsa, S., Shahin, I., Iraqi, Y., Damiani, E., Nassif, A.B., Werghi, N.: Speaker identification from emotional and noisy speech using learned voice segregation and speech VGG. SSRN Electron. J. **224**, 119871 (2022). https://doi.org/10.1016/j.eswa.2023.119871

7. Aucouturier, J.J., Johansson, P., Hall, L., Segnini, R., Mercadié, L., Watanabe, K.: Covert digital manipulation of vocal emotion alter speakers' emotional states in a congruent direction. Proc. Natl. Acad. Sci. U.S.A. **113**(4), 948–953 (2016)

8. de Lope, J., Graña, M.: An ongoing review of speech emotion recognition. Neurocomputing **528**, 1–11 (2023). https://doi.org/10.1016/j.neucom.2023.01.002

9. Huang, Z., Dong, M., Mao, Q., Zhan, Y.: Speech emotion recognition using CNN. In: Proceedings of the 2014 ACM Conference on Multimedia, MM 2014, pp. 801–804 (2014)

10. Qamhan, M.A., Meftah, A.H., Selouani, S.A., Alotaibi, Y.A., Zakariah, M., Seddiq, Y.M.: Speech emotion recognition using convolutional recurrent neural networks and spectrograms. In: Canadian Conference on Electrical and Computer Engineering, August 2020 (2020)

11. Ando, A., Mori, T., Kobashikawa, S., Toda, T.: Speech emotion recognition based on listener-dependent emotion perception models. APSIPA Trans. Sig. Inf. Process. **10**, e6 (2021)

12. Pandey, S.K., Shekhawat, H.S., Prasanna, S.R.: Attention gated tensor neural network architectures for speech emotion recognition. Biomed. Sig. Process. Control **71**(PA), 103173 (2022). https://doi.org/10.1016/j.bspc.2021.103173

13. Anvarjon, T., Mustaqeem, Kwon, S.: Deep-Net: a lightweight CNN-based speech emotion recognition system using deep frequency features. Sensors (Switzerland) **20**(18), 1–16 (2020)

14. Jiang, P., Fu, H., Tao, H., Lei, P., Zhao, L.: Parallelized convolutional recurrent neural network with spectral features for speech emotion recognition. IEEE Access **7**, 90368–90377 (2019)

15. Praseetha, V.M., Vadivel, S.: Deep learning models for speech emotion recognition. J. Comput. Sci. **14**(11), 1577–1587 (2018)

16. Guizzo, E., Weyde, T., Tarroni, G.: Anti-transfer learning for task invariance in convolutional neural networks for speech processing. Neural Netw. **142**, 238–251 (2021)

17. Teixeira, F.L., Costa, M.R., Abreu, J.P., Cabral, M., Soares, S.P., Teixeira, J.P.: A narrative review of speech and EEG features for Schizophrenia detection: progress and challenges. Bioengineering **10**(4), 1–31 (2023)

18. Mannepalli, K., Sastry, P.N., Suman, M.: Emotion recognition in speech signals using optimization based multi-SVNN classifier. J. King Saud Univ. Comput. Inf. Sci. **34**(2), 384–397 (2022). https://doi.org/10.1016/j.jksuci.2018.11.012. https://linkinghub.elsevier.com/retrieve/pii/S1319157818307158

19. Mirsamadi, S., Barsoum, E., Zhang, C.: Automatic speech emotion recognition using recurrent neural networks with local attention. In: IEEE International Conference on Acoustics, Speech, and Signal Processing, ICASSP 2017, pp. 2227–2231 (2017). https://doi.org/10.1016/j.specom.2019.09.002

20. Liang, R., Tao, H., Tang, G., Wang, Q., Zhao, L.: A salient feature extraction algorithm for speech emotion recognition. IEICE Trans. Inf. Syst. **E98D**(9), 1715–1718 (2015)

21. Özseven, T.: Investigation of the effect of spectrogram images and different texture analysis methods on speech emotion recognition. Appl. Acoust. **142**, 70–77 (2018)

22. Mao, Q., Dong, M., Huang, Z., Zhan, Y.: Learning salient features for speech emotion recognition using convolutional neural networks. IEEE Trans. Multimedia **16**(8), 2203–2213 (2014)
23. Zheng, W.Q., Yu, J.S., Zou, Y.X.: An experimental study of speech emotion recognition based on deep convolutional neural networks. In: 2015 International Conference on Affective Computing and Intelligent Interaction, ACII 2015, pp. 827–831 (2015)
24. Zhao, J., Mao, X., Chen, L.: Speech emotion recognition using deep 1D & 2D CNN LSTM networks. Biomed. Sig. Process. Control **47**, 312–323 (2019). https://doi.org/10.1016/j.bspc.2018.08.035
25. Li, P., Song, Y., McLoughlin, I., Guo, W., Dai, L.: An attention pooling based representation learning method for speech emotion recognition. In: Proceedings of the Annual Conference of the International Speech Communication Association, INTERSPEECH 2018, September 2018, pp. 3087–3091 (2018)
26. Satt, A., Rozenberg, S., Hoory, R.: Efficient emotion recognition from speech using deep learning on spectrograms. In: Proceedings of the Annual Conference of the International Speech Communication Association, INTERSPEECH 2017, August 2017, pp. 1089–1093 (2017)
27. Badshah, A.M., Ahmad, J., Rahim, N., Baik, S.W.: Speech emotion recognition from spectrograms with deep convolutional neural network. In: Proceedings of the 2017 International Conference on Platform Technology and Service, PlatCon 2017, pp. 1–5 (2017)
28. Yenigalla, P., Kumar, A., Tripathi, S., Singh, C., Kar, S., Vepa, J.: Speech emotion recognition using spectrogram & phoneme embedding. In: Proceedings of the Annual Conference of the International Speech Communication Association, INTERSPEECH 2018, September 2018, pp. 3688–3692 (2018)
29. Alluhaidan, A.S., Saidani, O., Jahangir, R., Nauman, M.A., Neffati, O.S.: Speech emotion recognition through hybrid features and convolutional neural network. Appl. Sci. (Switzerland) **13**(8), 4750 (2023)
30. Costantini, G., Iadarola, I., Paoloni, A., Todisco, M.: EMOVO corpus: an Italian emotional speech database. In: Proceedings of the 9th International Conference on Language Resources and Evaluation, LREC 2014, pp. 3501–3504 (2014)
31. Burkhardt, F., Paeschke, A., Rolfes, M., Sendlmeier, W., Weiss, B.: A database of German emotional speech. In: 9th European Conference on Speech Communication and Technology, May 2014, pp. 1517–1520 (2005)
32. Costantini, G., Iaderola, I., Paoloni, A., Todisco, M.: EMOVO corpus: an Italian emotional speech database. In: Proceedings of the Ninth International Conference on Language Resources and Evaluation, LREC 2014, Reykjavik, Iceland, May 2014, pp. 3501–3504. European Language Resources Association (ELRA) (2014). http://www.lrec-conf.org/proceedings/lrec2014/pdf/591_Paper.pdf
33. Livingstone, S.R., Russo, F.A.: The Ryerson audio-visual database of emotional speech and song (RAVDESS): a dynamic, multimodal set of facial and vocal expressions in North American English. PLoS ONE **13**(5), e0196391 (2018). https://doi.org/10.1371/journal.pone.0196391
34. Haq, S., Jackson, P.: Machine audition: principles, algorithms and systems. In: Multimodal Emotion Recognition, pp. 398–423. IGI Global, Hershey, August 2010
35. Shah Fahad, M., Ranjan, A., Yadav, J., Deepak, A.: A survey of speech emotion recognition in natural environment. Digit. Sig. Process. Rev. J. **110**, 102951 (2021). https://doi.org/10.1016/j.dsp.2020.102951

36. Silva, L., Bispo, B., Teixeira, J.P.: Features selection algorithms for classification of voice signals. Procedia Comput. Sci. **181**(2020), 948–956 (2021). https://doi.org/10.1016/j.procs.2021.01.251
37. Singh, V., Prasad, S.: Speech emotion recognition system using gender dependent convolution neural network. Procedia Comput. Sci. **218**, 2533–2540 (2023). https://doi.org/10.1016/j.procs.2023.01.227. https://linkinghub.elsevier.com/retrieve/pii/S1877050923002272
38. Rossetti, D.: Projetando o espectro do som no espaço: imagens-movimento de parciais e grãos sonoros. Orfeu **5**(1), 571–594 (2020)
39. Fernandes, J., Teixeira, F., Guedes, V., Junior, A., Teixeira, J.P.: Harmonic to noise ratio measurement - selection of window and length. Procedia Comput. Sci. **138**, 280–285 (2018). https://www.sciencedirect.com/science/article/pii/S1877050918316739. cENTERIS 2018 - International Conference on ENTERprise Information Systems/ ProjMAN 2018 - International Conference on Project ANagement / HCist 2018-International Conference on Health and Social Care Information Systems and Technologies, CENTERIS/ProjMAN/HCist 2018
40. Fernandes, J.F.T., Freitas, D., Junior, A.C., Teixeira, J.P.: Determination of harmonic parameters in pathological voices-efficient algorithm. Appl. Sci. (Switzerland) **13**(4), 2333 (2023)
41. Abbaschian, B.J., Sierra-Sosa, D., Elmaghraby, A.: Deep learning techniques for speech emotion recognition, from databases to models. Sensors (Switzerland) **21**(4), 1–27 (2021)

Exploring the Role of OR/MS in Cancer Research

A. Teixeira[1,2](✉) [ID] and R. Almeida[1,2] [ID]

[1] University of Trás-os-Montes e Alto Douro, Quinta de Prados, 5001-801 Vila Real, Portugal
{ateixeir,ralmeida}@utad.pt
[2] Mathematics Centre CMAT, Pole CMAT – UTAD, Vila Real, Portugal

Abstract. This study aims to explore and analyze the significant role of Operations Research/Management Science (OR/MS) in the field of cancer research. The purpose of this work is to identify and highlight the various applications, methodologies, and contributions of OR/MS techniques in advancing cancer research, as well as to establish how OR/MS can effectively contribute to the development of innovative strategies, optimization of treatment protocols, decision-making processes, and overall improvement in cancer treatment.

Fifteen papers with an extensive diversity of motivations were explored. Optimization of radiation therapy treatment plan, cancer prevention and personalized cancer therapy were some of the objectives of these works. Robust optimization, multi-objective optimization, Mixed Integer Programming, simulation and optimal control are some of the OR/MS techniques applied to cancer analysis.

Keywords: OR/MS · Methods · Modeling · Cancer research

1 Introduction

Cancer has been the subject of attention by scientists for a long time. In 1855 a major discovery was made when the cellular nature of cancer was established. Scientists proposed that cancer originated from abnormal growth and division of cells within the body [1], thus, making room for further investigations into the underlying mechanisms of cancer formation and progression. Another key finding was the introduction of tissue staining techniques in [2], that allowed to visualize cancerous tissues under the microscope, leading to the identification of distinct cellular characteristics associated with cancer. Furthermore, in the late 1800s, improvements in surgical techniques and anesthesia, allowed to explore radical approaches to remove cancerous tumors [3].

Nonetheless, at the beginning of the 20th century, cancer was still a poorly understood disease. Physicians struggled to differentiate between different types of cancer, and treatment options were limited. However, in the early 1900s, several pivotal developments took place laying the foundation for the modern field of cancer research. Works like the ones developed by [4–9] allow us to perceive the contributions made during the early 1900s in this area. Namely, the rise of radiation therapy as a potential treatment option, with researchers like Marie Curie [4], the discovery of a transmissible form of

A. I. Pereira et al. (Eds.): OL2A 2023, CCIS 1981, pp. 249–268, 2024.
https://doi.org/10.1007/978-3-031-53025-8_18

cancer in chickens, which provided early insights into the viral nature of certain cancers, was described in [5]; the effects of surgical removal of tumors in experimental animals, contributing to analyze the tumor growth and the significance of surgical interventions were investigated by [6]; the discoveries concerning the altered metabolism of cancer cells, emphasizing the glucose consumption increase and the role of cellular respiration in cancer, presented in [7]; the concept of chromosomal abnormalities as a possible origin of cancer analyzed by [8]; and, the investigation of [9] on cancer immunotherapy and the use of immune cells to combat cancer, among others.

While the progress made during the early 1900s was groundbreaking, cancer research still faced numerous challenges. Funding and resources were limited, and the interdisciplinary collaboration that characterizes modern cancer research was only in its infancy.

Mathematics plays an important role in cancer research. Works like the ones of [10–16] represent significant early contributions to the field of mathematical modeling in cancer research, covering various aspects such as carcinogenesis, chemotherapy, tumor growth dynamics, diffusion in tumors, and the spread of cancer. Namely, [10] presents a multi-stage theory of carcinogenesis, proposing that cancer development occurs through a sequence of genetic changes over time, and explores the age distribution of cancer cases. In 1958, a mathematical model was proposed by Fisher [11] to describe the spatial spread of advantageous genetic traits, as well as factors related to the growth and progression of cancer cells. [12] discussed the use of quantitative parameters and mathematical models to assess the effectiveness of chemotherapy drugs, helping in the design of treatment protocols. A mathematical model, based on the Gompertz function, was developed by Norton [13] to describe the growth dynamics of human breast cancer tumors, providing insights into tumor growth rates and response to treatment and [14] provides insights into tumor growth and highlights the importance of diffusion in understanding tumor development and explores various mathematical techniques to solve the models and discusses the results of simulations. It also examines how nutrients and waste products diffuse within the tumor and proposes mathematical equations to represent this process. In [15] the authors use optimal control theory to improve chemotherapy protocols for IgG multiple myeloma and present a mathematical model that considers tumor growth, immune system interactions, and the effects of chemotherapy drugs is presented; the best timing and dosage of chemotherapy for maximizing treatment effectiveness while minimizing side effects is determined.

A two-stage model for understanding the development of breast cancer in females from an epidemiological perspective is proposed in [16]. Epidemiological data on breast cancer is used to estimate parameters and investigate the relationship between various risk factors and the development of the disease.

In recent decades, there has been a significant rise in the publication of papers employing mathematics techniques for cancer analysis, as exemplified by the works [17–23].

In [17] a simulation study to investigate the most effective dosage and scheduling of chemotherapy drugs to achieve optimal tumor response while minimizing toxic side effects was conducted. A mathematical model that incorporates the pharmacokinetics of the drug, describing its absorption, distribution, metabolism, and excretion, as well as the pharmacodynamics, representing the drug's effect on tumor growth is proposed. [18] present mathematical models that simulate tumor invasion and metastasis, offering insights into the mechanisms and dynamics of cancer spread. Hybrid models that combine mathematical and computational approaches to study tumor growth are discussed by [19]; their usefulness in understanding complex aspects of cancer biology is highlighted. A mathematical model that investigates the tumor-immune evasion mechanism and studies the effects of siRNA treatment in enhancing immune response against cancer cells is proposed by Arciero et al. [20]. A mathematical model to study the effect s of cancer immunotherapy and its synergy with radiotherapy, offering insights into optimizing combination treatment strategies, was presented by Serre et al. [21]. In [22] a mathematical model that describes the dynamics of cancer growth, considering the fractional-order derivatives to capture the memory and long-range effects in the system is proposed. A vaccine strategy as an intervention to control cancer growth and investigate its impact on the model dynamics is incorporated. The findings contribute to the understanding of cancer dynamics from a mathematical perspective and offer potential strategies for utilizing vaccines in cancer treatment. [23] applies fractional calculus in cancer modeling and treatment. The authors provide valuable insights into the use of fractional calculus in cancer modeling and highlights the potential implications of this research for cancer treatment and patient outcomes.

Important and interesting reviews on the application of mathematics in cancer analysis can be found in the literature, such as the works by: Sfakianakis and Chaplain in [24], that provides an overview of the mathematical models that have been developed to understand the mechanisms and dynamics of cancer invasion. Different modeling techniques, such as ordinary differential equations, partial differential equations, and agent-based models, that have been employed to investigate tumor invasion; Dehingia et al. [25], that focus on the application of mathematical modeling techniques in understanding the disease and developing treatment strategies. The role of mathematical models in studying various aspects of cancer, including tumor growth, metastasis, treatment response, and drug optimization is discussed. The significance of mathematical approaches in advancing the understanding of cancer and developing innovative strategies for its treatment is highlighted; and West et al. [26] that identify key challenges and open questions in the field of adaptive therapy. Topics such as treatment schedules, dosing strategies, patient selection criteria, and the role of mathematical modeling in guiding adaptive therapy approaches are explored. The paper emphasizes the importance of bridging the gap between mathematical models and clinical practice in the context of adaptive therapy. Nonetheless, the authors believe that further analysis is necessary to gain a better understanding of the progress made in this area; thus, this work aims to gain a better understanding of the mathematical models and methods that have been used in the study of cancer.

Due to space limitations, the authors decided to focus specifically on contributions in the Operations Research/Management Science (OR/MS) field. OR/MS approaches can provide treatment protocols tailored to individual patients, improving the chances of successful outcomes while minimizing unnecessary treatments and side effects, optimize resource allocation, ensuring that limited resources are used efficiently to accommodate the increasing demand for cancer care, and help in identifying cost-effective strategies for acquiring new medical technologies and treatments, making cutting-edge therapies more accessible to patients. In this context, a selection of studies that exemplify the evolving landscape of this research area and demonstrate how OR/MS have contributed to an enhanced comprehension of tumor development is presented. In Sect. 2 the methodology is presented, in Sect. 3 the results are described, and finally, in Sect. 4 conclusions are drawn.

2 Methodology

This paper will focus on the publications referenced in the ISI Web of Science (WoS) database, as it is recognized for its high standard of quality in the publications it indexes. Furthermore, we will only analyze publications categorized as OR/MS in this database.

A document search in the "Web of Science Core Collection" using the Boolean sentence ("cancer" AND "math*") in ("Title" OR "Abstract" OR "Keyword Plus ®") was performed; a total of 8072 documents were found. After this, a refinement was performed using the following restrictive filters: ("Open Access"), ("Article" OR "Proceeding Paper" OR "Review Article") and Languages: "English"; this search yielded 4192 results.

In order to reduce the number of documents to be analyzed and also achieve the goal, the authors focused on the WoS category "Operations Research/Management Science" (OR/MS), obtaining 16 manuscripts.

3 Results

In this section the results of this investigation are presented. Figure 1 has a TreeMap chart catalogation, retrieved by the Web of Science database, of the 16 papers cataloged as OR/MS by the WoS database, where it can be seen the different areas to which the WoS also fits them.

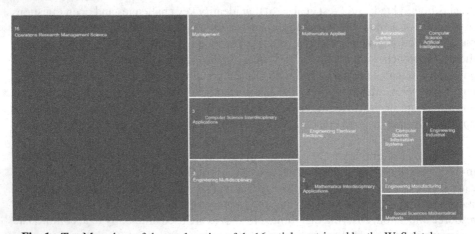

Fig. 1. TreeMap chart of the catalogation of the 16 articles retrieved by the WoS database.

One of the papers was excluded as its main aim was not cancer research and cancer was only mentioned as an example; thus, a total of 15 documents were analyzed. The elementary characteristics of these studies are presented in Table 1.

In [27] an optimization of radiation therapy (RT) treatment plan, based on the acquired mid-treatment biomarker information and adapt the remainder of the treatment course accordingly, was studied. An adaptive treatment-length optimization problem as a 2-stage problem was formulated. Unfortunately, the biomarker data obtained during treatment is prone to uncertainties, arising from measurement errors as well as imprecision in converting measured data into relevant model parameters. To address the inexactness of biomarker information it was used Adjustable Robust Optimization (ARO) techniques [42, 43]. ARO ensures that the treatment plan implemented during the initial treatment phase (before acquiring biomarker information) is designed in order to enabling greater flexibility when adapting treatment course. ARO operates under the assumption that the disclosed information is exact, to address the case when revealed information is not exact and only provides an approximation of the true parameters it was used the ARO methodology introduced in [44]. Explicit optimal decision rules for a challenging yet highly relevant ARO problem that involves nonconvex and mixed-integer elements, was provided. Furthermore, it was demonstrated that in the worst-case scenario, there exist multiple optimal solutions, which exhibit different performances in non-worst-case scenarios. To address this, the concept of Pareto ARO solutions specifically for 2-stage robust optimization problems (a generalization of Pareto Robustly Optimal from [45]) was introduced. Using patient data from lung cancer cases, a computational investigation was conducted to ascertain the ideal moment for obtaining biomarker information, considering potential improvements in biomarker quality over time. The delaying biomarker acquisition also imposes limitations on adaptability, and striking the optimal balance depends on the rate of improvement.

The authors of [28] focus on the RT planning for prostate cancer, which involves 2 stages: phase I, where the treatment focuses on irradiating the prostate and the surrounding organs affected by the cancer; and phase II only prostate will be irradiated. To initiate the planning process, cases are extracted from the database utilizing case-based reasoning, specifically targeting cases that bear similarity to the new case in question. These extracted cases are evaluated using Technique for Order Preference by Similarity to an Ideal Solution (TOPSIS) developed by Hwang and Yoon in [46]. TOPSIS is as a Multi-Criteria Decision-Making (MCDM) process that facilitates the balancing of treatment success rate, maximizing the dose to cancerous cells, and the potential side effects. Subsequently, utilizing the parameters of the most optimal case identified through the TOPSIS methodology, the dosage for both phase I and phase II of the treatment is determined via the Multi-Objective Integer Goal Programming (GP) approach. The proposed method had a success rate of 87.6%, with 57 out of 65 cases indicating that the recommended dose plan matches or surpasses the prescription provided by the oncologist; thus, generating an improved dose plan in 29 of these cases,

A mathematical proof-of-concept for the feasibility of mechanical deliverability constraints for an intensity-modulated radiation therapy (IMRT) treatment plan can be seen in [29]. A mixed integer programming (MIP) for integrating robust and direct aperture

Table. 1 Elementary characteristics of the analyzed publications.

Pub	Study Aim	Cancer Type	Data	Techniques	Main Findings	Limitations
[27]	To optimize radiation therapy treatment plan, based on the acquired mid-treatment biomarker information	Lung	Real data	Pareto Adjustable Robustly Optimal (PARO); Multiple optimal solutions are ARO stage-1 solutions to the EDP	• Construction of a mathematical tool based on ARO, which allows us to adjust the dose per fraction and the duration of treatment after acquisition of biomarker information at mid-treatment, as well as to analyze the impact of uncertainty in biomarker information • Explicit optimal decision rules for a challenging but with practical significance ARO problem • For the worst-case scenario it is demonstrates the existence of multiple optimal solutions, they perform variably under non-worst case scenarios. In order to address this variability, the concept of PARO was introduced to two-stage robust optimization problems. If the acquired biomarker information is precise, PARO solutions are obtained • To determine the optimal timing for acquiring biomarker information, in case the quality of biomarkers improves with time, a computational study was performed using real data from lung cancer patients	No limitations were presented by the authors

(continued)

Table. 1 (*continued*)

Pub	Study Aim	Cancer Type	Data	Techniques	Main Findings	Limitations
[28]	To optimize the dose plan of radiotherapy (RT) treatment using the oncologists' previous experiences	Prostate	Real data from Nottingham City Hospital	Multi Criteria Decision Making (MCDM): Technique for Order Preference by Similarity to Ideal Solution (TOPSIS); Multi-objective integer goal programming (GP) method	• Experiments revealed that the proposed system not only aids oncologists in balancing various decision-making criteria but also assists in determining the optimal dosage plan for treatment • The proposed method's treatment plans typically match or outperform those prescribed by experienced oncologists • The proposed method achieves a success rate of 87.6%. Out of 65 cases, it matches or surpasses the dose plan prescribed by the oncologist in 57 cases, with 29 cases showing a notably improved dose plan • To demonstrate the effectiveness of TOPSIS and goal programming methods, they were compared with CBR and CBR–TOPSIS. The results indicate that CBR–TOPSIS goal programming outperforms the other approaches, highlighting its superior performance	No limitations were presented by the authors

(*continued*)

Table. 1 (*continued*)

Pub	Study Aim	Cancer Type	Data	Techniques	Main Findings	Limitations
[29]	To establish a mathematical proof-of-concept for the feasibility of mechanical deliverability constraints for an intensity-modulated radiation therapy (IMRT) treatment plan	Generic, experimental results applied to breast cancer	Real data from Princess Margaret Cancer Centre in Toronto, Canada	Mixed Integer Programming (MIP) for integrating robust and Direct Aperture Optimization (DAO) constraints; Candidate Plan Generation (CPG) heuristic; Fluence Map Optimization (FMO)	• The establishment of a MIP framework that effectively integrates robust and DAO constraints • The introduction of a novel formulation designed to address five distinct types of mechanical deliverability constraints • An exploration of symmetry-breaking techniques specifically for aperture-angle assignments • The development of a heuristic approach capable of swiftly generating high-quality and feasible robust DAO treatments • The formulation of an algorithm that converts these feasible robust DAO treatments into initial incumbent solutions, which can be employed as a warm start for commercial solvers	• Although the CPG method did produce feasible and implementable plans, both as standalone solutions and warm-start contexts, they lacked the surgical precision desired from an optimization methodology. This can be attributed to the presence of significant optimality gaps in the reported solutions • The CPG methodology performed very well in generating stand-alone plans, but it fell short in its intended purpose as a warm start for the more precise RDAO model, failing to bring it to optimality as expected

(*continued*)

Table. 1 (*continued*)

Pub	Study Aim	Cancer Type	Data	Techniques	Main Findings	Limitations
[30]	To explore the impact of socio-demographic factors on the growth of cancer tumors	Colon	SEER database from 2004 until 2015 for four different races	Line graph approach and applies ordinary least squares regression; Quantile regression	• The findings strongly suggest that age significantly influences the growth of identified tumors, particularly in cases of young individuals diagnosed with colon cancer	No limitations were presented by the authors
[31]	Analyze and discuss results obtained by applying nonlinear optimal control tools to biomedical problems, in particular for cancer treatments	Generic	Real data	Optimal control problem for a general dynamical system	• Constructing an optimization criterion, using information from the fundamental principles of biology or relevant medical constraints • Identification of some obstacles to be avoid, while also incorporating valuable simplifications in both the Dynamics and the objective of the modeling process	No limitations were presented by the authors
[32]	To examines the growth of heterogeneous tumors, focusing on the interactions between sensitive cells, which respond to treatment, and resistant cells that are unaffected by it	Generic	In vitro tumor	Dynamical programming, nonlinear optimal control, reachability analysis, Hamilton-Jacobi equations	• A reconstruction algorithm designed for control problems that involve state constraints was introduced • The convergence of this algorithm was demonstrated and empirical evidence of its effectiveness through multiple numerical simulations was provided	While this study is suitable for in vitro tumor experiments, it may not be appropriate for medical applications with longer-term goals

(continued)

Table. 1 (*continued*)

Pub	Study Aim	Cancer Type	Data	Techniques	Main Findings	Limitations
[33]	To develop a mathematical optimization model aimed at addressing the challenges associated with the combined beam angle and dose distribution problems when confronted with multiple objectives, for radiotherapy treatment	Prostate	Erasto Gaertner Hospital (Curitiba, Brazil)	Multi-objective optimization model; Matheuristic based in Tabu Search; Goal Programming	• A novel approach utilizing Goal Programming to develop a multi-objective optimization model for effectively solving the combined beam angle and dose distribution problem • A matheuristic called Tabu Search (TSrad) that is designed for solving the proposed model, was development • The generation of optimal solutions for individual computed tomography slice instances but also offers viable solutions for more complex 3D problems, addressing the challenges of higher-dimensional scenarios	No limitations were presented by the authors
[34]	To propose a dynamic view of the Analytic Hierarchy Process (AHP) methodology for the assessment of tangible and intangible elements in a long-term decision-making scenario, specifically in the context of Health Technology Assessment for Biosensing Optoelectronics in Oncology	Thyroid	Real historical data Simulated data, created using Poisson distribution	Integrated approach combining Analytic Hierarchy Process with a System Dynamic simulation technique	• The proposed approach based on System Dynamics modeling and simulation can be an effective tool for evaluating and comparing different diagnostic methods in healthcare systems • The developed simulation models were able to capture the complexity of the healthcare system and provide insights into the performance of different alternatives • The importance of considering multiple criteria, including technical, organizational, clinical, economic, and social-ethical-legal aspects when evaluating diagnostic methods is highlighted • A multi-criteria decision-making approach based on System Dynamics modeling and simulation can be a valuable tool for decision-makers in healthcare systems	The study relies on historical data for one alternative and simulated data for the other two alternatives, which may introduce bias or inaccuracies in the results

(continued)

Table. 1 (*continued*)

Pub	Study Aim	Cancer Type	Data	Techniques	Main Findings	Limitations
[35]	Present a solution to the job shop scheduling problem with custom constraints, such as recurring and optional activities, and time window constraints for scheduling recurring RT appointments in an ion beam facility. The objective is to minimize the operation time of the bottleneck resource, the particle beam, while minimizing any penalties arising from violations of time window constraints	Generic	Randomly generated problem instances of varying sizes, based on real information/characteristics	Mixed-integer linear programming (MILP) to model the radiotherapy scheduling problem Genetic algorithm (GA) with tailor-made feasibility-preserving crossover operators, an iterated local search (ILS), and a combination of the two previous approaches	• The proposed scheduling model can efficiently solve the radiotherapy scheduling problem, resulting in reduced patient waiting times and increased machine utilization • The MILP formulation of the scheduling problem provides optimal solutions for small instances with GA and ILS, while the hybrid algorithm approach is more suitable for larger instances • The simulation-based approach used to generate problem instances provides a diverse set of instances for testing the scheduling model and can be used to evaluate the performance of other scheduling models • The paper provides optimal and robust schedules for real-world instances	Not using stochastic approach optimization techniques, as many parameters of the underlying problem are subject to intense uncertainty

(*continued*)

Table. 1 (*continued*)

Pub	Study Aim	Cancer Type	Data	Techniques	Main Findings	Limitations
[36]	To provide a survey of recent work on prostate cancer predictive modeling using computational intelligence approaches, to provide a broader perspective of the area, and to consider challenges that remain to be addressed	Prostate	Real data	Artificial Neural Networks, Deep Learning, Fuzzy approaches, Support Vector Machines, Metaheuristic optimization, Ensemble learning algorithms, Bayesian approaches, Markov models, regression models	• The review underscores the potential of various approaches for prostate cancer predictive modeling. It notes that computational intelligence methods show promise in achieving efficient and accurate predictions, supported by sufficient evidence in the literature. However, despite their potential, these approaches have not been as extensively utilized in prostate cancer detection compared to other diseases. The review highlights the importance of further research to bridge this gap and facilitate the translation of these approaches into clinical practice. In contrast, statistically-based nomograms are more commonly adopted in clinical settings	The methodology of the study is not referenced in the article
[37]	To use Infinitesimal Perturbation Analysis (IPA) to explore the tradeoff between system optimality and robustness thus providing valuable insights on modeling and control of cancer progression	Prostate	Real and simulated data	Threshold-based policy and IPA to derive unbiased estimators of the cost metric gradient Evaluation of the sensitivity estimates with respect to model parameters	• A new methodology for personalized cancer therapy design that explores the tradeoff between system optimality and robustness is proposed • Identifying curative and uncontrollable growth scenarios in the simulated Intermittent Androgen Suppression therapy scheme requires determining specific model parameter values • The conclusion suggests that prioritizing increased system stability over strict optimality might be of potential interest	• There may be other potentially critical parameters in the model that were not included in the sensitivity analysis. • The generalizability of the findings to other types of cancer or diseases that progress in stages is limited

(*continued*)

Table. 1 (*continued*)

Pub	Study Aim	Cancer Type	Data	Techniques	Main Findings	Limitations
[38]	To provide a natural-history simulation of breast cancer screening for older women, using a combined DES/SD model	Breast	Real data from Breast Cancer Surveillance Consortium (BCSC), 2010 Simulation-generated natural histories of untreated breast cancer	Combined DES/SD model, Discrete-Event Simulation (DES) and System Dynamics (SD) modeling	• A two-phase simulation modeling framework was developed to evaluate the effectiveness of breast cancer screening policies for US women aged 65 and above. Individualized sub-models were created to represent the incidence and progression of the disease, enabling precise and sharp comparisons of various breast cancer screening policies	• Model just intended s for evaluating US women aged 65+ • Risk factors, other than age, are assumed constant over time • In certain situations, a more accurately calibrated predictive model may be necessary • Insufficient information about the behavior of ductal carcinoma in situ and its progression to invasive breast cancer, as well as the relationship between tumor growth characteristics and a woman's age
[39]	To identify remote homologies with other proteins by generating a homology model of P-glycoprotein	Generic	Real data from protein data bank:	Sequence alignment algorithms (BLAST) Modeler	Alignment and matching sequencing was achieved. The required template was discovered	The model was not 3D

(*continued*)

Table. 1 (*continued*)

Pub	Study Aim	Cancer Type	Data	Techniques	Main Findings	Limitations
[40]	To describe the use of operations research (OR) and cost-effectiveness analysis to support the development of cost-effective interventions for hepatitis B in the United States and China	Liver	Real data	Decision analysis (DA) and Markov models	DA and Markov models and, in particular, the proposed are useful tools for evaluating the cost-effectiveness of different interventions and for informing policy decisions related to hepatitis B prevention and control Targeted screening, treatment, and vaccination programs can be cost-effective and can significantly reduce hepatitis B, particularly in high-risk populations	No limitations were presented by the authors
[41]	To develop a robust approach to the management of motion uncertainty in the optimization of intensity modulated radiation therapy treatments	Generic, experimental results applied to lung cancer	Real data	Robust formulation, Intensity-modulated radiation therapy (IMRT) optimization model using probability density functions	Development of a IMRT robust optimization model for respiratory motion uncertainty that was able to generate treatment plans that were robust to respiratory motion uncertainty and that the resulting plans were able to achieve the desired dose coverage while minimizing the dose to healthy tissue This model was able to generate treatment plans that were more robust than those generated by a conventional optimization model	Small sample size used in the study, only the data from five patients was considered in the study. Only focus on lung cancer patients, so it is unclear whether the model would be effective for other types of cancer

optimization (DAO) constraints was developed. Five types of mechanical deliverability constraints were formulated. An exploration of symmetry-breaking techniques for aperture-angle assignments was presented. A candidate plan generation (CPG) heuristic, for rapidly generating high-quality, feasible, robust DAO treatments, was also proposed. Additionally, an algorithm for converting feasible robust DAO treatments into initial incumbent solutions for warm starting commercial solvers, was introduced. The computational analysis, conducted using clinical patient datasets encompassing motion uncertainty, demonstrates the advantages of incorporating the CPG technique. The results highlight the improved quality of both the initial solution and the final output plan, but the achieved plans did not exhibit the surgical precision expected from an optimization methodology. Moreover, the CPG methodology fell short of its intended purpose to effectively warm-start the more precise RDAO model towards optimality.

In [30] a mathematical and statistical modeling to analyze the relationship between tumor sizes and age across four different races (Caucasians (88.9%), African Americans (10.4%), American Indians (0.3%) and others (0.4%)). It was used a line graph approach and applied an ordinary least squares regression to determine a model for predicting the average tumor growth based on age. A quantile regression was used to develop more robust models that focus on specific quantiles using tumor size and age as dependent and predictor variables. Surveillance Epidemiology and End Results Program (SEER) database, considering colon cancer data from in period 2004 until 2015, was used [47]. The results highlight the role of age in the growth of identified tumors, particularly in cases where individuals are diagnosed with colon cancer at a young age.

Results of applying nonlinear optimal control tools to biomedical problems were discussed for cancer treatments in [31]. Aspects of dynamics modeling, such as growth and interaction factors, are taken into account, as well as treatment modeling, which includes drug pharmacometrics. A critical aspect involves carefully selecting the objective functional that needs to be minimized. This choice plays an essential role in determining numerous properties of the optimal solutions. To address this limitation, methods to improve the selection process by considering the underlying biology of the problem were explored. Some obstacles to be avoid, while incorporating valuable simplifications in the dynamics and objective of the modeling process were identified.

The primary objective in [32] is to maintain the size of a benign tumor below a specific threshold, medically determined. When it cannot be achieved, the aim is to identify an effective strategy to reduce the tumor volume, allowing for subsequent maintenance below the size threshold. These challenges are referred to as stability or reachability problems. To address this, control problems and seek solutions within the framework of Hamilton-Jacobi equations were formulated. The model examines the growth of heterogeneous tumors, specifically focusing on the interactions between 2 populations of cancerous cells: sensitive cells, which respond to treatment, and resistant cells that are unaffected by it was explored. The biological model used involves in vitro experiments, previously studied in [48], and to keep track of the toxicity a model inspired in [49].

In [33], a multi-objective optimization model aimed to address the challenges associated with the combined beam angle and dose distribution problems, for RT treatment, is introduced. To tackle realistic large-scale instances, a matheuristic based on Tabu Search

(TSrad) is developed. To assess the effectiveness of the matheuristic, a series of experiments were conducted on two different instances. The findings strongly indicate that Probabilistic TSrad holds significant promise in facilitating RT planning, it consistently generates superior solutions within the prescribed computational time limits.

[34] aims to evaluate and compare the effectiveness of different diagnostic methods in healthcare systems. It uses MCDM approach based on System Dynamics modeling and simulation to evaluate the performance of 1 currently employed method and 2 prototype systems. The simulation models are developed based on time-dependent variables and Poisson distribution to model technical, organizational, clinical, economic, and social-ethical-legal aspects. It uses historical data for 1 alternative and simulated data for the other 2 alternatives. It concludes that the proposed approach can be an effective tool for evaluating and comparing different diagnostic methods in healthcare systems. It suggests that a MCDM approach based on System Dynamics modeling and simulation can be a valuable tool for decision-makers in healthcare systems.

A mixed-integer linear programming formulation of the radiotherapy patient scheduling problem in ion beam is presented in [35]; 3 heuristic solution methods, 2 stand-alone methods (genetic algorithm and iterated local search method) and 1 hybrid algorithm involving both of them, are proposed to solve the problem. This approach is tested on a diverse set of real-world based generated problem instances; the results show that the stand alone methods provide optimal solutions for small instances, while the hybrid approach is more suitable for larger instances. Robust and efficient schedules are obtained, resulting in reduced patient waiting times and increased machine utilization.

Article [36] is a review of recent work on computational intelligence approaches for prostate cancer predictive modeling. Recent advances in computational intelligence algorithms, including Artificial Neural Networks, Deep Learning, Fuzzy approaches, Support Vector Machines, metaheuristic optimization, Ensemble learning algorithms, Bayesian approaches, and Markov models are surveyed. Challenges that need to be addressed in developing accurate approaches for diagnosing, predicting the diagnosis and therapeutic responsiveness, as well as outcomes of prostate cancer are discussed. It also considers the potential of these approaches for clinical practice and emphasizes the need for further research to translate them into clinical practice. It concludes that now it is the time to widely apply these approaches to develop cancer prediction models which learn from large and big multimodal data and which can benefit clinical practice.

Article [37] proposes a new methodology for personalized cancer therapy design that explores the tradeoff between system optimality and robustness in the context of designing an ideal protocol for Intermittent Androgen Suppression therapy for advanced prostate cancer patients. The evaluation includes sensitivity estimates of various model parameters to identify critical parameters and assess the model's robustness against them. The findings indicate that the system is more sensitive to changes in the Hematopoietic Stem Cell proliferation and apoptosis constants compared to changes in the Colorectal Cancer proliferation and apoptosis constants. Moreover, 2 sets of model parameter values were identified: 1 in which the simulated Immune Activation Strategy therapy scheme is essentially curative, and another where the prostate tumor grows uncontrollably. It was also discovered that prioritizing increased system stability over optimality can be of interest in certain cases, suggesting the potential benefits of relaxing optimality.

The significance of applying the proposed methodology on an individual patient basis is emphasized, supporting recent efforts to develop personalized cancer therapies rather than relying on traditional treatment approaches generated for a group of patients on average. This highlights the importance of validating recent endeavors that favor personalized cancer therapies, opposed to conventional treatment schemes typically designed for a cohort of patients and may only be effective on average.

A 2-phase simulation modeling framework is proposed in [38] to assess the effectiveness of breast cancer screening policies for women aged 65 and above in the United States. The framework uses a natural-history simulation model that captures the occurrence and advancement of untreated breast cancer in randomly selected individuals from the specified population of older American women. The natural-history simulation incorporates a Discrete-Event Simulation model comprising sub-models for population growth, incidence, progression, and survival. The simulation generates a comprehensive database of natural histories of untreated breast cancer, which subsequently informs the screening-and-treatment simulation. The simulation, tailored to each individual in the simulated population, incorporates personalized sub-models for screening, treatment, survival, and cost accumulation. The study indicates that regardless of the adopted intervals, screening should commence early in life and continue into late adulthood, demonstrating the benefits of screening older women. However, it is important to note some primary limitations of this model. The model assumes: Markovian disease progression, implying certain simplifications, mammography as the sole method for disease detection, failing to differentiate between regional and distant (advanced) disease stages, and the analysis solely relies on mortality as the measure of medical effectiveness, potentially overlooking other relevant factors.

Article [39] focuses on the application of homology modeling to detect remote protein homologies for P-glycoprotein, with the intention of enhancing the understanding of its structure and functional relationships with other proteins, and role in cancer tissue.

The authors of [40] attribute the success of their projects to: a multidisciplinary team, development of an appropriately complex model on an accessible platform, and establishment of an extensive outreach and connections with policy makers. They found that hepatitis B, can derive to liver cancer, is a significant public health problem in both China and US, and that targeted screening, treatment, and vaccination programs can be cost-effective. They concluded that combination strategies including multiple interventions can be more effective and cost-effective than single ones. Also, they argue that the proposed approach can be useful tools for evaluating the cost-effectiveness of different interventions and for informing policy decisions related to hepatitis B prevention and control. Their findings had a deep impact, leading to significant changes in both US public health policy regarding hepatitis B screening and the decision by Chinese policymakers to offer free catch-up vaccination for hundreds of millions of children.

Article [41] presents a robust optimization model for intensity-modulated radiation therapy that accounts for respiratory motion uncertainty; real patient data was used to test the model. Varian's real-time position management system was used to gather data from five patients by recording their breathing patterns in every treatment fraction over the course of their entire treatments. Probability density functions derived from the patient data was used to construct the uncertainty set and test the resulting optimized solutions.

The authors found that their model was able to generate treatment plans that were robust to respiratory motion uncertainty and that the resulting plans were able to achieve the desired dose coverage while minimizing the dose to healthy tissue.

4 Conclusion

In this section, a brief summary of the analyzed documents is presented, both in terms of the mathematical techniques used and their main objective.

It is aimed to analyze mathematical techniques, with focus in OR/MS, that are applied to cancer research; 15 documents were considered. From these, 2 are proceeding papers [37, 39], 1 is a review article [36], and the remaining are articles. Several of them aim to optimize radiation therapy treatment plan, namely [27–29, 33, 35] and [41], others, like [38] and [40] focus on cancer prevention, [37] verse about personalized cancer therapy and the remaining ones have a wide variety of motivations.

A robust optimization model is proposed in [27, 29] and [41], while [28] and [33] use GP to develop a multi-objective optimization. A MIP formulation is used in [29] and [35], and both simulation and system dynamics approaches are applied in [34] and [38]. Statistical analysis is applied in [30] to study the association of age and the growth of identified tumors. In articles [31] and [32] the main results were obtained applying optimal control tools.

This study just focuses on the WoS database and only 15 papers were analyzed. The authors intend to extend the search to other scientific recognized databases in order to not only increase the number of studied documents but also to analyze the application of emerging OR/MS techniques, as artificial intelligence and big data analytics, to cancer research; thus, gaining better insight concerning this topic.

Acknowledgments. The research was partially financed by the Portuguese Funds through FCT (Fundação para a Ciência e a Tecnologia), within the Projects UIDB/00013/2020 and UIDP/00013/2020.

References

1. Virchow, R.: As based upon physiological and pathological histology: cellular pathology. Nutr. Rev. **47**(1), 23–25 (1989)
2. Ehrlich, P.: On staining tissues. A methodological contribution. Proc. R. Prussian Acad. Sci. **17**, 627–633 (1891)
3. Halsted, W.S.: The results of operations for the cure of cancer of the breast performed at the Johns Hopkins Hospital from June 1889 to January 1894. Ann. Surg. **20**(5), 497–555 (1894)
4. Curie, M.: Radioactive substances and their application in therapy. Nobel Lecture (1904)
5. Rous, P.: A transmissible avian neoplasm (sarcoma of the common fowl). J. Exp. Med. **13**(4), 397–411 (1911)
6. Bashford, E.F., Murray, J.F., Murray, C.D.: The growth and extension of tumours: II. An experimental study of the effect of surgical removal. Proc. R. Soc. Lond. Ser. B, Containing Pap. Biol. Charact. **88**(606), 241–264 (1915)
7. Warburg, O.: The Metabolism of Tumors. Richard R. Smith, Inc. (1925)

8. Boveri, T.: Concerning the origin of malignant tumors. J. Cancer Res. **1**(1), 1–19 (1914)
9. Ehrlich, P.: On Immunity with Special Reference to Cell Life. J.H. Chambers & Company (1909)
10. Armitage, P., Doll, R.: The age distribution of cancer and a multi-stage theory of carcinogenesis. Br. J. Cancer **8**(1), 1–12 (1954)
11. Fisher, R.A.: The wave of advance of advantageous genes. Ann. Hum. Genet. **22**(4), 223–229 (1958)
12. Skipper, H.E., Thomsom, H., Schabel Jr, F.M.: Experimental evaluation of potential anticancer agents. XI. Quantitative response of the Sa180 system to deoxypyridoxine. Cancer Chemother. Rep. Part 1 **29**, 63–76 (1963)
13. Norton, L.: A Gompertzian model of human breast cancer growth. Cancer Res. **36**(7 Part 1), 2229–2235 (1976)
14. Greenspan, H.P.: Models for the growth of a solid tumor by diffusion. Stud. Appl. Math. **55**(4), 317–340 (1976)
15. Swan, G.W., Vincent, T.L.: Optimal control analysis in the chemotherapy of IgG multiple myeloma. Bull. Math. Biol. **39**, 317–337 (1977)
16. Moolgavkar, S.H., Day, N.E., Stevens, R.G.: Two-stage model for carcinogenesis: epidemiology of breast cancer in females. J. Natl. Cancer Inst. **65**(3), 559–569 (1980)
17. Barbolosi, D., Iliadis, A.: Optimizing drug regimens in cancer chemotherapy: a simulation study using a PK–PD model. Comput. Biol. Med. **31**(3), 157–172 (2001)
18. Anderson, A.R., Chaplain, M.A., Newman, E.L., Steele, R.J., Thompson, A.M.: Mathematical modelling of tumour invasion and metastasis. Comput. Math. Methods Med. **2**(2), 129–154 (2000)
19. Rejniak, K.A., Anderson, A.R.: Hybrid models of tumor growth. Wiley Interdisc. Rev. Syst. Biol. Med. **3**(1), 115–125 (2011)
20. Arciero, J.C., Jackson, T.L., Kirschner, D.E.: A mathematical model of tumor-immune evasion and siRNA treatment. Discrete Continuous Dyn. Syst. Ser. B **4**(1), 39–58 (2004)
21. Serre, R., et al.: Mathematical modeling of cancer immunotherapy and its synergy with radiotherapy. Cancer Res. **76**(17), 4931–4940 (2016)
22. Farman, M., Akgül, A., Ahmad, A., Imtiaz, S.: Analysis and dynamical behavior of fractional-order cancer model with vaccine strategy. Math. Meth. Appl. Sci. **43**(7), 4871–4882 (2020)
23. Azeem, M., Farman, M., Akgül, A., De la Sen, M.: Fractional order operator for symmetric analysis of cancer model on stem cells with chemotherapy. Symmetry **15**(2), 533 (2023)
24. Sfakianakis, N., Chaplain, M.A.J.: Mathematical modelling of cancer invasion: a review. In: Suzuki, T., Poignard, C., Chaplain, M., Quaranta, V. (eds.) MMDS 2020. SPMS, vol. 370, pp. 153–172. Springer, Singapore (2021). https://doi.org/10.1007/978-981-16-4866-3_10
25. Dehingia, K., Sarmah, H.K., Jeelani, M.B.: A brief review on cancer research and its treatment through mathematical modelling. Ann. Cancer Res. Ther. **29**(1), 34–40 (2021)
26. West, J., et al.: A survey of open questions in adaptive therapy: Bridging mathematics and clinical translation. Elife **12**, e84263 (2023)
27. ten Eikelder, S.C.M., Ajdari, A., Bortfeld, T., den Hertog, D.: Adjustable robust treatment-length optimization in radiation therapy. Optim. Eng. **23**, 1949–1986 (2022)
28. Malekpoor, H., Mishra, N., Kumar, S.: A novel TOPSIS–CBR goal programming approach to sustainable healthcare treatment. Ann. Oper. Res. **312**, 1403–1425 (2022)
29. Ripsman, D.A., Purdie, T.G., Chan, T.C.Y., Mahmoudzadeh, H.: Robust direct aperture optimization for radiation therapy treatment planning. INFORMS J. Comput. **34**(4), 2017–2038 (2022)
30. Machavaram, V.B., Veeramachaneni, S.: Age dependent analysis of colon cancer tumours using mathematical and statistical modelling. Int. J. Math. Eng. Manage. Sci. **6**(3), 944–960 (2021)

31. Ledzewicz, U., Schattler, H.: On the role of the objective in the optimization of compartmental models for biomedical therapies. J. Optim. Theory Appl. **187**, 305–335 (2020)
32. Carrere, C., Zidani, H.: Stability and reachability analysis for a controlled heterogeneous population of cells. Optim. Control Appl. Meth. **41**, 1678–1704 (2020)
33. Obal, T.M., et al.: Development and evaluation of a matheuristic for the combined beam angle and dose distribution problem in radiotherapy planning. IMA J. Manag. Math. **30**, 413–430 (2019)
34. Improta, G., Converso, G., Murino, T., Gallo, M., Perrone, A., Romano, M.: Analytic hierarchy process (AHP) in dynamic configuration as a tool for health technology assessment (HTA): the case of biosensing optoelectronics in oncology. Int. J. Inf. Technol. Decis. Mak. **18**(5), 1533–1550 (2019)
35. Vogl, P., Braune, R., Doerner, K.F.: Scheduling recurring radiotherapy appointments in an ion beam facility. J. Sched. **22**, 137–154 (2019)
36. Cosma, G., Brown, D., Archer, M., Khan, M., Pockley, A.G.: A survey on computational intelligence approaches for predictive modeling in prostate cancer. Exp. Syst. Appl. **70**, 1–19 (2017)
37. Fleck, J.L., Cassandras, C.G.: Personalized cancer therapy design: robustness vs. optimality. In: IEEE 55th Conference on Decision and Control, pp. 5041–5046 (2016)
38. Tejada, J.J., Ivy, J.S., Wilson, J.R., Ballan, M.J., Diehl, K.M., Yankaskas, B.C.: Combined DES/SD model of breast cancer screening for older women, I: natural-history simulation. IIE Trans. **47**(6), 600–619 (2015)
39. Pal, A., Mishra, D., Mishra, S., Satapathy, S.K.: Homology modeling of P-glycoprotein for detecting remote protein homologies. Procedia Eng. **38**, 1778–1782 (2012)
40. Hutton, D.W., Brandeau, M.L., So, S.K.: Doing good with good or: supporting cost-effective hepatitis b interventions. Interfaces **41**(3), 289–300 (2011)
41. Bortfeld, T., Chan, T.C.Y., Trofimov, A., Tsitsiklis, J.N.: Robust management of motion uncertainty in intensity-modulated radiation therapy. Oper. Res. **56**(6), 1461–1473 (2008)
42. Ben-Tal, A., Goryashko, A., Guslitzer, E., Nemirovski, A.: Adjustable robust solutions of uncertain linear programs. Math. Program. **99**, 351–376 (2004)
43. Yanıkoğlu, I., Gorissen, B.L., den Hertog, D.: A survey of adjustable robust optimization. Eur. J. Oper. Res. **277**, 799–813 (2019)
44. De Ruiter, F.J.C.T., Ben-Tal, A., Brekelmans, R.C.M., den Hertog, D.: Robust optimization of uncertain multistage inventory systems with inexact data in decision rules. Comput. Manag. Sci. **14**(1), 45–77 (2017)
45. Iancu, D.A., Trichakis, N.: Pareto efficiency in robust optimization. Manag. Sci. **60**(1), 130–147 (2014)
46. Hwang, C. L.; Yoon, K.: Multiple Attribute Decision Making. Lecture Notes in Economics and Mathematical Systems, vol. 186, Springer, Heidelberg (1981). https://doi.org/10.1007/978-3-642-48318-9
47. Howlader, N., Noone, A.M., Krapcho, M.: SEER cancer statistics review, pp. 1975–2013. National Cancer Institute, Bethesda, MD (2016)
48. Carrère, C.: Optimization of an in vitro chemotherapy to avoid resistant tumours. J. Theor. Biol. **413**, 24–33 (2017)
49. Barbolosi, D., Freyer, G., Ciccolini, J., Iliadis, A.: Optimisation de la posologie et desmodalités d'administration des agents cytotoxiques à l'aide d'un modèle mathématique. Bull. Cancer **90**(2), 167–175 (2003)

On the Use of VGs for Feature Selection in Supervised Machine Learning - A Use Case to Detect Distributed DoS Attacks

João Lopes[1]([envelope]) [ID], Alberto Partida[2] [ID], Pedro Pinto[1,3,5] [ID],
and António Pinto[4,5] [ID]

[1] ADiT-Lab, Instituto Politécnico de Viana do Castelo, Viana do Castelo, Portugal
jmanuellopes@ipvc.pt, pedropinto@estg.ipvc.pt
[2] Data, Complex Networks and Cybersecurity Sciences Technological Institute, Rey
Juan Carlos University, Madrid, Spain
alberto.partida@dcncsciences.com
[3] Universidade da Maia, Maia, Portugal
[4] CIICESI, ESTG, Instituto Politécnico do Porto, Felgueiras, Portugal
apinto@estg.ipp.pt
[5] INESC TEC, Porto, Portugal

Abstract. Information systems depend on security mechanisms to detect and respond to cyber-attacks. One of the most frequent attacks is the Distributed Denial of Service (DDoS): it impairs the performance of systems and, in the worst case, leads to prolonged periods of downtime that prevent business processes from running normally. To detect this attack, several supervised Machine Learning (ML) algorithms have been developed and companies use them to protect their servers. A key stage in these algorithms is feature pre-processing, in which, input data features are assessed and selected to obtain the best results in the subsequent stages that are required to implement supervised ML algorithms. In this article, an innovative approach for feature selection is proposed: the use of Visibility Graphs (VGs) to select features for supervised machine learning algorithms used to detect distributed DoS attacks. The results show that VG can be quickly implemented and can compete with other methods to select ML features, as they require low computational resources and they offer satisfactory results, at least in our example based on the early detection of distributed DoS. The size of the processed data appears as the main implementation constraint for this novel feature selection method.

Keywords: Artificial intelligence · Machine Learning · Supervised Learning · Denial of Service attack · Visibility Graph · Cybersecurity

1 Introduction

Successful cyberattacks not only result in significant financial losses but also inflict reputational damage upon the affected companies [21,22]. In particular, single or distributed threat actors launch Denial of Service (DoS) attacks

A. I. Pereira et al. (Eds.): OL2A 2023, CCIS 1981, pp. 269–283, 2024.
https://doi.org/10.1007/978-3-031-53025-8_19

with a considerable degree of anonymity. Their aim is to exhaust all computing resources available in the attacked system, impairing the usual functioning of the business process that they support. They are popularly known by their acronyms, i.e., DoS (denial of service) and DDoS (distributed denial of service), respectively.

An increasing number of network-based intrusion detection systems (NIDS) implement Machine Learning (ML) algorithms to detect these attacks [34]. These NIDS use network traffic, i.e., data and protocols in the form of bits flowing between IT systems throughout time, as input data to identify potential attacks.

In general, time series data is often used as input in ML algorithms [5,28]. When ML algorithms are used, it is essential to assess and select input data features that could boost the performance and output quality of these algorithms. This article proposes a novel two-phased approach to identify valid features for ML algorithms used in network-based intrusion detection. First, it converts network traffic into a time series, and second, it transforms this time series into a complex network using Visibility Graphs (VGs). Specifically, this article studies how a complex network, resulting from applying visibility graphs to a time series, may support the feature pre-processing stage in ML algorithms.

Complex network analysis has found application in various fields that require the study of systems consisting of numerous interacting nodes exhibiting nonlinear behaviors. These fields include biology, economics, and social sciences [8,9,39,41,42,48]. There are several proposals to transform a time series into a complex network [52], such as the VGs, proposed by Lacasa et al. [29]. VGs provide valuable insights into the underlying dynamics of the time series data, leveraging the comprehensive set of tools available in complex network analysis. A potential application of VGs that is worth exploring is its use in anomaly detection and prediction.

ML is an area of study that develops algorithms capable of learning and making decisions based on the analysis of input data using different algorithms. It consists of four consecutive stages: data collection, data pre-processing, splitting the data into training and test sets, and applying a specific algorithm that would facilitate decisions or predictions. Collecting input data with sufficient quality is crucial to train machine learning (ML) algorithms. This training constitutes the basis to obtain reliable results. According to Smith et al., the quality of the input data is a determining factor for the success of the learning process [46]. After collection, data pre-processing plays an important role in cleaning, transforming, and normalising the raw input data to improve its quality and relevance [26]. Breaking down the data into training and testing sets is essential to assess the model's ability to generalise to previously unseen data [10]. Finally, the application of suitable algorithms allows the model to learn from the training data and make predictions or take decisions based on the test data [19]. The combination of a set of data, an algorithm, and output predictions constitutes an ML model.

Figure 1 depicts all the stages present in ML [14,27]. Our objective is to complement, or even to replace, traditional techniques used in feature selection such as correlation analysis, recursive resource elimination, random forest or support vector machine (SVM) [1,17,24], with visibility graphs. The proposal consists of building VGs to identify, in a fast way, the most informative IP network-related features that would help supervised ML-based Intrusion Detection Systems (IDS) detect DoS attacks. The IP protocol (Internet Protocol) is the network layer communications protocol used in the Internet.

The remainder of this article is organised as follows. Section 2 provides a detailed review of the work related to using ML to detect DoS attacks. Section 3 introduces and introduces VGs and how they are built. Section 4 describes the use case considered in this study, including data collection and feature selection. Section 5 presents the methodology and the results of the tests that have been carried out. Finally, Sect. 6 discusses those obtained results and summarises the main conclusions of this work, including future research paths.

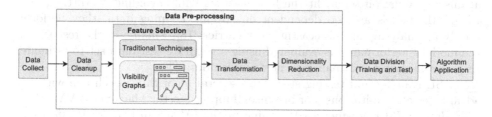

Fig. 1. ML stages. The focus of this research is to improve feature selection for ML.

2   Related Work

ML is an area within Artificial Intelligence (AI) that focuses on the development of algorithms and models capable of extracting insights from data and making informed decisions and predictions. ML can be categorised into four main types based on the approach to learning: Supervised Learning (SL), Unsupervised Learning (UL), semi-supervised learning, and reinforcement learning [20].

Among these types, SL stands out as the most prevalent form of ML [38]. SL involves learning from labelled data. The algorithm learns from a labelled dataset. Each input data point is associated with a corresponding output value. The goal is to train the algorithm to map input data to the correct output based on the provided labels. This labelled data is then used to train the model. The algorithm learns from the labelled data by adjusting its internal parameters. Once trained, the algorithm is capable of making predictions or classifications when presented with new input data. The key stages of SL encompass data preparation, model training, validation, and testing [23].

Unsupervised learning entails learning from unlabeled data, i.e., without any predefined output values. UL algorithms learn patterns without explicit output values. They discover patterns or relationships within the data on their own.

They are mostly used to cluster data, to identify anomalies, or to discover hidden patterns or structures in the data. All these actions are really useful to reduce the dimensionality of data.

A challenge in processing high-dimensional data is the difficulty of analysing and extracting meaningful information from datasets with many variables. Dimensionality reduction via UL tackles this issue [20]. It involves techniques that seek to project data into a smaller space, keeping as much relevant information as possible [11].

During the SL data preparation stage, data is cleaned, pre-processed, and divided into training and test sets. The process starts with a training dataset, composed of labelled examples, where the inputs are the features and the outputs are the corresponding labels [7]. In the model training stage, the algorithm is trained on the labelled data to learn the relationship between the input features and the output variable. In the validation stage, the trained model is evaluated against a validation set to fit the best features while avoiding overfitting, i.e., when ML models are too dependent on specific training data, they perform poorly at analysing and forecasting new entries [18]. Finally, in the test stage, the model's performance is evaluated using a separate test data set to estimate its generalisation performance on new, unseen data [40].

In SL training and testing stages use several algorithms, each one with its advantages and limitations. For instance, Support-Vector Machines (SVM) classifies data. SVM is a supervised learning method that can handle classification and regression problems with high precision [12]. Linear Regression predicts a continuous numerical value. Logistic Regression is used in binary classification tasks. Naive Bayes classifies input such as text [33]. Linear Discriminant Analysis (LDA) aims to maximise the separation between classes and reduces dimensions [16]. Decision Trees classify and generate decision-making rules [37]. The N-Nearest Neighbour algorithm (KNN) classifies data when the decision boundary is non-linear [13]. Multilayer perceptron (MLP) neural networks recognise patterns in learning complex patterns in image and speech processing applications [43]. Similarity Learning, used in both SL and UL understands relationships between instances in a dataset [18,35,36]. There is a vast number of Machine Learning algorithms [2].

Feature selection plays a key role in the SL data preparation stage. The aim is to identify the optimal set of features that provide the best performance, in terms of speed and quality, in the validation set. Feature selection can use several techniques. Table 1 includes grid search, random search and Bayesian optimization. These techniques provide flexible approaches to select the most relevant features in the SL, allowing for improved performance and model generalisation [6,15,47]. Grid search is a straightforward, yet computationally demanding, approach that exhaustively explores all possible combinations of features within a predefined range. It systematically evaluates the performance of the model for each combination of features, allowing the selection of the best ones. However, due to its exhaustive nature, grid searching consumes significant time and resources. Random search, however, offers a more efficient alternative. It randomly samples different combinations of features from a predefined collection. This approach reduces computational costs while providing a good chance of discovering well-performing feature sets. Alternatively, Bayesian optimisation presents a more sophisticated method for feature selection. It uses probabilistic models to efficiently search for the most promising combinations of features that lead to optimal model performance. Through the iterative selection and evaluation of subsets of features based on their expected utility, Bayesian optimization maximises the efficiency of the search process.

VGs are intuitive representations that convert a time series into a connected network structure. They provide a valuable means to explore the underlying dynamics and characteristics of a time series through the analysis of a complex network. VGs are constructed by transforming the time series into a collection of points, i.e., a value (or height) per time unit along a time axis. For each of those values (heights), if they "see each other", i.e., if a line can be drawn between them without crossing the vertical line created by any other intermediate point, then there is a direct line of visibility between them. In complex network terms, such visibility means that an edge is created between the two points and thus the VG is formed. VGs spawn a complex network whose properties, such as degree distribution, can be studied using the entire network analysis toolkit available to characterise complex systems [31,41,42,51]. The hypothesis of this article is that VGs can be useful artefacts to select supervised machine learning features.

Table 1. Comparison between supervised machine learning feature selection techniques, including our VG proposal.

Techniques	Information
Grid Search	The most simple and straightforward
	Non-iterative and uninformed search method
	Computationally demanding
	Exhaustive exploration
	All possible feature combinations.
Random Search	Iterative but uninformed search method
	Random sampling
	Reduced computational costs
	Good feature discovery probability.
Bayesian Optimization	Iterative and informed search method
	Probabilistic feature selection.
	Based on utility
	Maximises efficiency.
Visibility Graphs	Non-iterative and uninformed search
	Fast, visual and with low computing requirements
	No probability work required
	Alternative to traditional methods.

3   Visibility Graphs

VGs capture the visible relationships between points in a time series dataset [25]. For each point along a time axis, its height represents the values of the time series. If there is the possibility to link two of those values via a straight line (for VGs) or a horizontal line (for HVGs), then this line is drawn, creating a collection of "rays" that join visible values from the time series [29,30].

Creating a VG usually involves the following steps:

1. Collection of the dataset;
2. Identification of the feature to analyse;
3. Treatment of the data, i.e., creation of the time series. This involves cleaning the dataset so that it only has the expected feature, deleting the empty lines, transforming the categorical data into numeric data (if necessary), and creating a list with the already cleaned feature values to be introduced in the next step;
4. Identification of the edges connecting the visible points;
5. Building the graph based on the determined edges. This process can be performed in different ways, in this case, the VGs were created using the Python language with libraries such as Pandas, sklearn, pyplot, numpy, visibility_graph.

As an example, a dataset composed of four features, *"Time"*, *"Source"*, *"Destination"* and *"Protocol"* is loaded into a computing environment where the VGs will be created, based on one feature, i.e., on one of the columns in the dataset that is selected for analysis.

Selecting the feature "Protocol" to create the VG means that the processed values are *"TCP"* or *"HTTP"*. First, dataset lines with empty values are deleted. Second, the values, as they are categorical and not numeric, are transformed into corresponding numerical values. Third, a list with a series of values is created. This list constitutes the input data for the VG building library. It provides as output the collection of edges that connect the visible points to each other and build a complex network. Finally, an ad-hoc script coded in Python plots the VG.

VGs are a useful tool to analyse and visualise data. They provide important information about the structure and relationships present in the dataset. They facilitate the identification of highly visible points, i.e., nodes connected to many points. They also highlight specific connection patterns [41,42,49]. Furthermore, the visual representation of these VGs facilitates the analysis of ray trajectories and density. If different types of traffic produce different types of graphs, then VGs can be used to identify specific types of traffic, for instance, those types present in specific network attacks such as DoS.

4   Use Case: ML to Detect DoS Attacks

As a use case, this study utilises the distributed DoS application layer data set available in Kaggle [50]. This data set consists of network records of benign and malignant traffic and is composed of 77 resource columns and 1 target column, in *csv* format, as shown in the data set details in Kaggle. Each record represents a network packet and is labelled with a tag. The tag differentiates the type of traffic. The following three types are distinguished:

- *Slow loris DDoS*: IP network traffic present in an attack carried out by opening numerous TCP connections towards the target and keeping them open for an indefinite period of time, using these connections to repeatedly make HTTP requests [45].
- *Hulk DDoS*: IP network traffic typical of an attack that spoofs the UserAgent field and sends a high volume of HTTP GET requests, agnostic to the target, making the attack go undetected [3].
- *Benign*: benign IP network traffic without any DDOS (distributed DoS) attack.

A study carried out by Sarcevic et al. [44] in 2022 identifies ML features to classify network traffic using explainable artificial intelligence (XAI). XAI, also known as interpretable AI, uses white-box ML algorithms. In contrast to black box algorithms, their reasoning can be described and understood by human beings. Specifically, their study calculates the contributions of each of the features used in an if-then decision tree through the SHApley Additive exPlanations (SHAP) approach. The decision tree is a supervised ML algorithm that classifies options based on statistics [37]. The SHAP approach is a mathematical method, based on game theory, that provides an understanding of how each feature contributes to the performance of an ML model [4]. It calculates the importance of each feature and shows how much it influences the overall prediction of the model [32]. Sarcevic et al.'s research identifies ML features that are useful to detect DoS and DDoS attacks, as Table 2 illustrates. The objective of this study is to confirm the validity of those ML features identified by Sarcevic et al. using an alternative method that is easy to implement: visibility graphs (VGs).

Table 2. Best ML features for detecting DoS and DDoS attacks, according to [44].

No.	Feature	Description
1	Init Win bytes forward	The total number of bytes sent in the initial window in the forward direction
2	Flow IAT Mean	Average time between two packets sent in the stream
3	Destination Port	Destination port of a package
4	Min Seg Size Forward	Minimum observed segment size in forward direction

5   Assessing VGs for ML Feature Selection

The analysis carried out with the proposed dataset focuses on how VGs can help in the selection of the best input features for ML algorithms to detect distributed DoS attacks.

Table 2 presents four of the best features to detect DoS attacks, both distributed and non-distributed, based on the study by Sarcevic et al. [44].

Table 3 describes the usefulness of the mentioned selected features according to the work by Sarcevic et al. [44]. Finally, Table 4 shows how the same features, using visibility graphs, also provide relevant discriminating information. This table summarises the results of this study: VGs can be used to improve the classification/detection of (D)DoS using machine learning.

Table 3. Conclusions on the ML features identified by Sarcevic et al. [44].

No.	Feature	Info
1	Init Win bytes forward	High values (+ destination port 80) indicate benign traffic, while low values indicate DDoS attacks.
2	Flow IAT Mean	High values (+ destination port 80), compared to benign traffic, indicate DoS attacks.
3	Destination Port	Top feature in classifying benign traffic and brute force traffic and second top classifying DoS and DDoS attacks.
4	Min Seg Size Forward	High values (+ destination port 80) indicate a high probability of a DoS attack while low values of a DDoS attack.

Table 4. Conclusions on the ML features identified by visibility graphs in this study.

No.	Feature	Info
1	Init Win bytes forward	High values (and many edges) indicate benign traffic, while low (0) values (and no edges) indicate DDoS attacks.
2	Flow IAT Mean	Higher values in DDDoS attacks, compared with values in benign traffic.
3	Destination Port	Port value changes in benign traffic (and many edges) while just one port, normally port 80 (and very few edges) in DDoS attacks.
4	Min Seg Size Forward	Changes in the values (many edges) indicate a high probability of benign traffic while DDoS attack traffic shows no change in values (no edges)

Figures 2, 4, 5 and 6 depict the resulting VGs for the features identified in Table 3. The left side figures show the graphical representations of benign traffic and the right side pictures show the graphical representations for the DDoS attack traffic. Figure 3 represents the zoomed graph of Fig. 2.

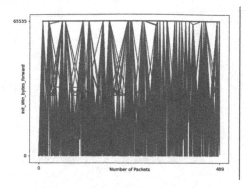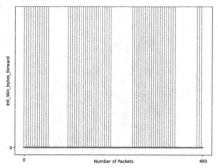

Fig. 2. VG Results - Comparing 500 network packets from Feature *Init Win Bytes Forward.* The left side corresponds to benign traffic and the right side corresponds to traffic from a DDoS attack. There is a clear difference in the number of edges present in each type of traffic. Benign traffic displays many edges.

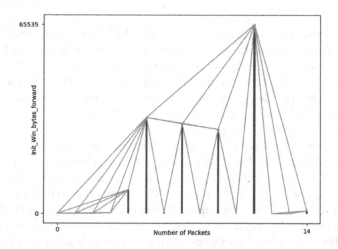

Fig. 3. Zoomed graph representing the first 15 nodes of the VG obtained in Fig. 2 of the benign traffic of the feature *Init Win Bytes Forward.*

Figure 2 shows the comparison of the *"Init Win Bytes Forward"* feature. This feature relates to the number of bytes present in the initial sending time window. It is observable that the maximum value reached by this feature in the case of benign traffic is 65,535, while in the case of malignant traffic, it remains at 0. In addition to the maximum value, the number of edges in the case of benign traffic (left graph) is much higher than with traffic present in an attack (right graph). This result confirms the usefulness of this feature to quickly distinguish between the two types of network traffic present in our dataset.

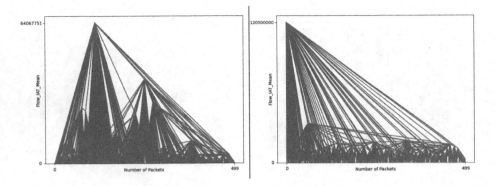

Fig. 4. VG Results - Comparing 500 network packets from Feature *Flow IAT Mean*. The left side corresponds to benign traffic and the right side corresponds to traffic from a DDoS attack. The maximum value for the distributed DoS attack is much higher than for benign traffic.

Figure 4 shows the comparison of the *"Flow IAT Mean"* feature. This feature displays the mean value of the inter-arrival time of network flows in both directions. The element that distinguishes the two types of traffic is the maximum value. Although in this case, the differentiation is quantitative and not so much visual, the maximum value of the average time between two sent packets is considerably higher in the case of a DDoS attack (120,000,000) than when dealing with benign traffic (64,067,751).

Figure 5 shows the comparison of the *"Destination Port"* feature. When it comes to an attack, the destination port does not change, e.g., port 80, the traditional HTTP port, in the studied dataset. However, in the case of benign traffic, port numbers change frequently. The number of edges in the case of benign traffic (left graph) is consequently much higher than with traffic present in a DDoS attack (right graph). This result confirms the usefulness of this feature to quickly distinguish between the two types of traffic: benign and DDoS.

Figure 6 shows the comparison of the feature *"Min Seg Size Forward"*. This feature relates to the minimum segment size of the IP network packet. While this feature is useful to distinguish between DoS and DDoS attacks in the study by Sarcevic et al. [44], the VG study shows that is also useful to discriminate between DDoS traffic and benign traffic. The minimum value and the maximum value differ in both traffic types. Additionally, the number of edges in the case of benign traffic (left graph) is much higher than with traffic present in an attack (right graph). This result suggests that a quick distinction can be made between the two types of traffic.

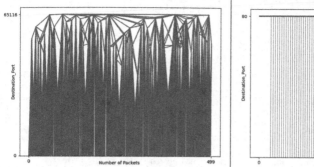
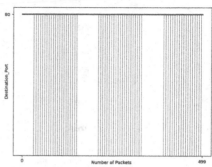

Fig. 5. VG Results - Comparing 500 network packets from Feature *Destination Port*. The left side corresponds to benign traffic and the right side corresponds to traffic from a DDoS attack. There is only one destination port in distributed DoS attacks while, in benign traffic, the number of ports varies.

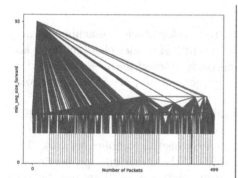

Fig. 6. VG Results - Comparing 500 network packets from Feature *Min Seg Size Forward*. The left side corresponds to benign traffic and the right side corresponds to traffic from a DDoS attack. There is a clear difference in the number of edges present in each type of traffic. Benign traffic displays many edges.

The obtained results show the different visibility patterns that benign and distributed DoS network traffic produce. Figures 2, 4, 5 and 6 and Table 4 summarise the conclusions on the ML features studied using visibility graphs. They confirm the hypothesis presented in this study: VGs are useful to select features for supervised machine learning models. At least, in this example, VGs distinguish distributed DoS attacks from benign network traffic.

Additionally, it was observed in the laboratory work of this research that there is a linear relation between the number of packets analysed to create the time series and the computing time required to plot the corresponding visibility graph, as Fig. 7 shows. Consequently, computing requirements are directly proportional to the size of the dataset to study.

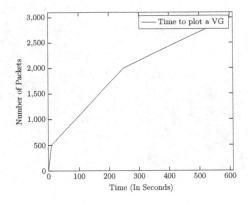

Fig. 7. Time spent plotting a Visibility Graph taking into account the number of network packets

6   Conclusion

Optimal feature selection is a crucial aspect to develop efficient machine learning (ML) models, as it directly influences the quality of model classifications and predictions. This article proposes a new approach to select features in supervised machine learning: using VGs as an easy-to-implement and low in computational cost feature search technique.

The proposal to use VGs as a feature selection tool in supervised ML offers significant advantages over traditional approaches. VGs are mathematical structures that represent visually a time series as a connected complex network. This graphical representation facilitates the analysis of the underlying properties and dynamics of the data, revealing patterns and relationships that may be very relevant when used as input features in a supervised ML model.

One of the main advantages of VGs is their ease of implementation and low computational cost. Unlike more complex and computationally intensive feature selection methods, VGs can be quickly built from time series data. This means that it is possible to perform feature selection in a fast way, even on complex datasets. The analysis of the visibility patterns in the VGs contributes to the reduction of complexity in the ML model.

However, the use of VGs for feature selection also has some limitations. The computation time needed to build the VGs increases linearly with the size of the dataset and, consequently, with the length of the time series. Therefore, the construction of a VG from a very lengthy time series, coming from a large volume of data, requires first a computational feasibility study.

In summary, the proposal to use VGs as a feature selection tool in supervised ML seems promising and paves the way for new research and applications in several domains, such as in the detection of other network attacks or even to detect fraud in payment transactions. Analysing patterns in VGs identifies features that build more effective and robust ML models.

Acknowledgements. This work was partially supported by the Norte Portugal Regional Operational Programme (NORTE 2020), under the PORTUGAL 2020 Partnership Agreement, through the European Regional Development Fund (ERDF), within the project "Cybers SeC IP" (NORTE-01-0145-FEDER-000044).

References

1. Abbas, L.B., Sadiq, M.A., Ahmad, M.O.: Machine learning-based detection of DDoS attacks: a review. Futur. Gener. Comput. Syst. **111**, 799–811 (2020)
2. Alpaydin, E.: Introduction to Machine Learning. MIT Press, Cambridge (2010)
3. Asonye, EA., Anwuna, I., Musa, S.M.: Securing Zig-Bee IoT network against HULK distributed denial of service attack. In: 2020 IEEE 17th International Conference on Smart Communities: Improving Quality of Life Using ICT, IoT and AI (HONET), pp. 156–162 (2020). https://doi.org/10.1109/HONET50430.2020.9322808
4. Bagheri, R.: Introduction to SHAP Values and their Application in Machine Learning. Towards Data Science (2022). https://towardsdatascience.com/introduction-to-shap-values-and-their-application-in-machine-learning-8003718e6827
5. Barrera-Animas, A.Y., et al.: Rainfall prediction: a comparative analysis of modern machine learning algorithms for time-series forecasting. Mach. Learn. Appl. **7**, 100204 (2022). ISSN 2666-8270. https://doi.org/10.1016/j.mlwa.2021.100204
6. Bergstra, J., Bengio, Y.: Random search for hyper-parameter optimization. In: International Conference on Learning Representations (2012)
7. Bishop, C.M.: Pattern Recognition and Machine Learning. Springer, New York (2006)
8. Boccaletti, S., et al.: Complex networks: structure and dynamics. Phys. Rep. **424**(4), 175–308 (2006). ISSN 0370-1573. https://doi.org/10.1016/j.physrep.2005.10.009
9. Boccaletti, S., et al.: Complex networks: structure and dynamics. Phys. Rep. **424**(4–5), 175–308 (2006)
10. Brown, C.: Data division strategies in machine learning. In: Proceedings of the International Conference on Machine Learning, pp. 234–245 (2017)
11. Chippalakatti, S., Renumadhavi, C.H., Pallavi, A.: Comparison of unsupervised machine learning Algorithm F or dimensionality reduction. In: 2022 International Conference on Knowledge Engineering and Communication Systems (ICKES), pp. 1–7 (2022). https://doi.org/10.1109/ICKECS56523.2022.10060625.
12. Cortes, C.: Support-vector networks. Mach. Learn. **20**(3), 273–297 (1995). https://doi.org/10.1007/bf00994018
13. Cover, T., Hart, P.: Nearest neighbor pattern classification. IEEE Trans. Inf. Theor. **13**(1), 21–27 (1967). https://doi.org/10.1109/TIT.1967.1053964
14. Domingos, P.: A few useful things to know about machine learning. Commun. ACM **55**(10), 78–87 (2012)
15. Falkner, S., Klein, A., Hutter, F.: BOHB: robust and efficient hyperparameter optimization at scale. In: Proceedings of the 35th International Conference on Machine Learning, pp. 1436–1445 (2018)
16. Fisher, R.A.: The use of multiple measurements in taxonomic problems. Ann. Eugenics **7**(2), 179–188. 1469-1809 (1936). https://doi.org/10.1111/j.1469-1809.1936.tb02137.x.
17. Gani, A., Ullah, S., Khan, K.: Detection of Denial of Service (DoS) attacks using machine learning techniques. In: 2019 International Conference on Computer and Information Sciences (ICCIS), pp. 1–6. IEEE (2019)

18. Géron, A.: Hands-On Machine Learning with Scikit-Learn, Keras, and TensorFlow: Concepts, Tools, and Techniques to Build Intelligent Systems. O'Reilly Media (2019)
19. Gonzalez, M.: Algorithm Applications in Machine Learning. Springer, Heidelberg (2019)
20. Goodfellow, I., Bengio, Y., Courville, A.: Deep Learning. MIT Press (2016)
21. Gupta, B.B., Badve, O.P.: Taxonomy of DoS and DDoS attacks and desirable defense mechanism in a Cloud computing environment. Neural Comput. Appl. **28**(12), 3655–3682 (2017). ISSN 1433–3058. https://doi.org/10.1007/s00521-016-2317-5
22. Gupta, B., Gupta, R., Tyagi, S.K.: Taxonomy of DDoS attacks and their prevention techniques: a review. J. Netw. Comput. Appl. **126**, 48–73 (2019). ISSN 1084-8045. https://doi.org/10.1016/j.jnca.2018.10.009
23. Hastie, T., Tibshirani, R., Friedman, J.: The Elements of Statistical Learning. SSS, Springer, New York (2009). https://doi.org/10.1007/978-0-387-84858-7
24. Islam, S.M.R., et al.: Detecting DDoS attacks with machine learning techniques. Inf. Sci. **254**, 1–14 (2014)
25. Johnson, M., Smith, L.: Visibility graphs: a survey. IEEE Trans. Vis. Comput. Graph. **21**(8), 933–952 (2015)
26. Jones, M., Brown, E.: Data pre-processing techniques in machine learning. Int. J. Data Sci. **8**(2), 789–804 (2016)
27. Kelleher, J.D., Tierney, B., Tierney, B.: Data Science: An Introduction, 2nd edn. CRC Press (2018). Chap. 5
28. Khosravi, A., Machado, L., Nunes, R.O.: Time-series prediction of wind speed using machine learning algorithms: a case study Osorio wind farm, Brazil. Appl. Energy **224**, 550–566 (2018). ISSN 0306-2619. https://doi.org/10.1016/j.apenergy.2018.05.043
29. Lacasa, L., et al.: From time series to complex networks: the visibility graph. Proc. Natl. Acad. Sci. **105**(13), 4972–4975 (2008)
30. Liu, J., Chen, J.: Visibility graphs for analyzing complex systems: a review. Chaos Interdisc. J. Nonlinear Sci. **28**(4), 041101 (2018)
31. Lucas, T., da Fontoura Costa, L., da Rocha, L.E.C.: Visibility graph analysis: a review. J. Stat. Mech. Theor. Exp. **2014**(8), 08001 (2014)
32. Mangalathu, S., Hwang, S.-H., Jeon, J.-S.: Failure mode and effects analysis of RC members based on machine-learning-based SHapley Additive exPlanations (SHAP) approach. Eng. Struct. **219**, 110927 (2020). ISSN 0141-0296. https://doi.org/10.1016/j.engstruct.2020.110927
33. McCallum, A., Nigam, K.: A comparison of event models for Naive Bayes text classification. In: AAAI-98 Workshop on Learning for Text Categorization, vol. 752, pp. 41–48 (1998)
34. Mishra, D.K., Singh, V.P., Tripathi, R.: Network security situation awareness using visibility graph. J. Netw. Comput. Appl. **58**, 49–62 (2015). ISSN 1084-8045. https://doi.org/10.1016/j.jnca.2015.09.007
35. Müller, A.C., Guido, S.: Introduction to Machine Learning with Python: A Guide for Data Scientists. O'Reilly Media (2016)
36. Murty, M.N., Raghava, R.: Support Vector Machines and Perceptrons. Learning, Optimization, Classification, and Application to Social Networks. SCS, Springer, Cham (2016). https://doi.org/10.1007/978-3-319-41063-0
37. Myles, A.J., et al.: An introduction to decision tree modeling. J. Chemom. J. Chemometr. Soc. **18**(6), 275–285 (2004)

38. Nasteski, V.: An overview of the supervised machine learning methods. In: HORI-ZONS.B 4, pp. 51–62, December 2017. https://doi.org/10.20544/HORIZONS.B. 04.1.17.P05

39. Newman, M.E.J.: The structure and function of complex networks. SIAM Rev. **45**(2), 167–257 (2003)

40. Ng, A.: Machine learning yearning. Draft (2018). https://www.mlyearning.org/

41. Partida, A., Criado, R., Romance, M.: Visibility graph analysis of IOTA and IoTeX price series: an intentional risk-based strategy to use 5G for IoT. Electronics **10**(18) (2021). ISSN 2079-9292. https://doi.org/10.3390/electronics10182282

42. Partida, A., et al.: The chaotic, self-similar and hierarchical patterns in Bitcoin and Ethereum price series. Chaos Solitons Fractals **165**, 112806 (2022). ISSN 0960-0779. https://doi.org/10.1016/j.chaos.2022.112806

43. Rumelhart, D.E., Hinton, G.E., Williams, R.J.: Learning representations by back-propagating errors. Nature **323**(6088), 533–536 (1986). https://doi.org/10.1038/323533a0

44. Šarčević, A., et al.: Cybersecurity knowledge extraction using XAI. Appl. Sci. **12**(17) (2022). ISSN 2076-3417. https://doi.org/10.3390/app12178669

45. Shorey, T., et al.: Performance comparison and analysis of Slowloris, GoldenEye and Xerxes DDoS attack tools. In: 2018 International Conference on Advances in Computing, Communications and Informatics, ICA CCI 2018, pp. 318–322 (2018). https://doi.org/10.1109/ICACCI.2018.8554590

46. Smith, J., Johnson, S.: Data collection for machine learning. J. Mach. Learn. Res. **12**(4), 1234–1256 (2018)

47. Snoek, J., Larochelle, H., Adams, R.P.: Practical Bayesian optimization of machine learning algorithms. In: International Conference on Neural Information Processing Systems (2012)

48. Stefano, B.: Multiscale vulnerability of complex networks. Chaos **17**(4), 175–308 (2007). https://doi.org/10.1063/1.2801687

49. Wang, X., Zhang, W.: Visibility graph analysis: a novel approach for network traffic modeling. In: Proceedings of the International Conference on Communications, pp. 123–130 (2017)

50. Warda: Application-Layer DDoS Dataset (2020). https://www.kaggle.com/datasets/wardac/applicationlayer-ddos-dataset?select=test_mosaic.csv

51. Xiang, J., Small, M.: Visibility graphlet approach to chaotic time series. Phys. Rev. E **92**(6), 062817 (2015)

52. Zhang, J., Small, M.: Complex network from pseudoperiodic time series: topology versus dynamics. Phys. Rev. Lett. **96**, 238701 (2006). https://doi.org/10.1103/PhysRevLett.96.238701

Learning Algorithms in Engineering Education

Accuracy Optimization in Speech Pathology Diagnosis with Data Preprocessing Techniques

Joana Filipa Teixeira Fernandes[1,2](✉) (iD), Diamantino Rui Freitas[2] (iD),
and João Paulo Teixeira[1,3] (iD)

[1] Research Centre in Digitalization and Intelligent Robotics (CeDRI), Instituto Politécnico de
Bragança (IPB), 5300 Bragança, Portugal
{joana.fernandes,joaopt}@ipb.pt
[2] Faculty of Engineering, University of Porto (FEUP), 4200-465 Porto, Portugal
dfreitas@fe.up.pt
[3] Associate Laboratory for Sustainability and Technology (SusTEC), Instituto Politécnico de
Bragança, Campus de Santa Apolónia, 5300-253 Bragança, Portugal

Abstract. Using acoustic analysis to classify and identify speech disorders non-invasively can reduce waiting times for patients and specialists while also increasing the accuracy of diagnoses. In order to identify models to use in a vocal disease diagnosis system, we want to know which models have higher success rates in distinguishing between healthy and pathological sounds. For this purpose, 708 diseased people spread throughout 19 pathologies, and 194 control people were used. There are nine sound files per subject, three vowels in three tones, for each subject. From each sound file, 13 parameters were extracted. For the classification of healthy/pathological individuals, a variety of classifiers based on Machine Learning models were used, including decision trees, discriminant analyses, logistic regression classifiers, naive Bayes classifiers, support vector machines, classifiers of closely related variables, ensemble classifiers and artificial neural network classifiers. For each patient, 118 parameters were used initially. The first analysis aimed to find the best classifier, thus obtaining an accuracy of 81.3% for the Ensemble Sub-space Discriminant classifier. The second and third analyses aimed to improve ground accuracy using preprocessing methodologies. Therefore, in the second analysis, the PCA technique was used, with an accuracy of 80.2%. The third analysis combined several outlier treatment models with several data normalization models and, in general, accuracy improved, obtaining the best accuracy (82.9%) with the combination of the Greebs model for outliers treatment and the range model for the normalization of data procedure.

Keywords: Outliers · Normalization · Speech Pathologies · Speech Features · Machine Learning · Vocal Acoustic Analysis

1 Introduction

This research aims to develop a straightforward artificial intelligence model that can distinguish between healthy and pathological subjects with high accuracy rates and can be implemented in a system for the early detection of vocal pathologies. In its initial

A. I. Pereira et al. (Eds.): OL2A 2023, CCIS 1981, pp. 287–299, 2024.
https://doi.org/10.1007/978-3-031-53025-8_20

trial stage, this technology will be installed in hospitals, where it will be used to record people's voices and determine if they are healthy or pathological.

Some unique data points differ significantly from other observations in a dataset. These observations are called outliers. Finding these outlying/anomalous observations in datasets has recently attracted much attention and is significant in many applications [1, 2].

As a rule, the appearance of outliers in databases is mainly due to human errors, instrument errors, population deviation, fraudulent behaviour and changes or failures in the system's behaviour. Some outliers can be observed as natural data points [3]. Detecting outliers in a dataset is important for many applications, such as network analysis, medical diagnostics, agricultural intelligence and financial fraud detection [4]. The statistics-based outlier detection methods model the objects using mean and standard deviation for a Gaussian distribution dataset or the median and inter-quartile range for non-Gaussian distribution [5–8].

Because normalization operations are designed to reduce issues like data redundancy and skewed results in the presence of anomalies, several modelling techniques, like Neural Networks, KNN, and clustering, benefit from improved performance [9].

The data set underwent some modifications. Making a scale to stabilize variance, lessen asymmetry, and bring the variable closer to the normal distribution is therefore what is needed [9].

In sets of searches with excessive information due to the inclusion of many features, issues like high dimensionality, overfitting risk, and biased results are dealt with by the selection of features. Low relevance and redundant input data have an impact on learning algorithms [10, 11].

As a result, the initial data set's size is reduced, computational costs are decreased, and the forecast accuracy of the predictors is increased as a result of the selection and elimination of less important attributes. The search direction, the search methodology, and the stopping criterion are the three dimensions that make up the selection of features [12].

This work intends to find a classification model and optimize the accuracy in the classification between healthy and pathological subjects. Therefore, it is necessary to treat and correct the anomalies identified in the automatically extracted feature values available in systems related to the diagnosis of voice pathologies, which have as input parameters relative jitter, absolute jitter, RAP jitter, PPQ5 jitter, absolute shimmer, relative shimmer, APQ3 shimmer, APQ5 shimmer, Fundamental Frequency, Harmonic to Noise Ratio (HNR), autocorrelation, Shannon entropy, logarithmic entropy and the subject's sex [13–17].

This work includes 4 section, the first being the introduction. The second describes the database, extracted parameters, outlier identification and treatment methods, data normalization and main component analysis. In the third chapter, the results and discussion are described. Lastly, the conclusion.

2 Materials and Methods

In this section, the Database used, the parameters used, the outliers identification methods, the normalization methods, Principal Component Analysis (PCA) and evaluation measurements will be described.

2.1 Database

The German Saarbrucken Voice Database (SVD), made available online by the Institute of Phonetics at the University of Saarland, was used as the source for the speech files [18].

The collection includes voice signals from more than 2000 individuals with both healthy voices and vocal problems. Each subject has recordings of the German greeting "Good morning, how are you?" with the phonemes /a/, /i/, and /u/ in the low, neutral/normal, and high tones and shifting between tones. The sound files have a duration of between one and three seconds, were recorded in mono at a sample rate of 50 kHz, and have a resolution of 16 bits [19]. Table 1 includes the mean age and standard deviation as well as the distribution of subjects by various pathologies (19 diseases, a total of 708 diseased subjects, and 194 control subjects).

2.2 Feature Extraction

In this section, the various parameters that will be extracted from the speech signal will be described.

Jitter is the glottal fluctuation between vocal cord vibration cycles. Higher jitter values are typically observed in subjects who have trouble modulating their vocal cords. Absolute Jitter (jitta), Relative Jitter (jitter), Relative Average Perturbation Jitter (RAP), and Five-point Period Perturbation Quotients Jitter (PPQ5) will be used as input features [15, 17, 19].

Shimmer is the amplitude variation over the glottal periods. Variations in glottal magnitude are mostly caused by lesions and decreased glottal resistance. Reduced glottal resistance and injuries can result in higher shimmer values, which can change the glottal magnitude. Absolute Shimmer (ShdB), Relative Shimmer (shim), Three-Point Amplitude Perturbation Quotient Shimmer (APQ3), and Five-Point Amplitude Perturbation Quotient Shimmer (APQ5) will be used as the shimmer measurements [15, 17, 19].

Fundamental Frequency (F0) is thought to correspond to the vibration frequency of the vocal cords. The Autocorrelation method is used to calculate the F0, with a frame window length of 100 ms and a minimum F0 of 50 Hz [20].

Harmonic to Noise Ratio (HNR) enables for assessing the relationship between the harmonic and noise components of a speech signal. Different vocal tract topologies result in various amplitudes for the harmonics, which can cause the HNR value of a signal to change [16, 21–24].

Table 1. Groups used for the study, sample size, mean and standard deviation of the ages.

Groups		Sample size		Average Ages	Standard Deviation Age
		subjects	%		
Control		194	21.51	38.06	14.36
Pathological	Dysphonia	69	7.65	47.38	16.27
	Chronic Laryngitis	41	4.55	49.69	13.47
	Vocal Cord Paralysis	169	18.74	57.75	13.77
	Cyst	3	0.33	47.50	15.56
	Vocal Strings Polyp	27	2.99	52.28	13.41
	Carcinoma of Vocal Strings	19	2.11	57.00	6.60
	Laryngeal Tumor	4	0.44	53.50	8.17
	Granuloma	2	0.22	44.50	4.50
	Intubation granuloma	3	0.33	53.00	11.22
	Hypopharyngeal Tumor	6	0.67	59.50	9.29
	Fibroma	1	0.11	46.00	0.00
	Dysplastic Larynx	1	0.11	69.00	0.00
	Reinke's edema	34	3.77	56.10	11.37
	Functional Dysphonia	75	8.31	47.12	14.54
	Hypofunctional Dysphonia	12	1.33	41.63	15.07
	Hyperfunctional Dysphonia	127	14.08	42.32	13.62
	Hypotonic Dysphonia	2	0.22	49.50	12.50
	Psychogenic Dysphonia	51	5.65	51.40	9.40
	Spasmodic Dysphonia	62	6.87	57.15	15.75

Autocorrelation.
The autocorrelation gives an indication of how similar succeeding phonatory periods that are repeated throughout the signal are to one another. The signal's periodicity increases as the autocorrelation value rises [19, 21, 25].

Entropy.
In order to quantitatively quantify the level of unpredictability and uncertainty of a particular data sequence, it takes into account the energy that is present in a complex system. Entropy analysis makes it feasible to precisely evaluate the nonlinear behavior characteristic of voice signals [26].

2.3 Identification and Treatment of Outliers

The basic methods for finding outliers can be distinguished by the criteria used, such as classification, distance, densities, clusters, and statistics [3].

The calculation of mean, standard deviation and histograms is affected by outliers. As a result, it distorts generalizations and inferences about the studied data set. As a result, the inclusion of outliers in the dataset can result in incorrect interpretations [3].

In the **Median** method, Outliers are items that deviate more than three MED from the median. Equation 1 provides the MED scale's definition.

$$c * \text{median}(|A - \text{median}(A)|) \tag{1}$$

where A is the data and c is described by Eq. 2, where erfcinv is the inverse complementary error function [27].

$$c = \frac{-1}{\sqrt{2} * \text{erfcinv}\left(\frac{3}{2}\right)} \tag{2}$$

The **Mean** method defines Outliers by the Mean method as components that deviate from the mean by more than three standard deviations. This approach is quicker but less reliable than the median approach [8, 27, 28].

In the **Quartile** method, items with more than 1.5 inter-quartile range above the upper quartile (75%) or below the lower quartile (25%), are considered outliers. This approach is advantageous when the data has not a normal distribution [27, 28].

The Grubbs test, which eliminates one outlier per iteration based on the hypothesis test, is used by the **Grubbs** method to identify outliers. The data will be assumed to have a normal distribution for this method [27].

By employing the Grubbs test, which eliminates one outlier per iteration based on the hypothesis test, the **Gesd** technique finds outliers. According to this strategy, the data should have normal distribution [27].

Once an outlier has been identified, filling is the procedure used to handle it. The limit value, which is determined in accordance with the selected method, takes the place of the outlier.

When new subjects (samples) are included in the dataset, the recognition process must be verified using the threshold value that was previously established using the original data set.

2.4 Normalization

Some modeling tools, such as neural networks, the k-nearest neighbors algorithm (KNN), and clustering, benefit from normalization since these normalizing operations aim to reduce issues such data redundancy and skewed findings in the presence of anomalies. The dataset underwent several modifications. Therefore, the goal is to create a scale that will stabilize a variance, reduce asymmetry, and approach the variable's normal distribution [3].

The **Z-Score** calculates a data point's distance from the mean, related to standard deviation,. The original data set's shape characteristics are preserved in the standardized data set (same skewness and kurtosis), which has a mean of 0 and a standard deviation of 1 [29, 30].

The general definition of the P-norm of a vector v with N elements according to the **P-Norm** technique is: where p is any positive real value, Inf or -Inf. Typical values of p include 1, 2, and Inf [29, 30].

- The sum of the absolute values of the vector elements is the 1-norm that results if p is 1.
- The vector magnitude, or Euclidean length of the vector, is determined by the 2-norm that results if p is 2.
- When p is Inf, then $\|v\|_\infty = max_i(|v(i)|)$.

By stretching or compressing the points along the number line, the **Resizing** method modifies the distance between the minimum and maximum values in a data collection. The data's z-scores are kept, therefore the statistical distribution's form is unaltered. The formula for scaling data X to a range [a, b] is: If A is constant, normalize returns the interval's lower limit (which is 0 by default) or NaN (when the range contains Inf) [29, 30].

A data set's **Interquartile Range** (IQR) describes the range of the middle 50% of values after sorting the values. In this case, the median of the data would be Q2, the median of the lower half would be Q1, and the median of the upper half would be Q3. When the data contains outliers (extremely big or very tiny values), the IQR is typically favored over examining the entire range of the data because it excludes the largest 25% and smallest 25% of values in the data [30].

The median value of the absolute deviations from the median of the data is known as the **Median Absolute Deviation** (MAD) of a data collection. As a result, the MAD illustrates how variable the data are in regard to the median. When the data contains outliers (extremely big or very tiny values), the MAD is typically favored over using the standard deviation of the data since the standard deviation squares differences from the mean, giving outliers an excessively significant impact. In contrast, the MAD value is unaffected by the deviations of a few outliers [30].

2.5 Principal Component Analysis (PCA)

This technique uses mathematical concepts such as standard deviation, covariance of eigenvalues and eigenvector. To determine the number of principal components, eigenvectors and eigenvalues must be determined starting from the covariance matrix. Then, calculating the cumulative proportion of the eigenvalues is all that is required. As a result, the first eigenvectors that correspond to 90% or 95% of the collected percentage will be chosen, meaning that the first eigenvectors account for 90% or 95% of the data. The final step is to multiply the fitted data by the inverse of the chosen eigenvector matrix [31].

2.6 Evaluation Measurements

In order to evaluate the performance, accuracy will be used. This measure is observed in Eq. 3. However, the data used are unbalanced, hence the need to present 4 measures in addition to accuracy, namely precision, sensitivity, specificity and F1-score. These measures are presented in Eq. 4, 5, 6 and 7 respectively. Where TP stands for True Positive, FN stands for False Negative, FP is False Positive, TN is True Negative, P stands Precision and S is Sensibility.

$$\text{Accuracy} = \frac{\text{TP} + \text{TN}}{\text{TP} + \text{FN} + \text{FP} + \text{TN}} \tag{3}$$

$$\text{Precision} = \frac{\text{TP}}{\text{TP} + \text{FP}} \tag{4}$$

$$\text{Sensibility} = \frac{\text{TP}}{\text{TP} + \text{FN}} \tag{5}$$

$$\text{Specificity} = \frac{\text{TN}}{\text{TN} + \text{FP}} \tag{6}$$

$$\text{F1} - \text{score} = 2 \times \frac{\text{P} \times \text{S}}{\text{P} + \text{S}} \tag{7}$$

3 Results and Discussion

In this chapter the results are presented as well as a discussion about them.

3.1 Results

For the analysis, 9 sound files were used per subject, and 13 parameters were extracted from each file (relative jitter, absolute jitter, RAP jitter, PPQ5 jitter, absolute shimmer, relative shimmer, APQ3 shimmer, APQ5 shimmer, fundamental frequency, HNR, autocorrelation, Shannon entropy and logarithmic entropy), giving 117 parameters per subject, to which sex was added. Therefore, the input matrix is composed of 118 lines × N number of subjects.

Having the input matrix, the classification between healthy and pathological began. As classifiers we used Decision Trees, Discriminant Analysis, Logistic Regression Classifiers, Naive Bayes Classifiers, Support Vector Machines, Nearest Neighbor Classifiers, Ensemble Classifiers and Artificial Neural Network. The cross-validation technique of 10 folds was applied during the training process.

The classifier that obtained the best result without any data pre-processing, with a binary output (control/pathological) was the Ensemble Subspace Discriminant [32] with an accuracy of 81.3%. This model had 30 learners and subspace dimension 59.

In order to improve this accuracy, the technique of reducing the dimension was used, using Principal Component Analysis (PCA). This analysis was applied to the 118 parameters, with a variance of 95%, resulting in 7 new features and an accuracy of 80.2% was obtained.

Given that the accuracy obtained with the PCA technique is lower than those obtained without any feature dimension reduction and considering the work of Silva et al. 2019 [3], where it obtained an improvement of up to 13 percentage points, an attempt was made to understand whether, with the treatment of outliers and data normalization, the accuracy of the classifier increased. Therefore, in Table 2 it is possible to observe the result of the various combinations between the various models for treating outliers with the various models for normalizing the data. In this analysis, PCA was not used, since there was a loss of accuracy. In the normalization using the range model (resizing method), the data were normalized between [−1, 1].

Table 2. Accuracy using the Ensemble Subspace Discriminant model with the various outlier detection and data normalization techniques.

Accuracy (%)		Normalization method					
		zscore	norm	scale	range	center	medianiqr
Outliers method	Median	82.3	82	82.3	81.6	81.6	82.4
	Mean	81.6	81.2	82	81.9	82.2	81.5
	Quartiles	82.3	82.0	82.4	82.5	82.5	82.5
	Grubbs	82.5	81.7	82.3	**82.9**	82.3	82.2
	Gesd	82.2	82.0	81.2	81.8	82.3	81.6

Table 2 shows that using the outlier identification method and data normalization allows for improvements in accuracy over the baseline accuracy of 81.3%.

The combination between the outlier identification method and the data normalization method that obtained the best results was with the Grubbs method for outliers and the range method for data normalization, which obtained an accuracy of 82.9%. In this way, an improvement of 1.6 percentage points was achieved compared to the result where there was no data pre-processing, and an improvement of 2.7 percentage points compared to the accuracy obtained by the PCA method.

In Fig. 1, it is possible to see that the Area Under Curve (AUC) improved considerably, changing from 0.78 to 0.82.

3.2 Discussion

Comparing the results obtained in this work with those obtained by Silva et al. 2019 [3], it is possible to notice that the results obtained in this work are similar. In both works,

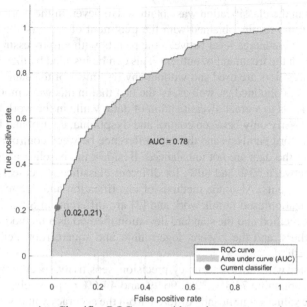

a)   Classifier ROC curve without data pre-processing.

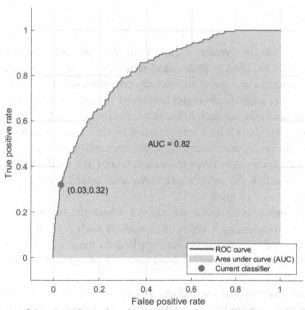

b) ROC curve of the classifier using the outliers and normalization method with better accuracy.

Fig. 1. a) Classifier ROC curve without data pre-processing; b) ROC curve of the classifier using the outliers and normalization method with better accuracy.

an improvement in the classification was obtained. However, in the work developed by Silva et al. 2019, the results obtained with the treatment of outliers showed a greater improvement at a percentage level between the results without processing outliers and those obtained with the treatment of outliers. This can be justified by the classifier used, since different classifiers are used and without any treatment of the data, in this work a higher accuracy was obtained, as well as, by the fact that in this work more pathologies are used, which leads to a great diversification of data, while in the work by Silva et al. 2019 [3] try to classify only between control and dysphonia, control and laryngitis and control and vocal cord paralysis and the data difference between control and pathology is smaller, that is, the data are not unbalanced. Besides, the baseline accuracy used in [3] was lower, between 63% and 80%, for different classification cases, leaving more space for improvements. Also, the methods of identification and treatment of outliers and data normalization used in this work and [3] are different. In Silva et al. 2019 [3] used the boxplot method and the standard deviation method as a method of identifying and treating outliers, and the z-score, logarithmic and square root method as a data normalization method.

For the situation with the best accuracy, precision, sensitivity, specificity and F1-score were calculated, obtaining 73.8%, 32%, 96.9% and 44.6% respectively.

The F1-score value is significantly different from the accuracy value, since the dataset is not balanced.

4   Conclusion

In order to try to obtain greater accuracy in the subject classification process (healthy/pathological) we tried to understand whether the results were better with the data from the input matrix in 3 ways: without any pre-processing, with PCA and without PCA with technique of identification and treatment of outliers and data normalization. Therefore, for this analysis we had 708 sick participants and 194 control individuals were used in this study, since it took into account 19 different pathologies.

Each subject comprises nine sound files, corresponding to three vowels and three tones, where 13 parameters were taken from each sound file, totalling 117 input features for each subject, to which the subject's sex was also added. The input matrix is thus made up of N subjects x 118 lines.

In this work, a first classification was started where the input matrix did not have any type of data pre-processing 8 types of classifiers with several models. The cross-validation technique of 10 validations was applied to these classifiers.From this first analysis, an accuracy of 81.3% was obtained for the Ensemble Subspace Discriminant classifier.

Then a second analysis was carried out where the Principal Component Analysis (PCA) technique was applied to the input matrix. In this analysis, only the classifier that obtained the best accuracy was used, but the accuracy results were not better, as an accuracy of 80.2% was obtained.

In work by Silva et al. 2019 [3], using different outlier treatment methods and data normalization, improved accuracy by up to 13 percentage points from a lower baseline accuracy. In this way, an analysis was initiated in which 5 outlier treatment models were combined with 6 data normalization models without the use of PCA, for the same classification model. Therefore, an improvement of 1.6 percentage points was achieved, with an accuracy of 82.9%. This accuracy was obtained with the combination of the grubbs model in the treatment of outliers, with the range model in the normalization of the data.

As future work, it is intended to classify the types of signals. In signal classification there are 3 types of signals. In type 1 the signals are periodic, in type 2 they have some periodicity and in type 3 the signals are chaotic. Signals that are classified as type 3 cannot use these parameters since they are signals without any type of periodicity, which leads to extremely high jitter and shimmer values, thus impairing the classification. Later, it is intended to identify the pathology and the degree of severity.

In order to increase the database, this system is implemented in a hospital in order to collect more speech signals.

Acknowledgements. The work was supported by the Foundation for Science and Technology UIDB/05757/2020, UIDP/05757/2020 and 2021.04729.BD and by SusTEC LA/P/0007/2021. The authors acknowledge the financial support for FEUP for this publication.

References

1. Toller, M.B., Geiger, B.C., Kern, R.: Cluster purging: efficient outlier detection based on rate-distortion theory. IEEE Trans. Knowl. Data Eng. **35**(2), 1270–1282 (2023). https://doi.org/10.1109/TKDE.2021.3103571
2. Abhaya, A., Patra, B.K.: An efficient method for autoencoder based outlier detection. Exp. Syst. Appl. **213**, 118904 (2023). https://doi.org/10.1016/J.ESWA.2022.118904
3. Silva, L., et al.: Outliers treatment to improve the recognition of voice pathologies. Procedia Comput. Sci. **164**, 678–685 (2019). https://doi.org/10.1016/J.PROCS.2019.12.235
4. Du, X., Zuo, E., Chu, Z., He, Z., Yu, J.: Fluctuation-based outlier detection. Sci. Rep. **13**(1), 2408 (2023). https://doi.org/10.1038/s41598-023-29549-1
5. Grubbs, F.E.: Procedures for detecting outlying observations in samples. Technometrics **11**(1), 1–21 (1969). https://doi.org/10.1080/00401706.1969.10490657
6. Atkinson, A.C., Hawkins, D.M.: Identification of outliers. Biometrics **37**(4), 860 (1981). https://doi.org/10.2307/2530182
7. Yang, X., Latecki, L.J., Pokrajac, D.: Outlier detection with globally optimal exemplar-based GMM. In: 2009 9th SIAM International Conference on Data Mining. Proceedings in Applied Mathematics, vol. 1, pp. 144–153. Society for Industrial and Applied Mathematics (2009). https://doi.org/10.1137/1.9781611972795.13
8. Seo, S., Marsh, P.D.G.M.: A review and comparison of methods for detecting outliers in univariate data sets (2006). http://d-scholarship.pitt.edu/7948/
9. Pino, F.A.: A questão da não normalidade: uma revisão. Rev. Econ. Agrícola **61**(2), 17–33 (2014)
10. Guyon, I., Elisseeff, A.: An introduction to variable and feature selection. J. Mach. Learn. Res. **3**, 1157–1182 (2003)
11. Rodrigues, P.M., Teixeira, J.P.: Classification of electroencephalogram signals using artificial neural networks. In: Proceedings of the 2010 3rd International Conference on Biomedical Engineering and Informatics, BMEI 2010, vol. 2, pp. 808–812 (2010). https://doi.org/10.1109/BMEI.2010.5639941

12. Silva, L., Bispo, B., Teixeira, J.P.: Features selection algorithms for classification of voice signals. Procedia Comput. Sci. **181**, 948–956 (2021). https://doi.org/10.1016/J.PROCS.2021. 01.251
13. Teixeira, J.P., Freitas, D.: Segmental durations predicted with a neural network. In: International Conference on Spoken Language Processing, Proceedings of Eurospeech 2003, pp. 169–172 (2003)
14. Teixeira, J.P., Freitas, D., Braga, D., Barros, M.J., Latsch, V.: Phonetic events from the labeling the European Portuguese database for speech synthesis, FEUP/IPB-DB. In: International Conference on Spoken Language Processing, Proceedings of Eurospeech 2001, pp. 1707–1710 (2001). 8790834100, 978-879083410-4
15. Teixeira, J.P., Gonçalves, A.: Algorithm for jitter and shimmer measurement in pathologic voices. Procedia Comput. Sci. **100**, 271–279 (2016). https://doi.org/10.1016/J.PROCS.2016. 09.155
16. Fernandes, J., Teixeira, F., Guedes, V., Junior, A., Teixeira, J.P.: Harmonic to noise ratio measurement - selection of window and length. Procedia Comput. Sci. **138**, 280–285 (2018). https://doi.org/10.1016/J.PROCS.2018.10.040
17. Fernandes, J., Junior, A.C., Freitas, D., Teixeira, J.P.: Smart data driven system for pathological voices classification. In: Pereira, A.I., Košir, A., Fernandes, F.P., Pacheco, M.F., Teixeira, J.P., Lopes, R.P. (eds.) Optimization, Learning Algorithms and Applications: Second International Conference, OL2A 2022, Póvoa de Varzim, Portugal, October 24–25, 2022, Proceedings, pp. 419–426. Springer, Cham (2022). https://doi.org/10.1007/978-3-031-23236-7_29
18. Pützer, M., Barry, W.J.: Saarbruecken Voice Database. Institute of Phonetics at the University of Saarland (2007). http://www.stimmdatenbank.coli.uni-saarland.de. Accessed 05 Nov 2021
19. Fernandes, J., Silva, L., Teixeira, F., Guedes, V., Santos, J., Teixeira, J.P.: Parameters for vocal acoustic analysis - cured database. Procedia Comput. Sci. **164**, 654–661 (2019). https://doi. org/10.1016/J.PROCS.2019.12.232
20. Hamdi, R., Hajji, S., Cherif, A., Processing, S.: Recognition of pathological voices by human factor cepstral coefficients (HFCC). J. Comput. Sci. **16**, 1085–1099 (2020). https://doi.org/ 10.3844/jcssp.2020.1085.1099
21. Fernandes, J.F.T., Freitas, D., Junior, A.C., Teixeira, J.P.: Determination of harmonic parameters in pathological voices—efficient algorithm. Appl. Sci. **13**(4), 2333 (2023). https://doi. org/10.3390/app13042333
22. Teixeira, J.P., Fernandes, P.O.: Acoustic analysis of vocal dysphonia. Procedia Comput. Sci. **64**, 466–473 (2015). https://doi.org/10.1016/J.PROCS.2015.08.544
23. Teixeira, J.P., Fernandes, J., Teixeira, F., Fernandes, P.O.: Acoustic analysis of chronic laryngitis statistical analysis of sustained speech parameters. In: 11th International Joint Conference on Biomedical Engineering Systems and Technologies, BIOSTEC 2018, vol. 4, pp. 168–175 (2018). https://doi.org/10.5220/0006586301680175
24. Boersma, P.: Accurate short-term analysis of the fundamental frequency and the harmonics-to-noise ratio of a sampled sound. In: IFA Proceedings 17, vol. 17, pp. 97–110 (1993). http:// www.fon.hum.uva.nl/paul/papers/Proceedings_1993.pdf
25. Boersma, P.: Stemmen meten met Praat. Stem-, Spraak- en Taalpathologie **12**(4), 237–251 (2004)
26. Araújo, T., Teixeira, J.P., Rodrigues, P.M.: Smart-data-driven system for alzheimer disease detection through electroencephalographic signals. Bioengineering **9**(4), 141 (2022). https:// doi.org/10.3390/bioengineering9040141
27. NIST/SEMATECH: e-Handbook of Statistical Methods. http://www.itl.nist.gov/div898/handbook/. Accessed 14 Jun 2023
28. Unwin, A.: Exploratory data analysis, 3rd edn. In: International Encyclopedia of Education, pp. 156–161. Elsevier, Amsterdam (2010). https://doi.org/10.1016/B978-0-08-044894-7.013 27-0

29. Triola, M.F.: Introdução à estatística, 12th edn. In: Elementary Statistics. Pearson Education INC, Rio de Janeiro (2017)
30. MathWorks: Normalize. https://www.mathworks.com/help/matlab/ref/double.normalize.html#d124e1046230. Accessed 14 Jun 2023
31. Teixeira, J.P., Alves, N., Fernandes, P.O.: Vocal acoustic analysis: ANN Versos SVM in classification of dysphonic voices and vocal cords paralysis. Int. J. E-Health Med. Commun. **11**(1), 37–51 (2020). https://doi.org/10.4018/IJEHMC.2020010103
32. Ashour, A.S., Guo, Y., Hawas, A.R., Guan, Xu.: Ensemble of subspace discriminant classifiers for schistosomal liver fibrosis staging in mice microscopic images. Health Inf. Sci. Syst. **6**(1), 21 (2018). https://doi.org/10.1007/s13755-018-0059-8

Application of Pattern Recognition Techniques for MathE Questions Difficulty Level Definition

Beatriz Flamia Azevedo[1,2]([✉]) [iD], Roberto Molina de Souza[3] [iD],
Maria F. Pacheco[1,2] [iD], Florbela P. Fernandes[1] [iD], and Ana I. Pereira[1,2] [iD]

[1] Research Centre in Digitalization and Intelligent Robotics (CeDRI), Instituto
Politécnico de Bragança, 5300-252 Bragança, Portugal
{beatrizflamia,pacheco,fflor,apereira}@ipb.pt
[2] Laboratório Associado para a Sustentabilidade e Tecnologia em Regiões de
Montanha (SusTEC), Instituto Politécnico de Bragança, 5300-253 Bragança, Portugal
[3] Federal University of Technology - Paraná, 80230-901 Curitiba, Brazil
rmolinasouza@utfpr.edu.br

Abstract. Active learning is a modern educational strategy that involves students in the learning process through diverse interactive and participatory activities. The MathE platform is an international online platform created to support students and lecturers in the Mathematics teaching and learning process. This platform offers a tool to aid and engage students, ensuring new and creative ways to encourage them to improve their mathematical skills. The study proposed in this paper refers to a comprehensive investigation of the patterns that may exist within the set of questions available on the MathE platform. The objective is to investigate how to evaluate the student's opinions about the question's difficulty levels based on the variables extracted from student answers collected through surveys applied among the platform's users. Moreover, a comparative study between variables is performed using correlation and hypothesis tests. Furthermore, based on the results obtained for samples of different sizes, it was possible to define the most appropriate number of answers that should be considered to categorize the question's difficulty level. The results demonstrated that the variables extracted could be used to carry out the question level, and 30 answers are the most appropriate number of questions that must be used to categorize the question level.

Keywords: active learning · e-learning · higher education · Mathematics

This work has been supported by FCT Fundação para a Ciência e Tecnologia within the R&D Units Project Scope UIDB/05757/2020, UIDP/05757/2020, SusTEC LA/P/0007/2021 and Erasmus Plus KA2 within the project 2021-1-PT01-KA220-HED-000023288. Beatriz Flamia Azevedo is supported by FCT Grant Reference SFRH/BD/07427/2021.

A. I. Pereira et al. (Eds.): OL2A 2023, CCIS 1981, pp. 300–315, 2024.
https://doi.org/10.1007/978-3-031-53025-8_21

1   Introduction

We live in a time characterized by extraordinary and rapid changes. There is a continuous emergence and evolution of new knowledge, tools, and methods for practicing and communicating mathematics, even more regarding digital tools and artificial intelligence resources. The importance of understanding and utilizing mathematics in everyday life and the professional sphere has never been greater and will continue to grow. In this dynamic world, individuals with mathematical proficiency will have significantly enhanced opportunities and choices for shaping their futures. A solid foundation in mathematics opens doors to productive pathways, while a lack of mathematical competence limits those opportunities. All students should be given the opportunity and necessary support to learn meaningful mathematics with depth and comprehension [11].

Although mathematics is a cornerstone of many higher education courses and essential for understanding the world, comprehending its concepts, even basic ones, is seen by many as an insurmountable hurdle. While some people have a positive view of mathematics, considering it a fascinating and challenging discipline, most individuals report difficulty grasping its concepts, finding it abstract and uninteresting, and feeling intimidated and often incapable of understanding the calculations and formulas involved. These negative complaints may be linked to many individuals who have had negative experiences in mathematics education, such as a lack of adequate support or non-engaging and demotivating teaching approaches, contributing to a negative perception of the subject.

One way to change people's negative views about Mathematics is by offering an education based on active learning methods. Active learning is a student-centered pedagogical technique that promotes student learning more effectively than traditional or lecturer-centered approaches [6,8]. The fundamental role of active learning is to encourage students to participate in their education by analyzing, debating, researching, and producing, either in groups or individually. In this way, the student is no longer just a listener and becomes an active participant in the learning ecosystem [5].

The development of learning capabilities and the learning process is strongly dependent on the active involvement of students in their education [1]. Case study research shows that active teaching strategies increase lecture attendance, engagement, students' acquisition of expertise on the discipline and engagement improves students' capabilities [1,5,7,9]. Besides, students who are trained through active learning methodologies express a high level of satisfaction [1,5].

Thereby, the implementation of active learning methods involves challenges, and the incorporation of digital educational tools in classes is one way to support lecturers and students throughout the process. In this sense, the MathE platform (mathe.pixel-online.org) was created to provide not only in-class resources, but also an alternative way to teach and study Mathematics, alone, in groups, in or outside the classroom.

Since the platform was created, several works have been carried out to improve the platform, aiming at refining the platform system to offer a customized platform that meets the needs of its users [2,4]. In [4], it was identified that dividing the difficulty level of the questions into basic and advanced was not enough to categorize the questions according to the student's needs since the error rate in questions considered basic was usually very high. In addition, since many students had poor performance on the basic level questions, they rarely attempted to answer the advanced level ones, causing a certain demotivation in using the platform. Thus, the work [3] investigated the classification of questions into different difficulty levels using clustering algorithms through hierarchical and partitioning techniques. To categorize the questions through clustering, only the question's success rate was considered as an input variable for the clustering algorithms. However, since this rate is calculated using a binary output (0 - incorrect answer or 1 - correct answer), the success rate of the questions tends to converge to 0.5 over time, making it impractical to use it to define the question's level.

To define the questions' level, weighing the students' and lecturers' opinions about the question's difficulty is important. Besides, based on previous research, it is known that for some question marked as easy for a lecturer is considered difficult for the student, and vice-versa. To explore the student's opinions about the question's difficulty level, a more in-depth study is proposed in this work. Thereby, the occurrence of correct and incorrect answers for each question is evaluated to identify question patterns and classify them into different difficulty levels. First, a temporal study is proposed to analyze the number of correct and incorrect answers for each question over time. After that, a comparative study is conducted among the obtained variables, considering different answers quantities. These results will help define new variables to address the issues detected in previous works, and will also be crucial in identifying the most appropriate number of answers representing the student's perspective about the question classification.

This paper is organized as follows. After the introduction, Sect. 2 describes the main functionalities and resources available at the MathE platform. After that, Sect. 3 presents the methodologies proposed to extract the parameters and compare the data sample. The database utilized is defined in Sect. 3.3. Section 4 presents the results and the discussion of the work. Finally, Sect. 5 concludes the paper by establishing the future direction for this work.

2　MathE Platform

The MathE platform (mathe.pixel-online.org) is an online educational system designed to assist students who face challenges in learning college-level mathematics, as well as those seeking to enhance their understanding of a wide range of mathematical topics, all at their own pace. This platform provides free access to various resources, including videos, exercises, practice tests, and pedagogical materials, covering various areas of mathematics taught in higher education courses. Additionally, MathE maintains a presence on YouTube and social media platforms such as Facebook and Instagram.

Until May 2023, the platform has already attracted participation from 109 lecturers and 1435 students from 14 nationalities. Its current structure consists of three sections, as demonstrated at Fig. 1: **Student's Assessment**, which encompasses topic-specific multiple-choice questions categorized into two difficulty levels (basic and advanced) predetermined by lecturers associated with the platform; **MathE Library**, an extensive collection of valuable and diverse materials about the covered topics and subtopics, including videos, lessons, exercises, training tests, and other formats; and **Community of Practice**, a virtual space that facilitates interaction and collaboration among lecturers and students, allowing them to work together towards shared objectives and fostering a robust networked community.

Fig. 1. MathE platform illustration.

MathE includes fifteen topics in Mathematics, among the ones that are in the classic core of graduate courses: Linear Algebra (5 subtopics: Matrices and Determinants, Eigenvalues and Eigenvectors, Linear Systems, Vector Spaces, and Linear Transformations), Fundamental Mathematics (2 subtopics: Elementary Geometry and Expressions and Equations), Graph Theory, Differentiation (including 3 subtopics: Derivatives, Partial Differentiation, Implicit Differentiation and Chain Rule), Integration (5 subtopics: Integration Techniques, Double Integration, Triple Integration, Definite Integrals, and Surface Integrals), Analytic Geometry, Complex Numbers, Differential Equations, Statistics, Real Functions of a Single Variable (2 subtopics: Limits and Continuity, and Domain, Image and Graphics), Probability, Optimization (2 subtopics: Linear Optimization and Nonlinear Optimization), Real Functions of Several Variables (2 subtopic: Limits and Continuity, Domain, Image and Graphics), and Numerical Methods. It is essential to mention that the platform's content is constantly updated, and other topics and subtopics may be created whenever necessary.

3   Methodology

As previously mentioned, the variable question success rate is not enough to categorize the level of the questions since it over time tends to be 0.50 for all questions. Then, this section describes the methods applied in this work to obtain other parameters through the information of the type of answer (correct or incorrect) provided by the students. Moreover, these parameters are compared considering different data samples.

3.1   Obtaining Parameters

An analysis of the distribution of correct and incorrect answers to questions over time is proposed to obtain new parameters from the answers collected. However, there is no information regarding the data and time when the questions were answered on the platform. On the other hand, obtaining the sequence of entries for the students' answers is possible, allowing for determining the order of the solutions obtained for each question. Considering this, Fig. 2 aims to illustrate the proposed concepts by analyzing three questions represented by colored asterisks: question 1 - green, question 2 - blue, and question 3 - red.

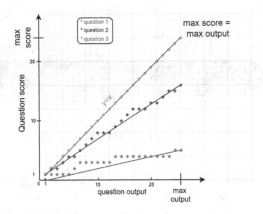

Fig. 2. Example of question answers over time (Color figure online).

Since correct answers are represented by the value 1 and incorrect answers by 0, 1 is added to the current question score for each correct answer. Similarly, for each incorrect answer, 0 is added. The higher the number of correct answers, the higher the score of the question, with the maximum score obtained if all answers to the question are correct, as illustrated by question 1 (green). Thereby, the x-axis represents the chronological order of the answers to the questions over time, where a coordinate closer to $x = 1$ indicates an earlier response recorded by the platform. Meanwhile, the y-axis represents the score obtained by the question, considering a certain number of outputs. This allows for an analysis of the answers over time. Consider the example of question 3 (red), where the answers vector is represented by $\mathbf{v3} = [0, 1, 0, 0, 0, 1, 1, 0, 0, 0, 0, 0, 0, 1, 0, 0, 0, 0, 0, 0, 0, 0, 0, 1, 0]$, which means that the first answer to question 3 was incorrect (0), the second answer was correct (1), the third, fourth, and fifth responses were incorrect, and so on.

With this data distribution for each question, it is possible to obtain the line that describes the points on the graph through linear interpolation [13], where $P(x)$ is the interpolating polynomial and m represents the angular coefficient of the line obtained by P, as shown in Eqs. 1 and 2, respectively. Here, y_1 and y_0 are the scores of the questions, and the number of questions' outputs is x_1 and x_0.

$$P(x) = y_0 + m(x - x_0) \tag{1}$$

$$m = \frac{y_1 - y_0}{x_1 - x_0} \tag{2}$$

When the maximum score is achieved (as in question 1, in the previous figure), we have $y = x$. In the other cases, we have variations in the slope of this line. Therefore, through the linear equations of each question, it is possible to evaluate the angular coefficient m of the line. Thus, questions with more incorrect answers will have smaller angular coefficients and are considered more difficult than those with larger coefficients.

Through this method, it is also possible to calculate the cumulative scores (cs) for each question so that questions with lower cumulative scores are more difficult than those with a higher cs value. In Fig. 2, question 1 has an angular coefficient of $m = 1$, and the highest possible cumulative score cs for the maximum number of outputs considered since all the answers were correct. This indicates that question 1 can be considered an easy-level question. On the other hand, question 2 has an intermediate value of the angular coefficient, suggesting it is an intermediate-level question. In turn, question 3 has the lowest angular coefficient classifying it as a difficult-level question. Considering this method, it is possible to obtain two new variables to analyze the question levels, the cumulative score cs, and the angular coefficient m of each question.

3.2   Sample Data Comparison Methods

In order to compare the variables extracted by the methodology proposed at Subsect. 3.1, two analyses are performed: the correlation analysis and the Hypothesis test. The correlation evaluates if the variables cs and m could replace the success rate variable without compromising the results. The Hypothesis test is used to evaluate the sample's most appropriate size, which is the number of answers, into the question categorization.

Correlation Analysis. To compare the correlation between the obtained parameters, the Pearson method is applied. The method aims to check if the variables cs and m when used instead of the success rate does not imply significant changes in the results for classifying the difficulty level of the questions.

Hypothesis Test. To evaluate the most suitable sample size of data to determine the difficulty level of the question, a hypothesis test is considered. In this case, it is intended to investigate whether a parameter collected using different sizes samples has equal means or not. Thereby, the t-Student test [10] is used to determine if there is a significant difference between the means μ_1 and μ_2 composed of 30 and 50 answers per question, respectively. So, the two hypotheses are considered:

$$H_0 : \mu_1 = \mu_2$$
$$H_1 : \mu_1 \neq \mu_2$$
(3)

in which, H_0 assumes that there is no difference between μ_1 and μ_2, whereas H_1 affirms there is difference between μ_1 and μ_2.

Thereby, to perform the t-test a significance level of 0.05 is considered. So, if the p-value found is less than the chosen significance level ($p < 0.05$), the null hypothesis is rejected, suggesting a difference between the means of the samples compared. But, if the p-value is greater than or equal to the significance level, the null hypothesis is not rejected suggesting that there is not enough evidence to support a difference between the means of the samples compared [10]. It is essential to point out that before applying the t-Student test, it is necessary to verify the normality of the data distribution. For this, the Kolmogorov-Smirnov test [10] was used, also with a significance level of 0.05.

3.3   Data Base

Currently, the MathE platform has 1824 questions available, distributed between 15 topics and 24 subtopics, in which the subtopics Vector Space and Linear Transformation are the two most used subtopics of the platform. Both of them belong to the Linear System topic. Table 1 describes the data considered per subtopic. So, column $N.$ *questions* shows the number of questions considered in this work; column $N.$ *Answers* presents the total number of answers obtain, and the column $N.$ *students* represents the number of different students that answered the questions since one question could be answered more than one time for the same student. However, for applying the methods used in this study, only the questions that received at least 50 responses were considered, which reduced that number of questions to 21 Linear Transformation questions and 24 questions at the Vector Space subtopic.

Table 1. Data base description.

Subtopic	N. questions	N. Answers	N. students
Linear Transformation	60	2067	31
Vector Space	61	2738	96

4   Results and Discussion

As previously mentioned, the information currently available on the MathE platform refers to the type of answer provided by the students (1 - correct or 0 - incorrect). Thus, this is an equiprobable sample space, with a success rate equal to 0.5, which makes this variable impracticable for classifying the questions in different difficulty levels. In this way, the need to extract other information from the available information was observed. Thus, with the methodology described in Sect. 3.1, it is possible to obtain the variables denominated by the cumulative score of the question (cs) and the angular coefficient (m). The variables obtained are analyzed through correlation and t-Student hypothesis methods. The results are presented below for the two most used subtopics of the platform: Linear Transformations (Sect. 4.1) and Vector Spaces (Sect. 4.2).

4.1   Linear Transformations Results

The Linear Transformations (LT) subtopic currently comprises 60 questions. However, only 21 questions have at least 50 answers collected since the MathE platform has been online. For this reason, these questions were selected to be analyzed since they have the minimum number of answers for applying the methods considered in this work.

Thereby, to provide a comparison between students' and lecturers' question level definition, the 21 questions of the Linear Transformation subtopic are classified into three groups by a lecturer, according to their knowledge. Each group means a difficult level, starting in the 1 - most basic level and 3 - most difficult level. After that to be better analyzed, three questions were randomly selected, one of each difficulty level provided by the lecturer. In this case, questions 287 is selected from level 1, questions 784 is selected from level 2, and questions 384 is selected from level 3. Figure 3 presents the profile of these questions, considering a maximum output equal to 50 (x-axis). And consequently, 50 is the maximum score to be achieved in case all answers provided are correct.

Based on the results presented at Fig. 3, the student's classification of the questions based on the question's success rate is equal to the classification provided by the lecturer for these three questions. But this is not always the case, sometimes while the lecturer indicates that the question 325 is basic, there were many incorrect answers, indicating that this question is not really basic from the student's point of view. However, it is important to highlight that they are some situations in which the classification of the student and lecturer are different. Such results demonstrate the reason for analyzing the two options: the

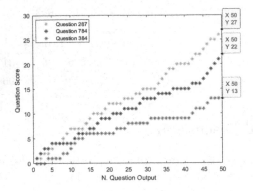

Fig. 3. Example of questions behavior 287, 784, and 384.

student's classification provided by the question success rate and the lecturer's classification based on their experience.

Considering the analysis proposed at Sect. 3.1, the linear interpolation was performed, and the parameter's cumulative score cs, angular coefficient m, and the success rate for each question were obtained. For this analysis, different quantities of answers were considered to analysis the behavior of consider different amount of data to extract the previously mentioned parameters. Thereby, Table 2 presents the data extracted for the three questions of Fig. 3. Considering different numbers of outputs (answers), it is 10, 20, 30, 40, and 50 for each question, it is noticed that the success rate, even in questions belonging to different difficulty level, tend to be close to 0.5 over time.

Table 2. Success rate for different numbers of outputs for the three LT questions.

Question ID	Level given by lecturer	Number of Output				
		N10	N20	N30	N40	N50
Question 287	1	0.90	0.60	0.50	0.50	0.54
Question 784	2	0.40	0.45	0.43	0.38	0.44
Question 384	3	0.30	0.30	0.26	0.23	0.26

On the other hand, Table 3 presents the values referring to the variable cumulative score, cs, also considering samples of different sizes. Besides the value, it is also presented the normalized value of the variable for a better understanding of the position of the question in the range of values between 0 and 1 and the definition of the most appropriate level of difficulty for the question.

Comparing Tables 2 and 3, there is a greater gap between the classes of the cs normalized values and success rate values. For the case of 50 answers, in Tables 2, we have a difference of 0.18 between the question of level 3 and level 2, and a difference of 0.1 between the question of level 2 and level 1; whereas, in Table 3,

Table 3. Cumulative score for different numbers of output for the three LT questions.

Question ID	Level given by lecturer	Number of Output				
		N10	N20	N30	N40	N50
Question 287	1	35 (0.63)	126 (0.69)	259 (0.63)	438 (0.63)	673 (0.68)
Question 784	2	33 (0.58)	105 (0.51)	217 (0.43)	359 (0.39)	539 (0.40)
Question 384	3	11 (0.04)	67 (0.18)	142 (0.08)	232 (0.00)	348 (0.00)

this difference is approximately 0.3 for the question of level 1 and 2, and 0.4 to questions of level 2 and 3.

Table 4 presents the three questions' angular coefficient m. As we can see, the m values are very similar to the success rate values, indicating that the variable cs is the most appropriate to replace the success rate variable at the questions level definition.

Table 4. Angular coefficient for different numbers of output for the three LT questions.

Question ID	Level given by lecturer	Number of Outputs				
		N10	N20	N30	N40	N50
Question 287	1	0.66	0.60	0.48	0.48	0.53
Question 784	2	0.33	0.42	0.41	0.36	0.42
Question 384	3	0.33	0.31	0.27	0.23	0.27

Considering that the MathE Platform is a world-class platform and through previous studies, a sample of 10 or 20 answers is too small to define the level of difficulty of the questions, that represent the opinion of student worldwide. So, a more deep analysis involving the sample of 30 and 50 answers is proposed. In this way, the Pearson correlation and the hypothesis test between the samples composed of 30 and 50 answers were performed.

The Pearson correlation was used to compare the correlation between the success rate, angular coefficient m, and cumulative score cs variables, for the 21 questions in the study. The result is shown in Table 5. As can be seen, there is a high correlation, over 0.8, between all variables independent of the number of outputs considered. This indicates that variables cs and m can substitute the success rate variable. However, as previously mentioned the m values are very similar to the success rate values. So, using the m variable, the tendency of the variable comes close to 0.5 is kept. Thus, the cs results are more expressive to the used in the question level definition.

Finally, the most appropriate size of the data was investigated. First, the questions were divided into 3 levels of equal sizes for each number of outputs

Table 5. Correlation between the variables of the LT.

N. Outputs	success rate & cs	cs & m	success rate & m
N30	0.93	0.89	0.99
N50	0.90	0.88	0.99

considered. In the case of the subtopic Linear Transformations, each level is composed of 7 questions, using the values of the variable cs. Thus, the first 7 questions with the lowest cs are at level 1, the following at level 2, and level 3 are the questions with the highest cs. This process was done for each sample independently. Since the lecturers classified the same questions, it is possible to compare the number of questions at the same level according to the lecturer's opinion with the classification provided by the students through the questions' answers. The results of this analysis are shown in Table 6. Each value in the table represents the number of questions at the intersection between one sample and another, 2 to 2 (Table 6a), and the similarity rate between the samples, in terms of question levels categorization (Table 6b). In other words, it means the number of questions that keeps at the same difficulty level in both numbers of output.

Table 6. Question levels comparison at LT subtopic.

(a) Number of questions at the intersection.

Sample	Lect.	N30	N50
Lect.	21	11	9
N30		21	17
N50			21

(b) Similarity rate between the levels.

Sample	Lect.	N30	N50
Lect.	21	0.52	0.43
N30		21	0.81
N50			21

As we can see, there are 17 questions that remain at the same levels, considering both a sample of 30 and 50 answers, which results in a similarity rate equal to 0.81. Regarding the classification of the lecturer and the students, we have 0.52 and 0.43 similarity rates between the classifications considering the samples composed of 30 and 50 answers. These results were already expected, given the knowledge of previous work that pointed to several divergences between the opinion of students and lecturers.

After checking whether the data follows a normal distribution, the hypothesis test was applied to compare the statistical means between the 30 and 50 samples. Through this, it is possible to define whether the observed sample differences are real or casual. It is important to clarify that the cs values were normalized to be compared by the hypothesis test approach. The results are shown in Table 7, in which the p-value model test equals 0.39. Considering a significance level equal to 0.05, the final decision considers not rejecting the null hypothesis (Sect. 3.2) since the p-value found are greater than 0.05. Therefore, there is no significant difference between the means of the two samples.

Table 7. t-Student test results for LT questions.

t	Degree of Freedom	Standard Deviation	p-value	Confidence Interval (95%)
−0.86	40	0.25	0.39	[−0.22, 0.09]

4.2 Vector Spaces Results

The Vector Spaces (VS) subtopic is composed of 61 questions, but only 24 had more than 50 answered computed, so only these were considered. The process applied to the Linear Transformations subtopic was replayed to the Vector Spaces subtopic. This way, a lecturer analyzed the 24 questions and categorized them into three groups. Figure 4 describes the profile of 3 questions randomly selected, 1 for each group, being the question 417 belongs to level 1; question 421 belongs to level 2; and question 453 belongs to level 3.

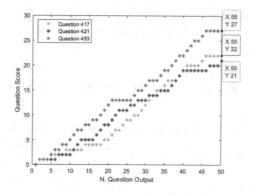

Fig. 4. Example of questions behavior 417, 421, and 453.

These questions were chosen to be better analyzed. So, Tables 8, 9 and 10 presents the value of the variable's success rate, the cumulative score cs, and the angular coefficient m, respectively, for the three questions.

Table 8. Success rate for different numbers of outputs for the three VS questions.

Question ID	Level given by lecturer	Number of Outputs				
		N10	N20	N30	N40	N50
Question 417	1	0.30	0.25	0.40	0.47	0.44
Question 421	2	0.40	0.45	0.40	0.37	0.36
Question 453	3	0.20	0.40	0.43	0.47	0.42

Considering the results of Table 8, the variation between the success rate of the three questions is quite small. In the case of 30 outputs, it is noteworthy that the three questions have a success rate of approximately 0.4. Similar results are obtained in Table 10.

Table 9. Cumulative score for different numbers of output for the three VS questions.

Question ID	Level given by lecturer	Number of Outputs				
		N10	N20	N30	N40	N50
Question 417	1	16 (0.28)	55 (0.27)	144 (0.34)	305 (0.43)	516 (0.46)
Question 421	2	21 (0.39)	82 (0.46)	180 (0.49)	315 (0.45)	483 (0.40)
Question 453	3	13 (0.21)	69 (0.37)	184 (0.49)	341 (0.52)	536 (0.50)

On the other hand, analyzing the Table 9 results, there is a more expressive difference between the values of the questions, even when we consider normalization.

Table 10. Angular coefficient for different numbers of output for the three VS questions.

Question ID	Level given by lecturer	Number of Outputs				
		N10	N20	N30	N40	N50
Question 417	1	0.33	0.26	0.41	0.49	0.44
Question 421	2	0.44	0.47	0.41	0.38	0.36
Question 453	3	0.22	0.42	0.45	0.49	0.42

Again, the correlation between the variables was evaluated. Thus, Table 11 presents the correlation between the three variables: success rate, cumulative score cs, and angular coefficient m, for the 24 Vector Spaces questions.

As occur in the Linear Transformations questions, both combinations of variables presented high correction, over 0.80, which indicates that the success rate variable could be replaced by the other two variables cs or m, without compromising the results. But, the success rate values are practically the same as the m values, so cs is the most appropriate variable for the question classification.

For the analysis of the most appropriate size of the data, it is, the number of questions to be used to define the cs values, the 24 Vector Spaces questions were categorized into 3 levels of equal size, in this case, 8 questions per level. Table 12 presents the results, considering the number of questions belonging to each sample's intersection, it is the same difficulty level, considering the lecturer classification and the different numbers of output (answers), 2 to 2 (Table 12a),

Table 11. Correlation between the variables of the VS.

N. Output	Success rate & cs	cs & m	Success rate & m
N30	0.84	0.81	0.99
N50	0.90	0.89	0.99

and the similarity rate between the questions difficult level (Table 12b). Again, a higher similarity between the sample of 30 outputs and the sample of 50 was found, equal to 0.83; while in the other cases, this similarity is not so higher, below equal to 0.46 for the comparison between the lecturer and 50 answers, and also between the sample of 30 and 50 answers.

Table 12. Question levels comparison at VS subtopic.

(a) Number of questions at the intersection.

Sample	Lect.	N30	N50
Lect.	24	11	11
N30		24	20
N50			24

(b) Similarity rate between the levels.

Sample	Lect.	N30	N50
Lect.	24	0.46	0.46
N30		24	0.83
N50			24

Finally, after the Kolmogorov-Smirnov test indicates that the data is normal, the t-Student test was performed considering the cs normalized variable for the samples composed of 30 and 50 answers. As presented in Table 13, the p-value found is 0.93. In this way, considering a significance level equal to 0.05, the final decision considers not rejecting the null hypothesis (Sect. 3.2) since the p-value found is greater than 0.05.

Table 13. t-Student test results for VS questions.

t	Degree of Freedom	Standard Deviation	p-value	Confidence Interval (95%)
−0.08	46	0.22	0.93	$[-0.13, 0.12]$

5   Conclusion

The MathE platform has been online since 2019. The necessity for some improvements on the platform has been identified in previous studies, such as question difficult level definition and the optimum way to reorganize the resources available on the platform [2–4]. The insights gained from prior research have guided the developers of the MathE platform in implementing intelligent features, leveraging optimization algorithms and machine learning techniques. These advancements will enable the platform to autonomously make personalized decisions tailored according to the needs of each user. This work investigated different variables to be used to define the question's difficulty level. Furthermore, the most appropriate number of answers to obtain the variable's information was also investigated.

Through previous works, it is known that the success rate variable is not enough to categorize the questions, taking into account that the information considered is a binary variable (1 - correct, and 0 - incorrect), the success rate of the answers to the questions is 0.5, and this is observed by computing responses over time. Thus, two new variables were extracted for each question: the angular coefficient m, and the cumulative score cs. Taking into account that the angular coefficient and the success rate have a high correlation and therefore present the same problem as the success rate variable, it is defined that the cumulative score variable is the most recommended to be used in the question classification task, and represent the students' opinions about the difficulty of each question. Regarding the number of samples to be used, although the sample 30 and 50 answers have no significance, it was established that 30 answers are the most appropriate value to obtain cs values and represent the students' opinions. Besides, from the literature, it is known that 30 samples are considered a minimal quantity to obtain trustful in the data analysis results [12].

From previous work, it is known that the opinion of students and lecturers, about the complexity of the questions is often divergent. While for a lecturer, a question may be very basic, for the student the same question may be considered very difficult, and vice-versa. Thus, it is important to give appropriate weight to the opinion of both students and lecturers, in order to obtain the most accurate classification. Thus, the focus of this work was the exploration of the best way to extract the students' opinions, which will be combined with the lecturer's opinion in future works. Thereby, the values of these opinion combinations will, in the future, be considered for the final classification of the questions.

References

1. Alhawiti, N.M.: The influence of active learning on the development of learner capabilities in the college of applied medical sciences: mixed-methods study. Adv. Med. Educ. Pract. **14**, 87–99 (2023)
2. Flamia Azevedo, B., Rocha, A.M.A.C., Fernandes, F.P., Pacheco, M.F., Pereira, A.I.: Evaluating student behaviour on the mathe platform - clustering algorithms approaches. In: Simos, D.E., Rasskazova, V.A., Archetti, F., Kotsireas, I.S., Pardalos, P.M. (eds.) Learning and Intelligent Optimization, LION 2022. LNS, vol. 13621, pp. 319–333. Springer, Cham (2022). https://doi.org/10.1007/978-3-031-24866-5_24
3. Azevedo, B.F., Amoura, Y., Rocha, A.M.A.C., Fernandes, F.P., Pacheco, M.F., Pereira, A.I.: Analyzing the MathE platform through clustering algorithms. In: Gervasi, O., Murgante, B., Misra, S., Rocha, A.M.A.C., Garau, C. (eds.) Computational Science and Its Applications, ICCSA 2022 Workshops, ICCSA 2022. LNCS, vol. 13378, pp. 201–218. Springer, Cham (2022). https://doi.org/10.1007/978-3-031-10562-3_15

4. Azevedo, B.F., Pereira, A.I., Fernandes, F.P., Pacheco, M.F.: Mathematics learning and assessment using MathE platform: a case study. Educ. Inf. Technol. **27**, 1747–1769 (2021)
5. Deslauriers, L., McCarty, L.S., Miller, K., Callaghan, K., Kestin, G.: Measuring actual learning versus feeling of learning in response to being actively engaged in the classroom. Proc. Nat. Acad. Sci. **116**(39), 19251–19257 (2019)
6. Dunkle, K.M., Yantz, J.L.: Intentional design and implementation of a "flipped" upper division geology course: improving student learning outcomes, persistence, and attitudes. J. Geosci. Educ. **69**(1), 55–70 (2021)
7. Gu, X., et al.: Active versus passive strategy in online creativity training: how to best promote creativity of students with different cognitive styles? Think. Skills Creat. **44**, 101021 (2022)
8. Indorf, J.L., et al.: Distinct factors predict use of active learning techniques by pre-tenure and tenured stem faculty. J. Geosci. Educ. **69**(4), 357–372 (2021)
9. Keiler, L.S.: Teachers' roles and identities in student-centered classrooms. Int. J. STEM Educ. **5**(1), 34 (2018)
10. Montgomery, D.C.: Design and Analysis of Experiments. Wiley, Hoboken (2017)
11. NCTM: Principles and Standards for School Mathematics, vol. 1. National Council of Teachers of Mathematics (NCTM) (2000)
12. Pagano, M., Gauvreau, K.: Principles of Biostatistics. Duxbury Press (2000)
13. Weisstein, E.W.: Linear interpolation. From MathWorld - A Wolfram Web Resource. http://mathworld.wolfram.com/LinearInterpolation.html

Machine Learning and Data Analysis
in Internet of Things

Predicting Flood Events with Streaming Data: A Preliminary Approach with GRU and ARIMA

Rodrigo Moura[1], Armando Mendes[1,2]($\boxtimes$)(iD), José Cascalho[1,2], Sandra Mendes[3], Rodolfo Melo[3], and Emanuel Barcelos[3]

[1] FCT, University of the Azores, Ponta Delgada, Portugal
armando.b.mendes@uac.pt
[2] IS²E Research Nucleus and LIACC Research Centre, Porto, Portugal
[3] Direção Regional do Ordenamento do Território e dos Recursos Hídricos, Secretaria Regional do Ambiente e Alterações Climáticas, Ponta Delgada, Portugal

Abstract. The most frequent flooding situations in the Azores are caused by torrential rainfall, which is difficult to predict due to its characteristics. Using data collected by sensors, rainfall and stream flow values, from natural occurring flood events, we describe results from learning RNNs, ARIMA time series forecast model, and a warning system that can empower civil protection decision-makers to safeguard property and lives. For dealing with all the difficulties resulting from forecasting rare events undersampling are used to get a richer sample of positive events, combined with simulation of new events. GRU and ARIMA models performed better than LSTM, using the hit hate measure and 30% of the positive events as test sample and 70% for learning sample. Even though the alert messages are sent by SMS to relevant deciders, two apps were developed to deploy the forecast models. An WWW application to manage the alerts and the sensors spread by all the islands, and a mobile app for operational staff working in all Azores archipelago.

Keywords: Flood forecast · IoT data · RNN · ARIMA · Azores

1 Introduction

1.1 The Problem

For an effective management of water in the Azores, promoting integrated planning of regional water resources and implementing measures for the rehabilitation, conservation, and correction of the hydrological network is crucial. To achieve this, it is essential to deepen the understanding of the hydrological cycle, comprehend and analyze the behavior of water systems, and therefore obtain meteorological, hydrological, and udometric records through the implementation of a hydrometeorological monitoring network.

In the Azores, the Regional Secretariat for the Environment and Climate Change, through the Regional Directorate for Spatial Planning and Water

A. I. Pereira et al. (Eds.): OL2A 2023, CCIS 1981, pp. 319–332, 2024.
https://doi.org/10.1007/978-3-031-53025-8_22

Resources, is responsible for implementing the hydrometeorological network and developing surveillance and basic information systems for hydrological risk alert.

Until 2009, the Regional Government of the Autonomous Region of the Azores had a hydrometeorological network with data collection being carried out weekly or daily by local observers. In 2010, the network was expanded with the installation of new stations and facilities, as well as the restructuring of existing ones, in order to transmit data automatically and in real-time, significantly reducing logistical and operational difficulties. This network allows the acquisition and provision of real-time information at appropriate time intervals. The collected information represents a significant improvement in knowledge for water resource management, maximising the benefits derived from permanent, updated technical and scientific knowledge available to any citizen for personal, professional, and scientific purposes. Hydrometeorological data also serve as fundamental information for predictive models, which constitute a mitigation measure for risk factors such as floods, inundations, and mass movements, enabling civil protection entities and other organisations to take action in defence of populations, infrastructure, and the environment.

The most frequent flooding situations in the Azores are mostly caused by torrential rainfall, which is difficult to predict due to its characteristics, and their sudden occurrence hampers reactive action based on warning systems (Fig. 1).

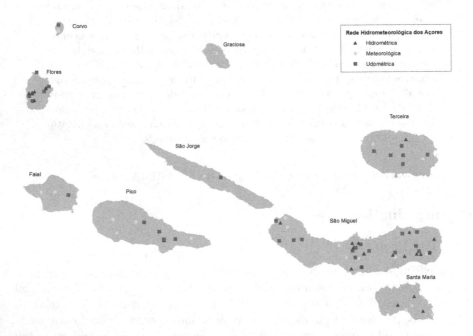

Fig. 1. "Hydrometeorological network in Azores" blue hydrometric, green meteorological and red udometric.

Currently, there are a total of 103 automatic stations strategically distributed across the nine islands of the archipelago. In spite of the fact that many data points are available, only 11 natural occurring positive events are recorded, which makes this problem a forecasting rare events situation.

1.2 Focastiong Rare Events

Fortunately floods are rare events in the Azores region. Since 2010 only 11 events are registered. Rare events have characteristics that make forecasting challenging [11].

First, they possess extreme outlier status i.e., they lie outside the realm of regular expectations since historical information can't be enough to indicate its possibility of occurring. Second, its impacts can last for several days. Natural systems are largely interconnected, so a small fault or imbalance may turn into a cascading impact if timely action is delayed. Third, data with an event is sparse and inbalanced classes by construction. It amplifies the computation effort of training forecasting models.

It has been well-documented that machine learning training is severely impaired by imbalanced class sizes [9,10]. In this text, we propose to handle this by undersampling the training set. Only a fraction of non-flood samples are used. A natural starting idea is to ensure, on average, an equilibrium on the 3 classes used, but not equality. These characteristics will play an important role in selecting a methodology for forecasting rare events.

When it comes to rare events, there are three different methods of forecast [14]:

- Point-in-time-independent probabilistic forecasts: Forecasts that provide a probability estimate for the event occurring in a given time-frame, but with no distinction based on the point in time. In other words, the forecast may say "there is a 5% chance of an earthquake higher than 7 on the Richter scale in this geographical region in a year" but the forecast is not sensitive to the choice of year.
- Point-in-time-dependent probabilistic forecasts: Forecasts that provide a probability estimate that varies somewhat over time based on history, but aren't precise enough for a remedial measure that substantially offsets major losses. For instance, if I know that an earthquake will occur in San Francisco in the next 6 months with probability 90%, it's still not actionable enough for a mass evacuation of San Francisco. But some preparatory measures may be undertaken.
- Predictions made with high confidence (i.e., a high estimated probability when the event is predicted) and a specific time, location, and characteristics: Precise predictions of date and time, sufficient for remedial measures that substantially offset major losses (but possibly at huge, if much smaller, cost). The extreme weather events are in this category.

Forecasting for floods in water streams has improved quite a bit over the last century, and falls squarely within Category 3. In The Signal and the Noise,

Nate Silver [12] notes that the probability of an American dying from lightning has dropped from 1 in 400,000 in 1940 to 1 in 11,000,000 today, and a large part of the credit goes to better weather forecasting causing people to avoid the outdoors at the times and places that lightning might strike.

This significant improvements are due to several statistic and physics developments and specially machine learning algorithms [1]. Machine learning has now been used for decades in climate and weather forecast sciences with various goals, such as post-processing, data assimilation, physical analysis, etc. Recently, deep neural networks were used with noticeable successes for prediction purpose [2–4]. While deep learning-based prediction performance remains far from challenging the prediction capabilities of physics modelling-driven procedures [4], they prove useful to improve physics models or their parameter tuning, to complementing them for analysis or pattern recognition, or to performing tasks not achievable with physics models.

Deep learning has also been used for extreme weather event prediction [5] or severe weather risk assessment [6]. In [5], it is shown that the CapsNet deep neural network is a fast and efficient tool, for predicting hot days several days ahead. In [7], it is shown that Long Short-Term Memory neural networks, focused this time on time series, are efficient in temperature prediction. As far as we now, no machine learning approach has been used so far to study floods in small streams with sensor data.

Transfer Learning [8] was chosen, in this work, as one technique used for flood events with streaming data. It is defined as the process of training a neural network on latest data while commencing it with pretrained weights derived from training on historic information.

For the development of the data models the transfer learning is used in conjunction with variants of Recurrent Neural Networks (RNN) [13]. RNN or Recurrent Neuronal Network are a type of artificial neural network architecture that is specially designed to process sequential or temporal data. Unlike traditional neural networks that process data in isolation, RNNs are able to keep data in memory in order to create a "context" and thus make predictions based on the sequence of data. These networks consist of layers composed of several processing units usually called cells or neurons. These cells have cyclic connections to each other, allowing previous outputs to be used as input in the next iteration, thus retaining previous information in the network's memory. Simply put, it is these cyclical connections that allow the creation of the "context" mentioned above. RNNs are suitable for tasks involving sequential data, such as time series prediction, speech recognition, and natural language processing.

The RNN is a big family of networks. In this work we tested two type of RNN, namely Long Short-Term Memory (LSTM) and Gated Recurrent Unit (GRU). The LSTM is a little more complex than classical RNN's. This added complexity allows to solve one of the big problems of RNN's, which is the difficulty of keeping the information for long periods of time. So this variant has a system that allows the network to decide whether to forget, update or issue the information from the internal memory. LSTMs are commonly used in natural language processing tasks, such as machine translation and sentiment analysis.

GRU networks are very similar to the previous one, but it was designed to be simpler, to have best performance and still keeping good results while consuming fewer resources. In short, GRU networks also aim to solve the problem of keeping information for long periods of time, but in a more optimised way [13]. GRUs are also used in natural language processing tasks.

Finally, and keeping in mind the strong limitation of applying neural networks to only 11 flood events a statistical method of forecast was also tested. Autoregressive Integrated Moving Average (ARIMA) is a time series prediction model that is widely used and considered to have high performance on this type of data [15]. It is composed of three main components like the autoregressive component (AR), this value is based on the idea that the past values of the time series have an influence on future values, so it relates the current value to a fixed number of previous observations. The integrated component (I) is used to keep the time series stable, this is important because most of these models assume the mean and variance as fixed values over time, and this component serves exactly to eliminate inconstant patterns in the data. Finally, the moving average (MA) component considers the influence of past forecast errors on the current values of the series. It relates the current observation to the residual errors generated by the moving averages of previous observations. ARIMA is a powerful tool for analyzing and forecasting time series, allowing the capture of complex patterns and providing valuable insights for decision-making.

2   Data Preprocessing

The Azores archipelago is divided into hydrographic basins. Some of these basins are located in different islands, and so, the distance between them justifies independent models for each basin. In these way each model can learn the characteristics and particularities of each hydrographic basin. Thus, each model will predict the events of a single basin, which makes the training and test data different in each situation, since the events of each basin concern only the respective basin. Additionally, since this monitoring network is still in its early stages and are plans to grow considerably, we were unable to obtain all the learning data necessary for developing models in some basins, such as streams flow levels and rainfall intensity. In fact, there are basins where only one feature is used for making predictions, when rainfall values or stream flow values are missing in that basin. As a result, we arrived at the following Fig. 2 that relates the floods in the region to the stations and sensors available.

Therefore, undersampled real data where selected, corresponding to short time periods, usually less than a month, during which these events occurred. We then aggregated the data by hydrographic basin, creating five data frames, each corresponding to one basin, containing the events related to it. With this data in hand, we proceeded to verify the presence of outliers and/or null values, ensuring a consistent and "clean" structure for our data. Thus, we verified the

data	hydrographic basin	island	meteorological or udometric station	hydrometric station
10 de novembro de 2020	Ribeira da Povoação	São Miguel	Monte Simplicio	Purgar
25 de junho de 2021	Ribeira da Povoação	São Miguel	Monte Simplicio	Purgar
21 e 23 de novembro de 2021	Ribeira da Povoação	São Miguel	Monte Simplicio	Purgar
22 de dezembro de 2012	Ribeira Grande	São Miguel	Salto do Cabrito	Pernada
28 de fevereiro de 2013	Ribeira Grande	São Miguel	Salto do Cabrito	Pernada
27 de setembro 2021	Grota dos Milhafres	São Miguel	Mosteiros	-
7 de outubro de 2021	Grota dos Milhafres	São Miguel	Mosteiros	
2 de janeiro de 2022	Ribeira da Agualva	Terceira	Lameiro	Gramas
16 de setembro de 2018	Ribeira das Nove	Terceira	Santa Barbara/ Ribeira das Nove	-
26 de setembro de 2018	Ribeira das Nove	Terceira	Santa Barbara/ Ribeira das Nove	
16 de junho de 2019	Ribeira das Nove	Terceira	Santa Barbara/ Ribeira das Nove	-

Fig. 2. Recorded flood events used. Each colour refers to a basin.

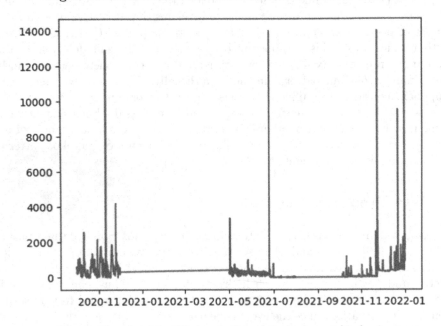

Fig. 3. Flow level in Ribeira da Povoação hydrographic basin.

absence of null values and found that the values outside the normal range of the data corresponded to peaks in rainfall intensity or river flow levels on specific days. Therefore, no major corrections were necessary for cleaning data at this stage (Figs. 3 and 4).

With the processed data, we proceeded to the development and training of the models. However, we quickly realised that due to the low occurrence of floods in the region during the recorded data period, the number of events would not be sufficient to train a model satisfactorily. This forced us to revisit the data modelling phase. To address this situation, a oversampling technique was used. This was made by multiplying the data for each basin (2 to 4 times, depending

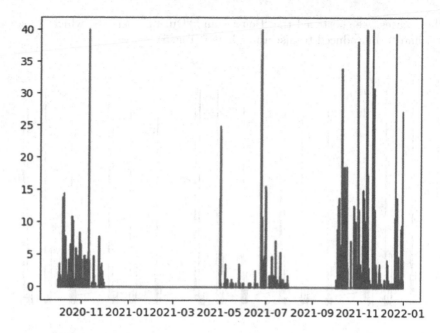

Fig. 4. Rainfall intensity Ribeira da Povoação hydrographic basin.

on the data scarcity in each basin) in order to increase the number of positive events. Additionally, to avoid overfitting, some noise was added to the duplicated data. Random values between zero and the standard deviation of each feature were added or subtracted.

With the prepared data, we proceeded to the modelling stage. First and foremost, the class feature was coded corresponding to the state in which the basin is at a given moment. Therefore, we defined three states:

- "Normal" → normal state of the stream, corresponding to a no danger situation;
- "Antes" or "Alerta" → alert state for a flood, indicating that if the current conditions persist in the next few hours/days, a flood will occur. This state was coded until three days before the flood occurs;
- "Durante" or "Cheia" → flood state, indicating that a flood is currently happening. This state was coded with all the values recorded for the day when the flood occurs.

With the class feature defined, we initially determined that the "Durante" state would encompass the entire day of the flood occurrence, the "Antes" state would cover the three days preceding the occurrence, and the "Normal" state would include all other records. This initial definition was in place; however, as the project progressed, some models faced difficulties in producing acceptable results. In such cases, we returned to the initial phase to adjust these patterns. Therefore, in these cases, we shortened the "Before" and "During" periods, which, in some cases, had to be reduced to just a few hours (Fig. 5).

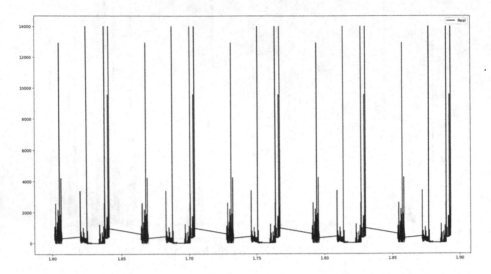

Fig. 5. Flow level after multiplying the data Ribeira da Povoação hydrographic basin.

In the previous figure, the data show periodicity because the graph shows the dataFrame resulting from the oversampling procedure. As some noise was added to the data, but the dates remained unaltered, the result was similar curves as pictured in the figure.

In an attempt to explore the data and obtain some useful rules from all the data available from the recorded values in the hydrometeorological network stations of the Azores that lead to flood and inundation alerts, several decision trees were learned (Fig. 6).

3   Classification Trees for Data Exploration

For this trees the pre-processing of data were quite different. Firstly, the precipitation values, intensities from meteorological and udometric stations, and in some cases, the flow levels from hydrometric stations were selected in a similar way as described before. But, in this case, some temporal aggregations, using time windows to accumulate rainfall in several periods were used to taken in account some memory effects. Some delays were also introduced in the data, in order to understand if the rainfall of previous periods influence the rules for predicting flood events in the following periods of time. The raw data were in 10-minute time intervals over a period of six days before and after a specific recorded occurrence. This process resulted in a set of conditions/rules corresponding to the behaviour of various factors that can indicate the occurrence of

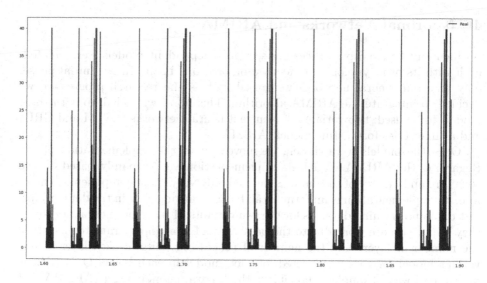

Fig. 6. Intensity after multiplying the data Ribeira da Povoação hydrographic basin.

floods or inundations. The results were presented in the form of decision trees and rule tables. One of the rules table is presented in Fig. 7.

After the analysis, a result was obtained with a set of rules corresponding to 405 out of a total of 463 interval records that exhibit "During Flood" behaviour. The rule with biggest support, 60 of the records, correspond to the following rule: "A flood event is highly probable if a Continuous rainfall time value is greater than 115 and less than or equal to 985 min, and accumulated rainfall times are less than or equal to 485 min, and intensity on a 10 min period is greater than 11.7 mm/h".

Row ID	S Condition	S	D	D	D R...	D Nu...
Row1	($Precipitação Acumulado$ <= 8.594999999999999 AND $Tempos Acumulados$ <= 375.0 AND $Intensidade (mm/h) (periodo anterior 1)$ <= 4.71 AND $Intensidade (mm/h) (periodo ante...	Não	?	?	2,381	2,370
Row2	($Tempos Acumulados$ <= 115.0 AND $Precipitação Acumulado$ > 8.594999999999999 AND $Tempos Acumulados$ <= 375.0 AND $Intensidade (mm/h) (periodo anterior 1)$ <= 4.71 AN...	Sim	?	?	17	13
Row3	($Tempo Continuo$ <= 45.0 AND $Tempos Acumulados$ <= 255.0 AND $Precipitação Acumulado$ <= 13.894999999999998 AND $Precipitação Acumulado$ <= 15.329999999999997 AND...	Não	?	?	25	19
Row4	($Tempo Continuo$ > 45.0 AND $Tempos Acumulados$ <= 255.0 AND $Precipitação Acumulado$ <= 13.894999999999998 AND $Precipitação Acumulado$ <= 15.329999999999997 AND $...	Sim	?	?	8	8
Row5	($Tempos Acumulados$ > 255.0 AND $Precipitação Acumulado$ <= 13.894999999999998 AND $Precipitação Acumulado$ <= 15.329999999999997 AND $Tempo Continuo$ <= 65.0 AND $...	Não	?	?	30	30
Row6	($Precipitação Acumulado$ > 13.894999999999998 AND $Precipitação Acumulado$ <= 15.329999999999997 AND $Tempo Continuo$ <= 65.0 AND $Intensidade$ <= 6.9 AND $Precipitaçã...	Sim	?	?	11	10
Row7	($Precipitação Acumulado$ > 15.329999999999997 AND $Tempo Continuo$ <= 65.0 AND $Intensidade$ <= 6.9 AND $Precipitação Acumulado$ <= 35.425 AND $Tempos Acumulados$ > 1...	Não	?	?	33	32
Row8	($Tempo Continuo$ > 65.0 AND $Intensidade$ <= 6.9 AND $Precipitação Acumulado$ <= 35.425 AND $Tempos Acumulados$ > 115.0 AND $Precipitação Acumulado$ > 8.594999999999999...	Não	?	?	209	204
Row9	($Intensidade$ > 6.9 AND $Precipitação Acumulado$ <= 35.425 AND $Tempos Acumulados$ > 115.0 AND $Precipitação Acumulado$ > 8.594999999999999 AND $Tempos Acumulados$ <...	Sim	?	?	8	6
Row10	($Precipitação Acumulado$ > 35.425 AND $Tempos Acumulados$ > 115.0 AND $Precipitação Acumulado$ > 8.594999999999999 AND $Tempos Acumulados$ <= 375.0 AND $Intensidade (...	Sim	?	?	6	6
Row11	($Tempos Acumulados$ > 375.0 AND $Intensidade (mm/h) (periodo anterior 1)$ <= 4.71 AND $Intensidade (mm/h) (periodo anterior 3)$ <= 12.030000000000001 AND $Intensidade$ <= ...	Não	?	?	29,04...	29,041...
Row12	($Intensidade (mm/h) (periodo anterior 1)$ <= 9.030000000000001 AND $Precipitação Acumulado$ <= 29.894999999999996 AND $Tempos Acumulados$ <= 415.0 AND $Intensidade (mm...	Não	?	?	124	105
Row13	($Tempo Continuo$ <= 105.0 AND $Intensidade (mm/h) (periodo anterior 1)$ > 9.030000000000001 AND $Precipitação Acumulado$ <= 29.894999999999996 AND $Tempos Acumulados$ ...	Não	?	?	24	21
Row14	($Tempo Continuo$ > 105.0 AND $Intensidade (mm/h) (periodo anterior 1)$ > 9.030000000000001 AND $Precipitação Acumulado$ <= 29.894999999999996 AND $Tempos Acumulados$ <...	Sim	?	?	28	19
Row15	($Tempo Continuo$ <= 940.0 AND $Precipitação Acumulado$ > 29.894999999999996 AND $Tempos Acumulados$ <= 415.0 AND $Intensidade (mm/h) (periodo anterior 1)$ > 4.71 AND $I...	Sim	?	?	14	14
Row16	($Tempo Continuo$ > 940.0 AND $Precipitação Acumulado$ > 29.894999999999996 AND $Tempos Acumulados$ <= 415.0 AND $Intensidade (mm/h) (periodo anterior 1)$ > 4.71 AND $Int...	Não	?	?	5	5
Row17	($Tempos Acumulados$ > 415.0 AND $Intensidade (mm/h) (periodo anterior 1)$ > 4.71 AND $Intensidade (mm/h) (periodo anterior 3)$ <= 12.030000000000001 AND $Intensidade$ <= 11...	Não	?	?	365.017	362.017
Row18	($Precipitação Acumulado$ <= 5.92 AND $Tempos Acumulados$ <= 495.0 AND $Intensidade (mm/h) (periodo anterior 3)$ > 12.030000000000001 AND $Intensidade$ <= 11.7)	Não	?	?	40	37
Row19	($Tempo Continuo$ <= 100.0 AND $Tempo Continuo$ <= 940.0 AND $Precipitação Acumulado$ > 5.92 AND $Tempos Acumulados$ <= 495.0 AND $Intensidade (mm/h) (periodo anterior 3)...	Não	?	?	12	10
Row20	($Tempo Continuo$ > 100.0 AND $Tempo Continuo$ <= 940.0 AND $Precipitação Acumulado$ > 5.92 AND $Tempos Acumulados$ <= 495.0 AND $Intensidade (mm/h) (periodo anterior 3)$...	Sim	?	?	66	63
Row21	($Tempo Continuo$ > 940.0 AND $Precipitação Acumulado$ > 5.92 AND $Tempos Acumulados$ <= 495.0 AND $Intensidade (mm/h) (periodo anterior 3)$ > 12.030000000000001 AND $Int...	Não	?	?	17	14
Row22	($Tempos Acumulados$ > 495.0 AND $Intensidade (mm/h) (periodo anterior 3)$ > 12.030000000000001 AND $Intensidade$ <= 11.7)	Não	?	?	69.006	68.006
Row23	($Tempos Acumulados$ <= 45.0 AND $Tempo Continuo$ <= 115.0 AND $Tempo Continuo$ <= 985.0 AND $Tempos Acumulados$ <= 485.0 AND $Intensidade$ > 11.7)	Sim	?	?	9	7
Row24	($Tempos Acumulados$ > 45.0 AND $Tempo Continuo$ <= 115.0 AND $Tempo Continuo$ <= 985.0 AND $Tempos Acumulados$ <= 485.0 AND $Intensidade$ > 11.7)	Não	?	?	17	17
Row25	($Tempo Continuo$ > 115.0 AND $Tempo Continuo$ <= 985.0 AND $Tempos Acumulados$ <= 485.0 AND $Intensidade$ > 11.7)	Sim	?	?	251	241
Row26	($Tempos Acumulados$ <= 175.0 AND $Tempo Continuo$ > 985.0 AND $Tempos Acumulados$ <= 485.0 AND $Intensidade$ > 11.7)	Sim	?	?	14	10
Row27	($Tempos Acumulados$ > 175.0 AND $Tempo Continuo$ > 985.0 AND $Tempos Acumulados$ <= 485.0 AND $Intensidade$ > 11.7)	Não	?	?	18	18
Row28	($Precipitação Acumulado$ <= 190.37999999999994 AND $Tempos Acumulados$ > 485.0 AND $Intensidade$ > 11.7)	Não	?	?	83.012	83.012
Row29	($Precipitação Acumulado$ <= 379.12 AND $Precipitação Acumulado$ > 190.37999999999994 AND $Tempos Acumulados$ > 485.0 AND $Intensidade$ > 11.7)	Sim	?	?	8	8
Row30	($Precipitação Acumulado$ > 379.12 AND $Precipitação Acumulado$ > 190.37999999999994 AND $Tempos Acumulados$ > 485.0 AND $Intensidade$ > 11.7)	Não	?	?	10	10

Fig. 7. Rules Table obtained with KNIME open source software.

4   Neuronal Networks and ARIMA

As mentioned in the pre-processing section independent models were created, each with its own typology and focused on only one basin. In the initial phase, only recurrent neural networks were used, but as the research progressed, we decided to integrate the ARIMA algorithm. Therefore, we ended up with three models to be used: two variants of recurrent neural networks (LSTM and GRU) and a time series forecasting model (ARIMA).

Once the models were chosen, we moved on to the implementation phase. Regarding the ARIMA model, its implementation varies mainly based on the structure and quality of the data, as we used only very short components. Therefore, its implementation is uniform for all basins, varying only in the data groups: test data and training data. As for the two variants of recurrent neural networks, they required more work due to the possibility of changing parameters, such as the number of layers and the number of processing units in each layer. Thus, various model formats were tested for each model in each basin. Our ARIMA model used was as simple as possible with all parameters being 1 (AR, MA and I). So we can guarantee that our model only takes into account the last moment to be able to predict the next event.

To assess the performance of the models, the mean squared error measure was used. It is important to note that a significant amount of time was spent on model optimisation during this phase of the project, as training the models could take from ten to twenty minutes depending on the data volume. After conducting all the tests and optimising the models, we arrived at the following table, which shows the different performances and structures of the models used (Fig. 8).

To better understand the table, we need to understand that the "Number of Neurons" indicates the number of processing units in the first layer, and the subsequent layers have twice the number of units as the previous layer.

A quick analysis of the results shows that the LSTM model, in general, performed much worse than the other models, consistently being the worst-performing model for each basin. Therefore, we decided to proceed only with the other two models for real-time testing.

A script capable of running all fifty models (two models for each basin, with five basins in total) was created. This script can access the real-time database, input the data into the models, receive notifications, analyse the predictions, and based on these predictions an alert is sent if both models agree in the forecast of a different state than "Normal". Initially, the alert was sent via email. The reading of the database was done every ten minutes. If the system detects a failure in obtaining new data, it will check the database every five minutes for new data. This search ends in two ways: either when the database is updated and the system resumes checking every ten minutes, or if there are no new data after one hour, the system sends a possible malfunction alert to the responsible decision-maker.

To finalise the prediction process, we had to create a script that includes all the functions created for each basin. To run all the functions in parallel, we

island	hydrographic basin	Model	nº layers	Number of Neurons	minimum loss value
S. Miguel	Ribeira da Povoação	ARIMA	X	X	0,00128
S. Miguel	Ribeira da Povoação	GRU	2	64	0,23125
S. Miguel	Ribeira da Povoação	LSTM	2	64	4,38384
S. Miguel	Grota dos Milhafres	ARIMA	X	X	0,00319
S. Miguel	Grota dos Milhafres	GRU	3	32	0,67993
S. Miguel	Grota dos Milhafres	LSTM	2	32	32,4
S. Miguel	Ribeira Grande	ARIMA	X	X	0,00101
S. Miguel	Ribeira Grande	GRU	2	32	0,18794
S. Miguel	Ribeira Grande	LSTM	3	32	8,13549
Terceira	Ribeira das Nove	ARIMA	X	X	0,00068
Terceira	Ribeira das Nove	GRU	2	32	0,73795
Terceira	Ribeira das Nove	LSTM	3	32	0,86085
Terceira	Ribeira da Agualva	ARIMA	X	X	0.00226
Terceira	Ribeira da Agualva	GRU	2	32	0,28236
Terceira	Ribeira da Agualva	LSTM	2	64	0,33179

Fig. 8. Testing results.

use threads. We assigned one thread to each function and then started the five created threads. During this phase, the program went through a testing period where we had the system make predictions for two days. At this point, we could see that all basins were being monitored correctly.

The models developed were used in an alert application that can use the learned model to make predictions and, also, learn with new data resulting from sensors.

5   Simulation and Real Time Tests

The tests were carried out in two different ways, first we put the models to analyse the data in real time for five days and we analysed the forecast results in the database in order to verify the results. The vast majority of the results were good, however some basins had to undergo some changes in terms of training and compiling the models so that we could increase their performance (remove low values of rainfall intensity and flow level to avoid model confusion). As these tests were carried out at a time when there was not much rain, we only get the "Normal" result. So, to try to obtain results with other states, we tried to remove from the database time intervals in which the rains had been more intense in order to force the models to predict the remaining states. In this way, we were able to test the functioning of the models in different states and possible situations to ensure that they functioned correctly.

6   An Alert Application

Besides the alerts sent on-time by SMS to 2 or 3 top deciders, and in order to be able to monitor real-time forecast results and ensure that workers have access to alerts, a simple mobile application was developed. Through this application, users can view a map showing which stations are on alert and which ones have possible malfunctions. To achieve this, some database adjustments were made since the sensor data could only be accessed through the local network. Therefore, a new database had to be created to allow access through an external network. The models take the data, make predictions, and only these predictions are made available to the application, thus overcoming the accessibility issue.

In addition to the map, the application also provides users with a historical overview of each basin, including all previous alerts, as well as a list of all basins currently on alert as an alternative to the map (Fig. 9).

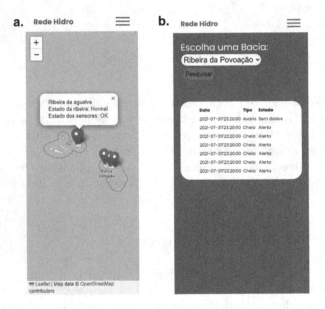

Fig. 9. a. Map in the Application, b. list of past events

7   Conclusions

In this work we describe the development of models capable of forecasting flood events in 5 hydrological basin in the Azores archipelago. This is done using two learned models a GRU and an ARIMA, which are used in a vote process to alert decision-makers in advance of an event occur. This models were developed using undersample of "normal" class and oversample of the other two classes considered: "before" and "during" from only 11 recorded events of flood in these 5 basins.

For the future of our project, it is important to prioritise the expansion and improvement of the hydrometeorological network in our region. This would allow us to address many of the issues related to the limited coverage of basins and the lack of data. By doing so, we can enhance both the size and quality of our network.

In spite of the fact that only a few positive data points were available the GRU and ARIMA models performed well and the application is usable and useful. Off course, with the actual plans of growing the IoT network for collecting data, the models and even the methods used for developing this models must be revised for full beneficial of the new data. We are aware that this results must be much more tuned and new methods should be tested, but for that longer time series are needed and more flood events should be recorded.

In fact, transfer learning was not completely applied in this work because of the historical data, in spite of the fact that a lot of points are available, many of than have zero or low figures of precipitation. So the tuning phase did most of the work. We intend to improve on this, still using undersampling and making the sample richer in heavy running periods, with or without flooding events.

Regarding the mobile application, it is important to continue working on both the design aspect and adding more functionality to it. This would further enhance its capabilities. As for the web application, it would be beneficial to develop a management-oriented application specifically designed for overseeing the network. This would allow for the addition of more basins, models, and recipients for alerts, simplifying tasks that are currently more complex to perform.

References

1. Jacques-Dumas, V., Ragone, F., Borgnat, P., Abry, P., Bouchet, F.: Deep learning-based extreme heatwave forecast. Front. Clim. **4**, 789641 (2022). https://www.frontiersin.org/articles/10.3389/fclim.2022.789641
2. Dueben, P.D., Bauer, P.: Challenges and design choices for global weather and climate models based on machine learning. Geosci. Model Dev. **11**(10), 3999–4009 (2018). https://doi.org/10.5194/gmd-11-3999-2018
3. Scher, S., Messori, G.: Weather and climate forecasting with neural networks: using general circulation models (GCMs) with different complexity as a study ground. Geosci. Model Dev. **12**(7), 2797–2809 (2019). https://doi.org/10.5194/gmd-12-2797-2019
4. Weyn, J.A., Durran, D.R., Caruana, R.: Can machines learn to predict weather? Using deep learning to predict gridded 500-hPa geopotential height from historical weather data. J. Adv. Model. Earth Syst. **11**(8), 2680–2693 (2019). https://doi.org/10.1029/2019MS001705
5. Chattopadhyay, A., Nabizadeh, E., Hassanzadeh, P.: Analog forecasting of extreme-causing weather patterns using deep learning. J. Adv. Model. Earth Syst. **12**(2), e2019MS001958 (2020). https://doi.org/10.1029/2019MS001958
6. McGovern, A., et al.: Using artificial intelligence to improve real-time decision-making for high-impact weather. Bull. Am. Meteor. Soc. **98**(10), 2073–2090 (2017). https://doi.org/10.1175/BAMS-D-16-0123.1

7. Karevan, Z., Suykens, J.A.K.: Transductive LSTM for time-series prediction: an application to weather forecasting. Neural Netw. **125**, 1–9 (2020). https://doi.org/10.1016/j.neunet.2019.12.030
8. Pratt, L., Thrun, S.: Guest editors' introduction. Mach. Learn. **28**(1), 5 (1997). https://doi.org/10.1023/A:1007322005825
9. Krawczyk, B.: Learning from imbalanced data: open challenges and future directions. Prog. Artif. Intell. **5**(4), 221–232 (2016). https://doi.org/10.1007/s13748-016-0094-0
10. Johnson, J.M., Khoshgoftaar, T.M.: The effects of data sampling with deep learning and highly imbalanced Big Data. Inf. Syst. Front. **22**(5), 1113–1131 (2020). https://doi.org/10.1007/s10796-020-10022-7
11. Yadav, S., Jain, A., Sharma, K.C., Bhakar, R.: Load forecasting for rare events using LSTM. In: 2021 9th IEEE International Conference on Power Systems (ICPS), December 2021, pp. 1–6 (2021). https://doi.org/10.1109/ICPS52420.2021.9670200
12. Silver, N.: The Signal and the Noise. Penguin Books (2013)
13. Kelleher, J.D.: Deep Learning. The MIT Press Essential Knowledge. The MIT Press, Cambridge (2019)
14. VipulNaik: Forecasting rare events. https://www.lesswrong.com/posts/Yb26htyo6SMirnzqt/forecasting-rare-events. Accessed 12 Jun 2023
15. Mills, T.C.: Time Series Econometrics - A Concise Introduction, 1st edn., vol. 1. Palgrave Macmillan (2015)

Digital Twin for Regional Water Consumption Simulation and Forecasting

Matheus Galvão[1,2], Pedro Rici[1,2], and Rui Pedro Lopes[1,2(✉)]

[1] Research Center in Digitalization and Intelligent Robotics (CeDRI),
Instituto Politécnico de Bragança, Bragança, Portugal
{matheusgalvao,pedrorici,rlopes}@ipb.pt
[2] Laboratório Associado para a Sustentabilidade e Tecnologia em Regiões de
Montanha (SusTEC), Instituto Politécnico de Bragança, Bragança, Portugal

Abstract. Water scarcity is a global concern due to population growth, climate change, and industrialization. Accurate water consumption simulation and forecasting are essential for understanding consumption patterns and predicting future demand. The control and visualization of how different aspects such as precipitation, season, and population affect water consumption can be a way for public agencies to plan actions that minimize waste and assist in the correct use of water. Technology, and especially Machine Learning and Digital Twin, can be used as tools for this. In light of this, this project aims to develop a system for simulating and forecasting water consumption in the Bragança region using a Digital Twin. In order to accomplish this, a comprehensive analysis is conducted to determine the necessary requirements for designing the system. This analysis encompasses the evaluation of hardware, software, data, machine learning models, web interface, as well as security and performance requirements. Furthermore, the architecture of this system and how it will be configured is analyzed, proposing a system with Training Data Sources, Training Process, Updated Data Sources, Digital Twin, Web Interface and Monitoring System. The system described in this article is under development and it is hoped to achieve as a result the full design of the Digital Twin and User Interface systems.

Keywords: Water · Consumption · Simulator · Web

1 Introduction

Water is vital for all living beings and plays a crucial role in our daily lives. It is used for basic needs such as drinking, cooking, and hygiene, as well as in agriculture, industry, and energy generation. Additionally, water is essential for maintaining aquatic ecosystems and biodiversity. Given its undeniable importance, it is imperative that we conserve and responsibly manage water resources to ensure its availability and quality for future generations. According to the World Health Organization (WHO) [11], 25% of the global population lacks access to clean drinking water, which raises concerns about water consumption.

A. I. Pereira et al. (Eds.): OL2A 2023, CCIS 1981, pp. 333–346, 2024.
https://doi.org/10.1007/978-3-031-53025-8_23

It is the responsibility of public authorities to plan actions for controlling water usage and reducing wastage.

Water scarcity is a pressing issue that affects numerous regions across the globe. The combination of population growth, climate change, agricultural expansion, and industrialization has exerted immense pressure on our limited freshwater resources, leading to an urgent need for effective solutions. Accurate simulation and forecasting of water consumption can play a crucial role in understanding the factors influencing consumption patterns and predicting future water demand in different scenarios. This paper proposes the development of an interactable system to monitor, simulate, and forecast water consumption in several urban and environmental scenarios.

At the core of this proposed system lies the concept of a Digital Twin (DT), which serves as a virtual representation of a physical object or process [6]. The DT is capable of collecting real-time information from the environment, validating its representation, and simulating its present and future behavior. By leveraging the power of Machine Learning (ML) models, the aim of this project is to construct a reliable DT specifically for water consumption. The ML models will be trained using vast amounts of historical data on water consumption, weather conditions, and social and economic characteristics, which have been previously collected and cleaned as part of a study conducted by [7]. The initial data used was collected in the city of Bragança, Portugal, and is related to 10 years of water consumption records, rain statistics and social and economic characteristics. Through this training process, the models will learn consumption patterns and establish relationships between water usage and various influencing factors.

In addition to the development of the DT model, this project also focuses on integrating it into a user-friendly web interface. This interface will not only provide access to the DT and real-time monitoring data but also facilitate easy manipulation and interaction with the system. By designing an intuitive interface, the system aims to ensure that relevant stakeholders, such as the responsible government agencies, can easily access and utilize the valuable insights provided by the DT.

The successful development of the proposed system could potentially contribute to a better understanding of water usage patterns. The system is expected to provide accurate simulations, forecast future water demands, and offer valuable information for decision-making processes related to water resource management. Although it is not within the scope of this project to suggest or present behavioral or governmental measures and changes to reduce water consumption, the tools presented here can be used by governments and responsible authorities to analyze and inform relevant decisions on the subject. Ultimately, this project aims to address the challenges of water scarcity by leveraging innovative technologies that could provide actionable insights to support sustainable water management practices and serve as a valuable tool for the region's infrastructure.

This paper is structured in 5 sections, starting with this introduction. Section 2 makes a bibliography review of the state-of-the-art, and Sect. 3 presents the system requirements that provide the support for the architecture definition. Section 4 describes the architecture proposed for the whole system and the paper ends, in Sect. 5 with some conclusions and perspectives for future work.

2   Related Work

The rise in the number of applications based on DTs has been creating a significant impact on real-world problems, combining the emergent power of modern ML frameworks and the massive amount of data collected by newly implemented IoT (Internet of Things) technologies, capable of providing real-time data from multiple different systems.

A DT can be defined as a virtual representation of a physical object or process capable of collecting information from the real environment to represent, validate and simulate the physical twin's present and future behavior [2]. DTs integrate ML and data analytics to create digital simulation models that are able to learn and update from multiple sources, and to represent and predict the current and future conditions of physical counterparts [10].

The concept of Smart Cities has become more popular in recent years as IoT devices are evolving and gaining adoption, multiple works have studied the use of DT models to simulate systems in the urban environment, such as infrastructure of buildings and cities [10], natural gas pipelines [17], urban mobility [15], water infrastructure [12]. Several other projects describe the application of DTs to Smart Agriculture, for instance, [4] proposes a framework to determine the optimal amount of fertilizers to be used.

Regarding applications that simulate water systems, studies have implemented systems in both urban and countryside spaces. On the urban level, studies include the work from Pesantez et al. [12] that develops a DT to explore the new patterns of water consumption in cities observed during the Covid-19 pandemic, and the work of Zekri et al. [16] on building a system of water management for price policy identification using a DT agent. In the agricultural environment, studies such as the one conducted by Alves et al. [1] are included, which develops a DT system focused on irrigation with real-time communication to an IoT platform, which enables farmers to evaluate the behavior of different irrigation systems before implementing in their farms.

ML algorithms play a crucial role in the construction and advancement of DT systems. These algorithms work hand to hand with DT frameworks to extract valuable insights from potentially large amounts of data and enhance the accuracy and effectiveness of virtual replicas. By leveraging ML techniques such as DL (Deep Learning), DTs can capture complex relationships, patterns, and behaviors within the physical systems they represent. Therefore the choice of efficient ML models enables more accurate predictions and optimization of system performance. Among the most recent relevant studies on water consumption forecasting, DL models have been broadly applied, especially DL architectures designed to handle sequential data, proving in most cases to be capable of outperforming other methods.

For instance, the work of Kavya and Mathew [8] compares various algorithms for the forecasting of urban water consumption, using a univariate approach that relied on consumption data to predict demand, and a multivariate approach incorporating consumption data, climatic parameters, and calendar inputs, concluding that DL models, particularly LSTM (Long Short-Term Memory), exhibited the highest performances. Another study on short-term forecasting of water consumption was conducted by Cao et al. [3], in which the performance of three DL architectures were evaluated in different forecasting horizons, including models such as LSTNet, AutoSTG and ASTGCN (Attention-based spatial-temporal graph convolutional network), which showed that all three models can outperform traditional benchmark algorithms.

Within applications with DT, the use of web applications for user interface and manipulation of the simulation parameters is a possibility to make the use of these systems more dynamic and to facilitate the contact with the final users [9]. Web applications present several advantages for projects involving the DT concept. Primarily, they enable remote access and interaction with the DT through a web browser. This aspect implies that geographically dispersed teams can collaborate in real time, view and manipulate DT data from any location in the world, without requiring specialized software or complex configurations [13].

Integration with other systems and technologies is another benefit of web applications. It simplifies the connection the DT to sensors, IoT devices, and management systems, feeding it real-time data and accurately reflecting the conditions and behaviors of the real object, as is done in the work of Wolf et al. [14]. In this paper, a DT is performed for a smart city in multi-agent incident management by collecting sensor data, simulating it, and displaying it in a web application.

Web applications also provide the ability to visualize and analyze historical data and future trends, allowing you to track the progression of variables over time, identify patterns, and anticipate scenarios. This predictive ability is of significant value for operations optimization, predictive maintenance, and strategic decision-making. The work by Alves et al. [1], realizes a system with DT for smart farming with the goal of reducing water consumption through irrigation management. The data collected by the system is stored in a database using MySQL and is displayed in the form of a dashboard for users using Grafana.

Another work that performs a web application of DT is that of Fonseca et al. [5], which applies DT for the maritime industry in order to simulate the operation of a boat in a real environment and monitor the global motion response. Two web applications were created, using the WebSocket protocol for communication with the modeling systems, one to monitor and control an experiment as it occurs and the other to repeat an experiment based on stored data.

In conclusion, the rise of applications based on DTs has had a significant impact on addressing real-world problems. These applications leverage the power of modern ML frameworks and the abundance of data collected by IoT technologies. Numerous studies have explored the application of DTs in various domains, such as urban infrastructure, natural gas pipelines, urban mobility, water infrastructure, and smart agriculture. Machine learning algorithms, particularly DL models, have played a crucial role in enhancing the accuracy and performance of DT systems, especially in water consumption forecasting. Furthermore, web applications have emerged as a valuable tool for interacting with DTs, providing remote access, visualization, analysis of historical data, and integration with other systems and technologies. These advancements have contributed to the optimization of operations, predictive maintenance, and informed decision-making processes. The research on such technologies and implementations provides valuable insight for the development of the proposed system, however, requirements should be addressed to accomplish the expected goal, as presented in the following section.

3   System Requirements

In order to successfully develop an interactable system for simulating and forecasting water consumption, it is crucial to comprehensively define the system requirements. These requirements encompass various aspects, including hardware and software components, data considerations, machine learning (ML) models, web interface design, security measures, and scalability/performance considerations. By carefully addressing these requirements, the proposed system can effectively utilize its resources to simulate water consumption patterns, forecast water demand for different scenarios, and provide valuable insights to end-users through a user-friendly and efficient graphical interface.

The requirements are structured in hardware, software, data, machine learning, user interface, security and scalability.

Hardware requirements should provide sufficient computational power to handle data processing and model training. This may include a high-performance server or cloud-based infrastructure. It should also have adequate storage capacity to store historical data and model parameters as well as reliable internet connectivity for data retrieval and web interface access.

Among the software requirements, the development of each different part of the system requires proficiency in programming languages commonly used for data analysis and ML, such as Python, as well as languages used for web development, such as Javascript. Utilization of ML libraries and frameworks like PyTorch for training and deploying robust models. Tools focused on Web development should be employed on building a web interface, such as HTML, CSS, JavaScript, and a suitable web framework like React. A database management system (DBMS) is needed to store and retrieve data efficiently, popular options include PostgreSQL, MySQL, or MongoDB. Data visualization libraries are another important component for presenting insights and trends in an interactive and visually appealing manner. Finally, the system should have access to web hosting services to deploy the web interface and make it accessible to users, requiring proprietary servers or third-party services.

The system requirements for data can be summarized as follows: The system must have access to a substantial amount of clean historical data, which will be used as the training dataset for the ML models. Additionally, the system should be able to access both historical and real-time water consumption data specific to the city of Bragança, Portugal, along with weather condition data. These datasets are necessary for training, simulating, and monitoring purposes.

Regarding the ML models, the system should utilize appropriate models capable of learning consumption patterns from the available historical data. The selection of models will be based on the specific requirements of the problem, which may include regression models, time series analysis, or deep learning architectures. Requiring access to adequate training infrastructure, including computational resources such as GPUs, if required, to ensure efficient model training.

Requirements regarding the web interface include a user-friendly platform design to allow users to easily access and manipulate the DT model. The interface should be designed with a responsive layout and intuitive navigation, ensuring rapid learning of how to use it for all parties involved. Furthermore, the interface should effectively present relevant information and insights, empowering users to make informed decisions regarding water consumption.

In terms of security and privacy, the system should incorporate sufficient measures to safeguard against unauthorized access or manipulation of both the system itself and the collected data. Privacy considerations should be given high priority, especially when dealing with sensitive data, to ensure compliance with relevant data protection regulations.

In order to ensure optimal functionality, the system must be designed with a focus on scalability and performance. It should possess the ability to seamlessly handle increasing amounts of data and adapt to growing computational demands over time. Additionally, the system should exhibit excellent performance in terms of response time and computational efficiency, especially when responding to the needs of multiple users concurrently. By prioritizing these factors, the system can provide a reliable and efficient user experience.

In this section, it was presented the main system requirements necessary regarding software, hardware, data, machine learning models, web interface, security, privacy, scalability and performance. These requirements are essential to carry out the proposal efficiently, reaching the expected goals. With such requirements ensured, it is possible to move on to the system architecture, which must respect and achieve the aforementioned requirements.

4   System Architecture

The Digital Twin is a virtual representation of a physical system that accurately simulates performance and predicts potential issues using real-world data and computational models. Based on this simulation, informed decisions can be made to optimize the system. Additionally, the digital twin enables testing of hypothetical scenarios, enhancing efficiency and safety. In summary, it is a valuable tool for monitoring and improving complex systems.

The system architecture is responsible for defining the structure, components, and interactions among the various technological layers that constitute the system. This architecture is designed to ensure efficient and reliable integration of data from the real physical object in order to create an accurate and up-to-date digital replica.

The system is developed in two main phases. First, it is necessary to train the necessary models to be able to estimate, later, the output according to changes in the input. The input may result from human interaction or as a result of real-time data retrieved from city resources sensors (Fig. 1).

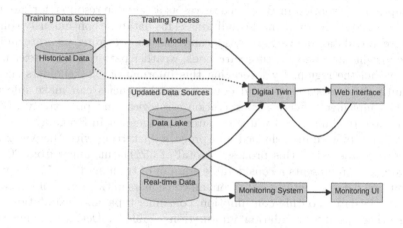

Fig. 1. System Architecture Diagram

The first essential component of the architecture is the Training Data Sources, which is responsible for providing the necessary data to train the system and produce a digitally faithful representation of reality. The system is trained with the following datasets:

- water consumption records from 2013 to 2020
- weather and rain data from 2013 to 2020
- population in each county of the Bragança district
- social-economic index of each county

This data is then forwarded to the next layer of the system.

The Training Process is where the stored raw data is processed and transformed into meaningful information. Signal processing algorithms, machine learning, and modeling techniques are applied to filter, organize, and structure the data.

The Updated Data Sources is a database with updated information in real time about climate, temperature, precipitation and consumption.

The Web Interface is responsible for presenting the information from the DT to users in an intuitive and understandable manner. Interactive graphical interfaces and web applications are used to enable users to explore and interact with the digital model. This layer plays a crucial role in data analysis, decision-making, and performance monitoring of the physical object.

Finally, the Monitoring System is responsible for displaying real-time information from the Updated Data Sources via a user interface, enabling user-friendly visualization of weather, temperature, and other data.

4.1   Training Data Sources

A real-time updated database incorporating temperature, weather, and water consumption information in Bragança serves as a valuable resource for monitoring and analyzing environmental conditions. This database continuously collects and aggregates data from various sensors and sources, providing accurate and up-to-date insights into temperature variations, weather patterns, and water usage trends within the region. By leveraging this information, stakeholders such as local authorities, researchers, and environmental agencies can make informed decisions, implement effective conservation strategies, and proactively address issues related to climate and water resource management in Bragança.

The datasets were first cleaned and processed, starting with the water consumption records. After this process, a total of 352944 instances from 2013 to 2020 were kept, represents a considerable amount of training data [7]. The water consumption dataset contains data from all consumers in the region of Bragança, regarding the date, monthly consumption, consumer type, and installation zone, among other specific installation information (Table 1). Despite having these types of information, information such as the consumer number and installation number will not all be used in the DT training process. This data is confidential and cannot be viewed. Because of this, the actual information has been hidden in the Table 1 to maintain data confidentiality.

Table 1. Sample of the water consumption dataset

Year	Month	Consumer_number	Consumer_type	Zone	Consumption	Installation_number
2013	1	***	1	4	0	***
2013	1	***	2	6	5	***
2013	1	***	1	6	6	***
2013	1	***	1	6	1	***
2013	1	***	1	6	13	***
...	...	...	...	...	...	...
2020	12	***	9	64	0	***
2020	12	***	9	22	0	***
2020	12	***	9	48	0	***
2020	12	***	1	4	14	***

Precipitation data was made available by the Portuguese Institute for Sea and Atmosphere (http://www.ipma.pt) and includes the amount of rain in Portugal recorded each month from January 2010 to December 2020 (Table 2).

Table 2. Sample of the precipitation dataset

Year	Month	QPRtot (mm)
2010	1	133,4
2010	2	201,2
2010	3	59,5
2010	4	106,9
2010	5	65,7
2010	6	104,8
...	...	...
2020	10	111,5
2020	11	119,6
2020	12	76,4

Finally, the population records were obtained from the Statistics Portugal Institute (http://censos.ine.pt) and register the residents in each of the Bragança's counties (Table 3).

Table 3. Sample of the resident population

Place of residence	Total
0402:Bragança	34582
040201:Alfaião	164
040203:Babe	209
040204:Baçal	460
040206:Carragosa	162
040209:Castro de Avelãs	430
040210:Coelhoso	279
...	...
040253:União das freguesias de Parada e Faílde	539
040254:União das freguesias de Rebordainhos e Pombares	148
040255:União das freguesias de Rio Frio e Milhão	287
040256:União das freguesias de São Julião de Palácios e Deilão	319
040257:União das freguesias de Sé, Santa Maria e Meixedo	22689
040249:Zoio	141

4.2 Data Processing

Prior to the application of the available data into the models, processing must be undergone in order to properly format the inputs and the representing relationship with the desired target. The process includes joining the datasets, removing irrelevant features, converting strings to numbers, and finally performing operations to achieve a format in which is possible to extract the total consumption information of each consumer type in each zone for multiple months, as displayed in Table 4. Such a dataset does not include any consumer-identifying data, as it provides the consumption information for a whole group in a specific region.

Table 4. Sample of processed dataset

Month	Consumer_type	Installation_zone	Count	mm	Total_Consumption
1	0	0	1415	142.0	10384
1	0	1	777	142.0	4979
1	0	2	1031	142.0	7335
1	0	41	1	142.0	11
1	1	0	193	142.0	2031
...	...	...	...	...	...
12	17	1	9	76.4	0
12	17	2	11	76.4	0
12	18	0	33	76.4	1484
12	18	1	15	76.4	1634
12	18	2	23	76.4	1432

4.3 Training Process

With the objective of creating an accurate model to be used as a DT, a carefully thought training process is necessary. Using the available data and a proper training methodology, different models shall be developed and tested to determine the best architecture, format, and hyperparameters. The project aims to leverage the capabilities of modern neural network architectures to develop models suited for the data and problem, evaluating their performances to find the most suited. The process should be available for further improvement and updated with newly available data to produce up-to-date models. A mechanism present in the API should identify updates in the database available to the model and trigger a retraining process, enabling the model to learn from more examples and adapt to possible data drifts.

Nevertheless, the DT is to be used by municipal authorities to simulate 'what-if' scenarios, so classification and estimation models are expected. The classification models should be able to:

- Identify anomalies in water consumption
- Classify water consumption patterns according to consumer type
- Suggest increasing or reducing the water supply to certain parts of the city

Similarly, the estimation models should be able to:

- Estimate the amount of water consumption by precipitation, population and consumer type
- Estimate water consumption by holidays and festivities

4.4   Digital Twin

The DT serves as the core component within the system architecture. Once the optimal machine learning (ML) models for the above mentioned simulations have been defined and trained, the DT is generated and made accessible as an Application Programming Interface (API) service hosted in a dedicated server. This API service allows the DT to be interacted with through requests initiated from the Web Interface. Through this seamless integration, users can effectively manipulate and harness the capabilities of the DT, enabling them to monitor, analyze, and make informed decisions based on the simulations provided by the DT. The availability of the DT as an API service enhances the system's flexibility, scalability, and usability, facilitating seamless communication between the Web Interface and the powerful analytical capabilities of the DT (Fig. 2).

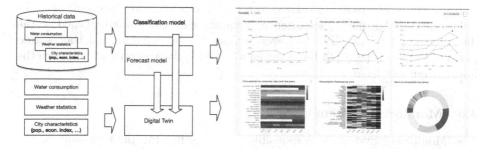

Fig. 2. Digital Twin architecture diagram

Furthermore, the DT should be open for updates on its training as new data becomes available, working in a cycle (Fig. 3). The system as a whole could be improved to deal with surging conditions and new patterns from additional data.

4.5   Web Interface

The Web Interface is the component of the architecture that enables the control of DT parameters and the visualization of the data generated by it. In this stage, an interface will be created with parameter manipulators, allowing the user to choose variables such as month, consumer type, population, and others.

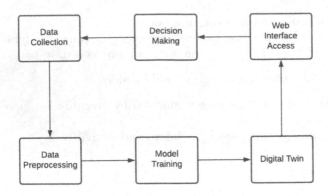

Fig. 3. Digital Twin Cycle

These parameters are sent to the DT, which will respond with the generated data for those parameters. The interface itself will display the generated data, showing simulated water consumption data. In addition to the data generated by DT, historical data will be displayed through graphs of water consumption, population and precipitation.

This interface empowers the user to have full control over the parameters used in the DT, enabling the analysis of different scenarios and the retrieval of generated information. Furthermore, the visualization of the generated data within the interface simplifies the understanding of the results, allowing the user to intuitively evaluate the simulated water consumption. This approach provides an interactive and efficient experience, facilitating decision-making based on the data generated by the DT. However, access will be restricted to the desired persons only, and there will be an authentication system to protect and keep the information restricted.

4.6 Monitoring System

The Monitoring System is responsible for accessing the data present in the Updated Data Sources and displaying it to the user. This is achieved through a user interface in the form of a dashboard, which presents real-time updated climate data such as temperature and precipitation, as well as water consumption in the Bragança region.

By accessing the updated data sources, the Monitoring System gathers relevant information to provide to the user. This data is presented in an intuitive and real-time manner through a dashboard that showcases information such as the current temperature and rainfall in the region. Additionally, the system also offers data on water consumption in the Bragança area, enabling users to efficiently track and monitor the utilization of this resource.

5   Conclusions

A proper water usage and the resolution of scarcity issues are urgent challenges we currently face. Technology plays a fundamental role in seeking effective solutions. The implementation of advanced systems, such as digital twins and real-time data analytics, enables a more precise understanding of consumption patterns and helps identify areas of waste and inefficiency. Furthermore, technology can assist in continuous monitoring of water resources, facilitating early detection of issues and the implementation of corrective measures. Technology plays a crucial role in optimizing water consumption, reducing waste, and ensuring a sustainable future for water resources.

This article presents a proposal for utilizing a Digital Twin system with a web interface to facilitate parameter manipulation and enhance the comprehension of water consumption in the city of Bragança. Moreover, the system incorporates real-time monitoring of weather conditions and water consumption within the city. By adopting this approach, users will have access to current information regarding water consumption and weather conditions, thus providing a comprehensive and real-time perspective of the water situation. The user-friendly web interface allows for seamless interaction, enabling users to adjust parameters and visualize pertinent data, thereby fostering a deeper understanding of water consumption in the city.

The implementation of the aforementioned system poses several challenges that need to be addressed. Firstly, developing an accurate and reliable Digital Twin model that can accurately simulate water consumption patterns and forecast future demands is a complex task. It necessitates the collection and analysis of large volumes of historical data, as well as the application of advanced machine learning algorithms to identify meaningful patterns and relationships.

Furthermore, integrating the Digital Twin system with a user-friendly web interface presents usability and design challenges. The interface needs to be intuitive, visually appealing, and responsive, allowing users to easily manipulate parameters and access relevant information. Usability testing and iterative design processes will be crucial to ensure an optimal user experience.

Acknowledgments. This work has been supported by FCT - Fundação para a Ciência e Tecnologia within the Project Scope: DSAIPA/AI/0088/2020.

References

1. Alves, R.G., Maia, R.F., Lima, F.: Development of a digital twin for smart farming: irrigation management system for water saving. J. Clean. Prod. **388**, 135920 (2023)
2. Botín-Sanabria, D.M., Mihaita, A.S., Peimbert-García, R.E., Ramírez-Moreno, M.A., Ramírez-Mendoza, R.A., Lozoya-Santos, J.D.J.: Digital twin technology challenges and applications: a comprehensive review. Remote Sens. **14**(6), 1335 (2022)

3. Cao, L., Yuan, X., Tian, F., Xu, H., Su, Z.: Forecasting of water consumption by integrating spatial and temporal characteristics of short-term water use in cities. Phys. Chem. Earth Parts A/B/C **130**, 103390 (2023). https://doi.org/10.1016/j.pce.2023.103390. https://www.sciencedirect.com/science/article/pii/S1474706523000347

4. Cesco, S., Sambo, P., Borin, M., Basso, B., Orzes, G., Mazzetto, F.: Smart agriculture and digital twins: applications and challenges in a vision of sustainability. Eur. J. Agron. **146**, 126809 (2023)

5. Fonseca, Í.A., Gaspar, H.M., de Mello, P.C., Sasaki, H.A.U.: A standards-based digital twin of an experiment with a scale model ship. Comput. Aided Des. **145**, 103191 (2022)

6. Fuller, A., Fan, Z., Day, C., Barlow, C.: Digital twin: enabling technologies, challenges and open research. IEEE Access **8**, 108952–108971 (2020)

7. Gubareva, R.: Extracting temporal patterns from smart city data. Master's thesis (2022). https://bibliotecadigital.ipb.pt/handle/10198/25870. Accepted 02 Sept 2022

8. Kavya, M., Mathew, A., Shekar, P.R., P, S.: Short term water demand forecast modelling using artificial intelligence for smart water management. Sustain. Cities Soc. **95**, 104610 (2023). https://doi.org/10.1016/j.scs.2023.104610. https://www.sciencedirect.com/science/article/pii/S2210670723002214

9. Liu, X., et al.: A systematic review of digital twin about physical entities, virtual models, twin data, and applications. Adv. Eng. Inform. **55**, 101876 (2023)

10. Lu, Q., et al.: Developing a digital twin at building and city levels: case study of west Cambridge campus. J. Manag. Eng. **36**(3), 05020004 (2020)

11. World Health Organization: State of the world's drinking water: an urgent call to action to accelerate progress on ensuring safe drinking water for all (2022)

12. Pesantez, J.E., Alghamdi, F., Sabu, S., Mahinthakumar, G., Berglund, E.Z.: Using a digital twin to explore water infrastructure impacts during the covid-19 pandemic. Sustain. Urban Areas **77**, 103520 (2022)

13. Tao, F., Xiao, B., Qi, Q., Cheng, J., Ji, P.: Digital twin modeling. J. Manuf. Syst. **64**, 372–389 (2022)

14. Wolf, K., Dawson, R.J., Mills, J.P., Blythe, P., Morley, J.: Towards a digital twin for supporting multi-agency incident management in a smart city. Sci. Rep. **12**(1), 16221 (2022)

15. Yeon, H., Eom, T., Jang, K., Yeo, J.: Dtumos, digital twin for large-scale urban mobility operating system. Sci. Rep. **13**(1) (2023). https://doi.org/10.1038/s41598-023-32326-9. https://www.scopus.com/inward/record.uri?eid=2-s2.0-85151176448&doi=10.1038%2fs41598-023-32326-9&partnerID=40&md5=a596bf448f95164776c3ee18d1f2182a. All Open Access, Gold Open Access, Green Open Access

16. Zekri, S., Jabeur, N., Gharrad, H.: Smart water management using intelligent digital twins. Comput. Inform. **41**(1), 135–153 (2022)

17. Zhang, X., et al.: Real-time pipeline leak detection and localization using an attention-based LSTM approach. Process Saf. Environ. Prot. **174**, 460–472 (2023). https://doi.org/10.1016/j.psep.2023.04.020. https://www.scopus.com/inward/record.uri?eid=2-s2.0-85152937802&doi=10.1016%2fj.psep.2023.04.020&partnerID=40&md5=3ab0978b41f5b91613e529429b1c7bdd

Automatic Fall Detection with Thermal Camera

Rebeca B. Kalbermatter[1,2,4]([✉]) [iD], Tiago Franco[1] [iD], Ana I. Pereira[1,2] [iD], António Valente[3,4] [iD], Salviano Pinto Soares[5,6,7] [iD], and José Lima[1,2,3] [iD]

[1] Research Centre in Digitalization and Intelligent Robotics (CeDRI), Instituto Politécnico de Bragança, Campus de Santa Apolónia, 5300-253 Bragança, Portugal
{kalbermatter,tiagofranco,apereira,jllima}@ipb.pt
[2] Laboratório Associado para a Sustentabilidade e Tecnologia em Regiões de Montanha (SusTEC), Instituto Politécnico de Bragança, Campus de Santa Apolónia, 5300-253 Bragança, Portugal
[3] INESC Technology and Science, Porto, Portugal
[4] Universidade de Trás-os-Montes e Alto Douro, Vila Real, Portugal
avalente@utad.pt
[5] School of Sciences and Technology-Engineering Department (UTAD), Vila Real, Portugal
salblues@utad.pt
[6] Institute of Electronics and Informatics Engineering of Aveiro (IEETA), University of Aveiro, 3810-193 Aveiro, Portugal
[7] Intelligent Systems Associate Laboratory (LASI), University of Aveiro, Aveiro, Portugal

Abstract. People are living longer, promoting new challenges in healthcare. Many older adults prefer to age in their own homes rather than in healthcare institutions. Portugal has seen a similar trend, and public and private home care solutions have been developed. However, age-related pathologies can affect an elderly person's ability to perform daily tasks independently. Ambient Assisted Living (AAL) is a domain that uses information and communication technologies to improve the quality of life of older adults. AI-based fall detection systems have been integrated into AAL studies, and posture estimation tools are important for monitoring patients. In this study, the OpenCV and the YOLOv7 machine learning framework are used to develop a fall detection system based on posture analysis. To protect patient privacy, the use of a thermal camera is proposed to prevent facial recognition. The developed system was applied and validated in the real scenario.

Keywords: Fall detection · Pose model · Ambient assisted-living

1 Introduction

Life expectancy is growing worldwide. In 2000, the life expectancy in the European Union was 77 years, whereas in 2020 was around 80 years old[1]. In Europe,

---

[1] https://data.worldbank.org/indicator/SP.DYN.LE00.IN?locations=EU.

A. I. Pereira et al. (Eds.): OL2A 2023, CCIS 1981, pp. 347–359, 2024.
https://doi.org/10.1007/978-3-031-53025-8_24

it is expected in 2050 the population of geriatric age, i.e. over 65 years old, will be around 170 million[2]. With this rising life expectancy and the increase in population over 65, the want of elderly people to live in their homes instead of an elderly care home. In Portugal, the preference for getting old was observed in their residence [5]. This desire is possible through public and private solutions enabling home care assistance.

Furthermore, it is important to observe that elderly people tend to have pathologies of this period that, at different levels of severity, hinder the autonomy in performing daily tasks [15]. More is rising the studies about Ambient Assisted Living (ALL), defined by the ALL Europe Group as "the use of information and communication technologies in a person's daily living and working environment to enable them to stay active longer, remain socially connected and live independently into old age"[3].

Fall detection using artificial intelligence is already present in AAL studies. Tools for posture estimation have been allied to these studies since they promote detection through the position of the monitored patient. Currently, one of the most used tools for computer vision is OpenCV, which includes algorithms for image filtering and geometric transformations and can be used for posture estimation.

The proposed system by this work uses, besides OpenCV, a YOLOv7 machine learning framework to develop a robust fall detection system based on the posture of the monitored patient. Moreover, the concern involving the security of the data collected through the monitoring camera is addressed, bringing an approach using a thermal camera to keep the patient anonymous, not having the possibility to recognize the person through the captured image.

The remainder of the paper is organized as follows: following the introduction are the works related to the present development in Sect. 2. Next, Sect. 3 presents the system description. Section 4 demonstrates the methodologies, followed by Sect. 5 to present the results obtained until now. Finally, Sect. 6 concludes the results and points to future work.

2   Related Work

About 30% of the geriatric population has experienced falls. According to the National Institute for Health and Care Excellence in London, 14–50% of people cannot get up independently after a fall. The main reasons for falls in the elderly are related to the environment, such as low light and slippery floors, among others [2,14]. Besides physical problems, such as joint dislocations, fractures, and trauma, falling also affects the self-confidence of the elderly, impairing their independence with long-term treatments [6]. Even more severely, falls are one of the most common causes of accidental death, as highlighted by [8], increasing the need to monitor and seek quick help for the elderly.

---

[2] https://population.un.org/wpp/Graphs/Probabilistic/POP/65plus/900.
[3] https://www.aal-europe.eu/.

Technology has been an ally in creating tools and solutions for better monitoring old age, triggering a series of research and projects focused on the subject. Currently, it is possible to find solutions based on two perspectives: one where the user needs to act through an emergency button on watches or similar, or real-time monitoring through video cameras. The significant disadvantage of the need for action by the patient is the inability of the older adult to call for help in case of loss of consciousness in the fall or because they forgot to press the alarm button after the fall [3]. For this reason, several studies have focused on monitoring through images, respecting the individual's privacy, and creating alert systems for help.

The problem of blind spots in real-time camera monitoring has been addressed in the works of Lee [7] and Nait-Charif [13]. Lee used the analysis of the person's 2D shape and speed. Nait-Charifi presumes a fall when the monitored individual is detected inactive outside a specified zone for that, such as a sofa or bed.

In 2006, Miaou et al. [11] relied on the relationship between the monitored object and the bounding box of the moving object. For this work, a 360° camera was used to eliminate blind spots in the field of view. The work presented two approaches, one using only the observed image and the other using user data such as weight, height, and heart history provided to adjust the algorithm's sensitivity. Were observed an accuracy of 79.8% and 68%, respectively.

De Miguel et al. [12] demonstrate that a low-cost system using the Raspberry Pi 2 and an attached camera module is sufficient to create a fall detection prototype based on machine vision algorithms. When a fall occurs, a photo and an alert are sent to the previously configured device, as well as the detection that the individual was able to get up after the fall. The fall detection is performed based on three variables, the angle, ratio, and ratio derivative of an ellipse and a rectangle surrounding the moving object. The system showed an accuracy and precision of 96%.

Some difficulties are encountered in detecting the elderly's falls, whether wearable or not. The first to highlight is the elderly's rejection of wearing the video and the idea that the system is invading their privacy. Regarding solutions to the privacy concerns associated with cameras, Ma et al. [9] used a thermal camera to locate faces and an RGB camera to detect falls. The faces of the subjects were blurred using the mask pattern on the spatial light modulator.

3   System Description

This section is destined to present the specifications of the camera used, the algorithm for pose estimation, namely YOLOv7, and the system specification utilized to run the approach. The methodologies to apply these tools are described in Sect. 4.

3.1 Thermal Camera

The *Seek Compact Pro* thermal camera is a compact, handheld device that uses advanced thermal imaging technology to detect and visualize heat patterns. By converting infrared radiation into a visible image, it accurately measures temperature differences and displays them as a color gradient. With high thermal sensitivity, it is widely used in wildlife observation and home security, the focus of this approach. Smartphone and tablet integration allows easy capture and sharing of thermal images and videos, making it a versatile tool. This thermal camera was chosen to help with the privacy issue of the individual being monitored, as it only outputs color gradient images and does not allow for facial recognition. Furthermore, it allows monitoring both day and night without adding polarizing or infrared filters.

3.2 Pose Estimation

The pose estimation *You Only Look Once version 7* (YOLOv7) is a single-stage real-time object detector [10]. The positions and classes are predicted with bounding boxes that should be created around each object. To achieve the forecast, YOLO performs a post-processing procedure known as non-maximal suppression (NMS). The structural diagram of the YOLOv7 network can be divided into three distinct components, the input, the backbone, and the head networks. The detailed process of the YOLOv7 can be read in [4,10]. The YOLOv7 was chosen for this work because it has more efficient model training and presents more efficiency in multiple object detection. The approach of YOLOv7 can read 10 FPS and detect 17 key points in the human body.

3.3 Dataset

The approach used three different datasets for training, testing and evaluation. The first, for training, is a dataset with a total of 575 figures with fall and not fall situations[4]. The second dataset was used on the testing process, from *Multiple Cameras Fall Dataset* [1]. This dataset comprised videos with fall, not fall and confounding events, and was chose 24 videos for the validation phase. For the final stage and focus of the approach, the third dataset consists of 30 videos recorded with the thermal camera with volunteers and was used for the evaluation phase.

3.4 System Specification

The experiments were done on two different machines. One was on a normal personal computer with Windows 10 operating system. The computer contains an Intel Core i7 CPU, an NVIDIA GEFORCE GPU, and 8 GB RAM. And the second is a virtual machine with Ubuntu MATE 1.26.0, AMD EPYC 7351 processor, and 8 GB RAM.

---

[4] https://github.com/Y-B-Class-Projects/Human-Fall-Detection/tree/master/fall_dataset/images.

3.5 Privacy License

Due to the policies of the General Data Protection Regulation[5] in Portugal, the participants involved in the tests were asked if they would volunteer for the test and signed a consent form giving the consensual use of the images for the purpose of the study involved. The signatures were scanned and archived to preserve and maintain open access for all, following the Open Access policy. The record of the videos was made in a controlled ambient and the safe of the participants was guaranteed.

4 Methodology

This section discusses the methodology for developing a posture estimation system for fall detection using YOLOv7 and OpenCV. The proposed methodology is divided into four stages: data collection, preprocessing, training, and evaluation.

The data collecting, at the moment for validation purposes, is done using a thermal camera connected to a smartphone. The video is recorded and imported for the repository to be read for the algorithm. The Seek Compact Pro thermal camera has a dedicated interface to access the images on the smartphone. To validate the algorithm, the recorded videos were manually transferred from the smartphone to the computer. Real-time integration between the camera and the algorithm is the object of study for the continuation of this approach. As described before, the thermal camera was chosen because it helps to hide the face of the monitored user, as shown in Fig. 1. For the test, three filters of the thermal camera were tested, and were not observed interference between them in the fall detection. The chosen filter, which is based on the color white for lower temperatures, was made because it keeps the patient's face more blurred, aiding in non-face identification through the image. Figure 1 presents an image of videos with the filters in order, black gradient, white gradient, and spectral. The second stage is to preprocess the data, including steps to resizing, converting the images to grayscale, and applying augmentation techniques.

The training was made with a deep learning pipeline on the preprocessed data to estimate human posture and estimate the fall or not. The pipeline used in this study, as described before, was the YOLOv7. The dataset for training used 349 images for fall and 226 images for not fall and was made with 300 epochs. The last stage, to evaluate the proposed system, was made with the videos collected in an open-source dataset and collected by the thermal camera. The evaluation metric used was the mean average precision (mAP).

Figure 2 describes the workflow of the architecture of the algorithm used for the approach. The methodology utilized in this project involved open-source frameworks, YOLOv7, OpenCV, and NumPy, to perform computer vision deductions on sensory data, facilitate the input of the video camera, and trigonometric calculations, respectively.

---

[5] Regulamento Geral sobre a Proteção de Dados (RGPD).

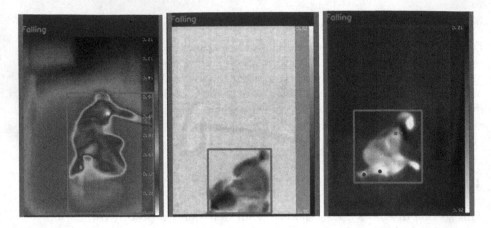

Fig. 1. Examples of the filters used in the thermal camera.

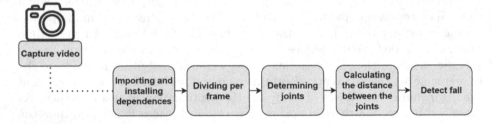

Fig. 2. Flowchart of the Architecture.

For the detection of the key points, the first step is to capture the video to the framework, where a deep learning model detects the body parts and identifies with the machine learning algorithms the key points or landmarks. In this approach, the key points are the shoulders, middle of the body (or hip), and feet. Figure 3, which shows the key points, namely shoulder right and left in red, body right and left in green, and foot right and left in blue. The process of detection involved setting up the YOLOv7, as the image is pre-processed, resized to $640 \times 640 \times 3$, and inputted to the backbone network. Then, the length and width of the feature map are successively cut in half by the Computational Block Scaling (CBS) composite module, the Efficient Layer Aggregation Network (ELAN) computational block, and the Max-Pooling (MP) module. The video is processed frame per frame and recolored first to RGB and after to BGR before rendering the key points detection.

Once the key points are detected, the coordinates can be used to perform further calculations and analysis, in this case, the distance between key points. The calculation is based on the Euclidean distance between shoulders and body and between shoulders and feet. Figure 3 represents the Euclidean distances utilized to detect the fall, namely "f_e" represented in cyan for the distance between

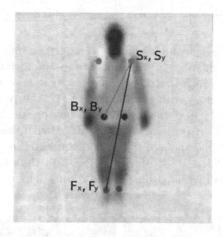

Fig. 3. Representative images for the key points joints and the Euclidean distances between shoulder to the body (yellow) and to the foot (cyan). (Color figure online)

shoulder to foot, and "b_e" represented in yellow for the distance between shoulder to the body, and calculated by Eqs. (1) and (2). Each key point has an associated value of cardinal coordinates x and y, and where s_x and s_y are the coordinates of the shoulder, f_x and f_y are the coordinates of the foot, and b_x and b_y are the coordinates of the body. The calculation is made both for left and right side. The approach for detecting the fall is based on conditions of these distances and the positions of the key points of the joints.

$$f_e = \sqrt{(s_y - f_y)^2 + (s_x - f_x)^2} \tag{1}$$

$$b_e = \sqrt{(s_y - b_y)^2 + (s_x - b_x)^2} \tag{2}$$

Another condition used in the approach is to detect how many frames the fall occurs to trigger an alarm, which will be implemented in the future. It is important to emphasize that the work presented here is still in progress and the results obtained are still partial.

The tests for evaluating the precision of the approach were made in two parts. The first part with the Multiple Cameras Fall Dataset [1], which contains 24 videos including falls and confounding events, and the second part with a total of 30 videos recorded by the 10 volunteers of the test with the thermal camera. These two tests are evaluated using a ground truth label, with 0 when no fall occurs and 1 for fall detection. The algorithm's output is the video with the key points on the body and a box around the person that informs when the fall is detected and when the alarm is raised. The results will be discussed in the next section.

5   Results

Once the video is processed, the key points are marked and the fall is detected, the algorithm saves a video with these outputs in the format ".mp4". As mentioned before, this approach is still improving and it is a work in progress. In the first case of evaluation, with the dataset of [1], the results obtained prove the algorithm's efficiency in detecting the fall, having an mAP for the dataset of human fall of 83.33%. A positive result obtained with this approach is that it was possible to avoid blind spots of the person generated by the furniture of the scene, which is possible to observe in Fig. 4(a), and the event of fall detection even though there are different people in the room, demonstrated by Fig. 4(b).

(a) Example of blind spot.   (b) Example of people in the room.

Fig. 4. Representative images for the cases with furniture or more than one person in the room. Adapted from [1].

The process explored here is to improve fall detection without the need for wearable sensors or RGB cameras, keeping the face of the user monitored unidentified. The thermal camera, in comparison with what was made by [9] is not used only to blur the face but is implemented to be a useful tool for the elderly monitoring, keeping privacy, and further being a tool to evaluate other information about the patient, like the thermal comfort. The tests with the thermal camera have shown positive results and will continue to be tested in different scenarios. Figure 5 presents an example of the output when the approach detects the fall and if the alarm is activated. To prove the efficiency of the approach in different angles, the falls were recorded in two different ways, the first in front of the camera and the second in a side way to the camera, as observed in Fig. 6. For the tests made with the thermal camera, the result obtained was an mAP of 80%, meaning that in a dataset of 30 videos with falls, 24 were detected.

As a result of the algorithm applied to both datasets, the ground truth of true and false positives or true and false negatives, the results are summarized in Table 1, and indicate that some adjustments are still observed to be necessary to eliminate these false positives or negatives. Although presenting an accuracy below the work developed by [12], the approach developed here differs in that

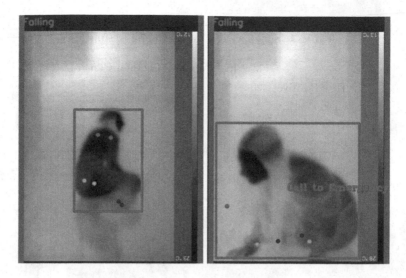

Fig. 5. Output of the approach when detected fall and then activates the alarm.

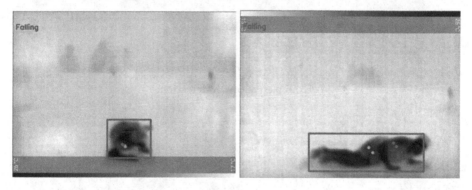

Fig. 6. Representative of the ways to fall: the first one to fall in front of the camera, and the second one perpendicular to the camera.

it uses the thermal images to have no identification, there is no need to change the background for the detection of the person, and there is no need to send the image to the alert system. These distinctions were applied precisely as tools to help the acceptance of the monitoring system by the elderly population.

Examples of the videos recorded with the thermal camera are shown in Fig. 7. In the first example, Fig. 7(a), the fall was a little quick, and the detection was made correctly. In the second example, Fig. 7(b), the fall occurred with more time in the flow, and the detection was correct. Finally, in the third example, Fig. 7(c), the fall lasted more time and caused the alarm to be activated, with the alert of "Call the emergency" in the red box.

Difficulties have been encountered and will be addressed in future work. One of them is related to the optical aperture of the camera. The tests with the

Table 1. Summary of True and False Results.

	Multiple Camera	Thermal Camera
True Positive	20	24
False Positive	2	0
True Negative	0	0
False Negative	2	6

(a) Example (1) of fall detection.

(b) Example (2) of fall detection.

(c) Example (3) of fall detection and alarm.

Fig. 7. Examples of fall detection with the thermal camera.

thermal camera were done in a purpose-designed environment, with the camera positioned at a distance of about 3 m from the person and at a height of about 1.60 m. The difficulty of fixing it at a higher height was an obstacle for further tests and will be one of the objectives for the continuation of this work. Another observation to be discussed is the small aperture angle of the thermal camera, only 32°. Despite having a long-range with accurate temperature measurement, up to 550 m distance between the camera and the object, the small optical aperture may influence the presence of blind spots in the room, as the optical aperture would need to be wider for larger environments.

The compatibility of the common alternatives to the YOLOv7, namely MediaPipe has also been explored at a research level. Some points of the difference between the approaches made the MediaPipe was discarded at the beginning of the validation of the algorithm, highlighted in Table 2. It is important to note that both alternatives present relevant features for pose estimation, but in the case studied and tested here, YOLOv7 presented better qualities and was therefore taken as the main tool. New tests will be addressed in other environments to ensure the quality of YOLOv7 in different situations.

Table 2. Comparison between YOLOv7 and MediaPipe.

	Workflow	GPU Support	Multi-Person Detection
YOLOv7	Runs for all frames	Both CPU and GPU	Both Multi and Single-Person
MediaPipe	Runs once followed by tracker until occlusion occurs	Only CPU	Only Single-person

6 Conclusion and Future Work

Due to the exponential growth of artificial intelligence in various areas, the required time for creating AI-based tools has been reduced. Technologies similar to YOLO, CNN, and others have been researched for their accuracy in person detection up to the joint level. The goal of this research is to provide a system based on pose estimation to detect falls without using wearable sensors or RGB cameras. The proposed methodology for developing fall detection using a thermal camera provides a solid foundation for future work. Due to the factor of using a self-authored dataset with the thermal camera, there was a limited number of videos used for the tests. Despite this, the accuracy was high, and it is expected that in the continuation of this work, the results will be further improved. The thermal camera shows a positive result in this approach, being a tool that the authors will explore more. Due to the commercialism that thermal cameras have demonstrated, the easy access to this type of technology already allows the approach presented here to have a viable implementation both in facility and cost. Also, the fact that it allows visual occlusion without the need to modify the image virtually to blur or erase objects that will not be monitored decreases the required processing power of the device to be used. In particular, future work is planned for this approach and pointed out here. The first is to conduct the research to implement the read of the thermal camera in real-time experiments, using appropriate tools to process the algorithm in real-time. Also, improve the position of the camera, checking the better position and the necessity or not to use more than one camera in the room. Furthermore, combining different position categories to eliminate false positives and improve the precision of fall detection, enabling the algorithm to recognize daily-life actions, like sitting, eating, or pick-up something. And finally, test the approach in a real environment to evaluate the usability of home assistance for the elderly, integrating the development of an alert system to notify the medical services, healthcare institutions or family of the elderly.

Acknowledgment. The authors are grateful to the Foundation for Science and Technology (FCT, Portugal) for financial support through national funds FCT/MCTES (PIDDAC) to CeDRI (UIDB/05757/2020 and UIDP/05757/2020) and SusTEC (LA/P/0007/2021).

References

1. Auvinet, E., Rougier, C., Meunier, J., St-Arnaud, A., Rousseau, J.: Multiple cameras fall dataset. DIRO-Université de Montréal, Technical report, 1350, p. 24 (2010)
2. Berg, R.L., Cassells, J.S.: The second fifty years: promoting health and preventing disability (1992)
3. Chen, M., Ma, Y., Song, J., Lai, C.F., Hu, B.: Smart clothing: connecting human with clouds and big data for sustainable health monitoring. Mob. Netw. Appl. **21**, 825–845 (2016)
4. Dewi, C., Chen, A.P.S., Christanto, H.J.: Deep learning for highly accurate hand recognition based on yolov7 model. Big Data Cogn. Comput. **7**(1), 53 (2023)
5. Fonseca, A.M.: Aging in place, envelhecimento em casa e na comunidade em portugal. Public Sci. Policies **6**(2), 21–39 (2020)
6. Freeman, S., et al.: Olfactory stimuli and enhanced postural stability in older adults. Gait Posture **29**(4), 658–660 (2009)
7. Lee, T., Mihailidis, A.: An intelligent emergency response system: preliminary development and testing of automated fall detection. J. Telemed. Telecare **11**(4), 194–198 (2005)
8. Lord, S.R., Ward, J.A., Williams, P., Anstey, K.J.: An epidemiological study of falls in older community-dwelling women: the randwick falls and fractures study. Aust. J. Public Health **17**(3), 240–245 (1993)
9. Ma, C., Shimada, A., Uchiyama, H., Nagahara, H., Taniguchi, R.I.: Fall detection using optical level anonymous image sensing system. Opt. Laser Technol. **110**, 44–61 (2019)
10. Maji, D., Nagori, S., Mathew, M., Poddar, D.: Yolo-pose: enhancing yolo for multi person pose estimation using object keypoint similarity loss. In: Proceedings of the IEEE/CVF Conference on Computer Vision and Pattern Recognition, pp. 2637–2646 (2022)
11. Miaou, S.G., Sung, P.H., Huang, C.Y.: A customized human fall detection system using omni-camera images and personal information. In: 1st Transdisciplinary Conference on Distributed Diagnosis and Home Healthcare, 2006. D2H2, pp. 39–42 (2006). https://doi.org/10.1109/DDHH.2006.1624792

12. Miguel, K., Brunete, A., Hernando, M., Gambao, E.: Home camera-based fall detection system for the elderly. Sensors **17**, 2864 (2017). https://doi.org/10.3390/s17122864
13. Nait-Charif, H., McKenna, S.J.: Activity summarisation and fall detection in a supportive home environment. In: Proceedings of the 17th International Conference on Pattern Recognition, 2004. ICPR 2004, vol. 4, pp. 323–326. IEEE (2004)
14. Thangaraj, P.: Falls among elderly and its relation with their health problems and surrounding environmental factors in riyadh. J. Fam. Community Med. **25**(3), 222–223 (2018)
15. Tornero-Quiñones, I., Sáez-Padilla, J., Espina Díaz, A., Abad Robles, M.T., Sierra Robles, Á.: Functional ability, frailty and risk of falls in the elderly: relations with autonomy in daily living. Int. J. Environ. Res. Public Health **17**(3), 1006 (2020)

Image Transfer over MQTT in IoT: Message Segmentation and Encryption for Remote Indicator Panels

David Valente[1,2], Thadeu Brito[1,2,3,4]([✉]), Márcio Correia[5],
José A. Carvalho[1,2], and José Lima[1,2,3]

[1] Research Centre in Digitalization and Intelligent Robotics (CeDRI), Instituto Politécnico de Bragança, Campus de Santa Apolónia, 5300-253 Bragança, Portugal
{a40414,brito,jac,jllima}@ipb.pt
[2] Laboratório para a Sustentabilidade e Tecnologia em Regiões de Montanha (SusTEC), Instituto Politécnico de Bragança, Campus de Santa Apolónia, 5300-253 Bragança, Portugal
[3] INESC TEC - INESC Technology and Science, Porto, Portugal
[4] Faculty of Engineering of University of Porto, Porto, Portugal
[5] Displays & Mobility Solutions - DMS, Rua de Cidres 1444, 4455-442 Perafita, Portugal
marciocorreia@dmsdisplays.com

Abstract. The Internet of Things (IoT) has revolutionized how objects and devices interact, creating new possibilities for seamless connectivity and data exchange. This paper presents a unique and effective method for transferring images via the Message Queuing Telemetry Transport (MQTT) protocol in an encrypted manner. The image is split into multiple messages, with each carrying a segment of the image, and employ top-notch encryption techniques to ensure secure communication. Applying this process, the message payload is split into smaller segments, and consequently, it minimizes the network bandwidth impact while mitigating potential of packet loss or latency issues. Furthermore, by applying encryption techniques, we guarantee the confidentiality and integrity of the image data during transmission, safeguarding against unauthorized access or tampering. Our experiments in a real-world scenario involving remote indicator panels with LEDs verify the effectiveness of our approach. By using our proposed method, we successfully transmit images over MQTT, achieving secure and reliable data transfer while ensuring the integrity of the image content. Our results demonstrate the feasibility and effectiveness of the proposed approach for image transfer in IoT applications. The combination of message segmentation, MQTT protocol, and encryption techniques offers a practical solution for transmitting images in resource-constrained IoT networks while maintaining data security. This approach can be applied in different applications.

Keywords: Message Segmentation · Internet of Things · Message Payload Optimization · Transmission Encryption Algorithm

A. I. Pereira et al. (Eds.): OL2A 2023, CCIS 1981, pp. 360–373, 2024.
https://doi.org/10.1007/978-3-031-53025-8_25

1   Introduction

In today's world, the Internet of Things (IoT) has become an integral part of our lives, revolutionizing the way devices communicate with each other and exchange data [13]. Despite all the resources IoT has provided over the years, one important key feature is the possibility to transfer messages over Message Queuing Telemetry Transport (MQTT). This popular messaging protocol is often used by IoT and Industrial Internet of Things (IIoT) applications as a lightweight message broker [7]. For example, to support the exchange data from sensors or control messages that contain few bytes [1]. On the other hand, in some cases, images or large data transfer over MQTT can pose considerable challenges due to the limited payload size and the demand for encryption to guarantee security.

The challenge is further compounded when considering the hardware requirements on which the IoT application will be implemented. As is well known, the hardware cost is usually proportionate to the performance and features of certain devices. And for that reason, the selection of hardware will not always be seamless when scrutinizing for the best cost benefit. For instance, some low-cost device models do not have enough embedded memory to receive a payload message with images in one shot.

This work proposes a solution to address these challenges by introducing message segmentation and encryption techniques for sending messages via MQTT with low-cost solutions. By breaking down the image into smaller segments, it is possible to send them over the MQTT protocol without exceeding the payload size limit. Moreover, it is possible to ensure that the data remains secure during transmission through encryption techniques. The proposed approach aims to improve the reliability and security of image transfer over MQTT using a real case of updating a LED remote panel indicator (IoT application issue detailed in Sect. 3). Furthermore, a CRC algorithm implementation can support the identification of any errors during data transmission. The main contributions of this paper are as follows.

- Indicate a low-cost solution to update remote panel indicators.
- Develop a segmentation algorithm to optimize the data transmission regarding the MQTT limits.
- Encrypt each segmentation to secure the payload during the updating process.

This paper is organized as follows. After an introduction in Sect. 1, related works about secure image transfer techniques are presented in Sect. 2. In Sect. 3, the methodology is described. The tests and results are presented in Sect. 4. Finally, Sect. 5 concludes the paper and points out some future work directions.

2   State of the Art on Secure Image Transfer over MQTT in IoT

The rapid growth of the IoT has brought forth numerous challenges, including the secure transmission of data, particularly when it comes to image transfer

[9]. In recent years, researchers have focused on developing efficient and secure methods for transferring images over MQTT [4,5], a lightweight messaging protocol widely used in IoT applications. This section presents a state-of-the-art review of techniques and advancements in secure image transfer over MQTT in IoT.

One key challenge in image transfer is the efficient utilization of network resources. Researchers have proposed various message segmentation techniques to divide images into smaller segments for transmission over MQTT [8,10]. These techniques ensure optimal bandwidth utilization and handle potential packet loss or latency issues. Notable approaches include adaptive segmentation based on image content analysis and dynamic segmentation based on network conditions. In this sense, in [15], the proposed application uses a Compression and Image Recovery Algorithm (CIRA) for sending images regarding the network bandwidth.

To address the security concerns associated with image transfer, encryption techniques play a vital role [12]. Encryption ensures the confidentiality and integrity of image data during transmission [6]. In [3], the authors have explored symmetric and asymmetric encryption algorithms, such as Advanced Encryption Standard (AES) and Rivest-Shamir-Adleman (RSA), to secure image data over MQTT. Additionally, authentication mechanisms, digital signatures, and access control techniques have been proposed to prevent unauthorized access and tampering.

In conclusion, the secure transfer of images over MQTT in IoT has witnessed significant advancements in recent years. The combination of message segmentation techniques, encryption algorithms, and real-world validation has paved the way for efficient and secure image transfer in resource-constrained IoT networks. Ongoing research aims to further optimize performance, explore novel encryption methods, and address the unique challenges associated with diverse IoT applications.

3   Methodology Overview

Indicator panels on roads are valuable for informing drivers about traffic conditions, special events, and critical alerts. However, the task of updating these panels can present some challenges that require efficient and practical solutions. One of the challenges faced is sending a technician to the panel location to update the alerts (left side of Fig. 1). Depending on the panel's geographic location and weather conditions, dispatching a technician can be a time-consuming and expensive process. Furthermore, transportation logistics and technician safety can become additional concerns when the panel is located in remote or difficult-to-access areas.

One solution to mitigate this problem is to adopt remote communication technologies (right side of Fig. 1). Instead of depending on the physical presence of a technician, remote management systems can be used to update the panels. Through the IoT, it is possible to send update commands to the digital panels quickly and efficiently. In this context, some approaches use systems based on permanently dedicated communications, for example, it is common to find out some projects using the 4G network.

Fig. 1. Remote management. Left side, the presence of the technician is required. Right side, remote management access is used, reducing logistics constraints.

To overcome the challenges mentioned in updating digital panels on the roads, an efficient solution is to use a low-cost microcontroller that could connect via MQTT communication to receive and display updated images on the panels. The microcontroller is responsible for receiving the updated information, processing it, and controlling the digital panel. Its low-cost nature makes it an affordable option for large-scale deployment, allowing multiple panels to be updated simultaneously along roadways. In this sense, when the microcontroller receives a large payload, such as an image, it will need to be able to process and temporarily store this data before displaying it on the digital panel.

An essential characteristic to be considered is the limited available memory space to store large payloads, such as images. These microcontrollers often have limited (or need more) storage capacity, which can pose a challenge when dealing with extensive data. However, due to the volatile memory space constraint, the microcontroller storage capacity can become a bottleneck, making it impossible to process large payloads. A possible solution to outweigh this limitation is splitting the image into smaller parts, instead of sending the complete image simultaneously. Due to the complexity that involves this process, the following subsections are dedicated to explaining each step.

3.1 Microcontroller

Although the family Raspberry Pi is a popular and versatile platform for IoT and embedded computing projects, newer versions, such as the Raspberry Pi 4, can be considered unnecessary high-cost solutions for applications that require MQTT. Older versions of the Raspberry Pi, such as the Raspberry Pi 1, 2, and 3, provide enough processing and memory resources can be significantly lower in cost compared to newer versions. These older versions can be a viable option for low-cost projects with less demanding processing requirements. However, it is important to consider that older Raspberry Pi versions may not have built-in Wi-Fi connectivity (which may require external adapters or additional modules to achieve MQTT connectivity). Moreover, during the present global chip crises, some Raspberry Pi models can be unfeasible (sold out or expensive).

In the context of updating digital panels, where the primary demand is the reception and display of real-time MQTT data, low-cost microcontrollers with Wi-Fi or mobile network connectivity can be a more cost-effective and straightforward solution. These microcontrollers offer enough features to manipulate MQTT data (store and processing) and control the digital panel. Therefore, when considering the choice of the most suitable microcontroller for this specific application, it is recommended to explore more economical options. In this work, it is considered the most worldwide low-cost microcontrollers used: the ESP8266EX, ESP32, Arduino MKR1000, Raspberry Pi Pico (W version), and Sipeed Lichee Nano (WiFi module). Following in Table 1 are described the pros and cons of each mentioned device.

Table 1. Price list and main characteristics of eligible microcontrollers.

Microcontroller	CPU	RAM	Flash	Cost *
ESP8266EX (MCU)	160 MHz	50 KB	2 MB	2.82 €
ESP32 (S2 mini)	240 MHz	320 KB	4 MB	2.48 €
Arduino MKR1000 WiFi	48 MHz	32 KB	256 KB	41.14 €
Raspberry Pi Pico (W version)	133 MHz	264 KB	2 MB	7.49 €
Sipeed Lichee Nano (WiFi module)	900 MHz	256 KB	16 MB	10.70 €

* The costs are based on each of the microcontrollers' official web pages or official distributors.

When evaluating the microcontrollers for this work, two options were discarded due to high cost, they are the Arduino MKR1000 WiFi and the Sipeed Lichee Nano (WiFi module). Therefore, comparing the ESP8266EX, the ESP32, and the Raspberry Pi Pico (W version), the choice was the ESP32. This offers more powerful processing, with a frequency of up to 240 MHz, which allows it to handle larger and more complex payloads.

Additionally, the ESP32 has a larger memory capacity with up to 320KB of RAM which is crucial to ensure proper data handling. Overall, the ESP32 stood out for its combination of features, performance and affordability. The hardware design that will be developed is illustrated in Fig. 2. Essentially, the ESP32 will receive the payload from MQTT and store the information on an SD card. Once all the data is transmitted, the ESP32 will control the digital panel to display the final alert notification.

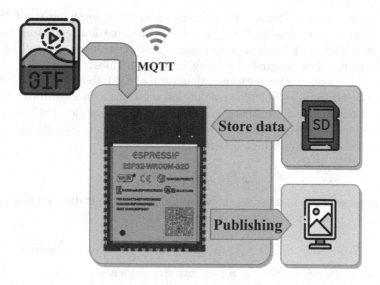

Fig. 2. High-level architecture for electronics development.

A significant challenge arises during image transmission using MQTT related to ESP32's limited ability to store large amounts of data in a single variable. An effective solution to this problem is partitioning the image into small segments before sending them via MQTT. Therefore, instead of transmitting the entire image, all at once, it can be broken into smaller pieces like blocks or lines, which are sent sequentially to the ESP32.

By partitioning the image, each segment can be temporarily stored on the SD card, allowing the gradual receiving and processing of data. This process is repeated until all segments have been transmitted and reconstituted in the ESP32, forming the complete image. In addition to overcoming the memory constraint of ESP32, the image partitioning approach also offers advantages regarding transmission reliability. If any interruption occurs during the sending process, only the current segment needs to be retransmitted, reducing bandwidth usage and improving communication efficiency.

When implementing image transmission using MQTT and partitioning as a solution, it is crucial to consider factors such as maximum segment size, correct transmission order, and adequate transmission rate to ensure accurate and efficient image reconstitution in ESP32.

3.2 Upload and Encode

When transmitting an image over a communication, it is essential to ensure data integrity during transfer. An efficient way to check integrity is to use the

Cyclic Redundancy Check (CRC) algorithms. CRCs are a widely used error-checking mechanism that adds extra bits to data to detect possible changes or corruption [11].

In the context of splitting an image, the process of applying the CRC can be divided into steps. The first step involves uploading and encoding one GIF image as a MQTT payload. This step ensures efficient transmission of the image data and ensures data integrity by using CRC algorithms.

The upload phase begins with the calculation of the CRC CCITT 16-bit value for the entire GIF image file. This calculation serves as a checksum to verify the integrity of the image data during transmission. The key idea behind it is the use of polynomial division. The CRC-16-CCITT algorithm uses the polynomial demonstrated by the following equation [2].

$$x^{16} + x^{12} + x^5 + 1 \tag{1}$$

The process of calculating it involves dividing the input data by this polynomial, and the remainder obtained is the CRC checksum.

$$CRC - 16 - CCITT(x) = remainder(x \times 2^{16}, polynomial) \tag{2}$$

For this purpose, in Eq. 2 x represents the sequence of bits being checked, and the **remainder** function calculates the remainder of dividing $x \times 2^{16}$ by the polynomial used in the CRC-16-CCITT algorithm. By applying the CRC-16-CCITT algorithm, we obtain a unique value that represents the image's content [2].

Next, to facilitate the transmission process, the total payload is divided into smaller parts, in the developed work, 100 characters were used. Breaking the payload into manageable chunks allows for efficient transfer and processing on the ESP32 microcontroller (as mentioned before, due to ESP32 limitations). Each part will have its own CRC value calculated later in the process.

To ensure compatibility and ease of transmission, the payload is converted into a `Base64` format. Although `Base64` encoding will increase the character length by, approximately, 1/3, we choose it as the transmission file format because it provides a textual representation of binary data, allowing for reliable and straightforward transfer through MQTT [14]. This encoding format simplifies the handling of non-textual data, such as images, in the messaging protocol. The resulting `Base64` payload is then sent to the ESP32 microcontroller using the MQTT protocol.

To facilitate the organization and identification of the payload parts, a `JSON` format is adopted. Each part is represented as a `JSON` file containing the following information: the file name, the total number of parts, the part number in the payload, the CRC value of the part in the payload, the CRC value of the total image, and the associated payload data.

By employing this methodology, we enable one reliable and efficient transmission of GIF images data through MQTT. The calculated CRC values provide a means of ensuring data integrity throughout the transmission process, while the payload organization and JSON representation facilitate the proper identification and processing of each payload part. Figure 3 represents the message upload and encoding process in flowchart mode.

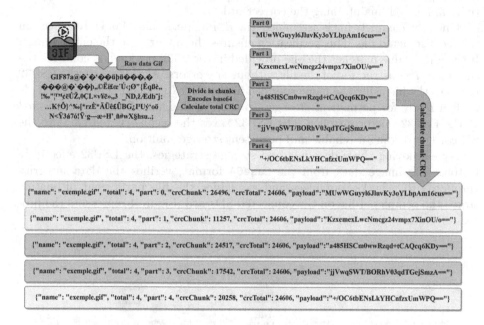

Fig. 3. Message upload and encoding procedure flowchart.

3.3 Decoding and Storage Strategies

In the decoding and storage strategies, firstly, we focus on the processes involved in decoding the `Base64` format, then performing CRC checks. Next, the temporary file is stored, and finally each part is merged into a single file and saved in an SD card connected to the ESP32.

Upon receiving the payload, the ESP32 initiates the decoding process by converting the `Base64` encoded payload back to its original format. This step allows the retrieval of the actual image data contained within the payload. By decoding the `Base64` representation, the microcontroller can restore the image to its original state. Following the next process, the ESP32 performs CRC calculations on the decoded data. This involves calculating the CRC value of each individual part and comparing it to the CRC value provided in the `JSON` payload. If any CRC values do not match, it indicates a transmission error or data corruption, and appropriate measures can be taken, such as requesting a retransmission of the affected part.

To simplify the handling and reassembly of the payload parts, the ESP32 temporarily stores each part in separate files. These temporary files provide a mechanism for organizing data until the complete file is successfully reconstructed. If the CRC checks for all parts pass, indicating data integrity, the ESP32 proceeds to create a new temporary file to which each part is sequentially appended, maintaining the correct order.

Once the complete file is assembled, the ESP32 performs a final CRC check on the reconstructed file. This verification ensures the integrity of the entire image. If the CRC value matches the one provided in the JSON payload, it confirms the successful reconstruction of the file without any errors. At this stage, the ESP32 renames the file using the name specified in the JSON payload. The renamed file is then ready for permanent storage. To achieve this, an SD card is connected to the ESP32 microcontroller. The ESP32 saves the reconstructed file onto the SD card, providing a reliable and persistent storage solution.

By employing these decoding and storage strategies, the ESP32 effectively restores the image data from the Base64 format, verifies the data integrity through CRC checks, organizes and assembles the file parts, and ultimately stores the completed file on the connected SD card. Figure 4 represents the process of downloading and decoding messages in flowchart mode.

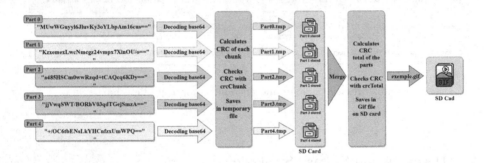

Fig. 4. Message download and encoding procedure flowchart.

4   Results

The performance and effectiveness of the system developed to send images via MQTT were evaluated by tests using a GIF dataset. This choice allows the simulation of various animated images that can be found in practice, representing a more realistic data transmission scenario. The dataset contains a collection of GIFs with different resolutions, file sizes, and complexities. This dataset version contains approximately 102 000 files in URL format with heterogeneous file sizes.

The main goals of the tests were to validate multiple file uploads and the ability to handle different sizes, with and without noise. Therefore, a Python script was created to download each GIF file, resize them to 75×75 pixels, and keep them at up to 0.1 s of duration. Then, a random selection of 100 GIFs was made. These 100 random GIFs have sizes from 3 to 2077 KBytes.

During the tests, each of the 100 GIFs was individually selected to be transmitted sequentially through the implemented system, using MQTT communication to send the data to the destination. At the end of each test, the integrity of the received images was reviewed using a binary file check program. With this software, it was possible to compare the 100 randomly chosen GIFs (sent files) with the files saved on the SD card after the test (received files). During all tests, the average time to send one GIF was 12 min. It is important to note that the total time of transmission varied based on the size of each randomly selected GIF, therefore, it will not be considered in our evaluation. The validation of the proposed system was conducted in two phases, following each one is described.

4.1   Sending Without Created Noises

The first test consists of sending the 100 randomly chosen GIFs without intentionally manipulating the data, that is, sending without simulating noise. Figure 5 demonstrates an example of the process for submitting a file through a GUI. The user can be notified if the upload process was completed successfully (Fig. 5a) or if there was a failure during the upload, and which part is faulty (Fig. 5b).

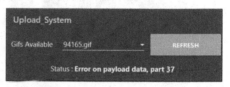

(a) Feedback's GUI when the message is successfully transmitted.

(b) Feedback's GUI when the error transmission appears.

Fig. 5. GUI examples that inform the user of the transmission status.

After sending all the 100 GIFs, as mentioned above, the binary file check program compares each one of the files transmitted with those received (stored on the SD card). Figure 6 displays the graph obtained after this first test, and it has the total sends, received, and error values.

4.2   Sending with Added Artificial Noises

In the process of developing a GIF transmission system using MQTT, it is essential to ensure the integrity of the data being exchanged. One crucial aspect is the detection of errors that may occur during the transmission, to address this concern, a testing procedure was conducted to evaluate the system's robustness and the effectiveness of the CRC implementation.

The testing procedure involved simulating various scenarios to assess the system's ability to detect errors introduced intentionally into the payloads. Figure 7

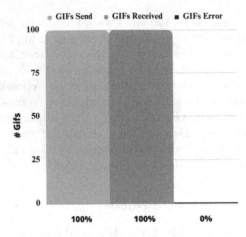

Fig. 6. Graph exhibiting the number of messages sent, received, and errors found.

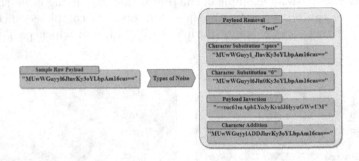

Fig. 7. Flowchart displaying the different types of artificially added noise in graphic mode to evaluate the proposed system.

indicates the intentional manipulation of data graphically, and the following are their descriptions:

- Payload Removal: In this test, the payload was deliberately removed from one of the parts of the GIF. The objective was to evaluate whether the CRC could detect the missing data and raise an error.
- Character Substitution: To assess the system's resilience to data corruption, a single letter in one part of the payload was replaced intentionally. The letter has been replaced by another letter, number, or nothing at all. The CRC calculation was expected to detect the altered data, signaling an error.
- Payload Inversion: The system's ability to identify payload inversion was tested by intentionally flipping the payload of one of the parts of the GIF. The CRC check was anticipated to detect this inversion, indicating a transmission error.
- Character Addition: To evaluate the system's sensitivity to data expansion, additional letters were introduced into one part of the payload. The CRC

validation was expected to detect the mismatched data length, signifying an error.

The implementation of CRCs within the GIF transmission system proved successful in detecting errors introduced during the testing process. In all the deliberate error scenarios mentioned above, the CRC calculations accurately identified the inconsistencies within the payloads. Whenever an error was detected, a message would return with the warning error and which part of the payloads was wrong. The data presented in Fig. 8 provides a comprehensive overview of the total sends, received, and error values gathered during the test with intentional noise.

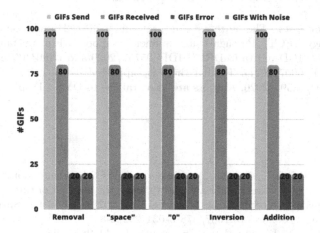

Fig. 8. Graph indicating the number of messages sent, received, and errors found after adding artificial noises.

5   Conclusions and Future Work

This paper presented a method for transferring images via the Message Queuing Telemetry Transport (MQTT) protocol with Encryption. The original image is split into multiple messages and an encryption technique top-notch is applied to ensure secure and confidentiality communication. This procedure minimizes the network bandwidth, since some equipment used for this purpose have their own communication limitations. Moreover, an error checking mechanism using Cyclic redundancy check was used to detect errors in transmission. The developed system was applied in a real-world environment involving remote indicator panels with LEDs to verify the approach.

Furthermore, the system was tested for its ability to handle different formats and sizes of GIFs. This included GIFs with different resolutions, aspect ratios and frame rates. By performing these tests using the GIFs dataset, it was possible to verify the robustness and efficiency of the developed system to send images via MQTT. The obtained results provided valuable insights into the performance, capacity and limitations of the system regarding the transmission of animated image data.

As future work, the proposed methodology will be implemented in different indicator panels with different types of messages. Moreover, it could be helpful to perform a full evaluation of algorithms for compacting or different types of encryption in the images before sending them. Regarding transmission performance, the development of a list with the image received could be used inside the ESP32 as a support manager and inform the server that the image is already stored in the SD card. Different communications technology, such as LoRA, is also pointed out for remote locations deployments.

Acknowledgements. The authors are grateful to the Foundation for Science and Technology (FCT, Portugal) for financial support through national funds FCT/MCTES (PIDDAC) to CeDRI (UIDB/05757/2020 and UIDP/05757/2020) and SusTEC (LA/P/0007/2021). Thadeu Brito is supported by FCT PhD Grant Reference SFRH/BD/08598/2020. Authors are also grateful to DMS - Displays & Mobility Solutions.

References

1. Biondo, E., Brito, T., Nakano, A., Lima, J.: A WSN real-time monitoring system approach for measuring indoor air quality using the internet of things. In: Pereira, T., Impagliazzo, J., Santos, H. (eds.) IoECon 2022, pp. 76–90. Springer, Cham (2022). https://doi.org/10.1007/978-3-031-25222-8_7
2. Chi, M., He, D., Liu, J.: Fast software-based table-less algorithm for CRC generation. In: 2018 21st International Symposium on Wireless Personal Multimedia Communications (WPMC), pp. 544–549 (2018). https://doi.org/10.1109/WPMC.2018.8713103
3. El Aidi, S., Bajit, A., Barodi, A., Chaoui, H., Tamtaoui, A.: An advanced encryption cryptographically-based securing applicative protocols MQTT and CoAP to optimize medical-IOT supervising platforms. In: Saeed, F., Mohammed, F., Al-Nahari, A. (eds.) IRICT 2020. LNDECT, vol. 72, pp. 111–121. Springer, Cham (2021). https://doi.org/10.1007/978-3-030-70713-2_12
4. Gonzalez-Zapata, A.M., Tlelo-Cuautle, E., Cruz-Vega, I., León-Salas, W.D.: Synchronization of chaotic artificial neurons and its application to secure image transmission under MQTT for IoT protocol. Nonlinear Dyn. **104**(4), 4581–4600 (2021)
5. Guillén-Fernández, O., Tlelo-Cuautle, E., de la Fraga, L.G., Sandoval-Ibarra, Y., Nuñez-Perez, J.C.: An image encryption scheme synchronizing optimized chaotic systems implemented on raspberry PIS. Mathematics **10**(11), 1907 (2022)
6. Gupta, V., Khera, S., Turk, N.: MQTT protocol employing IoT based home safety system with ABE encryption. Multimedia Tools Appl. **80**(2), 2931–2949 (2021)
7. Huang, G., Yi, J., Zhao, R., Chen, J., Huang, M., Wang, J.: Application of MQTT in power distribution internet of things. In: 2021 3rd International Conference on Electrical Engineering and Control Technologies (CEECT), pp. 98–103 (2021). https://doi.org/10.1109/CEECT53198.2021.9672327

8. Kim, J., Jenkins, J., Seol, J., Kwak, M.: Extending data transmission in the multi-hop LoRa network. Issues Inf. Syst. **23**(3) (2022)
9. Lombardi, M., Pascale, F., Santaniello, D.: Internet of things: a general overview between architectures, protocols and applications. Information **12**(2) (2021). https://doi.org/10.3390/info12020087. https://www.mdpi.com/2078-2489/12/2/87
10. Sahlmann, K., Clemens, V., Nowak, M., Schnor, B.: MUP: simplifying secure over-the-air update with MQTT for constrained IoT devices. Sensors **21**(1), 10 (2020)
11. Sobolewski, J.S.: Cyclic Redundancy Check, pp. 476–479. John Wiley and Sons Ltd., GBR (2003)
12. Su, W.T., Chen, W.C., Chen, C.C.: An extensible and transparent thing-to-thing security enhancement for MQTT protocol in IoT environment. In: 2019 Global IoT Summit (GIoTS), pp. 1–4 (2019). https://doi.org/10.1109/GIOTS.2019.8766412
13. Villamil, S., Hernández, C., Tarazona, G.: An overview of internet of things. Telkomnika (Telecommun. Comput. Electron. Control) **18**(5), 2320–2327 (2020)
14. Wei, C.C., Su, P.Y., Chen, S.T.: Comparison of the LoRa image transmission efficiency based on different encoding methods. Int. J. Inf. Electron. Eng. **10**(1), 1–4 (2020)
15. Zhang, J.Y., Yeung, B.L., Wong, J.C., Cheung, R.C., Lam, A.H.: Lorawan-based camera with (CIRA) compression and image recovery algorithm. In: 2021 IEEE 7th World Forum on Internet of Things (WF-IoT), pp. 136–141 (2021). https://doi.org/10.1109/WF-IoT51360.2021.9595674

Optimization

An Extension of a Dynamic Heuristic Solution for Solving a Multi-Objective Optimization Problem in the Defense Industry

Khwansiri Ninpan[1][(✉)], Kirill Kondratenko[1][iD], Shuzhang Huang[1],
Alexandra Plancon[1], Arthur Aumont[1], Lucas Artaud[1], Mouna Baker[1],
Emir Roumili[1], Francesco Vitillo[1], Lies Benmiloud Bechet[1], and Robert Plana[2]

[1] Digital Excellence Center, Assystem, Courbevoie, France
{kninpan,kkondratenko,shuang,aplancon,aaumont,lartaud,mbaker,eroumili,
fvitillo,lbenmiloud}@assystem.com
[2] Technology & Innovation, Assystem, Courbevoie, France
rplana@assystem.com

Abstract. Project scheduling in a real-life scenario often involves multiple-criteria decision-making in which no single solution exists. To solve such a problem, a multi-objective optimization method has been applied to define the satisfying trade-off between different criteria. In this paper, we focus on a specific use case in the defense industry in which the overall mission is to generate a maintenance plan for the transfer operations of power grid consumers to the new service area. The project objectives include restricting the outage duration during transfer operations, grouping operations concerning the proximity between them, moderating the allocation of supporting resource, and regulating human resources intervention outside business hours. To solve this problem, we propose a combination of heuristic approaches starting by defining a sequence of activities based on their complexities to be scheduled. Concerning the obtained order, a serial-schedule generation scheme (S-SGS) is then implemented by iterating through each activity to define the best time period to proceed the operation in accordance with project's multiple objectives. Finally, the output is transferred to our existing parallel scheme-based solver, Optimizio, to finally justify the project planning. The proposed S-SGS solution provides a feasible schedule of 110 transfer operations in 2 s with solution evaluation analysis and information of a Pareto frontier in approximately 15 min. The set of Pareto optimal solutions allows the expert to explore potential trade-offs between criteria. Together with a fast execution time of the algorithms that benefits a multi-scenario simulation, our tool demonstrates a potential capacity to get the optimum outcome of the multi-objective optimization project.

Keywords: Serial-Schedule Generation Scheme · Multi-Objective Programming · Heuristic Algorithms · Resource-Constrained Project Scheduling Problem

A. I. Pereira et al. (Eds.): OL2A 2023, CCIS 1981, pp. 377–390, 2024.
https://doi.org/10.1007/978-3-031-53025-8_26

1   Introduction

The Resource-Constrained Project Scheduling Problem (RCPSP) is one of the most widely studied scheduling problems [1], which aims to construct a feasible planning with a minimized project makespan. It can be described as the following components: a set of resources $R = \{R_1, ..., R_q\}$ that are demanded by the activities and with a limited capacity a_k at the same time; a series of n activities in a project $J = \{J_1, ..., J_n\}$. Each of the activity J_i has a duration d_i and a set of required units $(r_{i,k})_{k \in [1,q]}$, where each $r_{i,k}$ means the required units of resource R_k by activity J_i.

Despite minimizing the project finish time while respecting the critical industrial constraints is a pivotal perception, project planning in real-world problems often associates with multiple criteria to be considered, such as minimizing the risk of investment, maximizing productivity, optimizing the design for the best performance, etc. [2–4]. For this purpose, the multi-objective optimization (MOO) method can be used to define the optimum balance in the trade-offs between criteria.

The compromise solutions are the solutions in which any criteria cannot improve without worsening at least one of the remaining criteria - in other words, they are not worse than other solutions in any criteria and there are no other solutions better than them for at least one criterion. This type of solutions dominates the others and they are known as Pareto optimal, Pareto efficient, or non-dominated solutions. The set of these solutions is known as the Pareto front (i.e., Pareto set, Pareto frontier, or Pareto curve) [5,6]. It can be visualized in the N-dimension in order to narrow choices of efficient criterion to aid in further analysis of the whole model (Fig. 1).

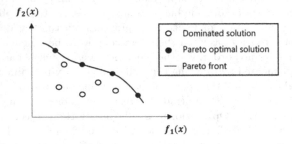

Fig. 1. Example of Pareto optimal solutions and Pareto front in a two-dimensions objective space.

Several methods have been purposed to find optimal solutions and assess the Pareto front in the MOO [7] which could be mainly grouped into scalarization and evolutionary techniques. While scalarization techniques combine multi-objectives into one single objective function by using different methods such as weighted aggregation (weighted-sum method) or keeping only one objective to be optimized and convert others as set of constraints (ε-constraint method), evolution techniques like non-dominated sorting genetic algorithm (NSGA-II) and Multi-objective Particle Swarm Optimization (MOPSO) select a set of the best solutions in a population with additional processes like crossover and mutation to ensure the diversity before feeding to the next generation.

To model the combination of the scheduling problem in a large-scale industrial case, we propose Optimizio [8]. Our proposed method uses a greedy heuristic: assigns dynamic scores to all the unscheduled tasks at each time step with the cost function. Based on the score and constraints satisfaction, we schedule feasible tasks as many as possible at each time step, thus getting a feasible and relatively optimal schedule at last. Our solution has been tested in a large-scale industrial scheduling problems in different domains [9] such as nuclear, defense, and construction industries. The user feedback shows that the tool's efficiency allows for high robust planning studies and to test hypothesis that go beyond conventional scheduling methods in these domains. Yet the latest case we were asked to solve poses a new challenge. Besides a wide variety of constraints, this project composes of multiple criteria to be considered. Since the tool's original approach is not designed to solve a multi-objective optimization as in this case, finding and developing a new approach is therefore critical to answering this issue and addressing a common problem of the industry. Due to the high computational cost of evolutionary methods which is not suit for the large-scale industrial case; thus, one of the most commonly used scalarization approaches, the weight-sum method [10, 11], is selected for this study.

The paper is organized as follows. The problem statement and the demonstrated instance are presented in Sect. 2. Section 3 explores the implementation of certain algorithms in our proposed solution. The optimization results of the selected algorithms are shown in Sect. 4 and, finally, the major findings together with future research are discussed in Sect. 5.

2   Use Case

2.1   Statement of the Problem

The main objective of this use case is to plan the transfer of the existing power grid consumers to the new distribution infrastructure on a large industrial site. Consumers are connected to the low-voltage general distribution boards, which are in turn connected to a high-voltage distribution substation (Fig. 2). The transfer of consumers (further referred to as "*transfer operation*" in the manuscript) requires the electrical isolation of the original and destination distribution boards. In order to limit the duration of isolation, it is necessary to group the transfers of all consumers from the same distribution board. However, each consumer may have specific requirements in terms of possible isolation options. These constraints may be specific dates or particular weekdays on which isolation is possible, precise isolation schedule (during the day, at night, for example), impossible isolation operation which then requires prior implementation of temporary power supply by generator, the capacity of the company carrying out the transfers in terms of workforce and therefore the number of transfers, etc. The constraints of different consumers are likely to change regularly depending on the site's operational constraints. It is also necessary to take into account the actual progress of transfers. This requires regular re-planning of all remaining tasks.

The optimization objectives could be formulated as follows:

Maximize: $F(x) = [w_1 f_1(x), \ldots, w_k f_k(x)]$
such that $\sum_{i=1}^{k} w_i = 1$ and $w_i \geq 0, i = 1, \ldots, k$
subject to: $x \in Z$,
where k is the number of objective functions, $f_i(x)$ is a vector of objective function, $x \in R^n$ is a vector of decision variables, and Z is the set of feasible solutions. To obtain this set of solutions, the simple weighted sum method is used by applying w as a user-defined scalar weights.

For this use case, the objective functions are as follows:

1. Minimize duration (*Makespan objective*, $f1$): all operations must be completed as soon as possible.
2. Maximize proximity of transfer operations (*Proximity objective*, $f2$): activities corresponding to the same distribution substation should be scheduled with a minimal time lag.
3. Minimize supporting resource manipulation (*Support resource objective*, $f3$): activities that require a supporting resource should be scheduled together to minimize the costs of transportation and the immobilization of generators.
4. Minimize non-standard working hours assignments (*Shift distribution objective*, $f4$): avoid scheduling activities during night and weekend shifts.

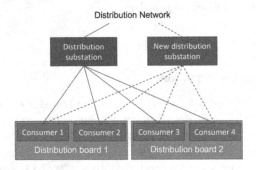

Fig. 2. The organization scheme of the distribution infrastructure.

2.2   Problem Instance

In order to clarify the problem scheme, a planification for approximately 100 transfer operations is demonstrated in this paper. Each high-voltage distribution substation provides power to around 10 grid consumers (we will refer to this consumer group as *"cluster"* further in this manuscript). Each consumer represents a transfer operation to be dispatched. All consumers contain information on feasible dates, days, and time intervals for scheduling the transfer operation together with a list of forbidden dates when the transfer procedure is not allowed. Due to variations in the electricity framework that powers the grid, consumers may require different durations of electrical isolation. Some might demand an additional generator for a temporary power supply during the transfer process. In addition, considering the limited resource capacity of the operating company, the maximum number of transfer operations that can be conducted in parallel is restricted to only 5 operations simultaneously.

3   Proposed Solution

With a quick and simple problem-solving algorithm, a heuristic technique is known to be an efficient practical approach for building a feasible project schedule. There are two alternative schedule methods that are commonly used to define a priority of each project activity, a serial-, and a parallel-schedule generation scheme (SGS) [12]. While a serial-SGS (S-SGS) iterates through activities to define the earliest possible time period that the activities can be scheduled [13], a parallel-SGS (P-SGS) follows a time-incrementation to schedule a set of activities in which all constraints are respected [14].

Our existing P-SGS-based solver aims to schedule the tasks as early as possible and as much as is feasible for each time point [8]. However, to find a solution that satisfies multiple objectives as in this use case, the implementation of an additional optimization algorithm is required. In this study, a coupling of our modular heuristic solution and implementation of the weighted-sum method in the S-SGS scheme is evaluated.

3.1   Serial-Schedule Generation Scheme (S-SGS)

The S-SGS algorithm's performance greatly depends on the order of the tasks in the sequence to dispatch [15]. It is possible to reduce the initial search space for the algorithm by attributing the priority to the tasks which will allow us to reorder the list accordingly.

We may consider options for this preprocessing such as user-defined priority, precedence relationships, or available time window. In our case, the transfer operations (i.e., tasks) are equivalent to each other, and no user-definable priority or precedence relationships exist. We have developed a simple heuristic for this purpose: every task in the list is evaluated according to its complexity (i.e., "difficulty" to plan). The scores will be summed for the tasks which belong to the same optimization cluster (absolute value is used to account for the number of tasks in the cluster). This score is going to be used to sort the tasks inside the cluster itself to allow the most complex tasks to be planned first.

As described in Algorithm 1, the following criteria are used to score the tasks: (i) available time slots count (inversely proportional to the number of timeslots which are eligible for this task); (ii) work shift (add a penalty for the tasks which require restricted working hours); (iii) support resource (add a penalty for the special resource requirements) and (iv) duration of the task (complexity score proportional to the length of the operation). This procedure allows us to maximize the options for the tasks which have the strictest requirements and reduce the variance of the optimization outcome.

Algorithm 1. Heuristic for task sequence sorting

1: Group transfer operations in list J based on the cluster of the distribution infrastructure. Let C represents all clusters in the distribution framework. There are total $C = \{1, 2, ...n\}$ clusters with J_c as operations per individual cluster c.
2: Define the level of difficulty of the transfer operations:
3: **for** each cluster c **do**
4:     **for** each operation activity j in J_c **do**
5:         Calculate the available timeslot score
6:         Calculate the work shift score
7:         Calculate support resource score
8:         Calculate duration score
9:         Define the complexity, $cost(j, c)$ $cost(j, c)$ = available timeslot score + work shift score + support resource score + duration score
10:     **end for**
11:     Sort activities in J_c based on $cost(j, c)$
12:     Sum the score of all transfer operations in the optimization cluster c as cpx_c
$$cpx_c = \sum_{j=1}^{n} cost(j, c)$$
13: **end for**
14: Sort the list J based on the level of complexity cpx_c
15: **return** J

After retrieving the sequence of transfer operations to dispatch based on the level of complexity, S-SGS is implemented to define the possibility to process each operation at each time step along the project horizon considering multiple objectives of the project (Algorithm 2).

The algorithm iterates over the list of unplanned tasks J and attempts to dispatch these tasks sequentially. For each task, it evaluates every available timeslot (which is not included in the forbidden date list and follows the work shift requirements of the transfer operation). This evaluation is performed with objective functions in list L at step 5 (see Sect. 2.1 for the objective definitions)

Algorithm 2. Decoding procedure to define the most suitable time period for each transfer operation

---
1: Set empty list PT for planned activities
2: **while** $PT \neq J$ **do**
3:    **for** each timeslot t in list T **do**
4:        **if** t is not in forbidden timeslots **then**
5:            **for** each objective l in L **do**
6:                Calculate objective score
7:                Multiply the score by the weight
8:            **end for**
9:            Sum the score
10:        **end if**
11:    **end for**
12:    Sort timeslots
13:    Assign a timeslot with the highest suitable score to the activity j
14:    Add activity j to the list PT
15:    Update timeslot attributes
16: **end while**
17: **return** PT

---

which results are multiplied by the corresponding weight and summed at step 8 such that $F(x) = \sum_{i=1}^{k} w_i f_i(x)$.

After every available timeslot is evaluated, we sort the timeslot list by the score and assign the timeslot with the highest score to task j (the task itself is placed in the list PT). After this, the corresponding attributes of the timeslot (such as remaining resource capacity) are updated at step 15.

When performing a search of optimal simulation parameters, it is necessary to have a fast way of proposed planning evaluation [16]. The objectives stated in Sect. 2.1 in fact have different measurement units which makes it difficult for the end user to observe how well the algorithm performs on the supplied data. To facilitate this task, we have decided to convert these values to a dimensionless metric (between 0 and 1) for ease of evaluation and visualization:

Metric for $f1$: assign a score inversely proportional to the length of the resulting makespan
Metric for $f2$: the assigned score is inversely proportional to the mean ratio of optimization cluster makespans to the project makespan (provides a higher score if the cluster makespans are short)
Metric for $f3$: first, we perform kernel density estimation (KDE) for the timeslots which were used for tasks with support resource requirements. This allows us to find 1D "clusters" of the support resource usage in the project. To calculate the metric score, we perform a calculation similar to the Proximity objective evaluation in order to score how tightly support resource usage is grouped around the maxima of the KDE.

Metric for f4: the score is inversely proportional to the sum of the used timeslot weights and the total timeslot weights.

3.2   Parallel-Schedule Generation Scheme (P-SGS)

After sorting and assigning the most suitable time period to each transfer operation, the S-SGS output was fed into the existing solver based on P-SGS algorithm for feasibility verification. At each decision point during the simulation, the solver will evaluate unscheduled operations considering their expected start dates and times, levels of criticality based on a dynamic cost function [8], and constraints to be respected. A set of transfer operations that satisfy all requirements will be scheduled given the current decision point as their starting time.

4   Results and Discussions

4.1   Schedule Generation

Initial schedule generation with S-SGS algorithm took about 2 s for a dataset of 110 transfer operations on a 8 core CPU. Figure 3 demonstrates an example of S-SGS algorithm output: plot of transfer operations per cluster as a function of the planned date. Here we have assigned the maximal weights for the objective f_1 (Fig. 3,a) and objective f_2 (Fig. 3,b) respectively.

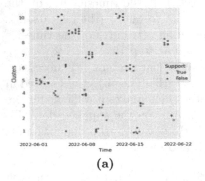
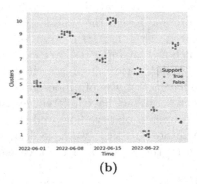

(a)   (b)

Fig. 3. Plots for dispatched tasks per cluster as a function of time from the SGS-S algorithm for various optimization objectives: (a) makespan and (b) operations proximity. Marker color corresponds to the usage of support resources.

When applying the weighted sum approach to the MOO problem, it is important to understand how sensitive the simulation outcome to the user-defined weight is applied to the objective functions. Figure 4 assembles the solution evaluation metrics obtained for 4 different weight combinations: the corresponding objective from the legend was set to 1 while others were set to 0 (i.e., not considered).

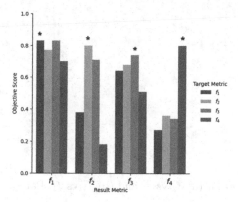

Fig. 4. Solution evaluation of all objectives for the single target objective of the SGS-S algorithm

The target metric is marked with an asterisk. From this picture one can notice that the target metric is always greater or equal to metrics related to other weight combinations, meaning that each of the individual objective functions can influence the simulation outcome. It also allows us to obtain an estimate of the upper bound of the solution reachable by this method for each individual objective. It is important to underline that the individual objective score can tend to 1 but often it cannot reach a perfect score of 1 due to the constraints provided by the input data (i.e., some operations requiring night intervention or mutually exclusive date ranges for neighboring operations which belong to the same cluster).

4.2 Pareto Optimal Solutions Analysis

In order to obtain desirable optimization outcome in case of multiple objectives, we have to resort to constructing Pareto optimal subspace of the objective space, where no solution is dominated by others. To explore the region of feasible solutions, we run the algorithm with varying objective weights between 0 and 1 with a step of 0.25 ($5^4 = 625$ solutions).

Figure 5 presents 2 examples of 2D Pareto fronts computed from the set of 625 solutions. It is possible to notice that the points on the Pareto front (and in general in the remaining solution set) are not distributed uniformly despite the uniform distribution of the objective weights. This behavior is not uncommon in the case of the weighted sum approach [17]. One possible explanation includes that the scalarization methods in general are unable to map the nonconvex regions of the Pareto curve, which explains the observed discontinuity [18]. It is also worth noting that the data corresponding to the f_1 objective score has discrete values (i.e., dates) which may also contribute to this apparent "binning" effect).

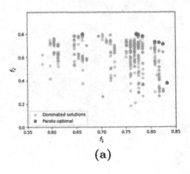
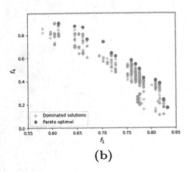

Fig. 5. Objective spaces for (a) f_2 vs f_1 and (b) f_4 vs f_1. Pareto-optimal solutions are highlighted in red.

From Fig. 5(a) we may conclude that the Pareto front for these 2 objectives has a convex shape characteristic for the case of maximizing the objective functions [19], and a larger number of optimal solutions are reachable for maximizing f_2 (than compared to f_1), meaning that the S-SGS algorithm is able to construct solutions which consistently reach high score for the proximity objective for a variety of makespan lengths. This makes it possible to select an optimal solution without a significant trade-off for the makespan objective. On the other hand, the Pareto front for the f_4 vs f_1 objectives (Fig. 5,b) has a more linear shape which signifies the direct relationship between these 2 objectives (by optimizing for the f_4, the algorithm avoids placing the activities in the night and weekend timeslots, thus increasing the makespan).

These plots display a subset of the real 4D Pareto front by projecting it onto 2 objective functions. This approach provides some insights into the shape of the Pareto subspace' and allows the end user to identify some useful trade-offs between different pairs of objectives and compare the performance of different weight sets. However, it does not fully represent the structure of the 4D Pareto since it may not demonstrate potential disconnected or concave regions [20]. This approach is also heavily influenced by the choice of the 2 objective functions. In order to better understand the underlying relations between the objectives, we have to employ additional visualization techniques such as parallel coordinate plots and 3D scatter plots which provide additional information on the shape of Pareto plot.

In order to better understand the effect of objective weight distribution on the optimization outcome, we have explored the solutions in the form of parallel coordinate plot [13] (PCP, Fig. 6). It represents the solution in the form of a line which crosses equally spaced axes. Each axis corresponds to an objective and the intersection with it provides the corresponding metric value for the solution in scope.

This plot allows us to evaluate the variance of reachable solutions for each objective. For f_1 objective, the majority of the values are distributed between 0.6 and 0.9 which corresponds to 30% of the available optimization project

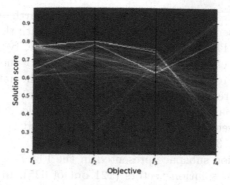

Fig. 6. 2D histogram in PCP for solution metrics. The density of the lines corresponds to the number of solutions in the given region of objective space.

timespan. The f_2 objective corresponding to the proximity of transfer operations demonstrates significant variance which may be expected due to the combinatorial nature of this objective. Interestingly, objective f_3, though having similar evaluation metric to the f_2, displays significantly lower variance (lowest in the given solution set) which can be explained by the input data (operations which require support resources have similar complexity score). On the other hand, the f_4 objective displays the highest variance due to the significant number of options (a relatively small number of operations have requirements which exclude normal working hours from the possible time slots list).

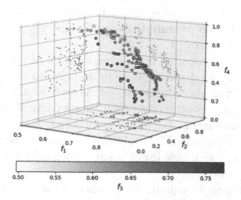

Fig. 7. f_1 vs f_2 vs f_4 3D scatter plot of Pareto optimal space for the set of 625 solutions. The values of f_3 objective are indicated with color (see the colorbar at the bottom for reference). Individual 2D fronts are projected onto the planes of the plot (Color figure online)

The 3D plot is another way of visualizing the optimization results. Figure 7 demonstrates a 3D plot of Pareto subspace of the solution set. We project the 3D data on the three axes and use color to represent the fourth objective. We choose f_3 values to be represented by color (as the objective with the least variance) for illustration purpose. This plot allows us to indirectly verify the convexity of the Pareto front [21]. We can clearly identify the 3D shape of the Pareto surface and select some potential regions of interest depending on the nature of the trade-off which the end user is ready to make. One way of facilitating this task would be to introduce an additional quantifiable metric (for example, operational expenses) and bin the solution set as a function of this metric in order to construct multiple 2D Pareto fronts in a 3D space [22].

The Pareto solution subspace presented in the Fig. 7 represents about 20% of the total generated solution vectors (121 out of 625). In order to select the final solution, it is necessary to filter the solution set further. The user may elect to experiment with the objective weights further by generating a solution set over a finer objective weight grid. To do so, one can identify first the potential regions of interest in the solution set for acceptable trade-offs and evaluate the density of solutions in this subset (by using indicators such as crowding distance [23]). By mapping the objective weights to the neighborhood of this subset, it is possible to deduce the range of weights which produce the desired trade-off.

5   Conclusion and Future Works

This paper describes the application of S-SGS algorithm to the multi-objective optimization of the RCPSP covered in this complex industrial use case. The described approach provides the end user with a modular solution which can be easily adapted according to the identified operational needs. We have demonstrated that it is possible to construct a Pareto front for 4 objectives which is sufficient to identify the potential trade-offs and get a lower bound on the expected outcome of the project.

An important point to consider is the execution speed [24]. The end user has a multitude of options in the decision space in addition to the weight adjustment, which include modifying the constraint set as well as the input data (which includes hiring additional contractors or shifting a particularly problematic and constrained cluster to another batch of operations). Fast algorithm execution (around 15 min for the presented 625 solution set) allows the user to re-generate the feasible solution set with new input assumptions and significantly facilitates the decision-making process.

The selection process is equally as important as the solution generation. We have demonstrated the classic techniques used for exploration of a Pareto-optimal solution subset such as 2D Pareto front, PCP and 3D approximation of the Pareto surface. This, however, does not provide us with a straightforward way to select the solution based on the user requirements. One possible approach to alleviate this limitation is to cluster the solutions based on their density in the solution space (visualized in the PCP Figure) to map the optimal weight combinations to the optimization outcome which is directly accessible for the user. However, it is unknown how sensitive this method is to the input data variance and how well it can scale with increasing complexity of the dataset (higher number of operations and larger available timespan) and/or additional constraints. Additional work needs to be performed to properly evaluate these scenarios.

The S-SGS algorithm could be further improved by performing local search on the generated solution. This could include the introduction of a heuristic that attempts permutations of the planned activities in the generated schedule to improve the final outcome. This approach might be beneficial for objectives with a significant combinatorial component (for example, f_2 and f_3 of the present use case). Another challenge that could be addressed in future works is the generalization of this approach. Current implementation relies heavily on objective function engineering which is based directly on the information extracted from the requirements submitted by the project stakeholders. It is necessary to develop an array of generic objective functions and find simple and intuitive ways to construct specific objective functions similar to popular MOO frameworks.

References

1. Coelho, J., Vanhoucke, M.: Going to the core of hard resource-constrained project scheduling instances. Comput. Oper. Res. **121**, 104976 (2020)
2. Tapia, M.G.C., Coello, C.A.C.: Applications of multi-objective evolutionary algorithms in economics and finance: a survey. In: 2007 IEEE Congress on Evolutionary Computation, pp. 532–539 (2007)
3. Gunasekara, R.C., Mehrotra, K.G., Mohan, C.K.: Multi-objective optimization to identify key players in social networks. In: 2014 IEEE/ACM International Conference on Advances in Social Networks Analysis and Mining, ASONAM 2016, pp. 443–450 (2014)
4. Sessarego, M., Dixon, K.R., Rival, D.E., Wood, D.H.: A hybrid multi-objective evolutionary algorithm for wind-turbine blade optimization. Eng. Optim. **47**, 1043–1062 (2015)
5. Ramirez-Rosado, I.J., Bernal-Agustin, J.: Reliability and costs optimization for distribution networks expansion using an evolutionary algorithm. IEEE Power Eng. Rev. **21**, 70 (2001)
6. Carrano, E.G., Soares, L.A.E., Takahashi, R.H.C., Saldanha, R.R., Neto, O.M.: Electric distribution network multiobjective design using a problem-specific genetic algorithm. IEEE Trans. Power Deliv. **21**, 995–1005 (2006)
7. Marler, R.T., Arora, J.S.: Survey of multi-objective optimization methods for engineering. Struct. Multidiscip. Optim. **26**, 369–395 (2004)
8. Rai, A., et al.: A dynamic heuristic optimization for condition-based maintenance planning. Preprint (2020)
9. Rai, A., et al.: A modular solution for large-scale critical industrial scheduling problems with coupling of other optimization problems. Int. J. Mech. Ind. Eng. **16** (2022). https://publications.waset.org/abstracts/search?q=Khwansiri%20Ninpan
10. Das, I., Dennis, J.E.: A closer look at drawbacks of minimizing weighted sums of objectives for Pareto set generation in multicriteria optimization problems. Struct. Optim. **14**, 63–69 (1997)
11. Kim, I.Y., de Weck, O.L.: Adaptive weighted-sum method for bi-objective optimization: pareto front generation. Struct. Multidiscip. Optim. **29**, 149–158 (2005)

12. Kolisch, R.: Serial and parallel resource-constrained project scheduling methods revisited: theory and computation. Eur. J. Oper. Res. **90**, 320–333 (1996)
13. Baur, N.-F., Rieck, J.: A serial schedule generation scheme for project scheduling in disaster management
14. Artigues, C., Lopez, P., Ayache, P.-D.: Schedule generation schemes for the job-shop problem with sequence-dependent setup times: dominance properties and computational analysis. Ann. Oper. Res. **138**, 21–52 (2005)
15. Kim, J.-L., Ellis, R.D.: Comparing schedule generation schemes in resource-constrained project scheduling using elitist genetic algorithm. J. Constr. Eng. Manag. **136**, 160–169 (2010)
16. Chiandussi, G., Codegone, M., Ferrero, S., Varesio, F.E.: Comparison of multi-objective optimization methodologies for engineering applications. Comput. Math. Appl. **63**, 912–942 (2012)
17. Caramia, M., Dell'Olmo, P.: Multi-objective Management in Freight Logistics. Springer, London (2008). https://doi.org/10.1007/978-1-84800-382-8
18. Marler, R.T., Arora, J.S.: The weighted sum method for multi-objective optimization: new insights. Struct. Multidiscip. Optim. **41**, 853–862 (2010)
19. Santos, W.G.: Discrete multiobjective optimization applied to the spacecraft actuators command problem and tested in a hardware-in-the-loop rendezvous simulator (2015)
20. Nagar, D., Ramu, P., Deb, K.: Visualization and analysis of Pareto-optimal fronts using interpretable self-organizing map (iSOM). Swarm Evol. Comput. **76**, 101202 (2023)
21. Null, S.E., Olivares, M.A., Cordera, F., Lund, J.R.: Pareto optimality and compromise for environmental water management. Water Resour. Res. **57**, e2020WR028296 (2021)
22. Smith, S., Southerby, M., Setiniyaz, S., Apsimon, R., Burt, G.: Multiobjective optimization and Pareto front visualization techniques applied to normal conducting rf accelerating structures. Phys. Rev. Accel. Beams **25**, 062002 (2022)
23. Peng, G., Fang, Y.-W., Peng, W.-S., Chai, D., Xu, Y.: Multi-objective particle optimization algorithm based on sharing-learning and dynamic crowding distance. Optik **127**, 5013–5020 (2016)
24. Caramia, M., Dell'Olmo, P.: Multi-objective Optimization. In: Multi-objective Management in Freight Logistics, pp. 21–51. Springer, Cham (2020). https://doi.org/10.1007/978-3-030-50812-8_2

BHO-MA: Bayesian Hyperparameter Optimization with Multi-objective Acquisition

Vedat Dogan[1]($\boxtimes$)(iD) and Steven Prestwich[2](iD)

[1] Confirm Centre for Smart Manufacturing, School of Computer Science and Information Technology, University College Cork, Cork, Ireland
vedat.dogan@cs.ucc.ie

[2] Insight Centre for Data Analytics, School of Computer Science and Information Technology, University College Cork, Cork, Ireland
s.prestwich@cs.ucc.ie

Abstract. Good hyperparameter values are crucial for the performance of machine learning models. In particular, poorly chosen values can cause under- or overfitting in regression and classification. A common approach to hyperparameter tuning is grid search, but this is crude and computationally expensive, and the literature contains several more efficient automatic methods such as Bayesian optimization. In this work, we develop a Bayesian hyperparameter optimization technique with more robust performance, by combining several acquisition functions and applying a multi-objective approach. We evaluated our method using both classification and regression tasks. We selected four data sets from the literature and compared the performance with eight popular methods. The results show that the proposed method achieved better results than all others.

Keywords: Bayesian Optimization · Multi-objective Optimization · Hyperparameter Tuning

1 Introduction

Machine learning (ML) algorithms have been used in various application domains such as recommender systems, natural language processing, behaviour analytics, and computer vision [18]. The construction of an effective ML model is a time-consuming and complex process. Effective ML models have achieved great success in a wide range of practical problems but the performance depends on correctly setting the many parameters. We can categorize the ML parameters considering the setting procedure. Model *parameters*, such as neural network weights, are learned during the training process. In contrast, *hyperparameters* (HPs), such as the number and size of neural layers, must be set before training.

This publication has emanated from research conducted with the financial support of Science Foundation Ireland under Grant number 16/RC/3918.

Tuning HPs is a crucial step when building an ML model. There is a wide range of possibilities that need to be explored to build an effective and optimal ML model. The process of HP tuning differs among different ML models according to their different types of HP, which can be categorical, discrete, or continuous. A traditional approach is manual tuning, which requires expertise and a deep understanding of the chosen ML algorithms. It is not effective for most problems because of the high number of HPs, model complexity, the time-consuming nature of evaluations, and the convexity of HP interactions. This has motivated research in the field of hyperparameter optimization (HPO), which aims to find optimal HPs for a given model. The main goal of HPO is to build automated systems and allow non-expert users to effectively apply ML models to practical problems. It also reduces human effort, as ML experts often spend a great deal of time on HP tuning, especially when working with complex ML models. Thus HPO improves the performance of ML models, as HPs might have different optima for different problems.

Many optimization techniques have been applied successfully to HPO problems. Bayesian optimization (BO) is an iterative global optimization method to optimize expensive-to-evaluate black-box functions [17]. BO uses a surrogate model, typically Gaussian process (GP) [25], and an acquisition function to evaluate future points based on previous observations. While the surrogate model aims to fit all current observations into the objective function and obtain a probability distribution, the acquisition function determines the next optimal evaluation by balancing exploration and exploitation. It works by updating the surrogate model after each iteration until reaching a near-optimal solution. BO can usually detect near-optimal HP configurations within a few iterations [11]. Several BO approaches focused on surrogate models have been developed for HPO. Besides GP, commonly used surrogate models include Random forest (RF) [33] and the tree Parzen estimator (TPE) [12]. As we shall discuss in Sect. 2, there has been much recent progress in the HPO field and the methods have strengths and weaknesses according to their constraints. However, surprisingly few works have focused on improving the next point selection process by modifying the acquisition function of the HPO problem.

The main contribution of this paper is to combine the strengths of several methods to obtain more robust results. Ensemble learners [8] have proven to be effective in a wide variety of ML applications, especially when diverse methods are combined. We apply this idea to BO by using more than one acquisition function, to obtain a more intelligent search strategy for hyperparameter optimization. As stated in [14] no single acquisition function always outperforms others. We propose a new Bayesian hyperparameter optimization method using a multiobjective acquisition function, which we call BHO-MA. Our proposed BHO-MA method seeks robust selection by trading off acquisition functions with different search strategies for hyperparameter optimization tasks. To the best of our knowledge, this idea has not previously been applied to HPO. Our contributions can be considered as three-fold. First, we use multiple acquisition functions for hyperparameter tuning and solve the multi-objective problem with a genetic algorithm to obtain the best trade-off. Second, we show empirically how using the multi-acquisition approach affects HPO performance and obtains near-optimal configurations. Also, BHO-MA provides another insight into the benefit of combining multi-objective optimization and preference learning literature, as there is no single optimal solution for multiple objectives. It provides the user with the freedom of choosing the next selection according to his/her preference after the Pareto-front is obtained and explored by the automated machine learning regime while optimizing the hyperparameters of the preferred ML model.

The rest of the paper is organized as follows. Related works on HPO are surveyed in Sect. 2. The preliminaries of multi-objective problems and Bayesian optimization are given in Sect. 3. BHO-MA method is explained in Sect. 4. In Sect. 5 the experimental setup is described, and Sect. 6 follows with results and discussions. Finally, Sect. 7 concludes the paper and proposes future work.

2   Related Work

Several methods have been successfully applied to the HPO problem over the years. Grid Search (GS) [2] and Random Search (RS) [3] are relatively simple decision-theoretic approaches. While RS samples hyperparameters randomly from a configuration space, GS evaluates the Cartesian product of a set of values for each hyperparameter. Neither scales well to large-scale search spaces, and each HP configuration is treated independently. Because of computational resource limitations, multi-fidelity optimization algorithms are improved to solve these problems. Hyperband [20] is a bandit-based optimization technique that generates small data sets and sets the specific budget for each HP combination. It can be considered an improved version of RS. Metaheuristic techniques have been successfully applied to large-scale, complex HPO problems, including genetic algorithm (GA) [32] and particle swarm optimization (PSO) [22]. They can locate near-optimal solutions well but are expensive in terms of function evaluations. Bayesian optimization (BO) determines the next sample of HP value based on previously observed HPs [21], thus reducing function evaluations compared to other methods. BO uses the distribution of the objective function as the surrogate function. Examples of surrogates are Gaussian process (BO-GP), random forest (BO-RF) [33], and tree-structured Parzen estimators (BO-TPE) [12].

In recent years, the research community has focused on building systems that continuously improve over time, especially in automated HPO tasks [16]. In some works, reinforcement learning is successfully employed in solving HPO problems [9,36]. Meta-learning techniques received increased attention in recent works by combining other optimization techniques for HPO problems [7,15,24]. Applying HPO techniques to tune hyperparameters of ML models can greatly improve their performance on practical problems. [6] worked on the health estimation problem of lithium-ion batteries and improved the estimation accuracy by optimizing convolutional neural network (CNN) hyperparameters with BO.

Another HPO application of CNN hyperparameters can be found in [29]. They worked on the facial emotion recognition problem and improved the algorithm performance by applying the RS algorithm to the HPO problem. HPO of artificial neural networks was used by [5] for designing software sensors. For the prediction problem of passengers at a metro station using deep neural networks, [28] explored different HPO techniques such as GD and PSO. In [13] heuristic techniques for the HPO problem worked well for deep learning models for genomic prediction problems.

We believe BO is a very promising global optimization method, especially after the interesting work of [31] for applying BO in high-dimensional space. In this work, we focus on improving BO by using a multi-objective acquisition approach. We shall describe our BHO-MA method and compare it with various HPO methods in the literature.

3   Preliminaries

We now provide some necessary background.

3.1   Multi-objective Optimization

Multi-objective optimization (MOO) aims to optimize a vector-valued objective function $\mathbf{f}(\mathbf{x}) \in \mathbb{R}^n$ over a bounded set $\mathcal{X} \subset \mathbb{R}^d$. There are multiple objectives to optimize when we consider the multi-objective optimization problems. It is formulated as

$$\underset{\mathbf{x} \in X}{\text{minimize}} \ \mathbf{f}(\mathbf{x}) = (f_1(\mathbf{x}), \dots, f_n(\mathbf{x})). \tag{1}$$

Because of different possible trade-offs between objectives, there is no single best solution. The main goal is to approximate the *Pareto-optimal solution set* which is a set of optimal objective trade-offs. The *Pareto-optimal* solution set is a set of non-dominated solutions that trade-off objectives. Let us say that $\mathbf{f}(\mathbf{x})$ *dominates* another solution $\mathbf{f}(\mathbf{x}')$ if $\mathbf{f}^{(i)}(x) \succ \mathbf{f}^{(i)}(x')$ for all $i = 1, 2, \dots, M$ and there exists $i' \in \{1, 2, \dots, M\}$ such that $f^{i'}(x) \succ f^{i'}(x')$. So we can express the *Pareto-optimal* by $P^* = \{\mathbf{f}(\mathbf{x}) \ s.t. \ \nexists \mathbf{x}' \in X : \mathbf{f}(\mathbf{x}') \succ \mathbf{f}(\mathbf{x})\}$ and $X^* = \{\mathbf{x} \in \mathbf{X} \ s.t. \ \mathbf{f}(\mathbf{x}) \in P^*\}$. A solution set is Pareto-optimal if it is not dominated by any other point and it dominates at least one point. The Pareto-set the set of all Pareto-optimal points, and a set of Pareto-optimal points is called a Pareto-front. The existence of multiple feasible optima, namely the Pareto-front, provides freedom to the decision-maker to choose an objective trade-off according to their preferences. *Hypervolume* is a metric for measuring the quality of the frontier which is bounded from below by a reference point that bounds a region of interest in objective space [30]. It is commonly assumed to be known by the decision-maker.

3.2 Bayesian Optimization

Bayesian optimization (BO) is a method to optimize expensive-to-evaluate black-box functions. BO uses a probabilistic surrogate model, typically Gaussian Process (GP) [25], $p(f|\mathcal{D})$ to model the objective function f based on previously observed data points $\mathcal{D} = \{(\mathbf{x}_1, y_1), \ldots, (\mathbf{x}_n, y_n)\}$. GPs are models that are specified by a mean function $\mu(\mathbf{x}; \{\mathbf{x}_n, y_n\}, \theta) : \mathbb{R}^d \to \mathbb{R}$ and predictive variance function $\sigma(\mathbf{x}; \{\mathbf{x}_n, y_n\}, \theta) : \mathbb{R}^d \times \mathbb{R}^d \to \mathbb{R}$ where $\mathbf{x} \in \mathbb{R}^d$. Surrogate model $p(f|\mathcal{D})$ is assisted by an acquisition function $\alpha : \mathcal{X} \to \mathbb{R}$. We represent an acquisition function depending on the previous observations by $\alpha(\mathbf{x}; \{\mathbf{x}_n, y_n\}, \theta)$ where θ is Gaussian parameters such as kernel for the model. Because the objective function is expensive to evaluate and the surrogate-based acquisition function is not, it can be optimized much more quickly than the true function to yield $\mathbf{x}_{new}$. Gaussian process uses the acquisition function to select the $\mathbf{x}_{new}$ Then it evaluates the objective function $y_{new} = f(\mathbf{x}_{new})$ and updates the data set with new observations $\mathcal{D} \leftarrow \mathcal{D} \cup (\mathbf{x}_{new}, y_{new})$. It continues until the budget criterion is met.

4 Method

We now describe our proposed method which uses multi-objective acquisition optimization to take advantage of different search strategies of different acquisition functions during Bayesian optimization. First, we will present the problem statement and then the adaptation of multi-objective acquisition optimization to hyperparameter optimization.

4.1 Problem Statement

Let us assume that we have an ML algorithm $\mathcal{A}$ with M hyperparameters. If we denote the m-th hyperparameter by Λ_m, the configuration space can be denoted by $\mathbf{\Lambda} = \Lambda_1 \times \Lambda_2 \times \ldots \times \Lambda_M$. Also, define the set of hyperparameters as a vector and denote by $\lambda \in \mathbf{\Lambda}$ and $\mathcal{A}_\lambda$ represents the algorithm $\mathcal{A}$ with hyperparameters λ. For a given data set $\mathcal{D}$, our goal is to find [16]:

$$\lambda^* = \underset{\lambda \in \mathbf{\Lambda}}{\operatorname{argmin}} \; \mathbb{E}_{(\mathcal{D}_{tr}, \mathcal{D}_{vl}) \sim \mathcal{D}} \mathbf{V}(\mathcal{L}, \mathcal{A}_\lambda, \mathcal{D}_{tr}, \mathcal{D}_{vl}), \qquad (2)$$

where $\mathbf{V}(\mathcal{L}, \mathcal{A}_\lambda, \mathcal{D}_{tr}, \mathcal{D}_{vl})$ represents the loss of the model generated by algorithm $\mathcal{A}$ with HPs λ on training data $\mathcal{D}_{tr}$ and evaluated on validation data $\mathcal{D}_{vl}$.

4.2 Acquisition Functions

There are several popular choices of acquisition functions. Different acquisition functions have different characteristics according to their structure and point selection strategy. Improvement-based strategies rely on the best selection so far at each iteration. For example, the probability improvement (PI) function value decreases when the difference between the mean function and the best objective value is far below zero. The expected improvement (EI) function value at sampled points would always be worse than the EI values at pending decision points. Uncertainty-based acquisition functions, for instance, upper-confidence-bound (UCB), increase as $\sigma(\mathbf{x}; \{\mathbf{x}_n, y_n\}, \theta)$ increases. The formulations of the acquisition functions used in this work are provided as follows. $\Phi(\cdot)$ will denote the cumulative distribution function of the standard normal, and $\phi(\cdot)$ will denote the standard normal density function.

Probability of Improvement (PI). The strategy of the PI acquisition function is to maximize the probability of improvement over the best current value. Given the minimum objective function value τ in the data set, the formulation is given in Eq. 3 as in [19].

$$\alpha_{PI}(\mathbf{x}; \{\mathbf{x}_n, y_n\}, \theta) = \Phi(\gamma(\mathbf{x})), \quad \gamma(\mathbf{x}) = \frac{\tau - \mu(\mathbf{x}; \{\mathbf{x}_n, y_n\}, \theta)}{\sigma(\mathbf{x}; \{\mathbf{x}_n, y_n\}, \theta)} \tag{3}$$

Expected Improvement (EI). The EI strategy maximizes the expected improvement over the current best observation [27]. The corresponding formulation can be expressed as in Eq. 4.

$$\alpha_{EI}(\mathbf{x}; \{\mathbf{x}_n, y_n\}, \theta) = \sigma(\mathbf{x}; \{\mathbf{x}_n, y_n\}, \theta)(\gamma(\mathbf{x})\Phi(\gamma(\mathbf{x})) + \phi(\gamma(\mathbf{x}))),$$
$$\gamma(\mathbf{x}) = \frac{\tau - \mu(\mathbf{x}; \{\mathbf{x}_n, y_n\}, \theta)}{\sigma(\mathbf{x}; \{\mathbf{x}_n, y_n\}, \theta)} \tag{4}$$

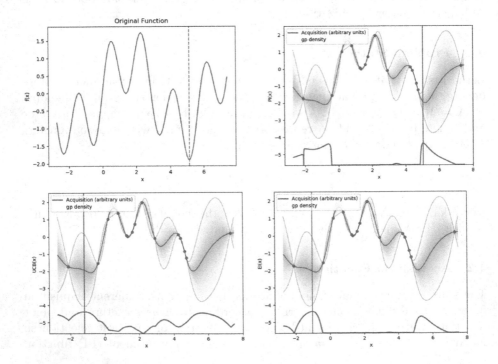

Fig. 1. Illustration of the difference of acquisition function search strategies.

Upper Confidence Bound (UCB). This is not an improvement-based strategy like EI and PI. Instead, it tries to guide the search from an optimistic perspective. The formulation is given in Eq. 5,

$$\alpha_{UCB}(\mathbf{x}; \{\mathbf{x}_n, y_n\}, \theta) = \mu(\mathbf{x}; \{\mathbf{x}_n, y_n\}, \theta) + \beta\sigma(\mathbf{x}; \{\mathbf{x}_n, y_n\}, \theta) \qquad (5)$$

where β is a parameter that represents the exploration-exploitation trade-off. We fix $\beta = 0.1$.

4.3 Multi-objective Acquisition Adaptation to Hyperparameter Optimization

For an illustration of the acquisition function search strategy difference, we use a multimodal problem in Fig. 1. Multimodal problems can have more than one global optimal point with several local optima. The red line on the top-first graph represents the optimal point. The PI, UCB and EI acquisition function strategies can be seen on the other three graphs. As shown in Fig. 1, different acquisition functions suggest different candidates after initializing on 15 data points. While the PI acquisition function is trying to make the next decision around global optima, the EI and UCB acquisition functions are exploring the other points at the current iteration.

In the proposed BHO-MA method, we use the MOO approach during the next point selection process, according to the different selection strategies explained above and in Sect. 4.2. We aim to find the best trade-off between acquisition functions with different search strategies. This is called the Pareto-front solutions of acquisition functions. Acquisition functions are the key point in Bayesian optimization. It is expected to be cheap to solve compared with the true objective function, and easier to optimize. It also includes information on uncertainty and estimated values everywhere in the search space. So modifying the acquisition optimization step on the Gaussian process improves the global optimization process significantly. This is the main reason that the literature has worked on creating various acquisition functions such as q-knowledge gradient (qKG) [34], and predictive entropy search (PES) [26]. Each acquisition function may not agree to sample the same points as each of them has a different search strategy. Reconstructing the acquisition function with multiple acquisition functions gains us the information to use the benefits of different acquisition search strategies.

For the purpose declared above, we constructed the data set $\mathcal{D}$ with the finite collection of hyperparameters $\lambda_1, \lambda_2, \ldots, \lambda_n \in \Lambda$ and $f(\lambda_1), f(\lambda_2), \ldots, f(\lambda_n) \in \mathbb{R}$ is the evaluation results of the loss function defined in Eq. 2, where n represents the number of initial data points. Let us define the variable $\mathbf{x}_n = [\lambda_1, \ldots, \lambda_n]$ and $y_n = [f(\lambda_1), \ldots, f(\lambda_n)]$ with the GP parameters θ, the optimization problem of the multi-objective acquisition function is constructed as follows:

$$\min_{\mathbf{x} \in \mathcal{X}} \left\{ \begin{array}{l} -\alpha_{EI}((\mathbf{x}; \{\mathbf{x}_n, y_n\}, \theta)) \\ -\alpha_{PI}((\mathbf{x}; \{\mathbf{x}_n, y_n\}, \theta)) \\ -\alpha_{UCB}(\mathbf{x}; \{\mathbf{x}_n, y_n\}, \theta) \end{array} \right\} \qquad (6)$$

Algorithm 1. The Bayesian optimization algorithm via multi-objective acquisition function for HPO task.

Initialize the number of iterations N. Initialize the size of sample size n for beginning the algorithm. Select random hyperparameters $\lambda_1, \ldots, \lambda_m$ with the size of m from the configuration space.

Obtain the evaluation results of the loss function of the selected ML model $f(\lambda_1), \ldots, f(\lambda_m)$ that is defined in Equation 2.

1: Construct *Gaussian model* with the observations
2: **for** i $= 0 : N$ **do**
3:     Construct the acquisition functions according to the Equation 6
4:     Find non-dominated solutions of multi-objective acquisition problem using the NSGA-II algorithm
5:     Make a random selection from the non-dominated solution set
6:     Calculate the evaluation results of the loss function
7:     Update Gaussian Process model with new observations
8: **end for**
9: **Return** Best hyperparameter λ^* and corresponding evaluation results

---

Solving MOO problems is computationally more difficult and time-consuming. But as acquisition functions are easy-to-solve functions, the multi-objective structure of the problem does not have a significant effect on algorithmic performance, especially when the learner being tuned is applied to a large problem. The objective of HPO is to minimize the number of executions of the learner. However, wall-clock times are provided in Table 4.

Instead of a random selection of acquisition functions during the optimization process, the Pareto-front allows us to use trade-offs between these different search strategies. It allows the decision maker to pick the most preferred solutions from this set. The advantage is the decision maker does not have to specify the preferences before optimization, which is an acquisition function in BO literature. The MOO problem defined in Eq. 6 is solved by the popular NSGA-II algorithm [10]. The NSGA-II algorithm is a successful algorithm for solving MOO problems. At each iteration, we constructed the multi-objective acquisition function by using Eq. 6. We constructed the population of 100 with current acquisition values and terminated the algorithm after 100 generations. After we obtained the final population, we used random sampling for the next iteration. The details can be found in Algorithm 1.

5   Experiments

This section presents experiments applying the popular HPO techniques on ML algorithms on two benchmark data sets. Firstly, the experimental setup is discussed. Secondly, the results of the BHO-MA are compared with those of other popular methods and analyzed.

5.1   Experimental Setup

We evaluated BHO-MA's performance on four tasks selected from the sklearn library [23]. Firstly, the Modified National Institute of Standards and Technology (MNIST) and IRIS data sets are selected for the classification problem. MNIST is a hand-written digit recognition data set which has 1797 instances with 64 attributes, used for multi-classification problems. Iris data set is a classification data set which has 150 instances with 4 attributes, that contain three classes and each class refers to a type of iris plant. The Boston housing and diabetes data sets are chosen as regression problem benchmarks where the Boston housing includes 506 instances with 13 attributes while diabetes data set has 442 instances with 10 attributes.

Support vector machines (SVM), K-nearest neighbour (KNN), and random forest (RF) are three ML algorithms that are chosen as targets for HPO problems according to the type of their hyperparameters. They can be applied to regression and classification problems and are popular in the ML community to solve practical problems. We implemented 3-fold cross-validation to evaluate the HPO methods for each experiment. For the classification problems, the accuracy metric is selected for performance comparison while the mean squared error (MSE) is chosen for the regression problems. Accuracy measures the proportion of correctly classified data. MSE calculates the average squared difference between predicted and actual values. The highest accuracy and the lowest MSE value are returned for each experiment. The maximum number of iterations for all HPO methods is set to 50 for the selected ML models. Thus, all learners are tuned based on 50 executions, for a fair comparison with the results presented in [35]. All experiments are repeated 10 times with different random seeds, and report the average results with standard deviations. We compared our results with 8 different popular approaches in the literature. We presented the details of our approaches in Sect. 2. The algorithm implementation is made by considering the settings mentioned in Sect. 5.1.

Table 1. Configuration space for the HPs of tested ML models.

Model	Hyper-parameter	Type	Search Space
RF Classifier	n_estimators	Discrete	[10,100]
	max_depth	Discrete	[5,50]
	min_samples_split	Discrete	[2,11]
	min_samples_leaf	Discrete	[1,11]
	criterion	Categorical	['gini', 'entropy']
	max_features	Discrete	[1,64]
SVM Classifier	C	Continuous	[0.1,50]
	kernel	Categorical	['linear', 'poly', 'rbf', 'sigmoid']
KNN Classifier	n_neighbors	Discrete	[1,20]
RF Regressor	n_estimators	Discrete	[10,100]
	max_depth	Discrete	[5,50]
	min_samples_split	Discrete	[2,11]
	min_samples_leaf	Discrete	[1,11]
	criterion	Categorical	['mse', 'mae']
	max_features	Discrete	[1,13]
SVM Regressor	C	Continuous	[0.1,50]
	kernel	Categorical	['linear', 'poly', 'rbf', 'sigmoid']
	epsilon	Continuous	[0.001,1]
KNN Regressor	n_neighbors	Discrete	[1,20]

5.2 Parameters

All experiments are conducted on a single core of 1.4 GHz Quad Core i5, 8 Gb 2133 MHz LPDDR3 RAM. We constructed the selected ML models using the *sklearn* library [23] by using the parameters in Table 1. To make the comparison fair, we used 3-fold cross-validation for each experiment. The number of iterations is selected as the budget for each ML model. For the stopping criterion, the default tolerance value 10^{-3} is used for all algorithms. For scoring the final performance, *neg_mean_squared_error* is used for regression and *accuracy* is used for classification tasks. We set the *n_jobs* parameter to −1 cause being able to use the all processors. Other parameters are left as default.

The *BoTorch* library is used for Bayesian optimization [1]. The method initialized 20 Sobol points to construct the initial GP model. *MaternKernel* is used to compute the covariance matrix with parameter $\nu = 2.5$ and other parameters taking default values. After constructing the GP model, the acquisition functions are initialized with the parameters below. The current best selection is important to the EI acquisition function to select the next point successfully. So in each iteration, the selections are analyzed and set to the *best_f* parameter of EI. The selection of β is important for UCB acquisition function tuning and we set it to 0.1. The PI acquisition function is constructed with the default hyperparameters as well.

After we obtained the multi-objective acquisition function with the parameters above, we used a genetic algorithm called Non-dominated Sorting Genetic Algorithm (NSGA-II) to solve the MOO problem. For the NSGA-II algorithm [10] we used the *PyMOO* library [4]. *pop_size* is selected as 100 at each iteration and *n_gen* as 100. We set *eliminate_duplicates = True* to discard unnecessary function evaluations. After we obtained the Pareto-optimal solution set, we used a random selection process.

Pre-processing is important during the machine learning process, but we did not focus on it for our experiments as it is not our main aim.

6   Results and Discussion

We compared our results with those of 8 different HPO methods in the literature and present our results in Table 3 and Table 2. We also shared the wall-clock time comparison of the best performances of all Bayesian-related algorithms in Table 4. It can be seen that our algorithm is relatively slower than others from Table 4. We believe the main reason is its use of MOO during acquisition optimization. However, the difference will be negligible when the classification or regression tasks involve big data. The aim of BO is to optimise an objecting while minimising the number of black-box function evaluations, and a modest increase in runtime is not a drawback Please see Fig. 2 and Fig. 3 for more details of experimental results.

The KNN search space of HPs has discrete, RF has categorical and continuous, and SVM has discrete and categorical variables. The SVM regressor's parameters are the regularization parameter C, the kernel type, and ϵ which determines the width of the tube around the estimated function (hyperplane). The selected parameter for the KNN regressor is the discrete-valued $n\_neighbors$ as it is the most important parameter for this ML model. The RF algorithm has the largest parameter space. The mean value of accuracy and MSE scores are presented with the standard deviations of ten runs. We can see that using the default HP configurations does not yield the best model performance in our experiments which shows that optimizing hyperparameters are crucial.

The Models Performance on Boston-Housing Dataset. In this experiment, we evaluated the BHO-MA performance for optimizing the three selected regression ML models for predicting housing prices. We experimented with the BHO-MA method for optimizing the KNN, RF and SVM regressors. As we can see from the MSE score which is shared in Table 2, the proposed BHO-MA method for optimizing the ML models selected from the literature reached the minimum and the best score compared to the other algorithms. The closest algorithm to optimize the regressor's parameters is BOHB which combines the Bayesian optimization and Hyperband method. As the black-box approach works well with low-dimensional feature spaces, it makes sense to have similar results with them. In terms of the whole performance analysis of the selected three ML algorithms, the best result was obtained from the RF model which has the minimum MSE score compared with all. It also has the biggest parameter spaces including discrete and categorical variables. Also, we can observe that all of the methods outperformed GS at the end of the budget. It is clear that the BHO-MA technique for the HPO problem worked well among the other techniques for the Boston housing data set for the regression task.

Table 2. The performance of optimizing KNN, RF and SVM algorithms for regression and classification tasks on Boston-housing and MNIST data sets over 10 different runs.

Hyperparameter Optimization Algorithm	Regressor's MSE Mean ± Std. (Boston-housing data set)			Classifier's Accuracy (%) Mean ± Std. (MNIST data set)		
	KNN	RF	SVM	KNN	RF	SVM
BHO-MA	**80.75 ± 0.0300**	**25.24 ± 0.2100**	**58.45 ± 0.0217**	**97.60 ± 0.0264**	**93.96 ± 0.0412**	**97.45 ± 0.0032**
BOHB	80.77 ± 0.1322	25.56 ± 0.7812	59.67 ± 1.1484	97.44 ± 0.0034	93.38 ± 0.0054	97.44 ± 0.0136
GA	80.77 ± 0.0014	26.95 ± 0.4355	60.17 ± 0.8733	96.83 ± 0.0003	93.83 ± 0.0032	97.44 ± 0.0004
Hyperband	80.87 ± 0.2654	26.14 ± 0.5471	73.44 ± 3.4956	96.22 ± 0.0034	93.38 ± 0.0005	97.44 ± 0.0023
BO-GP	80.99 ± 0.3365	26.44 ± 0.6812	59.70 ± 1.1694	96.54 ± 0.0024	93.35 ± 0.0075	97.40 ± 0.0002
BO-TPE	81.06 ± 0.3137	26.38 ± 0.6258	62.09 ± 4.2994	96.29 ± 0.0025	92.92 ± 0.0072	97.41 ± 0.0003
PSO	81.01 ± 0.2835	26.73 ± 0.4541	60.26 ± 1.0675	95.54 ± 0.0024	92.46 ± 0.0058	97.39 ± 0.0001
GS	81.49 ± 0.0004	28.06 ± 0.3970	67.07 ± 0.0030	96.82 ± 0.0122	93.60 ± 0.0015	97.38 ± 0.0142
RS	80.99 ± 0.2731	26.80 ± 0.4438	60.88 ± 2.0768	96.64 ± 0.0021	92.98 ± 0.0046	97.40 ± 0.0004
Default HPs	81.48 ± 0.0010	29.57 ± 0.3762	77.43 ± 0.0008	96.27 ± 0.0014	92.97 ± 0.0363	96.99 ± 0.0018

Table 3. The performance of optimizing KNN, RF and SVM algorithms for regression and classification tasks on Diabetes and Iris data sets over 10 different runs.

Hyperparameter Optimization Algorithm	Regressor's MSE Mean ± Std. (Diabetes data set)			Classifier's Accuracy Mean ± Std. (Iris data set)		
	KNN	RF	SVM	KNN	RF	SVM
BHO-MA	**3190.66 ± 0.0003**	**3074.17 ± 2.1634**	**3030.71 ± 12.626**	**0.9893 ± 0.0046**	**0.9683 ± 0.0028**	**0.9819 ± 0.0002**
BOHB	3198.38 ± 5.3243	3103.67 ± 6.5465	3047.37 ± 14.722	0.9733 ± 0.0087	0.9667 ± 0.0017	0.9801 ± 0.0065
GA	3193.54 ± 2.5412	3099.82 ± 3.6587	3039.88 ± 1.4529	0.9766 ± 0.0023	0.9666 ± 0.0054	0.9803 ± 0.0006
Hyperband	3194.07 ± 1.4476	3098.32 ± 5.4284	3038.68 ± 2.4354	0.9820 ± 0.0043	0.9670 ± 0.0089	0.9810 ± 0.0002
BO-GP	3197.04 ± 7.4451	3112.87 ± 22.979	3049.30 ± 21.657	0.9806 ± 0.0058	0.9660 ± 0.0021	0.9813 ± 0.0042
BO-TPE	3195.07 ± 7.9000	3120.69 ± 18.835	3056.60 ± 26.128	0.9801 ± 0.0062	0.9644 ± 0.0066	0.9770 ± 0.0035
PSO	3194.09 ± 3.6494	3121.81 ± 9.6953	3052.89 ± 5.4383	0.9813 ± 0.0061	0.9613 ± 0.0048	0.9803 ± 0.0031
GS	3241.33 ± 0.0000	3102.64 ± 0.0000	3040.91 ± 0.0000	0.9802 ± 0.0000	0.9666 ± 0.0000	0.9733 ± 0.0000
RS	3200.33 ± 19.332	3135.33 ± 26.122	3048.28 ± 10.857	0.9840 ± 0.0046	0.9646 ± 0.0032	0.9806 ± 0.0037
Default	3619.27 ± 0.0000	3354.91 ± 46.426	3895.66 ± 0.0000	0.9805 ± 0.0000	0.9633 ± 0.0035	0.9609 ± 0.0000

The Models Performance on MNIST. The popular MNIST is an image-processing data set that is created for recognizing handwritten digits. It has been worked on with various classification algorithms over the years. In our experiment, we evaluated the accuracy of three ML models explained in Sect. 5. The accuracy of the KNN, RF and SVM models is shared as a percentage the Table 2. As we can see from Table 2, the BHO-MA method reached the highest accuracy compared with the other algorithms implemented. The second best HPO algorithm for KNN and SVM is BOHB and GA for RF. As the RF has the largest parameter space, it is understandable that the genetic algorithm works better than the black-box approach in this experiment. The worst algorithm performance is with the default HPs for all algorithms which shows the importance of the HPO problem in ML literature. Among all ML algorithms, the KNN classifier got the best accuracy.

Table 4. The best surrogate-assisted accuracy results and wall-clock time duration (s) for regression and classification tasks on all data sets over 10 different runs.

Hyperparameter Optimization Algorithm	Regressor's MSE Mean ± Std. (Boston-housing data set)		Classifier's Accuracy (%) Mean ± Std. (MNIST data set)		Regressor's MSE Mean ± Std. (Diabetes data set)		Classifier's Accuracy (%) Mean ± Std. (Iris data set)	
	RF	Time (s)	KNN	Time (s)	SVM	Time (s)	KNN	Time (s)
BHO-MA	**25.24 ± 0.2100**	6.1	**97.60 ± 0.0264**	7.6	**3030.71 ± 12.626**	10.8	**0.9893 ± 0.0046**	11.1
BOHB	25.56 ± 0.7812	**4.9**	97.44 ± 0.0034	3.4	3047.37 ± 14.722	9.8	0.9733 ± 0.0087	6.9
Hyperband	26.14 ± 0.5471	6.2	96.22 ± 0.0034	4.8	3038.68 ± 2.4354	**7.6**	0.9820 ± 0.0043	**5.4**
BO-GP	26.44 ± 0.6812	12.3	96.54 ± 0.0024	**2.6**	3049.30 ± 21.657	9.4	0.9806 ± 0.0058	7.9
BO-TPE	26.38 ± 0.6258	5.9	96.29 ± 0.0025	3.7	3056.60 ± 26.128	11.3	0.9801 ± 0.0062	2.3

The Models Performance on Diabetes Dataset. The diabetes data set includes information about patients who have diabetes, such as age, sex, blood pressure, etc. We used the data set for the regression problem and the same ML models for the HPO task. We shared the MSE score in Table 3 with the standard deviation over ten runs. As we can see, the proposed BHO-MA method optimized the ML models better than other HPO methods. The best ML model is SVM which has the minimum score compared with RF and KNN. The genetic algorithm and hyperband method seem the second and third-best HPO methods to optimize the HPs. We found the worst performance with SVM using default HPs. As we can observe from the difference between the best and the worst score from all experiments, the proposed HPO method significantly improves the final MSE score.

The Models Performance on Iris Dataset. The iris data set is relatively small compared with other data sets selected for the experiments. It is maybe the best-known data set in pattern recognition literature and a multi-class classification data set, and we used it for classification problems with the same three ML models to optimize their HPs. The target is classifying the iris plants according to predictive attributes. The accuracy for the classification problem is shared in Table 3. As we can observe, the BHO-MA method reached the best accuracy among all ML models selected for the HPO task. The best accuracy is obtained by the KNN algorithm with optimized parameters by the proposed BHO-MA method. As the KNN algorithm is successfully studied over the years for classification problems, we are not surprised by this result. The variation in the SVM classifier accuracy score shows how important HPO is in ML. The performance improvement is more than 2% between the default hyperparameters and the optimized model.

Our approach reached the best scores for both classification and regression tasks. It also gives the freedom to the user to choose the next preferred hyperparameter values from the Pareto-optimal solution set according to the trade-off between three different acquisition functions. Several popular acquisition functions have been described in the literature, and the proposed application can be extendable by using multiple acquisition function search strategies.

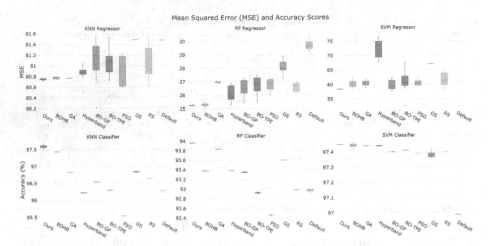

Fig. 2. Comparisons of the accuracy and mean squared errors between ours and the other methods on 2 different data sets with 3 different algorithms over 10 different runs.

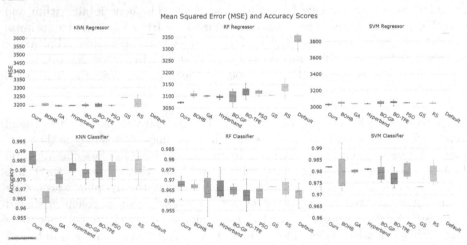

Fig. 3. Comparisons of the accuracy and mean squared errors between ours and the other methods on 2 different data sets with 3 different algorithms over 10 different runs.

We shared the box plots of the experiments for each data set in Fig. 2 and Fig. 3. We can observe from the figures the mean and standard deviations of the performance metrics over 10 different runs.

7   Conclusion

We introduced BHO-ML, a hybrid and effective method for hyperparameter optimization. To the best of our knowledge, the first approach uses a multi-objective acquisition function for hyperparameter optimization tasks. It achieved strong performance on a diverse set of benchmarks including both classification and regression tasks, and also we compared it with several state-of-the-art approaches.

Our work can be extended in various directions. It would be interesting to consider exploring the preferences of decision-makers during Bayesian optimization in terms of multiple acquisition options. Various kinds of multi-criteria decision-making methods can be applied to our work to improve hyperparameter optimization tasks for point selection during the Gaussian process. This could potentially extend our approach into the domain of preference learning. Furthermore, there are various kinds of acquisition functions in the literature and they can be applied to our presented idea for the hyperparameter optimization task.

Finally, a more in-depth analysis of the relationship between the acquisition functions and tuned machine learning rate could provide insight into how acquisition function selection improves performance.

Limitations and Future Work. MOO problems are expensive to evaluate and time-consuming most of the time. It might cause a lack of performance during the acquisition optimization process of the proposed algorithm. Also, the Pareto-optimal solution set does not always provide the optimal solution for all objectives but still exploring the trade-off between acquisition functions improves the performance compared with various existing methods as we can see from Sect. 5. In future work, we shall explore the use of preferences during the optimization process. Moreover, we will look to gain some information by analyzing the relationship between acquisition selection and optimization results.

Acknowledgements. This publication has emanated from research conducted with the financial support of Science Foundation Ireland under Grant number 16/RC/3918 which is co-funded under the European Regional Development Fund. For the purpose of Open Access, the author has applied a CC BY public copyright licence to any Author Accepted Manuscript version arising from this submission.

References

1. Balandat, M., et al.: BoTorch: programmable Bayesian optimization in PyTorch. CoRR abs/1910.06403 (2019). http://arxiv.org/abs/1910.06403
2. Bergstra, J., Bardenet, R., Bengio, Y., Kégl, B.: Algorithms for hyper-parameter optimization. In: Shawe-Taylor, J., Zemel, R., Bartlett, P., Pereira, F., Weinberger, K. (eds.) Advances in Neural Information Processing Systems, vol. 24. Curran Associates, Inc. (2011). https://proceedings.neurips.cc/paper/2011/file/86e8f7ab32cfd12577bc2619bc635690-Paper.pdf
3. Bergstra, J., Bengio, Y.: Random search for hyper-parameter optimization. J. Mach. Learn. Res. **13**, 281–305 (2012)
4. Blank, J., Deb, K.: pymoo: Multi-objective optimization in Python. IEEE Access **8**, 89497–89509 (2020)

5. Blume, S., Benedens, T., Schramm, D.: Hyperparameter optimization techniques for designing software sensors based on artificial neural networks. Sensors **21**(24), 8435 (2021). https://doi.org/10.3390/s21248435. https://www.mdpi.com/1424-8220/21/24/8435

6. Bockrath, S., Lorentz, V., Pruckner, M.: State of health estimation of lithium-ion batteries with a temporal convolutional neural network using partial load profiles. Appl. Energy **329**, 120307 (2023). https://doi.org/10.1016/j.apenergy.2022.120307. https://www.sciencedirect.com/science/article/pii/S0306261922015641

7. Bohdal, O., Yang, Y., Hospedales, T.: EvoGrad: efficient gradient-based meta-learning and hyperparameter optimization. In: Ranzato, M., Beygelzimer, A., Dauphin, Y., Liang, P., Vaughan, J.W. (eds.) Advances in Neural Information Processing Systems, vol. 34, pp. 22234–22246. Curran Associates, Inc. (2021). https://proceedings.neurips.cc/paper/2021/file/bac49b876d5dfc9cd169c22ef5178ca7-Paper.pdf

8. Bühlmann, P.: Bagging, boosting and ensemble methods. In: Gentle, J., Härdle, W., Mori, Y. (eds.) Handbook of Computational Statistics. Springer Handbooks of Computational Statistics, pp. 985–1022. Springer, Heidelberg (2012). https://doi.org/10.1007/978-3-642-21551-3_33

9. Chen, S., Wu, J., Liu, X.: EMORL: effective multi-objective reinforcement learning method for hyperparameter optimization. Eng. Appl. Artif. Intell. **104**, 104315 (2021). https://doi.org/10.1016/j.engappai.2021.104315. https://www.sciencedirect.com/science/article/pii/S0952197621001639

10. Deb, K., Pratap, A., Agarwal, S., Meyarivan, T.: A fast and elitist multiobjective genetic algorithm: NSGA-ii. IEEE Trans. Evol. Comput. **6**(2), 182–197 (2002). https://doi.org/10.1109/4235.996017

11. DeCastro-García, N., Muñoz Castañeda, A.L., Escudero García, D., Carriegos, M.V., Sánchez Lasheras, F.: Effect of the sampling of a dataset in the hyperparameter optimization phase over the efficiency of a machine learning algorithm. CompLex **2019**, 1–16 (2019). https://doi.org/10.1155/2019/6278908

12. Eggensperger, K., Hutter, F., Hoos, H.H., Leyton-Brown, K.: Efficient benchmarking of hyperparameter optimizers via surrogates. In: Proceedings of the Twenty-Ninth AAAI Conference on Artificial Intelligence, AAAI 2015, pp. 1114–1120. AAAI Press (2015)

13. Han, J., Gondro, C., Reid, K., Steibel, J.: Heuristic hyperparameter optimization of deep learning models for genomic prediction. G3-Genes Genomes Genet. **11** (2021). https://doi.org/10.1093/g3journal/jkab032

14. Hoffman, M., Brochu, E., de Freitas, N.: Portfolio allocation for Bayesian optimization. In: Proceedings of the Twenty-Seventh Conference on Uncertainty in Artificial Intelligence, UAI 2011, pp. 327–336. AUAI Press, Arlington (2011)

15. Hospedales, T., Antoniou, A., Micaelli, P., Storkey, A.: Meta-learning in neural networks: a survey. IEEE Trans. Pattern Anal. Mach. Intell. **44**(9), 5149–5169 (2022). https://doi.org/10.1109/TPAMI.2021.3079209

16. Hutter, F., Kotthoff, L., Vanschoren, J. (eds.): Automated Machine Learning. TSSCML, Springer, Cham (2019). https://doi.org/10.1007/978-3-030-05318-5

17. Injadat, M., Salo, F., Nassif, A.B., Essex, A., Shami, A.: Bayesian optimization with machine learning algorithms towards anomaly detection. In: 2018 IEEE Global Communications Conference (GLOBECOM), pp. 1–6 (2018). https://doi.org/10.1109/GLOCOM.2018.8647714

18. Jordan, M.I., Mitchell, T.M.: Machine learning: trends, perspectives, and prospects. Science **349**(6245), 255–260 (2015). https://doi.org/10.1126/science.aaa8415. https://www.science.org/doi/abs/10.1126/science.aaa8415

19. Kushner, H.J.: A new method of locating the maximum point of an arbitrary multipeak curve in the presence of noise. J. Basic Eng. **86**, 97–106 (1963)

20. Li, L., Jamieson, K.G., DeSalvo, G., Rostamizadeh, A., Talwalkar, A.: Efficient hyperparameter optimization and infinitely many armed bandits. CoRR abs/1603.06560 (2016). http://arxiv.org/abs/1603.06560

21. Lindauer, M., Feurer, M., Eggensperger, K., Biedenkapp, A., Hutter, F.: Towards assessing the impact of Bayesian optimization's own hyperparameters. CoRR abs/1908.06674 (2019). http://arxiv.org/abs/1908.06674

22. Lorenzo, P.R., Nalepa, J., Kawulok, M., Ramos, L.S., Pastor, J.R.: Particle swarm optimization for hyper-parameter selection in deep neural networks. In: Proceedings of the Genetic and Evolutionary Computation Conference, GECCO 2017, pp. 481–488. Association for Computing Machinery, New York (2017). https://doi.org/10.1145/3071178.3071208

23. Pedregosa, F., et al.: Scikit-learn: machine learning in Python. J. Mach. Learn. Res. **12**, 2825–2830 (2011)

24. Raghu, A., Lorraine, J., Kornblith, S., McDermott, M., Duvenaud, D.K.: Meta-learning to improve pre-training. In: Ranzato, M., Beygelzimer, A., Dauphin, Y., Liang, P., Vaughan, J.W. (eds.) Advances in Neural Information Processing Systems, vol. 34, pp. 23231–23244. Curran Associates, Inc. (2021). https://proceedings.neurips.cc/paper/2021/file/c3810d4a9513b028fc0f2a83cb6d7b50-Paper.pdf

25. Rasmussen, C.E.: Gaussian processes in machine learning. In: Bousquet, O., von Luxburg, U., Rätsch, G. (eds.) ML -2003. LNCS (LNAI), vol. 3176, pp. 63–71. Springer, Heidelberg (2004). https://doi.org/10.1007/978-3-540-28650-9_4

26. Shah, A., Ghahramani, Z.: Parallel predictive entropy search for batch global optimization of expensive objective functions. In: Cortes, C., Lawrence, N., Lee, D., Sugiyama, M., Garnett, R. (eds.) Advances in Neural Information Processing Systems, vol. 28. Curran Associates, Inc. (2015). https://proceedings.neurips.cc/paper/2015/file/57c0531e13f40b91b3b0f1a30b529a1d-Paper.pdf

27. Srinivas, N., Krause, A., Kakade, S.M., Seeger, M.W.: Gaussian process bandits without regret: an experimental design approach. CoRR abs/0912.3995 (2009). http://arxiv.org/abs/0912.3995

28. Tsai, C.W., Fang, Z.Y.: An effective hyperparameter optimization algorithm for DNN to predict passengers at a metro station. ACM Trans. Internet Technol. **21**(2) (2021). https://doi.org/10.1145/3410156

29. Vulpe-Grigoraşi, A., Grigore, O.: Convolutional neural network hyperparameters optimization for facial emotion recognition. In: 2021 12th International Symposium on Advanced Topics in Electrical Engineering (ATEE), pp. 1–5 (2021). https://doi.org/10.1109/ATEE52255.2021.9425073

30. Wada, T., Hino, H.: Bayesian optimization for multi-objective optimization and multi-point search (2019). https://doi.org/10.48550/ARXIV.1905.02370

31. Wang, Z., Hutter, F., Zoghi, M., Matheson, D., de Freitas, N.: Bayesian optimization in a billion dimensions via random embeddings (2013). https://doi.org/10.48550/ARXIV.1301.1942. https://arxiv.org/abs/1301.1942

32. Wicaksono, A.S., Supianto, A.A.: Hyper parameter optimization using the genetic algorithm on machine learning methods for online news popularity prediction. Int. J. Adv. Comput. Sci. Appl. **9**(12) (2018)

33. Wu, J., Chen, X.Y., Zhang, H., Xiong, L.D., Lei, H., Deng, S.H.: Hyperparameter optimization for machine learning models based on Bayesian optimization b. J. Electron. Sci. Technol. **17**(1), 26–40 (2019). https://doi.org/10.11989/

JEST.1674-862X.80904120.   https://www.sciencedirect.com/science/article/pii/S1674862X19300047

34. Wu, J., Frazier, P.I.: The parallel knowledge gradient method for batch Bayesian optimization (2016). https://doi.org/10.48550/ARXIV.1606.04414. https://arxiv.org/abs/1606.04414

35. Yang, L., Shami, A.: On hyperparameter optimization of machine learning algorithms: theory and practice. Neurocomputing **415**, 295–316 (2020). https://doi.org/10.1016/J.NEUCOM.2020.07.061

36. Zhang, B., et al.: On the importance of hyperparameter optimization for model-based reinforcement learning. In: Banerjee, A., Fukumizu, K. (eds.) Proceedings of The 24th International Conference on Artificial Intelligence and Statistics. Proceedings of Machine Learning Research, 13–15 April 2021, vol. 130, pp. 4015–4023. PMLR (2021). https://proceedings.mlr.press/v130/zhang21n.html

Prediction of Health of Corals *Mussismilia hispida* Based on the Microorganisms Present in their Microbiome

Barry Malick Barque[1,4] , Pedro João Soares Rodrigues[3,4] ,
Pedro Luiz de Paula Filho[1,4] , Raquel Silva Peixoto[2,4] ,
and Deborah Catharine de Assis Leite[1,4(✉)]

[1] Federal Technological University of Parana, Curitiba, Brazil
deborah.leite@gmail.com
[2] Polytechnic Institute of Bragança, Bragança, Portugal
[3] King Abdullah University of Science and Technology (KAUST),
Thuwal, Saudi Arabia
pjsr@ipb.pt
[4] Institute of Microbiology Professor Paulo de Goes - Federal University
of Rio de Janeiro, Rio de Janeiro, Brazil
raquelpeixoto@micro.ufrj.br

Abstract. One of the most diverse and productive marine ecosystems in the world are the corals, providing not only tourism but also an important economic contribution to the countries that have them on their coasts. Thanks to genome sequencing techniques, it is possible to identify the microorganisms that form the coral microbiome. The generation of large amounts of data, thanks to the low cost of sequencing since 2005, provides an opening for the use of artificial neural networks for the advancement of sciences such as biology and medicine. This work aims to predict the healthy microbiome present in samples of *Mussismilia hispida* coral, using machine learning algorithms, in which the algorithms SVM, Decision Tree, and Random Forest achieved a rate of 61%, 74%, and 72%, respectively. Additionally, it aims to identify possible microorganisms related to the disease in question in corals.

Keywords: Coral reef · Microbiome · Machine learning algorithm

1 Introduction

Coral reefs, mentioned by [1], are remarkable for their diversity and productivity, with an estimated annual economic contribution ranging from thirty to three hundred and seventy-five billion dollars. In addition to their economic value, these ecosystems play a crucial role as natural barriers against storms, erosion, and cyclones.

© The Author(s), under exclusive license to Springer Nature Switzerland AG 2024
A. I. Pereira et al. (Eds.): OL2A 2023, CCIS 1981, pp. 409–423, 2024.
https://doi.org/10.1007/978-3-031-53025-8_28

However, over the past few decades, coral reefs have been heavily impacted by climate change and pollution caused by human activities. These factors have significantly affected the health of corals, which harbor complex communities of microorganisms, including dinoflagellates, fungi, bacteria, and archaea, collectively known as the coral microbiome [1].

The microorganisms present in coral reefs play a crucial role in maintaining coral health and ecosystem resilience in the face of environmental stress. However, they can also contribute to positive feedback cycles that intensify the decline of coral reefs, as mentioned by [1,2]. To identify such microorganisms in corals, genetic sequencing techniques, such as Metabarcoding, are often employed. The gene encoding the 16S region present in bacterial ribosomes is widely used in these Metabarcoding techniques when identifying the bacteria present in a given sample [3].

Complete DNA sequencing began in the 1970s, but it was only since 2008 that DNA sequencing became more common, resulting in large volumes of data to be processed [4]. Currently, bacteria are grouped into Amplicon Sequence Variants (ASVs) through software like QIIME. QIIME is an open-source software widely used in the field of bioinformatics for sequence processing, alpha and beta diversity analysis, and construction of phylogenetic trees [5].

The complete sequencing process, leading to the identification of bacteria, is illustrated in Fig. 1 [6]. Initially, the sequences are read by the machine, generating two files representing the forward and reverse reads. Then, the initial reads, known as primers, are removed, followed by sequence clustering by size and exclusion of ambiguous sequences. The resulting sequences are stored in a database, from which chimeric or incorrect reads are subsequently removed. In the following steps, the sequences are grouped and identified as Amplicon Sequence Variants (ASVs), and finally, the phylogenetic tree and abundance table of each ASV in organisms A and B are generated [6].

The increasing generation of information from massive DNA sequencing has posed a significant challenge for humans in terms of dealing with this colossal amount of data. Genomics sequence analysis yields vast amounts of detailed information about individuals and their genetic characteristics. However, due to the voluminous and complex nature of these data, it becomes virtually impossible for humans to process them and extract relevant insights efficiently. To overcome this limitation, advanced machine-learning techniques have been widely adopted. Through these methods, powerful algorithms can be trained to identify patterns, perform predictive analyses, and classify genomics information on a large scale. The application of these techniques allows for a more agile and accurate approach to interpreting and understanding DNA sequencing data, empowering genomics research and driving advancements in areas such as personalized medicine, disease diagnosis, and drug discovery.

In this context, the main objective of this study is to utilize binary classification algorithms, such as Support Vector Machines (SVM), Decision Trees, and Random Forest, to predict the health of corals based on the microorganisms found in their structure. Additionally, the aim is to identify key microorganisms strongly associated with the relevant diseases through the decision tree and

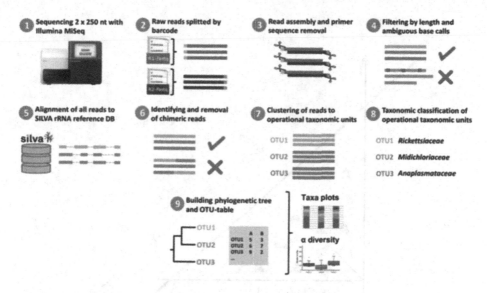

Fig. 1. Representation of the 16S RNA sequencing process.

Random Forest. As a result, the obtained findings may guide the field of microbiology towards a more in-depth study of these disease-related microorganisms, seeking a better understanding and control of the related diseases.

2 Classifiers

In this section, we will describe and introduce the classifiers that were used in this study.

2.1 Support Vector Machines (SVM)

Support Vector Machines (SVM) is a machine learning algorithm commonly used for classification tasks with linearly separable data. In some cases, SVM can also be applied to non-linearly separable data by utilizing hyperplanes [7]. Given an input dataset X and the output represented by the set $-1, 1$, a hyperplane is defined by Eq. 1, where $w \cdot x$ denotes the dot product between vectors w and x, and b represents a real number. Equation 1 can be used to divide the input data using Eq. 2, as illustrated in Fig. 2 [7].

$$h(x) = w \cdot x + b \tag{1}$$

$$y = \begin{cases} 1 & se \ w.x + b > 0 \\ -1 & se \ w.x + b < 0 \end{cases} \tag{2}$$

For non-linearly separable data, SVM employs two concepts. The first concept is called "One vs Rest", where each classifier C_i is responsible for classifying

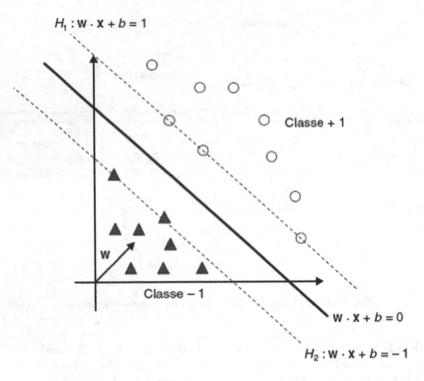

Fig. 2. Illustration of canonical hyperplanes and a separator.

class i against the others. Given a new value x, it belongs to the classifier that achieves the highest score among all n classifiers, as shown in Eq. 3 [8].

$$C(x) = \arg \max_{1 < i < n} (C_i(x)) \tag{3}$$

The second concept is "All vs All", where the new value x belongs to the class with the highest number of votes after a voting system [8].

2.2   Decision Tree

A decision tree is a machine learning algorithm commonly used for classification and regression tasks. It is a type of directed graph in which each node generates two or more leaf nodes. Each branch of a node is defined by a condition characterized by a logical operator (such as $>$, $<$, $=$) and an attribute value from the domain. In classification, the attribute is chosen using a splitting criterion called "goodness of split", which determines how well the attribute represents the class, as shown in Fig. 3 [9].

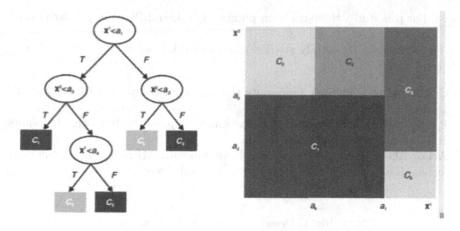

Fig. 3. A decision tree and decision regions in the object space.

2.3 Random Forest

Random Forest is a machine learning algorithm that combines multiple decision trees to build a more robust and accurate predictive model. Each decision tree is trained on a random sample from the original dataset and is used to make predictions. The final prediction is obtained by averaging the predictions of all individual trees [10].

The construction of decision trees in Random Forest is performed using the bootstrap method, which involves randomly sampling the original dataset with replacement to generate new subsets of data for training the individual trees. Additionally, at each node of the tree, a random sample of attributes is selected to determine which attribute will be used to split the data at that node [11].

The random selection of attributes and the use of multiple trees reduce the correlation between predictions and improve the model's generalization to new data. Random Forest also allows for measuring the importance of each attribute in the prediction, which can be useful for understanding the model's behavior and selecting relevant attributes for analysis.

3   Methodology

This study used sequencing data from the research conducted by Leite et al. [12], which focused on the coral *Mussismilia hispida* collected from five reefs located near a marine protected area (Parque Natural Municipal do Recife de Fora) in Porto Seguro, Bahia, Brazil. The sequencing data, with accession numbers (SAMN08391548-SAMN08391636), were retrieved from the Sequence Read Archive (SRA) database at NCBI. The five sampling points are as follows: the first point is located approximately 2 km from the Buranhém River mouth (P1), the second point is 4 km away (P2), the third point is 6 km away (P3), the fourth point is 8 km away (P4), and the fifth point is 9.4 km away (P5), as shown in

Fig. 4. For this study, the data from points P1, P3, and P5 were primarily used, as suggested by Leite et al. [12].

The samples in this study are described in Table 1 according to the following pattern:

- C followed by a number represents the season of the year, with a total of 4 seasons (2 rainy and 2 dry);
- P followed by a number represents the sampling point, with a total of 3 points;
- HH indicates a healthy coral sample;
- AH or AG indicates a diseased coral sample, with AH representing the unaffected tissue and AG representing the affected tissue.

Table 1. Descriptive table of the samples

Sample	Description
C1P1AG3	Replica 1 of a coral sample with affected tissue, collected at point 1, during the first rainy season
C1P1HH1	Healthy coral sample, replica 1, collected at point 1, during the first rainy season

The data provided in Leite et al. [12] were analyzed using QIIME 2.0 software (2023.2), as described by the authors. The result includes an abundance table of Amplicon Sequence Variants (ASVs) and a phylogenetic tree containing the 9,488 ASVs found in the 68 coral samples collected from three different points and four seasons, as shown in Fig. 5.

The first step in the data preprocessing is to replace each sample identification with 0 for diseased coral samples and 1 for healthy coral samples.

After this step, the abundance table is divided into two parts: the first part consists of 47 samples for training (70%), including 33 healthy samples and 14 diseased samples, and the second part consists of 21 samples for testing (30%), including 12 healthy samples and 9 diseased samples.

After preprocessing the data, Support Vector Machines (SVM), decision trees, and Random Forest classifiers were used, as they are common machine learning algorithms for classification tasks. The classifiers were initially trained with predefined parameters and then trained again with parameter optimization using GridSearchCV. The best parameters found for SVM were: $C = 100$, degree $= 2$, gamma $=$ scale, and kernel $=$ poly. For Random Forest, the best parameters were: n_estimators $= 100$, min_samples_split $= 10$, min_samples_leaf $= 1$, max_features $=$ log2, and max_depth $=$ None. For the decision tree, the best parameters were: criterion $=$ 'gini', max_depth $= 7$, min_samples_leaf $= 1$ and min_samples-_split $= 6$.

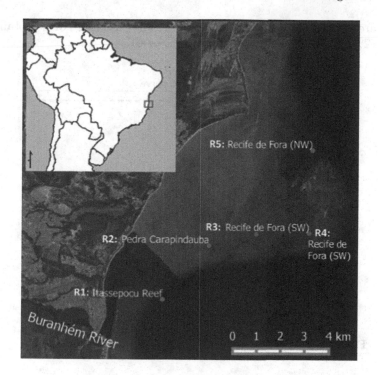

Fig. 4. Map showing the location of the Parque Municipal Marinho do Recife de Fora.

Amostras	4bccbdb96fb331b5bd8aec33cbb8a34e	c9b702e51c8e9a8d7235f376ae865078	7be1e1d42e8842852c036f3c1e7d1fd8
0	C1P1AG1	1185	0	686
1	C1P1AG3	1335	0	3279
2	C1P1AH2	1490	0	1687
3	C1P1HH1	535	0	211
4	C1P1HH2	49	0	53

Fig. 5. Abundance table of bacteria.

Finally, the obtained results are compared to determine the most efficient approach for this dataset.

4   Results and Discussion

The obtained results were based on a comparative analysis of the SVM, decision tree, and Random Forest algorithms regarding the classification of healthy and diseased corals.

After training the algorithms with the specified parameters, an evaluation was performed using the ROC curve and the confusion matrix. In the ROC curve (Fig. 6), it can be observed that the decision tree achieved the best performance, with an area under the curve (AUC) of 74%. The Random Forest obtained an AUC of 72%, followed by SVM with an AUC of 61%.

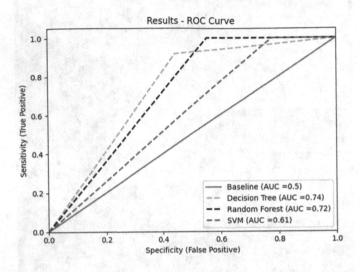

Fig. 6. ROC Curves - SVM, Decision Tree, and Random Forest

Analyzing the confusion matrix (Fig. 7), it can be seen that both the decision tree and SVM achieved an accuracy rate of 100% for the category of healthy corals, correctly classifying all samples. The Random Forest achieved the best accuracy rate for the diseased samples, correctly classifying 5 out of 9 samples (55.5%).

In addition to the confusion matrix, decision trees were also generated for the Random Forest and decision tree classifiers, represented in Fig. 8 and Fig. 9, respectively.

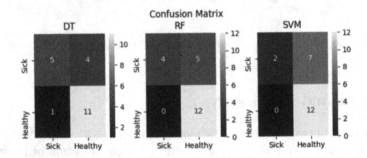

Fig. 7. Confusion Matrix - SVM, Decision Tree, and Random Forest

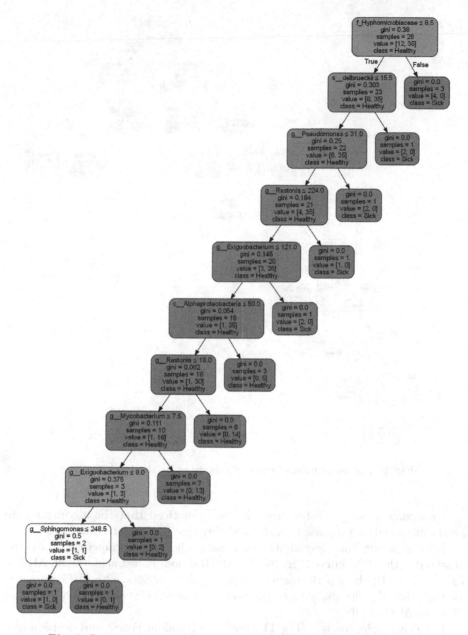

Fig. 8. Representation of the tree generated by the Random Forest

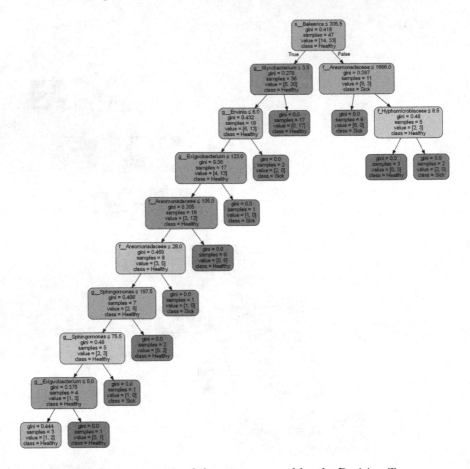

Fig. 9. Representation of the tree generated by the Decision Tree

Analyzing these generated trees, it can be noticed that the algorithms are better at identifying diseased corals, probably due to the data imbalance.

By comparing the algorithms again using the new parameters, it can be observed in the ROC curve (Fig. 10) that the Random Forest achieved an AUC of 72%, which is the best performance compared to the others. The AUC decreased for the other algorithms, with the decision tree presenting an AUC of 68% and SVM an AUC of 56%.

In the confusion matrix (Fig. 11), both the Random Forest and decision tree achieved an accuracy rate of 100% for the category of healthy corals, correctly classifying all samples. The Random Forest and decision tree obtained the best accuracy rate for the diseased samples, correctly classifying 4 out of 9 samples (44.4%).

Once again, the decision tree and Random Forest trees were provided with the optimized parameters, as seen in Fig. 12 and Fig. 13, respectively.

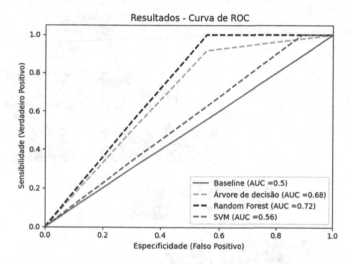

Fig. 10. ROC Curves with GridSearchCV - SVM, Decision Tree, and Random Forest

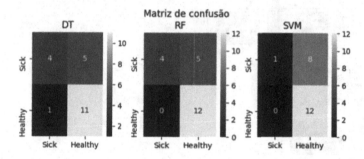

Fig. 11. Confusion Matrix with GridSearchCV - SVM, Decision Tree, and Random Forest

It can be observed once again that with optimized parameters, both the decision tree and Random Forest trees are similar to those without parameter optimization, especially the branches identified as key for classifying coral health.

These results suggest that both the decision tree and Random Forest are promising for the classification of healthy and diseased corals, demonstrating superior performance compared to SVM. It is also noticeable that the trees generated by the classifiers identified some key microorganisms related to the disease in question. Additionally, it can be observed from the confusion matrix that most algorithms tend to classify healthy samples better, likely due to the

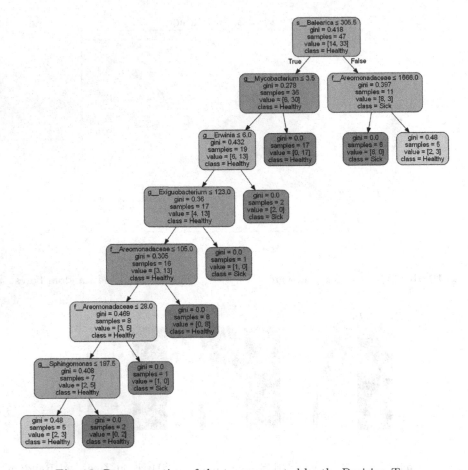

Fig. 12. Representation of the tree generated by the Decision Tree

data imbalance. However, it is important to note that the choice of the most suitable algorithm depends on the specific characteristics of the dataset and the classification objectives, and optimizing parameters does not always guarantee improved algorithm performance.

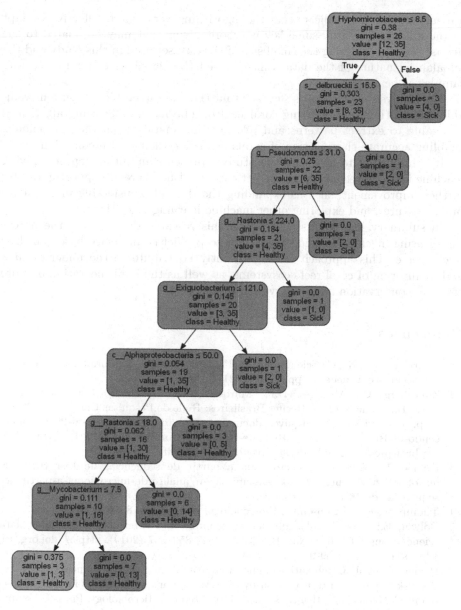

Fig. 13. Representation of the tree generated by the Random Forest

5   Conclusion

In conclusion, this study explored the application of machine learning algorithms in predicting coral health based on their microbiome. The obtained results demonstrated an accuracy rate (specify the metric used for accuracy) of 74% for the decision tree, 72% for the Random Forest, and 61% for SVM. These results are encouraging and indicate that the algorithms were able to effectively adapt to the data and identify some key microorganisms that may be related to the disease, even considering the small size of the dataset used in this study and the imbalanced nature of the data, which caused the classifiers to tend to classify samples as healthy.

The analysis of the results suggests that the coral microbiome contains valuable information for predicting coral health. The machine learning algorithms were able to extract patterns and relevant information from the microbiome, enabling accurate classification of corals regarding their health condition.

It is important to note that this study represents an initial step in applying machine learning techniques to predict coral health. There are opportunities for further improvement, such as expanding the dataset, considering more microbiome features, and exploring other machine learning algorithms.

In summary, the results achieved in this research demonstrate the potential of using machine learning algorithms to predict coral health based on their microbiome. This approach can significantly contribute to the understanding and monitoring of coral reef ecosystems, as well as the implementation of more effective conservation and preservation measures.

References

1. Courtial, A., Furla, C., Scientifique, D., Paola, F., Marine, S.: Coraux: les ingenieurs des océans sont menacés, pp. 1–10 (2021)
2. Zilberberg, C., Abrantes, D.P., Marques, J.A., Machado, L.F., Marangoni, L.F.d.B.: Conhecendo os Recifes Brasileiros: Rede de Pesquisas Coral Vivo (2016). http://coralvivo.org.br/arquivos/documentos/Livro-Zilberberg-et-al-2016-Conhe cendo-os-Recifes-Brasileiros-Rede-de-Pesquisas-Coral-Vivo.pdf. http://coralvivo.org.br/wp-content/uploads/arquivos/2308file-3.pdf
3. Riyuzo, R.: Analise de microbioma a partir de sequências de 16sr rna: Asv ou otu? (2020). https://blog.varsomics.com/analise-de-microbioma-a-partir-de-sequencias-de-16sr-rna-asv-ou-otu/
4. Thompson, F., Thompson,C.: Biotecnologia marinha, p. 855 (2020)
5. Bolyen, E.: Reproducible, interactive, scalable and extensible microbiome data science using QIIME 2. Nat. Biotechnol. **37**, 852–857 (2019). https://doi.org/10.1038/s41587-019-0209-9
6. Regier, Y., et al.: Combination of microbiome analysis and serodiagnostics to assess the risk of pathogen transmission by ticks to humans and animals in central Germany 11 Medical and Health Sciences 1108 Medical Microbiology. Parasit. Vectors **12**(1), 1–17 (2019)
7. Haykin, S., Neurais, R.: Princípios e Prática. Artmed (2007). https://books.google.com.br/books?id=bhMwDwAAQBAJ
8. Goncalves, A.R.: Fundamentos e Aplicacões de Técnicas de Aprendizado de Maquina (2008). https://andreric.github.io/posts/2018/05/blog-post-2/
9. Faceli, K., Lorena, C., Gama, J., Almeida, A.D.: Inteligencia ˆ artificial: uma abordagem de aprendizado de maquina. Grupo GEN (2021). https://integrada.minhabiblioteca.com.br/books/9788521637509
10. Breiman, L.: Random forests (2001)

11. Ali, J., Khan, R., Khan, R., Ahmad, N., Maqsood, I., Maqsood, I.: Random forests and decision trees (2012)
12. Leite, D.C.A., et al.: Coral bacterial-core abundance and network complexity as proxies for anthropogenic pollution. Front. Microbiol. **9**, 833 (2018). https://www.frontiersin.org/article/10.3389/fmicb.2018.00833
13. Zilberberg, C., et al.: Conhecendo os Recifes Brasileiros: Rede de Pesquisas Coral Vivo [s.n.], 360 p. (2016). ISBN 978-85-7427-057-9

The Consistent Vehicle Routing Problem: An Application to the Pharmaceutical Supply Chain

Manuel Eusébio[1] , Telmo Pinto[1,2(✉)] , and Miguel Vieira[1,3,4]

[1] CEMMPRE, ARISE, University of Coimbra, Coimbra, Portugal
`telmo.pinto@uc.pt`
[2] Centro ALGORITMI/LASI, University of Minho, Braga, Portugal
[3] RCM2+, Universidade Lusófona, Lisboa, Portugal
[4] CEGIST, Instituto Superior Técnico, Universidade de Lisboa, Lisboa, Portugal

Abstract. With increasingly competitive markets, companies have turned their strategies towards process optimization to better respond to customer demands. The vehicle routing problem has gained greater prominence in this paradigm shift since, through its resolution, it can be obtained gains in improving the use of resources. In this paper, we developed a route planning methodology for a pharmaceutical distributor company that has recently changed the structure of its operations, thus being necessary to redefine its entire service to the different pharmacies, based in real instances. The proposed methodology combines an exact method with cluster-first, routing-second approach to solve a consistent route planning problem with multiple customers, time window constraints, heterogeneous fleet, and different delivery periods. It was possible to apply the method for large set of customers, achieving results with relatively low computational effort. The results demonstrate the methodology's potential to reduce operational costs and improve overall service fulfillment.

Keywords: Consistent Vehicle Routing Problem · Cluster based approach · Pharmaceutical Supply Chain

1 Introduction

Within the broad scope of supply chain management, the general problem of route planning in today's logistic systems is becoming increasingly important. The interest in this problem by companies in the distribution area arises to reorganize the main element of its value stream, the transportation system, efficiently. Due to extensive experience in field operations, some choose to develop their routes through intuitive methods. However, through mathematical formulations and with the support of common calculation machines, it becomes possible to reach reliable solutions with much less effort compared to the first approach.

In the case of the pharmaceutical sector, in the last two decades, customers have been changing their behavior, showing appreciation for buying in smaller volumes, more frequently, and with a shorter response time. To adjust to these changes without penalizing their service level, distribution companies have been forced to increase their inventory or even restructure their supply chain, constantly searching for a balance between costs and regulated services provided. Regarding the distribution, this attitude forces an increase in the frequency of deliveries and greater attention to service, especially when there is strong competition [1].

Given these logistical challenges, this paper developed a route planning methodology for a pharmaceutical wholesaler that intends to redefine its entire service structure to different pharmacies, given an increase in its market share. Through the analysis of delivery data, it was proposed to develop an accurate model that reflects the overall goal of placing the right products, in the right quantity, at the right time and in the right place. Since this is an extremely competitive supply chain, this proposition becomes even more important, considering the need to balance the demand for customer service with the optimization of resources.

This paper is organized as follows: in Sect. 2, the literature background related to routing problems is discussed; in Sect. 3, the case study is presented with its pharmaceutical context, followed by the problem description in Sect. 4; in Sect. 5, the proposed approach is detailed along with the mathematical formulation; and finally, in Sect. 6, the results are discussed, leading to the conclusion in Sect. 7.

2 Background

2.1 Routing Problems and Its Variants

Distribution route planning, typically known by Vehicle Routing Problem (VRP) is a combinatorial problem belonging to the NP-Hard class, which involves route planning for a fleet of vehicles supplying a set of customers, taking into consideration certain constraints. VRP focuses on the face-to-face distribution of products and services, considering the character of the goods transported, the quality provided, and the characteristics of the customers and vehicles [2].

Currently, there is a growing trend to incorporate constraints that bring theoretical models closer to real situations. Varying travel times (based on traffic behavior), time windows for both pickup and delivery, fleet multiplicity, among other inputs that change scenarios dynamically over time constitute a pragmatic yet intricate answer, increasing model complexity. Heuristics and meta-heuristics are the approaches that best fit real-world applications, since these types of problems are considerably larger. The application of exact methods is efficient for smaller cases, and the study of VRP has been the lever for major developments of these algorithms [3].

The basic vehicle routing problem usually considers a homogeneous fleet. By varying the capacities of the vehicles, the problem evolves into Heterogeneous

Fleet VRP (HFVRP), also known as Mixed Fleet VRP [4,5]. In the VRP with Time Windows (VRPTW), duration is added in the arcs, and the deliveries must occur within a time interval for each customer. In the VRP with pickups and deliveries (VRPPD), and for each order, an origin and a destination are required with the particularity that both operations can occur in the same location [6]. Another common extension is the VRP with backhauls (VRPB) reverse logistics, in which pickups and deliveries are combined into a single trip. However, all delivery requests need to be made before the start of the pickup of goods at customer locations [7]. Otherwise, the different customers are mixed (VRP with Mixed backhauls) [8].

In the development of most VRP models, it is assumed that vehicle capacity is translated by a simple one-dimensional measure. However, the way customer orders are distributed in the cargo bay can be considered, and so loading-constrained VRP (L-VRP) addresses cases in which customer requests and the vehicles' own measurements are expressed in two or three dimensions: two-dimensional loading VRP (2L-VRP) [9,10] or three-dimensional loading (3L-VRP) [11,12], respectively.

2.2   Consistent VRP

The Consistent VRP was introduced by [13] as a variant of VRP in which it is guaranteed that customers are always visited by the same driver and at the same time of day [14]. This problem was introduced due to the importance of providing high customer service in small package distribution. As stated in [15], in this type of supply chain, it is preferred to offer the same level of service to a broad group of customers, than to generate familiarity with a single geographical area, even more so because it is a type of distribution characterized by low and constant service times. The same authors refer that the consistency of a service is related to customer satisfaction, and with the growth of markets comes the need to balance low-cost route design with a high-quality type of route planning that prioritizes end-customer satisfaction. [16] states that from the point of view of distribution companies, having consistent routes also improves driver satisfaction and their own productivity since they gain knowledge of the territory they are driving through and, above all, of the very procedures that the final customer assumes at the time of delivery, improving the informal driver-customer relationship. This level of knowledge also allows for improvements in distribution to overcome difficulties resulting from incidents in transit or with consumers.

In resume, there are two models that can be used in distribution systems: flexible routes, which are designed dynamically, based on the orders at that moment that must be delivered; or consistent routes, where the set of customers that must be served per route are defined a priory. The first option, in theoretical terms can lead to better fleet sizing and more optimized routes. However, it ignores that the orders in the type of distribution in question are sometimes known only a few hours before the start of the route. On the other hand, using consistent routes increases the driver's familiarity with his own means of operation, ultimately improving his competence. In addition, this consistency also allows for an easier and more stable way of managing delivery planning and unlocks the possibility of delivering to customers at approximately the same times of the day.

3   Case Study

3.1   Company Context

The scope of this work is based on the operations of a pharmaceutical distribution company whose objective was to determine the optimal planning of the routes of its vehicles in the distribution of medicines to pharmacies. The company is responsible for supplying, storing, and distributing medicines in the shortest possible time. In addition to the distribution, it is also responsible for collecting damaged or expired products. The company has witnessed in recent years a strong growth in its market share which has resulted in a greater number of pharmacies to supply, units transported, operating costs, and, above all, more significant challenges.

The pharmaceutical context is highly regulated, and several processes are imposed by the regulatory authority, thus allowing little flexibility to the distribution conditions [17]. The margins for each of the players in the chain, from suppliers to pharmacies, are stipulated by the national regulator. With these tight margins and the pressure to transport increasingly fractional, smaller, and more frequent orders, distributors need to optimize their supply chains to reduce operating costs while guaranteeing high service standards.

3.2   Scope Characterization

In this type of logistic distribution, consumption patterns generally present low variability, given the constant need for goods and services in the pharmaceutical area, minimizing the complexity of transporting more than 10,000 different units' references. On the other hand, this particularity requires an increase in the level of service offered to the various customers. To supply the demand of 384 customers weekly, there are two delivery times, which are divided into the morning and afternoon periods (Fig. 1). Of all the pharmacies supplied, 60% have 2 daily visits and the remaining 40% are entitled to only one visit, with the morning period being the most demanding. The process of defining the number of deliveries to be made to each customer is directly related to their order volume and their own location.

To optimize the distribution process, the company has adopted plastic boxes for the packaging of medicines. The fleet of vehicles is also heterogeneous and consists of 3 types of vehicles (capacity for 50, 100, and 150 boxes).

The main objective is to provide decision support to allow the optimization of distribution routes and the company fleet of vehicles. Through the adaptation

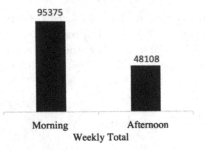

Total Pharmacies	384
Daily average demand	285
Daily min	70
Daily max	346

Fig. 1. Characterization of demand (daily average and weekly total units).

of a consistent route planning model, it is intended to minimize costs related to the distribution operation, ensuring that all customers are served, on time and in the quantities required.

The capacity of the vehicles, the warehouse working hours, and the drivers' working hours limit are also constraints that will affect the development of the model and that will bring it closer to reality, so that it will be possible, when completed, for it to have practical applications.

4   Problem Description

The problem can be defined by a graph $G = (N, A)$, where N is the set of nodes $N = \{0, \ldots, n+1\}$, connected by a set of arcs $A = \{(i, j) : 0 \le i, j \le n+1, i \ne j\}$. The nodes 0 and $n + 1$ correspond to the warehouse, in which k vehicles of c different types of vehicles are available, each $C = \{1, \ldots, c\}$ characterized by a capacity C_c and limited by the set $S_c = \{c_1, \ldots, c_k\}$ which refers to the set of vehicles available for each type. The remaining set $V = N \backslash \{0, n+1\}$ corresponds to the customers required to visit and deliver a certain quantity $q_i \in Q$ in the course of the service time s_i. At each vertex $i \in N \backslash \{0, n+1\}$ is associated with a time window, in most cases rigid, $[a_i, b_i]$, where a_i and b_i represent the lower and upper limits at which a vehicle can reach the vertex i, respectively.

For each vehicle k, there is a variable cost α_c (monetary units/km), associated with each arc $(i, j) \in A$ and each vehicle $k \in K$, for all $c \in C$, directly dependent on the distance d_{ij} traveled. One route $R = \{0, i_1, \ldots, i_h, n + 1\}$ having at least one vertex i is a simple circuit belonging to G that passes through the warehouse, visits the h customers, fulfilling the respective time windows, and returns to the warehouse, considering the following constraints:

- Each customer is visited exactly once.
- When a customer is visited, it is guaranteed that the visiting vehicle is also part of that node.
- The total demand of the customers visited by a given vehicle cannot exceed the maximum capacity of that same vehicle, C_c.

- Each vehicle can only leave the warehouse after the instant A it visits all the clients foreseen in the route R and returns to the warehouse before the instant B, where $[A, B]$ is the warehouse opening hours.
- Finally, the duration of each route must be less than DM, which is the maximum working hours defined by legislation for a driver.

The following is the mathematical formulation for the problem involving two types of decision variables:

- X_{ij}^k corresponds to a binary variable, which takes value 1 if the arc (i, j) is traveled by the vehicle k, and takes value 0 otherwise.
- w_i^k corresponds to a continuous variable, which specifies the beginning instant of time of the service in the node i when served by the vehicle k.

The parameter α_c is responsible for converting the sum of the distances traveled into a cost. Its value was previously determined by the company and was the one applied in this work, being indicated by 0.46 monetary units/km.

The problem can be formulated as follows:

$$\min \sum_{c \in C} \sum_{k \in S_c} \sum_{(i,j) \in A} \alpha_c d_{ij} X_{kij} \tag{1}$$

Subject to:

$$\sum_{k \in K} \sum_{j \in V} X_{ij}^k = 1, \quad \forall i \in N \tag{2}$$

$$\sum_{j \in V} X_{0j}^k \leq 1, \quad \forall k \in K \tag{3}$$

$$\sum_{i \in V} X_{in}^k \leq 1, \quad \forall k \in K \tag{4}$$

$$\sum_{i \in N} X_{ip}^k - \sum_{j \in N} X_{pj}^k = 0, \quad \forall p \in V, \, k \in K \tag{5}$$

$$\sum_{i \in V} \sum_{j \in N} q_i X_{ij}^k \leq C_c, \quad \forall k \in K, \, c \in C \tag{6}$$

$$X_{ij}^k \left(w_i^k + S_i + t_{ij} - w_j^k \right) \leq 0, \quad \forall k \in K, \, i \in V, \, j \in N \tag{7}$$

$$\sum_{j \in V} a_i X_{ij}^k \leq w_i^k \leq \sum_{j \in V} b_i X_{ij}^k, \quad \forall k \in K, \, i \in V \tag{8}$$

$$\sum_{i \in N} \sum_{j \in N} (t_{ij} + S_i) X_{ij}^k \leq DM, \quad \forall k \in K \tag{9}$$

$$A + t_{0j} \leq w_j^k + M(1 - X_{0j}^k), \quad \forall k \in K, \, j \in V \tag{10}$$

$$w_j^k + S_j + t_{j0} \leq B + M(1 - X_{0j}^k), \quad \forall k \in K, \, j \in V \tag{11}$$

$$\sum_{k \in S_c} \sum_{j \in V} X_{0j}^k \leq |S_c|, \quad \forall c \in C \tag{12}$$

$$w_i^k \geq 0, \quad \forall k \in K, i \in N \tag{13}$$

$$X_{ij}^k \in \{0,1\}, \quad \forall k \in K, (i,j) \in A \tag{14}$$

The objective function (1) aims to minimize the total cost of the operation by minimizing the total distance traveled, considering a heterogeneous fleet. Constraint (2) ensures that each customer must be visited exactly once, while constraints (3) and (4) together prevent that a node $i \in V$ can be assigned more than one vehicle. Inequalities (5) ensure flow conservation by guaranteeing that if a vehicle is assigned to a particular customer, it must also depart from that same node when the service is finished. Constraints (6) limit the amount transported to the maximum capacity of the model C_c in use, while (7) and (8) guarantee that the time windows are respected. Constraints (9) limit the duration of each route to labor legislation. Conditions (10) and (11) concern the coordination of the departure and arrival of the vehicles at the warehouse, with their respective opening hours. Constraints (12) are the imposition of a limit to the number of available vehicles of each type $c \in C$. Finally, constraints (13) and (14) define the values of the decision variables that serve as a basis for the formulation.

In this formulation, a non-linear expression (7) was presented. However, through the linearization presented in [17], it was possible to replace it with the following linear expression:

$$w_i^k + S_i + t_{ij} - w_j^k \leq (1 - X_{ij}^k) \cdot \max\{b_i + S_i + t_{ij} - a_j, 0\}, \quad \forall k \in K, (i,j) \in A \tag{15}$$

This constraint (15) also solves the subtour problem, and this methodology was extended to the development of expressions (10) and (11) (representation displayed in Fig. 2).

5   Proposed Approach

The proposed methodology for the given VRPTW problem combines exact solution procedures through a solver, with a set of valid inequalities for confining the solution space through cutting planes, and a decomposition-based approach $cluster - first, routing - second$.

5.1   Strengthening the Model

The formulation of the mixed integer programming problem (1)–(15) guarantees that no valid solution allows cycles to exist. However, through the explicit definition of this type of elimination, a reinforcement of the linear programming

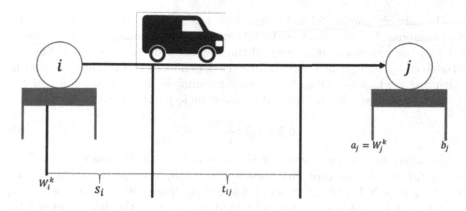

Fig. 2. Representation of parameters and variables imposed on the model

constraints is noted. Since this is a problem that precludes the existence of displacements in the arcs in both directions, through the following constraint, the existence of this type of cycles can be eliminated, limiting the search space and, consequently, reducing the computational effort:

$$X_{ij}^k + X_{ji}^k \leq 1, \quad \forall k \in K, \forall (i,j) \in V \tag{16}$$

Despite the assignment of time windows to each client, in [18] it was discussed through computational analysis that in a large number of cases, when considering an arc (i,j), the linear relaxation of (14) translates $X_{ij}^k > 0$, however, $w_j^k > w_i^k$. These situations are called inverse flow of X_{ij}^k within the circuit considered, which may give rise to many infeasible solutions, even respecting the set of constraints defined. It is also noted that the existence of reverse flow may lower the efficiency indexes of some subroute constraints. Thus, a new constraint is introduced that considers time windows and complements constraint (8):

$$(1 - X_{ij}^k)(b_j - a_i + s_i + t_{ij}) + w_i^k \geq w_j^k + s_j + t_{ji} + (1 - X_{ji}^k)(a_i - b_j - s_j - t_{ji}),$$
$$\forall k \in K, \forall (i,j) \in A \tag{17}$$

To strengthen constraints (2), (3), and (4), the following constraint is added:

$$\sum_{k \in K} X_{ij}^k \leq 1, \quad \forall (i,j) \in V \tag{18}$$

A parameter $D_{\max}$ is created, which defines the maximum distance allowed to each arc. This assignment implies that a given arc can only be traversed by any vehicle if its distance is limited to $D_{\max}$ kilometers. In practical terms, applying this procedure prevents that in a route, a pharmacy distances from other pharmacies at a distance higher than $D_{\max}$.

$$X_{ij}^k d_{ij} \leq D_{\max}, \quad \forall k \in K, \forall (i,j) \in V \tag{19}$$

The service time considered is based on the work of [19], and consists of a fixed component, which involves the action of parking, loading the various bays, going to the pharmacy, and filling all the necessary documents. Regarding the variable component, it is a portion directly dependent on the number of bumps transported, which is divided by the average number of boxes that a driver can load simultaneously (in this case, 6) in the vehicle-pharmacy route, as follows:

$$S_i = 2.5 + 1.5 \left\lceil \frac{q_i}{6} \right\rceil, \quad \forall i \in V \tag{20}$$

To determine the parameters of the demand, given the consistency of the problem, it was defined through an arithmetic mean, based on the weekly behavior over a month. On the other hand, for the implementation of time windows, the company has defined that the delivery periods set for the daily commute for all clients are:

- Morning: 7 h 00–09 h 30 (order picking in the previous day);
- Afternoon: 13 h 30–16 h 30 (order picking in the morning).

5.2   Clustering Method

Due to the size of the problem, it is very challenging to determine optimal solutions using exact methods in a timely manner. Based on the algorithm developed by [20], a formulation was implemented that translates into an assignment of vehicles to different groups of customers. The main idea is to solve a generalized assignment problem of the vehicle routing problem to obtain an assignment of customers to vehicles. Therefore, the set of customers assigned to each vehicle are then sequenced using the proposed exact model. Therefore, this method relies in assigning a Cluster First-Routing Second approach.

To model this formulation, it is essential to consider the demand of the different customers, q_i, and the capacity of the vehicles C_c. However, it assumes as the main objective the minimization of a distance $d_{i_k} = d_{0j} + d_{ii_k} - d_{0i_k}$ which represents the cost of inserting a customer i to the route taken by vehicle k, which first moves from the warehouse to the customer and returns. The binary variable y_{ik} takes value 1 if customer i is assigned to vehicle k (and 0 otherwise).

The formulation is presented as follows:

$$\min \sum_{k \in K} \sum_{i \in V} d_{i_k} y_{i_k} \tag{21}$$

Subject to:

$$\sum_{i \in V} q_i y_{i_k} \leq C, \quad \forall k \in K \tag{22}$$

$$\sum_{k \in K} y_{0_k} = K \tag{23}$$

$$\sum_{k \in K} y_{i_k} = 1, \quad \forall i \in V \tag{24}$$

$$y_{i_k} \in \{0, 1\}, \quad \forall k \in K, i \in V \tag{25}$$

Constraints (22) ensure that the vehicle's maximum capacity is not violated, while constraint (23) equal the number of clusters to the fleet size. Constraints (24) ensure that each customer is assigned to each vehicle. Regarding the number of clusters, the number of daily routes currently applied by the company was used as a reference. Therefore, after data processing, the set i_k is composed of 23 clusters. As can be seen in restriction (22), the vehicle capacity is considered a constant. However, the company has a heterogeneous fleet; thus, to adapt the solution to this practical constraint, each cluster was initially assigned a vehicle with the maximum possible capacity of the fleet. From these results, the clusters that have not reached 2/3 of the maximum capacity of the vehicle or have a total number of customers served exceeding 30 are enforced to use one

Table 1. Clusters and Total Demand

Clusters	Morning		Afternoon	
	Number of customers	Total Demand	Number of customers	Total Demand
1	23	99	10	23
2	17	43	7	21
3	25	75	12	24
4	26	75	11	30
5	17	75	20	49
6	20	50	20	50
7	10	51	24	50
8	16	48	24	50
9	10	28	16	50
10	17	75	21	49
11	7	34	11	31
12	15	74	9	26
13	15	50	12	50
14	21	50	14	49
15	11	50	16	50
16	16	87	6	17
17	7	39	13	45
18	22	99	14	50
19	9	46	-	-
20	15	88	-	-
21	16	93	-	-
22	4	22	-	-
23	23	130	-	-

of the corresponding vehicles with less capacity. The summary of the various parameters analyzed in this problem is shown in Table 1.

6   Computational Results

In this section, the results obtained are derived from models implemented in OPL language in the commercial solver Ilog Cplex 12.10, using a computer with i7-4700MQ CPU 2.40 GHz with 12 GB of RAM.

One of the main objectives of this first analysis is to evaluate the computational times and respective optimal solutions given the order of magnitude of the global problem. These instances set, consisting of 5, 10, 25 and 50 clients, allowed us to evaluate the number of constraints and variables involved, the values of the objective function and, finally, the computational effort when different numbers of vehicles are applied. As displayed in Table 2, the need to reduce the problem size is recognized, and it is concluded that for instances with the size of the defined clusters the model performs well enough to achieve optimal solutions in a reasonable time.

Table 2. Validation of the developed exact model

Customers	No. of Vehicles	Gap (%)	CPU Time (s)	No. of Variables
5	1	0%	0.09	42
10	1	0%	1.25	156
25	3	27.1%	3600	2268
50	5	34.8%	3600	13780

For the proposed case study, solutions were presented for the total set of pharmacies, taking into account the respective constraints given demand, distance and time between customers, time windows, vehicle capacity, and service times. 354 pharmacies were considered, grouped into 17 clusters, referring to the morning and afternoon delivery periods, respectively. This determines the metrics obtained in the modelling phase in Table 3, and despite the two delivery periods consider a significantly different number of customers, the increase in costs is about 17%.

Table 3. Results obtained with the application of real instances

Period	Customers	Objective (m.u.)	Variables	CPU Time (s)	Gap (%)
Morning	354	1528.3	8384	3584.7	1.0%
Afternoon	231	1297.6	6230	1971.6	1.0%

Regarding the implementation of the methodology at the computational level, it obtained results within a reasonable gap of 1%.

In order to obtain a validation of the results, a comparison analysis was developed based on a historic solution reported by the distributor company for the same case, namely in the total distance traveled, number of vehicles, and operating costs (Table 4).

Table 4. Comparison of the proposed model with company indicators

Period	Proposed Model			Company Solution		
	Distance (km)	No. of Vehicles	Costs (m.u.)	Distance (km)	No. of Vehicles	Costs (m.u.)
Morning	3322.9	23	1528.3	3866.1	25	1778.4
Afternoon	2820.9	17	1297.6	3374.3	25	1552.2

It is possible to demonstrate that the proposed model allows, in general terms, an improvement of the resources needed for distribution operations. Regarding the number of vehicles used, which are linked to the number of routes, it was possible through the optimization methodology to reduce this metric by 8% in the morning period, with the afternoon period representing the greatest gains, with a 30% reduction. With this solution, it is possible to reduce the number of routes maintaining the levels of supply and cadence of the final customer, which represents a positive impact on the company's costs. Given the heterogeneous characteristics of the fleet, Table 5 also compares the solution given the different types of vehicle capacities considered, allowing a preference for larger capacity vehicles to save costs.

Table 5. Comparison of the required fleet of vehicles

Capacity Types	Proposed Model	Company Solution
50	17	43
100	22	5
150	1	2

Moreover, regarding the compliance with the time windows, the solution was achieved for the case of pharmacies supplied, which represents a positive aspect for the company's operation.

7 Conclusions

In this work, a combined methodology was developed for a consistent route planning problem with time windows and a heterogeneous fleet, applied to a case based on real data from the operation of a pharmaceutical distributor. Being this one of the fundamental parts of the supply chain management, given the large number of customers considered, in an initial phase, cutting plans were applied to reduce the solution space and achieve an optimal solution for the global problem with less computational effort. In a second phase, while maintaining the goal of reducing the computational effort, a Cluster First-Route Second methodology was implemented, which allowed the division of the total number of pharmacies supplied by the distributor into different clusters, subsequently applying the methodology developed in the previous phase. This approach led to achieving good results close to the optimal solution, with a relative computational effort.

By applying the proposed methodology to a real case of a pharmaceutical distributor, it was possible to optimize the resources of its transportation activity, resulting in a reduction in kilometers traveled, number of vehicles used, and higher occupancy rates of transport vehicles, thereby minimizing operating costs. Considering the importance of customer satisfaction in this supply chain, it is noteworthy that the proposed model generates route planning solutions while considering problem restrictions. This improvement may lead to a higher service level, a fundamental factor for logistic operations in an extremely competitive environment.

Funding Information. This work has been supported by FCT - Fundação para a Ciência e a Tecnologia within the R&D Units Project Scope UIDB/00319/2020.

References

1. Martins, S.S.B.: Configuração da cadeia logística de um grossista farmacêutico. Faculdade de Engenharia da Universidade do Porto (2014)
2. Baldacci, R., Mingozzi, A., Roberti, R.: Recent exact algorithms for solving the vehicle routing problem under capacity and time window constraints. Eur. J. Oper. Res. **218**(1), 1–6 (2012). https://doi.org/10.1016/j.ejor.2011.07.037
3. Laporte, G.: Fifty years of vehicle routing. Transp. Sci. **43**(4), 408–416 (2009). https://doi.org/10.1287/trsc.1090.0301
4. Koç, Ç., Bektaş, T., Jabali, O., Laporte, G.: Thirty years of heterogeneous vehicle routing. Eur. J. Oper. Res. **249**(1), 1–21 (2016). https://doi.org/10.1016/j.ejor.2015.07.020
5. Baldacci, R., Battarra, M., Vigo, D.: Routing a heterogeneous fleet of vehicles. In: Golden, B., Raghavan, S., Wasil, E. (eds.) The Vehicle Routing Problem: Latest Advances and New Challenges. Operations Research/Computer Science Interfaces, vol. 43, pp. 3–27. Springer, Boston (2008). https://doi.org/10.1007/978-0-387-77778-8_1
6. Parragh, S.N., Doerner, K.F., Hartl, R.F.: A survey on pickup and delivery problems: part ii: transportation between pickup and delivery locations. J. fur Betriebswirtschaft **58**(2), 81–117 (2008). https://doi.org/10.1007/s11301-008-0036-4
7. Pollaris, H., Braekers, K., Caris, A., Janssens, G.K., Limbourg, S.: Vehicle routing problems with loading constraints: state-of-the-art and future directions. OR Spectrum **37**(2), 297–330 (2015). https://doi.org/10.1007/s00291-014-0386-3

8. Pinto, T., Alves, C., Valério de Carvalho, J.: Variable neighborhood search algorithms for the vehicle routing problem with two-dimensional loading constraints and mixed linehauls and backhauls. Int. Trans. Oper. Res. **27**(1), 549–572 (2020). https://doi.org/10.1111/itor.12509

9. Iori, M., Salazar-González, J.J., Vigo, D.: An exact approach for the vehicle routing problem with two-dimensional loading constraints. Transp. Sci. **41**(2), 253–264 (2007). https://doi.org/10.1287/trsc.1060.0165

10. Côté, J.-F., Gendreau, M., Potvin, J.-Y.: The vehicle routing problem with stochastic two-dimensional items. Transp. Sci. (2013). https://doi.org/10.1287/trsc.2019.0904LNCS

11. Gendreau, M., Iori, M., Laporte, G., Martello, S.: A tabu search algorithm for a routing and container loading problem. Transp. Sci. **40**(3), 342–350 (2006). https://doi.org/10.1287/trsc.1050.0145

12. Moura, A., Pinto, T., Alves, C., Valério de Carvalho, J.: A matheuristic approach to the integration of three-dimensional bin packing problem and vehicle routing problem with simultaneous delivery and pickup. Mathematics **11**(3), 713 (2023). https://doi.org/10.3390/math11030713

13. Groër, C., Golden, B., Smith, R.H., Wasil, E.: The consistent vehicle routing problem. Manuf. Serv. Oper. Manage. **11**(4), 630–643 (2009). https://doi.org/10.1287/msom.1080.0243

14. Junqueira, L., Morabito, R., Yamashita, D.S.: Modelos de otimização para problemas de carregamento de contêineres com considerações de estabilidade e de empilhamento. Pesquisa Operacional **30**(1), 73–98 (2010). https://doi.org/10.1590/s0101-74382010000100005

15. Lespay, H., Suchan, K.: A case study of consistent vehicle routing problem with time windows (2019). http://arxiv.org/abs/1912.05929

16. Wong, R.T.: Vehicle routing for small package delivery and pickup services. Oper. Res. Comput. Sci. Interfaces Ser. **43**, 475–485 (2008). https://doi.org/10.1007/978-0-387-77778-8-21

17. Vieira, M., Pinto-Varela, T., Barbosa-Póvoa, A.P.: A model-based decision support framework for the optimisation of production planning in the biopharmaceutical industry. Comput. Ind. Eng. **129**, 354–367 (2019). https://doi.org/10.1016/j.cie.2019.01.045

18. Schmid, V., Ehmke, J.F.: An effective large neighborhood search for the team orienteering problem with time windows. In: ICCL 2017. LNCS, vol. 10572, pp. 3–18. Springer, Cham (2017). https://doi.org/10.1007/978-3-319-68496-3_1

19. Campelo, P., Neves-Moreira, F., Amorim, P., Almada-Lobo, B.: Consistent vehicle routing problem with service level agreements: a case study in the pharmaceutical distribution sector. Eur. J. Oper. Res. **273**(1), 131–145 (2019). https://doi.org/10.1016/j.ejor.2018.07.030

20. Fisher, M.: Vehicle routing. In: Handbooks in Operations Research and Management Science, vol. 8, no. C, pp. 1–33. Elsevier (1995). https://doi.org/10.1016/S0927-0507(05)80105-7

Using OR-Tools When Solving the Nurse Scheduling Problem

Márcia Oliveira[1], Ana Maria A. C. Rocha[1], and Filipe Alves[1,2,3](✉)

[1] ALGORITMI Research Centre/LASI, University of Minho, 4710-057 Braga, Portugal
pg49841@alunos.uminho.pt, {arocha,d12076}@dps.uminho.pt
[2] Research Centre in Digitalization and Intelligent Robotics (CeDRI), Instituto Politécnico de Bragança, Campus de Santa Apolónia, 5300-253 Bragança, Portugal
[3] Laboratório Associado Para a Sustentabilidade E Tecnologia Em Regiões de Montanha (SusTEC), Instituto Politécnico de Bragança, Campus de Santa Apolónia, 5300-253 Bragança, Portugal

Abstract. Scheduling of employees is a common problem that can be found in most organizations all over the world. One example is the nurse scheduling problem (NSP), which is a complex combinatorial opti-mization problem faced by healthcare institutions in assigning working and nonworking days. The NSP comprises constraints for the nurses, for the hospital and considers specific labor regulations, as well as the skills and preferences of workers. In summary, it involves hard and soft constraints. It is essential to create a quality timetable that can lead to a more contented and thus, more effec-tive and productive workforce. To improve this process, it can be used automated approaches and techniques. In this study, a litera-ture review about the nurse scheduling problem and how to use the Google OR-Tools software to solve it is performed. Moreover, an example of an NSP involving 10 nurses being assigned to three shifts a day, seven days a week is presented. Some condi-tions/constraints have been added in order to reproduce a real situation.

Keywords: Nurse scheduling problem · Constrained optimization · Google OR-Tools

1 Introduction

In most organizations, the service manager faces one of the critical tasks: the effective scheduling of its employees. The scheduling problem of shift workers, known as the shift scheduling problem (SSP), is considered a common problem in several sectors. A shift usually corresponds to a block of work periods to be performed, with or without a short meal or rest breaks [1]. It is a complex NP-hard integer programming problem, especially when many shifts and a large number of workers with several levels and skills are involved [2]. NP-hard is considered a complex class of decision problems that are intrinsically harder than those that can be solved by a nondeterministic Turing machine (mathematical model of computation) in polynomial time [3].

© The Author(s), under exclusive license to Springer Nature Switzerland AG 2024
A. I. Pereira et al. (Eds.): OL2A 2023, CCIS 1981, pp. 438–449, 2024.
https://doi.org/10.1007/978-3-031-53025-8_30

The SSP becomes more complex when employees can perform a lot of different tasks during the same shift. It seeks to assign workers to activities, work shifts and rest periods, considering specific labor regulations, legal and organization rules, policies and workers skills and preferences [2]. It is also necessary to comply with demand needs and other applicable requirements, such as different sensitive dimensions like flexibility, stability, predictability, or fairness. A good shift scheduling plan helps to maintain a desired service level during the day since this increases the on-job performance and, consequently, productivity and service quality. Therefore, employees' satisfaction with the shift schedule is essential because, in a good plan, work is assigned in the most effective manner. Besides that, it can fight overstaffing and understaffing, reducing costs and increasing profitability. All these attributes significantly impact the worker and can negatively affect his mental and physical health. For instance, stressful factors such as long shifts of work, short periods of rest and inadequate distribution between rest and work periods [1].

An example of SSP is the nurse scheduling problem (NSP), also known as the nurse rostering problem. In health institutions, nurses are one of many scarce resources, since they are on staff 24 h a day, seven days a week [4]. NSP is a complex combinatorial optimization problem that affects institutions personnel daily worldwide. The issue involves the assigning each shift to a worker, leading the nurses to have working and nonworking days, and determining which nurses should be on call during a rostering period, typically a month. It is also important to determine their working day's shift start and finish times [5]. However, it is not an easy task, since there are constraints related to the nurses and the hospital. So, it is necessary to find a schedule that respects the constraints of the nurses and fulfills the hospital requirements to ensure the proper functioning of the health institution. The best way to improve the timetabling process and quality of those timetables is to resort to automated and optimized approaches. To produce a variety of solutions, ensuring the quality of schedules and dividing work equally can be used mathematical or heuristic approaches [4]. It is necessary to have optimized solutions for several reasons. In addition to satisfaction, one of the most significant advantages is considerable time-saving for the personnel involved [6].

This project, which is being carried out in the scope of the master´s degree in Bioinformatics, intends to initially perform a literature review about the nurse scheduling problems. Hence, the first goal of this project is to understand the nurse scheduling problem and its surroundings, as well as to study and solve an optimized approach to nurse scheduling since NSP is a combinatorial optimization problem. This way, it will be used as a fast and portable software tool for optimization that helps solve the above mentioned problem. Therefore, to tackle the shift scheduling problem, a specific tool named Google OR-Tools [7] will be explored in order to solve the NSP. Finally, an example of a NSP involving three shifts per day, seven days a week, to be assigned to 10 nurses is presented. In addition, some constraints were added in order to mimic a real situation.

This paper is structured as follows: Sect. 2 presents the state of the art in this work.

The methodology and the procedure to solve the problem are presented in Sect. 3. Section 4 describes the results and discussion, while Sect. 5 concludes the paper.

2 State of the Art

2.1 Nurse Scheduling Problem (NSP)

Optimization is present in many aspects of everyday life and is considered an essential approach for solving problems in different areas, such as computer science and engineering [7, 8]. It is an essential tool in decision science and operational problems such as the Nurse Scheduling Problem.

Since the 1950s, scheduling problems have been extensively studied by the Operations Research community [4]. Operations Research consists of an analytical method of problem-solving and decision-making that is useful in the management of most organizations. The reported research on scheduling in this community is huge [10]. In this regard, there are literature reviews that provide studies on nurse scheduling problem such as Burke et al. [6] and Ernst et al. [11]. Today, scheduling is notably different than it was in its beginning, because many new features have been introduced [4]. Especially since the 1990s, nurse scheduling has become a very interesting area of research in several domains [12].

Nurse scheduling consists of creating a schedule for the nurses in healthcare organizations. The nurse scheduling problem is a common problem all hospitals face on a daily basis [13] and corresponds to the assignment of employees to shifts during a certain period, which implies some constraints (both organizational and personal). This task is particularly challenging due to various nurse requirements on different days and shifts [14]. There is a need to find a duty roster for a few nurses in such a way that the rosters comply with work regulations and meet the institutions' requests. Healthcare organizations advocate these good schedules, which improve the quality of care and the mental and physical health and social well-being of many workers. This is because different stressful factors can negatively affect the health of large numbers of employees [12]. The main objective varies between minimizing the costs of floating nurses or minimizing understaffing. On the other hand, maximizing the degree to which the nurses' requests are satisfied may also be an objective. In this case, it is necessary to consider the optimization of the steady flow of materials and the coordination of a sequence of resources such as staffing and scheduling of hospital resources [15].

Nurse scheduling classifications can be performed in several ways. For example, Burke et al. [6] recognized a classification based on the developed model. Bellanti et al. [16] proposed other models that consist of assigning morning, late or night shifts to full-time nurses with the same skills for a certain period. These models involved other conditions such as shift requirements, work regulations, part-time work, skill categories, legal constraints, and personal requirements, among others [12]. As already mentioned, nurse scheduling takes into account several constraints. Thus, the nurse scheduling problem has two types of constraints. Hard constraints are those that have to be satisfied in order to obtain a feasible schedule. These usually include physical resource restrictions and legal issues. On the other hand, soft constraints arise when requirements are desirable but not mandatory. In this way, these constraints are not necessary conditions for feasible schedules and are often used to evaluate the quality of these schedules. However, their violation causes a penalty due to nurses' dissatisfaction. There are many examples here, namely coverage demand, day-off requirements, weekend-off requirements, minimum and maximum staffing, etc. More precisely, a hard constraint is that a nurse cannot be assigned to a morning shift immediately following a night (late) shift because there has been rest time after a night shift. An example of a soft constraint could be a nurse who asks to have a certain day off on a certain day [4, 16].

Burke et al. [6] argued that hospital nurse scheduling has different approaches for various time horizons, such as short-term timetabling and long-term management. Specific terminology is also used, namely planning period, which is the time interval during which personnel has to be scheduled, the skill category, which determines who has a certain level of qualification, skill or responsibility, the shift type that corresponds to a well-defined start and end time, coverage constraints that express the number of workers needed for every skill category and for every shift or time interval during the planning period. These time-related constraints refer to all the restrictions on personal schedules. Other terms are also described, such as hard constraints, soft constraints and lastly, work regulations [6]. As an illustrative example of a nurse scheduling problem to illustrate the use of some of this terminology, it is considered a hospital supervisor that needs to create a schedule for four nurses over a period of three-days. The shift types correspond to the fact that each day is divided into three 8-h shifts. Coverage constraints concern the fact that each shift is assigned to a single nurse and that no nurse works more than one shift. Another coverage constraint is that each nurse is assigned at least two shifts during the three-day period [7].

2.2 Solution Approaches to the NSP

In recent decades, many strategies have emerged in the scientific literature to solve Nurse Scheduling Problem [6, 18]. Solution techniques can be divided into three categories: exact methods, heuristics and hybrid approaches. The first ones can be integer programming and constraint programming, so traditional mathematical algorithms are implemented. These methods guarantee convergence to optimality, but the computational times increase drastically as problem dimension increases. Most mathematical scheduling approaches use an optimized objective function subject to certain constraints [4, 6]. To solve the problem, researchers attempted to develop linear models. For example, Warner and Prawda [17] presented a mixed integer quadratic programming to find the number of nurses of a given skill category to perform a number of shifts per day. In the study, it is intended to minimize the difference between a given lower limit for the number of nurses and the variables. Trivedi and Warner [18] presented a branch and bound algorithm to organize the floating nurses (short-term assignment of nurses from different units) whenever there is a shortage of personnel. These mathematical approaches manage to face only small scale problems and that is why they are not relevant at the moment [6]. Santos et al. [19] described an integer programming formulation, i.e., a formulation with a polynomial number of constraints and variables for the problem in the International Nurse Rostering Competition (INRC). This formulation successfully models all the conditions, explicit or implicit, considered in the INRC instances. In this case, nurses are hired under different contracts and the soft constraints have been divided into two groups.

To solve these problems, exact optimization methods usually require significant computational time to produce optimal solutions. In contrast, heuristic approaches can provide high-quality results faster in reasonably short times. However, since the solutions are nearly optimal, solutions may need to be optimized by a local method. Note that this type of method focuses on solving cycle scheduling problems. Heuristics/metaheuristics can include many solution approaches, namely variable neighborhood search (VNS), tabu search (TS), simulated annealing (SA), or genetic algorithm (GA) [4, 18]. Many papers in the literature used heuristic approaches [23–26]. Curtois and Qu [24] presented an ejection chain and branch and price algorithms to solve the NSP, as well as Gurobi optimizer. They concluded that their results indicate that the branch and price method is effective only in smaller instances. This is due to the fact that it is inadequate on larger test data and runs out of memory at the same time [4]. TS is a search that moves iteratively from one solution to another by moving in a neighborhood space with the assistance of adaptive memory [15]. Dowsland [25] used TS with strategic oscillation in a big hospital to ensure enough nurses on duty at every moment while taking into account constraints. GA aims to find a genetic representation of the problem so that the "characteristics" are inherited. Randoly created solutions are more likely to be selected as better solutions to be recombined into new solutions.

One approach that involved hybrid solutions is made by Rahimian et al. [26]. Here, to solve the Nurse Scheduling Problem, researchers hybridized the VNS algorithm using integer programming. The initial solutions are created using a greedy heuristic and improved using the hybrid method. It reports new best-known results and compares them with studies already existing. Turhan and Bilgen [4] proposed an approach that integrates mixed integer programming (MIP) based Fix-and-Relax and Fix-and-Optimize heuristics with SA. A problem is divided into a set of sub-problems and each one is optimized. This is an iterative process that continues until all sub-problems are solved.

3   Methodology

In this paper, after presenting the inherent problem of nurse scheduling, an optimization approach will be used to obtain the scheduling solution for a given period. In [13], a constraint programming technique to solve the nurse scheduling problem is used, but the authors do not specify a step or sequence of steps to execute but rather the properties of a solution to be found. For this purpose, in the present work, a specific software named Google OR-Tools will be used. Compared to previous works, the use of Google OR-Tools can provide enhanced efficiency, modeling flexibility, integration with other tools and continuous improvements.

3.1   Google OR-Tools

The Google OR-Tools is an open-source software suite for combinatorial optimization and aims to provide various optimization techniques for finding the solution to a given problem. Usually, there is a large set of possible solutions and OR-Tools uses state of the art algorithms to narrow that set in order to find an optimal or near optimal solution. This software can be used to tackle different and more difficult problems that may exist in several areas. For example, vehicle routing problems, flow problems, integer and linear programming and constraint programming (CP). First, it is modeled the problem with the chosen programming language. The OR-Tools supports various programming languages, including C++, Python, DotNet (.NET) and Java. Then, the problem is solved using any of the solvers, such as commercial solvers (Gurobi or CPLEX) or the open-source solvers such as SCIP, GLPK, Google's GLOP or award-winning CP-SAT [7, 30].

In this study, Python programming language will be chosen, and the CP method will be used, which keeps track of the solutions that remain feasible when new constraints are added. This is the reason why this method is considered a powerful tool for solving large scheduling problems. In this way, Google provides ways to solve CP problems, among which will be chosen as the CP-SAT solver which corresponds to a constraint programming solver that uses SAT (satisfiability) methods [7, 30]. Therefore, this will be employed to solve a nurse scheduling problem with some specific constraints.

3.2 Solver

There are many different types of optimization problems and for each problem, different approaches and algorithms can be used to find an optimal solution. After identifying the type of problem of this work, a scheduling problem involving the assignment of nurses to perform a set of several tasks at specific times, a suitable solver will be chosen. In this case, the CP-SAT solver will be used, where the methods for building and solving CP-SAT models are described in Table 1. In this way, the first two columns show the main methods (CpModel and CPSolver) and additional methods (Constraint) used to build and solve these CP-SAT models. In the third column these same methods and their function are described.

Table 1. Methods for building and solving CP-SAT models.

Main methods	CpModel	Create models, including variables and constraints (e.g., Maximize)
	CPSolver	Solving a model and evaluating solutions (e.g., Objective Value)
Additional methods	Constraint	A few utility methods for modifying constraints created by CpModel through the Add methods (for example, OnlyEnforceIf)

3.3 Procedure

In order to use OR-Tools to solve a problem, several steps must be followed. The basic steps for setting up and solving the problem mentioned above, is shown in Fig. 1.

Thus, in the beginning of the process, it is necessary to define the data for solving the problem, namely the number of nurses ("num_nurses"), number of shifts ("num_shifts") and number of days ("num_days"). It is also important to add nurse requests for specific shifts (if any). Then, the solver must be selected. After creating the model, in Step

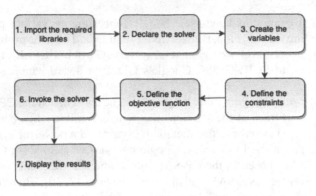

Fig. 1. Procedure to solve a problem using OR-Tools.

3, Boolean variable "shifts" are created for each combination of nurse, day and shift, generating an array of variables where the variable "shifts" [(n, d, s)] equals 1 if shift "s" is assigned to nurse "n" on day "d". Otherwise, this variable equals 0. Then, certain constraints are also selected and the assignment of shifts to nurses is defined as evenly as possible. If the total number of shifts and days is not evenly divisible by the number of nurses, then some nurses will be assigned more shifts than others. After this step, there is a need to define the objective function for the problem, where the goal is the number of assignment shifts that meet a request. In this way, it is generated a schedule that maximizes the number of requests that are met. For most scheduling problems, it is advisable to optimize an objective function because it is not practical to print out all possible schedules. In the end, the solver is invoked through "cp_model.CpSolver ()". The next step is to present the results, which contain an optimal schedule, the requested shift assignments, and the number of satisfied requests. The last step is the calculation of the associated statistics.

3.4 Problem Definition

In this study, a service manager in a long-term care unit needs to create a schedule for their sector, namely, for eleven nurses for seven days, since he schedules every week and is subject to several conditions. Each day is divided into three 8-h shifts (morning, afternoon, and night). In this example, shift 0 corresponds to the morning shift, shift 1 to the afternoon shift and shift 2 to the last shift in the night. There is a need to take into account the fact that one nurse is on vacation in this particular week, so a schedule will be created only for a total of 10 nurses. So, the number of nurses was defined as 10 (ranging from Nurse 0 to Nurse 9), the number of shifts as 3 and the number of days as 7 (ranging from Day 0 to Day 6).

Initially, nurses were assigned to shifts subject to the two general constraints. The first one ensures exactly that each shift is assigned to two nurses per day (Condition 1) and the second one guarantees that each nurse works at most one shift per day (Condition 2). When interpreting the results, it was found that the solutions obtained had three drawbacks: the nurse who works at the last shift (shift 2) on one day can work the morning shift (shift 0) the next day; the nurse who works the last two consecutive shifts can work any shift on the next day; the nurse who works on the last two days of the week (Day 5 and Day 6), referring to weekend days, can have more than two shifts during the week (from Day 0 to Day 4). These situations cannot happen because, in this service, these three specific particularities exist in the shifts.

So, there was a need to add three more constraints to ensure that these situations do not occur. In this way, the Conditions 3, 4 and 5 were included. More specifically, Condition 3 ensures that the nurse who works the last shift of one day does not work the next day's morning shift, as shown in Fig. 2. Condition 4 states that the nurse who works the last two consecutive shifts does not work any shift the next day (no shift) and Condition 5 establishes that the nurse who works the two weekend days (Day 5 and Day 6) has a maximum of 2 shifts on previous days (Condition 5).

There are also two requests from nurses for specific shifts and days, such as Nurse 1 wants to work the afternoon shift (shift 1) on the fifth day (identified as Day 4) and Nurse 9 who wants to work the morning shift (shift 0) on the first day (identified as Day 0).

```
for n in all_nurses:
    for d in range(num_days - 1):
        last_shift_of_day = shifts[(n, d, num_shifts - 1)]
        first_shift_of_next_day = shifts[(n, d+1, 0)]
        model.Add(last_shift_of_day.Not() + first_shift_of_next_day.Not() >= 1)

✓ 0.0s
```

Fig. 2. Condition 3 created to solve this specific problem.

In terms of programming the Condition 3, the "model.Add" function adds a constraint to the model that requires that at least one of the following conditions is true: either the last shift of the current day does not occur ("last_shift_of_day" is false) or the first shift of the next day does not occur ("first_shift_of_next_day" is false). In summary, it ensures that for each nurse, on each day, there is at least one rest period between the last shift of the current day and the first shift of the next day. In the fourth condition, the "model.Add" function also adds a constraint to the model. The constraint states that the sum of shifts worked in the three consecutive days (represented by the variables "last_shift_of_day_0", "last_shift_of_day_1", and "any_shift_of_day_2") should be at most 2. In resume, this code limits the maximum number of shifts worked by each nurse in a consecutive three-day period. Finally, in the fifth condition, the resulting sum is then constrained using "model.Add" to be less than or equal to 2, ensuring that nurses working on the last two days have a maximum of 2 shifts on the previous days.

4   Results and Discussion

All the code for obtaining the results is stored in an online repository (https://github.com/MarciaOliveira27/Project_OR-Tools_NSP). After executing the code, the solution containing an optimal schedule was displayed and this solution is shown in Fig. 3.

```
Solution:
Day 0
Nurse 0 works shift 1 (not requested).
Nurse 5 works shift 2 (not requested).
Nurse 6 works shift 0 (not requested).
Nurse 7 works shift 2 (not requested).
Nurse 8 works shift 1 (not requested).
Nurse 9 works shift 0 (requested).


Day 1
Nurse 1 works shift 0 (not requested).
Nurse 5 works shift 1 (not requested).
Nurse 6 works shift 0 (not requested).
Nurse 7 works shift 1 (not requested).
Nurse 8 works shift 2 (not requested).
Nurse 9 works shift 2 (not requested).


Day 2
Nurse 3 works shift 2 (not requested).
Nurse 4 works shift 1 (not requested).
Nurse 5 works shift 2 (not requested).
Nurse 6 works shift 0 (not requested).
Nurse 7 works shift 0 (not requested).
Nurse 8 works shift 1 (not requested).
```

Fig. 3. Part of the solution obtained from software OR-Tools.

Figure 3 shows the first 3 days of the nurses schedule for the long-term care unit. It is possible to see that each nurse is assigned to a specific shift and so to understand which nurse is on a day off. For example, on Day 0, which corresponds to the first day of the week, Nurse 6 and Nurse 9 are assigned to the morning shift (shift 0), Nurse 0 and Nurse 8 work the afternoon shift (shift 1), and Nurse 5 and Nurse 7 will do the night shift (shift 2). For the second day of the week (Day 1), Nurse 1 and Nurse 6 will work on the morning shift, Nurse 5 and Nurse 7 will be assigned to the afternoon shift and Nurse 8 and Nurse 9 will work the night shift. In that way, nurses 0, 2, 3 and 4 have a day off.

Finally, an Excel file was generated to visualize the solution data, using the Python programming language. Thus, the nurse schedule obtained using this software is presented in Fig. 4, where each shift is associated with a different color to make its interpretation easier. So blue corresponds to shift 0, pink to shift 1, green to shift 2 and yellow is associated with the non-working day. In this schedule, it can also be verified that the initially stipulated constraints have been fulfilled. For example, Nurse 7, when assigned to the night shift on the first day (day 0), will not work the morning shift (shift 0) on the next day, therefore, it satisfies Condition 3. Beyond that, Nurse 5 when he/she works two last consecutive shifts on third and fourth days (Day 2 and Day 3), has a day off on the next day, satisfying Condition 4. It should be noted that there were requests for two nurses, such as Nurse 1 wants to do the afternoon shift (shift 1) on the fifth day (identified as Day 4) and Nurse 9 wants to work the morning shift (shift 0) on the first day (identified as Day 0), that were achieved. In addition, it is possible to see that each shift is assigned to two nurses per day (Condition 1) and each nurse works at most one shift per day (Condition 2). And still Nurses 0, 1, 2, 3 and 4 who work on the last two days (Day 5 and Day 6) are assigned to 2 shifts on previous days (Condition 5). For last, each nurse is assigned to at least four shifts over the seven days, except for Nurse 6 and Nurse 9 that will work five shifts this week.

	Day 0	Day 1	Day 2	Day 3	Day 4	Day 5	Day 6
Nurse 0	shift 1	does not work	does not work	does not work	shift 2	shift 1	shift 0
Nurse 1	does not work	shift 0	does not work	does not work	shift 1	shift 1	shift 1
Nurse 2	does not work	does not work	does not work	shift 2	shift 1	shift 2	shift 2
Nurse 3	does not work	does not work	shift 2	does not work	shift 0	shift 0	shift 0
Nurse 4	does not work	does not work	shift 1	does not work	shift 0	shift 0	shift 1
Nurse 5	shift 2	shift 1	shift 2	shift 2	does not work	does not work	does not work
Nurse 6	shift 0	shift 0	shift 0	shift 1	does not work	does not work	shift 2
Nurse 7	shift 2	shift 1	shift 0	shift 1	does not work	does not work	does not work
Nurse 8	shift 1	shift 2	shift 1	shift 0	does not work	does not work	does not work
Nurse 9	shift 0	shift 2	does not work	shift 0	shift 2	shift 2	does not work

Fig. 4. Example of a nurse schedule made from OR-Tools solution in Excel.

At the end, there are some statistics that provide diagnostic information about the progress and performance of the solver, including the number of conflicts, the number of branches explored, and the total time taken. A conflict occurs when the problem constraints are not simultaneously satisfied, causing the solver to make choices and backtrack to find a valid solution. Branching refers to the process of making choices or decisions to explore different paths in the search space. The total time taken, defined by the elapsed time during the solving process in seconds, was equal to 0.041 s. Therefore, it is possible to verify that this process is super-fast and is always available in a quick way. Therefore, it becomes very useful for this service manager of a long-term care unit to program a nurse schedule every week.

5 Conclusion

In short, OR-Tools is highly optimized and designed to solve optimization problems efficiently. It comprises advanced algorithms that can handle large amounts of data and computational complexity, allowing to solve nurse scheduling problems more complex than the one presented. Another advantage of using this software is to obtain a fast response and that way, it is possible to create a schedule from one moment to another. This particularity can lead to faster and more effective decisions. This is crucial in an environment where nurse scheduling needs to be constantly updated to accommo-date unexpected changes. Getting a quick response saves time and resources, which is especially important in this sector.

In this paper, a small example for a scheduling of a week containing three shifts (morning, afternoon and night) to be assigned to a total of 10 nurses has been described. First, two constraints were defined in order to ensure that every day, each shift must have two nurses assigned, and that no nurse works more than one shift on any given day. Therefore, each nurse should be assigned to at least four shifts during the seven-day period to ensure that assignment of shifts to nurses is as fair as possible. Later, three more constraints were added to ensure that the nurse who works at the last shift on one day cannot work the morning shift the next day, the nurse who works the last two consecutive shifts cannot work any shift on the next day, and the nurse who works on the two days of the weekend, cannot have more than two shifts during the rest of the week.

Finally, after running the CP-SAT solver from the Google OR-Tools, the problem was solved and the nurses' calendar solution was presented. In this solution all the defined constraints were met. In addition, workload balance refers to the equitable distribution of tasks and responsibilities among individuals or teams to ensure a fair and manageable workload for all involved, which is crucial to, for example, optimizing efficiency, and avoiding burnout. It also ensures flexibility and adaptation, which are crucial factors in nurse scheduling to accommodate unforeseen changes, such as unexpected absences or changes in patient volume and ensure the efficient allocation of resources. It can take into consideration personal preferences and improved human resource management in a critical area of healthcare that contributes to employee satisfaction and overall efficiency.

In conclusion, this guarantees efficiency in resource allocation, which refers to optimizing the allocation of available resources while ensuring that the staffing levels meet the required demand. It causes a reduction of human errors that can have severe consequences, especially in such high-risk environments. In this way, healthcare organizations can enhance productivity, reduce costs, minimize overtime, and improve patient care.

Acknowledgments. The authors are grateful to the Foundation for Science and Technology (FCT, Portugal) for financial support through national funds FCT/MCTES (PIDDAC) to CeDRI (UIDB/05757/2020 587 and UIDP/05757/2020), SusTEC (LA/P/0007/2021) and ALGORITMI Research Centre/LASI (UIDB/00319/2020). Filipe Alves thanks the FCT for supporting its research with the PhD grant SFRH/BD/143745/2019.

References

1. Ferreira, M.S., Rocha, S.: The staff scheduling problem : a general model and applications Marta Soares Ferreira da Silva Rocha Faculdade de Engenharia da Universidade do Porto (2013)
2. Shuib, A., Kamarudin, F.I.: Solving shift scheduling problem with days-off preference for power station workers using binary integer goal programming model. Ann. Oper. Res. **272**(1–2), 355–372 (2019)
3. van Leeuwen, J.: Algorithms and Complexity 1. MIT Press, Cambridge (1998)
4. Turhan, A.M., Bilgen, B.: A hybrid fix-and-optimize and simulated annealing approaches for nurse rostering problem. Comput. Ind. Eng. **145**, 106531 (2020)
5. Glass, C.A., Knight, R.A.: The nurse rostering problem: a critical appraisal of the problem structure. Eur. J. Oper. Res. **202**(2), 379–389 (2010)
6. Burke, K.E., De Causmaecker, P., Berghe, G.V., Van Landeghem, H.: The state of the art of nurse rostering. J. Sched. **34**, 441–499 (2004)
7. Perron, L., Furnon, V.: OR-Tools. Google (2023)
8. Guenin, B., Könemann, J., Tunçel, L.: A Gentle Introduction to Optimization. University of Waterloo, Ontario (2014)
9. Nocedal, J., Wright, S.J.: Numerical Optimization. Springer, Heidelberg (2006)
10. Wiers, V.C.S.: A review of the applicability of OR and AI scheduling techniques in practice. Omega **25**(2), 145–153 (1997)

11. Ernst, A.T., Jiang, H., Krishnamoorthy, M., Owens, B., Sier, D.: An annotated bibliography of personnel scheduling and rostering. Ann. Oper. Res. **127**(1–4), 21–144 (2004)
12. Petrovic, S., Berghe, G.V.: Comparison of algorithms for nurse rostering problems. In: 7th International Conference on Practice Theory Automation, Timetabling, PATAT 2008, vol. 44, pp. 1–18 (2008)
13. Alade, O.M., Amusat, A.O., Adedeji, O.T.: Solving nurse scheduling problem using constraint programming (CP) technique. Asian J. Res. Comput. Sci. **1995**, 1–8 (2019)
14. Burke, E.K., Li, J., Qu, R.: A hybrid model of integer programming and variable neighbourhood search for highly-constrained nurse rostering problems. Eur. J. Oper. Res. **203**(2), 484–493 (2010)
15. Djordjević, J., Simić, D., Milutinović, D., Simić, S.: Challenges for nurse rostering problem and opportunities in hospital logistics. J. Med. Informat. Technol. **23**, 195–202 (2014)
16. Bellanti, F., Carello, G., Croce, F.D., Tadei, R.: A greedy-based neighborhood search approach to a nurse rostering problem. Eur. J. Oper. Res. **153**(1), 28–40 (2004)
17. Warner, D.M., Prawda, J.: A mathematical programming model for scheduling nursing personnel in a hospital. Manag. Sci. **19**(4-Part-1), 411–422 (1972)
18. Trivedi, V.M., Warner, D.M.: Branch and bound algorithm for optimum allocation of float nurses. Manag. Sci. **22**(9), 972–981 (1976)
19. Santos, H.G., Toffolo, T.A.M., Gomes, R.A.M., Ribas, S.: Integer programming techniques for the nurse rostering problem. Ann. Oper. Res. **239**(1), 225–251 (2016)
20. Burke, E., De Causmaecker, P., Vanden Berghe, G.: A hybrid tabu search algorithm for the nurse rostering problem. In: McKay, B., Yao, X., Newton, C.S., Kim, J.-H., Furuhashi, T. (eds.) SEAL 1998. LNCS (LNAI), vol. 1585, pp. 187–194. Springer, Heidelberg (1999). https://doi.org/10.1007/3-540-48873-1_25
21. Aickelin, U., Dowsland, K.A.: Exploiting problem structure in a genetic algorithm approach to a nurse rostering problem. J. Sched. **3**(3), 139–153 (2000)
22. Burke, E.K., Curtois, T., Post, G., Qu, R., Veltman, B.: A hybrid heuristic ordering and variable neighbourhood search for the nurse rostering problem. Eur. J. Oper. Res. **188**(2), 330–341 (2008)
23. Awadallah, M.A., Bolaji, A.L.A., Al-Betar, M.A.: A hybrid artificial bee colony for a nurse rostering problem. Appl. Soft Comput. J. **35**, 726–739 (2015)
24. Curtois, T., Qu, R.: Computational results on new staff scheduling benchmark instances. Technical Report, pp. 1–5 (2014)
25. Dowsland, K.A.: Nurse scheduling with tabu search and strategic oscillation. Eur. J. Oper. Res. **106**, 393–407 (1998)
26. Rahimian, E., Akartunalı, K., Levine, J.: A hybrid integer programming and variable neighbourhood search algorithm to solve nurse rostering problems. Eur. J. Oper. Res. **258**(2), 411–423 (2017)
27. Didier, F., Perron, L., Mohajeri, S., Gay, S.A., Cuvelier, T., Furnon, V.: OR-Tools' vehicle routing solver: a generic constraint-programming solver with heuristic search for routing problems, pp. 8–9 (2023)

Predicting the Solution Time for Optimization Problems Using Machine Learning
Case of Job Shop Scheduling Problem

Shaheen Pouya[1]([⊠]) [iD], Oguz Toragay[2] [iD], and Mehrdad Mohammadi[1] [iD]

[1] Industrial and Systems Engineering, Auburn University, Auburn, AL, USA
{shaheen.pouya,mzm0346}@auburn.edu
[2] Mechanical, Robotics, Industrial Engineering, Lawrence Technological University,
Southfield, MI, USA
otoragay@ltu.edu

Abstract. In organizations that use optimization and other computer-related problem-solving techniques, a better understanding of the required computational time is essential for efficient decision-making and resource allocation which also directly affects productivity and operational effectiveness. This study proposes the application of various Machine Learning (ML) methods to predict the computation time needed to solve job shop problems. Specifically, we implemented 11 ML models, including the Deep Neural Network (DNN), which delivered the most accurate results. The proposed approach involves utilizing a DNN algorithm to predict computation time for Integer Programming (IP) job shop problems, trained on synthetically generated data that indicate the gap-time correlation in a branch and bound tree. The developed model in this study estimates the total computation time with an accuracy of 92%. The model development process involves collecting data from a set of solved problems using the branch and bound method and training the ML models to estimate the computational time required to reach the optimal solution in unsolved similar problems.

Keywords: Machine Learning · Deep Neural Networks · Performance Evaluation · Job Shop Scheduling · Integer Programming · Branch and Bound Method · Computation Time Prediction

1 Introduction

Time is of utmost importance in the industrial landscape, particularly in the realm of optimization and computer-related problem-solving, as efficient and timely decision-making, directly impacts productivity, resource allocation, and overall operational effectiveness. Solving optimization problems poses challenges in modeling, setting constraints, and determining objective functions, with computation time being a crucial yet uncertain aspect, particularly in the context

A. I. Pereira et al. (Eds.): OL2A 2023, CCIS 1981, pp. 450–465, 2024.
https://doi.org/10.1007/978-3-031-53025-8_31

of Industry 4.0. In this study, we propose a DNN model that leverages historical data as gap-times pairs from solved problems and use that to accurately predict the total computation times required for the optimization problem. Having a good prediction of the total computation time for solving an IP (Job Shop problem in this case), could be of great help to schedule work in organizations. The job shop problem modeled as IPs are known to belong to the NP-hard group of optimization problems [15, 27]. For the mathematical model and detail of extracting the required data that we use for the training of the ML models in this study, we refer to the audience to our previous work [36]. Although many aspects of optimization problems have been utilized to train the ML models, to the best of the authors' knowledge there are no previous studies in the literature in which the training of the ML models can be done using the gap-time pair of data. In this regard, this study is unique and will pave the way for further investigation of these aspects of optimization models. The remainder of this study is structured as follows. We provide most related works from the literature in Sect. 2, then in Sect. 3 we discuss our methodology to prepare and scale the data in hand. In Sect. 4 we provide the detail of the ML methods and measures of accuracy that we use in this study and summarize the results of applied ML methods on the data. Also in Sect. 4, we further elaborate on the accuracy of the models in predicting the required computation time for job shop scheduling problems. We then conclude the paper by highlighting the main findings of the study and providing the potential extensions of this study for future work in Sect. 6.

2   Literature Review

Mathematical optimization problems involve finding the best solution from a set of candidates in a feasible region, considering specific criteria or constraints and one or more objectives. These models are widely applied across various fields, to improve efficiency, minimize costs, maximize performance, or optimize resource allocation. NP-hardness of mathematical optimizations reflects the computational challenges associated with finding optimal solutions. The scheduling problem, also known as the Job shop scheduling problem is one of the well-known combinatorial optimization problems that is known to be NP-hard and can be modeled as IPs. These problems involve determining the optimal sequence and timing for processing a given set of tasks on a group of machines while considering various constraints, including machine availability, job dependencies, and processing duration [10]. The objective typically revolves around minimizing certain types of costs, such as completion time, tardiness, or makespan. Alternatively, it may involve maximizing certain benefits, such as profit or earliness. For the mathematical model and more details about the problem at hand, we refer the reader to [36].

The branch and bound method (B&B) is a technique used to solve combinatorial optimization problems by systematically exploring the solution space and pruning branches that are guaranteed to yield sub-optimal solutions [24].

This iterative process requires sequential decision-making, such as node selection, i.e., selecting the next node to evaluate, and variable selection, i.e., selecting the variable by which to partition the node's search space [25]. It is particularly effective for problems with a large search space. B&B-based designed solvers, in each iteration, compare the best-found solution to the lower bound (minimization problem) and try to minimize the gap between the two solutions. In optimality, the gap is zero or negligibly small. Although B&B has been widely used to solve combinatorial optimization problems, including job shop scheduling problems, the size of the B&B tree and the required time to optimally solve the problem are unknown at the beginning of solving process.

There are many attempts in the literature to pre-calculate the size of the tree or the computation time of the optimization problems. For instance [14] investigates estimating the size of B&B trees for solving Mixed Integer Programming (MIP) problems. It proves limitations in approximating tree size and introduces a new measure called "leaf frequency". Various methods, including ML or Bayesian estimation, are explored to improve estimation accuracy [4]. Computational experiments demonstrate the effectiveness of the proposed approaches. Unlike [14], where the number of solved nodes in the B&B tree or time series have been suggested to estimate the tree size, in this work, we focus on the application of gap-solving time relation, and based on that, we estimate the computation time of a problem. Although the optimality gap is an important and useful measure of progress for the B&B method, authors in [31] in addition to gap define a measure called the sum of sub-tree gaps (SSG) which can be used for the predicting of computation time. Many benchmark problems have been solved using open-source solvers (CBC, SYMPHONY, and GLPK) because gathering the required data from commercial solvers simply is not possible. In this work, we gathered data from callback functions defined in Gurobi [13] commercial solver. Unlike [31], which is the closest in the literature to current work, we use only the gap values in specific intervals.

One of the first papers discussing the application of ML techniques in job shop scheduling is [30]. The paper discusses the importance of dynamically selecting scheduling rules for production line scheduling. Selecting the solving algorithm for the NP-Hard problem has been studied in [12]. The paper addresses the challenge of determining whether an instance of an NP-hard optimization problem is solvable or not, and if not, identifying the best approximate algorithm to solve it. Due to the difficulty of analytically characterizing the behavior of such algorithms, experimental methods have been employed. The paper presents an ML-based approach that utilizes algorithmic performance data to build models representing how performance relates to problem instance characteristics. An enhanced survey paper [39] discusses the use of ML for solving MIPs, which are known to be NP-hard. By leveraging ML techniques, researchers aim to provide solutions based on patterns learned from training data. The paper discusses the integration of ML and MIP, presents learning-based methods categorized as exact and heuristic algorithms, and explores future prospects for learning-based MIP solvers.

Regression models have been used to estimate tree size for instance in [14], where linear regression models with different numbers of features, regression tree, and random forest regression have been used. Applications of the ML techniques in the operations research literature primarily focus on three objectives: serving as heuristic solutions to optimization problems [2,29], enhancing the accuracy of solver algorithms, and estimating some aspects of optimization problems such as branch and bound tree in MIP models [14]. Authors in [5] survey various applications of ML in both solving combinatorial optimization problems as well as learning the best strategy in doing the branch and bound tree search (branching policies, node selection, etc.). In a study by Larsen et al. [23], a Neural Network is trained to predict solutions for a stochastic load planning problem. The researchers aim to address the problem's stochasticity caused by incomplete information and the need for tactical decision-making. They utilize operational solutions from a deterministic version of the problem and aggregate them to provide targets for the ML model. For scheduling problems early works such as [16] suggested using a Hopfield neural network to solve a general job-shop scheduling problem. [35] proposed a parallel neural network similar to the Hopfield network to solve the single-machine mean tardiness scheduling problem. They also categorized the existing literature on using neural networks for scheduling problems into three categories: Hopfield model networks, Competitive Networks, and Backpropagation networks. They define each job as a neuron and a network of $n \times n$ neuron matrix for which only one of the neurons is active in each row. In another attempt [3], the author explored the use of Artificial Neural Networks (ANNs) to model six heuristic algorithms for flow-shop scheduling problems with the makespan criterion. The objective is to minimize makespan by predicting job completion times on each machine. Fuzzy membership functions are employed to incorporate scheduling uncertainty. The trained networks offer a faster alternative to conventional iterative methods for generating solutions. To model the functional relationship between the input and output variables, multilayered feedforward networks (MFNs) trained with error backpropagation learning rules are used. Recently, the DNN has been applied to predict the optimal makespan of countless different problems [28] such as the job shop scheduling problem in [38]. Using Deep Learning reduces the time of finding optimal solutions to the problem, without much human effort, by up to 9% compared to the baseline method. Authors in [11] introduce a novel Graph Convolutional Neural Network (GCN) model that learns variable selection policies for branch-and-bound algorithms. This approach utilizes the inherent bipartite graph structure of MILPs, representing variables and constraints. By training our model using imitation learning from a strong branching expert rule, we show significant improvements over existing ML methods for branching. Moreover, our approach demonstrates the ability to generalize to larger problem instances beyond the training data, as evidenced by its performance on a series of challenging problems. The random-forest-based approach applied in [18] to learn dispatching rules in a flexible job shop scheduling problem. Authors, in three phases, first find the schedule using three existing solution approach. After identifying the best schedules, the process of rule learning involves transforming the schedules into training data by creating new attributes. This transformed data is then used to generate a dispatching rule through inductive learning. In the final step, the rule improvement phase enhances the dispatching rules using a genetic algorithm. This involves discretizing continuous attributes and adjusting parameters for the random forest algorithm, to minimize the average total weighted tardiness. Authors in [33] developed regression models and trained a neural network to predict the makespan of jobs in a batch process industry and compare the prediction results. They concluded that the estimation quality of the neural network models appears significantly better than the quality of regression models.

Tackling the difficulties in making decisions when B&B is used to solve the combinatorial optimizations, Khalil et al. in a series of papers proposed using the ML techniques for solving combinatorial optimization problems over graphs [20], and learning the branching decisions [21]. In [20] the proposed approach combines reinforcement learning and graph embedding and utilizes a learned greedy policy that acts as a meta-algorithm, gradually building a solution. The decision-making process is influenced by a graph embedding network that captures the current state of the solution. The framework proves to be versatile, as it can be applied to various optimization problems involving graphs. The approach effectively learns algorithms for problems such as Minimum Vertex Cover, Maximum Cut, and the Traveling Salesman problem. In [20] three branching strategies, i.e., Strong Branching (SB), Pseudocost Branching (PC), and ML-based branching where the learned weight vector is used to score variables (branching on the one with maximum score) have been compared and authors showed that ML-based strategy makes a significantly smaller search tree. In addition to exact methods ML techniques are also integrated into metaheuristic methods to improve their performance in terms of solution quality, convergence rate, and robustness in solving combinatorial optimization problems. An extended review paper [19] surveyed 136 papers on the intersection of ML and Metaheuristics (MH). In [37], the aim is to explore how ML tools can be used to predict the viability of a production plan. Typically, production schedules deviate from the initial plans because these plans do not consider all the specific requirements that arise during the scheduling phase. The study demonstrates that by using a decision tree to predict the feasibility of a production plan, a precision rate of approximately 90% can be achieved, surpassing the 70% precision rate typically obtained by classical capacity constraints in planning tools.

3   Methodology and Data

The main focus of this study is to use ML models to accurately estimate the required computation time for a job shop scheduling problem. Utilizing these models to predict the total computation time after the branch and bound process has reached a certain gap (such as 20%), provides valuable insights into the optimization processes. Especially in real-world implementations, knowing how long the solving of a problem is going to last, could be beneficial for better and more agile work orders. The codes and algorithms, as well as the feeding data, have been uploaded to the project's GitHub repository[1] and are publicly available and ready to be used for replication of the results and further investigations.

The feeding data that we used in the ML models are generated by a code specifically developed by the authors to extract computation times to reach certain gaps (20%, 10%, 5%, and 0% gap from global solution in which 0% meaning the total solution time) for randomly generated scheduling problems with a predetermined number of machines and jobs. The data has been collected from solving 12 different IP scheduling problems (based on a different combination of the number of machines and the number of jobs in the system) with 100 replication of each problem that in total, generated 1200 data points. While there are no missing points in the collecting process as well as the feeding data in this study, the ML models, especially regression models [26], can be affected by missing data [9]. Table 1 summarizes the collected data by providing the average of 100 replications of times to reach a specific gap in each row. As the given feeding data have been generated and gathered under precise and supervised conditions, there is no need to implement any kind of pre-processing or cleaning of the data to increase the accuracy of ML models' results. The only process that has been implemented for some of the ML models is scaling which we explained in detail in the following.

Table 1. The summary of feeding data.

Run	# of Machines	# of Jobs	20% Gap	10% Gap	5% Gap	0% Gap
1	5	8	0.3	1.1	2.1	2.5
2	5	9	0.9	5.5	22.6	49.3
3	5	10	7.5	160.4	1443.0	5368.2
4	6	8	0.2	0.9	1.8	2.3
5	6	9	0.6	4.8	19.5	43.9
6	6	10	5.2	118.8	1313.0	5585.5
7	7	8	0.1	0.8	1.9	2.6
8	7	9	0.4	3.8	18.5	73.1
9	7	10	3.2	64.5	634.8	3454.7
10	8	8	0.1	1.0	3.5	5.5
11	8	9	0.3	3.3	18.1	73.7
12	8	10	1.3	28.1	308.1	2657.0

Most of the regression techniques in ML require scaling the data before training the models. Feature scaling, also known as data normalization, is a technique used to adjust the range of independent variables or features in data [34]. It is

---

[1] https://github.com/oguztoragay/ML4JS.

commonly applied during data pre-processing to ensure a consistent and comparable scale for the features. The main reason for scaling the data in this research is to manage the magnitude of features which is an issue in the feeding data with a great range of numbers as computation times of the IP models. More specifically, the computation times that the problem instances reach the predefined gap values, are varied between 0.1 s to more than 100,000 s. On one hand, scaling has benefits such as enhancement of the gradient descent optimization process (especially for categorical-based regression algorithms), on the other hand, many regression models including linear regression and decision tree, perform poor under scaling condition [34]. In this research, to further understand the effect of scaling on the result of the implemented ML models, both scaled and real data are tested for all the models, and only the most accurate scores are reported.

Although in many studies, it is recommended to use the scaled normalization for skewed data [6,32] (and previous study by the authors [36] showed that the feeding data is skewed), for the deep learning model, the actual data were used since better results were obtained. Moreover, since the results from Standard Scaling were significantly better than the Normalization, only the scores using Standard Scaling are stated in the results section of this article. However, the normalization codes are available in the dedicated Github repository and ready to be tested. As we mentioned, the only criteria to use either standard-scaled data, normalized data, or actual data is the highest obtained accuracy from the models so in this work we report those results for each model that has the highest accuracy using different data types (among the three above mentioned). Focusing attention on the theoretical reasoning of differences between the accuracy of various models on various data is out of the scope of this article.

4   Results

In this section first, we explain the measures that we used to compare the accuracy of the models, then discuss the results in detail. Since the main motivation in this study is to predict the most accurate estimations of the computation times, two highly recognized and well-developed measurement methods are used to evaluate the accuracy of each model [22].

1. **Mean Absolute Percentage Error (MAPE):** This is a statistical metric used to measure the accuracy of a forecasting or prediction model [8]. It calculates the average percentage difference between the predicted values and the actual values using Equation (1):

$$\mathbf{MAPE} = \frac{1}{n} \sum_{i=1}^{n} \frac{|Actual_i - Predicted_i|}{Actual_i} \times 100 \tag{1}$$

MAPE is a percentage representation that signifies the discrepancy between the model's predictions and the actual observations. A smaller MAPE value implies a higher level of accuracy in the model's forecasting. MAPE allows for comparison of forecasting accuracy across different data sets or models, regardless of the scale or magnitude of the data [8].

2. **Mean R Squared Error (R^2):** This is a measurement that indicates how well a regression model fits the observed data. It ranges from 0 to 1, with higher values indicating a better fit. This accuracy measure is calculated using Equation (2):

$$\mathbf{R}^2 = 1 - \frac{SSR}{SST} \tag{2}$$

Where:
- SSR is the Sum of Squares Residual which represents the sum of the squared differences between the observed values and the predicted values.
- SST is the Total Sum of Squares that represents the sum of the squared differences between the observed values and the mean of the dependent variable.

Without loss of generality, for the sake of differentiating MAPE values from R^2 values, in this research, we use MAPE's real values (between zero and one) instead of expressing them as percentages.

For measuring the accuracy of each model, a test set was extracted from the data and then compared with the predicted numbers by that model. Using the test and predicted split functions, 20% of the data was assigned to the test set, and the remaining 80% was used for training the model. The data splitting function picked points for the train and test sets randomly using the related packages such as Scikit learn [32]. Since the range of the results (times) is so broad and the absolute error measurements (such as R^2) do not consider the relative error for each point [8], in this study, the main estimation to measure the accuracy is MAPE.

4.1 Applied Machine Learning Models

Each of the ML models that we employed in this research has its own set of assumptions, strengths, and limitations. The following set of models has been employed to predict the outputs in this study.

1. Linear Regression
2. Kernel Ridge Regression
3. Elastic Net Regression
4. Bayesian Ridge Regression
5. Gradient Boosting Regression
6. LGBM Regression
7. Decision Tree Regression
8. Polynomial approximation of Linear Regression
9. Support Vector Regression (SVR)
10. Multi-Layer Perceptron (MLP)
11. Deep Neural Network (DNN)

Although many of the listed models may yield better results with proper tuning of the model parameters, we avoid the fine-tuning, for the sake of simplicity, and focus more on the models with promising performance. Such fine-tuning endeavors are mostly conducted for the last three models which showed better performance even before the fine-tuning. For the first regression models, we have only tuned the depth parameter of the Decision Tree Regressor to 12 and for the Polynomial Regularization, we tried a set of degrees between 2 to 5 and found out that degree 3 has the best outcomes which then are selected as the parameter for Polynomial Regularization model.

Table 2. Accuracy measures of all the models

Features	Data	Models										
		(1)	(2)	(3)	(4)	(5)	(6)	(7)	(8)	(9)	(10)	(11)
		Scaled	Scaled	Scaled	Scaled	Scaled	Actual	Actual	Scaled	Scaled	Scaled	Actual
All	MAPE	1.00	0.82	0.83	0.92	0.35	0.79	0.36	0.99	0.32	0.59	0.23
	R^2	80.3%	74.5%	33.5%	75.6%	49.6%	19.7%	48.3%	-1724.0%	79.7%	80.9%	92.3%
Partial	MAPE	0.46	0.43	0.77	0.47	0.38	0.81	0.38	0.70	0.38	0.69	0.27
	R^2	75.6%	78.5%	42.2%	77.8%	48.9%	35.1%	37.1%	-2535.2%	74.1%	71.2%	83.2%

Table 2 summarizes the accuracy of all the models listed and numbered in 4.1. These ML models are applied to the full-featured data, (including all five features namely, all three gap times, the number of machines, and the number of jobs). The models also have been trained and checked on partially featured data (including only the three gap times) for which the results are given in the last two rows on Table 2 denoted by "Partial". Summarized results show that the best accuracy can be achieved by implementing the DNN model and accordingly most of the endeavors in this study are directed toward the perfection of that approach. On the other hand, there are many parameters to increase the accuracy of other model's results and probably the correct regularization function might lead to a more accurate prediction of the computation time. However, finding the perfect fit for all models regarding this data is out of the scope of this research.

For each run of each model, we implemented a cross-sectioning with $K = 25$ folds for the models to generate more accurate results. As mentioned before, both actual and scaled data were fed to all the models, and only the most accurate results are reported for each model. The best results (except for the last three models which will be investigated separately) are from the decision tree with a MAPE of approximately 0.36 on real data and Gradient Boosting Regression on Scaled data with a MAPE of 0.354. Considering the R^2 score, Linear Regression and Bayesian Ridge Regression seem to have the best results. On the other hand, eliminating two of the features, i.e., number of machines and number of jobs, does not seem to have a significant effect on the accuracy of the results for most of the regression models such as "Gradient Boosting" with MAPE of 0.35 when all features are used and 0.38 when the number of machines and jobs are not used. Even in some cases the MAPE and R^2 accuracy scores are better without those two parameters (for instance in the case of "Elastic Net Regression").

Note that throughout this study, the negative high percentages of the R^2 occur when the trained model's predictions are worse than the average test values. As shown in Table 2, the Polynomial Regularization model happens to have this problem, and it's negative R^2 indicates that even random results are better than that model's predictions. Even though ML models are widely applied in various fields and a fast pace research on their development boosts their accuracy, our results reveal that even for a relatively simple data set, the accuracy measures (here we applied two of them, MAPE and R^2) yield different outcomes answering the inquiry for the most accurate model. This lack of coherence in the developed accuracy measures, on one hand, is beneficial for the field as it encourages more in-depth research, and on the other hand is challenging for the applicants of those models to find the best combination of models, accuracy measures, fine-tuning, and hyperparameters to understand, analyze and predict their data with the highest possible accuracy.

In the next sections, a slightly deeper review of the two models (SVR and MLP) is presented and finally, the most accurate and promising model (DNN) is fully analyzed.

4.2   Support Vector Machine Regression

For the SVR model, in addition to the full-featured data, we also used several partially featured data sets. Preliminary results showed that for this model, the best outcomes are achieved after scaling the data. As a consequence, the MAPE scores are considerably lower than using the actual data (using full features, the MAPE of scaled data is 0.324 while the MAPE of actual data is 1.98). Using the available packages for tuning and testing different types of kernel functions, i.e., SciKit Learn package's tuner [32], it turns out that for our data set a prediction function of Radial Basis Function (a.k.a. 'rbf') performs the best while the Penalty parameter (C) is 1000, gamma (influence) is 0.0001 and epsilon (margin of tolerance) is 0.01.

The results were under cross-validation of 25 folds ($K = 25$). Table 3 indicates the results of implementing the SVR method on the full and partially featured data. Note that for each set of features, we report both MAPE and R^2 metrics. Based on the score results reported in Table 3, we observe that in the best case, SVR can predict the results with MAPE of 0.324 and R^2 of 79.7%.

4.3   Multi-layer Perceptron Regression

There are some fundamental differences between a Multi-Layer Perceptron (MLP) model and a DNN model such as (usually) having fewer hidden layers and especially implementing a feed-forward direction while DNNs are using loops with backpropagation [17]. Accordingly, the training time of MLPs is less than DNNs and requires less hyperparameter tuning and, they might generate results with lower accuracy. For this research, the standard scaled data generated the best results (for actual data MAPE was 1.079 and for scaled data, MAPE was 0.586 using full features). Using a similar package as SVR, the tuning process of MLP is also conducted using the GridSearch package by SciKit learn [32]. Fine-tuning resulted in the following parameters for MLP:

Table 3. Accuracy scores for SVR model implemented on full and partial data

Features for SVR	Measure	Score
All	MAPE	0.324
	R^2	79.7%
20% Gap time, 10% Gap time, 5% Gap time	MAPE	0.383
	R^2	74.1%
20% Gap time, 10% Gap time, Number of Machines and Jobs	MAPE	0.675
	R^2	51.4%
20% Gap time, 10% Gap time	MAPE	0.588
	R^2	46.9%
20% Gap time, Number of Machines and Jobs	MAPE	1.179
	R^2	5.8%
20% Gap time	MAPE	1.116
	R^2	8.5%

- The size of hidden layers: (50, 100, 50),
- Activation Function: Rectified Linear Unit (relu),
- Solver: adaptive moment estimation (adam),
- Alpha: 0.001, and 'Constant' learning rate.
- Maximum iteration was confined to 5000 (due to time constrain)

The hyperparameters were tuned for best performance using all available features. All scores are the results of cross-validation with $K = 25$ folds. Table 4 shows the accuracy scores using the fine-tuned MLP model on the full and partial feature data set.

Table 4. Accuracy scores for MLP model implemented on full and partial data

Features for MLP	Measure	Score
All	MAPE	0.586
	R^2	80.9%
20% Gap time, 10% Gap time, 5% Gap time	MAPE	0.691
	R^2	71.2%
20% Gap time, 10% Gap time, Number of Machines and Jobs	MAPE	1.392
	R^2	−8.4%
20% Gap time, 10% Gap time	MAPE	1.152
	R^2	0.9%
20% Gap time, Number of Machines and Jobs	MAPE	2.306
	R^2	−15.7%
20% Gap time	MAPE	1.795
	R^2	−8.5%

The results in Table 4 show that the accuracy is reduced drastically when fewer items are fed to the model. This observation might be related to the tuning of the model which has been conducted on the full-featured data. It turns out that, despite its more complicated network, MLP, cannot achieve a better MAPE score than Linear Regression or SVR while it is expected to predict more accurate results. A simple explanation for this phenomenon might be the linear behavior of this study's data while MLP models are usually best performing for categorization problems than regression problems.

Another observation during the measurement of accuracies using MLP models was that there were a great variety of good and bad results while running the codes for cross-validation. Despite the fact that the tuning process of MLP has been set with 2000 iterations and 25 folds, running the tuner at different times, generated different values as the best hyperparameters set. Moreover, during the cross-validation process, the reported MAPE and R^2 scores were indicating results with very high accuracy (as high as 0.083 MAPE or 98% R^2) while in many replications, the accuracy could not get even close to the accuracy of other models (such as MAPE of 2.58 for one run). Probably, with more data, the model could be better trained to have more homogeneous results.

4.4   Deep Neural Network

The last model that we developed and tested in this study is the DNN model [7] which (as expected) predicts the most accurate results. Assuming that there is a connection between the reported gap times and the final solution time, this model generates the closest predictions to the real computation times in the data set. Although 1800 observations could be a relatively small number for a model with more than 800 nodes; still this model was able to have the most accurate results with a close range for all runs. DNN's characteristics have been determined by using the "tuner" search package in TensorFlow [1] tool in Python. The best hyperparameters as well as the number and size of hidden layers are listed below:

- Number of Hidden Layers: 6 (options: 2 to 10 layers)
- Size of hidden layers: [224, 256, 96, 256, 32, 32] (options: 32 to 512 nodes, the step of 32)
- Activation function: Rectified Linear Unit (relu) (options: relu, elu, exponential, sigmoid, softmax, tanh, and linear)
- Last layer's activation function: linear
- Loss function: mean absolute percentage error
- learning rate: 0.002 (options: $1e-2$, $1e-3$, $1e-4$, $5e-2$, $5e-3$, $5e-4$, $2e-3$, $3e-3$, and $1e-4$)
- optimizer: adaptive moment estimation (adam)

The final layer utilizes a linear activation function since the model aims to forecast the computation time, which is a continuous numerical value, as opposed to a categorical value. The results of the model are summarized in Table 5. The

Table 5. Accuracy scores for DNN model implemented on full and partial data

Features for DNN	Measure	Score
All	MAPE	0.231
	R^2	92.3%
20% Gap time, 10% Gap time, 5% Gap time	MAPE	0.267
	R^2	83.2%
20% Gap time, 10% Gap time, Number of Machines and Jobs	MAPE	0.439
	R^2	49.6%
20% Gap time, 10% Gap time	MAPE	0.283
	R^2	80.4%
20% Gap time, Number of Machines and Jobs	MAPE	0.663
	R^2	2.7%
20% Gap time	MAPE	0.689
	R^2	−1.5%

model was set and tuned for the best performance under full features and each score is cross-validated with 25 runs.

Based on the reported results in Table 5, for our data set, the lowest MAPE as well as the highest R^2 can be achieved using the DNN model. The trend in the accuracy scores in Table 5 shows that fewer features indicate less accurate predictions. It is a valid conclusion that feeding larger and broader data sets to the model can generate more accurate predictions. This observation also suggests that using a few data points reporting the gap times in the B&B process (here we used only 3 data points for each observation) to train the model, could possibly generate a very accurate model in predicting the computation times.

It is worth noting that the observed trend in the feature-accuracy correlation in this model could be related to the fact that the model has been tuned using the full features data and accordingly fewer features might need another architecture of DNN. Moreover, a large neural network with 6 hidden layers might not be a suitable model when only two or three features are fed to the model. For instance, concerning the last row of the above table when only one feature (20% gap time) is fed to the model, a much simpler DNN model with only one 64-node hidden layer could predict scoring 0.71 for MAPE. Having the best accuracy requires tuning the model for each set of features that are being used to predict computation time which could be an interesting subject for future studies. Finally, since deep learning models are more complex than other ML models, they usually require more data which requires more generation of B&B computation times. It is a strong estimation that with more data points the power of prediction could be even better.

5   Discussion

By developing a DNN model, we managed to predict the total computation time to an acceptable state. Although the computation time is significantly dependent on the characteristics of each computer and each model, there is a possibility to add the concept of our presented code (available on Github) to the solvers or use the exact code for each computer to create data points and later use them to predict computation time. The applicability of this approach is not confined to scheduling or job shop problems but it also can be applied to any environment where data similar to the gap to the final solution (as in B&B) is yielded.

By investing more time into building a better model (such as adding it to any of the current solvers), and especially by recording more times (for instance recording the related times for every gap value from 20% to 0%), there is a discernible chance to improve the accuracy of the presented model. The following can be considered as possible extensions of this research: studying the effects of a larger data set on the accuracy of the models, the effects of missing data on each ML method, determining the most vulnerable method in case of having missing data, and finally studying the effectiveness of the same approach on other similar optimization problems.

6   Conclusion

The process of solving optimization problems has a lot of unknowns such as modeling, setting constraints, and objective functions. One of the biggest unknowns and challenges in this process is the computation time. Especially the new industrial revolutionized processes such as Industry 4.0 show the importance of addressing such problems even more. The simple progress in utilizing the B&B method to solve IPs could be seen as a great source of information. In this regard, using related times of initial gaps in the B&B process for predicting the final solution time could be considered the simplest example. On many occasions, engineers with a little experience in the B&B method, use "verbose" functions in the solvers to see the current gap to the ultimate solution while solving the real problems and empirically predict the final solution times just by using their implicit knowledge. In this situation and with the usage of existing data of the previous "solved" problems with their related gap times, we managed to predict the final solution time to a very accurate state.

Moreover, even if the computer is in a state where less than 5% of the gap to the ultimate solution is remaining, it is known that only around 25% of the total time (depending on the difficulty of the problem) [36] has passed and having a good estimation of the total computation time is gravely beneficial for industrial purposes. It could also be a great opportunity for the solvers to implement this algorithm into their systems and predict total computation times on the fly as a part of their report, especially since they can train their deep learning model very fast by a few data points and later reinforce it with newer data.

References

1. Abadi, M., et al.: Tensorflow: large-scale machine learning on heterogeneous distributed systems. arXiv preprint arXiv:1603.04467 (2016)
2. Abolghasemi, M., Abbasi, B., Babaei, T., HosseiniFard, Z.: How to effectively use machine learning models to predict the solutions for optimization problems: lessons from loss function. arXiv preprint arXiv:2105.06618 (2021)
3. Akyol, D.E.: Application of neural networks to heuristic scheduling algorithms. Comput. Ind. Eng. **46**(4), 679–696 (2004)
4. Asadi, N., Ghoreishi, S.F.: Bayesian state estimation in partially-observed dynamic multidisciplinary systems. Front. Aeros. Eng. **1**, 1036642 (2022)
5. Bengio, Y., Lodi, A., Prouvost, A.: Machine learning for combinatorial optimization: a methodological tour d'horizon. Eur. J. Oper. Res. **290**(2), 405–421 (2021)
6. Buitinck, L., et al.: Api design for machine learning software: experiences from the scikit-learn project. arXiv preprint arXiv:1309.0238 (2013)
7. Chien, J.T.: Chapter 7 - deep neural network. In: Chien, J.T. (ed.) Source Separation and Machine Learning, pp. 259–320. Academic Press (2019). https://doi.org/10.1016/B978-0-12-804566-4.00019-X. https://www.sciencedirect.com/science/article/pii/B978012804566400019X
8. De Myttenaere, A., Golden, B., Le Grand, B., Rossi, F.: Mean absolute percentage error for regression models. Neurocomputing **192**, 38–48 (2016)
9. Emmanuel, T., Maupong, T., Mpoeleng, D., Semong, T., Mphago, B., Tabona, O.: A survey on missing data in machine learning. J. Big Data **8**(1), 1–37 (2021)
10. Garey, M.R., Johnson, D.S., Sethi, R.: The complexity of flowshop and jobshop scheduling. Math. Oper. Res. **1**(2), 117–129 (1976)
11. Gasse, M., Chételat, D., Ferroni, N., Charlin, L., Lodi, A.: Exact combinatorial optimization with graph convolutional neural networks. Adv. Neural Inf. Process. Syst. **32**, 1–13 (2019)
12. Guo, H., Hsu, W.H.: A machine learning approach to algorithm selection for np-hard optimization problems: a case study on the MPE problem. Ann. Oper. Res. **156**(1), 61 (2007)
13. Gurobi Optimization, L.: Gurobi optimizer reference manual (2021)
14. Hendel, G., Anderson, D., Le Bodic, P., Pfetsch, M.E.: Estimating the size of branch-and-bound trees. INFORMS J. Comput. **34**(2), 934–952 (2022)
15. Hoorfar, H., Bagheri, A.: Np-completeness of chromatic orthogonal art gallery problem. J. Supercomput. **77**(3), 3077–3109 (2021)
16. Jain, A.S., Meeran, S.: Job-shop scheduling using neural networks. Int. J. Prod. Res. **36**(5), 1249–1272 (1998)
17. Jiang, M.R., Feng, X.F., Wang, C.P., Zhang, H., et al.: Robust color image watermarking algorithm based on synchronization correction with multi-layer perceptron and cauchy distribution model. Appl. Soft Comput. **140**, 110271 (2023)
18. Jun, S., Lee, S., Chun, H.: Learning dispatching rules using random forest in flexible job shop scheduling problems. Int. J. Prod. Res. **57**(10), 3290–3310 (2019)
19. Karimi-Mamaghan, M., Mohammadi, M., Meyer, P., Karimi-Mamaghan, A.M., Talbi, E.G.: Machine learning at the service of meta-heuristics for solving combinatorial optimization problems: a state-of-the-art. Eur. J. Oper. Res. **296**(2), 393–422 (2022)
20. Khalil, E., Dai, H., Zhang, Y., Dilkina, B., Song, L.: Learning combinatorial optimization algorithms over graphs. Adv. Neural Inf. Process. Syst. **30** (2017)

21. Khalil, E., Le Bodic, P., Song, L., Nemhauser, G., Dilkina, B.: Learning to branch in mixed integer programming. In: Proceedings of the AAAI Conference on Artificial Intelligence, vol. 30 (2016)
22. Kreuzberger, D., Kühl, N., Hirschl, S.: Machine learning operations (mlops): overview, definition, and architecture. IEEE Access **11**, 31866–31879 (2023)
23. Larsen, E., Lachapelle, S., Bengio, Y., Frejinger, E., Lacoste-Julien, S., Lodi, A.: Predicting tactical solutions to operational planning problems under imperfect information. INFORMS J. Comput. **34**(1), 227–242 (2022)
24. Lawler, E.L., Wood, D.E.: Branch-and-bound methods: a survey. Oper. Res. **14**(4), 699–719 (1966)
25. Lodi, A., Zarpellon, G.: On learning and branching: a survey. TOP **25**, 207–236 (2017)
26. Marcelino, C., Leite, G., Celes, P., Pedreira, C.: Missing data analysis in regression. Appl. Artif. Intell. **36**(1), 2032925 (2022)
27. Mohabbati-Kalejahi, N., Yoon, S.W.: Parallel machines scheduling problem for minimization of maximum lateness with sequence-dependent setup times. In: IIE Annual Conference, Proceedings, pp. 837. Institute of Industrial and Systems Engineers (IISE) (2015)
28. Morteza, A., Yahyaeian, A.A., Mirzaeibonehkhater, M., Sadeghi, S., Mohaimeni, A., Taheri, S.: Deep learning hyperparameter optimization: application to electricity and heat demand prediction for buildings. Energy Build. **289**, 113036 (2023)
29. Largani, S.M., Lee, S.: Efficient sampling for big provenance. In: Companion Proceedings of the ACM Web Conference 2023, pp. 1508–1511 (2023)
30. Nakasuka, S., Yoshida, T.: Dynamic scheduling system utilizing machine learning as a knowledge acquisition tool. Int. J. Prod. Res. **30**(2), 411–431 (1992)
31. Özaltın, O.Y., Hunsaker, B., Schaefer, A.J.: Predicting the solution time of branch-and-bound algorithms for mixed-integer programs. INFORMS J. Comput. **23**(3), 392–403 (2011)
32. Pedregosa, F., et al.: Scikit-learn: machine learning in python. J. Mach. Learn. Res. **12**, 2825–2830 (2011)
33. Raaymakers, W.H., Weijters, A.: Makespan estimation in batch process industries: a comparison between regression analysis and neural networks. Eur. J. Oper. Res. **145**(1), 14–30 (2003)
34. Raschka, S., Liu, Y.H., Mirjalili, V., Dzhulgakov, D.: Machine Learning with PyTorch and Scikit-Learn: Develop Machine Learning and Deep Learning Models with Python. Packt Publishing Ltd. (2022)
35. Sabuncuoglu, I., Gurgun, B.: A neural network model for scheduling problems. Eur. J. Oper. Res. **93**(2), 288–299 (1996)
36. Torağay, O., Pouya, S.: A monte carlo simulation approach to the gap-time relationship in solving scheduling problem. J. Turk. Oper. Manag. **7**(1), 1579–1590 (2023)
37. Tremblet, D., Thevenin, S., Dolgui, A.: Predicting makespan in flexible job shop scheduling problem using machine learning. IFAC-PapersOnLine **55**(10), 1–6 (2022)
38. Wang, T., Payberah, A.H., Vlassov, V.: Convjssp: convolutional learning for job-shop scheduling problems. In: 2020 19th IEEE International Conference on Machine Learning and Applications (ICMLA), pp. 1483–1490. IEEE (2020)
39. Zhang, J., et al.: A survey for solving mixed integer programming via machine learning. Neurocomputing **519**, 205–217 (2023)

Optimization in the SDG Context

Schedule Modeling in a Fire Station: A Linear Approach to Optimize Service and Human Resources

Ana Rita Silva[1] , Helena Sofia Rodrigues[1,2,4]($\boxtimes$) , and Ângela Silva[1,3,4]

[1] Instituto Politécnico de Viana do Castelo, Viana do Castelo, Portugal
{sofiarodrigues,angela.a}@esce.ipvc.pt
[2] CIDMA - Centro de Investigação e Desenvolvimento em Matemática e Aplicações, Universidade de Aveiro, Aveiro, Portugal
[3] ADiT-LAB, Instituto Politécnico de Viana do Castelo, Viana do Castelo, Portugal
[4] ALGORITMI Research Centre, University of Minho, Guimarães, Portugal

Abstract. Associations of Volunteer Firefighters form the basis of helping the Portuguese population. In these institutions, to guarantee the first line of assistance, there are volunteers and also a group of professional firefighters. However, there are not always enough funds to hire the human resources effectively needed, or even to guarantee the continuity of services provided 24 h a day. In this work, the linear programming method was used to study a schedule problem, and the simulations presented were carried out at Excel OpenSolver. The aim was to understand the minimum number of firefighters needed to meet the demands of the population and to guarantee a quick response to requests that may occur over the day. Even with some restrictions associated with the specific roles of each firefighter, it was possible to design several scenarios, involving different shifts, and left the decision of the best solution for the responsible of the fire station taking into account the trade-off between costs and provided service.

Keywords: Firefighter · Scheduling · Linear Optimization

1 Introduction

Health services in Portugal have seen a marked development, in order to meet the needs of the population and to adapt to the increased demands [1].

In Portugal, fire brigades are the agents of Civil Protection which have a higher level of activity, and the greatest geographic coverage [2]. In Portugal, the rescue of populations is essentially based on volunteer firefighters, who are prepared to respond immediately to needs and disasters, whether serious accidents

Supported by Portuguese Foundation for Science and Technology (FCT - Fundação para a Ciência e a Tecnologia).

or catastrophes, primarily at local level, articulating with a single command at district or national level [3]. Just a few corporations manage to guarantee a service of excellence in supporting the population by resorting only to professional firefighters, mainly due to the lack of financial resources.

Additionally, firefighter work plays a crucial role in creating sustainable cities and communities. Their intersects with various aspects of sustainable cities and communities, such as public safety, disaster risk reduction, urban fire management, collaboration, community engagement, and infrastructure protection [4].

In a natural way, is easy to connect the firemen work with the Sustainable Development Goals (SDG). The 2030 agenda, adopted by all Member States of the United Nations, consists of 17 sustainable development goals, which must be implemented [5]. Three goals are intrinsically related to firefighters.

SDG 3, "Good Health and Well-Being", intends to guarantee access to quality health and promote well-being for all, at all ages, taking as main points to reduce the mortality rate, reduce the number of deaths and injuries in road accidents. Through emergency medical response, fire prevention and safety education, disaster response and relief efforts, firefighters actively contribute to ensuring access to healthcare services, reducing injuries and deaths, and protecting public health [6].

SDG 11 "Sustainable Cities and Communities" is related to firemen works, because they contribute to creating sustainable cities and communities by ensuring public safety and emergency response. They play a crucial role in minimizing the impact of disasters, including fires, which can cause significant damage to urban areas [7].

Firefighting work also plays a significant role in achieving SDG 13, "Climate Action". They are on the front lines of combating the effects of climate change. As the frequency and intensity of wildfires increase due to climate change, firefighters work to suppress and manage these fires, protecting ecosystems, communities, and infrastructure [8].

For all these reasons, investing in fire stations that are efficient and committed to their community is a key factor in achieving a sustainable society. This investigation tend to answer the following research question: which is the minimum of firefighters required to ensure all services during the working period?

In Sect. 2, a literature review is carried out, explaining the different types of firefighters, as well as the entities in charge, and also the importance of teamwork. This section will also address the various types of shifts, as well as their main risks. Further, the dynamics of the current operation, as the number of operatives necessary for each task and their shifts is explained. Section 3 discusses the methodology used in this work, namely the use of linear programming, resorting to free software. The results of five scenarios are presented in Sect. 4, and the main conclusions and limitations of the study are exposed in Sect. 5.

2 Literature Review

2.1 Firefighters

According to data extracted from Pordata [9], in 2022, at the end of 2022 there are 465 fire departments and 26,123 firefighters in the Portugal. We can define a firefighter as being the individual who, professionally or voluntarily integrated into a fire department, has the activity of fulfilling the missions of the fire department, namely the protection of human lives and property in danger, through the prevention and fire extinguish. According to the Portuguese law, the following types of fire departments may exist:

- Professionals: include only professional collaborators and are created under the direct responsibility of the City Council;
- Mixed: made up of volunteer and professional firefighters, created under a Municipal Council or a Humanitarian Association of Firefighters;
- Volunteers: made up only of staff on a voluntary basis, however the legislation allows for a minimum number of professional firefighters
- Private: private fire brigades may be constituted and belong to a private legal person, with a view to protecting its activity or assets

Furthermore, in a fire station, there are operators who work on a fixed schedule, while other workers work on a shift schedule. Therefore, it is important to explain the main aspects and impacts of shift work.

2.2 Fixed vs Rotating Shifts

In today's society, more and more people work in shifts, as there are new economic and productive strategies, mainly due to the globalization of the market [10]. In this way, the organization and distribution of working hours becomes fundamental for a correct structuring of work among the various employees.

According to Moz [13], the distribution of employees by work shifts can be organized into 5 phases:

1. Staffing: determination of the number of workers needed for the normal functioning of the organization and work
2. Allocation: sizing of employees for each shift
3. Scheduling: creation of scales, in a certain period of time (weekly or monthly)
4. Rostering: Assignment of defined rosters to each worker
5. Rerostering: this phase may be optional, however it will consist of adapting the scale to the worker in the event of an unexpected event.

The different shifts can have a very different impact on the health and wellbeing of employees, especially when this involves night work. Fatigue and drowsiness affect the state of alertness and vigilance, jeopardizing their work and safety and that of everyone around them [10–12].

Thus, it is understood that the organization of working hours in rotating shifts may cause disturbances for the worker, both in terms of health and safety.

Rotating shifts often involve night work, making it even more complicated for the worker, since the body is geared towards rest during these hours [14].

Speaking of firefighters in Portugal and due to the level of demand that the profession demands, such as physical robustness, visual and auditory capacity, physical agility and a high level of concentration, it is crucial that professionals are in the full state of their abilities, which is why it is necessary to who perform and are entitled to the correct rest days [1].

In shift work, like all other jobs, there are also advantages, the main ones being: a different routine for the worker, easier family life, differentiated compensation and flexibility in personal life [15].

2.3 Team Work

In order to guarantee quality work, especially in the firefighter profession, it is essential to work as a team, guaranteeing its effectiveness. The effectiveness of teams has an impact on the satisfaction, viability and high performance of all members [16].

The effectiveness of teamwork depends on numerous factors, such as access to shared information, flexibility and communication between members, that is, it depends on the physical environment where it is inserted. Otherwise, it could lead to absenteeism, turnover and decreased employee satisfaction [16,17].

Furthermore, effective teams are only possible if they have adequate resources, if there is effective leadership, as well as a climate of trust between team members and hierarchical superiors [18].

2.4 In a Fire Station

Taking the knowledge acquired in a Portuguese fire station, the work of professional firefighters is usually divided into 4 teams: Call Center; Rescue Ambulance team; Non-Urgent Transport team; and Permanent Intervention Team. Some of the task requires special training and therefore, the fire fighters are usually permanently assigned to a function. Example given, a call center operator can not be part of the Rescue Ambuance team if does not have additional training.

The Call Center (CC) team should work 24 h per day, 7 days per week, in order to receive all the call that the population make. Usually works in rotating shifts.

The Non-Urgent Transport (NUT) team is the team responsible for non-urgent transport, that is, the one whose objective is to obtain the provision of health care for the user. These transports have their origin and/or destination at an establishment of the National Health Service, or with an agreement with the same, and can be used in case of: consultation; hospitalization or surgery, exams, complementary means of diagnosis and therapy. Usually it works in a fixed schedule, and it is only necessary one firefighter per ambulance.

The Rescue Ambulance (RA) team the emergence team. It is intended for the stabilization and transport of patients who need assistance during transport, thanks to the equipment they have that allow the application of basic life support measures. They aim to ensure a quick displacement of the crew, which must be trained in medical emergency techniques, and can always be complemented with other pre-hospital emergency means, as well as the transport of the victim to the most appropriate health unit. Each ambulance works with two specialized firefighters.

Finally, the Permanent Intervention team is a specialized force, and work with a fixed number of elements (one team leader and four firefighters). This team guarantees, at all times, assistance to the population in the following cases: fire fighting; assistance in case of floods, landslides, accidents or catastrophes; help for shipwrecked people; complementary help, in a second intervention; and minimization of risks in the event of a serious accident. Due to its specifications and hiring restrictions at the level of the competent authorities, this team will not be the object of study in this work.

3   Methodology

A linear optimization problem has been formulated for the fire station scheduling. Its objetive is to minimize the required amount of personal and posing retrictions on labour laws, minimum number of firefighters necessary to perform the specialized tasks.

Linear programming is a mathematical method used to solve operational research problems, regarding the optimization of resources in the different tasks or activities that must be carried out [19]. Linear programming is used to optimize decision problems and can be adapted to different realities. These models are made up of decision variables, the objective and the restrictions, which represent the conditions that have to be fulfilled [20].

The first approach to solve the problem was to use the Solver add-in of Excel [21]. It is a basic implementation of Simplex, in order to be able to solve linear programming studies. When applying Solver in real situations, it is frequent to realize that it is limited to a certain number of variables. Due to limitations of the number of constraints and variables, it was necessary to use a more robust version, OpenSolver. OpenSolver is an optimizer for Microsoft Excel that allows solving models in linear programming, offering better performance than Solver [22].

4   Mathematical Model

The objective of this work is to understand the smallest number of firefighters that, satisfying the labor laws and simultaneously seeking to guarantee the longest possible time of service provision.

Therefore 5 scenarios were carried out, which differ in the number of working hours of the teams, as well as in the schedules and/or shifts that each one ensures, night time and weekend time (see Table 1).

In the first scenario, there was a concern to ensure that all types of teams were available 24 h a day, every day of the week. However, not all services make sense to be permanently available (as is the case of non-urgent transport), so, other scenarios were taken to manage other types of schedules for some teams. Each scenario will be presented in detail in the following subsections.

Table 1. Schedule available for each team (CC - Call Center, RA - Rescue Ambulance, NUT - Non-Urgent Transport) in the different scenarios on working days

Scenario	Team	Hours (1–24)
A	CC	all hours shaded (1–24)
A	RA	all hours shaded (1–24)
A	NUT	all hours shaded (1–24)
B	CC	all hours shaded (1–24)
B	RA	all hours shaded (1–24)
B	NUT	all hours shaded (1–24)
C	CC	all hours shaded (1–24)
C	RA	all hours shaded (1–24)
C	NUT	shaded approx. hours 9–18
D	CC	all hours shaded (1–24)
D	RA	all hours shaded (1–24)
D	NUT	shaded approx. hours 9–18
E	CC	all hours shaded (1–24)
E	RA	all hours shaded (1–24)
E	NUT	shaded approx. hours 9–18

In the model, we assume that the fire station is equipped with a call center, an emergency rapid response ambulance, and three ambulances for scheduled and non-urgent services.

In a general way, it is necessary to define the two indices. The index $i \in I$ regards to the firefighter specialization task (teams), that are $1 = CC$; $2 = NUT$; $3 = RA$. The index $j \in J$ is concern to the staggered shift for firefighter, ranging from 1 to 4 or from 1 to 5, depending on the scenario. In scenarios A and E, where firefighter work more hours per week, j refers to $1 = $ night, $2 = $afternoon, $3 = $morning, and $4 = $day-off; in the other scenarios, it were considered 5 parts, namely $1 = $night, $2 = $afternoon, $3 = $morning, $4 = $dawn, and $5 = $day-off .

Additionally for each scenario were consider the decision variables:

x_{ij} : number of firefighters from team i on shift j

It is intended to minimize the number of firefighters used in each scale, so the objective function can be defined as the minimization of:

$$Z = \sum_{i \in I} \sum_{j \in J} x_{ij} \tag{1}$$

Additionally, we have several constraints:

– at least one operator/firefighter on each shift in the CC task

$$x_{1j} \geq 1, \forall j \tag{2}$$

– at least three operators in each NUT team for each shift

$$x_{2j} \geq 3, \forall j \tag{3}$$

– at least two operators in each RA team for each shift

$$x_{3j} \geq 2, \forall j \tag{4}$$

– the total number of available operators (N)

$$\sum_{i \in I} \sum_{j \in J} x_{ij} \leq N \tag{5}$$

– the total number of Call Center Operators (N_{CC})

$$\sum_{j \in J} x_{1j} \leq N_{CC} \tag{6}$$

– the total number of NUT Operators (N_{NUT})

$$\sum_{j \in J} x_{2j} \leq N_{NUT} \tag{7}$$

– the total number of NUT Operators (N_{RA})

$$\sum_{j \in J} x_{3j} \leq N_{RA} \tag{8}$$

5   Scenarios and Results

In this section, more details are given for each scenario, as well as the results of the minimum number of firefighters needed to satisfy the described model.

Table 2. Solution of OpenSolver for scenario A

x_{11}	x_{12}	x_{13}	x_{14}	x_{21}	x_{22}	x_{23}	x_{24}	x_{31}	x_{32}	x_{33}	x_{34}	Z
1	1	1	1	3	3	3	3	2	2	2	2	24

5.1   Scenario A

Scenario A considers that the three functions are present 24 h a day in the fire station, every day of the week, working in 8-h shifts. In this way, 4 shifts are required (NAMO): Night (N, from 11 pm to 7 am), Afternoon (A, from 3 pm to 11 pm), Morning (M, from 7 am to 3 pm), and Day-Off (O).

Since there are 3 types of operatives and all of them work in shifts, 12 variables will be needed to formulate the simulation.

After using OpenSolver, the obtained solution is depicted in Table 2

Given the obtained solution, one firefighter is guaranteed for each call center shift, three firefighters for each NUT team guaranteeing the operation of the three available ambulances and two firefighters for each RA team, allowing the full operation of the emergency ambulance. In this way, the total number of operatives needed to guarantee this service is 24 firefighters.

5.2   Scenario B

In scenario B, the teams also provide specialized services 24 h a day, 7 days a week. However, each firefighter only performs shifts of 6 h each, meets the work of 36 working hours per week. Therefore, it is necessary to have more shifts per day, namely NAMDO: Night (N, from 7 pm to 1 am), Afternoon (A, from 1 pm to 7 pm), Morning (M, from 7 am to 1 pm), Dawn (D, 1 am to 7 am), and Day-Off (O).

With these constraints the model have 3 specialized teams and 5 shifts, giving a total of 15 decision variables.

Table 3. Solution of OpenSolver for scenario B

x_{11}	x_{12}	x_{13}	x_{14}	x_{15}	x_{21}	x_{22}	x_{23}	x_{24}	x_{25}	x_{31}	x_{32}	x_{33}	x_{34}	x_{35}	Z
1	1	1	1	1	3	3	3	3	3	2	2	2	2	2	30

In Table 3 is possible to see the expected increase in firefighters needed to cover the entire week's service. It went from 24 firefighters in scenario A, to 30 firefighters in scenario B. Each specialized team had to increase one shift leading to an increase of 6 additional firefighters to be hired.

5.3   Scenario C

Observing the two previous scenarios, it appears that the firefighters assigned to non-urgent and scheduled transport are also working all night and early morning hours. Now this type of service is made to help people who cannot travel by their own means for routine consultations, means of diagnosis or even therapy services. Thus, these are hours that would not have served and would be incurring additional costs to the fire station.

In this scenario there are two teams with rotating shifts of 6 h each (CC and RA), with NAMDO scheme and two schedules with fixed shifts of 6 h each were defined for the NUT team: a fixed shift for the morning schedule (7 am to 1 pm) and a fixed for the afternoon schedule (1 pm to 7 pm). Additionally, these firefighters have to work on Saturdays, in order to complete their week schedule. A total of decision variables were design and solution is given in Table 4.

Table 4. Solution of OpenSolver for scenario C

x_{11}	x_{12}	x_{13}	x_{14}	x_{15}	x_{21}	x_{22}	x_{31}	x_{32}	x_{33}	x_{34}	x_{35}	Z
1	1	1	1	1	3	3	2	2	2	2	2	21

Even with the NUT service ensured from 07:00 to 19:00, which is the most usual period to guarantee non-urgent medical services, it was possible to considerably reduce the number of firefighters assigned to the fire station. Additionally, allowing fixed shifts may increase the quality of job satisfaction provided by these operators.

5.4 Scenario D

Having in mind that the simulations describes a small-sized firestation and that there are a small number of urgent calls during the night shift, it was decided to study this scenario with the call center teams with 6-h rotating shifts, over the course of all week (NAMDO scheme), the NUT teams with fixed 6 h shifts ensuring the service from 7 am to 7 pm, from Monday to Saturday, and the NUT teams with fixed 6 h shifts, guaranteeing a response from 7 am to 1 am. In this way, both the rescue ambulance team, which works in 3 fixed shifts (morning, afternoon and night), and the non-urgent transport team, which works in two fixed shifts (morning and afternoon), guarantee their service during the Saturday, with the right to be off on Sunday.

Table 5 shows that is only necessary to have 17 firefighters in the fire station to ensure this schedule.

Table 5. Solution of OpenSolver for scenario D

x_{11}	x_{12}	x_{13}	x_{14}	x_{15}	x_{21}	x_{22}	x_{31}	x_{32}	x_{33}	Z
1	1	1	1	1	3	3	2	2	2	17

It should be noted that this decrease in the hiring of human resources has an important price to bear in mind: the emergency service during the early hours of the morning (1 am to 7 am) on any day, as well as on Sundays, remains unanswered by this association of firemen. Thus, it is essential that there is a network of collaboration and a prompt response from nearby fire station so that the population can be helped in a timely manner.

5.5   Scenario E

Scenario E is perhaps the closest to the reality of a fire station in Portugal. Non-specialized teams, such as the call center and non-urgent transport, have 8-h shifts per shift, while specialized teams, such as the emergency ambulance, have 6-h shifts.

In this way, it was decided to simulate 8 h rotating shifts for the CC team (NAMO scheme), two fixed shifts for the NUT teams ensuring a schedule from 7 am to 7 pm and three fixed shifts for the RA teams, ensuring a schedule from 7 am until 1 am, from Monday to Saturday.

Table 6. Solution of OpenSolver for scenario E

x_{11}	x_{12}	x_{13}	x_{14}	x_{21}	x_{22}	x_{31}	x_{32}	x_{33}	Z
1	1	1	1	3	3	2	2	2	16

Table 6 shows that there was a decrease in a decision variable, compared to the previous scenario. This is due to the fact that firefighters assigned to the call center work 8-h shifts, reducing the need for an extra shift. Furthermore, despite not being seen in the model solution, there was an increase in the service time provided by the NUT teams by 2 h per day.

Thus, when drawing up the timetables assigned to each specialized task, the person in charge will always have to think not only of the human and material resources available, but also the best allocation of them to guarantee a quality service to the surrounding community.

Table 7 summarizes the solutions for the 5 scenarios. As expected, the reduction of shifts from 8 to 6 h leads to an increase in human resources to do the same work. Whenever there are rotating shifts, we have to take into account that there is a team that is on a given day off, and by the way, it has to be taken into account when accounting for human resources. The reduction of working hours, transforming rotating shifts into fixed shifts, may have added inconveniences, namely the obligation to work on Saturdays to complete the shift. But what is more worrying about withdrawing the 24-h service provided by the emergency team is the non-guarantee of quick assistance by a neighboring fire brigade, at times when the fixed shifts of this team do not operate (dawn and Sunday).

Table 7. Summary of distinct scenarios

Scenario	Team	Shift Scheme	Type of Shifts	Hours of service	No. firefighters per team	Total of firefighters
A	CC	NAMO	rotating	0 h–24 h	4	24
	NUT				12	
	RA				8	
B	CC	NAMDO	rotating	0 h–24 h	5	30
	NUT				15	
	RA				10	
C	CC	NAMDO	Rotating	0 h–24 h	5	21
	NUT	—	Fixed	7 h–19 h	6	
	RA	NAMDO	Rotating	0 h–24 h	10	
D	CC	NAMDO	Rotating	0 h–24 h	5	17
	NUT	—	Fixed	7 h–19 h	6	
	RA	—	Fixed	7 h–01 h	6	
E	CC	NAMO	Rotating	0 h–24 h	4	16
	NUT	—	Fixed	7 h–19 h	6	
	RA	—	Fixed	7 h–01 h	6	

6   Conclusions

Ensuring that the fire brigade covers a service of the highest quality and with an immediate response to the population is essential, so it becomes necessary to study the available schedules, as well as the length of service of each team in the firehouse. Thus, 5 different scenarios were simulated with the intention of understanding which one best fits the current requirements and needs of the population.

The number of required firefighters varies depending on the number of hours each firefighter can work, as well as the type of shift to be contracted (fixed or rotating).

Rotating shifts, ensuring all hours of the day and all days of the week lead to more costly solutions, while placing fixed shifts on only part of the day leads to less demand for human resources, but the concern of not ensuring an effective response at all times.

In order to decide the best scenario to adopt at a fire station, it is up to the corporation to verify, through the number of calls by the emergency services, the pertinence of ensuring night and early morning shifts, and the total effective firemen have to distribute in a responsible way the human resources.

The study presented has some limitations, in the 8-hour per shifts, only the NAMO schemes were considered, while in the 6-hour per shifts the NAMDO scheme were used. Considering that the number of requests and peak work remain stable, it is possible to use only these shifts. However, in the daily reality of a corporation there are absences from work (holidays, sick leaves), or even peaks at certain hours, or seasonal work peaks, making it necessary to create new shifts, or reinforce already used shifts. Additional schemes for the shifts, ensuring at the same time, the labour rights of the firefighters and their work break could be simulated in order to give more answers to the schedule of a fire station.

Acknowledgements. This work has been supported by FCT - Fundação para a Ciência e Tecnologia within the R&D Units Project Scope: UIDB/00319/2020. It is also supported by The Center for Research and Development in Mathematics and Applications (CIDMA) through the Portuguese Foundation for Science and Technology (FCT - Fundação para a Ciência e a Tecnologia), references UIDB/04106/2020 and UIDP/04106/2020. This research is part of Ana Rita Silva logistics master thesis.

References

1. Costa, F. J.: A saúde no trabalho: a realidade de quem socorre. Masther Thesis. Instituto Politécnico de Viana do Castelo (2015)
2. Moura, D., Oliveira, E.: Fighting fire with agents: an agent coordination model for simulated firefighting. In: Proceedings of the 2007 Spring Simulation Multiconference, vol. 2, pp. 71–78. Society for Computer Simulation International (2007)
3. Amaro, A.D.: O socorro em Portugal : organização, formação e cultura de segurança nos corpos de bombeiros, no quadro da Protecção Civil. PhD Thesis, universidade do Porto (2009)
4. United Nations Office for Disaster Risk Reduction. Sendai Framework for Disaster Risk Reduction 2015–2030 (2015)
5. United Nations.: Transforming our world: the 2030 Agenda for sustainable development (2016)
6. Devine, M., Bond, RR., Simms, V., Boyce, K. E., Kerr, DP.: Mapping the health, safety and wellbeing challenges of firefighting to wearable devices. In: Paper presented at British HCI Conference 2018, Belfast, Northern Ireland, pp. 1–5 (2018)
7. Raffer, C., Scheller, H., Peters, O.: The UN sustainable development goals as innovation drivers for local sustainability governance? examples from Germany. J. Public Sector Econ. **46**(4), 459–487 (2022)
8. Thangavel, K., Spiller, D., Sabatini, R., Marzocca, P., Esposito, M.: Near real-time wildfire management using distributed satellite system. IEEE Geosci. Remote Sens. Lett. **20**, 1–5 (2023)
9. Pordata. https://www.pordata.pt/portugal/numero+de+bombeiros-1188. Accessed 5 May 2023
10. Costa, G.: Shift work and occupational medicine: an overview. Occup. Med. **53**(2), 83–88 (2003)
11. Chiang, S.L., et al.: Impact of rotating shifts on lifestyle patterns and perceived stress among nurses: a cross-sectional study. Int. J. Environ. Res. Public Health **19**(9), 5235 (2022)
12. Zverev, Y.P., Misiri, H.E.: Perceived effects of rotating shift work on nurses' sleep quality and duration. Malawi Med. J. **21**(1), 19–21 (2009)
13. Moz, M., Pato, M.V.: An integer multicommodity flow model applied to the rerostering of nurse schedules. Ann. Oper. Res. **119**, 285–301 (2003)

14. Costa, D.: Trabalho por turnos e descanso semanal - A atualidade de uma antiga controvérsia. Masther Thesis. Universidade Católica Portuguesa (2020)
15. Domingos, C.S.: Impacto do trabalho por turnos na saúde dos trabalhadores Caso dos Polícias de Segurança Pública (PSP). Masther thesis. Universidade do Porto (2017)
16. Francisco, A. S. (2017). O impacto do ambiente físico na eficácia do trabalho em equipa. Masther thesis. ISCTE (2017)
17. Schmutz, J.B., Meier, L.L., Manser, T.: How effective is teamwork really? the relationship between teamwork and performance in healthcare teams: a systematic review and meta-analysis. BMJ Open 9(9), e028280 (2019)
18. Bação, A.S.: Desenvolvimento do trabalho em equipa num contexto de cultura de safety: Estudo de caso numa empresa da indústria mineira. Masther thesis. Universidade de Évora (2023)
19. Scalabrin, I., Mores, C.J., Enderli Bodanese, R., Oliveira, J. A.: Programação linear: estudo de caso com utilização do solver da Microsoft Excel. Em Revista Universo Contábil (pp. 56–66). Blumenau, Brasil: Universidade Regional de Blumenau (2006)
20. Teles, R.E.: Desenvolvimento de uma ferramenta de apoio à alocação de recursos humanos Aplicação ao centro de distribuição da FNAC Portugal. Masther Thesis. ISCTE (2018)
21. Kowalik, P., Rzemieniak, M.: Binary linear programming as a tool of cost optimization for a water supply operator. Sustainability 13, 3470 (2021)
22. Mason, J.: OpenSolver – an open source add-in to solve linear and integer progammes in excel. In: Operations Research Proceedings, pp 401–406 (2012)

Help us to Help: Improving Non-urgent Transport on a Portuguese Fire Station

Emanuel Lopes[iD], Eliana Costa e Silva[✉][iD], Óscar Oliveira[iD],
and Wellington Alves[iD]

CIICESI, ESTG, Politécnico do Porto, Felgueiras, Portugal
emanuellopes96@gmail.com, {eos,oao,wal}@estg.ipp.pt
https://ciicesi.estg.ipp.pt/

Abstract. In Portugal, the transport of non-urgent patients is mostly performed by fire stations. These non-profit organizations have tight budgets and cannot afford to buy expensive software to improve their services. Furthermore, it is not always easy to find open-source tools. In this research, an open-source solver, developed in Visual Basic for Applications, was used and adapted as a case study to analyze the case of a fire station in the North of Portugal. The modifications to the solver are presented and real instances are tested. An analysis of the environmental impacts that originated during transportation is presented, summarizing the main implications caused by this activity. The results show better use of the ambulances' capacity and significant reductions in the traveled distances and in the fire station's ecological footprint.

Keywords: OR in Practice · Vehicle Routing Problem · Sustainability

1 Introduction

The transport of non-urgent patients refers to the transportation of individuals who need to move between healthcare facilities and their homes for medical appointments (including all types of medical examinations and therapies) that are not considered emergencies. It also includes the transport to the homes of patients after discharge from the hospital or from an emergency episode [8].

However, despite the fact that the use of transportation is considered a strategic activity to ensure the flow of goods as well as the transport of non-urgent patients around the globe, this sector is responsible for a significant impact of global greenhouse gas (GHG) emissions (see [15]). According to [3], transportation accounts for 25% of global carbon emissions, and is the main contributor to global climate change. Thereby, the non-urgent transport service has a negative environmental impact, since it contributes to air and health pollution. As a consequence, improving the transport of non-urgent patients can contribute to reducing the environmental and social negative impacts of this activity, namely the impact on air and health.

Although several methods and software solutions have been developed to solve this issue, manual selection is still used in most Portuguese fire stations for planning appointments and routes for the transport of non-urgent patients. This procedure is time-consuming and does not guarantee the better possible use of the available resources, as the distances traveled by the vehicles may be larger than necessary and their capacity may be underused. Reducing the distance traveled by the ambulances will contribute to reducing the burned fuel and the vehicles' wear, and consequently reduce the environmental impact of this type of transport.

The transport of patients may be classified as primary or secondary. Primary transport is carried out between the location where the need is generated and the corresponding healthcare institution, while secondary transport is relative to the transport of patients between healthcare institutions. Furthermore, in any of the previous cases, the transport may be urgent or non-urgent. Thus, the following four categories are considered in Portugal, as well as in most countries [4], for patients' transport: (i) primary urgent; (ii) secondary urgent; (iii) primary non-urgent; and (iv) secondary non-urgent.

In Portugal, most of the transport of patients is performed by fire brigades, which can be categorized into three groups: professional, volunteers and mixed. Nonetheless, it is important to highlight that most of the firefighters are volunteers. In fact, less than 10% of the firefighters in Portugal do not belong to any volunteer fire station [7]. Volunteer and professional firefighters have equal knowledge and skills and, therefore, can perform the same activities. However, non-urgent transport is usually carried by professionals. The most common fire station type is hybrid. In these, the majority of the firefighters are paid[1] and the other firefighters are 100% volunteers. Sappers are fully paid and their fire stations are only present in large cities and belong to the City Council [7].

According to [12], to improve non-urgent transport it is necessary to create standards for quality and safety systems, as its implementation will decrease the risk of the operations and make it more efficient. According to these authors, new software and technologies should be used to improve patients' satisfaction. In fact, patients' satisfaction and perceived quality are very important for the healthcare sector, particularly for non-urgent transport [11]. Different aspects of non-urgent transport have been studied, and while some works focus on the accordance with the law [4] others focus on reducing costs and traveled distances [24].

The present work aims to provide an alternative to manual selection, focusing on primary transport of non-urgent patients, that can be used by fire stations. In particular, modifications of the open-source solver proposed in [10] are presented. Then, real instances extracted from real data provided by a fire station located in the north of Portugal are tested. Due to the importance of the environmental impact caused by the transport sector, the emissions caused during transportation are analyzed and discussed.

The fire station has in its facilities a physiotherapy clinic and provides transport for patients to and from their treatments. In this fire station, transport is carried out in nine-seat ambulances. Each ambulance driver receives a list of

---

[1] But they also have to do volunteer hours.

patients to transport and their appointment times[2]. Each driver departs from the fire station and collects the patients at their homes at most one hour prior to appointment time[3] and transports them to the clinic for the appointments. The service provided by this fire station is very appreciated, but the users report the need to improve the service in order to reduce the long waiting times that still occur frequently.

The remainder of this paper is organized as follows. The literature on non-urgent transport is reviewed in Sect. 2. Section 3 presents the methodology, more specifically, the modifications made to the solver are explained. Next, the numerical results, obtained on 20 instances extracted from real data provided by the (above-mentioned) fire station, are presented and discussed in Sect. 4. Finally, in Sect. 5, conclusions are drawn and future work is proposed.

2   Literature Review

In recent years, the healthcare transport sector has been the subject of considerable research. The focus has been on creating innovative tools, including software and techniques, to aid decision-making processes, ultimately benefiting the service provided by healthcare institutions involved in transportation.

Several approaches have been explored to address this issue, and a significant portion of them treat it as a Vehicle Routing Problem (VRP) – a classic optimization problem in the field of operations research and logistics [10]. The VRP involves finding the most efficient manner to satisfy the demand or provide services to a set of customers using a fleet of vehicles from a central location (i.e., the depot) minimizing the overall cost – typically represented as the distance traveled or time taken [6] – while satisfying certain constraints. The list of VRP variants is quite extensive as different objective(s) and/or constraints can be considered. For example, variations of the VRP include Time Windows (VRPTW), where specific time intervals are incorporated for visiting each location [27]. Another variant is the Capacitated Vehicle Routing Problem (CVRP), which takes into account the maximum capacity of the vehicles [6]. The Periodic VRP (PVRP) is another type. This involves assigning customers to routes in predefined time periods to meet specific service level requirements such as visit frequency or time lag constraints [19]. Lastly, the VRP with Simultaneous Pick Up and Delivery (VRPSPD), where items must be both picked up and delivered on the same route [2]. We refer to [14] for a review of the VRP variants.

Several tools exist to solve VRP and its variants. The tool presented in [1] was developed with CPLEX Optimization Studio and was able to find solutions for the PVRP. However, it has the drawback of requiring long computational times which is impractical for daily use in fire stations. In [17], transport of non-urgent patients was treated as a VRP and a Dial-a-Ride Problem (DARP).

---

[2] Note that, the appointment times are defined priory by the physical therapists.

[3] E.g., for a patient with an appointment at 11:00 a.m. the time window 10:00 a.m. to 11:00 a.m. is considered.

Using the general algebraic modeling language GAMS, the authors were able to achieve better results than those obtained by using manual selection.

In [21], a mathematical model and a heuristic were developed to minimize the costs of transporting non-urgent patients by reducing the distances. The model, based on Team Orienteering Problem, was intended to find several routes from the same depot to the different points that must be visited and returned to the depot. More specifically, the model was implemented in the algebraic modeling language AMPL and solvers from the NEOS Server[4] were used to solve different instances. However, due to limitations of memory usage, some points were not visited, since the solver stopped before finding a solution that included all the points. The heuristic procedure was based on the iterative resolution of problems with a single vehicle with a capacity of up to eight patients. According to the authors, this heuristic provided good accuracy and computational time results.

In [24], a single day of work, several vehicles, multiple depots, and destinations are considered in the transport of non-urgent patients. The objective was to find better routes to reduce costs. For that, a DARP-based model was developed for the case study. Furthermore, the authors recommended the usage of mathematical modeling languages and methods, for better decisions and planning in this type of organization.

Additionally, the possibility of introducing efficient routes can be seen as an alternative to reduce greenhouse gas. In fact, all types of vehicles, such as cars, SUVs, and small vans, can account for around 60% of GHG, which configures the most polluting economic sector [25]. Cao and Liu, in [3], analyzed the impact of population aging on CO_2 emissions in transportation. The authors refer that due to the significant amount of emissions caused during the transport of goods and passengers, the transportation sector is considered one of the sectors with the most significant impact on climate change. Therefore, it is imperative to develop initiatives to minimize the negative impacts on the environment and society.

Hanne et al. [13] refer to the fact that the transport of patients is often underestimated by many hospitals. In fact, the delay of a single patient could have a large impact on the hospital's costs, since, due to the snowball effect, other services in the organization can be delayed. In [13], the OPTI-TRANS – a software that plans the entire hospital logistics (from booking, scheduling, monitoring and final reporting) – was proposed. Treating the problem as a DARP, the software was able to find the best routes in terms of costs and time for transport between hospitals, demonstrating the benefits of using integrated logistic tools in the healthcare sector. In fact, communication between hospitals was improved and savings in non-urgent transport were achieved.

Smith et al. [26] state that scheduling the transport of non-urgent patients without criteria is a very expensive decision. Further, every aspect of the transport, namely, vehicles, depots, timetable, destination, return home and all the intervening parts, should be carefully contemplated. Moreover, most services are paid for through public money at minimal prices. Therefore, the institutions

---

[4] https://neos-server.org/neos/.

need to be as efficient as possible in order not to run into big losses, which may lead to their closure.

In [29], two approaches to optimize non-urgent transport routes were employed: an Integer Linear Programming (ILP) model and a heuristic approach. By utilizing these methods, they were able to determine the most suitable ambulance type for different transport scenarios, thereby maximizing the overall efficiency of the ambulance fleet while ensuring better routes. The authors argue that heuristic methods can be significantly beneficial as they offer practical solutions in a reasonable amount of time, in contrast to ILP, which tends to be more time-consuming and costly when applied to real-life situations. However, they emphasize that the increasing availability of software for solving optimization problems, including freely accessible ones, should not lead to the neglect of ILP models. Despite their drawbacks, ILP models still play a crucial role in addressing complex optimization challenges.

According to Koç et al. [14], Tabu Search (TS), Genetic Algorithms (GA), and Local Search meta-heuristics offer the most effective approaches for discovering optimal solutions in the context of non-urgent transport. In [18], the transportation of non-urgent patients is treated as a DARP, and developing a model using LINGO to achieve better routes and reduce waiting times compared to the procedures utilized by the Center for Addictive Behavior Health and Recovery Services. Initially, a Branch-and-Bound algorithm was applied to find optimal solutions; however, due to its extensive computational time requirements, it was less practical. Instead, they found improved results by employing the TS approach, which benefited non-urgent patient transport providers in terms of reduced travel time and waiting times.

Also using TS (and Fico Xpress 7.7), [20] developed a model to optimize ambulance routes. The results showed that with this solution method used daily, it was possible to decrease the waiting times of the patients. The solution method was based on the Unified Tabu Search (UTS) proposed by [5] for the VRPTW and for two generalizations: the PVRP and the multi-depot VRPTW.

The VRP Spreadsheet Solver[5] presented in [10] is a user-friendly open-source software that runs in Microsoft Office Excel. It aims at assisting institutions in solving several variants of VRP. It considers locations resorting to the Geographic Information System (GIS) and was capable to find solutions for many VRP variants with up to 200 customers. Results on the optimization of medicines distribution for healthcare organizations and on improving the visiting routes in the tourism sector are presented in [10]. The solver is tested using a benchmark dataset containing CVRP instances and distance-constrained VRP. The VRP Solver implements a variant of the Adaptive Large Neighborhood Search (ALNS) [22], a meta-heuristic that has been widely used for determining feasible solutions for scheduling VRP [23], including several variants, such as CVRP and VRPTW.

Despite the urgent need to address the environmental impact of transportation, the current literature still fails when discussing this impact for some sectors. This is the case with the transport of healthcare. For instance, the analysis of

---

[5] Available online at: https://people.bath.ac.uk/ge277/vrp-spreadsheet-solver/.

the environmental impact of freight transportation is widely discussed in the literature, in some cases the research conducted attention calls to stakeholders and practitioners to develop initiatives to mitigate the impact caused for these activities (see [15,28]).

From the literature review, the solver proposed in [10], shows the greater potential to be used by the fire station since it: (i) is an open-source tool, available online; (ii) allows solving VRP with time windows and capacity constraints; (iii) does not require the computation of the distances; (iv) is implemented in an environment that is familiar to the staff that works at the fire station, i.e. Excel. However, there is a limitation with the solver as it does not provide an option to specify the desired appointment time.

3 Methodology

The VRP Spreadsheet Solver, proposed in [10] and extended for multi-trip VRP (i.e., vehicles return to the depot between customer visits to load and unload), was employed in a previous study [16]. The authors used this solver to analyze five real instances derived from data obtained from a fire station located in the North of Portugal. The results of the study showed that approximately 50% of patients experienced delays. The median delay time for patients reaching their appointments was approximately one hour and 20 min, while the maximum delay observed was nearly three hours.

To address these challenges and make the VRP Spreadsheet Solver more user-friendly for the fire station personnel while reducing patient delays, several steps were taken after a thorough examination of the solver code was conducted to pinpoint areas requiring modifications.

First, as the goal was to implement changes that would minimize the number of patients arriving late for their appointments, the mathematical formulation was modified. Let set $V = \{o\} \cup V_C$, where o is the depot and V_C denotes the vertex set containing the patients to visit. For each patient $i \in V_C$ and for the depot o, there is a time interval $[a_i, b_i]$ and $[a_o, b_o]$, respectively. The profit of serving patient $i \in V_C$ is p_i. Let V_r be the set of patients to visit in route $r \in R$ of the ambulance. For each route r, f^r is the fixed cost of using the ambulance and c_{ij}^r is the travel cost from i to j, with $i, j \in V$. The decision variables are: x_{ij}^r which is 1 if on route r the ambulance travels from i to j, with $i, j \in V$, and zero otherwise; y_i^r is 1 if the ambulance serves patient $i \in V_C$ on route r and zero otherwise; and ν_i is the amount of violation of the time window of vertex $i \in V$. The objective is to maximize the total profit minus the travel cost of the vehicles, the fixed cost of using the vehicles and the penalty for violating time windows, i.e.:

$$\max \sum_{i \in V_C} \sum_{r \in R} p_i\, y_i^r - \sum_{(i,j) \in V^2} \sum_{r \in R} c_{ij}^r\, x_{ij}^r - \sum_{j \in V_C} \sum_{r \in R} f^r\, x_{o,j}^r - \Pi \sum_{i \in V} \nu_i, \qquad (1)$$

where Π is the penalty cost per unit of time. For the sake of brevity, the constraints are not presented here, however, they can be found in [10]. All constraints, with the exception that all patients must be visited, are soft constraints and their violation is penalized using a quadratic scaling method. The penalization of the time windows does not guarantee that they are respected. However, in practice, small violations (up to 10 min) of the time window's end are allowed since the personnel at the clinic can handle this. For guaranteeing a good service in terms of client satisfaction the patients should be picked up at most one hour before the treatment. Therefore, to overcome the large number of delayed patients and the delayed time to the appointments, the time windows constraints were reinforced as:

$$b_o = \min_{i \in V_r} b_i \tag{2}$$

This sets the "time windows end" of the depot, b_o, equal to the earliest "time window end" of the patient assigned to that route, b_i. Therefore, the ambulance must return to the clinic in time for the earliest appointment of the patient in that ambulance.

Then, customizations were performed on the solver to ensure that it complied with the specific needs and requirements of the fire station personnel. To facilitate the use of this tool, some of the parameters for this specific case study were set by default. More precisely, on the VRP Spreadsheet Solver console, the Bing Maps key, the depot address, the working time of the physiotherapy clinic, and the ambulances capacity, were fixed for the fire station reality. The objective was to simplify the required steps when planning the routes. Noteworthy that when importing the address of each patient it was not possible to specify the door number. Thus, the patient's home is considered at the central point of the street. This is not a significant limitation since, given the geographic characteristics, the majority of the streets is less than 1 km long.

Finally, to speed up the solution evaluation process, a macro was introduced into the solution spreadsheet. This macro would help facilitate quicker analysis and assessment of potential routes and schedules. After the VRP solver retrieves a solution, this macro computes and displays: the number of delayed patients, per route, and in total; the time of delay to the appointment, in minutes, per patient, and in total. In fact, it allows for a quick evaluation of the quality of the solution found, namely if it: (i) goes in line with the current objective; (ii) needs further improvements; (iii) fulfills further limitations or objectives that were not included on the VRP solver but have emerged.

In the present work, focusing the environmental analysis and aiming to draw attention to the importance of considering sustainable aspects during transportation, the following steps were carried out: i) analysis of the different types of pollutants emitted; ii) analysis of the real distances traveled by one ambulance and compared with those obtained using the proposed solver; iii) analysis of the amount of pollutants, apart from CO_2, for an illustrative scenario considering a route for the transport of five patients. For the environmental analysis, the Ecotransit Platform [9] was used as the main source of data. This platform is a well-known tool widely used to develop scenarios to better understand the negative environmental impacts related to freight transportation. In order to obtain the data from the type of emission, the vehicle classified as EURO 5 up to 26-4on tons was considered, and the calculation of energy consumption, air pollutants such as Sulphur dioxide (SOx), Nitrogen oxides (NOx), and Particular Matter (PM) were pointed out.

4 Results and Discussion

4.1 Routes Obtained for Real Instances

A dataset was compiled based on the fire station data containing information about 442 patients. The dataset also includes data from 10 d of work for one ambulance and one firefighter. The objective is to transport each patient from their residence to the physiotherapy clinic and then back home after treatment. For testing purposes, a total of 20 instances were used, representing both the morning and afternoon periods of each of the 10 d. These instances were evaluated using the VRP Spreadsheet Solver version 3.5.2, with the modifications detailed in Sect. 3. The computational experiments were conducted using a system with a 2.1 GHz AMD Ryzen 5 3500U processor and 8 GB 2133 MHz of RAM.

The dataset instances were labeled using a combination of the day of the month and whether it corresponds to the morning or afternoon period. For instance, 2M represents the morning period of May 2nd, while 2A pertains to the afternoon of May 2nd. The decision to distinguish between the morning and afternoon periods aligns with the standard operating procedure of the fire station. Specifically, from 11 a.m. to 1 p.m., the service is dedicated to transporting patients back to their respective homes after receiving treatment at the physiotherapy clinic. This practice ensures efficient patient care and transportation services during these designated time frames. The lunch period of the drivers is dependent on the specific service they have been assigned to. Usually, the lunch break occurs either from 12 a.m. to 1 p.m. or from 1 p.m. to 2 p.m. Adjustments to the list of patients assigned to each driver are sometimes necessary. Furthermore, considering morning and afternoon periods resulted in smaller (but realistic) instances that can be solved in a more competitive computational time.

The default values of the parameters were used with the exception of: (i) on the VRP Spreadsheet Solver console: the number of depots = 1; the number of customers varies between 14 to 30, depending on the instance; the average vehicle speed = 50 km/h; the number of vehicle types = 1; if the vehicles must return to the depot = yes; the time windows constraints = "hard"; the CPU time limit = 1 min; (ii) on the Vehicles spreadsheet: the capacity = 8; the work start time = 6 a.m.; the working time limit = 12 h; the fixed cost per trip = 0; the cost per unit distance = 1.00 euro.

Table 1 shows the results for the 20 instances. For example, on May 2nd morning, the 14 patients were transported in two routes. On the first route, six patients were transported, while on the second, the entire capacity of the ambulance was used. Thus, the used capacity of the ambulance was 75% and 100%, for the first and second routes, respectively, yielding a mean used capacity of 87.5%.

Table 1. Computational results for the 20 instances, where $i = jk$ is the identification of the instances with $j \in \{2, ..., 15\} \setminus \{4, 5, 11, 12\}$ and $k \in \{\text{"}M\text{"}, \text{"}A\text{"}\}$, and for each instance i, N_i is the number of patients to transport; n_i^r is an n-uplo with the number of patients transported in each route r of that instance i; $\bar{c}_i$ is the average used capacity of the ambulance.

i	N_i	n_i^r	$\bar{c}_i$	i	N_i	n_i^r	$\bar{c}_i$
2M	14	(6, 8)	88%	2A	25	(6, 8, 7, 4)	78%
3M	20	(5, 6, 8, 1)	63%	3A	26	(4, 8, 5, 4, 4)	65%
6M	17	(3, 7, 7, 7)	71%	6A	30	(8, 8, 5, 6, 3)	75%
7M	18	(1, 7, 8, 2)	56%	7A	25	(7, 8, 5, 5)	78%
8M	15	(2, 7)	56%	8A	26	(6, 7, 8, 5)	81%
9M	18	(3, 7, 8)	75%	9A	24	(7, 8, 7, 2)	75%
10M	20	(5, 6, 8)	79%	10A	29	(6, 7, 5, 4, 6)	70%
13M	20	(4, 7, 7, 2)	63%	13A	28	(7, 8, 4, 7, 2)	70%
14M	20	(4, 7, 8, 1)	63%	14A	24	(5, 8, 6, 5)	75%
15M	17	(5, 7, 5)	71%	15A	26	(5, 8, 7, 6)	81%

Further, the results show that, in 14 out of the 20 instances tested, the average used capacity of the ambulance is either equal to or greater than 70%. Additionally, in 44 out of the 77 routes examined, the used capacity exceeds 75%. Moreover, in 85% of the routes, at least half of the ambulance's capacity is utilized, as indicated in column $\bar{c}_i$ in Table 1.

Nonetheless, it is important to note that, unfortunately, a direct comparison of the results regarding the used capacity of the ambulances, the number of patients, and their delayed time cannot be made with real cases. This limitation arises from the unavailability of such information for reference or validation. Nevertheless, the computational experiments offer valuable insights into the performance and efficiency of the proposed approach based on the given instances and available data.

As the only available information for the real service is the number of kilometers at the end of each day, Fig. 1, presents a comparison between the distance traveled by the ambulance when using the solution found by the solver (indicated by the orange bars) and the actual distance covered during the real service (represented by the blue bars). Note that, it is of great importance to reduce the distance traveled by the ambulance since it leads to reductions in the expenses with fuel and maintenance of the vehicle. Also, it makes transport more eco-friendly by reducing the fuel burned to the atmosphere and the tire wearing.

For the 10 d under analysis, a daily average of approximately 44 patients are transported (442 in total) and 117 km (1.170 km in total) are traveled by the fire station's ambulance for performing the service (see Table 1 and Fig. 1). Using the solutions found with the VRP solver, a total of 1.112 km would be traveled,

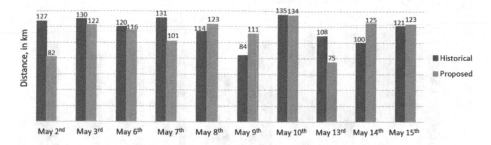

Fig. 1. Comparison of the real distance traveled by the ambulance (blue bars) and the distance traveled when using the proposed solver (orange bars), for the 10 days (Color figure online).

corresponding to a reduction of 58 km, i.e., 5%. Although this reduction seems small it presents a significant reduction of fuel consumption and vehicle wear.

Furthermore, for May 2nd, 7th and 13rd, reductions of 45 km (36%), 30 km (23%) and 33 km (31%), respectively, are observed. This corresponds to an average reduction of 30%. For May 3rd, 6th, 8th, 10th and 15th, the distance difference was very close to zero. However, for May 9th and 14th an average of 28.5% increase was observed (27 km, 32% and 25 km, 25%, respectively). In fact, these two days, correspond to the ones with the smallest distance traveled by the fire station's ambulance. For these, manual selection yielded a very good solution in terms of the distance traveled by the ambulance, mainly due to the large experience of the fire station's personnel. Furthermore, one may not forget that manual selection is quite time-consuming.

4.2 An Environmental Analysis of the Impact on Transportation

In this section, two main results are presented. First, a comparative analysis of the greenhouse gases CO2 emitted in the real scenario of transportation using the proposed methodology is presented. Then, a summary of the different types of toxic substances for a route selected to be analyzed is presented.

The results presented in Fig. 2, summarize the greenhouse gases CO2 emitted for the 10 d of analysis selected in this research. The conducted analysis showed that the results after the application of the proposed solver contribute to minimizing the environmental impact of transportation for May 2nd, 3rd, 6th, 7th, 10th, 13rd). Yet, it is important to highlight that for some cases the CO2 emitted for these transportation increases, which is the case on May 8th, 9th and 14th. This is justified by the fact that the real distance traveled is higher than the one proposed by the solver, which has a direct impact on emissions. The results also put in evidence the negative impact caused by transportation, namely the impact of global warming and climate change, which has been one of the main concerns for governments and companies worldwide. It is important to highlight that in the current literature there is several research focusing on the impact of transportation on the environment, especially when discussing

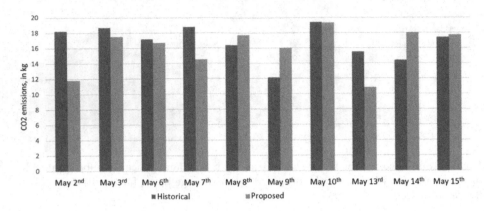

Fig. 2. Comparison between CO2 emission, for 10 days.

the transport freight and passengers, however, there is a gap when discussing the impact of patients' transportation which is widely used for long and short distances worldwide, contributing to environmental and social concerns.

Yet, the transportation of goods and different passengers has a significant impact not only on global warming and air pollution but also on human health, since several emissions are emitted during transportation. Table 2 shows the type of substances followed by the related impact on the environment and health.

Table 2. A summary of the main type of emissions caused during the transportation

Substances	Main negative impacts	Acronym
Nitrogen oxides	Contributes to summer smog, acidification, and cause damage to human health	N2O
Non-methane hydrocarbon	Contributes to summer smog and cause damage to human health	NOx
Sulphur dioxide	Contributes to acidification and causes damage to human health	SO2
Particulate matter	Causes damage to human health	PM

In this research, to illustrate the real impact of transportation of patients, considering the different types of emissions, a scenario that considers a route to transport four patients to the clinic was proposed, and the ECOtransit platform was used to get data regarding the pollutants. For this analysis, latitude and longitude were used for the origin and destination of every patient. Figure 3 shows the results of this analysis for each patient.

The results presented in Fig. 3 summarize the main pollutants generated during the transportation of non-urgent patients used in this research to illustrate the environmental impacts, namely Nitrogen oxides (N2O), Sulphur dioxide (SO2), Non-methane hydrocarbon (NOx), Particulate matter (PM) and CO2

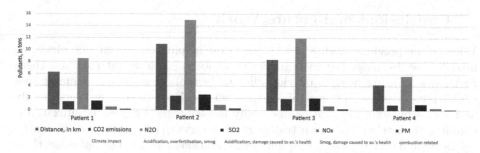

Fig. 3. Emissions caused during the transport of each of the four patients, by pollutants.

emissions. The results confirm that, for all patients, the N2O were the substance with the larger impact when transporting the patients. For this case, it is important to highlight that this pollutant has a significant impact on acidification, respiratory problems for human health. Regarding S02, it was also considered a pollutant with a significant impact. For this, beyond the impact on the environment, mainly on damage to trees and loss of ecosystems, this substance may also cause health problems such as eye irritation, nose congestion and throat infection.

Regarding the total emission for the transport of the four patients, Fig. 4 summarizes the results for this scenario putting in evidence the negative impact of non-urgent transport. Especially, N2O, SO2 and CO2 emissions have the greatest impact on the environment and on human health.

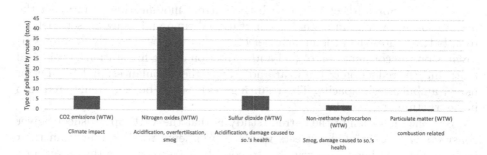

Fig. 4. Emission of different pollutants caused during the transport of four patients.

The analysis presented in this section brings to light the need to increase the discussion of the environmental and social impact caused by transportation over short distances, which is the case of patients' transport. This type of transport is not yet well discussed in literature, however, it is an important type of transport that is daily performed worldwide.

5 Conclusions and Future Work

While some previous studies have focused on helping non-profit organizations in reducing distances and costs in the transport of non-urgent patients, there remains a pressing need to develop affordable tools that do not demand specialized knowledge. The goal of the present work is to provide user-friendly and accessible solutions that can be easily implemented by these organizations, enabling them to enhance their transportation services effectively and efficiently. By developing such tools, non-profit organizations can further optimize their operations, reduce delays, and ultimately improve the overall quality of service for non-urgent patients. Also, they will assist in reducing the ecological footprint f these organizations.

The VRP Spreadsheet Solver, proposed in [10], aims to address this need. After customizing this solver to meet the specific requirements of the fire station being studied, the research findings indicate that this tool is indeed well-suited to assist the fire station in planning more optimal routes for non-urgent patient transport. This successful adaptation and utilization of the solver demonstrate its potential to be a valuable asset in improving transportation planning and enhancing service efficiency for the fire station and similar non-profit organizations.

The results obtained in the present work show that the total distance traveled by ambulances presents savings of approximately 5% (i.e., 58 km) for the 10 d used in the computational tests. This reduction may seem small, but it presents a significant reduction in fuel consumption and vehicle wear and tear. Further, it results in savings on fuel and maintenance of the ambulances by the fire station, as well as the reduction of its ecological footprint.

The VRP Spreadsheet Solver with the current modifications, can assist the fire station in finding, in a small computational time and using a user-friendly tool, better routes than the manual selection that it uses currently. It allows (i) savings on the consumption of fuel and reduction of the fire station's ecological footprint; (ii) reduction of the wear and tear of the ambulances; and (iii) better use of ambulances' capacity. The resulting savings can be, e.g., reinvested into infrastructure and vehicles.

Yet, one limitation of the current study is that the VRP Spreadsheet Solver considers the center of the streets where the patients reside rather than their specific door numbers. This was due to confidentiality concerns that prevented the inclusion of such detailed information. As a result, the distances calculated in the solver are approximations, as patients could live either at the beginning or the end of the streets. Despite this limitation, the approximations are still good, especially considering that the geographic area served by the fire station primarily comprises streets with lengths mostly below 1 km.

The research also calls attention to the increasing concerns regarding the negative impact of the transport sector on climate change. These concerns have forced companies and governments to develop initiatives to minimize the impact of these activities. However, in some cases, the impact on short distances is yet not well discussed. In this context, the present research sought out an analysis of the environmental and social impact of patients' transport over short distances. The results showed that, despite the reduced number of traveled kilometers when transporting patients between their homes and the clinics for treatment, there is a significant impact on both human health for local communities and also to the environment. The proposed analysis in the present research aimed to offer insights for efficient transportation, which will contribute then to minimizing these impacts and draw attention to disseminating this discussion between academics and governments.

Future work aims at reinforcing time constraints and relaxing the distance ones, as well as exploring different objective functions in order to further decrease the number of delayed patients, the delayed time and the ecological footprint of non-urgent patients' transport.

Acknowledgments. This work has been supported by national funds through FCT - Fundação para a Ciência e Tecnologia through project UIDB/04728/2020.

References

1. Alves, F., Alvelos, F., Rocha, A.M., Pereira, A.I., Leitão, P.: Periodic vehicle routing problem in a health unit. In: ICORES 2019 - Proceedings of the 8th International Conference on Operations Research and Enterprise Systems, pp. 384–389 (2019). https://doi.org/10.5220/0007392803840389
2. Campbell, A.M., Wilson, J.H.: Forty years of periodic vehicle routing. Networks **63**(1), 2–15 (2014). https://doi.org/10.1002/net.21527
3. Cao, P., Liu, Z.: The impact of population characteristics on transportation co2 emissions-does population aging important? Environ. Sci. Pollut. Res. 1–20 (2023). https://doi.org/10.1007/s11356-023-26465-9
4. Cardoso, R.: O modelo de transporte de doentes não urgentes: estudo do caso hospital geral de santo antónio. Universidade Nova de Lisboa, Escola Nacional de Saúde Pública, Trabalho final de especialização em administração hospitalar (2012)
5. Cordeau, J., Laporte, G., Mercier, A.: A unified tabu search algorithm for vehicle routing problems with soft time windows. J. Oper. Res. Soc. **59**(5), 663–673 (2008). https://doi.org/10.1057/palgrave.jors.2601163
6. Dantzig, G.B., Ramser, J.H.: The truck dispatching problem. Manag. Sci. **6**(1), 80–91 (1959). https://doi.org/10.1287/mnsc.6.1.80
7. Delicado, A.: Caracterização do voluntariado social em portugal. Intervenção Social **25**, 127–140 (2002)
8. DRE: Portaria n.º 142-a/2012, diário da república, 1.ª série - n.º 94–15 de maio de 2012, 2532-(2)–2532-(3) (2012)
9. ECOtransit: Emission calculator for greenhouse gases and exhaust emissions (2022)
10. Erdoğan, G.: An open source spreadsheet solver for vehicle routing problems. Comput. Oper. Res. **84**, 62–72 (2017). https://doi.org/10.1016/j.cor.2017.02.022

11. Ferreira, D.: Qualidade e Satisfação no transporte programado de doentes: o caso dos Bombeiros Voluntários da Póvoa do Varzim. Master's thesis, Escola de Economia e Gestão (2012)
12. Hains, I.M., Marks, A., Georgiou, A., Westbrook, J.I.: Non-emergency patient transport: what are the quality and safety issues? a systematic review. Int. J. Qual. Health Care J. Int. Soc. Qual. Health Care/ISQua **23**(1), 68–75 (2011). https://doi.org/10.1093/intqhc/mzq076
13. Hanne, T., Melo, T., Nickel, S.: Bringing robustness to patient flow management through optimized patient transports in hospitals. Interfaces **39**(3), 241–255 (2009). https://doi.org/10.1287/inte.1080.0379
14. Koç, C., Laporte, G., Tükenmez, I.: A review of vehicle routing with simultaneous pickup and delivery. Comput. Oper. Res. **122**, 104987 (2020). https://doi.org/10.1016/j.cor.2020.104987
15. lo Storto, C., Evangelista, P.: Infrastructure efficiency, logistics quality and environmental impact of land logistics systems in the EU: a dea-based dynamic mapping. Res. Transport. Bus. Manag. **46**, 100814 (2023). https://doi.org/10.1016/j.rtbm.2022.100814
16. Lopes, E., Costa e Silva, E.: Evaluation of an open source solver to assist on the non-urgent patients transport problem. In: Abraham, A., Hanne, T., Castillo, O., Gandhi, N., Nogueira Rios, T., Hong, T.-P. (eds.) HIS 2020. AISC, vol. 1375, pp. 375–384. Springer, Cham (2021). https://doi.org/10.1007/978-3-030-73050-5_38
17. Loureiro, M.: Optimização de Rotas de Transporte de Doentes Programados : O Caso da Cruz Vermelha Portuguesa Amadora - Sintra. Master's thesis, Instituto Superior Técnico (2010)
18. Melachrinoudis, E., Ilhan, A.B., Min, H.: A dial-a-ride problem for client transportation in a health-care organization. Comput. Oper. Res. **34**(3), 742–759 (2007). https://doi.org/10.1016/j.cor.2005.03.024
19. Mourgaya, M., Vanderbeck, F.: The periodic vehicle routing problem: classification and heuristic. RAIRO-Oper. Res. **40**(2), 169–194 (2006). https://doi.org/10.1051/ro:2006015
20. Oberscheider, M., Hirsch, P.: Analysis of the impact of different service levels on the workload of an ambulance service provider. BMC Health Serv. Res. **16**(1), 1–13 (2016). https://doi.org/10.1186/s12913-016-1727-5
21. Oliveira, J., Ferreira, J., Dias, L., Figueiredo, M., Pereira, G.: Non emergency patients transport - a mixed integer linear programming. In: International Conference on Operations Research and Enterprise Systems - ICORES, vol. 2, pp. 262–269. INSTICC, SciTePress (2015). https://doi.org/10.5220/0005214902620269
22. Pisinger, D., Ropke, S.: A general heuristic for vehicle routing problems. Comput. Oper. Res. **34**(8), 2403–2435 (2007). https://doi.org/10.1016/j.cor.2005.09.012
23. Shaw, P.: Using constraint programming and local search methods to solve vehicle routing problems. In: Maher, M., Puget, J.-F. (eds.) CP 1998. LNCS, vol. 1520, pp. 417–431. Springer, Heidelberg (1998). https://doi.org/10.1007/3-540-49481-2_30
24. da Silva, M.: Transporte de Doentes Não Urgentes: Elementos de Modelação Estatística e Melhorias Potenciais de Eficiência Via Otimização de Roteamento. Master's thesis (2019)
25. Silva, O., Cordera, R., González-González, E., Nogués, S.: Environmental impacts of autonomous vehicles: a review of the scientific literature. Sci. Total Environ. **830**, 154615 (2022). https://doi.org/10.1016/j.scitotenv.2022.154615
26. Smith, S., Fortnum, D., Ludlow, M., Mathew, T., Toy, L.: Challenges in methods and availability of transport for dialysis patients. Renal Soc. Aust. J. **11**(3), 118–125 (2015)

27. Solomon, M.M.: Algorithms for the vehicle routing and scheduling problems with time window constraints. Oper. Res. **35**(2), 254–265 (1987). https://doi.org/10.1287/opre.35.2.254

28. Tian, G., et al.: A survey of multi-criteria decision-making techniques for green logistics and low-carbon transportation systems. Environ. Sci. Pollut. Res. **30**(20), 57279–57301 (2023). https://doi.org/10.1007/s11356-023-26577-2

29. Van Den Berg, P.L., Van Essen, J.T.: Scheduling non-urgent patient transportation while maximizing emergency coverage. Transp. Sci. **53**(2), 492–509 (2019). https://doi.org/10.1287/trsc.2018.0823

Location of an Electric Vehicle Charging Station: Demographic Factor as Decision Making

Catarina Gonçalves[1] , Ângela Silva[1,2,3](✉) , and Helena Sofia Rodrigues[1,4]

[1] Instituto Politécnico de Viana do Castelo, Viana do Castelo, Portugal
{angela.a,sofiarodrigues}@esce.ipvc.pt
[2] ADiT-LAB, Instituto Politécnico de Viana do Castelo, Viana do Castelo, Portugal
[3] ALGORITMI Research Centre, University of Minho, Guimarães, Portugal
[4] CIDMA - Centro de Investigação e Desenvolvimento em Matemática e Aplicações,
Universidade de Aveiro, Aveiro, Portugal

Abstract. Infrastructure is referred as being one of the major drivers for the sound economic development of the country, however, the location of the same can become a crucial factor for the population that lives mainly in rural areas. This case study aims to identify the best point for the installation of a new electric charging station in the municipality of Viana do Castelo, Portugal. The method applied is the centre of gravity, using as data the coordinates of the parish councils, the total population, and the administrative division of 2011 and 2021. The goal is to find a central location, considering the population density and minimizing the distance between the location of the charging station and the parish councils. In this work, three scenarios were tested. The coordinates of all the parish councils belonging to the municipality were taken and analyzed, assuming the weight related to existing population in each parish. The results obtained, applying the gravity centre method directly, in the first two approaches, it was achieved were not a realistic point, since it represented a space in Lima River. In the last scenario, to promote the parishes that do not have any type of loading, it was found a central location near several parishes without charging point.

Keywords: electric charging stations · centre of gravity method · location

1 Introduction

It is notorious for the gradual growth that has been witnessed regarding electric vehicles in Portugal and many claim that this will be the future of electric mobility. As stated by [26], "Electrics grow 120% and break sales record in a month in Portugal. The beginning of the year was very strong with sales of all types of electric vehicles rising to 2509 units in the month of January." This is a new monthly record of electric vehicle sales across the country, which promises to be "a fantastic year for electric mobility in Portugal".

A. I. Pereira et al. (Eds.): OL2A 2023, CCIS 1981, pp. 498–515, 2024.
https://doi.org/10.1007/978-3-031-53025-8_34

According to studies conducted in January 2023, the sale of plug-in hybrid vehicles (PHEV) fell short of the sale of 100% electric vehicles because these increasingly have better ranges and are increasingly more efficient for what the customer wants.

With the increase of greater use of electric vehicles, it is necessary that there is an increase in the network of electric infrastructures so that it is possible to satisfy the needs of the customers. However, it should be noted that the cities' shape is increasingly associated with the availability of public services and facilities bringing to the population direct impacts on the quality of life, as cities grow, thus containing increasingly dispersed patterns of urbanization, which can bring some negative impacts on the ability of people to access these services and infrastructures and create some dependence on vehicular displacements, especially the population that is found in rural areas. In addition, research has pointed out impacts on the density of urban vitality, as [3] points out.

The year 2022 was also marked by the arrival of new charging stations in the public access network, more specifically, with the opening of 5600 new infrastructures, whereas at the end of 2022, there were 3100 active electric charging stations [26].

The objective of this work is to identify the best location for a new charging station in the city of Viana do Castelo considering the parish councils of the municipality and the total population of each parish. This study will be developed with the aid of the centre of gravity method to find the most viable location and more competitive positioning.

2   Literature Review

The role of transport in sustainable development was first recognized in 1992 by the United Nations. It was noted that over the next 20 years, transportation would be the main driving force behind a growing global demand, all due to energy [19].

Sustainable developments in the year 2002 once again played an important role in the achievement of the Johannesburg implementation plan, providing several reference points for sustainable transport in the context of infrastructure, transport systems, accessibility, and reduction of greenhouse gases, among many others. World leaders unanimously recognized that transport and mobility are crucial for sustainable development, achieving better integration into the economy, improving social equity, achieving better urban-rural connections, and even resilience in cities [19].

For sustainable development, by 2030, sustainable transport will be integrated into several SDGs and specific targets, especially related to food security, health, energy, economic growth, infrastructure, and cities. In the context of transport in climate action, it will play a particularly important role in the realization of the Paris Agreement, given that a quarter of global energy-related greenhouse gas emissions come from petrol transport and these emissions are expected to grow substantially in the coming years [19].

2.1 Infrastructures

The various infrastructural segments support the provision of public services, in addition to fostering population development. The concept of infrastructure can be defined as something that is linked to meeting both the needs of social life and the needs of companies. Transport infrastructures, in their various modes, constitute the main support for activities related to logistics [3].

The concept of logistics evolves from military use to the needs of goods destined for export, domestic market supply and military security. It consists of planning alternatives, as well as seeking to reduce costs caused by operational inefficiencies, legal, bureaucratic, and institutional obstacles. Difficulties in infrastructure compromise the efficiency of logistics chains [3].

In recent years, the geographical layout of logistics infrastructures has been analyzed in a more comprehensive way, receiving special attention, especially with the concerns of the potential growth of goods vehicles attributed to the movement of logistics facilities from the interior to the exterior of cities [6]. This logistical expansion has been analyzed in several cities such as Paris [6], Atlanta [7], Los Angeles and Seattle [5], Tokyo [23], Zurich [24], Berlin [14], Chicago [9], among many others.

In addition, logistics infrastructures entail high investment costs that may or may not have some growth effect, and this is an issue that will depend not only on the size and type of investment but also on a set of factors that can boost or hinder although this is widely studied for developed countries [11]. Thus, infrastructures constitute a set of production and non-production sectors and facilities that include logistical, scientific and industrial complexes, free economic zones and other forms of organization of regional economies [15].

In Portugal there is the Mobi.E network, which is a universal structure that covers charging stations installed in public spaces. It started with 1200 public charging stations and gradually expanded the network, depending on the demand for electric vehicles and the framework for electric mobility activities.

2.2 Decision on the Location of Recharging Stations

Location and infrastructure interact with each other and determine the direction and size of trade flows, they argue [17].

In the supply chain, location has the potential to become decision support and is defined as being a geographical location in which companies establish their physical facilities [18]. Locations are decided in a broad and lasting way, with a great impact on various operational and logistical decisions, always considering the high costs [11].

However, according to the authors [21], the problem of the location of infrastructures is related to the size and geographical characteristics of these facilities, whose objective is to minimize the total cost associated with supply chain operations while satisfying customer demand.

It should be noted that the location of the most efficient infrastructures depends mainly on the selection of the site, based on capital investments, labour and the minimization of costs and time.

The studies that exist on the location and characterization of logistics infrastructures and their impacts, tend to focus mainly on the flows of goods, ending within a specific area. The question of the location of logistics activities arose essentially, both from the point of view of logistic spatial dynamics and logistics expansion. This logistical expansion has led to changes in the geographical location of urban cargo, increasing mileage and affecting the displacement of logistics employment [1].

On the other hand, the authors [13], argue that there is a positive correlation between logistics infrastructures or interregional accessibility with the levels of economic indicators, such as GDP. Accessibility is one of the main factors of regional competitiveness and is influenced by geographical distances [11]. The way infrastructures affect accessibility, location and the consequent growth and development of regions, lead to an improvement in accessibility bringing advantage, and whose main restriction translates into the convergence of regions further from the centre/interior [25].

2.3   Centre of Gravity Method

The centre of gravity method allows for finding solutions for the best location, whether for a warehouse, terminal, plant or even for the provision of services [8]. The centre of gravity method is based on the costs of transportation between origins and destinations, to determine the best location, and the chosen point will be the one that will minimize costs. The centre of gravity is represented and weighted by the places of origin and destination to which the goods are transported.

The application of this method can be observed in different sectors in the literature, from the industrial to services.

For example, the authors [20], applied the centre of gravity method to determine the location of a company distributing drugs and hospital materials.

[22] applied the centre of gravity method to analyze the best location of a distribution centre. However, it is important to emphasize care when choosing this type of methodology [11]. As mentioned in the previous article, prepared by the authors [10], they describe how to proceed with the realization of the centre of gravity method. In the previous work, the authors studied the new location having in mind the already existing charging points.

The formula for minimizing the total cost is the sum of the flows, which can be quantity or cost, W_j, multiplied by the D_j distances (1) and to calculate the distances the formula that is represented in equation (7) is used.

$$Min \quad C = \sum_{j=1}^{n} W_j D_j \qquad (1)$$

According to [2], the process of finding the ideal location occurs in several stages, the first is designated by determining the initial solution of the centre of gravity method that consists of determining an initial location, thus determining the coordinates X^0 and Y^0 (Eq. (2) and Eq. (3)). The second step consists of calculating the D_j (Eq. (7)) from X^0 and Y^0 to all the other points (j). The third phase is to determine the total cost associated with this initial location (Eq. 1).

$$X^0 = \frac{\sum_{j=1}^n W_j X_j}{\sum_{j=1}^n W_j} \tag{2}$$

$$Y^0 = \frac{\sum_{j=1}^n W_j Y_j}{\sum_{j=1}^n W_j} \tag{3}$$

$$D_j = \sqrt{(X^0 - X_j)^2 + (Y^0 - Y_j)^2} \tag{4}$$

The method is an interactive one, using recurrence formulas. So, the fourth step is to find the new points of location based on the distances calculated, D_j (Eqs. (5) and (6)) X^i and Y^i.

$$X^i = \frac{\sum_{j=1}^n \frac{W_j X_j}{D_j}}{\sum_{j=1}^n \frac{W_j}{D_j}} \tag{5}$$

$$Y^i = \frac{\sum_{j=1}^n \frac{W_j Y_j}{D_j}}{\sum_{j=1}^n \frac{W_j}{D_j}} \tag{6}$$

$$D_j = \sqrt{(X^i - X_j)^2 + (Y^i - Y_j)^2} \tag{7}$$

The defined stopping criterion was the variation in the objective function value between iterations of less than 0.5%.

3   Methodology

Due to the intervention of the Troika, with whom the Portuguese government signed the Memorandum of Understanding on May 17, 2011, the Administrative Reorganization of the Territory of Parishes (RAFT) was implemented in 2013, which reduced from 4259 to 3092 the number of parishes in Portugal and the city of Viana do Castelo was no exception. This reduction was a way to reorganize and significantly reduce the number of parish councils, with the aim of strengthening the provision of public service, increasing efficiency, and simultaneously reducing costs.

The territory of the union of parishes of Viana do Castelo merges with the city itself. Its parishes contain a great cultural and architectural heritage and are installed businesses and companies of reference for the economic dynamics of Viana do Castelo in said territory.

In this way, the layout of the parishes of Viana do Castelo underwent in 2013 a change, coming to exist the so-called "union of parishes". Table 1 shows the before and one after the union of parishes for the years 2011 and 2021, data that were taken from the [12].

Table 1. Population in each parish of Viana do Castelo- administrative division of 2011 and 2021(Source:INE, 2023)

Parish 2011	Population 2011	Parish 2021	Population 2021
Afife	1632	Afife	1518
Alvarães	2623	Alvarães	2462
Amonde	293	Amonde	231
Anha	2415	Anha	2257
Areosa	4853	Areosa	4698
Barroselas	3927	Barroselas e Carvoeiro	4701
Carvoeiro	1104	Cardielos e Serreleis	2150
Cardielos	1309	Carreço	1737
Serreleis	1003	Castelo de Neiva	2719
Carreço	1759	Chafé	3447
Castelo de Neiva	2930	Darque	8003
Chafé	2841	Freixieiro do Soutelo	465
Darque	7798	Geraz do Lima	3046
Freixieiro de Soutelo	511	Lanheses	1517
Santa Maria de Geraz do Lima	875	Mazarefes e Vila Fria	2494
Santa Leocádia de Geraz do Lima	916	Montaria	450
Moreira de Geraz do Lima	597	Mujães	1422
Deão	951	Nogueira, Meixedo e Vilar de Murteda	1433
Lanheses	1645	Outeiro	1060
Mazarefes	1343	Perre	2772
Vila Fria	1327	Santa Marta de Portuzelo	3901
Montaria	549	São Romão de Neiva	1048
Mujães	1550	Subportela, Deocriste e Portela Susã	2250
Nogueira	916	Torre e Vila Mou	1092
Meixedo	467	Vila de Punhe	2064
Vilar de Murteda	214	Vila Franca	1688
Outeiro	1234	Viana do Castelo (Monserrate, Santa Maria Maior e Meadela)	25158
Perre	2956		
Santa Marta de Portuzelo	3805		
São Romão de Neiva	1225		
Subportela	1179		
Deocriste	776		
Portela Susa	597		
Torre	615		
Vila Mou	566		
Vila Franca	1757		
Monserrate	2390		
Santa Maria Maior	10645		
Meadela	9782		

Issues are increasing on the political and economic agendas of decision-making. Considering the population size of each parish and the existing infrastructures, it is intended to calculate the installation of a new electric vehicle charging centre taking into account 3 scenarios:

- Scenario A: regarding the political division of 2011 (without the union of parishes);
- Scenario B: structured based on the political division of 2021 (with the union of parishes);
- Scenario C: the ratio between the population of a parish of 2021 and the number of charging stations in that same parish was taken into account.

4   Results and Discussion

In this section, the results obtained with the centre of gravity will be presented and discussed, for each of the three scenarios described below.

4.1   Scenario A - 2011 Administrative Breakdown

In this scenario, the crucial factor used is the non-consideration of the union of parishes of the municipality of Viana do Castelo. As main variables, the total population and the coordinates of each parish council were used, emphasizing that the data taken from the population is from the year 2011 since it was the most recent data on the non-union of the parishes.

Study Characterization. The coordinates of each parish council's location were collected through the software google earth. Then, with the help of [12], a survey was made to find the total population of each parish.

Thus, Table 2 shows the coordinates of each parish council and its total population.

Table 2. Population and coordinates of parish councils (Source: (INE,2011)

Parish	W(2011)	X	Y
Afife	1632	41,780356	−8,858464
Alvarães	2623	41,643934	−8,742681
Amonde	293	41,786792	−8,756816
Anha	2415	41,662901	−8,793086
Areosa	4853	41,713796	−8,851511
Barroselas	3927	41,646554	−8,676654
Carvoeiro	1104	41,646554	−8,676654
Cardielos	1309	41,704204	−8,744478
Serreleis	1003	41,702814	−8,750722
Carreço	1759	41,749972	−8,863329
Castelo de Neiva	2930	41,623609	−8,795903
Chafé	2841	41,648464	−8,779629
Darque	7798	41,682212	−8,797554
Freixieiro de Soutelo	511	41,797819	−8,817046
Santa Maria de Geraz do Lima	875	41,704301	−8,679018
Santa Leocádia de Geraz do Lima	916	41,704301	−8,679018
Moreira de Geraz do Lima	597	41,704301	−8,679018
Deão	951	41,706184	−8,696927
Lanheses	1645	41,734694	−8,681353
Mazarefes	1343	41,678372	−8,767896
Vila Fria	1327	41,658327	−8,760301
Montaria	549	41,790364	−8,729197
Mujães	1550	41,657587	−8,712248
Nogueira	916	41,738253	−8,733013
Meixedo	467	41,758557	−8,705054
Vilar de Murteda	214	41,769201	−8,795903
Outeiro	1234	41,752601	−8,786772
Perre	2956	41,721632	−8,782472
Santa Marta de Portuzelo	3805	41,707238	−8,773203
São Romão de Neiva	1225	41,641575	−8,773054
Subportela	1179	41,693454	−8,723251
Deocriste	776	41,683204	−8,710838
Portela Susa	597	41,680917	−8,731367
Torre	615	41,719476	−8,709938
Vila Mou	566	41,727668	−8,700436
Vila Franca	1757	41,682511	−8,747598
Vila de Punhe	2273	41,656409	−8,729427
Monserrate	2390	41,688631	−8,834298
Santa Maria Maior	10645	41,701779	−8,824914
Meadela	9782	41,705402	−8,807532

Optimization Results. For this work, and to use the centre of gravity method, W1 was considered, having as value attributed to weight, the population size of each parish. Thus, after identifying the coordinates of the parish councils, the stopping criterion between lower iterations is 0.5%. Thus, the new optimum point found can be seen in Table 3. It only took a few iterations to get the coordinates of the new charging station.

It appears that the new charging station should be located at the point with the coordinates (41.693302; −8.791601). In Fig. 1, it is implied where the new charging station is, however, this new optimal point is not feasible since it is on the Lima River.

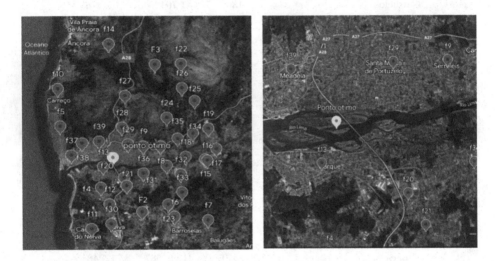

Fig. 1. Location of the new optimum point - Scenario A

Thus, since the point found is not feasible it was decided to choose the parish closest to the optimal point. Of the parishes closest to the optimum point we have: Meadela, Santa Marta de Portuzelo, Darque and Mazarefes the closest with 1,195 Km of distance, is the parish of Darque.

As shown in Fig. 2, once the parish closest to the optimum point has been found, it is necessary to find the objective function value, related to the viable solution. In this way, it is necessary to measure the distance from the viable point to the parishes belonging to the municipality of Viana do Castelo and finally calculate the objective function by adding the weights with the distances.

Table 3 shows the possible solution, obtained with the criterion of the nearest parish from the optimum point, away from the Lima River, where a charging station with the coordinates (41.682212; −8.797554) could be placed, which would cause a penalty of the objective function of 100.536888.

Table 3. Optimal solution and viable solution

	Search for the optimal solution				Viable solution
	1st iteration	2nd iteration	3rd iteration	4th iteration	
Coord. X	41,694035	41,693703	41,693445	41,693302	41,682212
Coord. Y	−8,779828	−8,766144	−8,789676	−8,791601	−8,797554
Total Cost	4584,746257	4516,883853	4494,419480	4487,556046	4588,092934
Variation	0%	1,48%	0,50%	0,15%	

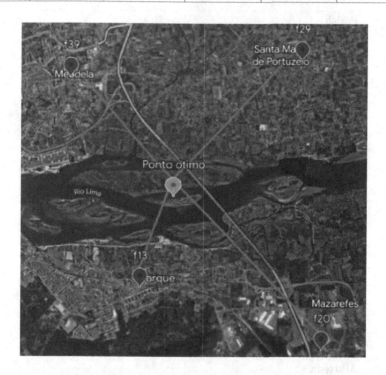

Fig. 2. Parish closest to the optimum point

4.2   Scenario B - 2021 Administrative Breakdown

In this scenario, the crucial factor used is the consideration of the union of parishes of the municipality of Viana do Castelo. As main variables, the total population and the coordinates of each parish council were used, highlighting that the data taken from the population are from the year 2021, the most recent data from the [12].

Study Characterization. For this model, it was necessary to find the total population corresponding to each parish, as well as the coordinates of the parish councils, as can be seen in Table 4, using support INE [12] and google earth software.

Optimization Results. After identifying the coordinates of the parishcouncils and considering that they all have a weight that is the population W1, the centre of gravity method was applied to obtain a new optimal point for the location of a charging station, considering the criterion of stopping variation between iterations of less than 0.5%. Thus, the new optimum point found can be seen in Table 5. It only took 4 iterations to get the coordinates of the new charging station.

Table 4. Population and coordinates of the union of parishes (Source: INE, 2023

Parish	W	X	Y
Afife	1518	41,780356	−8,858464
Alvarães	2462	41,643934	−8,742681
Amonde	231	41,786792	−8,756816
Anha	2257	41,662901	−8,793086
Areosa	4698	41,713796	−8,851511
Barroselas e Carvoeiro	4701	41,684035	−8,702497
Cardielos e Serreleis	2150	41,710556	−8,733629
Carreço	1737	41,749972	−8,863329
Castelo de Neiva	2719	41,623609	−8,795903
Chafé	3447	41,648464	−8,779629
Darque	8003	41,682212	−8,797554
Freixieiro de Soutelo	465	41,797819	−8,817046
Geraz do Lima e Deão	3046	41,705464	−8,680255
Lanheses	1517	41,734694	−8,681353
Mazarefes e Vila Fria	2494	41,676377	−8,770989
Montaria	450	41,790364	−8,729197
Mujães	1422	41,657587	−8,711764
Nogueira, Meixedo e VIlar de Murteda	1433	41,738993	−8,732719
Outeiro	1060	41,752601	−8,786772
Perre	2772	41,721632	−8,782472
Santa Marta de Portuzelo	3901	41,707238	−8,773203
São Romão de Neiva	1048	41,641575	−8,773054
Subportela, Deocriste e Portela Susã	2250	41,687943	−8,706793
Torre e Vila Mou	1092	41,728427	−8,824795
Vila de Punhe	2064	41,652181	−8,726508
Vila Franca	1688	41,683484	−8,747802
Viana do Castelo (Monserrate, Santa Maria Maior e Meadela)	25158	41,702127	−8,824795

It appears that the new charging station should be located at the point with the coordinates (41.692247; −8.796170). In Fig. 3, it is implied where the new charging station is (yellow point), however, this new optimal point is not feasible since it is on the Lima River.

Thus, since the point found is not feasible, the same criterion was used, choose the parish closest to the optimal point. Of the parishes closest to the optimum point, we have: Meadela, Santa Marta de Portuzelo, Darque and Mazarefes the closest with 1,195 Km of distance, is the parish of Darque as shown in Fig. 4 (yellow point).

In order to find the objective function, the distances from the optimum point to the nearest parish centre coordinates were determined and the objective function was calculated.

Table 5 shows a possible solution, obtained with the criterion of the nearest parish, away from the Lima River, where a charging station with the coordinates (41.682212; −8.797554) could be placed, which would cause a penalty of the objective function of 59.303624.

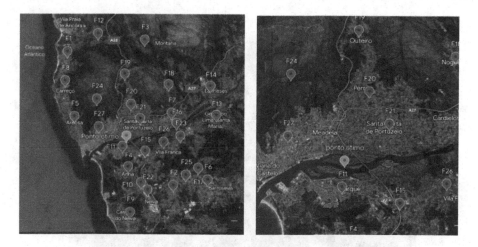

Fig. 3. Location of the new optimum point - Scenario B

Table 5. Optimal solution and viable solution

Search for the optimal solution					Viable Solution
	1st iteration	2nd iteration	3nd iteration	4nd iteration	
Coord. X	41,695307	41,693516	41,692626	41,692247	41,682212
Coord. Y	−8,785021	−8,791109	−8,794476	−8,796170	−8,797554
Total Cost	4517,399088	4447,085331	4424,983082	4419,375455	4478,679079
Variation	0%	1,56%	0,50%	0,13%	

4.3   Scenario C - Population to Be Divided by the Number of Posts (Union of Parishes)

In this scenario, the 2021 administrative division (with the union of parishes) was used. However, the focus was not only on the demographic factor but above all on access to the charging equipment already existing in the parish. Thus, the weight used for the centre of gravity was the ratio between the population and the number of charging stations already existing in the parish.

Study Characterization. In this scenario, the goal is to find the best optimal spot in the municipality of Viana do Castelo. However, as shown in Table 6, there are several parishes without any type of charging station. Thus, in order to promote the parishes that do not have any type of loading, it was decided to put the highest value of W existing for the other parishes, multiplied by 1000, that is, in this case, the largest W is represented by the number 4701, we have to multiply this number by 1000, thus giving 4701000 and replace this W in all parishes in which the number of posts is equal to 0.

Fig. 4. Parish closest to the optimum point

Optimization Results. After identifying both the coordinates of the parish councils and the population (W) that each of the parishes will have and the population W1, the centre of gravity method was applied to obtain a new optimal point for the location of a charging station, meeting the criterion of stopping variation between iterations less than 0.5%. Thus, the new optimum point found can be seen in Table 7. It only took 2 iterations to get the coordinates of the new charging station.

It appears that the new charging station should be located at the point with the coordinates (41.711594; −8.768219). In Fig. 5, it is implied that the new charging station is (yellow point), near the median and high school of Santa Marta de Portuzelo.

Table 6. Population and coordinates of the parishes

Parish	Resident Population 2021	Number of posts per parish	W	X	Y
Afife	1518	0	4701000	41,780356	−8,858464
Alvarães	2462	0	4701000	41,643934	−8,742681
Amonde	231	0	4701000	41,786792	−8,756816
Anha	2257	0	4701000	41,662901	−8,793086
Areosa	4698	1	4698	41,713796	−8,851511
Barroselas e Carvoeiro	4701	1	4701	41,684035	−8,702497
Cardielos e Serreleis	2150	0	4701000	41,710556	−8,733629
Carreço	1737	0	4701000	41,749972	−8,863329
Castelo de Neiva	2719	1	2719	41,623609	−8,795903
Chafé	3447	0	4701000	41,648464	−8,779629
Darque	8003	3	2667,667	41,682212	−8,797554
Freixieiro de Soutelo	465	0	4701000	41,797819	−8,817046
Geraz do Lima e Deão	3046	1	3046	41,705464	−8,680255
Lanheses	1517	1	1517	41,734694	−8,681353
Mazarefes e Vila Fria	2494	1	2494	41,676377	−8,770989
Montaria	450	0	4701000	41,790364	−8,729197
Mujães	1422	0	4701000	41,657587	−8,711764
Nogueira, Meixedo e VIlar de Murteda	1433	0	4701000	41,738993	−8,732719
Outeiro	1060	0	4701000	41,752601	−8,786772
Perre	2772	0	4701000	41,721632	−8,782472
Santa Marta de Portuzelo	3901	1	3901	41,707238	−8,773203
São Romão de Neiva	1048	0	4701000	41,641575	−8,773054
Subportela, Deocriste e Portela Susã	2250	0	4701000	41,687943	−8,706793
Torre e Vila Mou	1092	0	4701000	41,728427	−8,824795
Vila de Punhe	2064	0	4701000	41,652181	−8,726508
Vila Franca	1688	0	4701000	41,683484	−8,747802
Viana do Castelo (Monserrate, Santa Maria Maior e Meadela)	25158	29	867,517	41,702127	−8,824795

Table 7. New optimum point

	1st iteration	2nd iteration
Coord .X	41,713081	41,711594
Coord. Y	−8,770362	−8,7682194
Total cost	5617214,185	5608102,094
Variation	0%	0,16%

However, the goal in scenario C was that the new optimum point is positioned in a parish where there was no charging station, but this is not what happened. The positioning of this new optimal point is due to the fact that this parish is in the centre of the parishes around it that has no stations, and in this way, "pulls" the new point to the central parish, which in this case is the parish of Santa Marta de Portuzelo.

In addition to this, it would be more interesting and beneficial to implement another charging station in this parish, since compared to the parishes around it, it is a parish that has a higher population density, greater commercialization and is busier than the nearest parishes.

Fig. 5. Location of the optimum point for scenario C

5   Conclusions and Limitations of the Study

In this case study, we used as reference the population of the parishes and the latitude and longitude of the parish councils belonging to the municipality of Viana do Castelo, also highlighting the administrative division of the parishes of the years 2011 and 2021, presenting these as a very relevant factor for the decision of the new optimal point.

In this way and looking at the results obtained in scenarios A and B, it is possible to verify that the factor of the administrative division of the parishes proved to be a differentiating factor, although the optimal points obtained for the new location are non-viable points. However, after a new analysis of both scenarios, it is concluded that the new point should be positioned in the parish of Darque, which would be a good bet for the implementation of another charging station, since Darque presents itself as a large parish and its geographical location presents itself as a very positive factor, not having the people who take off or Viana or Mazarefes that are the nearest parishes with public loads.

Analyzing scenario C, the population density factor is shown to be the main factor of prominence, being crucial for this scenario. It was possible to conclude that the higher the population density, the greater the probability that the new optimum point will affect this parish. So, the goal of this scenario was to have a new location for a new charging station in a parish where there was no charging station which, according to the data obtained, did not happen, the optimal solution obtained was in a parish located in the centre of parishes with no stations. It may be, also, because the parish has a higher population density compared to those that surround it, making it more beneficial to implement a charging station in this parish, which is more numerous and with greater commercialization compared to the parishes that surround it.

As future work, it is intended to consider other variables for decision making. As weights attached to the parishes, such as localization coefficient of property tax (IMI) and the type of services available in each zone (residential, commerce, industry, public services).

Acknowledgements. This work has been supported by FCT (Fundação para a Ciência e Tecnologia within the R&D Units Project Scope: UIDB/00319/2020. It is also supported by The Center for Research and Development in Mathematics and Applications (CIDMA) through FCT, references UIDB/04106/2020 and UIDP/04106/2020. This research is part of Catarina Gonçalves logistics master thesis.

References

1. Aljohani, K. and Thompson, R.: Optimizing the establishment of a central city transshipment facility to ameliorate last-mile delivery: a case study in Melbourne CBD. Towards Sustain. Liveable Cities 23–46 (2018)
2. Ballou, R.: Gerenciamento da cadeia de suprimentos/Logística Empresarial. Bookman Editora, Porto Alegre (2006)
3. Barat, J.: Planeamento das Infraestruturas de Logística e transporte. In: Radar, pp. 10–13 (2009)
4. Curvelo, P.: Portugueses fizeram quase 2,5 milhões de carregamentos de carros elétricos em 2022. (2022). Accessed Janeiro 2023. https://www.jornaldenegocios.pt

5. Dablanc, L., Ogilvie, S., Goodchild, A.: Logistics sprawl: differential warehousing development patterns in Los Angeles, California, and Seattle, Washington. Transport. Res. Rec. 105–112 (2014). https://doi.org/10.3141/2410-12

6. Dablanc, L., Rakotonarivo, D.: The impacts of logistics sprawl: how does the location of parcel transport terminals affect the energy efficiency of goods' movements in Paris and what can we do about it? In: The Sixth International Conference on City Logistics, vol. 2, pp. 6087–6096 (2010)

7. Dablanc, L., Ross, C.: Atlanta: a mega logistics center in the piedmont atlantic megaregion (PAM). J. Transp. Geogr. 24, 432–442 (2012). https://doi.org/10.1016/j.jtrangeo.2012.05.001

8. Davis, M., Chase, R., Aquilano, N.: Fundamentos Da Administração Da Produção, 3rd edn. Bookman (2001)

9. Dubie, M., Kuo, K., Giron-Valderrama, G., Goodchild, A.: An evaluation of logistics sprawl in Chicago and Phoenix. J. Transp. Geogr. 88, 102298 (2020). https://doi.org/10.1016/j.jtrangeo.2018.08.008

10. Gonçalves, C., Silva, A., Rodrigues, H.S.: Centre of gravity method for locating an electric charging station - an initial approach for Viana do Castelo. Accepted to ICOTEM 2023 - Conferência Internacional de Gestão e Operações de Tecnologia Vila Nova de Famalicão, Portugal (2023)

11. Gonçalves, P.: Caraterizaçao das Infraestruturas Logísticas em Portugal. Master thesis in Business Sciences - Logistics management. Instituto Politécnico de Setúbal (2022)

12. INE. Censos 2021 (2023). https://www.ine.pt. Accessed Fevereiro 2023

13. Keeble, D., Offord, J., Walker, S.: Peripheral Regions in a Community of Twelve Member States. Office for Official Publications of the European Communities, Luxembourg (1988)

14. Klauenberg, J., Elsner, L.A., Knischewski, C.: Dynamics of the spatial distribution of hubs in groupage networks - the case of Berlin. J. Transp. Geogr. 88, 102280 (2020)

15. Kuhan, S.: Logistic infrastructure and its role in economic security of regions. Wspolczesne Problemy Zarzadzania 6(1(12), 177–190 (2018). https://doi.org/10.52934/wpz.113

16. Lappe, F., Santos, A.: A cidade dispersa e sua infraestrutura como consequência: um estudo para a cidade de Lajeado/RS. Destaques Acadêmicos, Lajeado 10(4), 260–278 (2018)

17. Limão, N., Venables, A.J.: Infrastructure, geographical disadvantage, and transport costs (1999). SSRN: https://ssrn.com/abstract=629195. Accessed 20 Apr 2016

18. Meijboom, B., Voordijk, H.: International operations and location decisions: a firm level approach. J. Econ. Social Geogr. 94, 463–476 (2003)

19. Nations, U. Sustainable transport. https://sustainabledevelopment.un.org. Accessed Dec 2022

20. Oi, R., Nogueira, D., Silva, P., Neto, J., khalil, R.: Aplicação do método de centro de gravidade para a localização de um CD de distribuição de medicamentos e materiais hospitalares. XXXVII Encontro Nacional De Engenharia De Producao, pp. 15 (2017)

21. Rich, N., Hines, P.: Quality function deployment: a decision support matrix for location determination. In: 2nd International Symposium on Logistics, pp. 295–300 (1995)

22. Rosa, I., Abreu, I., Pedrozo, I.: Avaliação da localização do centro de distribuição da empresa AES sul distribuidora Gaúcha de energia em relação aos depósitos

regionais. Revista de Administração da Universidade Federal de Santa Maria, pp. 356–370 (2016)

23. Sakai, T., Kawamura, K., Hyodo, T.: Spatial reorganization of urban logistics system and its impacts: case of Tokyo. J. Transp. Geogr. **60**, 110–118 (2017)

24. Todesco, P., Weidmann, U., Haefeli, U.: Logistics sprawl in the region Zurich. In: 16th Swiss Transport Research Conference (STRC 2016), Ascona, Switzerland, pp. 18–20 (2016)

25. Vickerman, R.: Location, accessibility and regional development: the appraisal of trans-European networks. Transp. Policy **2**(4), 225–234 (1996)

26. Welectric: Elétricos crescem 120% e batem recorde de vendas num mês em Portugal. https://welectric.pt/2023/02/08/eletricos-crescem-120-e-batem-recorde-de-vendas-num-mes-em-portugal/. Accessed 12 June 2023

Speeding up the Oscillation-Free Modified Heavy Ball Algorithm

Koba Gelashvili[1]([✉]) [iD] and Paata Gogishvili[2] [iD]

[1] St. Andrew the First-Called Georgian University of the Patriarchate of Georgia,
53a Chavchavadze Avenue, 0179 Tbilisi, Georgia
koba.gelashvili@sangu.edu.ge
[2] Ilia State University, 3/5 Kakutsa Cholokashvili Avenue, 0162 Tbilisi, Georgia
paata.gogishvili@iliauni.edu.ge
http://sangu.edu.ge, http://iliauni.edu.ge

Abstract. This paper presents modified, faster momentum minimization algorithms based on existing ones. The modified algorithms monotonically decrease the objective function and do not allow it to oscillate. The modification scheme aims to enhance momentum minimizers by incorporating contemporary line search procedures and restarts, akin to the state-of-the-art unconstrained minimizers. We also investigate the unique resource of oscillation-free momentum minimizers for their further acceleration. In particular, the wider range of variation in the friction-related coefficient within the model significantly impacts the performance time.

Our previously developed techniques can be used to prove the convergence of modified algorithms. In this paper, we focus on the technical and experimental aspects of these algorithms. To determine the efficiency of the new algorithms, numerical experiments were conducted on standard optimization test functions and on single-layer neural networks for several datasets.

Comparisons were made with the best unconstrained minimization algorithms – lcg, L-BFGS and ADAM. Oscillation-free momentum algorithms are significantly easier to design and implement than lcg and L-BFGS, while still being competitive in terms of performance. Collections of minimizers and test functions have been uploaded to GitHub.

Keywords: Polyak's heavy ball method · Nesterov's accelerated gradient method · L-BFGS · lcg

1 Introduction

The range of applications of artificial neural networks and their technologies has been expanding rapidly in the last decade. Unconstrained minimization is an essential component of the mathematics of neural networks, and the recent trend is to use minimization algorithms with momentum.

From the perspective of classical optimization, low-memory or limited-memory minimization algorithms (L-BFGS [1], and lcg [2]) have been shown

© The Author(s), under exclusive license to Springer Nature Switzerland AG 2024
A. I. Pereira et al. (Eds.): OL2A 2023, CCIS 1981, pp. 516–530, 2024.
https://doi.org/10.1007/978-3-031-53025-8_35

to be superior when considering a single objective function and working on a single pass with a predetermined accuracy.

Momentum-based minimizers (referenced in [3–6]) have gained widespread adoption in artificial neural networks due to the following reasons:

- Implementing and utilizing algorithms like lcg and L-BFGS can be challenging, requiring more memory compared to momentum-based algorithms.
- In neural network applications, there is often a requirement to restart the algorithm, running it again using the previous result as an initial condition. This need arises during transitions from epoch to epoch and from mini-batch to mini-batch. lcg and L-BFGS tend to perform multiple iterations relatively slowly after each iteration.
- During the development of a new model, it is convenient to employ lightweight optimization algorithms at the initial stages.

The modified heavy ball algorithm (MHB) has not yet been widely used, despite being incomparably faster than the classical momentum or heavy ball (HB) algorithm and competitive with L-BFGS and lcg. MHB can also be called an oscillation-free momentum algorithm because it is a sequence of restarts of the base algorithm (HB), with restarts managed as follows:

- When the values of the objective function in the base algorithm at the current iteration start to increase, the algorithm restarts. This guarantees that the value of the function decreases.
- At each iteration, a line search algorithm is used to increase the initial momentum and determine the learning speed coefficient.

Restarts and line search are techniques adopted from the L-BFGS and lcg algorithms, respectively. The practice of algorithms borrowing specific techniques from one another is widely accepted and common in the field. Despite belonging to different algorithm groups, L-BFGS and lcg share several common features. The remarkable speed exhibited by both algorithms can be attributed to their utilization of the following components:

- Periodical restarts: This approach involves periodically resetting the algorithm's state, which can help overcome issues such as getting trapped in local optima or slow convergence. By restarting the algorithm, it has the opportunity to explore new regions of the optimization landscape.
- Inexact Line Search: Line search is a fundamental optimization technique used to determine the step size at each iteration. Inexact line search allows for approximate solutions that still ensure sufficient progress is made. This balances the computational cost with the accuracy of the optimization process.
- Updating Search Directions: The search direction refers to the direction in which the optimization algorithm looks for improvements in each iteration. Efficiently updating the search direction can significantly impact the algorithm's speed. L-BFGS and lcg employ effective strategies to update the search directions, which contributes to their rapid convergence.

Furthermore, the lcg algorithm essentially uses preconditioning, - a technique used to transform the optimization problem into a more favorable form by applying suitable transformations or reparametrizations. This can enhance the convergence rate and numerical stability of the algorithm. By incorporating these components, L-BFGS and lcg achieve exceptional speed and effectiveness in solving optimization problems, despite their algorithmic differences.

In [7], the integration of restarts and line search was achieved effortlessly and seamlessly, resulting in an oscillation-free MHB (Modified Heavy Ball) approach. To simplify the implementation, a non-mutable value of $\beta = 1$ was adopted. In this paper, we explore additional methods for accelerating MHB, including preconditioning, updating descent directions, and considering alternative values for β. In the oscillation-free model, the β coefficient, which relates to friction, can assume values that would be inconceivable in the presence of oscillation. Through conducted experiments, the potential of leveraging this resource is evident. The main focus of this article is to provide a description of the experiments conducted and the corresponding results. It is worth noting that the approach outlined in [7] serves as a validation for the convergence of the proposed methods.

The first section of our paper focuses on presenting the test functions employed in our study and the implementation of the minimizers. It is worth noting that the design and implementation of these test functions differ from those discussed in other experiments, such as the ones outlined in [8], as well as from the typical C/C++ samples available on the Internet, for example, [9–11]. The primary distinction lies in the inclusion of a stopping condition and precision within the description of the test functions. This approach is intuitive since different tasks often require different stopping conditions based on their specific requirements.

Our test suite encompasses a diverse range of scenarios. It consists of 44 unconstrained minimization test functions, an unconstrained minimization problem related to a symmetric matrix game incorporating a quadratic penalty function, and 10 tests involving 10 neurons of the MNIST dataset (refer to [12]) within a logistic regression model with a single layer. By incorporating this varied collection of test functions, we aim to provide a comprehensive evaluation of the performance of the proposed minimizers in different optimization scenarios. The collection of minimizers includes minimizers MHB, MNAG, L-BFGS, ADAM, line search algorithm, collection of unconstrained minimization tests, and logistic regression model. The project is built in Visual Studio 22 in C++ language. On GitHub, it is located in the RawCollectionOfMinimizers folder.

The second section of the paper focuses on providing a detailed description of the Modified Heavy Ball (MHB) algorithm. Furthermore, it compares two versions of the algorithm: one with a β coefficient value of 1 and another with a β coefficient value of 0.001, with the implementation CG_DESCENT-C-6.8 of the lcg algorithm. This implementation has been incorporated into the corresponding GitHub repository along with new test functions.

The presented MHB model in this section is slightly more general compared to the one described in [7]. It allows the friction-related coefficient to take values greater than 1. Furthermore, we explicitly address the fact that the stopping condition can manifest in different forms, accommodating the varying requirements of different optimization tasks.

The third section is devoted to the issue of using preconditioners in momentum-based algorithms. An experiment on the use of a preconditioner in MHB is described, in which an incomplete Cholesky decomposition with limited memory is programmed (see [13]). The `std::vector<std::map<double> >` container is used to store sparse Hessians, which greatly simplifies the coding process, but at the same time significantly slows down the calculations. Nevertheless, for the 7 numerical test functions on which lcg had a significant advantage over MHB in the experiments conducted in [7], after adding the preconditioner, the results of preconditioned MHB became significantly better than lcg in the case of 6 functions. Only one case exhibited deterioration, accompanied by an increase in the number of iterations. This indicates that the deterioration was not solely a consequence of the sparse matrix implementation.

The experiment shows that the use of preconditioning has a perspective in momentum-based optimizers, although an efficient and sustainable implementation is not found in this first attempt.

The fourth section of the paper provides a detailed description of the Modified Nesterov Algorithm (MNAG) as it represents one of the options for updating the descent direction in MHB. The key difference between Heavy Ball (HB) and Nesterov's Accelerated Gradient (NAG) lies in their selection of the descent direction. MNAG, being a modification of NAG, is more intricate than MHB but considerably easier to implement compared to the basic NAG algorithm described in [14].

Both MNAG and MHB utilize the information obtained from the line search to automatically determine the learning rate or step length. Additionally, MNAG is compatible with a software add-in (refer to [8]) that eliminates the lower bounds of variables in Box-Constrained problems through transformation, without requiring the creation of new auxiliary variables. In this section, two performance profiles are presented. The first profile compares the results of the $\beta = 1.001$ version of MHB, the $\beta = 1$ version of MNAG, and CG_DESCENT-C-6.8. The second profile focuses on comparing the results of the $\beta = 1$ version of MHB and the $\beta = 1$ version of MNAG.

These performance profiles provide insights into the comparative performance of MHB, MNAG, and CG_DESCENT-C-6.8, shedding light on the efficacy and suitability of the different algorithms in various optimization scenarios.

All three performance profiles (Figs. 1, 3, 4) are constructed following the main methodology for benchmarking optimization software, as outlined in the article by E.D. Dolan and J.J. Moré titled "Benchmarking optimization software with performance profiles" (see [15]).

The last Sect. 6 evaluates results, makes conclusions and considers the possible directions of future research.

The results of the conducted experiments can be found at the following GitHub repository: github.com/kobage/experiments-on-numerical-optimization.

Additionally, the repository includes Python code that enables the reading of data from two or three files in order to construct a performance profile. The corresponding files used in the experiments are also available for download in the repository.

All calculations were performed on a laptop with the following specifications: Intel(R) Core(TM) i7-1065G7 CPU @ 1.30 GHz 1.50 GHz and 16.0 GB of RAM.

2   Collections of Tests and Minimizers

Our new collection of test functions significantly deviates from the one utilized in [7]. In [7], a collection of 44 functions was chosen from a larger set of 145 functions, primarily focused on high-dimensional optimization, as described in [2]. In our current work, we have expanded upon this collection by incorporating additional test functions.

To enhance the diversity and scope of the test suite, we introduced a quadratic penalty function that corresponds to a symmetric matrix game. Additionally, we integrated 10 new test functions, specifically designed for 10 neurons in a single-layer logistic regression model based on the MNIST dataset.

The inclusion of a simple single-layer logistic regression neural network model holds significance for benchmarking unconstrained minimization algorithms. After addressing some compatibility issues in the design, this model serves its purpose remarkably well. Firstly, it facilitates the loading of data from different datasets, such as irises or MNIST. Consequently, the model generates as many test functions as there are neurons present in the given dataset, ensuring a comprehensive evaluation of the optimization algorithms.

A model is designed by means of a class. It contains the same necessary minimalist functionality as unconstrained minimization test functions. Additionally, the model includes the necessary data for validation purposes, although we do not delve into this aspect at the current stage. Furthermore, a stopping condition is provided as a method within the class.

In addition to compatibility with optimizers, we have taken into account several points that are necessary for the efficient functioning of this model in the C++ language. Firstly, the class is templated, allowing for compatibility with different datasets or even alternative approaches for the same dataset. For instance, the MNIST dataset can be utilized with real numbers, as exemplified in these instances, or with different types of integers, which can enhance execution speed. While these details are not critical for our specific objectives, it is important to note one specific aspect. Unlike the commonly used formula $C = -y \cdot \log(\varphi(z)) - (1-y) \cdot \log(1-\varphi(z))$, we employ a modified version that utilizes a branching construction: if (y == 1) $C = -\log(\varphi(z))$; else $C = -\log(1 - \varphi(z))$;

In our tests, we deliberately increased the dimensions of the optimization tasks compared to those conducted in [7]. However, there is an exception with the function Penalty 2, where the objective function exhibits an exponential dependence on the dimension.

The optimization test functions in [7] corresponded to the samples implemented in the C/C++ available on the Internet. In such examples, representing a minimization problem often involves creating two functions: one for initializing the variables and another (with parameters such as variable vectors, derivative, and problem dimension) for calculating the value and gradient of the function. However, more sophisticated algorithms like CG_DESCENT-C-6.8 require four functions: value, gradient, value and gradient combined, and an initialization function. This time, we have introduced several innovations in the design of both the test collection and the solver program. Our aim was to create a more natural framework where the stopping condition and solution accuracy are intrinsic to the problem itself rather than being hardcoded in the solver program.

To achieve this, we have implemented a class-based approach where the minimization problem becomes an object of the corresponding class. This class encapsulates various methods, including the initialization and calculation of the value and gradient functions, as well as the function responsible for checking the stopping condition during the minimization process.

This design choice aligns closely with the mathematical formulation of the minimization problem and provides a more intuitive approach to constructing the test collection. For example, in our tests, we actively utilize two types of stopping conditions. For the unconstrained minimization tests taken from the CUTest collection, we focus on the smallness of the infinity norm of the gradient, while for the symmetric matrix game, we consider both the smallness of the objective function and penalties as the criteria for termination. In the case of the neural network used in our numerical experiments, we simplify the situation and emphasize the smallness of the infinite norm of the gradient, although in real-world scenarios, different stopping conditions may be required.

By integrating the stopping condition within the problem formulation itself, we enhance the flexibility and adaptability of the solver program, allowing for a more natural and comprehensive assessment of the optimization algorithms.

In our opinion, the issue of integrating the stopping condition into the minimization problem still needs to be worked out, although the difference between the old and the new approach is already visible. For example, we can consider the issue of how CG_DESCENT-C-6.8 takes the stopping condition into account. The main difficulty and inconvenience is that in order to use a different stopping condition in any problem, it becomes necessary to intervene in the algorithm code at the functionality level. To use the smallness of the infinity norm (of the gradient) as a stopping condition, we added the necessary instruction on line 1692 in the file "cg_descent.cpp" (which is copied from the software created by the authors of [13]. With such a primitive intervention, it becomes impossible to pass the tolerance (accuracy) to the stopping condition, and for a different value of EPS in another task, it becomes necessary to comment out the existing instruction and insert a new one with the appropriate EPS. This simple approach is unusable when we want the stopping condition to be the smallness (deviation) of the violation of certain inequalities or equalities. In such a case, an even deeper intervention is required: in the "cg_user.h" file (again in the author's text) in the cg_parameter structure, we add a field `Bool (*stop)()`; and then again in the specified place in the "cg_descent.cpp" file we replace the stopping condition by calling

```
if (Com->Parm->stop()) return 1;
```

Adding a new test to the test function collection is straightforward. For example, in the collection placed in the "problems.h" file, whose members are not implementing Hessian, there will be created a class corresponding to the new minimization problem (in direct analogy with the existing samples), then a smart pointer to the dynamically created object of this class will be added to the container of test-problems named problems_container. Suppose that the new test is called, for example, newTest. In order to add newTest in problems_container, in the implementation of the function `void makeDoubleTestsVector(void)` the following string should be added:

```
problems_container.emplace_back(make_unique<newTest>(1e-6));
```

Here, 1e-6 is passed to the constructor of the problem class as the solution precision for the given problem. It can be changed at this time, or later by referring to the appropriate public field. This can be seen, for example, in the file "log_regression.h", at the beginning of the implementation of the `void runANNTest()` function:

```
oneLayerLogRegr<double>* a = mnistLoader<double>
      (
              "Data/mnist/train-images.idx3-ubyte",
              "Data/mnist/train-labels.idx1-ubyte",
              "Data/mnist/t10k-images.idx3-ubyte",
              "Data/mnist/t10k-labels.idx1-ubyte"
      );
   a->EPS = 1e-0;
```

One issue that arises in the case of an unconstrained minimization problem represented as a class object is the issue of rendering it to the best existing solvers, such as CG_DESCENT-C-6.8. One possible solution we use is wrapping of the problem. As an example, let us consider the logistic regression model again, when we create an object corresponding to MNIST (see [11]) for a single-layer neural network and wrap it in the form required by lcg (CG_DESCENT-C-6.8). These codes are also uploaded on GitHub, so without going into details, we will focus on the main aspects. We will not focus on this issue anymore, because our adapted code of CG_DESCENT-C-6.8 is also uploaded on GitHub.

In our project "RawCollectionOfMinimizers," developed in Visual Studio 2022 using C++, we have incorporated several minimizers that we implemented, namely MHB, MNAG, L-BFGS, and ADAM. These minimizers are combined within the project, which serves as a unified framework for evaluating their performance. Additionally, we have included a line search algorithm, based on the principles outlined in [2], with its own default parameters. The importance of the line search algorithm cannot be overstated, as it plays a crucial role in achieving optimal performance for the minimizers. The detailed implementation of the line search algorithm can be found in [7], where we have extensively discussed our experiences with incorporating line search in momentum-based algorithms. This experimentation has yielded promising results.

However, in our specific numerical experiments, we have excluded ADAM and L-BFGS. The ADAM algorithm is relatively simple and slower compared to the other minimizers in our collection. As a result, we have opted to focus on the more advanced minimizers. For L-BFGS, because we use our own implementation, we have chosen to utilize the widely recognized CG_DESCENT-C-6.8 implementation, developed by reputable authors, as our benchmark for comparison. This decision was made to ensure consistency and align with established standards in the field of optimization.

3   A Specific Resource to Speed up Oscillation-Free Momentum-Based Algorithms

The Heavy Ball method is described by the following scheme:

$$x_{k+1} = x_k - \alpha g_k + \beta(x_k - x_{k-1}) \tag{1}$$

where $\alpha > 0, \beta >= 0$ are the parameters of the method (β is a parameter related to friction), and g_k represents the gradient at point x_k. $\beta < 1$ is necessary for the method to converge. However, in cases where the method is modified to eliminate oscillations, this condition becomes unnecessary for convergence and unnecessarily restricts the algorithm. In [7], we used $\beta = 1$ for simplicity. The results of the new experiments with $\beta = 1.001$ clearly demonstrate a significant improvement in the convergence speed of the modified Heavy Ball algorithm.

Now let's describe the current version of MHB. During any restarts, the learning rate is determined using a line search algorithm. Momentum is accumulated based on this coefficient. In each iteration, we utilize the antigradient from the current iteration for MHB. There are two differences from the version described in [7]. Firstly, the stopping condition is no longer solely based on the smallness of the gradient; it can be more flexible. Secondly, we reintroduce the β coefficient into the model.

For the sake of simplicity, let's assume the presence of a function called stoppingCondition(g), which may depend on the gradient, and it tests the algorithm's stopping condition, x_0 be initial iterate. Calling the swap(u0, u1) means that vectors u0 and u1 are changing their names: former u0 after call becomes u1 and vice versa. We use line search, described in [2]: in order to line search start its work correctly, x0, f0 (the initial itarate and the corresponding value of the objective function) and direction of (guaranteed) descent dir from x0 (in our case - g0) should be accessible. Line search finishes when it finds the vector $x_0 + t \cdot d$, at which the function $\phi(t) = f(x_0 + t \cdot d)$ satisfies the approximate Wolfe condition $(2\delta - 1)\phi'(0) \geq \phi'(t) \geq \sigma\phi'(0)$ and condition $\phi(t) \leq \phi(0) + \epsilon$. When it finished, $x_1 = x_0 + \alpha \cdot d, f_1, g_1$ (function value and gradient at the $x1$) should be accessible from the main program.

In the MHB, due to restarts, the objective function monotonically decreases along the iterates, therefore, we have no oscillation. This fact has been proven in [7] for the case where $\beta = 1$. It is important to note that the proof does not rely on the specific value of the β parameter. The convergence is a result of the information acquired from the line search, which remains independent of the β parameter. Every time when the standard step of HB is done (lines 8–14) a certain number of times (in our case 100000 times), or when at some iteration the objective function increases, MHB restarts. Each restart determines the parameter α on the basis of the line-search algorithm, in order to maintain the high-speed of the convergence. When restarting, MHB sharply changes its direction along its trajectory in the vicinity of the local minima (turns in the direction of the anti-gradient), but with preservation of high-speed of convergence (using line search).

```
1       g₀ = (f'(x₀))ᵀ ;        f₀ = f₁ = f(x₀);
2       if( stoppingCondition(g₀) )  return;
3       while(true)  {
4           if ( f₀ <= f₁ || counter == 100000 )
5               dir = g₀;
6               α = lineSearch();
7               counter = 0;
8           momentum = x₁ − x₀;
9           swap( x₀,x₁ );
10          swap( g₀,g₁ );
11          if( stoppingCondition(g₀) )  return;
12          f₀ = f₁ ;
13          x₁ = x₀ − α · g₀ + β · momentum;
14          f₁ = f(x₁);     g₁ = (f'(x₁))ᵀ ;
15          ++counter;
16      }
```

Listing 1. - MHB Algorithm

In our experiments, we conducted tests using different values of the β parameter. One value that consistently demonstrated superior performance is $\beta = 1.001$. The following figures present the results obtained from these experiments.

Figure 1 illustrates the performance profile for all 55 test functions, including the 10 tasks associated with the neural network, over the interval $[1,50]$. It is evident from the graph that MHB with a higher β value consistently outperforms the variant described in [7]. When examining the performance within the time interval $[1,10]$, MHB is even competitive with lcg.

Figure 2 focuses specifically on the results pertaining to the neural network tasks. The vertical axis represents the time taken in seconds. As depicted in the graph, the overall trend of improved performance with the higher β value is maintained.

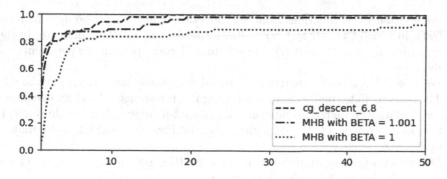

Fig. 1. Performance profile on [1, 50], based on CPU time

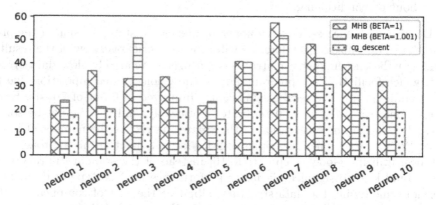

Fig. 2. CPU time

These figures provide a visual representation of the experimental results, clearly demonstrating the benefits of utilizing the $\beta = 1.001$ parameter and the enhanced performance of MHB over the previously described variant.

4   Preconditioned MHB

Preconditioning plays a crucial role in implementing efficient unconstrained minimizers. However, incorporating an effective preconditioner into an algorithm is a challenging task. Nonetheless, the impact of a preconditioner can be easily assessed by implementing the best optimizer without it and testing it on various test functions.

To investigate the effectiveness of preconditioning in MHB, we conducted the following activities:

- We selected 7 test functions from the collection of unconstrained optimization tests, in which CG_DESCENT-C-6.8 outperformed MHB significantly in the experiments presented in [7]. We conducted corresponding experiments on these tests.
- We developed a sparse matrix class based on `vector<map<int, double> >`. The class includes methods for computing the incomplete Cholesky decomposition of a given matrix, computing the limited-memory Cholesky decomposition as described in [13], and multiplying the inverse of the Cholesky matrix by a vector.
- We added a preconditioned solver to the MHB class, enabling the use of the preconditioner in the optimization process.
- We created a small test collection to compare the results of MHB with and without preconditioning.

Despite some success, we were unable to develop a stable version of the preconditioned optimizer. Therefore, we will provide a brief overview of the results. Although the chosen sparse matrix class utilized a relatively slow data structure, which facilitated the programming of the Cholesky decomposition due to its dynamic nature, the results significantly improved in 6 out of 7 tests. However, in one test, the results deteriorated noticeably, and this cannot be solely attributed to the implementation of the sparse matrix, as the number of iterations also increased. There is ample room for improvement in this approach. For instance, utilizing Google's cpp-btree [16] instead of the standard library map class would lead to significantly faster performance for this type of data. Furthermore, modifying the data structure, albeit at the cost of complicating the algorithms, is another avenue for exploration. However, it is important to note that the Cholesky decomposition approach, even in its most optimized form, may not yield superior results for all tests, and it is currently challenging to determine in advance which tests would benefit from this approach.

5   Experiments on Descent Directions - Oscillation-Free Modified Nesterov Accelerated Gradient Algorithm

The difference between MHB and MNAG is the standard step of the base algorithm. We can describe this difference in a simplified form as follows. Suppose at some iteration k, $momentum = x_k - x_{(k-1)}$, and g_k is the gradient at x_k. The next iteration for the classical momentum is determined by the formula:

$$x_{(k+1)} = x_k + momentum - \alpha g_k.$$

Let us split the operations on the right side into two. In HB, first the correction is made along the anti-gradient, and then the moment is added:

$$x_k = x_k - \alpha g_k, \qquad x_{(k+1)} = x_k + momentum.$$

In contrast, in Nesterov's accelerated gradient, the operations are permuted. First the moment is added, then the gradient is calculated and the correction is made:

$$x_{(k+1)} = x_k + momentum, \qquad x_{(k+1)}- = \alpha g_{(k+1)}.$$

For simplicity we omit the coefficient for the momentum term in MHB.

One possible form of the MNAG algorithm pseudocode is presented in Listing 2. Data transfer between line search algorithm and the solver is identical as for MHB.

Although one iteration of MNAG requires relatively more computations than one iteration of MHB, it is relatively fast in our test collection. In particular, Fig. 3 shows that MNAG performs uniformly better compared to MHB. Figure 4 is more interesting. It shows that speedup of MHB is possible with both approaches: via selecting the β coefficient and via changing the descent direction. Both of these changes give approximately the same improvement.

```
1      while(true) {
2          if( f_0 <= f_1 || counter == 100000)
3              if (1 != counter)
4                  g_0 = (f'(x_0))^T ;   f_0 = f(x_0);
5              if( stoppingCondition(g_0) )  return;
6              dir = g_0;
7              α = lineSearch();
8              counter = 0;
9          momentum = x_1 - x_0;
10         swap( x_0,x_1 );
11         swap( g_0,g_1 );
11         f_0 = f_1
13         x_1 = x_0 + momentum;
18         g_1 = (f'(x_1))^T
19         if( stoppingCondition(g_1) )  return;
20             swap( x_0,x_1 );
21             swap( g_0,g_1 );
22             return;
23         x_1 = x_0 - α · g_1 + β · momentum;      //default: beta = 1;
24         f_1 = f(x_1);
25         ++counter;
```

Listing 2. - MNAG Algorithm

6   Conclusions

Based on our previous publications, we have determined that MHB and CG_DESCENT-C-6.8 are competitive algorithms, although CG_DESCENT-C-6.8 still holds a slight advantage. However, this advantage is somewhat mitigated by the fact that MHB is relatively easy to implement and does not require additional memory. It should be noted that MHB cannot be classified as a lightweight algorithm due to its utilization of a complex line search procedure.

In our recent experiments, where the size of the test functions has been significantly increased, the performance gap between MHB and CG_DESCENT-C-6.8 has widened (although only slightly) in favor of the latter. Nevertheless, the results presented here demonstrate that there are several possible modifications to MHB that can lead to a significant improvement in its convergence speed. These modifications open up avenues for further optimization of MHB and highlight its potential for achieving even better performance.

Several avenues for improvement have been identified for further enhancing the performance of MHB. One notable modification is adjusting the coefficient related to friction, as depicted in Listing 1. Through experimental analysis, we have identified a value for this coefficient that proved effective across different test groups. However, there is room for further improvement by exploring other potential values based on theoretical research. An intriguing possibility is introducing mutability to the β coefficient, which could potentially enhance the algorithm's efficiency. For example, altering the α parameter of the model (1) during different restarts, determined through line search, resulted in a substantial acceleration by several orders of magnitude.

Figures 3 and 4 highlight the significance of studying descent directions. There may be parallels with the group of conjugate gradient algorithms, which differentiate themselves through their distinct descent directions. Exploring this aspect could lead to valuable insights and further improvements in MHB's performance.

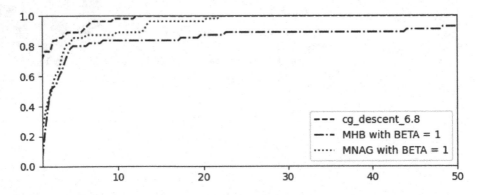

Fig. 3. Performance profile on [1,50], based on CPU time

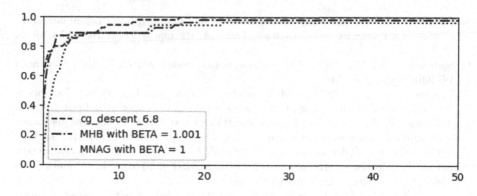

Fig. 4. Performance profile on [1,50], based on CPU time

To draw more informative conclusions, we believe it is essential to pursue additional research in two directions: conducting experiments on neural networks with more than two layers and developing more efficient non-oscillating momentum-based algorithms.

Of particular interest is the profile depicted in Fig. 4, which demonstrates that MHB can be accelerated through both approaches: adjusting the β coefficient and modifying the descent direction. Both of these changes yield similar levels of improvement. It is therefore logical to explore the possibility of implementing both changes simultaneously, with the expectation of achieving even greater advancements in performance.

Lastly, in order to popularize oscillation-free momentum-based algorithms, we have plans to create and share animations on GitHub for low dimensions (2 and 3) with carefully selected objective functions.

References

1. Liu, D.C., Nocedal, J.: On the limited memory bfgs method for large scale optimization. Math. Program. (Ser. B) **45**(3), 503–528 (1989)
2. Hager, W.W., Zhang, H.: The limited memory conjugate gradient method. SIAM J. Optim. **23**(4), 2150–2168 (2013)
3. Sutskever, I., Martens, J., Dahl, G., Hinton, G.: On the importance of initialization and momentum in deep learning. In: ICML'13: Proceedings of the 30th International Conference on International Conference on Machine Learning - Volume 28 June 2013, pp. III-1139-III-1147
4. Sebastian Ruder. An overview of gradient descent optimization algorithms. arXiv:1609.04747 [cs.LG], https://doi.org/10.48550/arXiv.1609.04747
5. Kingma, D.P., Ba, J.L.: Adam: a method for stochastic optimization. In: International Conference on Learning Representations, pp. 1–13 (2015)
6. Reddi, S.J., Kale, S., Kumar, S.: On the Convergence of Adam and Beyond. arXiv:1904.09237 [cs.LG.] https://doi.org/10.48550/arXiv.1904.09237
7. Gelashvili, K., Khutsishvili, I., Gorgadze, L., Alkhazishvili, L.: Speeding up the Convergence of the Polyak's Heavy Ball Algorithm. Trans. A. Razmadze Math. Inst. **172**(2), 176–188 (2018)

8. Gelashvili, K.: Add-in for Solvers of unconstrained minimization to eliminate lower bounds of variables by transformation. Trans. A. Razmadze Math. Inst. **173**, 39–46 (2019)

9. Source code for CG_DESCENT Version 6.8 (C code), March 7, 2015. Software | William Hager (ufl.edu)

10. Ernesto P. Adorio, U.P.: MVF-Multivariete Test Functions Library in C for Unconstrained Global Optimization. http://www.geocities.ws/eadorio/mvf.pdf

11. Alkhazishvili, L., Gorgadze, L.: A Collection of test functions for unconstrained optimization solvers with serial and parallel C++ implementations. http://eprints.tsu.ge/1206/1/A%20collection_%20%20%20%20L.Alkhazishvili_L.Gorgadze.pdf

12. LeCun, Y., Cortes, C., Burges, C.J.C.: THE MNIST DATABASE of handwritten digits. http://yann.lecun.com/exdb/mnist/

13. Lin, C.-J., Moré, J.J.: Incomplete Cholesky factorizations with limited memory. SIAM J. Sci. Comput. **21**(1), 24–45 (1999)

14. Nesterov, Y.: A method for unconstrained convex minimization problem with the rate of convergence o(1/k2). Doklady ANSSSR (translated as Soviet. Math. Docl.), 269, 543–547

15. Dolan, E.D., Moré, J.J.: Benchmarking optimization software with performance profiles. Math. Program. Ser. A **91**(2), 201–213 (2002)

16. cpp-btree. https://code.google.com/archive/p/cpp-btree/

Performance Comparison of NSGA-II and NSGA-III on Bi-objective Job Shop Scheduling Problems

Francisco dos Santos[1,2] (ID), Lino A. Costa[1,3(✉)] (ID), and Leonilde Varela[1,3] (ID)

[1] ALGORITMI Research Centre/LASI, University of Minho, Braga, Portugal
francisco_dos_santos@outlook.pt
[2] Polytechnic Institute, University Kimpa Vita, Uíge, Angola
[3] Department of Production and Systems, University of Minho, Braga, Portugal
{lac,leonilde}@dps.uminho.pt

Abstract. Job Shop Scheduling (JSS) problems emerge in many industrial sectors, where it is sought to maximize efficiency, minimize costs, minimize energy consumption among other conflicting objectives. Thus, these optimization problems involve two or more objectives. In recent years, new algorithms have been developed and proposed to tackle multi-objective problems such as the Non-dominated Sorting Genetic Algorithm II (NSGA-II) and the Non-dominated Sorting Genetic Algorithm III (NSGA-III), among others. The main goal of this work is to compare the performance of these algorithms on solving bi-objective JSS problems on unrelated parallel machines with sequence-dependent setup times. For comparison purposes, the results of the hypervolume performance measure are statistically analysed. The results obtained show that the performance of these two algorithms is not significantly different and, therefore, NSGA-III does not represent a clear advantage on solving bi-objective JSS problems.

Keywords: Multi-objective Optimization · Job Shop Scheduling · Algorithms

1 Introduction

The increase in computational capacity allows more robust and more realistic models for optimization problem in the industrial area. One of the important areas in the production process is production planning and programming, usually also known as Job Shop Scheduling (JSS) [12] in which different jobs are processed on different machines and each job comprises a sequence of tasks that must be executed in a certain time in order to maximize efficiency, minimize costs, minimize energy consumption among other conflicting objectives. Although single objective JSS problems have been solved using appropriate techniques [10],

This work has been supported by FCT - Fundação para a Ciência e Tecnologia within the R&D Units Project Scope: UIDB/00319/2020, and EXPL/EME-SIS/1224/2021.

A. I. Pereira et al. (Eds.): OL2A 2023, CCIS 1981, pp. 531–543, 2024.
https://doi.org/10.1007/978-3-031-53025-8_36

in practice, these problems involve many objectives to be simultaneously optimized that require the use of appropriate techniques to solve them [14,15]. So, a single objective optimization approach reveals to be insufficient to provide sufficient information to make decisions in industry and the use of multi-objective optimization approaches become crucial. In fact, most job shop scheduling (JSS) problems involve many objectives (more than three objectives) to be optimized simultaneously such as makespan, energy consumption, reduction of average task completion time, delay reduction, cost reduction, latency, among other objectives [1,16].

In recent years, new algorithms have be developed and proposed to tackle many objectives simultaneously [6]. The application of evolutionary algorithms have proven to be efficient in dealing with these complex multi-objective optimization problems [5]. Evolutionary algorithms such as GA and NSGA-II [7] have been used to solve different problems, whether single-objective or multi-objective problems. However, some studies show that these algorithms do not perform well when it comes to optimization problems with more than three objectives, because the selection pressure to pull the population to the Pareto front is lost. NSGA-III [11] was developed with the objective of solving problems with many objectives, where the search is oriented by a certain number of well distributed reference points [8]. Nevertheless, it is also important to study the performance of NSGA-III on problems with less than three objectives.

Several instances of JSS optimization problems with M unrelated machines, considering N tasks with sequence-dependent setup times have been successfully solved using a genetic algorithm (GA) to minimize the makespan [13]. In this work, bi-objective JSS problems are solved in which the goal is to find the best sequence of tasks in each machine that minimizes, simultaneously, the makespan and the average task completion time. A set of small instances is used to analyze and compare the performance of the NSGA-II and NSGA-III algorithms. So, the goal is to assess if there exist advantages of using NSGA-III when compared with NSGA-II for solving bi-objective JSS problems.

Therefore, this paper is organized as follows. In Sect. 1 an introduction is made stating the objectives and motivation of this work. Section 2 briefly presents some works on multi-objective JSS, the description of JSS problems, and the multi-objective algorithms. In Sect. 3, the experimental results are presented and discussed. Finally, Sect. 4 the conclusions and future work are addressed.

2   Multi-objective Job Shop Scheduling

The unrelated parallel machine scheduling problem is a JSS problem consisting on the scheduling of N jobs on M unrelated machines. The term span is generally used to define the completion time of a given machine, while the term makespan is generally used for the maximum completion time [2]. In spite of makespan being the most common objective to be minimized, there are other relevant conflicting objectives such as the average completion time [16]. So, problems arising from JSS can be considered multi-objective optimization problems since a large part of the problems in industry have more than one objective to be optimized. In this sense, there exist a set of trade-off solutions balancing differently among the objectives.

2.1   Problem Description

In the JSS problem, it is assumed that all M machines are continuously available, and each machine i can only execute one task j at each instant. Moreover, all N tasks are independent without any precedence restriction and available to be processed at the initial instant. Preemption is not allowed, that is, the processing of any task in a machine cannot be interrupted.

In the JSS problem formulation, $p_{i,j}$ is the processing time for task j on machine i, and $s_{i,j,k}$ is the setup time for task j after job k to be processed on machine i. The setup time for processing task j at the initial time on machine i is denoted by $s_{i,j,0}$. The feasible sequence of all tasks assigned to machines, π, is the vector of all feasible subsequences π_i on each machine i. For each machine i, $c_i(\pi)$ is the total completion time of tasks for the feasible sequence π.

The goal is to find feasible sequences of tasks that minimize simultaneously the makespan $(c_{max}(\pi))$ and the average completion time $(\bar{c}(\pi))$, considering machine sequence-dependent setup times. Mathematically, these objectives can be formulated as follows [14]:

$$c_{\max}(\pi) = \max_{i=1,\ldots,M} (c_i(\pi)) \tag{1}$$

and

$$\bar{c}(\pi) = \frac{1}{M} \sum_{i=1}^{M} c_i(\pi) \tag{2}$$

where $c_i(\pi) = \sum_{j \in \pi_i} p_{i,j} + \sum_{j \in \pi_i} s_{i,j,k}$ with k being the precedent task of task j in the subsequence π_i of the feasible sequence π. Note that if the task j is the first task in the subsequence π_i then k is zero and the setup time $s_{i,j,0}$ at the initial instant is considered.

Therefore, the bi-objective JSS optimization problem can be mathematical written as follows:

$$\min \mathbf{F}(\pi) = (f_1(\pi), f_2(\pi))^T = (c_{\max}(\pi), \bar{c}(\pi))^T \tag{3}$$

where π is a feasible sequence of size l belonging to the feasible set Ω (the set of all permutations of size l), and $\mathbf{F}(\pi)$ is the objective vector defined in the objective space.

Solutions are compared based on Pareto dominance. For any two solutions π_a and π_b of the feasible set Ω, a solution π_a is said to dominate a solution π_b $(\pi_a \prec \pi_b)$ if $\forall_{i \in \{1,2\}} : f_i(\pi_a) \leq f_i(\pi_b) \land \exists_{j \in \{1,2\}} : f_j(\pi_a) < f_j(\pi_b)$.

Since the different solutions are compared with respect to different objectives, there is no longer a single optimal solution. In this case, there exist a set of optimal solutions, generally known as the Pareto optimal set. The images of the Pareto optimal solutions define a Pareto front in the objective space, i.e., $\mathbf{PS} = \{\pi_{\mathbf{x}} \in \Omega \mid \nexists \pi_{\mathbf{y}} \in \Omega : \pi_{\mathbf{y}} \prec \pi_{\mathbf{x}}\}$. The Pareto front allows the identification of the trade-offs between the different solutions, thus facilitating decision making.

2.2   Multi-objective Algorithms

Multi-objective optimization deals with problems with two or more objective functions that need to be optimized at the same time. Usually, these objective functions are conflicting each other in such a way that improving one generally leads to degrading the others. The goal of a multi-objective optimization problem is to find a set of solutions that not only satisfies all imposed constraints, but also best balances the trade-off between the objectives [12]. From an algorithmic perspective, addressing multiple objectives and approximating the Pareto set that optimally balances them further increases the complexity of designing an efficient optimization techniques.

In the last decades, new algorithms have been developed to solve multi-objective optimization problems and, more recently, many-objective optimization problems. Evolutionary algorithms have proven to be efficient in dealing with these complex optimization problems [5]. These algorithms mimic the natural evolution of the species to guide the search. In this paper, NSGA-II [7] and NSGA-III [11] are used to solve bi-objective JSS problems for comparison purposes.

NSGA-II [7] is a well-known algorithm and has a good performance on problems with two or three objectives. However, when the number of objectives increases, its performance tends to decrease [9]. In this algorithm, the search starts from a population of chromosomes generated at random. Each chromosome represents a potential solution of the multi-objective optimization problem. All chromosomes are evaluated using a fitness measure that depends on a Pareto ranking and a crowding measure. In the Pareto ranking procedure, to all non-dominated individuals in the current population is assigned the best rank value. These solutions are then discarded from population for performing the next step of Pareto ranking. So, considering only the remaining solutions, to the non-dominated solutions is assigned the second best rank. This procedure is repeated until all solutions being ranked. A crowding measure is also computed for solutions to provide diversity. A binary tournament selection is used to select a set of parent solutions for reproduction. In the tournament, the solution with the best non-domination rank is preferred to the other. Otherwise, if both solutions have the same non-domination rank, the one with the highest crowding distance is selected. Next, genetic operators such as crossover and mutation are applied to create an offspring population. Then, the two populations are merged together and sorted according to the non-dominated fronts. If the size, of the first non-dominated front is smaller then the population size, all members of this front are copied to the population of the next generation. The remaining members of the population are chosen from subsequent non-dominated fronts in the order of their ranking.

NSGA-III [11] was developed to tackle many-objective optimization problems. NSGA-III seeks to maintain the diversity of solutions by using reference points. This algorithm has been developed after NSGA-II, differing from its ancestor by using reference points in the process of selecting solutions. The reference points are scattered on a hyperplane with a given dimension. The solution selection process in NSGA-III is done by associating each of the solutions to a reference point with the closest perpendicular distance, and if two of them are at the same point, the solution with the shortest distance is chosen, thus maintaining the diversity of solutions. In this manner, the search is guided toward the Pareto front. The rest of NSGA-III works similarly to NSGA-II.

3   Experimental Results

Several test problems were taken from previous works [2,3,14] to compare the performance of the NSGA-II and NSGA-III. Only small problems with balanced processing and setup time were considered for $M \in \{2,4,6,8\}$, and $N \in \{6,7,8\}$. For each combination of the number of machines and work, 15 different instances were solved. Two objectives were considered in each instance of the problems: minimization of the makespan $(c_{max}(\pi))$ and the average completion time $(\bar{c}(\pi))$.

3.1   Implementation Details

The implementation of NSGA-II and NSGA-III provided by the PYMOO framework [4] (in Python) were used. These implementations were adapted in order to solve the bi-objective JSS instances of the problem that has a combinatorial nature. Thus, a permutation representation was adopted to represent the feasible sequences of tasks on each machine π. A solution is represented by a chromosome which is a permutation of size $M + N - 1$, i.e., a sequence of integer values that can only occur once. In a chromosome, genes that are greater than N serve to separate the chromosome into M subsequences π_i that indicate the set of tasks and the corresponding order assigned to each machine i. In Fig. 1, the chromosome representation used is illustrated for $M = 2$ and $N = 6$. In this example, the chromosome is a permutation $\pi = < 4,6,7,5,2,3,1 >$ of size 7 since $M + N - 1 = 2 + 6 - 1 = 7$. The gene with value 7 (greater than $N = 6$) separates the chromosome in two parts that correspond to the subsequences of tasks for each machine, i.e., $\pi_1 = < 4,6 >$ and $\pi_2 = < 5,2,3,1 >$.

The selection operator used was the tournament selection operator to select the chromosomes for the application of the genetic operators. The genetic operators were chosen to ensure the feasibility of the solutions during the search: order-based crossover and inversion mutation. In the order-based crossover, two chromosomes are combined to generate offspring by selecting two positions at random and swapping the genes between them. Then the remaining empty positions are filled with the genes from the other parent, avoiding repeats. In the inversion mutation, two positions are randomly generated and the genes on the chromosome are reversed.

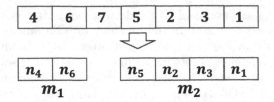

Fig. 1. Example of a chromosome for $M = 2$ and $N = 6$.

The population size used was 40 individuals on both algorithms. The stopping criterion was based on the maximum number of generations and the period without new improvements. Therefore, the total number of generations was set at 10,000 and the period at 100 generations.

Since the algorithms used are stochastic, 30 independent runs were performed. The hypervolume indicator (H) was used to assess the algorithms performance [17] since it measures the algorithm performance in terms of convergence to the Pareto front as well as the diversity of the solutions in the objective space. So, for each independent run, the hypervolume was computed considering the reference point $(1000, 1000)^T$. All hypervolume values were standardized into the interval $[0, 1]$. The higher the value of hypervolume, the best the performance of the algorithm.

The distribution of the hypervolume values for the 15 instances of the bi-objective JSS problem for each combination of M and N was statistically analyzed. In all statistical tests, a significance level of 5% was considered.

3.2   Results

The results are analysed in terms of the maximum hypervolume that indicates the best approximation to the Pareto fronts achieved by the algorithms for all 15 instances and the mean hypervolume that is related with the mean performance of the algorithms. It should be noted that for each instance, 30 independent runs were performed. Therefore, the maximum hypervolume corresponds to the best performance of the algorithms in all 30 runs. In addition, it is also considered the mean hypervolume that is a central tendency measure that reflects the average behaviour of the algorithms.

In Table 1, the statistics for the maximum hypervolume computed for the Pareto fronts obtained by the two algorithms for 15 instances of the bi-objective JSS problem are presented. These statistics are given in terms of each combination of M and N. In this table, $avg(H_{\max}^{II})$, $avg(H_{\max}^{III})$, $sd(H_{\max}^{II})$, $sd(H_{\max}^{III})$ are the average and standard deviation of the best hypervolume (maximum hypervolume) obtained, respectively. The difference between the best hypervolume of NSGA-II and the best hypervolume of NSGA-III, $avg(H_{\max}^{II}) - avg(H_{\max}^{III})$, and the p-values for the two-tailed paired t-student test are also provided.

In this table, it can be observed that the averages of the best hypervolumes for both algorithms are similar. It can be seen that NSGA-II was superior to

NSGA-III for the following combinations: **M2-N6, M2-N7, M4-N6, M4-N7,** and **M6-N8**. The opposite occurs for the remaining combinations. Nevertheless, the differences are not statistically significant since the p-values are all higher than 5% for all combinations of M and N. Thus, it can be said that there are no significant differences between the NSGA-II or NSGA-III in terms of the best hypervolumes achieved for all combinations of M and N.

Table 1. Statistics for the maximum hypervolume computed for Pareto fronts on bi-objective JSS problems using algorithms NSGA-II and NSGA-III.

M	N	$avg(H_{max}^{II})$	$sd(H_{max}^{II})$	$avg(H_{max}^{III})$	$sd(H_{max}^{III})$	$avg(H_{max}^{II}) - avg(H_{max}^{III})$	p-value
2	6	0.3754	0.0159	0.3753	0.0158	0.0001	0.1681
	7	0.2813	0.0142	0.2811	0.0141	0.0002	0.0664
	8	0.2388	0.0161	0.2389	0.0166	−0.0001	0.7709
4	6	0.6175	0.0081	0.6167	0.0083	0.0008	0.3205
	7	0.5898	0.0108	0.5888	0.0117	0.0010	0.2958
	8	0.5561	0.0063	0.5577	0.0079	−0.0016	0.3601
6	8	0.6442	0.0086	0.6441	0.0085	0.0001	0.6653

Table 2 presents the same statistics but in terms of the mean hypervolume computed for the Pareto fronts obtained by the two algorithms for the same 15 instances of the bi-objective JSS problem. In this table, $avg(H_{mean}^{II})$, $avg(H_{mean}^{III})$, $sd(H_{mean}^{II})$, $sd(H_{mean}^{III})$ are the average and standard deviation of the mean hypervolume (mean hypervolume), and $avg(H_{mean}^{II}) - avg(H_{mean}^{III})$ is the difference between the mean hypervolume of NSGA-II and the mean hypervolume of NSGA-III, respectively. Unlike the previous table, the results in this table are based on the mean hypervolumes of each instance in the case of the two algorithms. The differences between the performance of NSGA-II and NSGA-III are again very small. Now, it can be seen that NSGA-II was superior to NSGA-III for the following combinations: **M2-N6, M2-N7, M4-N7,** and **M6-N8**. The opposite occurs in the rest of the combinations. It should be noted that, for **M4-N6**, NSGA-III performed better than NSGA-II. All p-values are superior to 5% and, therefore, no significant differences exist.

Although this results could indicate that the performance of these two algorithms is similar on these problems, it is important to confirm if the number of objective function evaluations was not significantly different since it can vary due to stopping criteria adopted. Table 3 shows the number of objective function evaluations required by the two algorithms to obtain the results previously presented in Table 1 and Table 2. In this table, $avg(F^{II})$, $avg(F^{III})$, $sd(F^{II})$ and $sd(F^{III})$ are the mean and the standard deviation objective function evaluations for NSGA-II and NSGA-III, respectively. The p-value for the two-tailed paired t-student test is also indicated. It can be seen that, for all problems, NSGA-III required a large number of objective function evaluations than NSGA-II. Moreover, for the combination **M2-N8**, the difference is statistically significant since the p-value less than 5%. For all other cases, there are no statistically

Table 2. Statistics for the mean hypervolume computed for Pareto fronts on bi-objective JSS problems using NSGA-II and NSGA-III.

M	N	$avg(H_{\mathrm{mean}}^{II})$	$sd(H_{\mathrm{mean}}^{II})$	$avg(H_{\mathrm{mean}}^{III})$	$sd(H_{\mathrm{mean}}^{III})$	$avg(H_{\mathrm{mean}}^{II}) - avg(H_{\mathrm{mean}}^{III})$	p-value
2	6	0.3753	0.0159	0.3752	0.0158	0.0001	0.4687
	7	0.2803	0.0142	0.2800	0.0141	0.0003	0.2360
	8	0.2367	0.0165	0.2369	0.0168	−0.0003	0.4200
4	6	0.6154	0.0084	0.6155	0.0085	−0.0001	0.8336
	7	0.5864	0.0111	0.5861	0.0118	0.0003	0.6430
	8	0.5534	0.0090	0.5536	0.0088	−0.0002	0.4813
6	8	0.6400	0.0082	0.6391	0.0076	0.0009	0.3699

significant differences. As expected, it can also be observed that the number of required objective function evaluations grows with the dimension of the problem $(M + N - 1)$.

Table 3. Statistics for the average number of objective function evaluations for NSGA-II and NSGA-III.

M	N	$avg(\mathrm{F}^{II})$	$sd(\mathrm{F}^{II})$	$avg(\mathrm{F}^{III})$	$sd(\mathrm{F}^{III})$	$avg(\mathrm{F}^{II}) - avg(\mathrm{F}^{III})$	p-value
2	6	4650.18	395.02	4700.71	406.36	−50.53	0.1055
	7	5119.80	378.90	5199.89	449.38	−80.09	0.3820
	8	5627.73	611.52	6036.71	826.07	−408.98	0.0027
4	6	5184.90	413.60	5250.57	461.62	−65.67	0.4902
	7	6112.72	502.04	6226.22	365.63	−113.50	0.2193
	8	6733.91	600.14	6992.71	643.26	−258.80	0.0832
6	8	6693.33	580.75	6781.71	597.88	−88.37	0.3294

Figures 2a to 2g show the boxplots for the distributions of the differences between NSGA-II and NSGA-III for the 15 instances, in terms of the maximum hypervolume $(H_{\mathrm{max}}^{II} - H_{\mathrm{max}}^{III})$ and the average hypervolume $(H_{\mathrm{mean}}^{II} - H_{\mathrm{mean}}^{III})$ for each combination of M and N. Note the existence of outliers that indicate that there are some instances in which the performance of the algorithms differ greatly when compared with the other instances. In terms of $H_{\mathrm{max}}^{II} - H_{\mathrm{max}}^{III}$, taking into account the outliers, it can be observed that, when compared to NSGA-III:

- for **M2-N6**, NSGA-II is better on two instances;
- for **M2-N7**, NSGA-II is better on two instances;
- for **M2-N8**, NSGA-II is better on two instances and worse on one instance;
- for **M4-N6**, NSGA-II is better on two instances;
- for **M4-N7**, NSGA-II is better on one instance;
- for **M4-N8**, NSGA-II is better on one instance and worse on two instances;
- for **M6-N8**, NSGA-II is better on one instance.

Overall, NSGA-II performed better than NSGA-III in a superior number of instances for almost all combinations of M and N.

In terms of $H_{\text{mean}}^{II} - H_{\text{mean}}^{III}$, taking into account the quartiles, it can be observed that:

- for **M2-N6**, NSGA-II is worse than NSGA-III on about 25% of the instances;
- for **M2-N7**, NSGA-II and NSGA-III are similar since NSGA-II is better on about 50% of the instances and the opposite occurs on the other instances;
- for **M2-N8**, NSGA-II is worse than NSGA-III on about 25% of the instances;
- for **M4-N6**, NSGA-II is better on about 75% of the instances;
- for **M4-N7**, NSGA-II and NSGA-III are similar;
- for **M4-N8**, NSGA-II and NSGA-III are similar;
- for **M6-N8**, NSGA-II is better on more than 50% of the instances.

In general, NSGA-II performed better than NSGA-III. However, there are some exceptions that are highlighted by the existence of outliers. Thus, it is interesting to study these outliers, in particular, in terms of $H_{\max}$ differences. For this purpose, Figs. 3 and 4 depict the Pareto fronts for two of those outliers in terms of the maximum hypervolume observed in Figs. 2e and 2f. In the Pareto fronts, the trade-off solutions in terms of the minimization of the makespan and the average completion are shown.

Figure 3 shows the Pareto fronts obtained by the two algorithms for an outlier (instance 3) that corresponds to a better performance of NSGA-II (upper left outlier in Fig. 2e). The solutions obtained by NSGA-II and NSGA-III are represented by circles and triangles, respectively. Two of those solutions were found by both algorithms. However, solutions close to both extremes of the Pareto front were not found simultaneously by the two algorithms. NSGA-II achieved the solution with best value of average completion time, while NSGA-III was able to find solutions with better values of makespan. Furthermore, all solutions found by the two algorithms are non-dominated and, therefore, the best approximation to the Pareto set is obtained by joining these two sets. It can be seen that hypervolume of NSGA-II is larger then the hypervolume of NSGA-III.

Figure 4 shows the Pareto fronts obtained by the two algorithms for another outlier (instance 7) that corresponds to a worst performance of NSGA-II (lower left outlier in Fig. 2f). The solutions obtained by NSGA-II and NSGA-III are represented by circles and triangles, respectively. Almost all trade-off solutions were found by both algorithms with the exception of only one different solution for each algorithm. It can be seen that only NSGA-II found the trade-off solution corresponding to a makespan of 453.0 and an average completion time of 232.5. On the other hand, just NSGA-III has achieved to the solution with a makespan of 330.0 and an average completion time of 238.0. Again, all solutions found by the two algorithms are non-dominated and, therefore, the best approximation to the Pareto set is obtained by joining these two sets. In this case, the hypervolume of NSGA-III is superior than the hypervolume of NSGA-II.

In these two examples, it is clear that the approximations to the Pareto front obtained by these two algorithms separately are incomplete since all solutions are

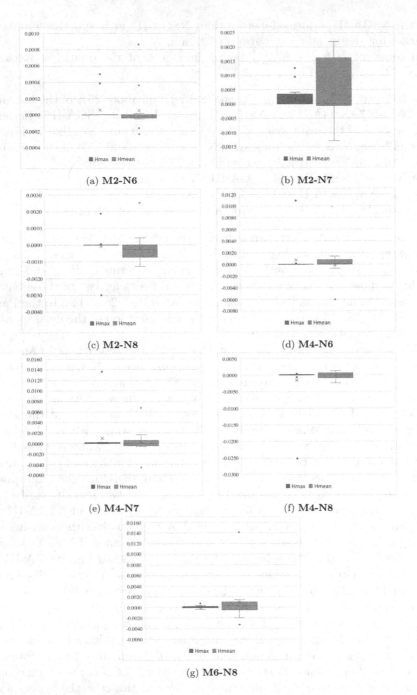

Fig. 2. Boxplots for the distribution of the differences between NSGA-II and NSGA-III in terms of the maximum and average hypervolumes for **M2-N6**, **M2-N7**, **M2-N8**, **M4-N6**, **M4-N7**, **M4-N8** and **M6-N8**.

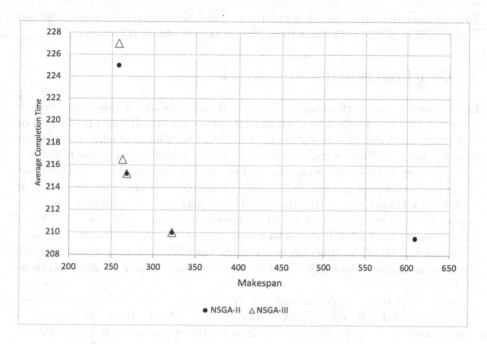

Fig. 3. Pareto front of the outlier instance from **M4-N7**.

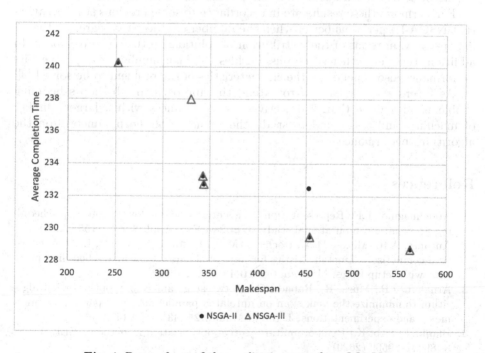

Fig. 4. Pareto front of the outlier instance from **M4-N8**.

non-dominated. This means that for this specific context the best approximation is obtained by joining solutions from NSGA-II and NSGA-III.

4   Conclusions and Future Work

In this paper, the performance of NSGA-II and NSGA-III was compared in terms of several bi-objective optimization job shop scheduling problems. For this purpose, 15 different instances with different number of machines and tasks were considered. The objectives were to minimize, simultaneously, the makespan and the average task completion time. The performance of the algorithms was statistically analysed in terms of the hypervolume measure. The results show that NSGA-II and NSGA-III achieved similar performance, although, in many cases, NSGA-II overcomes NSGA-III with respect to the maximum and average hypervolume. So, NSGA-II seems to be also preferable since it required in these problems less objective function evaluations than NSGA-III. However, overall, there are no statistically significant differences between these algorithms on these problems.

In spite of these results, it was observed that, in some instances, the algorithms obtained different approximations to the Pareto front. Joining these approximations, it is possible to obtain a better approximation to the Pareto front since all solution are non-dominated. This may suggest that further experiments must be carried out to tune the parameters of the algorithms.

Furthermore, these results are in accordance to some previous studies saying that NSGA-III performs better when the number of objectives is greater than 3 [6], specially, in terms of the distribution of solutions in the objective space. In addition, there are other situations, besides the high number of objectives, its performance also depends on the characteristics of the problem to be solved [9].

As future work, we intend to extend the approach to job shop scheduling problems with more than 2 objectives using instances with a larger number of machines and tasks, and to study the influence of the parameters on the algorithms performance.

References

1. Abdelmaguid, T.F.: Representations in genetic algorithm for the job shop scheduling problem: a computational study. J. Softw. Eng. Appl. **3**(12), 1155 (2010)
2. Antunes, A.R., Matos, M.A., Rocha, A.M.A., Costa, L.A., Varela, L.R.: A statistical comparison of metaheuristics for unrelated parallel machine scheduling problems with setup times. Mathematics **10**(14), 2431 (2022)
3. Arnaout, J.P., Musa, R., Rabadi, G.: A two-stage ant colony optimization algorithm to minimize the makespan on unrelated parallel machines-part ii: enhancements and experimentations. J. Intell. Manuf. **25**, 43–53 (2014)
4. Blank, J., Deb, K.: Pymoo: multi-objective optimization in python. IEEE Access **8**, 89497–89509 (2020)

5. Chaudhari, P., Thakur, A.K., Kumar, R., Banerjee, N., Kumar, A.: Comparison of NSGA-III with NSGA-II for multi objective optimization of adiabatic styrene reactor. Materials Today: Proc. **57**, 1509–1514 (2022)
6. Ciro, G.C., Dugardin, F., Yalaoui, F., Kelly, R.: A NSGA-II and NSGA-III comparison for solving an open shop scheduling problem with resource constraints. IFAC-PapersOnLine **49**(12), 1272–1277 (2016)
7. Deb, K., Pratap, A., Agarwal, S., Meyarivan, T.: A fast and elitist multiobjective genetic algorithm: NSGA-II. IEEE Trans. Evol. Comput. **6**(2), 182–197 (2002). https://doi.org/10.1109/4235.996017
8. Ibrahim, A., Rahnamayan, S., Martin, M.V., Deb, K.: EliteNSGA-III: an improved evolutionary many-objective optimization algorithm. In: 2016 IEEE Congress on Evolutionary Computation (CEC), pp. 973–982. IEEE (2016)
9. Ishibuchi, H., Imada, R., Setoguchi, Y., Nojima, Y.: Performance comparison of NSGA-II and NSGA-III on various many-objective test problems. In: 2016 IEEE Congress on Evolutionary Computation (CEC), pp. 3045–3052 (2016). https://doi.org/10.1109/CEC.2016.7744174
10. Katoch, S., Chauhan, S.S., Kumar, V.: A review on genetic algorithm: past, present, and future. Multimed. Tools Appl. **80**, 8091–8126 (2021)
11. Khan, B., Hanoun, S., Johnstone, M., Lim, C.P., Creighton, D., Nahavandi, S.: Multi-objective job shop scheduling using i-NSGA-III. In: 2018 Annual IEEE International Systems Conference (SysCon), pp. 1–5. IEEE (2018)
12. Para, J., Del Ser, J., Nebro, A.J.: Energy-aware multi-objective job shop scheduling optimization with metaheuristics in manufacturing industries: A critical survey, results, and perspectives. Appl. Sci. **12**(3), 1491 (2022)
13. Santos, F., Costa, L.: Multivariate analysis to assist decision-making in many-objective engineering optimization problems. In: Gervasi, O., Murgante, B., Misra, S., Garau, C., Blečić, I., Taniar, D., Apduhan, B.O., Rocha, A.M.A.C., Tarantino, E., Torre, C.M., Karaca, Y. (eds.) ICCSA 2020. LNCS, vol. 12251, pp. 274–288. Springer, Cham (2020). https://doi.org/10.1007/978-3-030-58808-3_21
14. dos Santos, F., Costa, L., Varela, L.: Multi-objective optimization of the job shop scheduling problem on unrelated parallel machines with sequence-dependent setup times. In: International Conference on Computational Science and Its Applications, pp. 495–507. Springer (2023)
15. dos Santos, F., Costa, L.A., Varela, L.: A systematic literature review about multi-objective optimization for distributed manufacturing scheduling in the industry 4.0. In: Computational Science and Its Applications-ICCSA 2022 Workshops: Malaga, Spain, July 4–7, 2022, Proceedings, Part II, pp. 157–173. Springer (2022)
16. Yenisey, M.M., Yagmahan, B.: Multi-objective permutation flow shop scheduling problem: literature review, classification and current trends. Omega **45**, 119–135 (2014)
17. Zitzler, E., Thiele, L., Laumanns, M., Fonseca, C.M., Grunert da Fonseca, V.: Performance assessment of multiobjective optimizers: an analysis and review. IEEE Trans. Evol. Comput. **7**(2), 117–132 (2003)

A Multiobjective Tuning of a Procedural Content Generator for Game Level Design via Evolutionary Algorithms

Vitor Gomes Soares Lins Peixoto[1] , Elizabeth Fialho Wanner[2] ,
and André Rodrigues da Cruz[1]([✉])

[1] Departamento de Computação, Centro Federal de Educação Tecnológica de Minas Gerais, Belo Horizonte, Brazil
dacruz@cefetmg.br
[2] School of Engineering and Applied Science, Aston University, Birmingham, UK
e.wanner@aston.ac.uk

Abstract. This work introduces a new multiobjective modeling approach for fine-tuning the parameters of a procedural game level generator in the platform game Infinite Mario Bros. The optimization problem aims to maximize three objectives related to game difficulty, including enemy placement, types of movements required, and time limits. The multiobjective problem is solved using two well-known evolutionary algorithms, NSGA-II and C-TAEA. In order to evaluate candidate parameter configurations, the averaged values of indicators returned by three artificial intelligent agents playing the levels are considered. A comprehensive computational experiment is conducted, and a statistical comparison using the Wilcoxon test is performed based on hypervolume values. The results include a nondomination analysis, an exploration of the distribution of final solutions, and the illustration of three levels from the final Pareto front. The key contribution of this work lies in the development of a multiobjective methodology that leverages evolutionary algorithms and incorporates agent-based evaluation, providing an effective approach for tuning procedural game level generators.

Keywords: Multiobjective optimization · Parameter tuning · Procedural game level generation

1 Introduction

A Procedural Content Generator (PCG) is a computational method that automatically creates content (levels, maps, assets, enemies, and so on) for digital games. PCGs have been used in the game industry to reduce costs and disk storage used by game assets, and increase replay value [11]. Within game content, a potential area of study is the generation of procedural levels. Different techniques can be used to generate content procedurally, like Evolutionary Algorithms (EAs), Generative and Context-Free Grammars, Cellular Automata, and Bayesian Neural Networks [2,10].

© The Author(s), under exclusive license to Springer Nature Switzerland AG 2024
A. I. Pereira et al. (Eds.): OL2A 2023, CCIS 1981, pp. 544–559, 2024.
https://doi.org/10.1007/978-3-031-53025-8_37

An example of the use of EAs is [12], which evolves a pool of new levels generated from the set of the puzzle-platform game Lode Runner. For the fitness function, the EAs run a Path Finding Algorithm on the level to ensure playability, resulting in variated levels for the game that can be beaten by a player.

The work [7] presents the Mario AI Framework, which is built upon the game *Infinite Mario Bros.*, a public domain clone of the game *Super Mario Bros.*. The game *Infinite Mario Bros.* involves traversing two-dimensional levels with a protagonist aiming to reach the end for victory. These levels are composed of various blocks, creating landscapes of valleys, mountains, and pits that the character must navigate by jumping. Additionally, the presence of enemies poses a threat to the character, as colliding with them can cause harm.

The Mario AI Framework provides a range of functionalities, including a textual representation of levels (encompassing map and enemies), AI agents that play levels and report their outcomes, and tools to facilitate level creation through generators. This work gives particular attention to the Notch Generator, an automated level generator that relies on a set of configurable parameter values. These parameters influence the composition of elements such as cannons, mountains, tubes, enemies, etc. By employing calculations with pseudo-random numbers, the generator constructs levels with a predefined length/height.

Understanding the impact of parameter adjustments on the generated levels can be challenging for game designers, so to automate the design step, this work proposes a multiobjective optimization model for tuning the parameters. Similarly to [12], we will evaluate the quality of generated levels to evolve them using EAs, but instead of checking playability directly with a Path Finding Algorithm, our fitness function runs AI agents on the levels considering interactions with all entities and collecting more data on their performance. The optimization process focuses on three key objectives that assess the difficulty of the generated levels. These objectives include evaluating the number of enemies defeated by the agents, the diversity of their movements, and the time required to complete the levels.

The parameters of the generator serve as the decision variables within a well-defined search space. To evaluate the black-box objectives, AI agents developed by participants of the Mario AI Competition have been integrated into the framework. These agents include an A* agent (Robin Baumgarten), a Neural Network-based agent (Sergey Polikarpov), and a State-Machines-based agent (Michael Tulacek) [13]. Each agent plays the generated level, and the resulting indicators are combined and averaged.

The selected EAs used in the tuning approach are the Nondominated Sorting Genetic Algorithm II (NSGA-II) [3] and the Constrained Two-Archive Evolutionary Algorithm (C-TAEA) [9]. To assess their performance, computational experiments have been conducted, focusing on comparing the hypervolume values achieved by each algorithm. The results obtained from these experiments not only present the final nondominated set of solutions obtained by all algorithm runs but also showcase illustrated solutions through graphical representations of the generated levels. Additionally, an analysis of the distribution of parameters used to generate the nondominated set solutions is provided.

The rest of this paper is organized as follows: Sect. 2 presents and explains the mathematical model that tunes the Notch Generator; Sect. 3 describes the methods, parameters, and tools used on the experiment; Sect. 4 shows the results we obtained after experimentation; and in Sect. 5 we conclude our work.

2   Mathematical Model

A multiobjective problem is a type of optimization problem where there are multiple conflicting objectives that need to be simultaneously optimized. The goal is to find a set of solutions that represent the best possible trade-offs among the competing objectives, rather than a single optimal solution. In the search space, this set is called Pareto set and encompasses solutions that are not dominated by any other solution. Given two solutions $\mathbf{a}, \mathbf{b} \in \mathbb{Z}^n$ and an objective vector $\mathbf{f} : \mathbb{Z}^n \to \mathbb{Z}^m$, $\mathbf{a}$ dominates $\mathbf{b}$ ($\mathbf{a} \preceq \mathbf{b}$) if and only if (i) $\forall i \in \{1, \ldots, m\}$ $f_i(\mathbf{a}) \le f_i(\mathbf{b})$ ($\mathbf{a}$ is not worse than $\mathbf{b}$ in any objective); and (ii) $\exists j \in \{1, \ldots, m\}$ $f_j(\mathbf{a}) < f_j(\mathbf{b})$ ($\mathbf{a}$ is strictly better than $\mathbf{b}$ in at least one objective).

Following an extensive examination of the generator, conducting thorough testing, and implementing certain modifications, we have established the decision variable vector, denoted as $\mathbf{x} \in \mathbb{Z}^{10}$, for the tuning problem. Within our model, we have chosen to retain the following discrete variables as parameters, as they already exist within the generator:

- $x_1 \in \{0, \ldots, 2\}$ – *Map type*: it defines the type of level to be generated. A value of zero enables the generation of mountains and values higher than zero enables the generation of a roof made of blocks.
- $x_2 \in \{0, \ldots, 15\}$ – *Difficulty*: it defines the difficulty of the map. This parameter influences the quantity, type, and variants of enemies generated (for example, enemies with or without wings), the likelihood of carnivorous plants being present within pipes, as well as the frequency at which pipes, holes, and cannons will appear throughout the map.
- $x_3 \in \{60, \ldots, 120\}$ – *Length*: it defines the length (in horizontal blocks) of the level. These values allow the generation of levels that fit on most screens and are easier to display on this paper.
- $x_4 \in \{16, \ldots, 32\}$ – *Height*: it defines the height (in vertical blocks) of the level.
- $x_5 \in \{30, \ldots, 300\}$ – *Time to complete*: it defines the time, in seconds, that the player has to complete a level.

In addition to the parameterizable variables, the generator incorporates several non-parameterizable variables with fixed values that determine the probability of generating specific structures. Since these constants have an impact on the generation of crucial elements within the maps, we have introduced additional variables that represent factors capable of modifying these constants, bringing more diversity to the levels:

- $x_6 \in \{-5, \ldots, 5\}$ – *Straight section generation factor*: by default, the generator uses a constant value of 20. After we add to this factor a variable ranged from 15 to 25.
- $x_7 \in \{-5, \ldots, 5\}$ – *Mountain section generation factor*: by default, the generator uses a constant value of 10. After we add to this factor a variable ranged from 5 to 15.
- $x_8 \in \{1, \ldots, 5\}$ – *Tube section generation multiplier*: by default, the generator uses a formula varying according to the difficulty, in the following format: $2 + x_2$. We add a discrete multiplier to the difficulty value so the formula is now defined by $2 + x_2 \cdot x_8$, and returns values ranging from 2 to 77.
- $x_9 \in \{1, \ldots, 5\}$ – *Hole section generation multiplier*: by default, the generator uses a formula varying according to the difficulty, in the following format: $2 \cdot x_2$. We add a discrete multiplier to the difficulty value so the formula is now defined by $2 \cdot x_2 \cdot x_9$, and returns values ranging from 0 to 150.
- $x_{10} \in \{0, \ldots, 10\}$ – *Cannon section generation multiplier*: by default, the generator uses a formula varying according to the difficulty, in the following format: $-10 + 5 \cdot x_2$. We add a discrete multiplier to the difficulty value so the formula is now defined by $-10 + 5 \cdot x_2 \cdot x_{10}$, and returns values ranging from -10 to 740.

The mentioned values serve as criteria for the generator to initially determine which structures can potentially be generated. The probability of selecting each of these structures is determined by Eq. (1), in which t represents the cumulative sum of nonnegative variables x_i, with i ranging from 6 to 10. If the generator happens to select multiple structures, the one with the highest index within the range of 6 to 10 is ultimately chosen and generated.

$$p_i = \frac{t + x_i - \sum_{j=6}^{i} x_j}{t}, \text{for } i = 6, \ldots, 10, \text{ and } t = \sum_{i=6}^{10} \max(0, x_i). \qquad (1)$$

During our investigation of the original version of the generator, we identified a specific implementation error. The code responsible for generating sections with mountains occasionally encountered a runtime error in specific scenarios where the generated mountain extended beyond the boundaries of the map. This error occurred due to the inadvertent passing of a negative threshold parameter to the random number generator, resulting in the runtime error. Although this issue occurred infrequently, it had the potential to impact our experiments, which involved generating multiple maps sequentially. We thoroughly analyzed the error and devised a solution. We leveraged existing logic within the function itself to detect and skip the generation of invalid structures. The correction follows a similar flow, ensuring that the mountain generation is bypassed if there is insufficient space within the map to accommodate its creation.

A constraint, represented by Eq. (2), is also applied aiming to guarantee a minimum time for the level to be completed based on its length. In this way, the level length, given a scale factor, is limited from above by the maximum time to pass it. The factor has been arbitrarily chosen and a further experimentation is needed for a better analysis.

$$0.2x_3 \leq x_5 \tag{2}$$

To quantify the quality of the maps, we have employed indicators derived from agents playing the levels generated by the Notch Generator. When instantiating the selected agents on a given map, the agents navigate the map and interact with the environment. During their attempt, the agents maneuver through the map, employing strategies to evade or combat enemies, while also leaping over gaps to reach the map's end within the allotted time. Upon completion of an agent's run, the framework generates a result, capturing various information regarding the agent's performance, such as the number of jumps executed, the count of enemies eliminated, the extent of damage sustained, and more. Consequently, executing an agent on a specific map yields a collection of informative data, which can be leveraged to assess the quality of the map in question. The black box indicators of performance that have been applied in this work are:

- $num\_jumps(\mathbf{x})$ – *Number of jumps*: the number of jumps the character performed during the level.
- $num\_kills(\mathbf{x})$ – *Number of monsters killed*: the number of monsters that were defeated during the level.
- $biggest\_jump(\mathbf{x})$ – *Longest jump*: the longest jump on the x axis, in pixels (each block is 16×16 pixels).
- $air\_time(\mathbf{x})$ – *Longest air time*: the longest time, in frames, between a jump and landing on the ground.
- $remaining\_time(\mathbf{x})$ – *Remaining level time*: the time remaining to complete the level at the end of the run, in miliseconds.

Combining the decision variables and the quality indicators, the objective function vector, $\mathbf{f} : \mathbb{Z}^{10} \rightarrow \mathbb{Z}^3$, is presented by Eq. (3). The objective function f_1 quantifies the difficulty of a level by considering the number of enemies defeated by the agent. This encompasses both enemy eliminations through jumping on top of them and utilizing collected power-ups. Our aim is to maximize f_1 to generate levels with a substantial presence of enemies that can be effectively overcome by the agent. This approach introduces both difficulty and variability to the levels. The objective function f_2 focuses on the agent's jumping behavior throughout a level, considering both the distance and frequency of jumps. Our aim is to maximize f_2 to create levels that feature a variety of jumps, including numerous jumps, long jumps, and high jumps. It introduces a level of difficulty that demands precision from players when executing these jumps. The objective function f_3 measures the time remaining, in milliseconds, for the agent to complete a level. By maximizing f_3, our objective is to generate levels that provide the agent with sufficient time to finish, effectively making them comparatively easier. The rationale behind this is to strike a balance between challenge and playability, ensuring that the levels are demanding but not insurmountable.

$$f_1(\mathbf{x}) = num\_kills(\mathbf{x})$$
$$f_2(\mathbf{x}) = num\_jumps(\mathbf{x}) + biggest\_jump(\mathbf{x}) + air\_time(\mathbf{x}) \qquad (3)$$
$$f_3(\mathbf{x}) = remaining\_time(\mathbf{x})$$

The evaluation of the objective function $\mathbf{f}$ involves three distinct agents: one based on A*, another utilizing a Neural Network, and a third employing State-Machines [13]. Each agent independently assesses the quality of a level by playing it, and their respective indicators are combined, averaged, and utilized within Eq. (3) to determine the overall quality of the parameter candidate $\mathbf{x}$ for the Notch Generator. Note that the evaluation of $\mathbf{f}$ is computationally expensive.

Let $\mathcal{X} \subseteq \mathbb{Z}^{10}$ be the feasible region for the decision vector bounds and Eq. (2). The resulting multiobjective model is presented by Eq. (4):

$$\max_{x} \quad \mathbf{f} = [f_1(\mathbf{x}), f_2(\mathbf{x}), f_3(\mathbf{x})]$$
$$\text{subject to:} \quad \mathbf{x} \in \mathcal{X} \qquad (4)$$

3   Experimental Design

Prior to solving Eq. (4), an essential step involved integrating the Mario AI Framework generator with the optimization algorithms. For this purpose, we have opted to utilize the Pymoo framework, a Python-based open-source framework specifically designed for mono and multiobjective optimization with evolutionary algorithms [1]. Pymoo provided us with the necessary implementations of NSGA-II and C-TAEA algorithms, along with valuable tools for model definition, experiment parameterization, graph generation, and result analysis. Furthermore, since the generator was developed in Java, establishing seamless communication between the generator and the optimizer required the incorporation of the Pyjnius library. Pyjnius, a Python library, facilitated the loading of Java classes and enabled the efficient exchange of information between the generator and the optimizer [8].

For the model implementation, Pymoo provides an interface that represents the problem we are going to optimize. The implementation consisted of defining the ten variables and their lower and upper bounds, the constraint, and the three objective functions. To evaluate each individual, the following procedure was performed: (i) A new map generator was instantiated using the decision variables from the individual as its parameters; (ii) The generator was utilized to create a map, which was subsequently stored for analysis; (iii) A run was conducted for each agent, with each agent playing and attempting to complete the generated map. The results from these attempts were recorded; and (iv) The constraints and objective values were computed by taking the average of the results obtained from all considered agents.

Two algorithms, NSGA-II and C-TAEA, are used to solve the multiobjective problem in Eq. (4). NSGA-II [3] is an evolutionary algorithm that aims to find a set of solutions that are not dominated by any other solution, representing the trade-off between different objectives. It utilizes a combination of genetic operators, including selection, crossover, and mutation, to evolve a population of candidate solutions over multiple generations. It incorporates a nondominated sorting mechanism that assigns a rank to each individual based on dominance relationships, enabling the preservation of diverse and Pareto-optimal solutions. It also introduces a density-estimation metric called crowding distance value in order to maintain a well-distributed set of solutions. This value is computed for each individual considering the average distance between its neighbors along each objective in the front level. Given the initial population, the usual binary tournament selection, recombination, and mutation operators are used to generate the children. The nondominated sorting mechanism sorts the individuals and then the crowding distance is calculated. The individuals with the best ranks are selected and if the last frontier considered does not fit completely on the next generation, its individuals with higher crowding distance are selected. That way, NSGA-II explores iteratively the solution space, promoting convergence towards a set of solutions that provide a comprehensive representation of the trade-off of the problem.

C-TAEA [9] is an evolutionary algorithm designed for solving multi-objective optimization problems with constraints. It employs a two-archive framework to handle the trade-off between optimizing multiple objectives and satisfying constraints. The algorithm maintains two separate archives: the main archive stores non-dominated solutions that are optimized in terms of the objectives, while the constraint archive stores solutions that violate one or more constraints. It also utilizes a diversity preservation mechanism to ensure wide coverage of the objective space in the main archive while also encouraging feasible solutions in the constraint archive. On the selection process, both archives are combined and the proportion of non-dominated solutions in each archive is considered. The first parent is selected from the archive with the higher proportion, and the second parent is chosen from the archives using a probability that favors the main archive when its proportion rises. Given the chosen archive, the parent solution is selected using a binary tournament selection that prioritizes feasibility; if both candidates are feasible the Pareto dominance is considered, otherwise the feasible candidate is chosen. If no candidate is feasible, the choice is random. The archives are then updated, but using different strategies: the main archive updates considering the Pareto domination between the previous population and the children that are feasible; the constraint archive does not consider feasibility and prioritizes areas where the main archive under-exploited by separating the individuals from both archives in subregions and checking whether there are already many solutions from the main archive on a region. Due to those characteristics, C-TAEA effectively explores the solution space, generating a set of high-quality solutions that not only optimize the objectives but also adhere to the given constraints.

NSGA-II and C-TAEA have been subjected to a series of experiments to compare their performance regard to the hypervolume indicator [6]. The hypervolume indicator serves as a quality indicator for sets of nondominated solutions.

It quantifies the volume occupied by the Pareto front space that is dominated by the given solutions. This indicator effectively measures the coverage and diversity of the solutions concerning an ideal or reference point. The hypervolume indicator takes into account the trade-offs between objectives, rewarding solutions that are not only closer to the reference point but also well-distributed across the objective space. A higher hypervolume value indicates a superior set of solutions, indicative of greater coverage and better spread across the objectives.

Due to the computational cost of the model, the experiment involves running each of the algorithms with a population of 20 individuals, and with a budget of 1000 objective evaluations. Both algorithms start with a randomly generated population and use the same crossover and mutation operators. The adopted crossover operator is the Simulated Binary Crossover [4]. This crossover operates on the decision variables of two parent individuals using a parameter, *eta*, that defines the resemblance that children will have to their parents. Higher values for the *eta* parameter generate individuals that are more similar to their parents, and lower values generate more diverse individuals. The default values of the Pymoo implementation are used for this operator, with the crossover probability being 90% and the *eta* being 30. The mutation operator is the Polynomial Mutation with a probability of 10% for our model.

Each algorithm has been executed 30 times, employing different seeds for the pseudo-random number generator in each run. During each execution, the nondominated solutions along with their corresponding function evaluations are stored for further analysis. In the end, a reference point is established, and a sample of 30 hypervolume indicators is computed for each algorithm. To determine the algorithm with the best performance, a statistical analysis is conducted to assess whether there existed a significant difference between the algorithms in terms of their hypervolume medians. The analyzed null hypothesis states that the algorithms have equal efficiency with respect to the hypervolume indicator, with a significance level (α) of 0.05. We employ the non-parametric Wilcoxon test, that does not rely on assumptions of normality and homoscedasticity, as these assumptions have not been satisfied by our result data [5].

In addition, we combine all the final solutions obtained from both algorithms and apply a nondominated sorting procedure to construct the final Pareto front. This allows us to observe the overall distribution of solutions and determine the number of final solutions contributed by each algorithm. We further analyze the characteristics of this final set, examining the distribution of solutions and evaluating their corresponding objective values. To provide a visual representation of the generated levels, we select a subset of solutions from the final Pareto front and illustrated their corresponding level designs. Additionally, we track the trajectory of an agent as it plays one of these generated levels.

4   Results

After all 30 runs, the hypervolume indicator values have been computed[1] The distribution samples, for each algorithm, are present in Fig. 1. This figure illustrates a hybrid visualization comprising violin and boxplot plots, with the average value represented by an orange dot. The statistics of the samples are presented in Table 1. The nondominated solution sets generated by C-TAEA exhibited a wider range of hypervolume values compared to NSGA-II. Notably, the hypervolume values achieved by NSGA-II generally outperformed those of C-TAEA, indicating superior performance. This conclusion is further supported by the results of the Wilcoxon test, which yielded a p-value of $4.41 \cdot 10^{-5}$-.

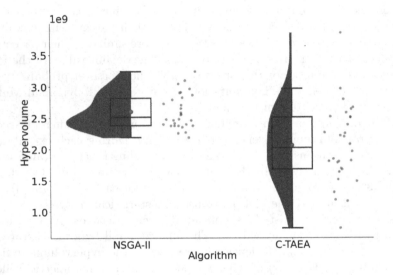

Fig. 1. Distribution of solution hypervolumes by algorithm.

Table 1. Statistics of hypervolume distribution per algorithm (multiples of $\cdot 10^9$).

	Min	Q1	Q2	Avg	Q3	Max
NSGA-II	2.1862	2.3734	2.5115	2.5988	2.8239	3.2350
C-TAEA	0.7356	1.6689	2.0174	2.0583	2.5078	3.8409

Figure 2 shows the final Pareto front, consisting of nondominated solutions obtained from all algorithm outputs. NSGA-II outcomes are denoted by blue dots, while C-TAEA ones are depicted as orange dots. Solutions enclosed by

---

[1] The source code can be accessed in https://github.com/VitorPeixoto/ol2a2023.

triangles indicate instances whose level maps will be illustrated shortly. It is possible to observe that both algorithms have generated a reasonably balanced number of nondominated solutions in the final set. NSGA-II contributed 82 solutions, whereas C-TAEA provided 60 solutions. Additionally, clusters can be observed, particularly in relation to the values of f_1 and f_3, wherein certain solutions exhibit similar behavior.

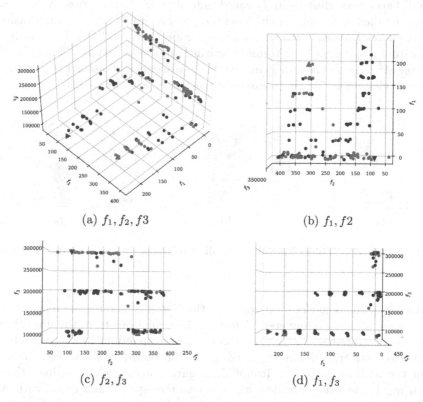

(a) $f_1, f_2, f3$

(b) $f_1, f2$

(c) f_2, f_3

(d) f_1, f_3

Fig. 2. Pareto front with all final nondominated solutions for NSGA-II (blue) and C-TAEA (orange). (Color figure online)

Figures 3 and 4 show the distributions of each objective and solution value within the final Pareto front, respectively. Table 2 presents statistics derived from these samples.

Figure 3 indicates the presence of clusters, particularly in relation to the objective f_1. For f_1, the majority of solutions exhibit values close to zero, suggesting that the agents either did not prioritize or struggled to eliminate enemies and progress through the levels effectively. The median value of 33.00 indicatesa reasonable number of enemies defeated, indicating some successful runs. The maximum value of 229.33 signifies that, on average, a significant number of enemies were defeated during the agents' runs, including instances where enemies may have fallen into pits or gone off-screen (e.g., bullet bills).

Regarding the distribution of f_3, distinct clusters are evident around 100, 200, and 300 s, representing the average remaining time that agents took to complete the levels. Considering that x_5 (maximum level time) predominantly hovered around 300 s, these clusters in f_3 could indicate various scenarios. Agents may have either died or completed the level too quickly, leading to f_3 values nearing 300 s. Conversely, some agents may have become stuck and failed to finish the level within a sufficient time frame, resulting in f_3 values approaching 0 s. The diversity of values observed in f_2 means that the agents had distinct requirements and strategies when it came to executing movements within the levels.

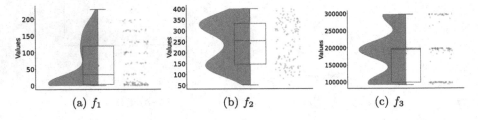

(a) f_1 (b) f_2 (c) f_3

Fig. 3. Distribution of objective values for all solutions in the final non-dominated set.

We depict the behavioral outcomes of the Notch Generator in creating three game levels, utilizing parameters determined by solutions from the final Pareto front, as illustrated in Fig. 5. The solutions corresponding to these levels are highlighted with triangles in Fig. 2. For each game level, we showcased an example of the path taken by the Robin Baumgarten agent, which utilizes the A* algorithm. These levels provide a glimpse into the agent's interaction with various entities within the game environment, including navigating around obstacles such as holes and strategically jumping on top of bullets to progress through the level.

We can see cannons and pipes distributed along Solution 1 (map type 0), Solution 2 (map type 1), and Solution 3 (map type 0). The A* agent managed to finish all of them. From Solution 2 map we can see that there were no pits, but there was a high drop that could influence f_2 since the air time is also considered.Solution 3 is an example where hills were created, a structure that

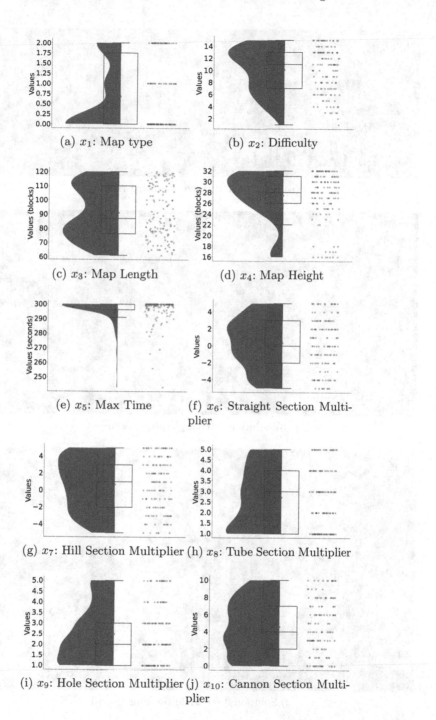

Fig. 4. Distribution of variable values for all solutions in the final non-dominated set.

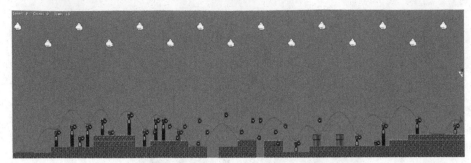

(a) Solution 1 (triangle pointing right).

(b) Solution 2 (triangle pointing up).

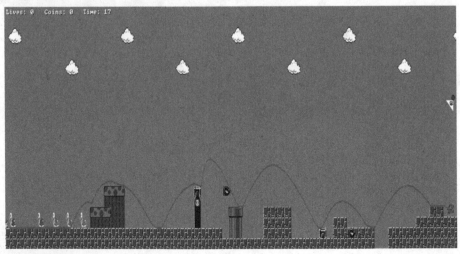

(c) Solution 3 (triangle pointing down).

Fig. 5. Levels from three solutions with an example A* agent path

Table 2. Statistics of decision variables and objective values in the final Pareto front.

	Min	Q1	Q2	Avg	Q3	Max
x_1	0	0	0	0.68	2	2
x_2	1	7	11	10.08	13	15
x_3	61	76	87	90.97	110	120
x_4	16	26	28	27.39	31	32
x_5	243	296	300	296.38	300	300
x_6	−5	−2	0	0.34	3	5
x_7	−5	−2	1	0.68	3	5
x_8	1	1	3	2.71	4	5
x_9	1	1	2	2.48	3	5
x_{10}	0	2	4	4.56	7	10
f_1	0.00	3.32	33.00	60.44	125.12	229.33
f_2	50.91	146.26	253.67	241.96	333.53	399.93
f_3	91746.67	98620.00	195380.00	182502.82	198064.00	298280.00

can influence the number and height of jumps. It is also possible to see enemies in Solution 3.

The Notch Generator generated three distinct game levels based on different solutions: Solution 1 (map type 0), Solution 2 (map type 1), and Solution 3 (map type 0). In Solution 2, although there were no pits, there was a notable high drop, which could impact the agent's performance in terms of f_2. This is because air time, which includes the time spent in the air during jumps, is considered in the evaluation. Solution 3 shows the creation of hilly terrain, introducing structures that influence the number and height of jumps required. Additionally, enemies were incorporated into this level.

5   Conclusions

We proposed a multiobjective methodology to fine-tune the parameters of a procedural game level generator designed for the platform game, Infinite Mario Bros. The optimization problem involved maximizing three conflicting objectives and was tackled using two distinct algorithms: NSGA-II and C-TAEA. The solutions were evaluated throught three artificial intelligent agents. These agents played the generated levels and provided outputs that were subsequently averaged.

In order to compare the efficacy of the evolutionary algorithms, it was conducted a planned computational experiment and a statistical comparison, via Wilcoxon test, of the evolutionary algorithms according to hypervolume values.

To assess and compare the effectiveness of the algorithms, a computational experiment was conducted. This experiment aimed to evaluate the performance of the algorithms and provide a statistical comparison between them using the hypervolume values. To ensure an in-depth analysis, a statistical approach was adopted. The Wilcoxon test, a non-parametric test for paired samples, was employed to compare the algorithms based on their hypervolume values.

The results showed that NSGA-II outperformed C-TAEA with statistical significance. This finding suggests that NSGA-II is better suited for the specific application at hand. However, it is worth noting that the final Pareto front consisted of solutions obtained by both NSGA-II and C-TAEA. This indicates that a combination of algorithms can yield improved results.

Based on the findings of our study, we can state that our model effectively tunes the parameter values of the Notch Generator, resulting in the generation of varied game levels that strike a balance between being challenging and yet not unbeatable. The parameter tuning process identified specific values for certain parameters, indicating their significant impact on the level generation. On the other hand, some parameters exhibited a more distributed range of values within their respective parameter space. These parameters are more flexible and may provide a wider range of configurations while maintain the desired level qualities.

Still, there is room to improve. In future works, evaluating the performance of the agents can help selecting better ones to reduce the runs where they get stuck. The objective f_1 can also be improved by considering only enemies that were defeated direct by agent action, like using power-ups or stomping them. Also, adding an objective that minimizes the number of hits the agents take can reduce the runs where the agents are killed.

Also, although the current implementation is not directly applicable to other platform games since the model is built considering entities specific to Infinite Mario Bros., the methodology of using evolutionary algorithms and agent-based evaluation on levels generated by a PCG could easily be reused on other games: All a new game would need is a PCG (from which a new model would be created) and at least one agent to run its levels. There are also many aspects of platform game levels that are similar, like width, height, enemies, collectibles, etc. A future work could explore the possibility of creating a model that leverages those similarities in a more generic way to be compatible with several platform games.

References

1. Blank, J., Deb, K.: pymoo: multi-objective optimization in python. IEEE Access **8**, 89497–89509 (2020)
2. Compton, K., Mateas, M.: Procedural level design for platform games. Proc. AAAI Conf. Artif. Intell. Interact. Digital Entertain. **2**(1), 109–111 (Sep 2021). https://ojs.aaai.org/index.php/AIIDE/article/view/18755
3. Deb, K., Pratap, A., Agarwal, S., Meyarivan, T.: A fast and elitist multiobjective genetic algorithm: NSGA-II. IEEE Trans. Evol. Comput. **6**(2), 182–197 (2002). https://doi.org/10.1109/4235.996017
4. Deb, K., Sindhya, K., Okabe, T.: Self-adaptive simulated binary crossover for real-parameter optimization. In: Proceedings of the 9th Annual Conference on Genetic and Evolutionary Computation, pp. 1187–1194. GECCO '07, Association for Computing Machinery, New York, NY, USA (2007). https://doi.org/10.1145/1276958.1277190

5. Derrac, J., García, S., Molina, D., Herrera, F.: A practical tutorial on the use of nonparametric statistical tests as a methodology for comparing evolutionary and swarm intelligence algorithms. Swarm Evol. Comput. **1**(1), 3–18 (2011)
6. Guerreiro, A.P., Fonseca, C.M., Paquete, L.: The hypervolume indicator: computational problems and algorithms. ACM Comput. Surv. (CSUR) **54**(6), 1–42 (2021)
7. Karakovskiy, S., Togelius, J.: The mario AI benchmark and competitions. IEEE Trans. Comput. Intell. AI Games **4**(1), 55–67 (2012). https://doi.org/10.1109/TCIAIG.2012.2188528
8. Kivy Team: Pyjnius (1.4.1). https://pyjnius.readthedocs.io/en/stable/ (2021)
9. Li, K., Chen, R., Fu, G., Yao, X.: Two-archive evolutionary algorithm for constrained multiobjective optimization. IEEE Trans. Evol. Comput. **23**(2), 303–315 (2019). https://doi.org/10.1109/TEVC.2018.2855411
10. van der Linden, R., Lopes, R., Bidarra, R.: Procedural generation of dungeons. IEEE Trans. Comput. Intell. AI in Games **6**(1), 78–89 (2014). https://doi.org/10.1109/TCIAIG.2013.2290371
11. Summerville, A., et al.: Procedural content generation via machine learning (pcgml). IEEE Trans. Games **10**(3), 257–270 (2018). https://doi.org/10.1109/TG.2018.2846639
12. Thakkar, S., Cao, C., Wang, L., Choi, T.J., Togelius, J.: Autoencoder and evolutionary algorithm for level generation in lode runner. In: 2019 IEEE Conference on Games (CoG), pp. 1–4 (2019). https://doi.org/10.1109/CIG.2019.8848076
13. Togelius, J., Karakovskiy, S., Baumgarten, R.: The 2009 mario ai competition, pp. 1–8 (08 2010). https://doi.org/10.1109/CEC.2010.5586133

Optimal Location of Electric Vehicle Charging Stations in Distribution Grids Using Genetic Algorithms

Eduardo Gomes[1], Adelaide Cerveira[2], and José Baptista[3]✉

[1] Department of Engineering, University of Trás-os-Montes and Alto Douro,
5000-801 Vila Real, Portugal
al68513@utad.eu
[2] Department of Mathematics, University of Trás-os-Montes and Alto Douro,
INESC-TEC, UTAD's Pole, 5000-801 Vila Real, Portugal
cerveira@utad.pt
[3] Department of Engineering, University of Trás-os-Montes and Alto Douro,
INESC-TEC, UTAD's Pole, 5000-801 Vila Real, Portugal
baptista@utad.pt

Abstract. In recent years, as a result of population growth and the strong demand for energy resources, there has been an increase in greenhouse gas emissions. Thus, it is necessary to find solutions to reduce these emissions. This will make the use of electric vehicles (EV) more attractive and reduce the high dependency on internal combustion vehicles. However, the integration of electric vehicles will pose some challenges. For example, it will be necessary to increase the number of fast electric vehicle charging stations (FEVCS) to make electric mobility more attractive. Due to the high power levels involved in these systems, there are voltage drops that affect the voltage profile of some nodes of the distribution networks. This paper presents a methodology based on a genetic algorithm (GA) that is used to find the optimal location of charging stations that cause the minimum impact on the grid voltage profile. Two case studies are considered to evaluate the behavior of the distribution grid with different numbers of EV charging stations connected. From the results obtained, it can be concluded that the GA provides an efficient way to find the best charging station locations, ensuring that the grid voltage profile is within the regulatory limits and that the value of losses is minimized.

Keywords: Fast electric vehicle charging stations · Genetic algorithm · Distribution network · Optimal placement · Power-Flow

1 Introduction

We are living in a time of change, where the main objective is to replace fossil fuels with clean energy sources. Since the transport sector is one of the most polluting, due to the emission of large amounts of greenhouse gases into the atmosphere, there is a need to create solutions to mitigate this problem. In addition, there is a legislative framework that increasingly promotes sustainable solutions for the sector. The solutions that can be adopted can be the construction of urban planning and mobility that reduce the demand for transport, and travel, instead of using the car, can be done on foot, by bicycle, or by public transport [1]. However, the transport factor is always present, and these can be powered by electricity or combustion. Since the intention is to reduce dependence on fossil fuels, electric vehicles are a great option in contrast to combustion vehicles, as they use electricity to charge their batteries, and this electricity can come from renewable energy sources [2]. In this way, it is necessary to create fast electric vehicle charging stations (FEVCS) so that owners can charge their vehicles in the shortest possible time. These DC-DC FEVCS (Mode 4) directly supply the vehicle's battery [3] and due to the high powers involved, typically greater than 22 kW, there is the appearance of voltage drops that impair the voltage profile of the network. According to standard NP EN 50160 [4], the minimum voltage cannot exceed 10% of the maximum voltage so that the voltage profile of the network remains within the regulatory limits.

Therefore, it is important to determine which are the best points in the network for the placement of FEVCS, in order to minimize the impact on the grid voltage. There are several researchers studying several solutions to solve this problem. In [5] there is a review of the optimization algorithms most commonly used for the optimal placement of FEVCS and good for solving objective multi-criteria problems. According to [6], GA can be applied to several fields, namely the resolution of optimization problems.

In the following papers, two optimization algorithms were used to obtain the optimal location of FEVCS, with the aim of minimizing a multi-objective problem. In [7] a GA was used and it is verified that in the mutation process, as there is alteration of genes of a chromosome, the diversity of the results is assured, and with the evolution of the generations the convergence for the minimization is remarkable of the objective function. In [8] a PSO is applied. [9] uses an approach that consists of mapping, through a graph, the streets of an urban area. A path is created between two nodes and, using Dijkstra's algorithm, the paths are weighted, and then a GA is applied to find the shortest distance between a FEVCS and a reference node of a path. In [10,11] hierarchical GAs are used in order to obtain the best location for a substation and the most favorable connections to wind turbines. In this process, a binary chromosome is used for the substation coordinates. In [12] an optimization algorithm is used that is based on the natural behavior and hunting techniques of gray wolves, this algorithm is called GWO. This algorithm can only be used to solve continuous problems, however, it is necessary to use binary numbers to determine the optimal location of FEVCS. In addition to the use of optimization algorithms, other solutions can be adopted to improve the profile of grid voltage. For example, in [13], a renewable energy source and a storage system were introduced and the results obtained were quite positive.

The main objective of this paper is to determine the best locations for FEVCS in order to minimize power losses and maintain the network voltage profile within regulatory limits. For this purpose, a genetic algorithm (GA) is used to solve the optimization model, having been applied to a case study of the IEEE 33 bus radial network. The use of GAs in this optimization problem has several advantages, starting with the simplification they allow in formulating and solving the problem, which involves a large number of variables and consequently solution spaces of high dimensions. Furthermore, in many cases where other optimization strategies fail to find a solution, the GA finds a very good solution. The novelty of this study, besides the calculation of the voltage drops in the different buses, is the minimization of the value of the power losses in the whole network.

The paper is organized as follows. In Sect. 2, the necessary calculations for the determination of the power losses in the distribution lines are presented, followed by the optimization model, where the objective function focuses on obtaining the minimum value of the power losses, followed by its constraints. Section 3 presents and describes the GA that will solve the problem of FEVCS placement. Section 4 presents the case studies, followed by an analysis of the results obtained. Finally, in Sect. 5, the conclusions are drawn.

2   Problem Formulation

This section presents the problem formulation, where the main objective is to determine the optimal location of FEVCS at locations that cause the least voltage drop in the distribution lines while ensuring that the voltage remains within the regulatory limits in order to minimize losses in the distribution network. This section consists of two subsections: one presenting the load flow calculations and another presenting the objective function and constraints of the problem.

2.1   Load Flow Calculation

To carry out a detailed study of the behavior of the network under investigation, it is necessary to examine how the main parameters evolve as a function of the load. Among these parameters, the effective value of the voltage on the buses and the energy losses in the different branches are particularly important. The mathematical modeling required to calculate the load flow is presented in this section.

The active and reactive power are calculated using the Eqs. (1) and (2). The voltage drops are calculated using the Eq. (3) and the power losses are calculated using the Eq. (4).

$$P_{i+1} = P_i - P_{Li+1} - R_{i,i+1} \cdot \left(\frac{P_i^2 + Q_i^2}{|V_i|^2} \right) \tag{1}$$

$$Q_{i+1} = Q_i - Q_{Li+1} - X_{i,i+1} \cdot \left(\frac{P_i^2 + Q_i^2}{|V_i|^2} \right) \tag{2}$$

$$|V_{i+1}|^2 = |V_i|^2 - 2.(R_{i,i+1}.P_i + X_{i,i+1}.Q_i)$$
$$+(R_{i,i+1}^2 + X_{i,i+1}^2).\left(\frac{P_i^2 + Q_i^2}{|V_i|^2}\right) \tag{3}$$

where P_i, Q_i, P_{Li}, Q_{Li}, V_i are the active power, reactive power, active load power, reactive load power, and voltage at node i, respectively. The parameters $R_{i,i+1}$ and $X_{i,i+1}$ are the resistance and reactance between the node i and $i+1$.

Figure 1 shows a typical distribution grid where node i is the emitter, and node $i+1$ is the receiver.

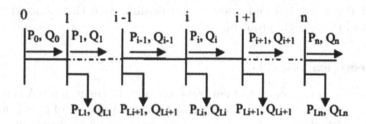

Fig. 1. Typical distribution grid model [14]

The power loss between bus i and bus $i + 1$, $P_{Loss(i,i+1)}$, is given by Eq. (4).

$$P_{Loss(i,i+1)} = R_{i,i+1}.\left(\frac{P_i^2 + Q_i^2}{|V_i|^2}\right) \tag{4}$$

When considering the entire grid with all buses $\{1, \dots, n\}$, the global power losses, $P_{T,Loss}$, is given by:

$$P_{T,Loss} = \sum_{i=1}^{n-1} P_{Loss(i,i+1)} \tag{5}$$

2.2 Objective Function and Constraints

The objective function to determine the minimum total power loss resulting from the placement of charging stations in a distribution network is given by Eq. (6).

$$\text{Minimization} \sum_{i=1}^{n-1} P_{T,Loss(i,i+1)} \tag{6}$$

The set of constraints is given by:

$$V_{Min,i} \leq V_i \leq V_{Max,i}, i \in \{1, \ldots, n\} \tag{7}$$

Constraints (7) assure that V_i should be greater than the minimum voltage, $V_{Min,i}$, and less than the maximum voltage, $V_{Max,i}$. The voltage cannot exceed a variation of 10% according to the standard NP EN 50160 [4].

3   Genetic Algorithm

The focus of this section is to understand how the Genetic Algorithm (GA) works in order to adapt it to solve the FEVCS placement problem. Therefore, this section is divided into two parts: a subsection dealing with the theoretical aspects of the algorithm and a subsection dealing with the adaptation of the algorithm to the specific problem.

3.1   Theoretical Aspects

A GA is based on the concept of natural evolution. In general, a GA is relatively easy to understand and it all starts with an initial population of individuals. The individuals with the best characteristics will have a higher chance of surviving and passing on their characteristics to their offspring. As a result, over generations, small changes are introduced into the characteristics of the offspring, driving the evolution of the species. These three processes are known as selection, crossover, and mutation.

An initial population is created in which each solution is represented as a chromosome and each position within the chromosome is called a gene. The performance of each chromosome is then evaluated. In the selection process, the chromosomes with the best performance values are selected. This selection can be done using various methods such as roulette wheel selection, scaling techniques, ranking methods or tournament selection.

Once the best chromosomes have been selected, the crossover process takes place. This involves randomly combining two chromosomes with efficient performance values, resulting in a descendant chromosome that inherits the best genes from both parents. Finally, there is the mutation process, in which a few genes undergo random changes with a low probability of mutation. This phase ensures both diversity and convergence of the chromosomes [15].

Since this algorithm is easy to adapt and highly effective in solving challenging problems, it is widely used in research, particularly for solving optimization problems that are difficult to solve exactly.

3.2   Methodology

To determine the optimal location of the FEVCS, a GA was adapted based on the parameters described in [16]. The methodology can be visualized through the flowchart shown in Fig. 2. The code implementation was done in MATLAB.

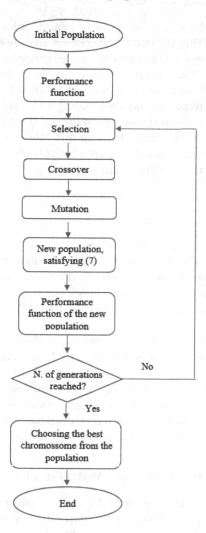

Fig. 2. Flowchart of the Genetic Algorithm used.

In the initial population, a binary population (0 and 1) is created with 100 chromosomes. Each position within the chromosome is called a gene, and each chromosome is limited by the total number of buses in a distribution network. n FEVCS are randomly assigned to each chromosome, and each charging station is represented by the value 1. Then, for each chromosome, the performance function is calculated, as shown in Eq. (5).

In the selection process, the performance values are sorted in ascending order, and the top 20% of chromosomes with the best values are selected. These chromosomes form the *elite* population. For the crossover process, two parents are selected from the entire population. Each parent is the best of two randomly selected chromosomes. A random crossover of genetic information from the parents is performed, resulting in new chromosomes that become part of the *offspring* population. In the mutation process, some genes undergo changes with a low probability of mutation. This involves exchanging information between two randomly selected positions. The probability of mutation is set to 2%.

Finally, the *elite* population and the *offspring* population are combined to obtain a new population. With the new population, the performance function is calculated again, (5), and the values that minimize the performance function (6) are stored, these three processes are repeated for 200 generations while ensuring that the values respect the condition imposed in Eq. (7).

4   Case Studies

In this section, two case studies are considered to analyze the impact of FEVCS on a distribution grid. The key aspects to be considered in each case are the FEVCS locations and the associated voltage drops. In the first case study, the behavior of the distribution network without charging stations is analyzed, while in the second case study, the impact of placing FEVCS on the distribution grid is addressed.

For this analysis, the IEEE 33-bus network, as shown in Fig. 3, is used. The load flow calculations were performed using MATLAB. The total active power of this distribution network is 3715 kW, and the total reactive power is 2300 kVar, with base power values of 100 MVA and a base voltage of 12.66 kV. Without FEVCSs, the distribution network has an active power loss of 176.367 kW and a reactive power loss of 117.43 kVar. The load values associated with this network, as well as the resistance and reactance values of the lines, can be found in [17].

4.1   Scenario 1: Distribution Grid Without FEVCS

In this scenario, the network without FEVCS was considered in order to understand its behavior and to facilitate the interpretation of the obtained results in this research. Figure 4 shows the voltage profile, in per unit (p.u.), of the network without FEVCS, clearly showing two minimum values on buses 18 and 33. The minimum voltage value is displayed in Table 1, along with the voltage limit, which is a fixed value that the minimum voltage should not exceed in order to comply with the regulatory limits imposed by the NP EN 50160 standard [4]. As the minimum voltage value approaches the limit, it can be concluded that the voltage drops in the distribution lines are significant, indicating that this network is highly constrained and problematic. With the placement of FEVCS, due to the high power involved, there will be significant voltage drops, leading to increased losses in the network and a decrease in the minimum voltage value. Determining the optimum locations for these stations is therefore critical to minimizing voltage drops and ensuring that network values remain within regulatory limits.

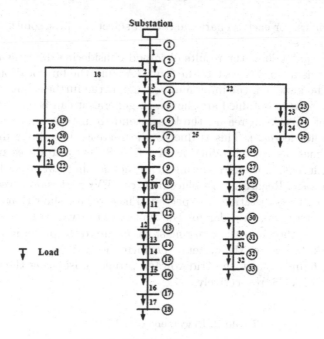

Fig. 3. IEEE 33-bus network

Table 1. Characteristics of the IEEE 33-bus network: base case.

Minimum voltage (p.u.)	Voltage limit (p.u.)
0.91947	0,90

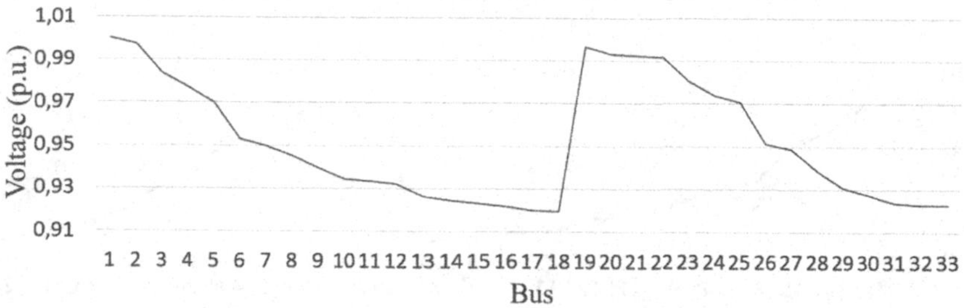

Fig. 4. Voltage profile of the IEEE 33-bus network: base case.

4.2 Scenario 2: Placement of FEVCS Using Genetic Algorithms

In this scenario, it was considered that each FEVCS has a power of 100 kW, and using the GA, the optimal locations of the charging stations are determined. In order to obtain the locations, the GA was executed four times to find the best possible solutions. As the genetic algorithm is not an exact algorithm, it provides a solution that is expected to be close to optimal, so it was decided to run the

algorithm 4 times, for each scenario, and then select the best solution according
to the objectives set.

Tables 2, 3 and 4 show the results obtained considering different numbers of
FEVCS to be installed. For each of the four GA runs, the bus location where the
FEVCS is to be installed, the minimum voltage at the furthest bus, bus 18, and
the total power losses obtained are shown. In general, it can be observed that as
the number of FEVCS increases, the losses tend to increase and the minimum
voltage tends to decrease. This is due to the increase in voltage drops in the
distribution lines, as the introduction of FEVCS also introduces more power
associated with these stations, resulting in an increase in total power losses and a
decrease in voltage. Regarding the placement of FEVCS, it is observed that they
are located near the substation as expected. These results show that in networks
with a radial structure, in order for the voltage drop values to remain within
regulatory limits, the closer the charging stations are to the power injection point
in the network, the better the system's performance will be.

Figures 5, 6 and 7 show the grid voltage profile considering the installation
of 4, 5, and 6 FEVCS, respectively.

Table 2. Placement of 4 FEVCS

Run	Location	Minimum voltage (p.u.)	Losses (kW)
1	1,2,19,21	0.91880	187.869
2	1,19,22,24	0.91757	204.603
3	1,2,4,20	0.91666	199.258
4	2,21,22,23	0.91734	210.422

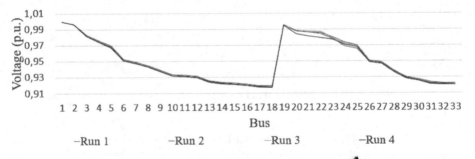

Fig. 5. Voltage profile of the 4 runs with 4 FEVCS.

Table 3. Placement of 5 FEVCS

Run	Location	Minimum voltage (p.u.)	Losses (kW)
1	1,2,21,24,25	0.91523	243.727
2	2,3,5,20,25	0.91115	257.577
3	3,19,21,22,24	0.91499	246.011
4	1,2,22,23,25	0.91528	236.322

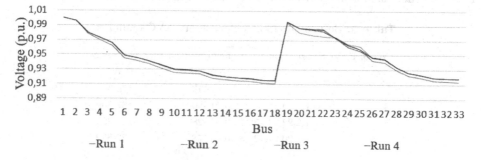

Fig. 6. Voltage profile of the 4 runs with 5 FEVCS.

Table 4. Placement of 6 FEVCS

Run	Location	Minimum voltage (p.u.)	Losses (kW)
1	2,3,21,23,25,28	0.90429	337.836
2	4,5,20,21,22,23	0.90778	322.822
3	2,5,19,24,25,26	0.90152	347.647
4	2,3,5,8,20,22	0.90005	324.367

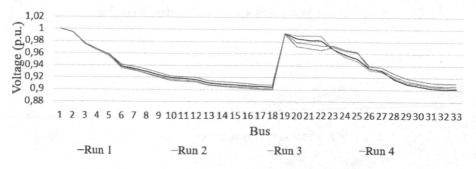

Fig. 7. Voltage profile of the 4 runs with 6 FEVCS.

In Table 5, the best results obtained are presented. From Fig. 8, a significant increase in loss values can be observed. As explained before, with the increase in the number of FEVCS, the installed power associated with these stations also increases, leading to a significant increase in voltage drops at the busbars where the FEVCS are located. By analyzing Fig. 9, it is evident that different voltage profiles are generated based on the different locations considered for the charging stations. However, none of the solutions exceed the limit value. It can also be seen in Figs. 10, 11 and 12 that for the best runs in Table 5, the FEVCS are located close to the substation.

Based on the obtained results, it can be concluded that the placement of 6 FEVCS differs significantly from the cases with 4 and 5 stations.

Table 5. Best solution for each case of FEVCS number

No. of FEVCS	Location	Minimum voltage (p.u.)	Losses (kW)
-	-	0.91947	176,367
4	1,2,19,21	0.91880	187.869
5	1,2,22,23,25	0.91528	236.322
6	4,5,20,21,22,23	0.90778	322.822

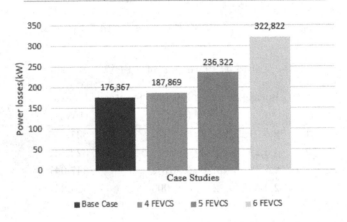

Fig. 8. Power losses values for the 4 studied scenarios

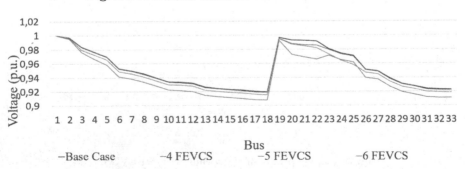

Fig. 9. Best voltage profile for the 4 studied scenarios

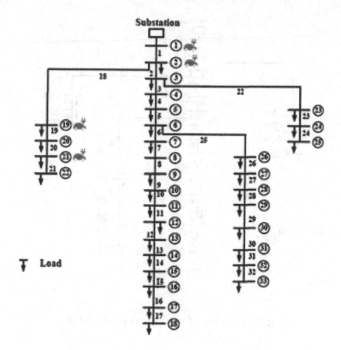

Fig. 10. Solution found for the 4 FEVCS

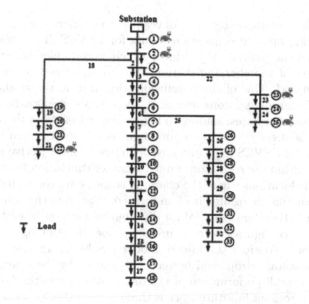

Fig. 11. Solution found for the 5 FEVCS

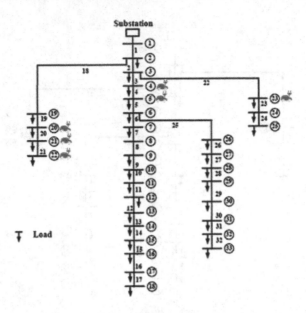

Fig. 12. solution found for the 6 FEVCS

5   Conclusion

In this research, a methodology was developed to support the decision-making process in finding optimal connection points for FEVCS. The chosen methodology was based on Genetic Algorithms, which were implemented to find the optimal location of the charging stations and to analyze their impact on the distribution network. One of the conclusions drawn from the studies is that as the number of charging stations increases, there is a corresponding increase in voltage drops between buses, leading to higher power losses. As the IEEE 33 bus radial network is already close to its minimum voltage limit, it can be concluded that the number of FEVCS to be installed is limited if the objective is to keep the voltage profile within the regulatory limits. Another conclusion from the study is that the specific locations where the charging stations are connected also have a significant impact on the results, both in terms of losses and the voltage profile of the network. It is therefore essential for distribution network operators to determine the optimal configuration to ensure the proper functioning of the network. Future work could consider the injection of renewable energy into the network to mitigate the voltage drops and power losses caused by the charging stations, improving the overall performance of the distribution network. Another aspect to be taken into account in future work is the study of other types of distribution network configurations in addition to the radial structure.

Acknowledgments. This work is financed by National Funds through the Portuguese funding agency, FCT - Fundação para a Ciência e a Tecnologia, within project LA/P/0063/2020.

References

1. Diretiva (ue) 2018/2002 do parlamento europeu e do conselho de 11 de dezembro de 2018 que altera a diretiva 2012/27/ue relativa a eficiência energética (2018).https://eur-lex.europa.eu/legal-content/PT/TXT/PDF/?uri=CELEX: 32018L2002
2. Diretiva (ue) 2018/2001 do parlamento europeu e do conselho de 11 de dezembro de 2018 relativa á promoção da utilização de energia de fontes renováveis (2018). https://eur-lex.europa.eu/legal-content/PT/TXT/ PDF/?uri=CELEX:32018L2001&from=ES
3. SGORME: Formas de carregamento de veículos elétricos em portugal (2011). https://www.uve.pt/page/wp-content/uploads/2016/02/Sgorme_formas_ carregamento_VEs.pdf
4. CENELEC, "Voltage characteristics of electricity supplied by public electricity networks, 2010." 1995, revised in 2010
5. Parah, S.A., Jamil, M.: Techniques for optimal placement of electric vehicle charging stations: a review. In: 2023 International Conference on Power, Instrumentation, Energy and Control (PIECON), pp. 1–5. IEEE (2023)
6. Anwaar, A., Ashraf, A., Bangyal, W.H.K., Iqbal, M.: Genetic algorithms: Brief review on genetic algorithms for global optimization problems. In: 2022 Human-Centered Cognitive Systems (HCCS), pp. 1–6 (2022)
7. Rajendran, A., Kumar, R.H.: Optimal placement of electric vehicle charging stations in utility grid-a case study of Kerala state highway network. In: 2022 IEEE International Conference on Power Electronics, Smart Grid, and Renewable Energy (PESGRE), pp. 1–6. IEEE (2022)
8. Singh, D.K., Bohre, A.K.: Planning of EV fast charging station including DG in distribution system using optimization technique. In: 2020 IEEE International Conference on Power Electronics, Drives and Energy Systems (PEDES), pp. 1–6. IEEE (2020)
9. Altundogan, T.G., Yildiz, A., Karakose, E.: Genetic algorithm approach based on graph theory for location optimization of electric vehicle charging stations. In: Innovations in Intelligent Systems and Applications Conference (ASYU), pp. 1–5. IEEE 2021 (2021)
10. Cerveira, A., Baptista, J., Pires, E.: Wind farm distribution network optimization. Integr. Comput. Aid. Eng. 23(1), 69–79 (2016)
11. Cerveira, A., Baptista, J., Solteiro Pires, E.J.: Optimization design in wind farm distribution network. In: Herrero, Á., et al. (Eds.) International Joint Conference SOCO 2013-CISIS 2013-ICEUTE 2013. AISC, vol. 239, pp. 109–119. Springer, Cham (2014). https://doi.org/10.1007/978-3-319-01854-6_12
12. Ahmad, F., Iqbal, A., Ashraf, I., Marzband, M., Khan, I.: Placement of electric vehicle fast charging stations using grey wolf optimization in electrical distribution network. In: 2022 IEEE International Conference on Power Electronics, Smart Grid, and Renewable Energy (PESGRE), pp. 1–6. IEEE (2022)
13. Ahmad, F., Ashraf, I., Iqbal, A., Khan, I., Marzband, M.: Optimal location and energy management strategy for EV fast charging station with integration of renewable energy sources. In: IEEE Silchar Subsection Conference (SILCON), pp. 1–6. IEEE 2022 (2022)
14. Tamilselvan, V., Jayabarathi, T., Raghunathan, T., Yang, X.-S.: Optimal capacitor placement in radial distribution systems using flower pollination algorithm. Alex. Eng. J. 57(4), 2775–2786 (2018)

15. Goldberg, D.E.: Genetic Algorithms in Search, Optimization and Machine Learning, 1st edn. Addison-Wesley, Boston (1989)
16. Su, C.-L., Leou, R.-C., Yang, J.-C., Lu, C.-N.: Optimal electric vehicle charging stations placement in distribution systems. In: IECON 2013–39th Annual Conference of the IEEE Industrial Electronics Society, pp. 2121–2126. IEEE (2013)
17. Wazir, A., Arbab, N.: Analysis and optimization of IEEE 33 bus radial distributed system using optimization algorithm. J. Emerg. Trends Appl. Eng. 1(2), 17–21 (2016)

Nonlinear Regression on Growth Curves for Placental Parameters in R

Daniela Lemos[1]([⊠])(iD), Ana Cristina Braga[2](iD), and Rosete Nogueira[3,4](iD)

[1] School of Engineering, University of Minho, 4710-057 Braga, Portugal
`pg45469@alunos.uminho.pt`
[2] ALGORITMI Research Centre, LASI, University of Minho, Campus de Gualtar, 4710-057 Braga, Portugal
`acb@dps.uminho.pt`
[3] Life and Health Sciences Research Institute (ICVS), ICVS/3B's - PT Government Associate Laboratory, Campus de Gualtar, 4710-057 Braga/Guimarães, Portugal
`rosete.nogueira@med.uminho.pt`
[4] CGC Genetics, Unilabs, Embryo-fetal Pathology Laboratory, R. Sá da Bandeira, 706, 1o, 4000-431 Porto, Portugal

Abstract. Growth charts play a crucial role in the evaluation and surveillance of paediatric populations, serving as indispensable tools for paediatricians and public health researchers. The development of these growth charts for fetal parameters has been extensively used in recent decades. However, investigation of placental parameters and their relationship with obstetric outcome has been relatively neglected, resulting in a significant gap in understanding their biological significance. This study presents an alternative approach for constructing reference growth curves specific to the placental parameter, Diameter 2. Our methodology uses the generalized additive models for location, scale, and shape (GAMLSS), offering distinct advantages over traditional quantile regression methods. One of the key advantages of GAMLSS is its flexibility to accommodate any statistical distribution, allowing for the modelling of various parameters that characterize the distribution of the response variable. Through the application of our proposed methodology, we demonstrated that by using P-splines as a smoothing function and Box-Cox t (BCT) as a distribution, we can achieve a representative growth curve for the Diameter 2 of the placenta throughout gestational age (GA). The resulting models demonstrated high representativeness, with R^2 values of 0.7608 and 0.7673 and AIC scores of 7953 and 7946 for the best two models, respectively. Moreover, our approach has the ultimate goal to facilitate early diagnosis of fetal complications, thereby providing valuable assistance to healthcare professionals.

Keywords: Placenta · Growth curves · Non-linear · Semi-parametric regression model · Smoothing functions · Distributions · GAMLSS · LMS

This work has been supported by FCT - Fundação para a Ciência e Tecnologia within the R&D Units Project Scope: UIDB/00319/2020.

A. I. Pereira et al. (Eds.): OL2A 2023, CCIS 1981, pp. 575–590, 2024.
https://doi.org/10.1007/978-3-031-53025-8_39

1   Introduction

Over the last decades, considerable attention has been dedicated to utilizing fetal and neonatal measurements as indicators of fetal development. However, there has been a recent surge of interest in exploring the biometric parameters of the placenta and their correlation with obstetric outcomes [18,22,31]. The placenta is an intricately complex organ that plays a crucial role in maintaining a healthy pregnancy, as it facilitates the transfer and exchange of oxygen and essential nutrients to the fetus [7].

As the fetus grows, the placenta undergoes significant transformations in its structure and function, reflecting the evolving needs of the fetus during different stages of development [2]. Consequently, any disturbance or deviation from the expected course of development and growth can result in notable disparities in both placental and fetal characteristics, making their monitoring vital. By closely assessing these intricately interconnected aspects, healthcare professionals can gain valuable insight into the general health and well-being of the fetus, thus ensuring appropriate management and optimizing pregnancy outcomes. Scientific evidence supports the notion that the morphology and dimensions of the placenta are statistically linked to pregnancy complications. These complications encompass fetal growth restrictions, diminished fetal movements, and long-term health consequences for the individual [3,13,38].

Yet, the placenta has not received as much attention in research compared to fetal studies, resulting in a significant knowledge gap concerning the biological implications of placental lesions within the neonatal and perinatal stages [23]. Portugal is an example where placental pathology remains an undervalued subspecialty within surgical pathology, inadequately managed, and not clinically shared. Hence, there has emerged a pressing need to investigate and devise methodologies for the assessment of placental biometric parameters.

The study of percentile growth curves plays a crucial role in the prediction and evaluation of placental parameters. Nonlinear regression models are widely employed in this context due to their robustness compared to linear regression models. Various researchers have conducted comparisons of nonlinear models to effectively fit a wide range of growth curves [5,23,24]. The advantage of these techniques lies in their ability to combine longitudinal measurements into a few easily interpretable parameters, simplifying the analysis [39].

Quantile regression [16] is a popular approach for fitting growth curves and has been applied in studies concerning placental parameters, such as the work conducted by Alves *et al.* (2022) [1]. This non-parametric method allows for fitting different quantiles of the distribution, as opposed to focusing solely on the mean as in standard regression [41]. However, a limitation of this methodology is that the estimation process may result in crossing quantile curves, as estimates for each quantile are determined independently [5]. Various attempts have been made in the literature to address this issue, yet these approaches frequently require supplementary endeavors and may lack suitability based on the particular problem being addressed. Additionally, centile curves estimated at the tails of the data distribution can manifest substantial instability, which adds complexity to their interpretation and compromises their reliability [19].

In this study, we employed a semi-parametric regression-type model within the generalized additive models for location, scale, and shape (GAMLSS) framework, as proposed by Rigby and Stasinopoulos (2005) [25], to accurately fit the reference growth curves for the placental parameter, Diameter 2 (length - largest diameter of the placenta). The main goal was to compare different smoothing functions and distributions within the GAMLSS framework to achieve the best centile growth curve for the placental parameter, Diameter 2.

This research makes significant contributions to the study of placental parameter analysis and growth curve modeling. It highlights the importance of placental biometric parameters in obstetric outcomes and fetal health. Additionally, we introduce the application of the GAMLSS framework for accurate and flexible estimation of centile growth curves for Diameter 2. The findings shed light on curve stability, especially at the tails of the data distribution, providing valuable information for clinical evaluation and improving pregnancy outcomes.

This paper is structured into five sections. Section 2 provides a comprehensive presentation of the dataset employed, along with a detailed description of the statistical methods used. Section 3 presents the obtained results, while Sect. 4, critically discusses these findings. Finally, in Sect. 5 we draw conclusions based on the results and outline avenues for future research.

2 Material and Methods

2.1 Dataset

In this study, we modeled and optimized growth curves for the placental parameter Diameter 2 as a function of GA (12 to 41 weeks), for the Portuguese population (Fig. 1). The data [17] to build and test the generated models was collected at Embryo-fetal Pathology Laboratory, Centro de Genética Clínica (CGC), Unilabs, Porto, Portugal, and contains information on a 4-year (2014–2017) placental pathological report. These data underwent a comprehensive preprocessing procedure in a previous study by Nogueira *et al.* (2019) [23]. The initial sample corresponded to 7321 placental histopathological reports, but after pre-processing only 1847 placentas were used to produce these percentile growth curves.

2.2 Statistical Methods

The estimation of growth curve distributions based on age commonly relies on the widely used approach of centile estimation [19]. These curves, which represent the growth patterns, are typically derived using two different sets of methods. One approach is the non-parametric method that utilizes quantile regression, as introduced by Koenker in 2005 [16]. The other approach is the parametric method initially pioneered by Cole in 1988 [10], which was later refined by Cole and Green in 1992 [9].

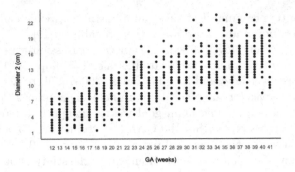

Fig. 1. Scatter plot depicting the relationship between GA (in weeks) and Diameter 2 of the placenta (in centimeters). Each data point represents an individual observation from a sample of 1847 placentas.

The selection of methods to construct centile growth curves for placental parameters should be guided by criteria that consider the characteristics of the dataset and the intended applications of future standards. Consequently, only methods that treat age as a continuous variable, rely on explicit distributional assumptions, and simultaneously estimate centiles were considered.

In this paper, we used a semiparametric regression-type model, known as GAMLSS [26, 27]. We also used the LMS method, which is a particular case of this method [9]. GAMLSS provides a highly flexible approach to modelling a univariate response variable (Diameter 2) in relation to an explanatory variable (GA). It also offers flexibility in employing a wide range of parametric distributions, including highly skewed and kurtotic continuous and discrete distributions [40]. Additionally, it allows for the incorporation of a non-parametric smoothing term to model distribution parameters based on an explanatory variable [19]. Maximum (penalized) likelihood estimation and the algorithm RS are used to fit the models [25].

In our modeling approach, we utilized the GAMLSS package in R [33, 36] to construct the models. This implementation allows for the use of distributions with maximum of four parameters, defined as μ, σ, ν, and τ. These parameters respectively describe the location, scale, skewness, and kurtosis shape of the distribution [40]. The GAMLSS model, originally formulated by Rigby and Stasinopoulos (2005) [25], is represented by Eq. 1, where the distribution parameters θ_k are related to the predictors η_k through monotonic link functions g_k:

$$g_k(\theta_k) = \eta_k = X_k\beta_k + \sum_{j=1}^{J_k} h_{jk}(X_{jk}) \tag{1}$$

Here, X_k corresponds to the matrix of explanatory variables, while β_k represents the matrix of parameters to be estimated for each specific parameter ($k = 1, 2, 3, 4$). The smooth functions h_{jk} capture the relationship between the explanatory variables X_{jk} and the distribution parameters, where $j = 1, ..., J_k$ represents the number of smooth functions for each parameter.

Smoothing Functions. Smoothers, being non-parametric techniques, let the data determine the relationship between predictor and explanatory variables. By avoiding assumptions about a specific parametric functional form, smoothers capture the underlying trend of the mean of a response variable y in relation to x [34]. Within the framework of the GAMLSS package, we have opted to utilize smoothing penalized univariate methods such as penalized splines (P-splines) and cubic splines. These methods control the level of smoothness, incorporating quadratic penalties [34]. We also tested other smoothing techniques like neural networks and loess that utilize alternative approaches, such as locality or non-quadratic penalties, to achieve smooth functions [34].

P-splines are a type of piecewise polynomial representation [12, 32]. They utilize B-spline basis functions within the explanatory variable, and the coefficients associated with these basis functions are subject to penalization to ensure adequate smoothness. Multiple approaches exist for estimating the smoothing parameter locally or globally. We used maximum likelihood (ML), generalized cross-validation (GCV), generalized Akaike information criterion (GAIC), and GAIC in conjunction with a local Schwarz Bayesian criterion (SBC) to select the most appropriate smoothing parameter for our analysis.

Cubic smoothing splines utilize basis functions akin to P-splines; however, they employ piecewise polynomials of degree 3. While both methods differ in two key aspects, in P-splines, equidistant knots are placed along the x-axis, and smoothness is controlled by applying a penalty to the model coefficients [34]. On the other hand, cubic smoothing splines have knots located at specific x-variable values, and smoothness is attained by applying a penalty that controls the curvature or bending of the function [34].

Neural networks represent highly flexible and overparameterized nonlinear models, granting them the ability to approximate nearly any continuous function [34]. In our analysis, we incorporated the argument "decay" as a smoothing parameter to aid the optimization process and potentially prevent overfitting.

Loess, also known as 'lowess', is a technique used for local regression smoothing. It utilizes one or several explanatory continuous variables to fit a polynomial curve or surface, which is adapted to the specific region of interest [32].

Distributions. The GAMLSS framework presents a significant advantage by accommodating a diverse range of distributions for the response variable [28]. It assumes a probability function $f(y|\theta)$ of the response variable y with up to four distribution parameters: $\theta = (\mu, \sigma, \nu, \tau)$ [34]. In this study, we utilized continuous distributions, including Box-Cox Cole and Green (BCCG), Box-Cox t (BCT), and Box-Cox power exponential (BCPE).

The **BCCG distribution** is appropriate for handling data with positive or negative skewness [32]. Cole and Green (1992) [9] were among the first to adopt this distribution, using it to model all three parameters through nonparametric smooth functions linked to a single explanatory variable [34]. Assuming Y is a positive random variable following the BCCG distribution (BCCG (μ, σ, ν)), we set the transformed random variable Z using Eq. 2 [28].

$$z = \begin{cases} \frac{1}{\sigma\nu}\left[\left(\frac{Y}{\mu}\right)^{\nu} - 1\right] & if \ \nu \neq 0 \\ \frac{1}{\sigma}\log\left(\frac{Y}{\mu}\right) & if \ \nu = 0 \end{cases} \tag{2}$$

Here, $0 < Y < \infty$, $\mu > 0$, $\sigma > 0$, and $-\infty < \nu < \infty$. It is presumed that the random variable Z is subjected to a truncated standard normal distribution [28]. The condition $0 < Y < \infty$ ensures Y^{ν} is real for all ν, leading to the range $-1/(\sigma\nu) < Z < \infty$ if $\nu > 0$ and $-\infty < Z < -1/(\sigma\nu)$ if $\nu < 0$. This requirement necessitates the standard truncated normal distribution for Z [28]. Consequently, the probability density function (pdf) of Y is given by Eq. 3 [32].

$$f_Y(y) = \frac{y^{\nu-1}\exp\left(-\frac{1}{2}z^2\right)}{\mu^{\nu}\sigma\sqrt{2\pi}\phi\left(\frac{1}{\sigma|\nu|}\right)} \tag{3}$$

The variable Z is determined by Eq. 2, and $\phi()$ represents the cumulative distribution function (cdf) of a standard normal distribution [32].

Consider Y as a positive random variable following the **BCT distribution** (BCT (μ, σ, ν, τ)) introduced by Rigby and Stasinopoulos in 2006 [27]. The distribution is characterized by the transformed random variable Z specified in Eq. 2, where Z follows a truncated t distribution with degrees of freedom $\tau > 0$, handled as a continuous parameter [32]. Equation 4 provides the pdf of Y.

$$f_Y(y|\mu, \sigma, \nu, \tau) = \frac{y^{\nu-1}f_T(Z)}{\mu^{\nu}\sigma F_T\left(\frac{1}{\sigma|\nu|}\right)} \tag{4}$$

For positive values of Y, with μ and σ being positive and $-\infty < \nu < \infty$, the random variable Z is determined by Eq. 2. The pdf and cdf of a random variable T, characterized by a standard t distribution with degrees of freedom parameter $\tau > 0$, are denoted as $f_T(t)$ and $F_T(t)$, respectively [32].

Consider a positive random variable Y with a **BCPE distribution** (BCPE (μ, σ, ν, τ)), Rigby and Stasinopoulos (2004) [26]. This distribution is described through the transformed random variable Z, given by Eq. 2, with Z assumed to follow a truncated standard power exponential distribution with power parameter $\tau > 0$, considered as a continuous parameter [32]. The pdf of Y, denoted by Eq. 4, is related to $f_T(t)$ and $F_T(t)$, the pdf and cdf of a variable T following a standard power exponential distribution [32].

Goodness-of-fit Criteria. In order to compare the effectiveness of the different smoothing functions and distributions applied to the placental parameter, Diameter 2, in function of the GA, several criteria were utilized:

- **Determination Coefficient** (R^2): is a measure of the proportion of explained variance present in the data [6]. Higher values of R^2 indicate a better model fit. It is calculated as $R^2 = 1 - (SSE/SST)$, where SSE represents the sum of squared errors and SST denotes the total sum of squares.

- **Mean Square Error (MSE):** combines both the bias and variance of an estimator, reflecting its accuracy [29]. A small MSE indicates a more precise estimator. It is calculated as $MSE = SSE/(n - k)$, where n is the number of observations, and k is the number of parameters.

- **Akaike's Information Criterion (AIC):** helps select the best fitting model by measuring how close it is to the true model [8]. Lower AIC values indicate better-fitting models. It is calculated as $AIC = n.ln(SSE/n) + 2k$.

- **Schwarz Bayesian Information Criterion (BIC):** selects the most parsimonious model that converges to the true model [21]. The model with the minimum BIC value is preferred. It is calculated as $BIC = n.ln(SSE/n) + k.ln(n)$.

- **Worm plot:** is a detrended QQ-plot used to detect regions in the data where the model may not accurately capture the underlying pattern [34]. Different shapes observed in the worm plot can indicate misfits in the model's assumptions related to mean, variance, skewness, and excess kurtosis of the residuals across specific age intervals [19]. Shapes like vertical shifts, slopes, parabolic curves, or S-shaped curves provide insights into potential discrepancies in different aspects of the model's fit [19].

3   Results

In this study, we analysed the relationship between the placental parameter, Diameter 2, and GA in order to produce reference centile growth curves ($\alpha = 3, 10, 25, 50, 75, 90, 97$). The sample consisted of 1847 placentas. To evaluate if there were statistically significant differences between the mean Diameter 2 for female (779 samples) and male (843 samples) fetuses at each GA, the t-student test, with a significance level of 0.05, was used. The results reveal varying degrees of significance at different gestational ages. At certain gestational ages, such as 12 (p-value = 0.02), 14 (p-value = 0.04) and 39 (p-value = 0.003) weeks, a statistically significant difference was observed in Diameter 2 between female and male genders, as indicated by the p-values below 0.05. The graphical representation of these results can be observed in Fig. 2.

Descriptive statistics like, sample size (N), mean, standard deviation (SD), minimum (Min), maximum (Max), median, skewness, and kurtosis of Diameter 2 across the GA (12–41 weeks) are presented in Table 1. Overall, we observed an increase in Diameter 2 as GA advanced, also seen in Fig. 1, demonstrating a positive relationship between the variables, and indicating a progressive development of the placenta. The mean of Diameter 2 was 4.375 ± 1.630 cm at week 12 and gradually increased to 16.261 ± 2.423 cm at week 41, also the variability tends to slightly increase with GA, as seen by the values of SD, indicating an increasing spread of the data. Additionally, it was also analysed the range and median values, which demonstrated a similar increasing trend, further supporting the notion of progressive growth. Notably, the skewness values

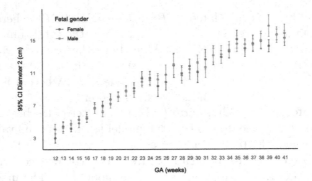

Fig. 2. The mean values and their corresponding 95% confidence intervals for the placental parameter, Diameter 2, are presented based on fetal gender at each GA.

indicated approximately symmetric distributions, because in general, the values are close to zero, implying a balanced development of Diameter 2. Furthermore, the observed positive kurtosis values suggested a slight peakedness in the distributions (leptokurtic), reflecting a degree of concentration around the mean.

In order to construct the growth curves, first it was evaluated the performance of different smoothing functions, as shown in Table 2. P-splines demonstrated good performance with R^2 values ranging from 0.7432 to 0.7452, indicating a strong fit to the data. The corresponding MSE values ranged from 4.400 to 4.402, indicating minimal deviation between the predicted and observed values. The AIC values ranged from 8110 to 8117, and the BIC values ranged from 8142 to 8157, suggesting good model fit and parsimony. Cubic splines also yielded satisfactory results, with R^2 values of 0.7442 and 0.7449, AIC values of 8113 and 8110, and BIC values of 8146 and 8152. Furthermore, neural networks demonstrated comparable performance, achieving a R^2 value of 0.7446, although it was accompanied by a slightly higher MSE of 4.427, indicating a small increase in prediction errors compared to other methods. The AIC value was 8133, and the BIC value was 8233. The Loess smoothing method displayed an R^2 value of 0.7437, an MSE of 4.401, and AIC and BIC values of 8115 and 8146, respectively.

After the most proper smoothing function was selected, different distributions were tested, as presented in Table 2 and Fig. 3. Fitting a GAMLSS model with the distributions BCCG, BCT, and BCPE demonstrated, in general, a good performance. The BCCG distribution had the highest value of R^2, 0.7644, closely followed by the distribution BCT with an R^2 of 0.7608. These distributions also exhibited relatively low MSE values of 4.330 and 4.328 and values of AIC and BIC of 7959 and 8049 for BCCG, and 7953 and 8051 for BCT. The BCPE seems to be the least promising distribution of the three with the lowest R^2 value of 0.7578, an MSE of 4.328, and AIC and BIC values of 7953 and 8051, respectively.

Upon analyzing the worm plots of these distributions in the GAMLSS, we can see that the BCT (Fig. 3b) and BCPE (Fig. 3c) distributions fit more adequately to the data, since they do not show a particular shape and 95% of the plotted data points are enclosed within the elliptical 95% pointwise interval bands. However, the distribution BCCG (Fig. 3a) presents an S-shape with the left bent down, indicating a deficiency in the fitted distribution.

When fitting the LMS model with the same distributions, the results were also promising. The BCT distribution had the highest value of R^2, 0.7673, in relation to all the distributions, including the GAMLSS method. It also had a low value of MSE, 4.329, AIC, 7946, and BIC, 8063.

Table 1. Descriptive statistics of Diameter 2 at each GA. The table includes the sample size (N), mean, standard deviation (SD), minimum (Min), maximum (Max), median, skewness, and kurtosis values.

GA	N	Mean	SD	Min	Max	Median	Skewness	Kurtosis
12	52	4.375	1.630	2.0	8.0	4.0	0.6543	2.672
13	58	4.957	1.612	1.5	9.0	5.0	0.5281	3.080
14	67	5.175	1.242	2.0	8.0	5.0	−0.1979	3.072
15	70	5.780	1.454	2.5	10.0	6.0	−0.0391	2.929
16	72	6.236	1.647	2.0	9.0	6.0	−0.2869	2.594
17	69	7.391	1.763	4.0	12.0	7.0	0.1551	2.353
18	72	7.282	1.752	2.0	11.0	7.0	−0.2817	2.840
19	71	8.232	1.942	3.0	12.5	8.0	−0.1931	3.149
20	69	8.804	1.698	4.0	12.5	9.0	−0.1618	2.809
21	69	9.472	1.793	4.0	13.0	10.0	−0.5473	3.237
22	69	9.638	2.130	5.0	15.0	10.0	−0.1506	2.715
23	71	10.775	2.126	5.0	16.0	11.0	−0.1910	2.977
24	66	10.962	2.149	7.0	18.0	11.0	0.5643	3.785
25	47	10.596	2.295	6.0	17.0	11.0	0.0172	2.962
26	41	10.915	2.358	6.0	16.0	11.0	0.2487	2.499
27	31	12.710	2.575	8.0	19.0	12.0	0.9498	3.493
28	59	11.661	2.445	7.0	18.0	12.0	0.1798	2.755
29	41	12.434	2.168	8.0	16.5	12.0	−0.0173	1.860
30	46	12.559	2.586	7.5	21.0	12.5	0.7403	4.356
31	51	12.922	3.017	6.0	23.0	12.0	0.7139	4.692
32	58	13.888	2.369	8.0	22.0	13.0	0.6878	4.297
33	65	13.794	2.475	8.0	21.0	14.0	0.0012	3.122
34	65	14.469	2.500	9.0	24.0	14.0	1.3151	6.647
35	66	15.583	2.629	11.0	23.0	15.0	0.7998	3.499
36	75	14.967	2.377	10.0	22.0	15.0	0.4033	3.535
37	64	15.009	2.151	11.5	23.0	15.0	1.3706	6.226
38	63	15.365	2.494	10.0	24.0	15.0	0.9666	4.938
39	65	15.492	2.594	12.0	23.0	15.0	0.9666	3.753
40	71	16.359	2.089	9.0	21.5	16.5	−0.4411	4.160
41	64	16.261	2.423	10.0	22.0	16.0	−0.0197	3.555

The BCCG also presented a good value of R^2, 0.7649, and low values for MSE, AIC, and BIC of 4.331, 7958, and 8056, respectively. Furthermore, the worm plots showed similar results to the ones for the GAMLSS method, BCT

(Fig. 3e) and BCPE (Fig. 3f) distributions fited more adequately, and the BCCG (Fig. 3d) revealed one more time an S-shape with the left bent down.

Centile curves for the best two models, GAMLSS (BCCT) and LMS(BCT), were obtained and displayed in Fig. 4. As a concluding model diagnostic, we present the sample percentages located at or below each of the fitted curves in Table 3. Notably, the close agreement between the nominal and sample percentages for both models suggests a strong fit of the centile curves.

To validate the effectiveness of the methodology employed in this study compared to quantile regression, we replicated the results of Alves et al. (2022) [1] for Diameter 2. The replicated results revealed an R^2 of 0.7049, MSE of 6.426, and AIC and BIC values of 8558 and 3526, respectively.

Table 2. Model performance metrics for different smooth functions and distributions. The table displays the coefficient of determination (R^2), mean squared error (MSE), Akaike information criterion (AIC), and Bayesian information criterion (BIC).

Smooth functions	R^2	MSE	AIC	BIC
P-splines (method ML)	0.7447	4.401	8111	8150
P-splines (method GCV)	0.7442	4.400	8112	8146
P-splines (method GAIC)	0.7452	4.402	8110	8157
P-splines (method GAIC, local SBC)	0.7432	4.400	8117	8142
Cubic spline	0.7442	4.400	8113	8146
Cubic spline (λ estimated)	0.7449	4.401	8110	8152
Neural networks	0.7446	4.427	8133	8233
Loess	0.7437	4.401	8115	8146
Distributions				
GAMLSS (BCCG)	0.7644	4.330	7959	8049
GAMLSS (BCT)	0.7608	4.328	7953	8051
GAMLSS (BCPE)	0.7578	4.328	7953	8051
LMS (BCCG)	0.7649	4.331	7958	8056
LMS (BCT)	0.7673	4.329	7946	8063
LMS (BCPE)	0.7597	4.326	7943	8055

4   Discussion

Over time, the development of percentile curves for fetal weight in relation to GA has been undertaken to provide valuable guidance to healthcare professionals and parents regarding the growth and development of fetuses and newborns [4, 15]. The findings of the present study show that is also possible to produce percentile curves for placental parameters like Diameter 2, to further make conclusions about the well-being of the fetus, since previous studies have demonstrated a statistically significant association between the shape and size of the placenta and complications during pregnancy, as well as the long-term health outcomes of individuals [20, 30]. Employing the GAMLSS method with the appropriate smoothing function, P-splines, and distribution, BCT, it was possible to achieve a good fit to the data.

Considering the known association between fetal gender and birth weight, it may be important to categorize the percentile curves into male and female-specific ones. Although some studies conclude that there were no significant differences in placental weight between male and female neonates [2, 23, 35]. We only found statistically significant differences between Diameter 2 and the genders for 12, 14, and 39 weeks. Hence, we opted to not categorize the percentile curves into male and female.

The descriptive statistics of Diameter 2 across the GA provided valuable insights into the overall patterns of placental growth. Our results demonstrated a positive relationship between Diameter 2 and GA, as evidenced by the increasing mean values of Diameter 2 as GA advanced. This observation aligns with previous research highlighting the progressive development of the placenta throughout gestation [37]. The presence of a positive kurtosis in the data indicates the need of using methods that can address it, like the GAMLSS method implemented, as a way to avoid distorted fitted centiles [5].

In order to construct the growth curves, it was important to select the best method to fit the data. According to the method selection criteria, GAMLSS and LMS methods were tested on the data. Firstly, different smoothing functions were evaluated because they are well known for their flexibility to fit curves without choosing in advance a rigid form for the underlying function [11]. The results showcased notable performance among the various smoothing functions. Nonetheless, the P-splines demonstrated competitive performance across all the evaluated criteria and were selected for inclusion in the model. P-splines offer advantages over other smoothers, such as cubic smoothing splines, due to their computational efficiency, allowing models to be fitted to larger datasets [11].

Once the most suitable smoothing function was identified, various distributions were tested. GAMLSS models employing the BCT and BCPE distributions exhibited good performance, as evidenced by their high R^2 values and relatively low MSE, AIC, and BIC. The worm plots further confirmed the adequacy of these distributions. Notably, when applying the LMS model with the same distributions, similar results were obtained, emphasizing the robustness of the findings.

Flatley *et al.* (2022) [14] conducted a recent study demonstrating the successful utilization of the GAMLSS method to create placenta weight reference curves. This work highlights the efficacy of the GAMLSS approach in analyzing placental parameters. In the study of Borghi *et al.* (2006) [5] for the construction of the World Health Organization child growth standards, the authors suggested the use of GAMLSS with these type of distributions due to its potential for yielding promising outcomes when age is treated as a continuous variable, similar to GA. In order to further validate this method, we made a comparison with a very famous method to fit centile growth curves, the quantile regression. The results showed that the GAMLSS method outperformed quantile regression, making it a favorable choice for the growth curves of placental parameters and even for other similar studies.

The resulting centile curves for the best two models, GAMLSS (BCT) with P-splines and LMS (BCT) with P-splines, offered valuable insights into the distribution of Diameter 2 values across different percentiles. And, as noted, all fitted centile curves with the BCT model exhibit a close alignment between nominal and sample percentages, indicating their effectiveness.

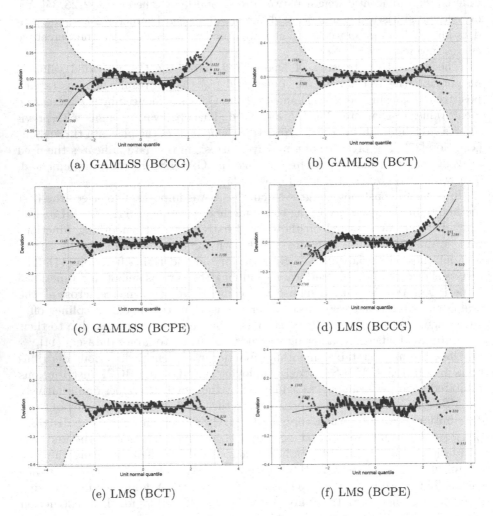

Fig. 3. Worm plots for the fit of distributions using the GAMLSS and LMS methods. Each subfigure represents a different distribution.

Consequently, the results suggest that both GAMLSS and LMS methods, combined with P-splines and the BCT distribution provide a strong fit for the

Table 3. Summary of the model's performance by comparing nominal and sample percentages at or below each centile.

Nominal Centile	3	10	25	50	75	90	97
GAMLSS (BCT)	3.194	9.637	24.85	50.19	75.04	90.47	96.48
LMS (BCT)	3.03	10.29	25.50	49.43	74.99	90.31	96.97

data, making them suitable for generating reference growth curves for placental parameters. These curves empower healthcare professionals to assess placental development effectively, as they can compare the Diameter 2 parameter against the 3% centile curve for any GA range. Such information proves invaluable in identifying any suboptimal placental development during pregnancy.

Lastly, it is important to highlight that this methodology can be applied in any study aiming to develop standard growth curves. For more comprehensive information on this approach, check [28, 34].

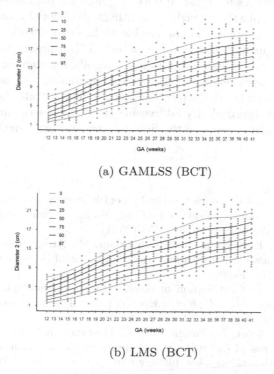

(a) GAMLSS (BCT)

(b) LMS (BCT)

Fig. 4. Observed Diameter 2 values plotted against GA along with seven fitted centile curves (3rd, 10th, 25th, 50th, 75th, 90th, and 97th).

5   Conclusions

This study introduced an innovative approach to create standard growth curves for placental parameters, specifically Diameter 2. Using the BCT distribution and P-splines within the GAMLSS framework, we achieved a robust fit to the data, evidenced by promising goodness-of-fit criteria and worm plots. These growth curves have the potential to enhance early recognition of fetal disorders, providing relief to families and improving perinatal success.

One of the main challenges encountered in this research was the relative dearth of existing studies in the area of placental biometric parameters. Prior to this study, the exploration of placental growth curves using GAMLSS had been largely unexplored. Therefore, limited literature and established methodologies in this specific field posed challenges in drawing comparisons and validating our results. Nonetheless, our pioneering approach fills a crucial gap in the literature, offering valuable insights into placental growth patterns and their clinical significance.

Looking ahead, our future work aims to extend this methodology to produce reference growth curves for other important placental parameters, such as placental weight ratio, placental weight, and others. Additionally, our ultimate goal is to develop a shiny application accessible to health professionals, facilitating better understanding and prevention of potential fetal problems.

In conclusion, this research represents a significant step forward in understanding placental parameters and their role in predicting fetal health outcomes. Despite the challenges faced, the results obtained demonstrate the feasibility and effectiveness of our approach. By addressing these challenges and extending our methodology, we aim to advance the field of perinatal medicine.

References

1. Alves, S., Braga, A.C., Nogueira, R.: Percentile growth curves for placenta measures: a dynamic shiny application. In: Computational Science and Its Applications - ICCSA 2022 Workshops, pp. 543–554 (2022)
2. Asgharnia, M., Esmailpour, N., Poorghorban, M., Atrkar-Roshan, Z.: Placenta weight and its association with maternal and neonatal characteristics. Acta Med. Iran. **46**, 467–472 (2008)
3. Ashwal, E., et al.: Contribution of second trimester sonographic placental morphology to uterine artery doppler in the prediction of placenta-mediated pregnancy complications. J. Clin. Med. **11**, 6759 (2022)
4. Aybuke, Y., Mehmet, B., Fatma Nur, S., Mustafa Senol, A., Omer, E., Evrim, A.D.: Comparison of different growth curves in the assessment of extrauterine growth restriction in very low birth weight preterm infants. Arch. Pediatr. **30**, 31–35 (2023)
5. Borghi, E., et al.: Construction of the world health organization child growth standards: selection of methods for attained growth curves. Stat. Med. **25**, 247–265 (2006)
6. Bucchianico, A.D.: Coefficient of Determination (R2). John Wiley & Sons Ltd., New York (2008)

7. Burton, G.J., Jauniaux, E.: What is the placenta? Am. J. Obstetr. Gynecol. **213**, S6.e1-S68 (2015)
8. Cavanaugh, J.E., Neath, A.A.: The Akaike information criterion: Background, derivation, properties, application, interpretation, and refinements. WIREs Comput. Statist. **11**(3), e1460 (2019)
9. Cole, T.J., Green, P.J.: Smoothing reference centile curves: the LMS method and penalized likelihood. Stat. Med. **11**, 1305–1319 (1992)
10. Cole, T.J.: Fitting smoothed centile curves to reference data. J. R. Stat. Soc. A. Stat. Soc. **151**, 385–406 (1988)
11. Currie, I.D., Durban, M.: Flexible smoothing with p-splines: a unified approach. Stat. Model. **2**, 333–349 (2002)
12. Eilers, P.H.C., Marx, B.D.: Flexible smoothing with B-splines and penalties. Stat. Sci. **11**, 89–121 (1996)
13. Eriksson, J.G., Kajantie, E., Thornburg, K.L., Osmond, C., Barker, D.J.: Mothers body size and placental size predict coronary heart disease in men. Eur. Heart J. **32**, 2297–2303 (2011)
14. Flatley, C., et al.: Placental weight centiles adjusted for age, parity and fetal sex. Placenta **117**, 87–94 (2022)
15. Grantz, K.L.: Fetal growth curves: is there a universal reference? Obstet. Gynecol. Clin. N. Am. **48**, 281–296 (2021)
16. Koenker, R.: Quantile Regression. Econometric Society Monographs. Cambridge University Press, Cambridge (2005)
17. Lemos, D., Braga, A.C., Nogueira, R.: Dataset placenta (2023). https://doi.org/10.5281/zenodo.8187507
18. Mohamed, M.L., Elbeily, M.M., Shalaby, M.M., Khattab, Y.H., Taha, O.T.: Umbilical cord diameter in the prediction of foetal growth restriction: a cross sectional study. J. Obstet. Gynaecol. **42**, 1117–1121 (2022)
19. Nakamura, L.R., et al.: Cattle reference growth curves based on centile estimation: a GAMLSS approach. Comput. Electron. Agric. **192**, 106572 (2022)
20. Naomi, M., et al.: Association between maternal hemoglobin concentration and placental weight to birthweight ratio: the Japan environment and children's study (JECS). Placenta **101**, 132–138 (2020)
21. Neath, A.A., Cavanaugh, J.E.: The Bayesian information criterion: background, derivation, and applications. WIREs Comput. Stat. **4**, 199–203 (2012)
22. Njeze, N.R., Ogbochukwu, J.O., Chinawa, J.M.: Correlation of ultrasound placental diameter & thickness with gestational age. Pak. J. Med. Sci. Q. **36**, 1058–1062 (2020)
23. Nogueira, R., et al.: Placental biometric parameters the usefulness of placental weight ratio and birth/placental weight ratio percentile curves for singleton gestations as a function of gestational age. J. Clin. Anat. Pathol. **4**(104), 1–15 (2019)
24. Numan, S., Asad, A., Imran, M., Nisar, A.: Evaluation of nonlinear models to define growth curve in Lohi sheep. Small Rumin. Res. **205**, 106564 (2021)
25. Rigby, R.A., Stasinopoulos, D.M.: Generalized additive models for location, scale and shape. J. Roy. Stat. Soc.: Ser. C (Appl. Stat.) **54**, 507–554 (2005)
26. Rigby, R.A., Stasinopoulos, D.M.: Smooth centile curves for skew and kurtotic data modelled using the box-cox power exponential distribution. Stat. Med. **23**, 3053–3076 (2004)
27. Rigby, R.A., Stasinopoulos, D.M.: Using the box-cox t distribution in GAMLSS to model skewness and kurtosis. Stat. Model. **6**, 209–229 (2006)

28. Rigby, R.A., Stasinopoulos, M.D., Heller, G.Z., Bastiani, F.D.: Distributions for Modeling Location, Scale, and Shape: Using GAMLSS in R. CRC Press, Boca Raton (2019)
29. Schluchter, M.D.: Mean Square Error. John Wiley & Sons, Ltd., New York (2005)
30. Shehata, F., et al.: Placenta/birthweight ratio and perinatal outcome: a retrospective cohort analysis. BJOG: Int. J. Obstet. Gynaecol. **118**, 741–747 (2011)
31. Siskovicova, A., et al.: Analysis of factors influencing ultrasound-based fetal weight estimation. Bratisl. Lek. Listy **124**, 25–28 (2023)
32. Stasinopoulos, M., Rigby, B., Akantziliotou, C.: Instructions on How to Use the GAMLSS Package in R, 2nd edn. CRC Press, Boca Raton (2008)
33. Stasinopoulos, M., Rigby, B., Voudouris, V., Akantziliotou, C., Enea, M., Kiose, D.: GAMLSS: generalised additive models for location scale and shape (2023). https://CRAN.R-project.org/package=gamlss. Accessed 2023
34. Stasinopoulos, M.D., Rigby, R.A., Heller, G.Z., Voudouris, V., Bastiani, F.D.: Flexible Regression and Smoothing. The R Series. Chapman & Hall/CRC, Philadelphia (2017)
35. Tamayev, L., Schreiber, L., Marciano, A., Bar, J., Kovo, M.: Are there gender-specific differences in pregnancy outcome and placental abnormalities of pregnancies complicated with small for gestational age? Arch. Gynecol. Obstet. **301**, 1147–1151 (2020)
36. TEAM, R.C.: R: A language and environment for statistical computing (2005). https://www.r-project.org/. Accessed 2023
37. Turco, M.Y., Moffett, A.: Development of the human placenta. Development **146**, dev163428 (2019)
38. Vişan, V., et al.: Morphological and histopathological changes in placentas ofpregnancies with intrauterine growth restriction. Rom. J. Morphol. Embryol. **61**, 477–483 (2020)
39. Vitezica, Z.G., Marie-Etancelin, C., Bernadet, M.D., Fernandez, X., Robert-Granie, C.: Comparison of nonlinear and spline regression models for describing mule duck growth curves. Poult. Sci. **89**, 1778–1784 (2010)
40. Voudouris, V., Gilchrist, R., Rigby, R., Sedgwick, J., Stasinopoulos, D.: Modelling skewness and kurtosis with the BCPE density in GAMLSS. J. Appl. Stat. **39**, 1279–1293 (2012)
41. Waldmann, E.: Quantile regression: a short story on how and why. Stat. Model. **18**, 203–218 (2018)

GLM's in Data Science as a Tool in the Prediction of *Delirium*

Alexandra Coelho[1]([✉])(iD), Ana Cristina Braga[2](iD), and José Mariz[3](iD)

[1] School of Engineering, University of Minho, 4710-057 Braga, Portugal
`pg45458@alunos.uminho.pt`
[2] ALGORITMI Research Centre, LASI, University of Minho, Campus de Gualtar, 4710-057 Braga, Portugal
`acb@dps.uminho.pt`
[3] ICVS - Life and Health Sciences Research Institute, 4700-057 Braga, Portugal

Abstract. *Delirium* is an acute neuropsychiatric dysfunction, prevalent in patients admitted to hospitals for inpatient and intensive care, being clinically characterized by attention deficit and clouding of the state of consciousness associated with cognitive disorders. Since this is a multifactorial manifestation that develops over a short period of time, it is usually underdiagnosed and neglected. Consequently, this disorder appears associated with high rates of mortality and morbidity, leading to a longer period of hospitalization. Additionally, *delirium* can be categorized, according to the motor activity profile, into two subtypes: hypo and hyperactive.

Currently, there are studies and assessment instruments for the study and prediction of the disease at an earlier stage, based on a set of risk factors. However, in the context of a hospital emergency, time is essential, as well as a correct and early diagnosis to intervene as quickly as possible. In this context, the goal of this paper arises, which aims to implement a diversity of techniques to preprocess the data to perform the multinomial logistic regression. The ultimate goal is to identify the most effective data balancing technique for accurate prediction of *delirium* occurrence and its subtypes, based on the methodology of generalized linear models (GLMs), specifically multinomial logistic regression (MLR).

Keywords: *delirium* · Generalized linear model · Multinomial logistic regression

1 Introduction

The area of data science has emerged as a way to address the increasing escalation of data, as well as the analytical and computational power it requires. When applied to medical research, the different approaches allow the exploration and

This work has been supported by FCT - Fundação para a Ciência e Tecnologia within the R&D Units Project Scope: UIDB/00319/2020.

A. I. Pereira et al. (Eds.): OL2A 2023, CCIS 1981, pp. 591–606, 2024.
https://doi.org/10.1007/978-3-031-53025-8_40

analysis of large data sets, with the aim of detecting patterns to obtain meaningful knowledge.

Globally, 25% of the population suffers from mental disorders. Based on the symptoms and associated risk factors, it is possible to implement methodologies that allow the detection and prediction of mental illnesses at an earlier stage, so it is in the medical interest to develop these predictive tools.

Currently, based on the definition in the DSM-V, *delirium* is a severe neuropsychiatric syndrome characterized primarily by disturbances in consciousness, incoherent thinking, attention deficit, and cognitive dysfunction, which sometimes can be accompanied by psychotic symptoms and mood alteration with fluctuations throughout the day [5,6,9]. Typically, *delirium* develops over a short period of hours or days [21], and there is evidence that the disturbance is a direct physiological consequence of a medical condition or multiple etiologies, which complicates the diagnostic process [5,25].

The symptomatology reflects deficits in three domains: cognitive, which is related to orientation, attention, short and long-term memory, and visuospatial perception; higher-level thinking domain, which involves impairment of language and thought processes; and circadian, which includes the sleep-wake cycle and disturbances in motor activity [27,31].

The prevalence of *delirium* varies from 3% to 52% depending on the studied population, the environment they are in [1,17], the type of hospitalization, as well as the detection method used [21]. The occurrence rate in the general community is less than 2%, but it increases with age [21]. The disorder is common among hospitalized older adults, representing a population of 23%, making them the highest-risk group [15].

Typically, patients with this disorder are subject to a combination of predisposing and precipitating risk factors. Predisposing factors are those that make an individual more susceptible to the development of *delirium*. On the other hand, precipitating factors occur when a patient experiences a specific event that contributes to the progression of the pathology.

The multifactorial model proposed by Inouye suggests that the greater the number of predisposing factors, the lower the number of precipitating factors, and vice versa [20]. Therefore, the prevention, detection, and treatment of *delirium* can be more efficient by addressing both the predisposing and precipitating factors.

Thus, *delirium* is the result of the interaction between vulnerability factors (predisposing) present before hospital admission and precipitating factors that overlap during hospitalization [21], contributing to distinct individual episodes [19]. This interaction explains the development of different subtypes and phenotypes of *delirium*.

According to Lipowski, *delirium* can be categorized into three clinically defined subgroups based on the profile of motor activity. These subgroups differ in terms of physiopathology, detection rates, and duration of the episode [26].

Individuals who exhibit the hyperactive subtype of *delirium* display a state of hyperarousal, often characterized by hypervigilance, agitation, hallucinations, verbal and physical confusion, aggression, hyperexcitability, and restlessness [11, 30]. On the other hand, the hypoactive subtype shows a decrease in alertness, lethargy, reduced awareness of the surrounding environment, apathy, and slow and inappropriate speech [14]. This form of *delirium* is the most common, but it significantly has a worse prognosis, resulting in a higher associated mortality rate [3]. Thus, mixed *delirium* is defined as the alternation between the hyperactive and hypoactive states within a single episode.

Based on what has been described, it is evident that there is a need to develop methods that enable the early diagnosis of *delirium*. In this regard, identifying high-risk patients becomes crucial to prevent the detrimental consequences of this disorder and improve the well-being of patients. By identifying individuals who are at greater risk of developing *delirium*, healthcare providers can implement preventive measures, such as proactive monitoring, interventions to address predisposing factors, and targeted management strategies.

In this context, the goal of this paper arises, which aims to identify the most effective data balancing technique for accurate prediction of *delirium* occurrence and its subtypes, based on the methodology of generalized linear models (GLMs), specifically multinomial logistic regression (MLR).

Multinomial logistic regression predictive models are often implemented to determine the variables that have the most significant influence, as they allow for modelling the relationship between multiple independent variables and a categorical dependent variable [7]. In the present case study, it will be used to estimate the probability of an individual presenting one of the subtypes of *delirium*. In order to obtain robust results for this classification problem, it is crucial to validate the developed model.

This article is structured into 6 sections, with the first section focusing on contextualizing the topic. It provides a comprehensive overview of *delirium*, emphasizing the urgency to develop a predictive model for accurately determining its occurrence. In the second section, the methods to be implemented are described, specifically focusing on multinomial logistic regression.

In the third section, we delve into the exploration of multinomial logistic regression models for the purpose of predicting *delirium* outcome. Furthermore, we present and analyse the dataset utilized in this specific case study, which serves as the foundation for implementing the model.

Regarding the fourth section, it provides a detailed description of the methodology implementation. This includes data preprocessing steps and the application of two different techniques for addressing data imbalance.

In the fifth section, we present and discuss the results obtained from the implementation of the multinomial logistic regression models using both feature engineering techniques. We analyse and interpret the performance of the models in relation to the predicted outcomes, and discuss any notable findings or trends observed.

Finally, the last section encompasses the conclusions drawn from the case study and discusses future prospects for improving the model to achieve better predictions. It summarizes the key findings and insights obtained from the study and highlights areas for further research and development to enhance the predictive capabilities of the model.

2   Methods

In order to achieve the main goal of this study, a machine learning algorithm will be implemented, the multinomial logistic regression.

2.1   Generalized Linear Models

Many data science models offer the option to specify the relationship used to describe the response variable. For example, a generic family of models that can represent a wide range of relationships between the input variables and the response variable is the generalized linear model (GLM) [23]. The term "generalized" refers to the dependence on potentially more than one explanatory variable, as opposed to simple linear models.

GLMs follow the structure of a linear model but allow for the response variable to have an arbitrary error distribution (rather than simply normal distributions). They allow for estimating regression models for univariate response data that follow a very general distribution family called the exponential distribution family, which includes Gaussian, Binomial, Poisson, and Gamma distributions. Each distribution serves a different purpose, and depending on the distribution and choice of the link function, the models can be used for prediction or classification, resulting in various types of models [10]. It is important to choose a specification of the response variable that best fits and aligns with the understanding of the domain being studied in order to ensure that GLMs produce physically meaningful results.

Each GLM consists of three components: the probability distribution of the response variable (also known as the random component), a linear predictor (systematic component) involving the predictor variables, and a link function that relates the linear predictor to the distribution mean. This allows for building a linear relationship between the response variable and the predictors, even if the underlying relationship is not linear [4]. Additionally, this algorithm allows the magnitude of the variance of each measurement to be a function of its predicted value [24].

There are numerous scientific studies where data come from distributions other than normal. Thus, GLMs are a sensible choice, assuming an appropriate specification of the distribution and link function, as long as the data consist of independent observations [22]. In the present case study, the focus will mainly be on multinomial logistic regression models, as they are often implemented to identify the most influential variables, as they model the relationship between multiple independent variables and a multicategorical dependent variable. It will be used to determine the most contributing variables for each subtype of *delirium* and, consequently, estimate the probability of an individual presenting one of the disorder's subclassifications.

2.2 Multinomial Logistic Regression

Multinomial logistic regression (MLR) is a statistical method used to estimate the probability of occurrence of a multicategorical outcome based on a set of explanatory variables. It also allows describing the influence of the considered factors on the dependent variable, which has at least three unordered categories [18].

The MLR model describes a qualitative, nominal, and multicategorical dependent variable. It allows estimating the probability of occurrence of one of the different possible outcomes of the response variable based on explanatory variables that can be ordinal, continuous, and/or categorical [28]. This approach not only enables solving classification problems, but also facilitates identifying factors that affect the dependent variable. The goal is to create a model that can explain the strength of the impact of these interactions in terms of relative risk [12].

Let's consider an outcome variable Y with J nominal categories and a collection of K predictors $X_1, X_2, \ldots, X_K$. The logit of the multinomial logistic regression model can be expressed as follows:

$$logit(Y_j) = \log \left(\frac{P(Y = j|X)}{P(Y = J|X)} \right) = \beta_{j0} + \beta_{j1}X_1 + \beta_{j2}X_2 + \ldots + \beta_{jK}X_K$$

where $j = 1, \ldots, J - 1$. Thus, the number of logit equations formed is $J - 1$ categories of dependent variables. Each is a linear function that models the logarithm of probability as having a response j to baseline category J [2]. $P(Y = j)$ represents the probability of the outcome variable Y being in category j. All logits are defined according to a predetermined baseline category. Regarding the lack of order among the J categories, it is possible to select any of them as the reference outcome. On the other hand, β_{j0} is a constant value that symbolizes the intercept coefficient for category j and β_{jK} represents the coefficients of the predictor variables $X_1, X_2, \ldots, X_K$ for the category j. In other words, it indicates the magnitude of change in the logit when there is a one-unit increase in the value of that predictor, assuming all other variables remain unchanged.

Regarding the interpretation of the model, the relative risk ratio (RRR) is a commonly employed measure, expressed as an exponential function of the regression coefficients. If the RRR is greater than 1, it indicates that the probability of the j-th category occurring is higher than the probability of the reference category J.

$$\frac{P(Y = j|X)}{P(Y = J|X)} = exp(\beta_{j0} + \sum_{K=1}^{K} \beta_{jK}X_K)$$

The sum of all probabilities of data belonging to a specific category of the outcome variable equals one, therefore it can be established that:

$$P(Y = j|X) = \frac{e^{\sum_{k=0}^{p} \beta_{jK}X_K}}{1 + \sum_{i=1}^{J-1} e^{\sum_{K=0}^{p} \beta_{iK}X_K}}$$

$$P(Y = J|X) = \frac{1}{1 + \sum_{i=1}^{J-1} e^{\sum_{K=0}^{p} \beta_{iK} X_K}}$$

Concerning the parameters β_{jK}, they are estimated by applying the maximum likelihood method, which aims to find the parameter values that maximize the probability of observing the given data, given the assumed model. To put it differently, the likelihood represents the probability of the observed data being generated according to the assumed model. Through the maximization of the likelihood, it seeks to identify the parameter values that offer the most accurate explanation and optimal fit to the observed data within the chosen model [18].

$$L(\beta) = \prod_{i=1}^{n} \prod_{j=1}^{J} P(Y = j)^{d_{ij}}$$

where

$$d_{ij} = \begin{cases} 0 & if \ Y_i \neq j \\ 1 & if \ Y_i = j \end{cases}$$

Thereby, test statistics based on the Wald coefficient are used to estimate the statistical significance of individual regression coefficients (β_K):

$$W_j = \frac{\hat{\beta}_j}{\hat{SE}(\hat{\beta}_j)}$$

To validate the suitability of the entire model built using the multinomial logistic regression algorithm, it is necessary to conduct the likelihood ratio chi-square test (G) and the Pearson chi-square statistic (X^2).

3   Case Study

This section exhibits related work on multinomial logistic regression models for predicting *delirium* outcomes. It also describes and analyses a database in a hospital context for later prediction of *delirium* diagnosis. Additionally, the techniques used for pre-processing as well as data balancing to improve its quality and effectiveness for modelling purposes will be presented.

3.1   Exploring Multinomial Logistic Regression Models for *delirium* Outcome

Indeed, all the aforementioned aspects suggest that multinomial logistic regression is widely used in various branches of science.

Based on what has been described, it is evident that there is a need to develop methods that enable the early diagnosis of *delirium*. In this regard, identifying high-risk patients becomes crucial to prevent the detrimental consequences of this disorder and improve the well-being of patients. Existing prediction models for *delirium* utilize different identification methods and risk factors to calibrate the model [29].

The PREdiction of DELIRium for Intensive Care patients (PRE-DELIRIC) model aims to predict the occurrence of *delirium* during the ICU stay. Through multinomial logistic regression, the model predicts the evolution of the disorder based on the 10 most influential factors (age, coma, urea, infection, metabolic acidosis, use of sedatives and morphine, diagnostic group, Acute Physiology and Chronic Health Evaluation-II (APACHE-II) score, and urgent admission) identified within the first 24 h of ICU admission. A study conducted in 2012 demonstrated that the model was validated with an accuracy of 0.87. Therefore, according to Liang, this model exhibits high predictive value, suggesting the implementation of this tool in the ICU setting to effectively and early prevent the disorder [8, 16].

On the other hand, in 2015, another model called Early PREdiction of DELIRium for Intensive Care patients (E-PRE-DELIRIC) was introduced in the intensive care setting to address the limitations of the previously presented model, particularly the requirement for predictors to be exclusive to the first 24 h after ICU admission. This model aims to predict the development of *delirium* throughout the entire ICU stay based on the available data at the time of ICU admission. The E-PRE-DELIRIC model includes nine predictors: history of alcohol abuse and cognitive impairment, urgent admission, blood urea level, diagnostic group, age, administration of corticosteroids, mean arterial pressure, and respiratory insufficiency [29].

In 2022, a computer-based tool was developed to identify *delirium* in the emergency department during patient admission. The model incorporates 26 predictors and combines the *SelectFromModel* method with the logistic regression algorithm. This model revealed that the most influential predictors for *delirium* prediction were age, glucose levels, and antipsychotic use. Although the developed application demonstrated reasonable predictive capability, it is suggested that with a larger dataset, the predictive model could achieve better results [13].

3.2 Database

A database collected between 2014 and 2016 from a Portuguese hospital, Braga's Hospital, was used to develop this case study.

Despite the current database presenting some years, its use is still suitable for this case study that aims to predict the diagnosis of *delirium* (absent or if present which of the subtypes). This is due to the fact that the population sample has remained the same in Portugal, with a predominance of older patients with this disorder.

The study comprises information about 434 individuals admitted to the emergency department and 112 variables. The study population varies between 18 and 100 years old. The outcome variable is multinomial and refers to the diagnosis of *delirium* determined using the Richmond Agitation-Sedation Scale (RASS). The response variable can display 3 possible categories: absence represented as 0, hypoactive as 1 and hyperactive as 2. Furthermore, the database available includes patient origin, admission category, patient characteristics, length of stay in the emergency department, diagnostic group, SIRS and RASS criteria, blood results (glucose, sodium, urea, creatinine, C-reactive protein (PCR), blood pH, partial pressure of oxygen (pO_2), partial pressure of carbon dioxide (pCO_2), ionized calcium and bicarbonate (HCO_3)), administered medications, alcohol dependence and the date of death.

As *delirium* can have multiple etiologies and can also result from a medical condition (such as an infection), the SIRS (Systemic Inflammatory Response Syndrome) criteria serve as an initial assessment method to identify patients who might be undergoing an acute inflammatory process or infection, when at least two criteria are met. These criteria refer to a collection of clinical indicators such as body temperature ($< 36\,°C$ or $> 38\,°C$), heart rate (> 90 beats per minute), respiratory rate (> 20 breaths per minute) and white blood cell count (> 12000 cells/mm^3 or < 4000 cells/mm^3). On the other hand, RASS is a standardized instrument employed to evaluate the degree of sedation or agitation in patients, using visual contact as a parameter. This scale ranges from -5 to +4, where -5 corresponds to deep sedation levels, 0 indicates a patient that is alert and calm, and +4 expresses combative behaviour.

4   Methodology

This section implements the methodology to perform raw data analysis and data balancing to, in the future, execute the multinomial logistic regression.

4.1   Pre-processing

Pre-processing involves applying a variety of methods to enhance model performance, avoid overfitting and reduce the complexity of the data, making them more amenable to analysis and interpretation. Therefore, data preparation is crucial for the purpose of obtaining more reliable and accurate results from machine learning algorithms, as it handles cleaning (missing values, outliers, and inconsistencies), transformation and data reduction.

In the original database, the categorical variables are encoded in a numeric form, where each feature is identified with numbers according to the respective categories. Although this is a critical step for most machine learning algorithms, multinomial logistic regression can handle numerical encoding as well as categorical predictors by creating dummy variables when fitting the model.

Primarily the dimensions and typology of the data were verified along with a graphic analysis, which also allowed to assess the number of missing values, as the first step to data cleaning. In the next step, each variable was analysed to understand the information it contained. Therefore, variables related to dates, times, lab results, criteria, and vital signs (such as temperature and heart rate) were converted into numerical values. In addition, the variable "date of death" was transformed into a binary variable, where 0 represents a person who is alive and 1 represents a deceased patient. The RASS variable was categorized into 3 categories. Negative values were assigned as -1, indicating a sedation state, positive values were assigned as 1, indicating an agitation state, while 0 corresponds to a calm state.

It is common for datasets to contain missing values, which can pose challenges when applying machine learning algorithms. Discarding them can lead to the loss of important information and violate assumptions of algorithms that assume complete data. This can ultimately impact the efficiency and performance of the model. The *missmap* function from the Amelia package allows for the visualization of missing data through visual representations, enabling the identification of different patterns of missingness. The variables in the blue colour scheme do not exhibit any missing values and are fully observed, whereas the variables in the white colour display one or more missing values that require imputation or the handling of missing data. Thereby, based on this visualization, the variables with the highest percentage of missing values, the white ones, were eliminated. These variables mainly consisted of dates, times, and other insignificant variables.

Then, the columns with redundant information were identified and eliminated. This included removing the duplicate variable 'HCO$_3$', as well as columns generated from the variables 'Origin', 'SU Location', and 'Diagnostic Group'. Additionally, columns related to the SIRS and RASS criteria were also excluded as they were not relevant to the analysis. After checking the columns, it was found that the variables designated as pharmacological groups did not contain the correct information regarding the medications that belong to each group, so it was decided to eliminate them.

After using the *unique* function to ensure there were not any duplicate rows, columns with unique values that did not have any information that could be used to model were left out, meaning there was zero variance. The identified and eliminated variables were 'Alverine' and 'Codeine', corresponding to two medications.

In the pre-processing phase, a thorough analysis was conducted on the remaining columns. Subsequently, it was determined that the patient identifier number and the 'ResultDelirium' variable, which is binary, should be removed. This decision was made because the case study primarily focuses on a multinomial problem. As a result, the 'Result' column, which encompasses multiple categories, was identified as the appropriate outcome variable. Taking into account the range and mean values, it was decided to exclude the length of stay in days in the ED instead of the number of hours. Thus, the resulting database comprises information about 434 individuals and 56 independent variables.

In the final step, dimensionality reduction techniques were applied to create a smaller set of variables corresponding to pharmacological groups, allowing the drugs to be categorized according to their respective groups. However, it was decided that pharmacological groups with a representation of less than 14 would be placed in a new pharmacological category called "Other drugs". Consequently, this led to a decrease in the number of independent variables to 29.

4.2   Data Imbalance Processing

Imbalanced data refers to a situation with a significant disparity in the number of instances across different classes, leading to an uneven distribution. This is particularly prevalent in emergency departments, where the majority of instances typically represent normal or non-urgent situations, whereas a minority of instances are associated with specific abnormal or emergency conditions.

The final database consisted of 342 patients without *delirium*, 74 patients with the hypoactive subtype and 18 with the hyperactive subtype. Given the imbalanced nature of the dataset, the use of a stratified split was deemed appropriate. This method ensures that classes with unequal representation are properly accounted for, as it preserves the class distribution in both the training and testing sets. After splitting the data, the train set contained 238 examples of the absence of *delirium*, 56 hypoactive cases and 10 hyperactive patients. Whereas the remaining examples were included in the test dataset.

Nevertheless, to balance the training dataset, methods were implemented to address this issue, with oversampling being the most suitable approach in this context of limited data, as it generates synthetic samples of the minority class. Thereby, two techniques were considered: SMOTE (Synthetic Minority Over-sampling Technique) and ADASYN (Adaptive Synthetic Sampling). The SMOTE algorithm creates new examples by interpolating features from existing examples, selecting an example from the minority class and finding its k-Nearest Neighbors. In contrast, the ADASYN algorithm generates synthetic examples by considering the density of samples surrounding the minority class examples. It adapts to the density of the data and produces more synthetic examples for minority class instances located in less dense regions.

In the next step, the numeric variables were scaled using the *preProcess* function with the range method from the caret package.

In general, the choice of the most suitable method and model typically depends on the main objective and specific application of the classifier, as well as the performance metrics employed to assess its effectiveness.

5   Results and Discussion

The main result of this study is a pipeline for multinomial logistic regression, which is schematized with the main steps and outputs (see Fig. 1).

The database used was previously pre-processed and transformed by the methods described in Sect. 4.1. The result was a dataset containing 434 individuals and 30 variables. Regarding the distribution of instances, it is worth mentioning that out of the total, 342 instances correspond to the absence of *delirium*, 74 patients exhibit the hypoactive subtype, and the remaining 18 patients display the hyperactive phenotype.

Through a graphical analysis of the distribution of the population based on age group and the occurrence of *delirium*, it becomes evident that this condition is more commonly observed in individuals aged 51 and above, particularly in

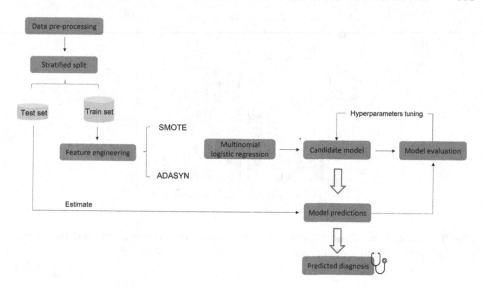

Fig. 1. Main steps of the pipeline to implement multinomial logistic regression to predict *delirium* outcome.

the elderly population. It is also noteworthy that the age range of 61–70 years exhibits the highest incidence of both hypoactive and hyperactive subtypes of *delirium* (see Fig. 2).

Prior to implementing multinomial logistic regression, the dataset was initially divided through a stratified split, allocating 70% of the data for training purposes and reserving the remaining 30% for testing.

Subsequently, to address the substantial class imbalance in the training set, two oversampling techniques, ADASYN and SMOTE, were evaluated for generating synthetic samples.

In the case of the SMOTE technique, the resulting training dataset comprises a total of 692 observations. Among these, 238 instances represent the absence of *delirium*, 224 instances correspond to the hypoactive subtype, and 230 instances pertain to the hyperactive subtype. On the other hand, the ADASYN technique yielded similar results, resulting in a training dataset of 696 instances. Out of these, there are 238 instances denoting the absence of *delirium*, 223 instances indicating the hypoactive subtype, and 235 instances pertaining to the hyperactive subtype (see Fig. 3). In summary, both methods ensured a more equal representation of the different categories in the dataset.

In the realm of machine learning, hyperparameter tuning plays a vital role as a crucial technique that unlocks the full potential of models by identifying the most effective hyperparameter combination for optimal performance through cross-validation. Through systematic exploration, accuracy is enhanced, ensuring adaptability across diverse datasets. The hyperparameters subjected to tuning were "decay" and "size". "Decay" regulates weight decay, specifically L2 regularization, while "size" determines the number of hidden units in the neu-

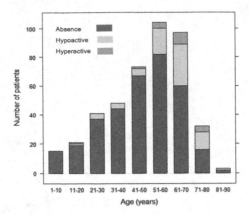

Fig. 2. Distribution of the population sample according to age group and the occurrence of *delirium* and its subtypes.

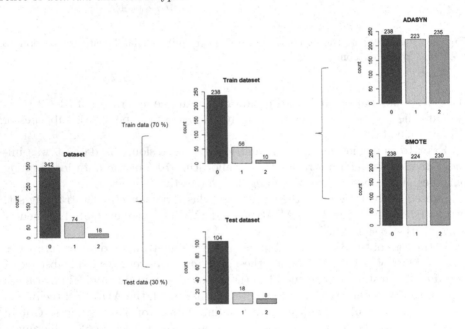

Fig. 3. Representative diagram of the data division through a stratified split and subsequent data balancing using two techniques, ADASYN and SMOTE.

ral network. By finding the best hyperparameter values, better generalization and improved predictive accuracy are achieved, making hyperparameter tuning essential for obtaining the best model candidate.

Finally, the multinomial logistic regression model was implemented using the optimal hyperparameters, with the reference category being the absence of *delirium*, to determine the best feature engineering technique that achieves the highest model performance. Once the model is trained, predictions are made on the test set and its performance is assessed using diverse performance metrics, such as accuracy, precision, recall, F1-score, AUC-ROC and AUC-PR. These metrics enable an evaluation of the model's ability to classify new instances and handle unseen data effectively. A strong performance on the test set indicates the model's proficiency in generalizing to novel situations. However, poor performance may suggest overfitting to the training data and a lack of adaptability to new scenarios.

Through the examination of Table 1 and Table 2, it becomes apparent that the ADASYN balancing technique consistently yields superior outcomes compared to SMOTE. This is particularly evident in relation to the F1-score, precision, AUC-ROC, and AUC-PR metrics. A higher F1 score indicates a well-balanced precision and recall, ensuring the accurate identification of positive instances while minimizing false positives. Improved precision indicates a more precise identification of positive instances, while higher AUC-PR demonstrates the model's ability to achieve both high precision and recall. When the AUC-ROC values are consistently higher for all classes, it signifies a heightened ability of the model to effectively discriminate and distinguish between the various categories, thereby demonstrating superior performance in classification tasks.

The results of this study demonstrate that ADASYN is a highly effective technique for improving model performance in imbalanced datasets. When compared to SMOTE, ADASYN consistently achieves higher levels of accuracy, precision, and discriminative ability. This improvement is evident in the higher values of F1-score, precision, AUC-ROC, and AUC-PR obtained with ADASYN. These findings provide strong evidence for the superiority of ADASYN in enhancing the performance of classification models in imbalanced data scenarios.

Table 1. Results obtained by the multinomial logistic regression for the ADASYN balancing technique.

	Accuracy	Recall	Precision	F1	AUC-PR	AUC-ROC
Hyperactive	0.65	0.19	0.33	0.24	0.10	0.49
Hypoactive	0.65	0.25	0.44	0.32	0.22	0.63

Table 2. Results obtained by the multinomial logistic regression for the SMOTE balancing technique.

	Accuracy	Recall	Precision	F1	AUC-PR	AUC-ROC
Hyperactive	0.63	0.10	0.12	0.11	0.11	0.45
Hypoactive	0.63	0.21	0.39	0.27	0.24	0.56

6 Conclusions and Future Work

Multinomial regression models are extensively used in the field of medicine due to their ability to assess the relative risk for a dependent variable with multiple categories. These models offer a more versatile approach compared to standard logistic regression, making them applicable to a wide range of medical research scenarios. The model presented in this paper is used to predict the *delirium* outcome, to anticipate the treatments and improve the quality of life of patients. In opposition to the existing methods, this article seeks to find the most effective data balancing technique for better predicting the occurrence of *delirium* and its subtypes. In the future, the goal is to identify the risk factors associated with *delirium* in an emergency department, as opposed to existing tools that focus on intensive care units. This occurs due to the possibility of encountering distinct variables in different environments. In one context, a specific factor may hold significant importance in triggering *delirium*, whereas in another setting, its impact might be relatively negligible.

This study demonstrated the importance of pre-processing the data in a machine learning algorithm to obtain more accurate predictions. The study compared the performance of two methods, ADASYN and SMOTE, for balancing imbalanced datasets. The results demonstrated that using ADASYN led to superior model performance in terms of F1 score, precision, AUC-ROC, and AUC-PR. Overall, these findings emphasize the importance of using ADASYN to improve classification model performance in imbalanced data scenarios.

In a future work perspective, feature selection methods should be implemented since lead to improved model performance, interpretability, and computational efficiency. Additionally, it helps identify the most relevant predictors, reduce dimensionality, and enhance the model's generalization capabilities. Afterwards, the main goal would be integrating this model into an application capable of assisting, in real-time, health professionals in the diagnostic process. Notwithstanding, another exciting feature to improve the model's predictive character could be adding more records, mainly related to the *delirium* subtypes, to the training dataset. Furthermore, as the database expands and new data is incorporated, there is also the possibility of including additional variables in the model.

References

1. Adamis, D., McCarthy, G., O'Mahony, E., Meagher, D.: Motor disturbances in elderly medical inpatients and their relationship to delirium. J. Geriatr. Psychiatry Neurol. **30**(4), 214–219 (2017)
2. Agresti, A.: An introduction to categorical data analysis second edition (2002)
3. Ali, M.A., Hashmi, M., Ahmed, W., Raza, S.A., Khan, M.F., Salim, B.: Incidence and risk factors of delirium in surgical intensive care unit. Trauma Surg. Acute Care Open **6** (2021)

4. Arnold, K.F., Davies, V., de Kamps, M., Tennant, P.W., Mbotwa, J., Gilthorpe, M.S.: Reflection on modern methods: generalized linear models for prognosis and intervention-theory, practice and implications for machine learning. Int. J. Epidemiol. **49**(6), 2074–2082 (2020)

5. Asken, M.J., Grossman, D., Christensen, L.W.: American Psychiatric Association. Diagnostic and statistical manual of mental disorders. arlington, va: American Psychiatric Publishing, 2013. archibald, herbert c., and read d. tuddenham. "Persistent stress reaction after combat: a 20-year follow-up." archives of general PSY. Therapy **45**(10), 2317–2325 (2007)

6. Assefa, M.T., Chekol, W.B., Melesse, D.Y., Nigatu, Y.A., Bizuneh, Y.B.: Incidence and risk factors of emergence delirium in elderly patients after general or spinal anesthesia for both elective and emergency surgery. Annal. Med. Surg. **84**, 104959 (2022)

7. Boateng, E.Y., Abaye, D.A., Boateng, E.Y., Abaye, D.A.: A review of the logistic regression model with emphasis on medical research. J. Data Anal. Inf. Process. **7**, 190–207 (2019)

8. Van den Boogaard, M., et al.: Development and validation of pre-deliric (prediction of delirium in ICU patients) delirium prediction model for intensive care patients: observational multicentre study. BMJ **344** (2012)

9. Bowman, E.M., Cunningham, E.L., Page, V.J., McAuley, D.F.: Phenotypes and subphenotypes of delirium: a review of current categorisations and suggestions for progression. Crit. Care **25**(1), 1–13 (2021)

10. Breslow, N.E.: Generalized linear models: checking assumptions and strengthening conclusions. Statist. Applicata **8**(1), 23–41 (1996)

11. Bulic, D., et al.: Cognitive and psychosocial outcomes of mechanically ventilated intensive care patients with and without delirium. Annal. Intens. Care **10**, 1–10 (2020)

12. El-Habil, A.M.: An application on multinomial logistic regression model. Pak. J. Statist. Oper. Res. 271–291 (2012)

13. Figueiredo, C., Braga, A.C., Mariz, J.: Early delirium detection using machine learning algorithms. In: Gervasi, O., Murgante, B., Misra, S., Rocha, A.M.A.C., Garau, C. (eds.) ICCSA 2022. LNCS, vol. 13377, pp. 555–570. Springer, Cham (2022). https://doi.org/10.1007/978-3-031-10536-4_37

14. Ghezzi, E.S., et al.: How do predisposing factors differ between delirium motor subtypes? Age Ageing **51**(9) (2022)

15. Gibb, K., et al.: The consistent burden in published estimates of delirium occurrence in medical inpatients over four decades: a systematic review and meta-analysis study. Age Ageing **49**(3), 352–360 (2020)

16. Ho, M.H., et al.: Diagnostic test accuracy meta-analysis of pre-deliric (prediction of delirium in ICU patients): a delirium prediction model in intensive care practice. Intensive Crit. Care Nurs. **57**, 14–22 (2020)

17. Hosie, A., Davidson, P.M., Agar, M., Sanderson, C.R., Phillips, J.: Delirium prevalence, incidence, and implications for screening in specialist palliative care inpatient settings: a systematic review. Palliat. Med. **27**(6), 486–498 (2013)

18. Hosmer, D.W., Lemeshow, S.: Applied Logistic Regression. Wiley, New York (2000)

19. Inouye, S.K.: Delirium-a framework to improve acute care for older persons. J. Am. Geriatr. Soc. **66**, 446–451 (2018)

20. Inouye, S.K., Charpentier, P.A.: Precipitating factors for delirium in hospitalized elderly persons: predictive model and interrelationship with baseline vulnerability. JAMA **275**, 852–857 (1996)

21. Inouye, S.K., Westendorp, R.G., Saczynski, J.S.: Delirium in elderly people. The Lancet **383**(9920), 911–922 (2014)
22. Janizadeh, S., et al.: Combination four different ensemble algorithms with the generalized linear model (GLM) for predicting forest fire susceptibility. Geomat. Nat. Hazards Risk **14**(1) (2023)
23. Karpatne, A., et al.: Theory-guided data science: a new paradigm for scientific discovery from data. IEEE Trans. Knowl. Data Eng. **29**(10), 2318–2331 (2017)
24. McCullagh, P.: Generalized Linear Models. Routledge (2019)
25. Morandi, A., et al.: Clinical features associated with delirium motor subtypes in older inpatients: results of a multicenter study. Am. J. Geriatr. Psychiatry **25**(10), 1064–1071 (2017)
26. Slor, C.J., Adamis, D., Jansen, R.W., Meagher, D.J., Witlox, J., Houdijk, A.P., de Jonghe, J.F.: Delirium motor subtypes in elderly hip fracture patients: risk factors, outcomes and longitudinal stability. J. Psychosom. Res. **74**, 444–449 (2013)
27. Tieges, Z., Evans, J.J., Neufeld, K.J., MacLullich, A.M.: The neuropsychology of delirium: advancing the science of delirium assessment. Int. J. Geriatr. Psychiatry **33**(11), 1501–1511 (2018)
28. Venkatesan, G., Sasikala, V.: A statistical analysis of migration using logistic regression model. Int. J. Sci. Technol. Res. **8**(10), 1331–1336 (2019)
29. Wassenaar, A., et al.: Multinational development and validation of an early prediction model for delirium in ICU patients. Intensive Care Med. **41**, 1048–1056 (2015)
30. Wilson, J.E., et al.: Delirium (2020)
31. Yaria, J., et al.: Delirium in elderly patients: frequency and precipitants in a tertiary hospital setting. West Afr. J. Med. **36**(2), 183–188 (2019)

Author Index

A. I. Pereira et al. (Eds.): OL2A 2023, CCIS 1981, pp. 607–609, 2024.
https://doi.org/10.1007/978-3-031-53025-8

Printed in the United States
by Baker & Taylor Publisher Services